With the battleship *Maine* being blown up in Havana Harbor, the Unit
States declares war on Spain. Commodore George Dewey and the U
fleet destroy the Spanish Armada in Manila Bay on I May. Aguina
back from exile in Hong Kong, declares independence on 12 Ju
Refusing to surrender to Filipinos, the Spanish agree to a mock ba
with the American forces, and surrender Manila to them 13 Augu
In December the Treaty of Paris is signed by Spain and
United States, whereby the latter take over the Philippi
and indemnifies Spain US$20 milli

Bonifacio and the
Katipunan start
the Philippine
Revolution
against Spain.
Emilio Aguinaldo
and his forces
take Cavite.
Accused by the
Spanish of help-
ing to foment the
revolution Rizal is
shot at dawn
30 December.

After two
hundred years,
the galleon
trade between
Mexico and
the Philippines
ceases.

Filipino clerics José Burgos,
Mariano Gomez, and Jacinto
Zamora are garroted by the
Spanish for their alleged role in
the Cavite Mutiny.

On his return from Europe, Rizal is
exiled to Mindanao. Andres
Bonifacio founds the Katipunan, a
revolutionary society dedicated to
the overthrow of the Spanish.

Manila is
occupied by
the British on
account of the
Seven Years' War.

1762-64

1815

1872

1892

1896

1796

1834

1877

1895

1897

The port of
Manila welcomes
its first U.S.
trading vessel.

The Spanish
colonial authorities
open up Manila to
global trade and
investment.

Noli me tangere,
José Rizal's first
novel and written in
Europe, provokes
controversy for its
account of Spanish
abuses and is imme-
diately condemned
by the authorities
in Manila.

The Cuban Revolution
against Spain begins.

Aguinaldo takes over the revolution by deposing
and ordering the execution of Bonifacio.
He establishes the independent Republic of the
Philippines in November at Biak-na-Bato.

Philippines declared liberated by MacArthur 5 July. On 6 August, the U.S. drops an atomic bomb on Hiroshima—the first use of atomic weaponry in history—and another one on Nagasaki on 9 August. Korea is divided into two, North and South, which later establish themselves as the Democratic Republic of Korea in the North and the Republic of Korea in the South.

ol. Frederick
unston, aided
y Macabebe
ercenaries cap-
ures Aguinaldo
n his Palanan,
abela hideout.
enceforth
nown as the
homasites,
merican
eachers arrive
board the
S Thomas on
3 August.

Macario Sakay, a revolutionary leader, is hanged by the Americans for alleged banditry.

The Philippine Commonwealth, with Quezon as president and Sergio Osmena as vice president, is established. Gen. Douglas MacArthur is posted to the Philippines as field marshal.

The Japanese form the Philippine Executive Commission 23 January. U.S. forces in Bataan capitulate to the Japanese 9 April. A new republic, with Jose Laurel as president is inaugurated on 14 October.

The Soviet-leaning *Partidong Komunista ng Pilipinas* is founded.

1907

1930

1938

1942

1945

1902

1922

1934

1941

1944

The Philippine-American War declared over on 4 July. Guerrilla warfare continues in much of the country.

Manuel L. Quezon emerges as the top Filipino politician.

The Tydings-McDuffie Act is passed by U.S. Congress, providing a ten-year transition period to independence.

Japan bombs Pearl Harbor and Clark Field, paving the way for the Japanese forces to land at Lingayen Gulf and a speedy takeover of the archipelago.

MacArthur returns to the Philippines, landing in Leye 20 October.

acknowledge the legitimacy of the Paris
naldo is sworn in as the first president of
e Republic on 23 January.

ry Willy Grayson, a Nebraska Volunteer,
kills a Filipino soldier, starting the
merican War.

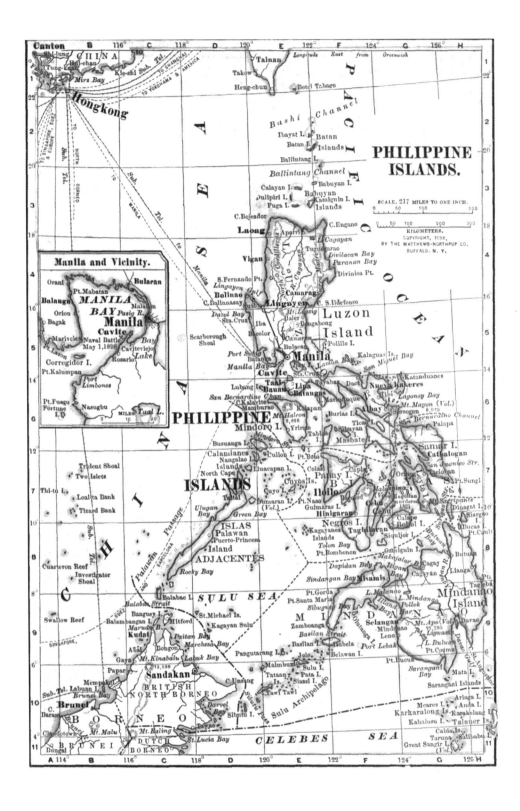

PHILIPPINE ISLANDS.

SCALE, 217 MILES TO ONE INCH.

KILOMETERS.
COPYRIGHT, 1898,
BY THE MATTHEWS-NORTHRUP CO.
BUFFALO. N. Y.

Manila and Vicinity.

Vestiges of War

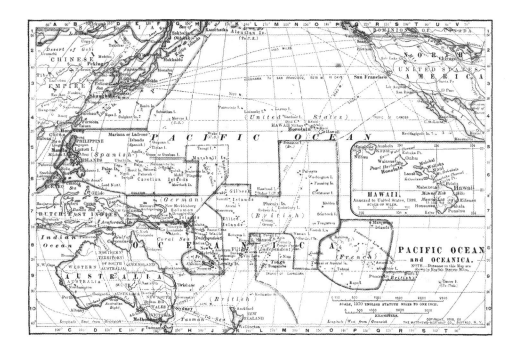

Vestiges of War

THE PHILIPPINE-AMERICAN WAR
and the
AFTERMATH *of an* IMPERIAL DREAM
1899 - 1999

EDITED *by* ANGEL VELASCO SHAW *and* LUIS H. FRANCIA

A Project of Asian/Pacific/American Studies Program and Institute, New York University

NEW YORK UNIVERSITY PRESS
Washington Square, New York

First Published in the U.S.A. in 2002 by
NEW YORK UNIVERSITY PRESS
Washington Square
New York, NY 10003

Library of Congress Cataloging-in-Publication Data
Vestiges of war: the Philippine-American war and the aftermath of an imperial dream, 1899-1999/
edited by Angel Velasco Shaw and Luis H. Francia
    p.cm.
"A project of Asian/Pacific/American Studies Program and Institute, New York University"
    Includes bibliographies and index.
ISBN 0-8147-9790-3 (cloth) – ISBN 0-8147-9791-1 (pbk.)
1. Philippines – History – Philippine-American War, 1899–1902.
2. Philippines – Foreign relations – United States.
3. United States – Foreign relations – Philippines. 4. United States – Politics and government –
20th century.
I. Shaw, Angel Velasco. II. Francia, Luis H.

DS679. V47 2000
959.91031—dc21

The printing of this book was partially funded by a grant to Anvil Publishing, Inc. from the National
Commission for Culture and the Arts of the Republic of the Philippines, with funds provided by
the Ford and Rockeller Foundations and the Asian/Pacific/American Studies Program and Institute,
New York University, United States of America.

Copyedited by L. R. Roa and Lorna Kalaw Tirol
Production Management by Ruth Roa, Balanghai Books
Book and cover design by John C. Woo and Yun Z. Wu
Cover art: *Free Trade* ©1998 by Santiago Bose, 177.8 x 152.4 cm, mixed media on canvas

THIS BOOK IS DEDICATED TO ALL THE INNOCENT CASUALTIES, LIVING OR DEAD, OF A WAR THAT SHOULD NEVER HAVE HAPPENED.

Contents

Exquisite Betrayal
ANGEL VELASCO SHAW

Forgetting is a form of death ever present within life… But forgetting is also the great problem of politics. When a big power wants to deprive a small country of its national consciousness it uses the method of organized forgetting… A nation which loses awareness of its past gradually loses its self.

—Milan Kundera[1]

ANXIETY OF MEMORY

The scene is the summer of 1980. Mount Kisco, New York, in Northern Westchester County. I am sixteen years old. My mother and I are sitting on our porch talking about the possibility of the United States reinstating the draft. She tells me that if this happens, she will arrange to have my brothers become Philippine citizens because she doesn't want them to ever fight in a war. This is what I remember. I didn't understand the power and importance of citizenship, the contradictions of national identity, and the conflicting brands of nationalism. Nor did I have an inkling about Philippine-U.S. history and current relations, despite the fact that I had already been to the Philippines four times and had seen visibly recognizable American influences on Filipino culture. This knowledge was to be gained cumulatively over half a lifetime later.

I have been seeking to understand war since this moment when my mother began telling me some of her Philippine World War II stories. I try to imagine her as a ten-year-old girl, a few months before liberation in 1945, running in the rice fields with my aunts, their daughters and sons, her grandmother, and her mother—running endlessly for days away from the Japanese guns, their blood-tipped bayonets. There are no maps for this terrain. There are no houses. There is nothing to hide in. The only shelter is the ground beneath their bare feet. They learned to make their bodies their home as I have been learning to do the same. My mother recalls that with bare hands, her mother dug ditches in which to hide her family. Eight feet deep. Perhaps some of this was my mother's imagination, part of her memory as a child during a time when her innocence was lost. She would wake up from nightmares until she was fifty years old. I wonder what the world was like for these women and children without the men who were off fighting. How often did they cry? How deep was their fear? Their strength? Their faith? Did my mother, her sisters, and her nieces and nephews ever play during those long war years when the Japanese occupied their country while waiting for General MacArthur to return?

I think about my father who supported his mother and four siblings while his father was incarcerated for being caught using a short-wave radio as a member of the guerrilla resistance. I imagine my father as a skinny little boy wandering the war-torn streets in Manila looking for any semblance of food. What did he see? Whom did he encounter? Did he know his childhood had ended? I search for these stories which he cannot share because he died when I was a baby. It is difficult to bring up the subject of war with my relatives who say they cannot remember or choose not to remember. When asked if they thought the severe treatment of the Filipinos by the Japanese had anything to do with the U.S.-Philippines relations, they answered with stories about the joyous day the American tanks rolled into Manila and about seeing packages of Spam and corned beef dropping from the sky. Two years later, in 1982, my older brother told me stories about the Philippine-American War, a war I never knew had taken place. On countless occasions I have had to ask myself—"Who is betraying whom?"

Over the course of fifteen years of living in Manila and New York, I was to discover that national identity was not in fact singular nor was history monolithic. All the light bulbs that went off in my head (more like electric shocks) led me to analyze the effects on identity constructs based on histories written from the perspective of the colonizers. My naïve internalization of identifying with the colonizer and not the colonized could not be fully comprehended until I read the mind-opening works of Frantz Fanon and other critical thinkers theorizing on the diverse impacts of colonialism.[2] This personally motivated historical investigation inspired my film and video work and was a significant factor in envisioning the *Vestiges of War* project.

Vestiges of War: The Philippine-American War and the Aftermath of An Imperial Dream, 1899-1999 is a part of this continuum of questioning. While researching in the National Archives in 1995, for a documentary on Filipinos in America, I came across over 250,000 photographs of the Philippine-American War, but it was called the "Philippine Insurrection." Thirteen years after first hearing about the war, what I finally saw evidence of was not an insurrection, but most definitely a war. There it was literally in black and white—a photograph taken by an American colonel of nearly naked Filipino prisoners bathing in a river; numerous images of American soldiers in firing lines, digging graves, standing on human bones; trenches of dead Filipinos, raggedy-clothed children staring up at smiling soldiers; American colonists lounging, socializing, and being served by their Filipino subjects.[3] What interested me most were the effects on the psyche, the aftermath of a bloody war, of two distinct forms of ceaseless colonial rule—Spanish and American, and imperialist agendas. The subtle violence of war haunted me more than I ever imagined it would.

My understanding of U.S.-Philippines relations and Philippine history, particularly of the late nineteenth century beginning with the Propagandist/Reformist Movement (1880-1895)[4] and early twentieth century, is grounded in a series of complicated contradictions of what I loosely interpret to be "betrayal narratives." These narratives that are repeated again and again in different eras with different characters, symbolize the complexity of whatever it means to be Filipino for

Filipinos in the Philippines, in the United States, and in other countries around the world.[5] The multiple ways individuals and a nation itself attempt to recover history, particularly one that is riddled with greed, intrigue, selective memory, and treachery, are microcosmic reflections of the conscious and unconscious quandary that Filipinos experience. It is not just Spaniards against Filipinos or the revolutionaries against the Spaniards, the Americans against the Filipinos, or the Filipinos against the Americans, but also Filipinos against Filipinos and Americans against Americans. The role played by individuals in a family, community, and region throughout history, how these histories got recorded, distorted, passed on, or forgotten are important factors. Some of the questions to ponder are—Were they freedom fighters, collaborators, or both with the Spanish, the Americans, and the Japanese? To whom did they pledge allegiance? Consequently, how did subsequent generations identify? With whom did they identify politically? How did they construct identity? Which perspectives did they align with—regionally, nationally, and transnationally—and why? The challenge is to get beneath the surface of events and characters, and to examine the details. *Vestiges of War* suggests that there are many details left to be found (not an easy task, however) and analyzed as distinct yet connective narratives in social, political, and cultural contexts.

CENTERING THE MARGIN

Collective and individual forms of forgetting took place in the Philippines as well as in the United States. Historian Reynaldo Ileto's essay, "The Philippine-American War, Friendship and Forgetting," presents a microhistory of the war in the Southern Luzon region, in which he critically examines the possible reasons for Philippine amnesia. He asks, "in the context of an emancipatory history of the twentieth century, a history of forward movement from what was pictured as Spanish medievalism toward a modern nation-state via an enlightened U.S. colonial regime, is it any surprise that the Philippine-American War became somewhat of a nonevent, a glitch in an otherwise smooth progression?" Depending on one's bias as pro-Filipino or pro-American, acknowledgment of such histories could be construed as a betrayal of what generations of Filipinos believed to be choosing the lesser of two evils—the Americans over the Spanish. This line of thinking would suggest that forgetting is better and less troublesome than remembering. Poet Alfrredo Navarro Salanga's thirteen poems propose that remembering would be a greater, although no less painful, form of liberty. Written from a place of rage, Salanga's words resonate with the powerful activist sentiment of the martial law days when he originally wrote them. This bridging across historical events and inclusion of what was happening in other parts of the Philippines decentralizes Manila and its inhabitants as the primary focus of politics, culture, and life. Along with Ileto and Salanga, contributors such as Erlyn Ruth Alcantara, Santiago Bose, Patricio Abinales, and Resil Mojares bring intertwining history and life experiences to what has usually been constructed as the margins of the archipelago into sharp focus—Baguio City, Benguet Province, Mindanao, and Cebu.

The marginalization and mainstream censorship of the Philippine-American War, American colonialism, subsequent U.S. interventions after colonial rule through to today, and the speaking out against them did not occur only in the

Philippines, but also in the United States. Legendary satirist Mark Twain's anti-Philippine-American War essay "To the Person Sitting in Darkness," and historian/Web site master Jim Zwick's "Mark Twain's Anti-Imperialist Writings in the 'American Century'" offer compelling criticism across the generations of what Twain labels "the blessings of civilization." Zwick alludes to the disappearance of Twain's anti-imperialist writings from Twain anthologies as one that coincides with the erasure of the Philippine-American War from American national memory, just as both reappear during the Vietnam War's antiwar movement.

Visual art is another area of cultural production where the recovery of buried voices is vibrantly expressed. Like Delacroix, Goya, Picasso, and other generations of artists whose works do not separate art from politics, the Filipino/American artists' visual essays in *Vestiges of War* depict the shifting world they live in, exploring the social and cultural dynamics of their time and challenging themselves to (re)present these narratives beyond deductive criticism of being Western-influenced. Ben Cabrera's eclectic "Philippine Album," for instance, is inspired by Spanish and American colonial history. With the blank space at the end of his canvas depicting the history of the Filipino people's struggle for independence, Antipas Delotavo's *Daantaon (Century)* supports our central thesis that these wars haven't ended. Delotavo's references in this painting to the war waged by the New People's Army and to the insidious nature of American cultural imperialism in other works reproduced here, embody social and political injustices denounced by many of the Philippine social realists. The women-centered works of Brenda Fajardo foreground the multiple struggles—urban, rural, and transnational roles of Filipino women over the past one hundred years, celebrating their undeniable contributions to the building and maintenance of an evolving nation.

Many of the contributors highlighted in this anthology examine the ongoing contradictions and variations of Philippine national consciousness within specific eras as well as across them. Such consciousness is not singular, but plural for a country like the Philippines that continues to struggle to become a unified nation, inclusive of those who identify as "Filipino" living elsewhere in the world. It is not enough to simply define oneself within a fixed context, but to know and embrace many selves that are fluid. If there is such a thing as national remembering, it lies in the quality and courage of how and what we remember and what we do with these memories when we pass them on.

ASSIMILATION BLUES

> It should be the earnest wish and paramount aim of the military administration to win the confidence, respect, and affection of the inhabitants of the Philippines by assuring them in every possible way that full measure of individual rights and liberties which is the heritage of free peoples, and by proving to them that the mission of the United States is one of Benevolent Assimilation substituting the mild sway of justice and right for arbitrary rule.
>
> — President William McKinley[6]

The forgetting of multiple acts of internal and external treachery and the selective remembering of McKinley's Benevolent Assimilation by way of road building, sanitation, and development of the social and political infrastructure in the Philippines are best seen in the legacy of the American educational system.[7] The late radical historian Renato Constantino's "The Miseducation of the Filipino" examines the differences between a powerful, established nation and an emerging nation within the primary context of how Filipinos were educated. Constantino calls for decolonization of the mind and a revamping of the Philippine educational system toward a nationalist consciousness promoting a more independent society, as opposed to the co-dependent nation that the Philippines has become. This task, however, may seem utopian, given the thoroughness of such an education that extended well beyond the formal classrooms, affecting those born and raised in the Philippines, as well as the descendants of former Philippine nationals. They must also grapple with this miseducation.

The ubiquity of popular American culture on the Philippine imagination is visualized in Australia-based artist Alwin Reamillo's mixed media collage/installation, and in the paintings of San Francisco-based artist, Manuel Ocampo. Both artists' visual essays are irreverently critical of the "Disneyfication"[8] of the Philippines and Spanish Catholicism as tools of colonialism. Their artworks clearly problematize the violence of colonialism and cultural imperialism. Santiago Bose's image and text piece, "Baguio Graffiti," addresses similar subject matter but viewed through a more personal lens. Bose shares stories of growing up in a northern pre-planned American colonial city. The collision of his neocolonial education within the Philippines' 1960s-1970s political climate of anti-American sentiments, and his growing interaction with Baguio City's indigenous culture, influenced his art and life in inseparable ways. These are acts of resistance, acknowledgments not merely of disturbing prevalent neocolonial mentalities, but of the struggles to raise consciousness about them and to transcend their alluring yet problematic rewards of aspiring to be American/European and all that this implies.

I wonder if McKinley ever thought about how the American assimilation of Filipinos in the Philippines would also affect Filipinos migrating to and being born in America. Did the words cultural schizophrenia, pain, alienation, anger, or betrayal ever come to mind? I doubt it. Gratitude resounds for those who were well educated under the colonial mission of benevolent assimilation. Nonetheless, even for the fearless and guilt-free Filipino/Americans, they too must do battle with who they think their redeemers really are.

CONVERGING IN THE DIASPORA

> *Identity: the singular naming a person, a nation, a race, has undergone a reversal of values. Effacing it used to be the only means of survival for the colonized and the exiled; naming it today often means declaring solidarity among the hyphenated people of the Diaspora... Identity is a way of re-departing. Rather, return to a denied heritage allows one to start again with different re-departures, different pauses, different arrivals.*
>
> —Trinh T. Minh-Ha[9]

Vestiges of War is borne of the heart and the mind that are often in conflict and sometimes in unison. At its core, it grew out of personal and professional experiences and out of the profound need to expose, and join together Filipino and Filipino

American histories, experiences, and critical cultural practices through the assemblage of artists, community activists, essayists, filmmakers, playwrights, poets, and scholars. This desire is deeply rooted in the quest to understand one's self in relation to an intricate and complicated matrix of social, cultural, and political structures and systems—not as separate generations, histories, experiences, peoples, and countries, but in direct relation to people spread across the globe who affect each other even if their paths never literally cross.

With migration, whether voluntary or forced, often come experiences and a web of complex emotions brought about by outsiderness, multiple identities, privileged mobility, displacement, and fleeting guilt. The romanticization and nostalgic imaginations of the American-born Filipino traveling to the Philippines are vastly different from those of the Philippine-born visiting or migrating to the United States. These differences, including curiosity and those of an economic nature, have largely to do with the reasons for movement in the first place. They are not simply questions of "home," racial/ethnic identity, or belonging somewhere that eventually become familiar. They are far more complex than this. There is, however, something difficult to name that joins these people together. Perhaps it is this feeling, however false it may actually be, that no matter where one settles, whether in the Philippines or the United States, that the person of Philippine descent assumes that she or he has a right to be there, wherever that "there" is. It is a dual sense of entitlement, but not necessarily one of citizenship or feeling as if one can claim to be a knowledgeable insider of the country or culture one is in. For both, it is a back-and-forth process in the mind and heart, and sometimes in the physical movement between the islands and the States. The people in these fixed and migratory spaces must come to peace with layers of internal and external forms of colonization that have become naturalized.

The narrator in Luis H. Francia's poem "A Manong Complains, as the Star-Spangled Banner is Played" recites "When my dark god comes/ When the sea spills out of the sky/ I'll be on a mountain of skulls/ Of those who christianized me/ Who english'd me/ Who split my speech and fed me/ The foul meat of false promise." The words of this Filipino old-timer, spoken through a Philippine-born American, echo across the decades, pulling the readers back to another forgotten era in Philippine-U.S. history. The young, mostly male Filipinos who sailed to the United States from the 1900s to the 1940s in ships named after U.S. presidents arrived in Hawaii, California, and the northwest regions in pursuit of a well-known dream. The urban and rural *manongs* and the few *manangs* experienced the hardships of survival, working in the fields and canneries, forming communities and re-creating cultural familiarity wherever they went. Others worked as houseboys, busboys, dishwashers, domestic helpers, ship and railway stewards. Unlike the other Asian groups, Filipinos had the right to migrate as colonial subjects, but like the Chinese, Japanese, Koreans, and Asian Indians, they were denied the right to buy land, to intermarry, and to become citizens.[10] The United States was not an extension of the Philippines, contrary to what they had grown up believing. "Who was betraying whom?"

Such distorted yet believable myths have also affected the American-born Filipinos who are minorities within a larger immigrant population of Filipino/Americans. They too, are betrayed by the allure of the American dream's attainability and by the naive belief that their lives are easier because they were born in the United States.

Alienation from their own cultural heritage, history, and knowledge about the relations between the Philippines and the United States often causes displacement, fragmentation, and an intense hunger to know more about who they are. Much to their surprise, their experiences, like the immigrant Filipino, are racialized as those of foreigners who speak really good English but are often perceived as not being "Asian" because of their westernization. *Dust Memories*, a poetic one-act play by Dionisio Velasco, embodies the bittersweet ambivalent temperament symbolic of the Filipino/American experience. A twenty-one-year-old Filipino-American filmmaker goes to a *manong* settlement in northern California to (re)claim his history by documenting their migrant stories in a rhapsodic monologue. Screening his newly shot film footage, the disappointed filmmaker says, "I've failed: the faces are dark, all you see is a collective silhouette, forms without detail or a definite shape. I look at this and it tells me nothing. I see nothing." The appearance of nothingness and silhouettes speak with contradictory clarity—the necessity of getting beneath the surface of events and characters, examining the details, and dispersing the knowledge.

For many Filipinos in the Philippines and in the United States, it is unfathomable that Filipinos and Filipino-Americans could be so ignorant of the Philippines, so Americanized, so indifferent, or so nationalistic at the same time. Sarita Echavez See's analysis of Ralph Peña's play *Flipzoids* in her essay "'An Open Wound'": Colonial Melancholia and Contemporary Filipino/American Texts," focuses on an examination of "melancholic jokes and imperial forgetting," emblematic of the unease Filipino/Americans experience in their constant search for something with which to identify. The characters in *Flipzoids* live in a contemporary, demystified America, surviving through self-deprecating humor. Conversely, novelist and play-wright Jessica Hagedorn exposes the internal forms of betrayal within a country and a family where the boundaries between familial ties, friendship, business, and politics blur with a stinging, ironic sense of humor. The scenes excerpted here from Hagedorn's play adaptation of her irreverent epic novel, *Dogeaters*, are set during the Marcos dictatorship era. The insidious nature of gossip, melodramatic indulgences, and duplicitous intrigues—all aspects of everyday Philippine life—are compressed in scenes between a television talk-show host and the first lady, two gossipy women, an opposition senator and his anxiety-filled beauty queen daughter, a radio soap opera, and in a golf game between an anti-Marcos senator and pro-Marcos associates. Contradictions abound and are no less difficult to confront than dual national ignorance and denial.

The differences between Filipinos and Filipino-Americans as well as within these groups, can be dividing. They can also converge in such spaces as the diaspora. Wigan Salazar sheds light on the little-known history of late nineteenth-century and early twentieth-century German life in the Philippines. Vicente Diaz deconstructs the word "Pappy," making personal and theoretical links to his upbringing in Guam, Filipino culture, and the Black South. The visual essays by Philippine-born artists Genara Banzon, Mariano del Rosario, and Christina Quisumbing Ramilo exemplify how they experience and create in the diaspora. Their diverse range of depictions challenge the reader to "read" their perspectives on Philippine heroes and revolution history, the collective effects of Spanish and American colonization, about the exportation of Filipino women's labor, and narratives of lesbian relationships in the Philippines.

If "identity is a way of re-departing," then naming oneself within an ethnic/racial diaspora also means to locate concretely how one is in solidarity with other people in these diasporic spaces. Rene Ontal's recounting of African-American soldier David Fagen's desertion from the U.S. Army to join the Filipino struggle for independence and the African-American responses to the Philippine-American War call important attention to an affinity of struggle across races often denied. Guillermo Gomez-Peña's performative texts draw out the connective nuances between two formerly colonized nations while focusing on Chicano experiences paralleling those of Filipino Americans treated as second-class citizens.[11] Paul Pfeiffer's image and text piece crosses the racialized boundaries of diaspora, theorizing about how marginalized people become "other," commodified, surveilled, and perceived as "evil" in words as well as in his own artworks reproduced here.

CREATING PRESENCE

Perhaps I will always have uncertain anxieties about colonialism, war, and the on-going cumulative effects unseen by the naked eye—whether it be the Philippine-American War, WWII in the Pacific, Korean and Vietnam Wars—contesting constructed and underrepresented histories and memories that they produce. Reconciling with the paradoxes of cultural visibility is a longer process that includes acknowledging and working with the slippage between truth, personal memory, and critically investigated documentation. Most Filipino-Americans interested in studying Philippine/Filipino-American history have had to engage, for the most part, in comparative studies within African, Caribbean, Latin, and Native American histories and cultures. This is because there is so little related scholarship available in the United States.[12] The exclusion of Filipino-Americans from political, academic, and cultural arenas led us to find ways to create presence for this absence in any way possible. I am fortunate to have been able to go to the Philippines to learn about the culture and history and to acquire the necessary books to conduct more in-depth studies. Nevertheless, this was part of the reason for the making of the *Vestiges of War* project.

The anthology as a whole is reflective of the coeditors' and contributors' processes—not just of remembering, recovering, reclaiming, representing, or re-examining, but also of politicizing and problematizing important events in the ongoing history of the Philippines and the United States. As is perhaps evident from the elliptical nature of this introduction, Luis H. Francia and I have faced many challenges along the way. At the top of the list was copublication in the Philippines and in the United States, outreaching to two interconnected yet divergent audiences. We risk printing much that Filipinos already know while enlightening an American readership. It is a risk we feel we need to take.

Through the conceptual design, visual essays, image and text pieces, and use of specific photographic images, we hope to further draw out the links across the sections which are contained here but whose issues are borderless. We have tried collaboratively with the contributors, publishers, and the book's designer, to create an anthology that breathes. We hope *Vestiges of War* will inspire others to embark on similar projects and expand on what we have tapped into in these pages.

CODA

March 7, 2002

It has been five months since the United States first began bombing Afghanistan in retaliation for the heinous terrorist attacks that occurred in New York City and Washington D.C. on September 11, 2001. My mother told me that she was having World War II nightmares again. I, on the other hand, immediately began to worry that the Philippines would become a part of this war against terrorism. Paranoia. Nationalism. Patriotism. These are what some people told me I was suffering from. I had this eerie gut feeling that history would come back in a different context, through another lens, because of circumstances in Mindanao, in Southeast and East Asia, and in the Middle East. These potentially connective links would be circular, subtle, and sometimes overt because the war(s) had not ended. The Philippines would resurface as a strategic location, this time for insuring global security and as an opportunity to rekindle U.S.-Philippines relations.

My airplane reading coming back to New York after spending the Christmas holidays in the Philippines confirmed my suspicions, but did not quite comfort my troubled mind and heart. The headlines of the January 15, 2002 *Philippine Daily Inquirer* read: "US troops to the rescue—Americans to participate in 6-12 month exercise." The color photograph was of a single file of Special Forces American soldiers moving in quick stride towards an awaiting U.S. Marines helicopter. On the left, stood the prominent figure of an American soldier with a camouflage painted face aiming what I think was a machine gun, in the direction of whom I don't know. A blurred figure next to him was squatting "ready, aim, fire." I couldn't see any recognizable Filipinos in the frame, just the top of a mountain peak in the distance. The article boasted that American and Filipino hostages taken by the Abu Sayyaf—suspected affiliates of the Al-Qaida and Osama bin Laden—would be freed and suggested that terrorism in the Asia/Pacific region would be eradicated. Knowledgeable journalists, government critics, and even President Arroyo herself say, however, that these ruffians from Mindanao are "bandits" and not terrorists. A lot remains to be seen.

As was true in the past, there are still many missing details and questions in need of investigation that remain largely absent in American media coverage. One hundred years after the official ending of the Philippine-American War, I am having another anxiety of memory. In my unease I recall lines from Mark Twain's journal, censored from publication during the Philippine-American War—"None but the dead have free speech. None but the dead are permitted to speak truth."[13]

As I write these sentences, *Vestiges of War* is finally about to go to press. It is our hope that the dead and those alive today will speak through this humble beginning.

NOTES:

Author's note: In 1997, Luis H. Francia invited me to collaborate with him on a film/video exhibition for the Guggenheim Museum in February 1999 called *Empire and Memory: Repercussions and Evocations of the 1899 Philippine-American War*. Around the same time, Jack Tchen, director of the Asian/Pacific/American Studies Program at New York University, gave me the opportunity to develop and coordinate a series of programs. The project consisted of public cultural events at the A/P/A Gallery and Joseph Papp's Public Theatre, a two-week conference at NYU, an art exhibition at the A/P/A Gallery which I co-curated with Didi Dee from Hiraya Gallery in Manila, and book-working sessions for the contributors attending the conference that took place in February-March 1999. Many of the participants, visual artists, and filmmakers in both exhibitions appear in this book as contributors. Other artists and essay contributors were later added to give the anthology even greater depth.

1. Marita Sturkin, *Tangled Memories: The Vietnam War, The Aids Epidemic, and The Politics of Remembering* (Los Angeles: University of California Press, 1997), 7. Milan Kundera, "Afterword: A Talk with the Author by Philip Roth" in *The Book of Laughter and Forgetting*, trans. Michael Henry Heim (New York: Penguin, 1980), 235.

2. Frantz Fanon's *Black Skin, White Masks*, trans. Charles Lam Markmann (New York: Grove Press, 1967) and Fanon's *The Wretched of the Earth: The Handbook for the Black Revolution That Is Changing the Shape of the World*, trans. Constance Farrington (New York: Grove Press, 1963). Some of the other early influences on my critical thinking about these issues in relation to my film/video projects were Edward Said's *Orientalism* (New York: Vintage Books, 1978); Benedict Anderson's *Imagined Communities: Reflections on the Origin and Spread of Nationalism* (New York: Verso Press, 1991); Gayatri Chakravorty Spivak's *The Post-Colonial Critic: Interviews, Strategies, Dialogues*, ed. Sarah Harasym (New York : Routledge, 1990); *Colonial Discourse and Post-Colonial Theory: A Reader*, eds. Patrick Williams and Laura Chrisman (New York: Columbia University Press, 1994); *Out There: Marginalization and Contemporary Cultures*, eds. Russell Ferguson, Martha Gever, Trinh T. Minh-Ha, and Cornel West (New York and Cambridge, Ma.: The New Museum of Contemporary Art and The MIT Press, 1990); Paulo Freire's *Pedagogy of the Oppressed*, trans. Myra Bergman Ramos (New York: Continuum, 1990); Trinh T. Minh-Ha's *Women, Native, Other: Writing Postcoloniality and Feminism* (Bloomington: Indiana University Press, 1989); and Trinh T. Minh-Ha, *When the Moon Waxes Red: Representation, Gender and Cultural Politics* (New York: Routledge, 1991); bell hooks, *Yearning: Race, Gender, and Cultural Politics* (Boston: South End Press, 1990) and bell hooks, *Black Looks: Race and Representation* (Boston: South End Press, 1992).

3. These are my descriptions of a range of photographs I saw in the files of the National Archives. The sources for these images came from records of the Office of the Chief Signal Officer List of Signal Corps. Albums, vol. 3 "Overseas Geographic File 1870-3055," DM. 2- Miscellaneous Collection, DM. 14- David L. Brainard Collection, DM. 20- Allen Webster Collection, DM. 21- John and Kate Evans Collection, and DM. 22- Charles N. Young Collection.

4. This movement was founded by the growing middle class made up of *ilustrados*, many of them the sons of wealthy and well-to-do Filipino families. Some of these young men migrated to Europe to study and organize politically. They were freer to meet, plan, and strategize than they had been in the Philippines. They initiated a campaign for reforms in the Spanish administration of the Philippines, and did not initially rally for independence when the 1896 Revolution broke out. It cannot be denied, however, that this movement influenced the leaders of the Katipunan and the Philippine Revolution. The reformists basically wanted the Philippines to become a province of Spain. They believed they would be better off if they were to become Spanish citizens so Filipinos could enjoy the right of and privileges of Spanish citizens. They thought they would be free of friarocracy and other Spanish authority abuses, and they wouldn't have to pay such unreasonable taxes. The reformists pushed for

Spanish assimilation. Those Filipinos who remained in the homeland secretly collaborated with those in Spain and founded nationalistic societies. For more information on the Propaganda/Reform Movement, see Teodoro A. Agoncillo, *History of the Filipino People* (Manila: R. P. Garcia Publishing Co., 1990); John N. Schumacher, S.J., *The Propaganda Movement: 1880-1895* (Quezon City, Phlippines: Ateneo de Manila University Press, 1997); and Renato Constantino, *The Philippines: A Past Revisited* (Manila: Renato Constantino, 1975).

5. For a deep critical reading of the Revolution, the betrayal of revolutionary leader Andres Bonifacio in relation to Philippine nationhood, see Reynaldo Ileto's essays, "The 'Unfinished Revolution' in Political Discourse" and "History and Criticism: The Invention of Heroes" in *Filipinos and their Revolution: Event, Discourse, and Historiography* (Quezon City, Philippines: Ateneo de Manila University Press, 1998) and Constantino, *The Philippines: A Past Revisited* (Manila: Renato Constantino, 1975) Vol.1(pre-Spanish 1941). I am indebted to historians Renato Constantino, Reynaldo Ileto, and Ambeth Ocampo, whose works have inspired much of my own theorizing about this history.

6. "Benevolent Assimilation Proclamation" by William McKinley (21 December 1898) in James H. Blount, *The American Occupation of the Philippines, 1898-1912* (New York: G. P. Putnam's Sons, 1913); available from Jim Zwick's Web site: http//www.boondocksnet.com/ (Sentenaryo/Centennial section).

7. See the three essays in Reynaldo C. Ileto's *Knowing of America's Colony: A Hundred Years from the Philippine War* (Philippine Studies Occasional Papers Series no. 13, Center For Philippine Studies School of Hawaiian, Asian and Pacific Studies, University of Hawai'i at Manoa, 1999) for more in-depth critical analyses of the effects of American colonial education and on American colonial discourses on Philippine Politics.

8. Henry Giroux, "Animating Youth: The Disneyfication of Children's Culture," *Fugitive Cultures: Race, Violence & Youth* (New York: Routledge, 1996), 89-113. Giroux analyzes the detrimental impact of Disney animation films and their character products on children's learning and on the shaping of their sense of values and ideals. Disney characters like Mickey Mouse, Donald Duck and the narratives in Disney-produced films like *Beauty and the Beast, Little Mermaid, Pocahontas,* and *The Jungle Book* take on other meanings when examined in the context of American cultural imperialism in the Philippines. In a country where these films are popularly viewed and their products blatantly adored, a closer look at the impact of "Disneyfication" on Philippine children's culture would be a worthwhile future study in order to gain a better understanding of the complicated mechanisms of (neo) colonial mentalities. Such films and the products they spawn clearly deter the Philippine film and television industries from producing more Filipino-animated narratives, as well as profiting from locally made toys, furthermore, they also present obstacles in teaching and learning.

9. Minh-Ha, *Moon Waxes Red*, 14.

10. For more information about the early migration and labor history of Filipinos in the United States, see Fred Cordova, *Filipinos: The Forgotten Asian-Americans, A Pictorial Essay, 1763-1963* (Dubuque, Iowa: Kendall/Hunt Publishing, 1983); Roberto V. Vallangca, *Pinoy: The First Wave, 1898-1941* (San Francisco: Strawberry Hill Press, 1977); Caridad Concepcion Vallangca, *The Second Wave: Pinay and Pinoy, 1945-1965* (San Francisco: Strawberry Hill Press, 1987); Craig Sharlin and Lilia V. Villanueva, *Philip Vera Cruz: A Personal History of Filipino Immigrants and the Farmworkers Movement* (Los Angeles: UCLA Labor Center, Institute of Labor Relations and UCLA Asian-American Studies Center, 1992); Marina E. Espina, *Filipinos in Louisiana* (New Orleans: A. F. Laborde & Sons, 1988); Marina Feleo-Gonzalez, *A Song For Manong* (Daly City, Ca: Likha Promotions, 1988); Yen Le Espiritu, *Filipino-American Lives* (Philadelphia, Pa.: Temple University Press, 1995); and Robert N. Anderson, *Filipinos in Rural Hawaii* (Honolulu: University of Hawai'i Press, 1984). For comparative Filipino-American history within a pan-Asian-American history see Ronald Takaki, *Strangers From A Different Shore: A History of Asian Americans* (New York: Penguin Books, 1989) and for specific Filipino migrant history, "Dollar A Day, Dime A Dance: The Forgotten Filipinos," and

Sucheng Chan, *Asian-Americans: An Interpretive History* (Boston: Twayne Publishers, 1991).

11. The fact that Spain governed the Philippines through Mexico points to the hierarchy of how Spain ruled in its colonies. Mexican and Philippine history intertwine not only through government, similarities in colonial implementation, although there are also some very real differences, but also in terms of Mexican/Chicano-Filipino American labor and migrant history.

12. This is not to suggest that no one is writing critically about Philippine and Filipino-American history in the United States. There are. Here are some of the books and essays I've happily come across specifically on the Philippine-American War, U.S. colonialism, and Philippine-U.S. relations: Stuart Creighton Miller, *Benevolent Assimilation: The American Conquest of the Philippines, 1899-1903* (New Haven, Conn.: Yale University Press, 1982); Leon Wolff, *Little Brown Brother: How the United States Purchased and Pacified the Philippines* (New York: Oxford University Press, 1991); Daniel B. Schirmer, *Republic or Empire: American Resistance to the Philippine War* (Cambridge, Mass: Schenkman Publishing Co., 1972); *Mark Twain's Weapons of Satire: Anti-Imperialist Writings on the Philippine-American War*, ed. Jim Zwick (Syracuse: Syracuse University Press, 1992); Daniel B. Schirmer and Stephen R. Shalom, eds., *The Philippines Reader: A History of Colonialism, Neo-colonialism, Dictatorship, and Resistance* (Boston: South End Press, 1987); Vicente L. Rafael, *Discrepant Histories: Translocal Essays on Filipino Cultures* (Pasig City, Philippines: Anvil Publishing, 1995); Vicente L. Rafael, *White Love and other Events in Filipino History* (Duke University Press, 2000); Stanley Karnow, *In Our Image: America's Empire in the Philippines* (New York: Ballantine Books, 1989); Howard Zinn, "The Empire and the People," *A People's History of the United States* (New York: Harper Perennial, 1990), 290-313; and Robert G. Lee, "Inner Dikes and Barred Zone," *Orientals: Asian-Americans in Popular Culture* (Philadelphia, Pa.: Temple University Press, 1999), 10-113. See also Amy Kaplan and Donald E. Pease, eds., *Cultures of United States Imperialism*, (Durham, N.C.: Duke University Press, 1993); and Lisa Lowe and David Lloyd, eds., *The Politics of Culture in the Shadow of Capital*, (Durham, N.C.: Duke University Press, 1997).

13. *Mark Twain's Weapons of Satire: Anti-Imperialist Writings on the Philippine-American War*, ed. Jim Zwick (Syracuse: Syracuse Univerity Press, 1992), excerpted from the chapter "Patriotic America" p. 162.

The Rind of Things

LUIS H. FRANCIA

IN THE BELLY OF THE BEAST

In 1970 as a Filipino new to the United States (though the United States was not new to me), new to New York City, I was very much in awe of a much-storied metropolis and the glorious traditions that it and the country represented. My arrival however coincided with newspapers and television screens filled with images of dead young American men in body bags, of Vietnamese cities under siege, and of massive protests in the U.S. and elsewhere against American involvement in the quagmire that was Vietnam. The passion and controversy generated by that war in Southeast Asia was especially brought home to me the day that I witnessed the well-publicized beating of antiwar protesters by hard hats in lower Manhattan. The sight of burly construction workers—many with pins declaring "America: Love It or Leave It"—roughing up young people, people my age, horrified me. I found myself asking, what happened to the notion of free speech and the right to peaceful protest, in a land that kept proclaiming itself the vanguard of democracy? And why was this war causing such pain and deep division all across America?

In Manila, it astounds me now to think, I had been largely indifferent to the war—if pushed hard enough I probably would have uttered some meaningless platitude about how its involvement in Vietnam exemplified, albeit paradoxically, America's commitment to democracy. But in Manhattan I could hardly afford the luxury of detachment: thanks to my mother, I was a citizen of the empire, draftable and hence potential fodder for this Pentagon-sponsored madness. What saved me ultimately was my high lottery number. Winding up as a grunt in Southeast Asia would have been cruelly ironic: having travelled across the Pacific only to recross it and fight an enemy with whom, like Muhammad Ali, I had no quarrel, with whom in fact I had more in common than my nominal, would-be comrades-in-arms.

At that time I had little interest in, and knowledge of, America's violent takeover and colonization of a newly emergent Philippine republic at the turn of the twentieth century, even though (or perhaps because of) in 1898 my *lolo*, my maternal grand-father, Henry Joseph Hunt, an *Amerikano* from the city of brotherly love, Philadelphia, had gone over as a soldier in a duplicitous army, and who may have traded shots with forebears on my father's side. Having seen action in Cuba he no longer was a raw recruit by the time he was shipped to Manila. He may have even killed some of those "damn insurrectos," as the Filipino revolutionaries were dismissively referred to at the time. In what I like to think of as a redemptive act, he wound up marrying the enemy, my *Lola* Agatona (whose mother refused to attend the wedding), and spent the rest of his life in the islands.

And so my family's history is emblematic, in so many ways, of two countries' star-crossed destinies—three, when one includes, as one must, Imperial Spain. Yet growing up I was barely cognizant of such confluences. Spain was all around me and in me, in the blood, in the medieval Catholic faith I grew up in, in the names we baptized ourselves with, in the Tagalog we spoke with its appropriated Castilian. Like a properly colonial and privileged subject I had no wish then to peer too closely at the underpinnings of that privilege or at a bowdlerized history. I knew something about our colonial past but that was no thanks to my university education, truly a sentimental one, concentrating as it did on the treasures of Western art and philosophy. I learned about the Magna Carta and the U.S. Civil War but not about the Malolos Republic or, say, about British rule in India. My peers and I read the English Romantics and engaged in exegeses of Kierkegaard and Heidegger. But where were Rizal's novels? Where were other Asian writers and our homegrown novelists, dramatists, and poets? The Philippines, much less Asia, rarely intruded into classrooms, possessing only a shadow reality. What shaped the knowledge thrust at us had more to do, as Foucault once pointed out, with relations of power rather than meaning. The question of how a young republic had sprung into existence only to see its independence quickly curtailed was never addressed. It was an area of darkness the curriculum shied away from. But America's continuing war on the Vietnamese quickly undermined my blithe disregard for my own history.

A blithe disregard, I might add, that arose partly from the fact that I grew up simply trusting the movies. John Wayne the Magnificent embodied America. If America and Wayne as the gung-ho soldier with a heart of gold were in Vietnam, as they were in the Philippines, why, there must be a damn good reason![1] He was there of course for no good reason, just as during the 1899 War men like Col. Frederick Funston and generals Arthur Bell and "Howling Jake" Smith were in the archipelago for no good reason: to make sure that beneath the velvety benediction of Benevolent Assimilation Filipinos felt its spiked fists.

Exposed in New York to perspectives completely different from those espoused by pro-American papers in Manila and the Marcos regime[2] I came to realize quickly enough not only how wrong and immoral the Vietnam War was, but how equally wrong and immoral its predecessor, with which it had many remarkable parallels and without which America's agonizing dilemma in Vietnam may never have occurred: the 1899 Philippine-American War. In my belated recognition was a clear case of the tail wagging the dog.

The interaction across the decades, between the Vietnam of the 1960s and '70s and the Philippines at the beginning of the twentieth century, with the United States as the common link, revealed how such categories as "past" and "present" were simply inadequate in encompassing the full range and depth of the ever-evolving narratives of three countries, with the "past" a convenient collection of musty relics, best set aside. It however made more sense to imagine time and its contents as a river of DNA coursing through and indelibly imprinted on our quotidian lives: the past as always present, the present as always past. Only from this perspective could the hybrid, labyrinthine Filipino and Filipino-American identity start to be understood. And only then would exploring—and deciphering—colonial histories acquire an urgency.

From that perspective then, every story points to other stories, and forgetting or ignoring one greatly increases the risk of misreading all the others: the American war on the Philippines presaging the Vietnam and Korean wars—as well as U.S. intervention in countries like the Dominican Republic in 1916 and Grenada in 1983—itself foretold by chronicles of slavery, the genocidal campaigns against Native Americans, and the annexation of Mexican territories in the enlargement of frontiers (and all with the remarkably consistent views of peoples of color as, variously, "niggers," "savages," and "gooks"). All these wars heralded the American Century with its two-headed offspring, industrial capitalism, and military hegemony.

The 1899 War then marks the leap of a fledgling empire to the Asia Pacific region. How convenient (and necessary) that it be forgotten for the sake of upholding the self-spun myth of a freedom-defending giant! Here is a war that lasted for a decade, cost so much more money and lives than the 1898 Spanish-American War, reduced in scale and intensity to a nonevent.[3] Such has been the fervent aim of a nation of apologists (including not a few scholars whose allegiance seems more to preserving America's aw-shucks good-guy image rather than to the facts). As Alfrredo Navarro Salanga so eloquently and caustically puts it in his "A Philippine History Lesson"—a poem that leads off this book—"We've been bitten off, excised/ from the rind of things."

Spurred on by the rise in 1972 of repressive rule in Manila and Washington's generous support of a tyrannical Marcos, I kept glimpsing the dark contradictions of a seemingly exemplary paradigm—that of a colony's smooth transition to democracy under American tutelage. But an expensive colonial education had done its job well, for a persistent inner voice kept uttering its disbelief that America could be less than benevolent. Not only was American goodwill assumed to be a self-evident truth, it was also the often reiterated premise of a Philippine society whose relationship to America even in a new era rested firmly in the neocolonial mold. The Philippines may have had its independence restored in 1946, but by then its leaders were indeed America's dutiful little brown brothers, its white oppressors transformed into saviors.

SEEN, YET NOT-SEEN

Every year, in a seminar I teach on Asian-American literature, as part of contextual backgrounding to the works of Filipino-American writers, I ask my students if they had ever heard of a war between the Philippines and the U.S. Two, at most three, hands (invariably belonging to Filipino-Americans) are raised, while the curious rest shake their heads. This simple fact attests to the near-absence of the war in U.S. official narratives and forms part of the mantle of invisibility that shrouds Filipinos and Filipino-Americans—an invisibility that unmoors and renders them contextless. It has been said often enough that Americans are in love with the present, fetishizing it not in any mystic-like sense of being here now, but out of fear of seeing the past gaining. They may suddenly realize the Filipino is *here* because they were *there*. This infatuation with ahistoricity has engendered a habit on my part of random cullings from different events and sources, filed in my mental archives over the years, to illustrate how pernicious and insistent such ahistoricity is—the treacherous, instinctive resistance of a society that wishes to see only the rosy hues of a bigger, better, brighter future.

Let me briefly cite three such items—all commonplace artifacts of late-twentieth- and early-twenty-first-century contemporary pop culture, all disconcertingly, simultaneously, funny and sad. In one, the gameshow *Jeopardy*, a question makes me lean forward: what islands in Asia did the United States win after defeating Spain in the 1898 Spanish-American War? I don't think any of the three contestants, two young men and a woman, know the answer but in fact one of the men does. The question resonated with comic irony, for, like late-model cars and vacations in Hawaii given away by shows like *Jeopardy*, imperial domains were simply recast as prizes to be sought. [4]

In the second, a turn-of-the-century photograph in *Century*—a massive coffee-table tome detailing in photographs a hundred years of American history—depicts a row of nine U.S. soldiers, raincoated and rifles in hand, a thatch hut and tropical foliage in the background.[5] The caption reads: "The presence of American troops in the Philippines foreshadows their future close involvement in the Far East." The innocuous language glosses over a bloody war; at the same time it raises inconvenient questions such as, where are the native bodies? There's that hut: are they in it, alive but afraid, or dead and no longer bound by fear? What the soldiers foreshadow is themselves, a murderous future already present in their very appearance. Even the benign, reductive "close involvement" alludes to later wars with Japan, Korea, and Vietnam, eliding the terrible costs of that involvement.

In the third, in early 1999, as part of the tail-end centennial celebrations of the Philippine declaration of independence, the Leyte Dance Troupe ends its program in downtown Manhattan with a virtuoso ensemble number where the dancers swirl various Katipunan flags and conclude with the Philippine national anthem, causing nationalist pride to ripple through the packed house. Then an odd thing happens: after a pause, the dancers commence singing "America the Beautiful."

I look on in disbelief. To commemorate the struggle for independence, then end on a paean to the very country that had aborted it! At that moment the whole troupe, along with a far more complex history tantalizingly glimpsed, had stepped back from an opening, sinking into the familiar embrace of anonymity. Seen, yet not-seen: the infuriating paradox of the Other. The mixed signals encoded in a heartfelt display excluded history, and symbolized an altogether depressing exercise in Pavlovian forgetting.

Seen, yet Not-Seen. Thus are a whole country, a whole history, and Filipino-Americans *desaparecido*, or in the '70s parlance of Marcos's martial-law era, "salvaged"—done in by death squads. Surely there's a crime here. But if a corpse does not exist, where's the crime? But we can speak, can we not, as James Baldwin does in *The Fire Next Time*, of "the crime of innocence"? Such "innocence" denies a people an identity, a history, even a pulse. *Seen, yet Not-Seen.* Can a nation absent from its own telling just be "gifted" with one, albeit as a kind of Trojan Horse? For what we have and continue to see are white narratives in brownface.

In truth, Filipinos have always raised their voices. But who has been listening? Whether we scream, whisper, admonish, orate, create, or write, we seem to do so from some distant star, hopeful that the signals we send impinge on some other civilization. A little more than a hundred years from the War, the Filipino/a is still rather like Chang, the displaced mestizo-Chinese father in *A Feather on the Breath of God*, Sigrid Nuñez's lyrical novel: "Not as one who would not speak but as one to whom no one would listen."[6]

ENLARGING THE BATTLEFIELD

From 1992 to 1998 commemorations (often tagged as "celebrations") of the different signal events of the nineteenth century took place in the Philippines, the U.S., and elsewhere; they form part of the matrix from which *Vestiges of War: The Philippine-American War and the Aftermath of an Imperial Dream, 1899-1999* arises. In a significant act of omission linking it to the dance troupe mentioned earlier, the Philippine government failed to mark the centennial of the 1899 War. What was abundantly clear in all the hoopla was the implied wish that one hundred years of independence be celebrated rather than just its declaration. That, and the desire on the part of the National Centennial Commission, the government body overseeing the celebrations, to have Tom Cruise play Dr. José Rizal in a feature film!

Oddly enough, one place where such a commemoration took place was at Manhattan's Solomon R. Guggenheim Museum. I was able, on the invitation and encouragement of John Hanhardt, its Senior Curator for Film and Media Arts, to put on a four-week program of films and videos, in February of 1999—a program for which I enlisted as my cocurator Angel Velasco Shaw (and who subsequently asked me to coedit this book). Titled "Empire and Memory: Repercussions and Evocations of the 1899 Philippine-American War," the program, like this book, was meant to not just view the war as historical artifact but examine its aftermath as the dominant subtext for contemporary perspectives in Filipino and Filipino-American affairs.[7]

The ideological continuum spanned in "Empire and Memory" stretched all the way from the white man's burden heroically shouldered by Gary Cooper and David Niven in the 1939 Hollywood feature *The Real Glory*, with its Orientalist tenor, to the quirky reimagining and critique of the 1904 St. Louis World's Fair in Marlon Fuentes's 1995 *Bontoc Eulogy*. The Guggenheim exhibition in part documented the colonizing gaze, the use of the camera as a genocidal weapon—a function and consequence Nick Deocampo investigates in his essay here, "Imperialist Fictions: the Filipino in the Imperialist Imaginary." The exhibition also revealed how war affects a whole society, and does not end simply because treaties are signed and armed hostilities cease. In the epilogue to his book, *The War Against the Americans: Resistance and Collaboration in Cebu, 1899-1906* (here reprinted as "The Hills Are Still There"), Resil Mojares points out that the war "assumes other forms, becomes an illusion of itself, a subversion of what it intends."[8] *Vestiges of War* continues to explore that premise, reframing not just the war but more significantly the war without bullets that goes on in classrooms, in literature, in the media, in popular culture— wherever the many pseudo- or incomplete assumptions about the War, about the history of Filipinos, their context, their ambivalent and often contradictory relationships with the United States, with the West, are accepted as self-evident truths.

By enlarging the battlefield, as it were, we begin to notice the multitude and variety of eloquent and subversive "weaponry." Thus, the range of works here, by a diverse group that includes not just scholars but poets, novelists, playwrights, visual artists, filmmakers, and community activists. In a war determined by aggressive colonial desire, and followed by occupation, the essence of a relationship that ensues—born out of conflict and the incommensurability of individual lives and nationalist aspirations with grand imperial ambition—cannot be grasped without an understanding of its human and psychic face.

The book considers socio/political/cultural dimensions—passed down not just by the War but by the weight of four hundred years of Spanish and American colonialism—in Filipino and Filipino-American communities, as well as in the ways Filipinos and Americans regard each other. When Doreen Fernandez in her "Food and War" reads Filipino cuisine as a multicultural text that distills various influences into a menu of a hybrid present; when Eric Gamalinda probes the condition of English in the Philippines in his wittily titled "English Is Your Mother Tongue/Ang Ingles Ay Tongue ng Ina Mo"; when Vicente Rafael provocatively notes the wry ironies and contradictions of the thoroughly conventional Philippine government celebration of 1898 in his "Parricides, Bastards, and Counterrevolution: Reflections on the Philippine Centennial"; when photographer Emilio Ganot frames his fellow expatriates in Austria in the melancholy embrace of the idea of "Home"; when artists such as the late Robert Villanueva (re)view modernity from a Cordilleran vantage point, and Christina Quisumbing considers the position, displacement, and queerness of today's Filipina in the diaspora—all engage in a necessary appraisal of our current condition: our intense, and intensely subjective, place in the world.

This book continues the process both of deconstruction and decolonization, in the spirit of the late nationalist historian Renato Constantino, who delineated quite accurately the imperative for doing so in his classic essay "The Miseducation of the Filipino" (reprinted here). I see another enlargement: the inclusion of the miseducated American, who at best has vague notions of his or her relationship vis-á-vis Filipinos. If he or she thinks of it at all, it's warm and fuzzy: legions of U.S. pooh-bahs have invariably invoked the deceptive label "special" in discussing that relationship, a word that at once absolves the sins inflicted on an emergent republic and elevates an erstwhile oppressor to privileged status.

Tellingly, a central figure in this so-called "special" relationship has been the American soldier—hardly a symbol of peace but historically entrusted to carry on "the charge of national symbolism and kinship," as Oscar Campomanes notes in his contribution here, "Casualty Figures of the American Soldier and the Other: Post-1899 Allegories of Imperial Nation-Building as 'Love and War'." By the end of World War II, in the eyes of the Filipino, he had been transformed from occupier to "liberator"—a metamorphosis looked at by Bienvenido Lumbera in "From Colonizer to Liberator: How U.S. Colonialism Succeeded in Reinventing Itself After the Pacific War." Arguably, in fact, the American GI has been the cornerstone of U.S. ties to Asian countries like Korea and Vietnam. (Linkages to these countries, cast as personal stories, are examined in this book's "Kindred Distance" by Yong Soon Min and "The Hairy Hand" by Nguyen Qui Duc.)

It may have seemed, with the 1991 rejection by the Philippine Senate of the bases treaty with the United States, that the deployment of the U.S. soldier as a leitmotif in the relationship between the two countries had ended. But in line with the U.S. maintaining its superpower status, that proved to be a temporary hiatus. The Visiting

Forces Agreement(VFA), forged in 1998 between the two governments, gives U.S. warships and troops access to Philippine ports—a deal Daniel Boone Schirmer connects to a dubious tradition of American hegemony in his essay here, "U.S. Racism and Intervention in the Third World, Past and Present."

In 2002, in the aftermath of the 9/11 tragedy, President Arroyo has invoked the VFA and the Mutual Defense Treaty to invite U.S. troops to help fight the Abu Sayyaf—a Mindanao gang that may have had ties to Al Qaeda but is now a kidnap-for-ransom outfit. The Philippine government and the Bush administration are using the so-called "global war on terrorism" as a Trojan horse, pushing their own agendas. Malacañang has offered another front in exchange for U.S. aid, which all but dried up with the 1991 rejection of the bases treaty. Washington sees the gang as an easy target, a possible opening for the Pentagon to regain control of the bases. D'Asia vu. Clearly, soldiers—old or not—never die; nor do they just fade away. With the complicity of Manila, they simply stay.

AGAINST THE DYING OF THE LIGHT

Is this book partisan? How can it not be? To acknowledge that the U.S. occupation of the Philippines was immoral and illegal right from the very beginning implies the necessary refusal to be silent about it (spurning thus the role of victim, rather than harping on it, as many are wont to interpret such truth-telling). It is simultaneously to resist the tremendous pressure to let the war go quietly into that Dylanesque good night, to instead "rage against the dying of the light." Above all, *Vestiges* is a multilayered act of resistance, that remembers, reimagines, and reinserts the War and its aftermath as a drama still playing out, this time with the Filipino/Filipino-American fullfleshed, onstage, onscreen, on the page.

Some may think resistance and scholarship incompatible, that scholarship must be unencumbered by politics or social realities, or any other agenda, except to tell like it is or was—though "objectivity" invariably acts as a synonym for insidious subjectivity. Having experienced institutional ignorance and racism first-hand; having read and learned from such scholars as Frantz Fanon, Edward Said, and Reynaldo Ileto; having contemplated and been moved by the writings of Pablo Neruda, James Baldwin, Mahmoud Darwish, and Emmanuel Lacaba; having seen (and continuing to see) America's obsessive paranoia—witness its irrational fixation on a missile-defense shield—and self-appointed role as global policeman and arbiter of human rights, I can only say that such a view is not merely anemic and irrelevant, it is indicative of a deeply rooted sense of denial.

The book I hope unsettles many readers, for its partisanship towards a fuller understanding of why precisely America came to figure so prominently in the lives of Filipinos—in their waking hours, their dreams and nightmares—over the last century. As for myself, I am inexorably motivated not just by the profound intersections between personal and public histories but by the desire—and the obligation—to see that the truths pointed to by this book endure, to more fully understand the milieu and history I find myself simultaneously burdened and blessed with. And so *Vestiges of War* is partisan in the way survivors are partisan, thankful they are alive, taking steps to assure not only that they continue, but that their stories blossom into vigilant insight and mercy.

And when we speak we are afraid
Our words will not be heard or welcomed
But when we are silent we are still afraid.
So it is better to speak remembering
We were never meant to survive.

        —Audre Lorde, from "A Litany of Survival"

NOTES:

1. I mean only that Wayne (1906-79) had been in the Philippines cinematically, in *They Were Expendable* and *Back to Bataan*, 1945 World War II films set in the Philippines. In the latter, Wayne leads the Filipino and American underground resistance to the Japanese. The ideologically curious screenplay has a guerrilla leader named Andres Bonifacio, an ironic nod to and dubious co-optation of nationialist aspirations. And the soundtrack mixes in the strains of the Philippine national anthem that would have in earlier times summoned Filipinos to fight American adventurers.

2. Marcos, with U.S. financing and eager to show his anti-Communist sympathies, authorized the sending of Philcag, a noncombatant unit of army engineers, to Vietnam in 1967, later expanded to five construction battalions.

3. And it was. In the Military Records Bureau of the National Archives in Washington, the War has been demoted to the footnote status of "the Philippine Insurrection." And yet, as Oscar Campomanes points out in his essay published in this anthology, the War saw the cumulative deployment of 126,000 men, cost $600 million, and entailed pension costs of $8 billion.

4. The price paid the Spanish for the archipelago, $20 million, as agreed-to in the 1898 Treaty of Paris, came to about $3 per Filipino, based on an estimated 7 million population, though not near enough to preserve the rights to life, liberty, and the pursuit of happiness, of between 250,000 and a million mostly civilian casualties. Applying the same ratio to the 2000 U.S. population of 290 million, the casualties would have been between an almost unimaginable 10 million and 40 million.

5. Bruce Bernard, ed., *Century* (New York and London: Phaidon Publishing, 1999), 19.

6. Sigrid Nuñez, *A Feather on the Breath of God* (New York: HarperPerennial, 1996), 22.

7. L. H. Francia, "Rising from the Trenches," program essay for "Empire and Memory," the Solomon Guggenheim Museum, Feb. 17-Mar.13, 1999. At the end of the 1980s, when the many thoughts I had on the War started to coalesce around tangible projects (one of which was to write a nonfiction book on the War, focused on my grandfathers) such as the program that eventually became "Empire and Memory," I had wanted the exhibition to include a set of essays in booklet form. Later Angel Velasco Shaw and I toyed with the notion of including films on Vietnam that had been shot in the Philippines—essentially to link the countries' violent experiences with the United States, and to point out how an Asian country that had once been invaded by U.S. troops was now being used to re-create conditions of another Asian country undergoing a similar conflict—Francis Ford Coppola's *Apocalypse Now* being a prime example. But format and budget limitations prevented such options.

8. Resil Mojares, *The War Against the Americans: Resistance and Collaboration in Cebu, 1899-1906* (Quezon City: Ateneo de Manila University Press, 1999), 205

The Object of Colonial Desire

A Philippine History Lesson

ALFRREDO NAVARRO SALANGA

It's history that
moves us away
from what we are

We call it names
assign it origins
and blame the might

That made Spain right
and America — bite.

This is what it amounts to:
we've been bitten off, excised
from the rind of things.

What once gave us pulp
has been chewed off
and pitted — dry.

The Philippine-American War: Friendship and Forgetting

REYNALDO C. ILETO

The 1899 Philippine-American War is not the sort of topic the Filipino public likes to talk about. To imagine Filipinos warring with Americans simply contradicts the dominant tropes of the Philippine-American relationship. In popular, and to some extent, official discourse as well, the Philippine-American relationship has been a special one, expressed in kinship terms like "compadre colonialism" and "little brown brother." "Mother America" is owed a lifelong inner debt, or *utang na loób*, by the Filipino people she nurtured.

Why is it so difficult to speak of the relationship in terms such as invasion, resistance (so readily applied to the Japanese in World War II), war, combat, colonialism, exploitation, discrimination? There are a number of explanations for this attitude, but from a historian's perspective the "problem" persists mainly because a special relationship with America has become an intrinsic part of the history of the Filipino nation-state's emergence and development. The recent Philippine centennial celebrations of the revolution against Spain in 1896 and the birth of the republic in 1898 show quite clearly how a war with the United States simply does not fit into the historical trajectory from colonialism to independence, tradition to modernity.[1] The goals of the *ilustrado* leaders of the 1898 revolution *were* apparently fulfilled through U.S. intervention. The repressive, anti-liberal regime of the Spanish friars *was* apparently replaced by U.S. tutelage towards eventual self-rule. Good government was established in Taft's New Era. By the time of Gov. Francis Burton Harrison's policy of Filipinizing the bureaucracy, and the passage of the Jones Bill promising eventual independence, it looked like the goals of the 1898 revolution were within reach through peaceful means rather than war.

In the context of an emancipatory history of the twentieth century, a history of forward movement from what was pictured as Spanish medievalism toward a modern nation-state *via* an enlightened U.S. colonial regime, is it any surprise that the Philippine-American War became somewhat of a nonevent, a glitch in an otherwise smooth progression?

The Philippine-American War broke out when the U.S. Army moved to take possession, in February 1899, of the territory it had procured from Spain two months earlier. The Filipino republican army fought a defensive war for the next three years. If successful, this action would have been taken as a demonstration of the nation-state's maturity. But, as we all know, it failed. The poorly trained and underequipped Filipino army was repeatedly beaten in setpiece battles, so that by late 1900 it had to shift to guerrilla warfare. By May 1901, Gen. Emilio Aguinaldo and most of the top brass of the army either had been captured or had heeded Aguinaldo's call to surrender and take the oath of allegiance to the United States. By May of the following year, 1902, Gen. Miguel Malvar and the rest of the army command in southern Tagalog, Ilocos, and Samar had surrendered.

From *Harper's History of War in the Philippines*

The process of turning the war into a nonevent began immediately after the official end of the war on 4 July 1902. In the earliest textbooks written for the newly opened public high schools, the revolution of 1896-98 and the Philippine-American War were clearly differentiated. American educators encouraged Filipinos to remember 1896-1898 as the time when Filipinos, inspired by the *ilustrados*, rose against their feudalistic colonial ruler, Spain. The 1898 republic was represented as the high point of Filipino development. It was also disparaged, however, as lacking in maturity. The U.S. takeover was deemed inevitable because the revolution, to paraphrase James Leroy, was led not by genuine revolutionaries but by local bosses or *caciques*; furthermore, U.S. observers liked to emphasize, the government and citizens alike had clashing views about what independence really meant. The most glaring evidence of lack was no less than the republican

Col. Cornelius Gardener, first colonial governor of Tayabas

government's resistance to U.S. occupation— the war itself. As textbook writer Barrows put it, the war (or rather, insurrection) was a great misunderstanding. If Aguinaldo and his generals had been mature or intelligent enough to understand the intentions of the United States (which was to help the Filipinos complete their revolution under their tutelage), they would not have put up a resistance.[2]

In short, the generations of Filipinos who learned their Philippine history in American colonial schools did not see the war as the U.S. suppression of their cherished revolutionary and nationalist dreams. Instead it was more of a misguided, even stupid, rejection of a gift of further enlightenment. The fact that many Filipino officers who had fought against the Americans came to hold public office under colonial rule, only reinforced the view that the war of resistance was a waste of effort, an event that was best forgotten.

On the American side, the myth generally persists that there was merely a "Spanish-American War" in 1898 which almost magically landed the Philippines on Uncle Sam's lap after some treaty in Paris and the payment of a check to Spain. Filipino resistance was termed an "insurrection" against duly constituted authority.

By 1902, any further resistance was termed *ladronism*, or banditry. Perhaps the myth of a "splendid little war" persists because it helps to conceal a profound contradiction. One of the senior officers in the Schwan expedition that invaded southern Luzon in early 1900 was Col. Cornelius Gardener, commanding the Thirtieth Infantry of U.S. Volunteers.[3] Gardener was no ordinary participant in these events. In a year's time, when it was thought that Tayabas had been "pacified," he would be appointed the first colonial governor of the province. A liberal and reformer, he also sympathized with the goals of his nationalist "enemy," reminding us that there were anti-imperialists even among the American troops. Gardener's private correspondence reveals the extent to which official justifications for the takeover of the islands had been internalized by members of the U.S. Army.[4]

Even as he was leading a regiment invading Tagalog towns in February 1900, Colonel Gardener was trying to clear his conscience. Something was not right when they were opposing a people whose goal was familiar to any American who knew his history. "Let us guarantee independence to Luzon," he wrote to his fellow libertarian, Governor Pingree of Michigan, for it is "in every way capable of self government... We then wait till the rest of the islands are more or less civilized." After granting independence, "let us apply the Monroe doctrine to the entire Philippine archipelago and say to the nations of Europe *hands off, this is our foster-child, a republic in Asiatic waters*. Let us become a leaven to overcome tyrants and monarchs in the orient, this our children will be more proud of than the role we are now playing." These words clearly echo the pronouncements of President McKinley and Philippine Commission Chief Schurman; these were the official, moral, and paternalistic justifications of the Philippine war.

Having engaged the Filipino revolutionaries in battle and tested their resolve, Gardener was sensitive to the ironies of the U.S. position: "When Spanish power was crumbling, when [the Filipinos] had taken prisoner every Spanish soldier on all these Islands, except Manila and one other place, there came a stronger power with limitless wealth to take Spain's place and undo all that had been done for independence. The thousands and tens of thousands who died for ultimate Filipino independence they now believe 'to have died in vain.'"

The remembering of a gruesome war of occupation and resistance would only undermine the myths of the special Philippine-American relationship that prevailed throughout the twentieth century. Gardener's liberal dilemma probably constitutes the limits of official remembering since it allows for the existence of an anti-imperialist position that neutralizes the brute facts of military occupation. But it would be well worth remembering, as well, the nonofficial matters that Gardener narrated in his private correspondence.

Grand questions about benevolent assimilation would have been too unreal or distant for the Filipinos defending their towns or hiding from the American cavalry. What they would have seen in the towns occupied by the Schwan expedition were American soldiers on the rampage. Gardener knew all too well the gap between the official discourse of a civilizing mission and the actual behavior of his army: "Of course the best houses in every town were occupied by them, and every hidden place ransacked in hope of the booty of Eastern lands, so often read of in novels; dreams of buried treasure in graveyards, churches or vaults."

I do not know that the American is worse than other soldiers, but surely it was bad enough, and a month's campaigning against the *Niggers* so-called is very demoralizing, and bad for discipline. *To the visitor belongs the spoils* as an aphorism, has perhaps done more harm than the saying that *No Indian is a good Indian, except a dead one*.[5]

Courtesy of Lorna Kalaw Tirol

Lt. Col. Norberto Mayo with the Kapisanan ng mga Veterano sa Lungsod ng Lipa (League of Veterans of Lipa City), 1959

Gardener claimed that one of the regiments in the Schwan expedition, all raw recruits, had set a bad example for his men; "they looted everything and destroyed for the fun of it. Every church and some graveyards were thoroughly gone through." These are the sort of details that remind us of the real war that gripped the towns of southern Luzon— similar to the experiences of the Japanese occupation which, in contrast, are well remembered.

In the sections that follow, I address further issues about the forgetting of the war by focusing on two of the towns initially occupied by Colonel Gardener's regiment: Tiaong and Candelaria. Whether the historical details about these towns and their leaders can be regarded as "representative" or not is beside the point. The myths of the "splendid little war" can be challenged effectively only by resurrecting local events and knowledges that have been marginalized or forgotten.[7]

AMIGO WARFARE

The years 1900-1902 constitute a lacuna in our knowledge of the war. In nationalist historiography the focus is on the fate of the republican government and army. By the end of 1899, many of the republic's wealthy and educated supporters had defected to the Americans, and its most capable military commander, Antonio Luna, had been assassinated by Filipino soldiers allegedly under orders from General Aguinaldo. Textbook histories generally trace the gradual retreat of Aguinaldo to the north until he is captured in early 1901 and takes the oath of allegiance to the United States in April.

The problem with presenting a history of the war at the regional and local level is that, in contrast to the Aguinaldo narrative, nothing much seems to have happened in terms of conventional warfare. For almost two years after the U.S. invasion of their region, the guerrilla columns of Lt. Cols. Norberto Mayo and Ladislao Masangcay dominated the hinterland of Tiaong and Candelaria. For a year the townspeople lived alongside them. But with the defeat of the anti-imperialist William Jennings Bryan in the November 1900 elections, most of them moved back to their homes. Mayo and Masangcay remained in the field throughout 1901, not to confront the Americans directly with their meager resources but hoping for succor — in the form of weapons from the Japanese, perhaps, or a German fleet that would come to the rescue, or an American shift in policy.

Question: What was the object of the insurrecto forces?

Lieutenant Cadiz: *What the insurrectos wanted was tranquility and independence.*

Q: So you preferred to gain independence by concealing yourselves every time you saw an American and to get your living from the poor people of the barrios?

Cadiz: *Because the lieutenant colonel [Masang-cay] told us to have patience and to hide ourselves; that this would not last long and we would be given our independence.*[6]

In such circumstances, much could easily be forgotten about the war, because the usual battle stories just were not there to memorialize.

What seems to be brought out in the local history of Tiaong and Candelaria is the Filipino experience of dealing with a superior force through various mechanisms, like feigning defeat, playing dead, shifting identities, allowing oneself to bend with the wind like the bamboo (to use a cliché quite common about Filipinos). Townspeople straddled both regimes, colonial and nationalist, with relative ease. The problem for the U.S. post commanders in so-called pacified towns was not that there was much danger of American soldiers being harmed by those pesky guerrilla bands which could not shoot straight, but that the Americans could not be certain that the friendly, cooperative *presidente*, or local mayor, they were dealing with in the daytime, was not the chairman of the town's revolutionary committee at night. This was not what the U.S. Army wanted or expected. The enemy had to be visible and stable, an object of confrontation that could be destroyed, yes, but possibly also turned into willing subjects and even friends. After all, the official ideology of the U.S. takeover of the islands was "benevolent assimilation"—conquest construed as a moral imperative to adopt and civilize the "Orphans of the Pacific."[7]

"Amigo warfare" was what the Americans derisively called the Filipino style of resistance. The Filipinos were friends during the day or when confronted, but at night or when no one was looking, they were guerrillas. When the cavalry approached, most of the enemy disappeared, or their uniforms were shed for peasant gear. Even more frustrating was when they donned American uniforms. In frustration, Brig. Gen. J. Franklin Bell, who took over the pacification of Southern Tagalog in November 1901, wrote: "In order to confuse their identity and thereby able them more safely to conduct their skulking operations, they have adopted the uniform of our Army and native troops without any plain, striking, and uniform mark of distinction of their own, in violation of section 63."[8] American patrols incurred several mishaps as a result of mistaken identity.

Knowing more about the dynamics of amigo warfare, the ability to shift identities in changing contexts, should enlighten us about the whole issue of collaboration—collaboration not just during the war itself but throughout the whole period of colonial rule. It might even explain why Filipinos today seem to be so adept at handling tricky situations that demand shifting or multiple identifications and commitments.

DESCRIBING LEADERSHIP: ILUSTRADOS AND CACIQUES

While there is no lack of national heroes stemming from the revolution of 1896-1898, Philippine-American War heroes are surprisingly sparse, considering that the war lasted almost three and a half years. Apart from Antonio Luna, Gregorio del Pilar,

Manuel Tinio, and perhaps a dozen others, the majority of leaders in the war have yet to be properly researched.[9] One obvious reason for their neglect is the very fact that they fought the Americans, "our" sentimental allies in World War II. Another reason is that both Filipino and American scholarship has tended to be critical of the *ilustrado principal* (rural gentry) or cacique origins of most of these military leaders. What is generally forgotten is that the U.S. Army itself, in justifying harsh measures in 1900-1902, deployed the notion that the ordinary guerrilla soldiers and their families needed to be emancipated from their despotic and feudal leaders.

Norberto Mayo, one of Tiaong's colonels, would be a good candidate for dismissal on the basis of social origins. If one were looking for a ready label to affix to him, then "mestizo" it must be— but not Chinese, nor Spanish, nor even a combination of both. His great-grandfather was an Irishman in the British expeditionary force that invaded the Philippines in 1762. He married a Chinese mestiza from Lipa and settled down there, making his fortune in the coffee industry.

Mayo is also described as "quite accomplished for a Filipino" and *con instrucción*, able to speak and write in both Tagalog and Spanish. A fourth-year enrolment record at the University of Santo Tomas reveals that he studied Spanish, Latin, geometry, trigonometry, and even a bit of English.[10] He was once spotted in the hills of Tiaong clutching his "little red book"— a copy of Rizal's seditious novel, *Noli me tangere*.[11] No doubt Mayo was an *ilustrado* or more accurately, a rural *ilustrado*.

The *ilustrados* of the Philippine-American War period have been punished in history owing to the "capitulation" in 1899 of many wealthy, highly educated, and mestizo legislators and officials of the republic.[12] The names Pedro Paterno, Felipe Buencamino, and Manuel Arguelles count among them. But this Irish-Chinese mestizo named Mayo represented another variety. Attached to the Banahaw Battalion, he saw action in many parts of the Southern Tagalog region and was seriously wounded in late 1899 (a fact which became well known).[13] After a period of recuperation, he was back in action in 1900, rising quickly through the ranks. Mayo acted as a rallying point for soldiers and officers being abandoned in the surrenders that took place in 1900 and 1901. He wisely based himself in the barrios of Tiaong where his brothers maintained the family ricelands. By 1901, his brother Martin, a schoolteacher, and his sisters Micaela and Amanda, were living in the relative security of the *poblacion*. Micaela was then caring for a little boy, a future vestige of the war, the feisty anticolonial politician Claro Mayo Recto.[14]

The other colonel of Tiaong, Ladislao Masangcay, equally begs forgetting on the grounds that he was a local boss. He hailed from an old family of Tiaong and bore a very *indio* surname. He owned some land, was a former headman, and became *gobernadorcillo* in 1892, all of which mark him out as a *principal*. But he neither spoke nor wrote in Spanish, so an *ilustrado* he was not. In fact, all of his correspondence was handled by a secretary. All of these qualities seem to mark him out as a cacique— a local chief.

But let us take a closer look. Caciques were not necessarily rapacious bosses or manipulative patrons. The problem in the existing literature on the subject is that we hardly ever hear these chiefs speak. The anti-Marcos literature on "guns, goons, and gold" has effaced the varieties of caciques that existed and the contexts in which they operated.[15]

Masangcay may have been ignorant of Spanish, but he was a proficient Tagalog speaker and so was able to rouse his men and keep up their morale. He was the original "filibuster" in the town, earning a reputation by squabbling with a Spanish lieutenant of the Guardia Civil in 1891 and joining the revolution early.[16] A commissioner from the capital, in confirming his election as revolutionary mayor in 1898, wrote that Masangcay was "the initiator of the revolution in this town, whose moral and material sacrifices offered up to the Motherland are most certainly worthy of this humble recommendation: he is and has always been a separatist through his political acts."[17] From mid-1900 through early 1902, Masangcay built up his column by attracting scattered soldiers who refused to surrender with their officers.[18] They all stood somewhat in awe, if not in fear, of this "man of prowess" they called "My Colonel" or "Capitan Islao."

WAR AND FRIENDSHIP IN PACIFIED TOWNS

The fact that just about all of the town centers or *poblacions* in the Philippines were under U.S. civil or military control by mid-1900 has facilitated the war's forgetting. For unlike the similar situation in 1942, when the Japanese army ruled the *poblacions*, only to be booted out two to three years later, U.S. control was not followed by a "liberation" phase that would have necessitated a recovery of war memories. Instead, U.S. pacification and education programs after 1902 managed to transform resistance in the "boondocks"[19] into a condition of banditry while the American towns came to signify progress and democratic tutelage.

The complexities of Filipino behavior in the "pacified" towns have yet to be brought to light. To start with, comparisons should be made with the "evacuation" period following the Japanese invasion. There is a ring of familiarity about the fact that only a fraction of the Tiaong evacuees returned to their homes in 1900. For almost a year after the Americans invaded, the bulk of them were still holding out in the hills and isolated barrios. As late as November, only fifty people could be found in the *poblacion*, not many more than the American soldiers themselves. The rest, as during "Japanese times," were in the guerrilla zones. Only in early 1901 did the populace return en masse to the town as a result of the ravages of malaria, the loss of William Jennings Bryan in the U.S. elections, and a conscious shift in guerrilla strategy.

The "pacified town" was, in reality, under a dual government—a companion strategy to amigo warfare. When the American government, either in its democratic zeal or because General Aguinaldo had finally been captured, allowed local elections to be called in mid-1901, the revolutionaries in the field realized that they could actually use electoral politics for their own ends. And so Malvar ordered his chiefs to go along with elections, but to see to it that they got the right officials in place, meaning "those who knew best how to get around the heads of the Americans."[20] Call this crass manipulation, or cacique democracy, but this was a time of war. The office of *presidente* was crucial because he had to deal with the commanding officer of the American garrison. After a couple of failed attempts to find a suitable person, young Pedro Cantos was finally elected *presidente* of Tiaong on 20 July.

Cantos was not a local "big man," but by 1890 he had gained a college education in Manila. He was a typical rural *ilustrado*, working in clerical posts in the colonial as well as republican bureaucracies. Since he had no military or revolutionary background— neither guns nor followers— one might ask why he became *presidente* in a time of war. In a real sense, he was meant to be a "secret weapon" of the guerrilla chiefs, as was shown a month after the election when he went to confer with Colonel Mayo, his patron, who urged him to "use all the influence he had to induce the people of the Pueblo to act against the Americans."[21]

What eventually made Cantos important in his own right was his growing influence (or at least his perceived influence) over the commanding officer of the local garrison. Working with Captain Moore could not have been easy, for this American was clearly disdainful of the ordinary *tao* or *hombre*. As he once explained to a visitor, *these black niggers would have to take their hats off when he passed*. He would walk over to anyone who failed to do so, pull off his hat and throw it to the ground, cursing in Spanish. This rule of saluting officers applied also to the *principales*, who detested it because "it reminded them so much of the arrogance of the Spanish government."[22]

Captain Moore's behavior partly confirms Gardener's allegation that "almost without exception, soldiers and also many officers refer to the natives in their presence as *niggers*."[23] But not all natives were lumped in this category. Moore was very friendly with the Spanish-speaking *poblacion* dwellers, some of whom were part Chinese or Spanish (or Irish). He was seen chatting with them often, attending their dance parties, getting caught up in relationships he only partly understood— for among themselves, the *principales* spoke in Tagalog. He got along particularly well with Cantos, whom he so trusted that he was heard to say— at a time when suspicions were growing about the "deception" of the town principales— "that as far as he observed Pedro Cantos, the latter was loyal."[24] Through this relationship, Moore's appalling behavior toward the *tao* was somewhat redeemed by the *presidente*'s mediation.

Being in touch with the "inside" as well as the "outside" of town, Cantos was regarded by Moore as a prime source of information. And he obliged, feeding the captain regularly with information about the *insurrectos*. But this was always misleading or dated; not a single guerrilla was captured in the expeditions of which Cantos himself sometimes acted as guide. Still, the *presidente* had to keep *both* Moore and the colonels relatively happy. At one point, when the provincial government was moving to assess the property of the guerrilla chiefs prior to confiscation, Cantos suggested the surrender of ten men and rifles "in order to gain the confidence of the Commander of the garrison." However, "Lt. Col. Masangcay refused to permit it, saying moreover that we were all stupid because they also were looking for rifles to buy and they could pay more than the Americans pay for the rifles surrendered."[25]

Even if Cantos was sincere about helping Captain Moore and the American government, there wasn't much he could do to sway the notables of the town. We can be sure that U.S. military pressure was taking its toll in late 1901; even members of the municipal council were beginning to have doubts. When revolutionary agent Ciriaco Gonzales announced at a council meeting in August that "Malvar was disposed to remain in the field although alone as Washington did in order to secure the independence of his people," an unidentified councilman quipped, *Malvar is very different because Washington was a wise man, who made laws and orders*.[26] Despite such misgivings, however, the council wasn't about to take positive measures against the guerrillas. Some believed in the cause of independence; others were simply scared. There was no explicit warning from the chiefs, but "by a rumor among the people" policeman Luciano Alabastro was convinced that if anyone gave information to the Americans of the *insurrectos*' presence, he would be killed.[27]

Once, Cantos got the *principales* to attend a meeting at his office but "none of them made proposals concerning the pacification of the pueblo." On another occasion, they "agreed to the job that had to be done but they left without complying." All this foot-dragging would have been frustrating when Moore was expecting results. *They are very indifferent*, complained Cantos, *they don't share in the work of good government and order.*[28]

Presidente Cantos played a delicate and often dangerous role in dealing simultaneously with the principales, the guerrilla chiefs, and the American commander. Ultimately, his goal was to keep the lines of communication open between the town and the countryside. Supplies, gifts, relatives, lovers, and even the soldiers themselves moved in and out of town, thus easing the burden of the increasingly difficult life *sa labas*, outside. *When we could no longer suffer the country, we came into town assured that we would not be informed upon.* (Cadiz)

"Dual government" meant straddling the divide between the colonial and revolutionary orders. Without adequate documentation, as we are privileged to have in relation to Cantos, it is difficult to determine whether characters like him were collaborators or freedom fighters. The linear history of either the revolutionary struggle or colonial progress is interrupted by the "duality" of much of Filipino behavior during this particular war. Thus the ease of its forgetting.

COUNTER-AMIGO WARFARE AND THE NEW COLONIALISM

What, then, to do when the natives constantly blurred the division between friend and foe? American solutions were often draconian, blatantly contradicting the imperial ideology of "benevolent assimilation" and other myths of a benign occupation. There were many frustrated army officers like Lieutenant Parker who proposed the following solution in May 1900: "Serve notice thoroughly that all who live in Dolores, Tiaong and San Pablo must return to their proper homes at once in order to prevent destruction; serve notice that hereafter all natives must stand and face American Soldiers, either to fight or in a friendly manner, and that all that do not, but run away, will be killed."[29] Sentiments like this help explain why the war is memorialized in U.S. textbooks as simply "the Spanish-American War," conjuring up images of armies and navies in battle rather than natives being shot on the run.

American frustrations intensified as the months wore on and "peace" was not in sight. Looking back on the latter part of 1901, Maj. Gen. Lloyd Wheaton concluded that the policy of "benevolent assimilation" had not worked because of certain intractable qualities in the Filipino psyche. "Surrounded by a dense population of semi-civilized natives belonging to a race whose every impulse is to treachery and perfidy, it was attempted to reduce them to obedience to law and order by the gentlest and most conciliatory methods." But the result of this benevolence was "a condition without parallel in the history of any country long occupied by an invading and conquering army."[30] To quell the guerrilla activity that flourished in the provinces of the Third Separate Brigade, General Bell, having successfully "pacified" the Ilocos provinces, was put in command at the end of November. He promptly announced that amigo warfare would be terminated,

> and to effect this every barrio in Batangas and Laguna will be burned, if necessary, and all the people concentrated in the towns.... Henceforth no one will be permitted to be neutral.... The towns of Tiaong, Dolores and Candelaria will probably be destroyed unless the insurgents who take refuge in them are destroyed.[31]

This was "a policy of permitting no neutrality"— meaning to say one had to be for or against, not just in words but in deed. *I realized that it would do no good to try to force the inhabitants to be our friends* (Bell).[32] The alternative was to force the inhabitants to stop aiding the resistance in order to save themselves from destruction. In order to apply pressure on them, they would be herded into "protected zones."

At first glance it appeared to be a voluntary thing. *As friendship cannot be created to order by force, I deemed it best not to compel the people to enter these zones... but merely to offer them the opportunity and permit them to decide for themselves whether they would be friends or enemies.*[33] Could they practice "free choice" and still save their skins? Bell assumed that those who didn't come in were either guerrilla supporters who would be treated accordingly, or were being forced against their will to stay outside the towns. An ominous discourse was developing in U.S. Army circles as to why many of the *tao* remained outside the American towns. Bell explains: "A reign of terror long existed in the mountains of Loboo, where *ladrone* (bandit) chiefs have held some of the people under domination as complete as ever existed in the days of feudalism." So the U.S. Army was to "hunt these intimidated people and bring them with their families into protected zones."[34] They were to liberate the masses and protect them from their oppressive caciques.

What we notice in Bell's speech is how a discourse of emancipation emerges alongside a discourse of native duplicity, despotism, and backwardness. One needed the other in the context of the imperial war. But the former is remembered as the precursor of the colonial hallmarks of "tutelage" and "development," while its complement of orientalism and racism are pointedly forgotten.

We also notice a play on the notion of friendship. Amigo warfare was an attempt to come to terms with the new colonizer— to deflect its massive power by being friends and negotiating with its representatives in the town centers, while maintaining commitment to the revolutionary project. Bell, in a pointed reference to amigo warfare, pronounced friendship to mean full submission to U.S. rule. One cannot force Filipinos to be friends, he says, but those who do not submit will be treated as enemies and destroyed. Since the Philippine-American relationship is celebrated today in terms of "friendship," it is hardly surprising that its disciplinary origins are best forgotten.

The establishment of "true" friendship required the delineation of firm boundaries between the American "inside"— the town centers— and the "outside" which would be turned into a no-man's land. Dual government would no longer survive if communications were totally cut. The U.S. Army, in a throwback to Spanish army methods in quelling the revolution in 1897, implemented a "protected zones" or "reconcentration" policy in December 1901. Bell ordered everyone to transfer to the town poblacions bringing all their food and property. Everything left outside would be either confiscated or destroyed.

The hub of the protected zone was the church and the U.S. garrison. On each of the streets surrounding the center a barrio was relocated, properly labeled and all.[35] It was like a theme park where a vast and variegated landscape consisting of barrios and sitios with their own histories and physical features, was reproduced in the pueblo center, the better to be watched and controlled by the U.S. Army. In one of the documents concerning the zones in Batangas, the word "concentration camp" appears but is crossed out.[36] While the benign term "protected zone" connotes protection against external threat—i.e., the bad insurgents—"concentration camp" more fittingly describes what the zones were all about. Within the bounded confines, the population could be systematically viewed and counted street by street. In such a controlled environment, dependency relations could be established by distributing food and other necessities. Individual houses and tents could be penetrated in the name of hygiene and sanitation.

General Bell reckoned, as well, that in the zones he and his fellow officers would be better appreciated without the alleged distortions of gentry influence. Lieutenant Colonel Crane in Lipa complained in late 1900 that benevolent American intentions were not getting through to the masses: "It is to the interest of the priest and of the rich to keep the black Tagalo in utter ignorance, and thus prolong the war."[37] Things would be different with reconcentration. Bell noted with satisfaction that hundreds of people were being brought into intimate contact with Americans, whom they had never seen or known before: "As a consequence no one will again be able to mislead them as to the real character of Americans."[38] The redemptive process could now begin.

Curiously enough, Bell seemed unaware that his actions were replicating what Spain and its missionaries had achieved two centuries earlier. Through the policy of *reducción*, scattered settlements were reconcentrated in Spanish-style pueblos dominated by a church-center. This center was the embodiment not just of a superior Hispanic-Christian order, but of civilization itself. By occupying the church-centers in the protected zones, the U.S. Army was in effect recolonizing the landscape. There the American commanders installed themselves as the new padres, representatives of a powerful nation bringing a new religion of modernity. An anonymous rural *ilustrado* in Candelaria penned the following description of the new era:

> By order of the Provost, every morning all of the town dwellers had to assemble in front of the Provost's headquarters to listen to his orders or speeches. This popular convocation, which the respectable Señor Provost regularly adorned with his victims, was preceded by the pealing of the church bells.[39]

A "HOWLING WILDERNESS"

The forgetting of the war has been helped along by the intervention of a new set of memories of war and occupation in which the Japanese loom as the clear enemy. Researchers in the 1960s and 1970s who interviewed veterans of the Philippine-American War noted with some exasperation that their accounts of atrocities, reconcentration, interrogation, and so forth were attributed to the Japanese invaders. The violence perpetrated by the U.S. Army in 1900, clearly evidenced in written records, seemed to have been purged from these veterans' memories by the acts of the Japanese Army in 1944. To top it all, Gen. Douglas MacArthur managed to install himself in the popular imagination as the returning hero, the Great Liberator of 1945. Could this same army of liberation have been the invaders and destroyers of 1900, led by Gen. Arthur MacArthur, the beloved Douglas's father?

Those who are at all aware of the real war that constituted the "Philippine insurrection" will have heard of the "Balangiga massacre." This was initially a reference to the treacherous killing, on 28 September 1901, of forty-five American soldiers in Balangiga, Samar, by guerrillas attached to Gen. Vicente Lukban. So enraged was the

American commander, Brig. Gen. Jacob Smith, that he ordered a "kill-and-burn" operation to punish the people at large—men, women, and children—for their crime. This was, or could be, another referent for the term *massacre*.

Balangiga was not an isolated incident. Other parts of the Philippines could be called a "howling wilderness"[40] in 1901 and 1902 but these have been obscured by the myth of "a splendid little war." From late December through early April, dozens of search-and-destroy operations were mounted throughout the jurisdiction of General Bell's Third Separate Brigade. For example, in one operation alone lasting twelve days, Lt. H. Richmond and his First Cavalry troop based in Lucena, in combination with infantry units, combed the countryside "destroying all livestock of every description, houses and supplies encountered." To be precise, a total of 540 houses, 5500 bushels of rice, 87 native ponies, 70 cattle, 14 carabaos, and 125 hogs were either confiscated or destroyed. By Richmond's own admission, it was usually a cavalry troop like his which was sent off the road, mounted or dismounted, "to burn a house or barrio, or kill animals, while waiting for the Infantry to rest."[41]

As early as December, complaints began to flood Governor Gardener's office in Lucena about "the bad treatment that the people of the barrios had received when the American officers wished to obtain news concerning the whereabouts of the *insurrectos*, or to secure arms.... The complaints were that not finding arms, the *gente* of the barrio were caught and detained in jail, or they put water in their mouth or their noses, and at times burned their houses."[42] This prompted Gardener to openly complain to Manila about the U.S. Army's atrocities in his province. He cited the "extensive burning of barrios in trying to lay waste to the country so that the insurgents cannot occupy it, the torturing of natives by so-called water cure and other methods, in order to obtain information, the harsh treatment of natives generally.... If these things need to be done, they had best be done by native troops so that the people of the U.S. will not be credited therewith."[43]

Let us be more specific. How many barrios of Tiaong were burned?, Masangcay was asked. *All the barrios.* Constabulary inspector Herrera actually witnessed American soldiers putting a Tiaong barrio to the torch. The same fate befell seven barrios of Candelaria. Gardener was right, the Ilocanos should have been made to do all of it. For by the end of the year the seeds of perpetual hatred against the Americans—to paraphrase the governor—had been sowed:

> From your conversations with the people of those towns (Tiaong, Candelaria, Sariaya, Tayabas) what could you say were their feelings towards the Americans in the latter part of 1901?
>
> Herrera: *The majority say they are displeased with the Americans.*
>
> Did you hear what was the cause of their displeasure?
>
> *The people say that the cause is the burning of some of the barrios of those towns and some tortures that they had in those places.*
>
> Are these cases of abuses generally known in those towns which you have visited?
>
> *That is what they say.*[44]

The "protected zones" were not necessarily immune from the horrors of war. In early April 1902, the local constabulary under the command of Inspector Julio

Herrera spread the word that Lieutenant Trent, Eighth Infantry, prosecuting attorney, was going to pass through Candelaria. Here was an opportunity for people to present their complaints against the military. It was not long before an anonymous Spanish document summarizing the abuses of the U.S. Army arrived at the headquarters of the Constabulary.[45] The Americans suspected that Herrera himself, an ex-revolutionary colonel now "collaborating" with them, had instigated the complaint. Whatever its provenance, the document contained damning accusations which the U.S. Army had to deal with, such as the following:

> The Provost of Candelaria, having brought about the incarceration of the whole Municipio and almost all of the pueblo, including a hundred or more women married, widowed, and single, submitted the men to cruel torture, forcing them to confess what he wanted, and proof of this is that no one who has been the victim of this cruel venting of fury, has denied his imaginary guilt owing to the sorrow and pain he has suffered...

During the interrogations almost all of the inhabitants of Candelaria proper had been detained, which meant that "the unfortunate young women of the *poblacion* were defenseless. They began to commit a thousand atrocities; the women were molested by officers and soldiers alike without any kind of consideration; those who resisted such barbarity were threatened with imprisonment, deportation, or death, and those who were disgraced had succumbed to force."

Looting was rampant, as well, when nearly no one was around to protect their homes. The best horses, furniture, household effects, saddles and trappings, and other property fell into the hands of the Scouts, and no one dared to reclaim them for fear of the threats which were actually carried out when the occasion warranted.

Names were given of some of the victims: Basilio Martinez, "shot dead because he did not confess what he was obliged to confess"; three other men who died after torture; two men with broken ribs and permanent injuries from being hit by rifle butts; eight women, raped. Many others had been killed, maimed, or raped but their cases had not come forward; meanwhile, enough had been said "to make the pueblo weep."

Finally, the complaint listed the names of fourteen citizens who had been sent into exile in Guam. One of them was Padre Gregorio Alma, whose main crime must have been setting a table in the church of Sariaya for the Virgin of the Immaculate Conception, their patron saint, on behalf of the *insurrectos* "to give them freedom and valor in their fight against the Americans." And there was a lone woman on the list, Serapia de Gala, an insurgent supporter, whose store had earlier been looted by American soldiers.

The detailed investigation subsequently conducted by the brigade provost marshall, Capt. D. H. Boughton, attempted to water down the complaints by pointing out inconsistencies in testimonies and exaggerated claims. Basilio Martinez was found to be very much alive still; perhaps he had survived the gunshot wound, we do not know. Others had allegedly been shot dead while trying to escape, or died of natural causes. Imprisonment was justified, said Boughton, "by the state of war existing at that time." The accusations of rape were sometimes twisted around so that the woman was held to blame, or the cases were left unresolved, passed on to higher authority. The thrust of Boughton's official investigation is not unexpected, but his findings are nonetheless valuable for their details about what the Candelarians went through in the protected zones.

The purpose of interrogations in the protected zones was not just to identify "elites" and "tao" so that the patron-client or "feudal" relations between them might be broken. It was also to exploit family ties, to take spouses and kin as hostage in order to force surrenders. Gregorio Mañibo was confined when it was discovered that he was the brother of soldier Eulogio, of Mayo's command. When Capt. Policornio de Luna's wife heard that the Tiaong authorities were arresting the families of *insurrectos*, she escaped and went back to the countryside, leaving her daughters in the *poblacion*. In Santa Rosa, they captured the wife of Col. Nicolas Gonzales, Malvar's second in command. Knowing that many guerrilla families had sought refuge in the Loboo mountains, the U.S. cavalry ferreted out a total of 495 women and children in a sweep of the mountains in March. They were herded into the protected zones, some to be used as hostages.[46]

Of the hundred or so women confined in Candelaria (and more in Tiaong), some had been charged with aiding or communicating with the *insurrectos*. Others were there as hostage while some male member of the family went in search of guns which he had confessed about. When Cayetano Umali, whose father was a soldier, was released in order to go out to secure a gun, he left his wife and his mother in the guardhouse.

Obviously, the women were vulnerable at different levels. According to investigator Captain Boughton, a rumor circulated that "if a scout presented himself at a house and a woman of his choice did not accede to his wishes, the husband, father, or male member of the family would be imprisoned, deported, or shot."

Laura L., whose husband was in the Malagi prison camp, claimed that "she had been violated by Scout Clement against her will by means of threats and intimidations." Boughton interviewed Clement who admitted that "he had on several occasions sent for women to be brought to his room at night but in no case was a carnal relation maintained against their will." Why did Laura L. visit Clement unaccompanied? Why didn't she make an outcry then? Raising such doubts, Boughton concluded that the charge was without merit. However, he did inform Lieutenant Trent, the prosecuting attorney, of the cases of Laura L. and three other women who had filed similar charges.

Another case was that of a thirteen-year-old girl who testified that an American lieutenant tried to rape her in his quarters but was foiled by her resistance. The lieutenant admitted the truthfulness of the statement, "with the exception of attempting to forcibly ravish the girl." The charges were repeated publicly by Rustica de Gala, acting as interpreter for the girl and her mother, in the presence of the accused, other army officers, and about seventy women of Candelaria who had assembled at Boughton's invitation to air their complaints. Mrs. de Gala declared that on the day following the occurrence of the alleged violation she found the girl and her mother hiding under her house. When asked why they were there, they informed Mrs. de Gala that "they were afraid of being taken to the officers' quarters for the purpose of administering to their carnal desires."

A more complex case involved the commanding officer of Candelaria himself. In late February, Alicia C. was confined by the provost judge as a hostage for the return of some relative who had been sent out to secure guns. While in prison, the girl was approached by the CO's interpreter, a Filipina, with the proposition that she become his mistress. "To this she finally consented, the relation being consummated after her release.... The father of this girl was a prisoner at the same time, and it appears that she requested his release from Lieutenant N. but was refused."

Alicia C.'s case is different from the rest because, although her story was initially brought up as a case of violation and became "public and notorious," Boughton's interviews of the woman, her parents, and the lieutenant seemed to point to the fact that "the relation was entirely voluntary on the part of Alicia and that she still wished it to continue." Her parents had furthermore given their consent. Therefore, concluded Boughton, there was no ground for the charge of violation.[47]

We should reflect further upon the meaning of Alicia C.'s case. It can be read as an allegory of the Philippine-American relationship as it was evolving at the turn of the century. Gardener's words in the early stages of the war were prophetic: the Philippines did become "our foster-child, a republic in Asiatic waters." Filipinos seemed in the end to accept America's tutelage willingly. Throughout the past century we have seen all sorts of variations on the theme of stewardship, tutelage, partnership, alliance, and the "special relationship." It seems voluntary, like Alicia C.'s relationship with Lieutenant N. which was ongoing as well. Yet we can easily forget that Alicia C.'s story began when she was in detention and then "invited" to be the white lieutenant's mistress. Her consent was followed by a request for the release of her father, also in detention. Hovering over the voluntary and special relationship are the circumstances of war.

SURRENDER, REDEMPTION, FORGETTING

Philippine history textbooks identify Miguel Malvar as the last Filipino general to surrender to the Americans. Sometimes the date is even mentioned: 16 April 1902. But not much else is said, for by this time the focus of attention is on the political campaigns of the pro-American Federalistas, and on the positive hallmarks of the new regime: sanitation, health, education, and political tutelage. Of course, there continued to be resistance and unrest of all sorts, but whatever cannot be assimilated into the discourse of national development is left to wallow in its colonial representations: banditry, religious fanaticism, ignorance, caciquism, and so forth.

In reconsidering this historical period, it would help us to remember the circumstances of Malvar's surrender: the imprisonment of guerrilla supporters or their relatives, mass destruction in the countryside, a cholera epidemic spreading out from Manila, people languishing in protected zones and unable to engage in agriculture, the spectre of famine. Surrender was not, this time anyway, a willing acquiescence to the benefits of tutelage and partnership with the United States.

> What broke up your forces and caused your soldiers to surrender their guns?
> Masangcay: *They could get no money to spend or food to eat and they had no clothes to put on.*[48]

Gabino Quizon came across his former chief, Masangcay, moving through the forest in the outskirts of barrio Pury, accompanied only by a lieutenant and five soldiers. He begged Masangcay to surrender, "protesting that the pueblo wished and begged for it and many more suffered enough in the *Calabosos* (jails)." *Masangcay replied each time that he wished to be faithful to his oath, that is to say, to be in the revolution until he dies in the field or is captured.* (Quizon)[49]

Masangcay was soon abandoned even by his sole lieutenant. He continued to hide out in the forest, living under the care of some *revolucionarios* who had been disarmed by their officers but had not surrendered. He finally presented himself to the commanding officer of Tiaong on 26 April. *I had only one gun and one revolver, because the rest were taken away from me by my soldiers.* (Masangcay)[50]

Norberto Mayo had surrendered in Lipa a week earlier. His revolutionary column had been doing well, he said, until "the American troops began to reconcentrate the people and... at the same time pursuing us constantly." *Our troops became disorganized and demoralized. At the time I surrendered on account of this demoralization I scarcely had thirty guns left with me.* (Mayo)[51]

Bernardo Marques, who had surrendered in Tiaong on 16 April, explained to his American interrogator why those who had sworn to resist "until they had accomplished their independence" eventually gave up as well: "They surrendered for various things; some because they were tired of staying in the field; some through fear and because they lost hope; because some of them had been injured or lost their health through life in the field; and some because their families obliged them to surrender. I do not know more."[52]

There was something about the way the war ended, at least in the area I have studied, that encouraged the forgetting of the experience. Much of the Southern Tagalog provinces was a wasteland by March of 1902. The rice stocks that could not be brought into the protected zones (fortified hamlets) were destroyed by the U.S. Cavalry. Granaries and houses were razed by the hundreds; one does not need to go beyond official U.S. Army reports to reconstruct the carnage. Furthermore, in April, at about the time General Malvar surrendered, cholera had spread from Manila to the provinces, facilitated by the movements of U.S. troops. An epidemic, coupled with a subsistence crisis, was about all that the populace of Batangas, Tayabas and Laguna could bear. The U.S. garrisons soon began receiving emotional letters from barrio heads pleading for assistance.[53]

What interests me here is the way that the U.S. Army was able to turn a situation of utter destruction and suffering, for which it was largely responsible, into a redemptive situation. With the destruction of crops, the loss of farm animals and implements, and the overall breakdown of agriculture, the Southern Tagalog region became dependent, for eight years at least, on the importation of food. Only the colonial regime, of course, was capable of importing food stocks, the commissaries in the U.S. posts becoming the local distribution centers.

In such a situation of utter dependence on the occupation forces for such basic necessities as rice and medicine, it is not difficult to imagine how "resistance" could be forgotten, and the generosity, the kindness, of the U.S. commissaries remembered. The U.S. Army played the role of benefactor extremely well. Sentiments of *utang na loób* then came into play as lives were actually saved through interaction with the Americans. When the population was on its knees, the use of force was lifted. There were no mass executions, no long-term imprisonment, just a rigorous disciplining as befitted a people under tutelage.

To understand the deeper implications of "surrender" in the towns of Tiaong and Candelaria, therefore, we have to look beyond the officers and soldiers who laid down their weapons in April 1902. We should note the wives and relatives of the hundreds of detainees who approached American officers, day or night, to seek their release; the townsfolk who lined up at the U.S. commissaries to receive their allocation of food. Ultimate surrender took the form of a rather quick forgetting. In the meeting where seventy women of Candelaria were told to file formal charges of violation against native scouts as well as their American officers, no one came forward. As Captain Boughton reports, "Some of the better class, when asked why it was that no complaint was made against any individual scout, replied that it was probably due to the fact that *the war being over, the people were disposed to let the dead past bury its dead.*"[54]

What does it mean to bury the past? At one level, it could mean that the women wished to erase a tragic and shameful event from public memory. But since this erasure seems to have been contingent upon "the war being over," it seems also to reflect the acceptance of a new era by the people of Candelaria. Señora de Gala's eloquent speech, the provost marshall's invitation to file complaints, the "collaborator" Inspector Herrera's behind-the-scenes work to get the investigation going, all indicate the extent to which communication had been established with the invading army. Forgetting the "dead past" can be taken to mean that the ravages of war had not diminished the Candelarian's ability to come to terms with another set of impositions from an outside power— to establish relationships of hierarchy and indebtedness with the Americans and thus, ultimately, to domesticate them.[55] One final explanation we might thus consider for the forgetting of the war is that the townspeople of Southern Tagalog could not be burdened by history as they commenced *still another* period of accommodation to colonial rule. Perhaps, with more research, we might even find the notion of "amigo warfare" useful in understanding this new period in Philippine history.

NOTES:

1. See Reynaldo C. Ileto, *Filipinos and Their Revolution; Event, Discourse, and Historiography* (Quezon City, Philippines: Ateneo de Manila University Press, 1998), epilogue.

2. See Reynaldo C. Ileto, *Knowing America's Colony: A Hundred Years from the Philippine War* (The Burns Chair Lectures, 1997). Occasional Papers Series, Center for Philippine Studies University of Hawai'i at Manoa, 1999, chapter 1.

3. The best account thus far of the Schwan expedition and of the various stages of the war in southern Tagalog, is Glenn A. May, *Battle for Batangas* (New Haven, Conn.: Yale University, 1991).

4. Gardener's confidential letter to Pingree, dated 21 February 1900, is published in Melvin Holli, ed., "A View of the American Campaign against 'Filipino Insurgents': 1900," *Philippine Studies 17*, 1 January 1969.

5. Ibid., 100.

6. Cadiz, Juan. Testimony. Lucena, 3 June 1902, United States National Archives (USNA) Record Group (RG) 94 Adjutant General's Office (AGO) 421607.

7. Vicente Rafael, "White Love: Surveillance and Nationalist Resistance in the U.S. Colonization of the Philippines," in Amy Kaplan and Donald Pease, *Cultures of United States Imperialism* (Durham, N.C.: Duke University, 1993), 185.

8. Bell, J. F. (Brig. Gen., Commanding 3rd Separate Brigade), Report, Batangas, December 1902, Washington: Government Printing Office 1903, w/ USNA RG94 AGO415839.

9. Recent examples are Resil Mojares, *The War against the Americans: Resistance and Collaboration in Cebu, 1899-1906* (Quezon City, Philippines: Ateneo de Manila University Press, 1999); Orlino A. Ochosa, *The Tinio Brigade: Anti-American Resistance in the Ilocos Provinces, 1899-1901* (Quezon City, Philippines: New Day, 1989). A good overview of the war is O. D. Corpuz, *The Roots of the Filipino Nation*, vol. II (Quezon City, Philippines: Aklahi Foundation, 1989), chapters 20-21.

10. *Libro de Matricula de Estudios Generales de Segundo Enseñanza*, 1890-1891, Archives of the University of Santo Tomas (AUST).

11. Concepcion Herrera vda de Umali, *Fragmentos de mi Juventud,* ms., 1977, Tomo II, 18.

12. The classic study of this is Teodoro A. Agoncillo, *Malolos: The Crisis of the Republic* (Quezon City: University of the Philippines Press, 1960).

13. The *Batallón Banahaw* was organized by Miguel Malvar shortly after the successful nationalist siege of the Spanish stronghold of Tayabas, capital of the province by that name, in August 1898. The experience of the siege had brought together revolutionaries from different towns in the region, including Tiaong. Appointed commander of the Battalion was Eustacio Maloles, Malvar's brother-in-law and a pharmacist by profession.

14. The information on Mayo is scattered throughout the US archival material. The most significant document is his testimony taken at Lucena, 9 May 1902, USNA RG94 AGO421607; see also Renato Constantino, *The Making of a Filipino* (Quezon City, Philippines: Malaya Books, 1989), 3.

15. Guns, goons and gold are the three evils said to obstruct the democratic process in the Philippines. The theme of cacique domination is persuasively developed in Benedict Anderson, "Cacique Democracy in the Philippines: Origins and Dreams," in Vicente L. Rafael, ed., *Discrepant Histories: Translocal Essays on Filipino Cultures* (Philadelphia, Pa.: Temple University Press, 1995), 3-50.

16. Historical Data Papers, Tiaong, Quezon province, 1952-53, National Archives, Manila.

17. Espediente instruido sobre eleccion de cargos publicos locales en el pueblo de Tiaong, siendo comisionado de elecciones Don Felix Arguelles. August 1898. Philippine Revolutionary Papers (PRP) 1101.8.

18. Masangcay, Ladislao. Testimony (Tagalog original). Lucena, 22-23 May 1902, RG94 AGO421607.

19. The Tagalog word *bundok* (mountain) was brought back to the United States by returning soldiers and as "boondock" has entered the American lexicon.

20. Malvar, Miguel. Testimony. Lucena, 02/6/16 to 02/6/19, RG94 AGO421607, 44 pp.

21. Pedro Cantos, Declaración, Tiaong, 25 February 1902, USNA RG395 E5495.

22. Bruin, Patrick (Inspector of Constabulary). Testimony. Lucena, 13 May 1902, RG94 AGO421607.

23. Gardener to Civil Governor of PI, Lucena, 16 December 1901, "Report of conditions in the

province since U.S. occupation," RG94 421607 encl. 99.

24. Herrera, Julio (Sariaya police Lt.) Testimony. Lucena, 23 May 1902, RG94 AGO421607.

25. Cantos, Declaración.

26. Trial of Sancho Capuli (Lt. of Police) and Councilors Cayetano Gonzales, Martin Mayo, Eulalio Recto. Court of First Instance (CFI), Tiaong, 19-26 April 1902, USNA RG94 Enc.4 to AGO42160.

27. Trial of Pedro Cantos, Zacarias Umali (Chief of Police) and Ysidro Dia (councillor). CFI Tiaong, 26-28 April 1902, USNA RG94 Enc.4 to AGO421607.

28. Cantos, Declaración.

29. Parker, John (Maj., 39th U.S.V.), "Report of a scout toward Tiaong and San Pablo," Tanauan, 24 May 1900, USNA RG395 E2408.

30. Wheaton, Lloyd (Maj. Gen. Commanding Dept. of Northern Philippines), Report, Manila, 6 May 1902 (w/ War Department Reports, 1902) in USNA RG 94 AGO439527.

31. Bell. J. F., Telegraphic circular no. 13, 21 December 1901, USNA RG94 AGO415839.

32. Bell Report, December 1902.

33. Ibid.

34. Ibid.

35. Wagner, Arthur., Col., Report on reconcentration in Tanauan and Sto. Tomas, 22 March 1902, USNA RG395 E2635 no. 7788.

36. Ibid.

37. Crane, E. J. (Lt. Col., CO, Lipa), Report of operations for October 1900, RG395 E2408 Box 2.

38. Bell Report, December 1902.

39. Attachment to Boughton, D. H. (Capt., Brigade Provost Marshall), Investigation of alleged abuses by U.S. personnel at Candelaria, 13 April 1902, USNA RG395 E2354 Box 4 OF367.

40. As Judge James Blount termed Balangiga after Smith's "punishment"; see Corpuz, II, 475.

41. Richmond, H. (1st Lt., 1st Cavalry), Report of operations in Candelaria, San Juan, and Loboo, 12 January 1902, USNA RG395 E2354 Box 2.

42. Unson, Gervacio (provincial secretary, Tayabas). Testimony. Lucena, 1-3 June 1902, USNA RG94 AGO421607.

43. Gardener, 16 December 1901.

44. Herrera, Testimony; Masangcay, Testimony.

45. Attachment to Boughton, Investigation.

46. List of confined soldiers and hostages, Tiaong, February-March 1902, USNA RG395 E5495; Insurrecto Officers of Tiaong, Descriptive List (in Spanish), n.d., RG395 E5495; N2521, N2526, 145.

47. Boughton, Investigation.

48. Masangcay, Testimony. Quizon, Gabino. (secretary to Masangcay) Testimony, 4 March 1902, USNA RG395 E5495.

50. Masangcay, Testimony.

51. Mayo, Testimony.

52. Marquez, Bernardo. Testimony. Lucena, 10 May 1902, USNA RG94 AGO421607.

53. See Reynaldo C. Ileto "Cholera and the Origins of the American Sanitary Order in the Philippines," in Rafael, ed., *Discrepant Histories*, 51-81.

54. Boughton, Investigation (my italics).

55. Recent work, particularly by Rafael, on the Spanish colonial period could be applied to the Philippine-American War; see Vicente L. Rafael, *Contracting Colonialism; Translation and Christian Conversion in Tagalog Society under Early Spanish Rule* (Durham, N.C.: Duke University Press, 1993).

Uneasy Observers:
Germans and the Philippine-American War

WIGAN SALAZAR

Counting more than two hundred people, the German community at the end of the nineteenth century was second only to the British community among the non-Spanish Europeans in the Philippines.[1] Having forged close ties to Philippine society—numerous German men were married to Filipino women, Chinese mestizas, or Philippine-born Spanish women—Germans found themselves in an awkward position when Philippine-American hostilities broke out early in 1899. Being neither colonizers nor colonized, they were not directly involved in the ensuing war, yet were forced to balance the maintenance of good relations to Filipinos with an accommodation to the new colonial power. Significantly, they obtained little support from the German government that had shown a keen interest in the colony during the Philippine Revolution, as manifest in the dispatch of warships to Manila Bay in 1896 and 1898—measures purportedly undertaken to protect German subjects against possible excesses of war.

With few exceptions, Germans living in the Philippines were primarily engaged in economic pursuits. By the end of the nineteenth century, German entrepreneurs had carved out several niches in the Philippine economy. Approximately a dozen German merchant houses, most of which specialized in the import business, traded in Manila. Numerous small- to middle-scale entrepreneurs, ranging from photographers and tailors to printers and lithographers, were also present. Moreover, German pharmacies operated in Manila, Vigan, Cebu, and Iloilo. Germans had additionally established a foothold in the tobacco industry. Several cigar factories in Manila, including the large and prestigious El Oriente, Alhambra, and Helios, were at least partly owned by Germans. Baer & Co., a large-scale tobacco leaf dealer since the 1860s, ran the tobacco hacienda Maluno in the Cagayan Valley in northern Luzon. Germans also participated in the unsuccessful mining boom of the 1890s, staking claims to mineral deposits in Bicol and Cebu.[2]

Socially, Germans in the Philippines were a very heterogenous group, comprising Protestants, Catholics, and Jews from diverse regional backgrounds. As the German merchant Carl Fressel repeatedly commented, differences between Germans were too marked for them to form a single united community. There nevertheless existed a loose form of social organization, first in the form of a German reading club and from the late 1880s with the Casino Union, a social club with a membership of Germans, Swiss, Dutch, Belgians, and Austrians. Few German women ventured to the Philippines, and among these, most came as wives of senior merchants. The small number of German wives can be linked to a propensity among German men to marry locally born Spanish, Chinese mestiza, or Filipino women. Despite the German community's apparent acculturation, there were divisions on the question of interracial marriages to mestiza or Filipino women. The case of Alfredo Rönsch, whose marriage to Rosario Abreu from Laguna prompted his father, a prominent merchant, to disinherit him, illustrates this rift.[3]

A Clash of Interests: German and American Territorial Ambitions

German territorial interest in the Philippines was initially restricted to the Sulu archipelago, where the merchant-adventurer Hermann Leopold Schück gained favor at the Sultan's court in the 1860s and attempted to initiate closer official ties between Germany and Sulu. The German government, however, did not aggressively pursue territorial gain in Sulu, although trading and land-owning privileges for German subjects were secured with the Anglo-German-Spanish treaties of 1878 and 1885. The first serious considerations of a possible German acquisition of Philippine territory can be dated to 1885, when Germany and Spain were engaged in a dispute over the Carolines. Anticipating a possible escalation of German-Spanish tension, Peter Kempermann, the German consul in Manila, dispatched a proposal for the annexation of Mindanao to Berlin. Kempermann's suggestion, however, seems to have been ignored, and it was only in the 1890s, a decade during which German foreign policy was at its most expansionist, that the Philippines reemerged on the agenda of German foreign policy.[4]

Spain's weak position in the Philippines at the outbreak of the Philippine Revolution in 1896 did not go unnoticed in Berlin. The German consul's request for a warship to protect German subjects in the Philippines thus offered an opportunity to assess the situation with an eye to possible locations for a base for the use of the German navy's East Asian Squadron. The German warship Arcona reached Manila on 24 November 1896 and was relieved on 25 December by the Irene, led by Vice-Admiral Alfred Tirpitz, the commander of the squadron, who stayed until 3 January 1897. Tirpitz's brief reconnaissance visit, however, did not mark the end of German government interest in the Philippines. In January 1897, a group of Hong Kong-based Filipinos presented a petition to the German consul, advocating an international intervention in the Philippines. This petition seems to have aroused the interest of the German emperor, who, convinced of the existence of a pro-German party in the Philippines, noted his intention to acquire the Philippines when an adequate opportunity arose.[5]

The further development of German government interest in the Philippines, treated in depth elsewhere, will only be broadly outlined here.[6] The German navy's desire for an outpost in Asia—one reason for Tirpitz's visit—was partly met by the seizure of Kiaochow, located on the Shantung Peninsula, from China in November 1897. However, as the three-day visit to Manila of the German warship Gefion in March 1898 indicates, surveillance of the Philippines remained on the agenda. The

German emperor's personal interest was revived when his brother Heinrich reported from Hong Kong on 11 April of the same year that the revolution in the Philippines was legitimate and that Filipinos wished to be protected by a European power, specifically by Germany. The German chancellor and foreign minister Bernhard von Bülow, skeptical of this analysis, more realistically judged that the revolution was directed against any form of foreign rule. Additionally, the Spanish-American War and the destruction of the Spanish fleet off Cavite by American warships on 1 May meant that an undisturbed German intervention was illusory. Acutely aware of Germany's inability to acquire the Philippines against possible British and American opposition, Bülow advocated a diplomatic solution that required either a partition or a neutralization of the Philippines by an alliance of nations. The German government resolved to dispatch the East Asian Squadron to Manila in order to assess the situation and to lay the basis for potential future claims on the archipelago. Two ships arrived in Manila in May, and the squadron's commander, Vice-Admiral Otto von Diederichs, arrived on 12 June. Later in the same month, the German fleet was supplemented by two cruisers and the transport ship *Darmstadt*, which carried 1,500 relief crewmen and stayed for three days. At this point, the German contingent constituted a larger force than the U.S. fleet.[7]

The American commander, Commodore George Dewey, seeing his blockade of Manila Bay disrupted, seems to have been profoundly irritated by the German presence. Although other neutral powers—France, Britain, Austria, and Japan—had also sent warships to Manila Bay, it was the German contingent that, as Terrell Gottschall notes, received Dewey's "special and resentful attention."[8] Friction between Germans and Americans in Manila, caused by a series of incidents, quickly became an issue of heated debate, particularly in the American press. However laden the atmosphere between German and American fleets may have been, there was apparently no intention on the part of Germany to interfere with American actions. Although interested in territorial expansion, the German government had no desire to provoke a conflict with the United States. Instead, Berlin made diplomatic advances to the U.S. government on a possible acquisition of part of the Philippines while secretly negotiating the purchase of other Pacific possessions, notably the Carolines, with Spain.[9] By the time the Philippine-American War began in February 1899, the German government had accepted that it stood no chance of acquiring part of the Philippines. Aware that territorial questions had largely been settled, the administration in Berlin strictly refrained from appearing to interfere in what was now deemed an internal American affair. In a move aimed at improving German-American relations, Bülow ordered that the squadron leave the Philippines in March 1899. This reticence on the part of the German administration was still evident in November 1901, when a German admiral's request to pay a courtesy call in Manila was rejected by Bülow, who feared that such a move might be misconstrued as intervention.[10]

AMERICAN RULE AND THE GERMAN COMMUNITY

The advent of American rule in the Philippines in 1898 was greeted with skepticism by the resident German community which was primarily based in Manila. According to Diederichs, German businessmen clearly preferred the installation of a British administration in the Philippines to American or even German rule. In hindsight, their hesitant attitude toward the Americans seems well-founded, as the renewed outbreak of war and the fact that the new rulers failed to introduce economic reforms was to prove detrimental to the German community's economic base.[11] According to the German consul Friedrich Krüger, German merchant houses had "suffered heavy losses and increasingly faced ruin" due to the Philippine Revolution.[12] They equally suffered from the Philippine-American War and the ensuing economic crisis that, epitomized in death and dislocation caused by the ravages of war, rinderpest and cholera epidemics, and a sharp decrease of the area of land under cultivation, affected the Philippine countryside in particular.[13] Between 1900 and 1902, four German firms were declared insolvent, escaping bankruptcy only because relevant Spanish laws had been declared void and the American bankruptcy act had not yet been introduced.[14]

Besides the more general effects of war, several difficulties German firms encountered can be ascribed to specific American actions. Company expenditure, for instance, rose through discriminatory attitudes of newly appointed officials. It had been standard practice under Spanish rule for foreign firms to employ Filipino clerks to handle errands with various authorities such as the Customs House. In the early years of American occupation, Filipino clerks were, however, routinely harassed by American officials—a treatment unheard of under Spanish rule. The tasks of dealing with the administration consequently had to be taken over by European staff or even by the owners themselves, which cost the companies money and for some clerks resulted in loss of employment.[15] A further example is the American bombardment of Iloilo which affected almost all German entrepreneurs residing in the city: the shop buildings of the firms A. Roensch & Co. and Wusinowski & Co., a pharmacy belonging to a certain Hermann Grimm, and two houses of the hacienda owner Ernst Oppen burned to the ground.[16] Finally, several German companies entered a legal conflict over the American extension of a wartime tariff, decreed in July 1898, for almost three years after the ratification of the Treaty of Paris (11 April 1899). One German import firm, Heinszen & Co., engaged in a lengthy and costly legal battle to reclaim duties it had paid during this period, bringing its case to the U.S. Supreme Court but eventually losing.[17]

Apart from economic woes, American rule brought about a factor of insecurity in the form of the American expeditionary forces who demonstrated a remarkable lack of discipline.[18] As the German consul Krüger reported in February 1899, few German families had been spared trouble. Crimes committed by American troops involving Germans included numerous burglaries in private homes, company offices, godowns, and the German consulate. More often than not, American soldiers reacted violently when confronted. A German employee of the Botica de Santa Cruz, a Manila pharmacy owned by Germans, was struck down by an American soldier who refused to pay for a bottle of soda water he had just consumed. The same fate befell E. Knauff, a foreman in the cigar factory El Oriente. Knauff had tried to protect female Filipino cigarette makers working in the factory from an American soldier who sexually assaulted them. One occurrence that particularly incensed the German consul involved a German woman who was stopped by American patrolmen and was touched and searched in what was described as an indecent manner. Remonstrations, as Krüger pointed out, were of no avail: "Her husband was given the answer that the guard thought the woman was a native, as though it were acceptable to reach under the skirts of Filipinas without being punished!"[19] These incidents were particularly astonishing as the victims were subjects of a neutral power. What is moreover noteworthy is that the soldiers involved were apparently not prosecuted.[20]

Encounters between German residents and American troops were not universally unpleasant. The American entrepreneur J. P. Heilbronn, who served as a U.S. Army soldier in 1898, retrospectively described an encounter of his company with two Germans in the early days of the occupation of Manila:

> One was Gustav Otto of Carmelo and Bauermann, the other was Friedrich Stahl of Botica Boie. Mr. Otto had three boxes of cigars under his arms and he gave them out to the soldiers.... He invited me to come to his lithographic establishment.... He introduced me to some Jamaica rum, and he was such a fine handsome generous young fellow that I took the sergeants and non-coms from my Company G to visit him, and they also enjoyed his hospitality, his cerveza, and rum.... Mr. Otto did more for the American Army of Occupation than any European I met in Manila.[21]

This cordial reception may be linked to the fact that Heilbronn spoke German. Fritz Rinne, a German geologist on a short-term visit to assay German-owned gold mines in the Paracale district near Daet in the province Ambos Camarines (Bicol), reported that many American soldiers were actually German immigrants who joyfully greeted their former compatriots.[22] Rinne nevertheless expressed his reservations about the American troops, pointing out that, apart from looting and robbing, they were known for making macabre jokes with the remains of killed Filipinos.[23]

The friendly attitude—toward Germans at least—of some German-American soldiers apart, the conduct of the American military contrasted sharply with that of the Philippine revolutionary troops, who were eager to demonstrate their ability to provide stability for foreign business and protection for foreigners. Philippine troops seem to have been dispatched to Masbate to protect the hacienda of the German merchant Emil Sackermann, who paid for this form of protection.[24] In the Cagayan Valley, Filipino forces tracked down thieves who had stolen $25,000 from German tobacco merchants near Aparri and even contributed money from their own funds in order to reimburse the full sum. The head of El Oriente, the company from which the sum had been stolen, was duly impressed and, according to Krüger, stated that "Aguinaldo's government has managed to gain respect and takes vigorous action."[25] Germans were not the only foreigners who recounted that they had been treated well. A London *Times* article reported the case of fifteen British refugees from Dagupan who confirmed that "the natives in the north of Luzon do sympathize with Aguinaldo's policy of war, but that they do not ill-treat foreigners." [26]

BETWEEN FILIPINOS AND AMERICANS

Germans were suspected of collusion with the Philippine independence movement ever since 1896, when Spanish and British sources alleged that German circles were inciting Filipinos to oppose Spanish rule. These rumors were principally fueled by the fact that José Rizal had published his seminal novel *Noli me tangere* in Berlin. Additionally, reference was made to the existence of German freemason lodges that purportedly assisted and influenced Philippine revolutionaries.[27] Available documents do not substantiate these claims, yet there seems to have been a degree of sympathy for the Philippine cause, at least among Manila's German community. In a report from the 1896 German expedition to the Philippines, Tirpitz, for instance, criticized what he perceived as an overly tolerant stance toward Filipino revolutionaries on the part of German merchants.[28] This possible affinity can be attributed to the establishment of family ties—after all, numerous Germans had married locally—and occasional friendships. The pharmacist and scholar Alexander Schadenberg, for instance, was, as a contemporary of his noted, a "personal friend" of José Rizal's.[29] Rizal himself studied in Germany and came into contact with numerous German scholars, including Fedor Jagor, who had traveled widely in the archipelago, and the scientist and liberal politician Rudolf von Virchow. Rizal's perhaps best-known European friend was Ferdinand Blumentritt, an Austrian school teacher who wrote extensively on Philippine affairs. Blumentritt in turn was in contact with numerous Philippine activists in Europe and in the Philippines as well as with Manila-based German and Swiss traders.[30] On another level, a link between Germans and the Philippine Revolution could be established through the Katipunan leader Andres Bonifacio, who according to contemporary accounts from September and October 1896 worked for the German firm Fressel & Co. But whereas this might have led to further recriminations against Germans, the fact that Fressel & Co. was German-owned was not stressed or may not have been widely known. Interestingly, Carl Fressel's letters to his brother from August to December 1896 suggest that he was oblivious to one of his former employees' involvement, let alone leading role, in the revolution.[31]

Germany and Germans seem to have been held in such high esteem in the Philippines that there were attempts, including the above-mentioned petition put forward by Hong Kong-based Filipinos in January 1897, to invoke German government support for the cause of the Philippine Revolution. However, as Blumentritt noted, much of the credit Germany possessed among Filipino leaders was lost in the course of the events of 1898. Despite a visit to Aguinaldo's headquarters in Cavite, the German squadron in Manila was perceived to be either pro-Spanish or pursuing German colonial ambitions.[32] Leading Filipinos discussed the specter of German colonial rule: Antonio Regidor, for instance, warned José Maria Basa, one of the Filipinos who petitioned the German government in 1897, not to "expect anything from the Germans but flogging."[33] Of significance also was the impression conveyed by Heinrich Spitz, a Catholic German merchant who acted as interim consul from 1896 to 1898. Spitz was closely linked to Manila's Spanish establishment and was reported to have business dealings with the clergy and the church savings and lending institution, the Obras Pias. To the chagrin of Admiral Diederichs, Spitz seems to have exploited his position as consul to circumvent the American blockade and sell provisions to Manila's Spanish community, thereby triggering rumors that the German fleet undermined the effectiveness of the American blockade.[34]

Suspicions concerning potential German colonial designs on the Philippines, the German-American naval rivalry in Manila Bay in 1898, and the sympathetic stance of Manila Germans toward Philippine independence bred American distrust that was to be fueled by several occurrences. In October 1898, three German subjects residing in the Philippines publicly expressed support for Philippine independence, voicing their opinion in an open letter to the revolutionary newspaper *La*

Independencia. The men in question were Otto Scheerer, the former proprietor of the cigar factory La Minerva who had retired to Benguet due to ill health, and the two pharmacists August Loher and Josef Roder. The publication of the letter, in which the humane treatment foreigners, and especially Germans, had received from Philippine troops was praised, incensed the German consul Krüger, who angrily summoned the three authors. Although issuing a statement denying any official endorsement of this letter, Krüger refrained from publicly denouncing Scheerer, Loher, and Roder. Aware of the fact that several Germans—notably ten tobacco planters in the Cagayan Valley—remained in the provinces, he did not wish to aggravate their situation by antagonizing Filipino public opinion.[35]

Krüger claimed that all important members of the German community were "outraged" by what he described as an "undignified declaration,"[36] but there is reason to believe that many shared the opinions expressed by Scheerer, Loher, and Roder yet preferred not to state them in public in order to preserve their business interests. During a visit to Blumentritt's Austrian home in June 1898, Karl Germann, who had spent thirty years in Manila working for the Swiss-German trading house Germann & Co., voiced his admiration for what he perceived as Aguinaldo's judicious use of authority.[37] Max Tornow, a shareholder in Germann & Co. and a further acquaintance of Blumentritt's, even went so far as to state in March 1899 that all foreign merchants wished that the Filipinos triumphed against the Americans, who, according to Tornow, had proved incapable of administering the country.[38]

In addition to the *La Independencia* letter, charges that a German firm based in China supplied Philippine troops with guns and ammunition with the aid of Germany's consul-general in Hong Kong in 1898 further strained German-American relations in the Philippines. Ironically, these weapons were probably shipped to the Philippines by the American merchant W. F. Sylvester, who purchased them from the Canton branch of the prominent German firm Siemssen & Co. in July 1898. According to German sources, Sylvester had secured a contract with the Chinese viceroy in Canton in order to acquire the arms legally but subsequently bribed Chinese authorities and diverted an arms shipment to Manila, where he sold 500 guns and 500,000 bullets to Philippine revolutionaries. Along with several other large China-based German firms, Siemssen & Co. denied any collusion in the deal. The suggestion that a German official may have been involved in arms smuggling operations had repercussions in Berlin, where chancellor Bülow vigorously refuted any such entanglement in a speech to the German parliament.[39] Another allegation put forward in the Manila-based American press was that Germans openly bankrolled Philippine troops. In an article titled "Germans Are in Sympathy with Aguinaldo" published in *The American* in January 1899, a certain Professor Irvine is said to have been "an eye-witness to a German Merchant paying into the hands of one of the insurgent commissioners $50, and Prof. Irvine states that the merchant accompanied his donations with best wishes for success."[40] An additional irritant was the presence of the German aristocrat Prinz Ludwig von Löwenstein, who arrived in Manila in 1897. Löwenstein, according to the German consul an adventurer seeking solace from a dispute with his wife, took an avid interest in the battles raging in the environs of Manila—an occupation that led to suspicions that he was a German spy. Whether Löwenstein engaged in espionage remains unclear, yet the fact that the secret German files on the Philippines do not contain reports from him seems to corroborate the German consul's assessment. Löwenstein died in March 1899, shortly after the outbreak of the Philippine-American War, caught between Philippine and American lines in Malabon.[41]

From the point of view of the American authorities, suspicions about German sympathy for Philippine independence were corroborated by a letter found in 1902 among the Malolos Republic papers captured by the United States Army.[42] Written by the German consulate's translator Gotthard Klocke to Aguinaldo's Secretary of the Interior Teodoro Sandico in January 1899, this document constituted Klocke's offer to serve the Philippine government as a special agent:

> As I desire to contribute to and join with the forward movement of the Filipino people, a movement which they have an absolute right to make, I am ready to renounce my career as a Consul (if I obtain the consent of my government) and to offer my services to the Filipino republic.

Klocke, moreover, offered to travel to Europe to assist in negotiations with European governments. In return, he requested consideration to serve "as an assistant to the future political representative of the Filipino government in Berlin" once independence materialized. In this role, Klocke suggested, he could attract German investors and scholars as well as "arrange for officers to instruct the army (as in Japan)."[43]

The nature of Klocke's relationship with the Philippine government is difficult to assess in light of the scant evidence available—the 1899 letter seems to have been the only document relating to Klocke that was seized by the Americans. Klocke arrived in the Philippines in August 1897 to work as a consular secretary and translator, a post he had previously held in Bucharest. A dispatch reporting a visit of German Navy officers to Aguinaldo's Cavite headquarters in July 1898 reveals that Klocke had encountered Sandico prior to writing his letter: accompanying the German officers, Klocke negotiated with Sandico over the release of a Spanish prisoner.[44] The revelation of Klocke's letter prompted a verbal note by the American government yet did not spark a diplomatic crisis. The German government's professions that Klocke acted clandestinely and the fact that he was neither a major consular officer nor an important German merchant may have convinced the American government that his was but an act of an individual.[45] It is indeed conceivable that Klocke's action was that of a maverick, especially in light of his apparent eagerness to leave the consular service for more glamorous and profitable pursuits. Klocke temporarily left his post at the German consulate to work for a Philippine mining syndicate but was forced to return when the syndicate went bankrupt in 1901. He left Manila for Managua in 1902, eventually returning to his former post in Bucharest.[46]

Interestingly, German consular dispatches make no reference to American concern about German-Philippine collaboration after 1899. This contrasts with the attention given to British merchants, some of whom were expelled from the island of Samar in 1901 for maintaining commercial ties with business partners in this region who had been branded as "insurgents," and for allegedly paying taxes to Philippine forces.[47] Rinne's account of the Philippine-American War, published in Germany in 1901, offers a rare insight into German encounters with Philippine forces. Together with two other mining engineers, including the Manila-born German subject Dr. Raphael Herrmann, who had a fluent command of Tagalog, Rinne worked beyond American lines in Paracale. His account reveals that sympathy for Germans was strong even far out in the provinces. It needs to be added that Herrmann, who led the mining group, not only functioned as an interpreter but also possessed a pass issued by Aguinaldo, which most probably smoothened the group's dealings with Filipinos.[48] On the whole, it seems that German merchants in particular discontinued any activities that may have been deemed suspicious in order to sustain their commercial interests—after all, the early years of American rule were a time not only of readjustment to new political constellations but also of economic crisis. Another possibility may have been a clandestine form of cooperation—this, however, is not supported by archival sources.

In light of the heterogenous nature of the German community in the Philippines, it is not surprising that not all Germans aligned themselves with the Filipino side. The aforementioned example of Gustav Otto shows that German men at times cooperated with the new regime. This was also the case with Edward Schück of Sulu—the son of the nineteenth-century adventurer Hermann Leopold Schück—who served as an interpreter for the American forces.[49] A more intriguing move into the colonial service can be observed in the case of a German advocate of Philippine independence. Otto Scheerer, a co-author of the 1898 letter to *La Independencia*, seems to have gained a sponsor in the colonial administrator Dean Worcester and embarked on a career in the service of the colonial state. By the time of the American occupation, Scheerer was one of the more experienced Germans residing in the Philippines. He had settled in Manila in 1882, first working for the merchant house Klöpfer & Co. and subsequently founding the cigar factory La Minerva. Scheerer married Margarita Asuncion, a Filipino woman with whom he had three children, learned to speak Tagalog, and used his spare time for extended explorations of Luzon. In 1896 a serious case of dysentery forced him to abandon Manila. Instead of returning to Europe, Scheerer chose to move to Benguet, experiencing the Philippine Revolution, as he intimated to Blumentritt, "as a Filipino."[50] Scheerer was in close touch with Filipino revolutionaries such as Apolinario Mabini and Pedro Paterno; the latter even purchased one of Scheerer's houses in Manila in 1895.[51] As the only European left in Benguet, Scheerer was immediately approached by the American authorities. Maj. Evan Johnson, the American commanding officer in La Trinidad, asked Scheerer to locate Paterno, who was in hiding.[52] Although not at all interested in being drawn into the matter, Scheerer reluctantly agreed to act as a mediator and got in touch with Paterno, but American officers remained suspicious of his acquaintance with Paterno and other revolutionaries. In spite of the military's misgivings, Scheerer, who had entertained the commissioners Luke Wright and Dean Worcester during their trip to the Cordillera, was appointed provincial secretary of the Mountain Province in 1900. The military's doubts still were not dispelled, and Scheerer became a regular target of allegations, including Gen. Arthur MacArthur's assertion that he was "known to have been an active cooperator with the insurgents."[53]

Whether allegations about Scheerer's supposed "collaboration" were true remains uncertain, but he resigned in 1901 and left for Japan, where he taught German and

remarried. Interestingly, his involvement with the top flight of the revolutionary movement is also evident during his Japanese sojourn as he was the neighbor of the revolutionary plenipotentiary Mariano Ponce, who encouraged Scheerer to establish contact with Blumentritt. During his stay in Japan, Scheerer was furthermore reported to have been connected with other Philippine exiles like Gen. Jose Lukban.[54] Scheerer was even mentioned in American intelligence reports, yet he astonishingly received a government appointment upon his return to the Philippines, becoming Lieutenant-Governor of the sub-province of Batanes and subsequently effecting the region's separation from Cagayan province. The choice of Scheerer for this post is particularly intriguing as this northernmost province was the Philippine region closest to Formosa, which Japan had acquired as recently as 1895, and was thus vulnerable to potential Japanese territorial ambitions.

Scheerer's career is clearly unique among Germans in the Philippines as he was not only a successful businessman but moreover had a stake in Philippine politics and in the administration of the Philippines, a country he referred to as his "adoptive 'fatherland.'"[55] Despite his friendship with Filipino revolutionaries, he struck a chord with several American administrators, thereby negotiating a space in which he could combine administrative work with his scholarly interest in the Philippines. His accommodation with the new status quo parallels the increasingly cooperative stance of the Western-educated *ilustrado* elite in the Philippines.[56] Yet in contrast to Filipino *ilustrados* who made use of the limited political opportunities offered by the

Otto Scheerer (far right), a German businessman and scholar, called for Philippine independence in 1899 but soon came to an accommodation with the Americans, serving the colonial state in numerous government functions. This photograph, taken in Benguet in July 1900, shows Scheerer with General Luke Wright, the Corporal Constabulary of Benguet, and unnamed Filipinos.

31

colonial state, the key to Scheerer's successful adaptation to the American regime seems to have been a withdrawal from anything that might have been construed as political activism. As he wrote to Blumentritt's son Friedrich in 1913: "My political opinions are of a purely personal nature and I do not have the slightest wish to publicize them."[57] Scheerer eventually pursued his academic interests full-time, joining the staff of the University of the Philippines as an instructor for German language in 1911. In 1923 he founded the university's Department of Oriental Languages together with Trinidad H. Pardo de Tavera. Scheerer retired from his academic posts in the early 1930s and died in Manila in 1938, leaving behind an impressive body of work on Philippine linguistics.[58]

In contrast to Scheerer, the majority of Germans preferred to assume a low profile during the Philippine-American conflict. For the German community as a whole, the main consequence of the Philippine-American War in general and American distrust and repeated infringements against Germans in particular seems to have been an increasing formalization and nationalization of their social organization. After all, apart from showing their disrespect to German subjects, American soldiers had torn down German flags posted on the Escolta shopfront of the tailor Ernst Meyer on the afternoon of the capitulation of Manila.[59] In March 1899, sixty-eight German men consequently founded the *Deutsch-Nationaler-Interessen-Verein* in Manila. In contrast to its predecessor, the Casino Union, essentially a social club with a cross-national, albeit German-speaking membership, this organization admitted only German nationals, a manifestation of nationalism that did not, however, result in the German community's isolation.[60] The relationship with the American rulers remained uneasy, yet the predominantly economic interests of Germans in the Philippines necessitated a pragmatic approach which entailed a cautious stance toward domestic political and military conflicts.

The German community in the Philippines eventually prospered in the 1900s and early 1910s. German merchant houses, cigar factories, and pharmacies profited especially from the trading boom that followed the lowering of tariff barriers between the Philippines and the United States. The community's social composition was slightly altered by the influx of Catholic missionaries and nuns in the 1900s, yet the majority of Germans remained connected to business pursuits. World War I, particularly the American entry into war in 1917, profoundly disturbed the prosperous life of the German community in the Philippines. Since no fighting took place in the archipelago, the damage inflicted on the community occurred on an economic rather than human level. In 1918 German property worth about P15 million was sequestered and numerous German subjects were deported to the United States. German business partly recovered in the 1920s, yet the loss of key firms in the pharmaceutical and tobacco sectors meant that the community failed to regain its former economic and social status. From the German community's point of view, World War I thus proved a far more unsettling experience than the Philippine-American War, which left Germans, who essentially remained observers, relatively unscathed.[61]

NOTES:

I am grateful to Kim Alidio, Stefan Rohde-Enslin, Richard G. Scheerer, and Zdenka Vasilijevová, who generously shared their material on Otto Scheerer. Comments from participants in the Vestiges of War conference at New York University—especially from Oscar Campomanes, Rey Ileto, Ruby Paredes, and the editors Luis Francia and Angel Shaw—prompted me to rethink (and, hopefully, refine) some of my ideas. Angus Campbell, Tobias Rettig, Volker Schult, and Karl-Heinz Wionzek commented on drafts of this essay, thereby contributing valuable information. Finally, A. B. Christa Schwarz was involved in numerous stages of this paper, commenting on it and acquiring much-needed material. The following abbeviations are used in this essay:

BA   -   Bundesarchiv, Berlin

LC   -   Library of Congress, Washington, D.C.

PA   -   Politisches Archiv, Auswärtiges Amt, Bonn

1. BA R 901/30875: Krüger to Bülow, Manila, 30 January 1902.

2. BA R 901/13058: Krüger to Hohenlohe, 8 July 1898; 1830-1930 *Centennial Memorial Botica Boie, Philippine-American Drug Co.* (Manila: n.p., 1930); Adolph Frankenthal, "Business Points for the Philippines," Advance Sheets of Consular Reports (Washington, D.C.) 11 October 1898: 3; Melinda Tria Kerkvliet, *Manila Workers' Unions, 1900-1950* (Quezon City, Philippines: New Day, 1992), 22; Wigan Salazar, "British and German Passivity in the Face of the Spanish Neo-Mercantilist Resurgence in the Philippines, c. 1883-1898," *Itinerario* 11 (1997): 137-38; BA R 901/13062: Krüger to Bülow, 16 and 22 November 1901.

3. There is one report from 1909, identifying the religious affiliation of Germans registered with the Manila consulate, according to which the German community consisted of 122 Protestants, 85 Catholics, 27 Jews, one Mennonite, and one atheist. Evangelisches Zentralarchiv, Berlin, EZA 5/3139: Heintze to Auswärtiges Amt, Manila, 15 March 1909, Fressel Papers, private collection, Hamburg: C. Fressel to parents, Manila, 28 November 1886 and C. Fressel to mother, Manila, 8 January 1887; *The German Club Manila, 1906-1986* (Manila: German Club, 1986), 15, 25; interview with Tony Bosch (grandson of A. Rönsch), Pasay City, 20 January 1998.

4. Volker Schult, "Sulu and Germany in the Late Nineteenth Century," *Philippine Studies* 48 (2000), forthcoming; L. R. Wright, "The Anglo-Spanish-German Treaty of 1885: A Step in the Development of British Hegemony in North Borneo," *Australian Journal of Politics and History* 18 (1972): 67-69; Richard G. Brown, "The German Acquisition of the Caroline Islands, 1898-99," *Germany in the Pacific and Far East, 1870-1914*, John A. Moses and Paul M. Kennedy, eds. (St. Lucia: University of Queensland Press, 1977) 138-40; PA R 19462: Kempermann to Bismarck, Manila, 14 September 1885; Winfried Baumgart, "German Imperialism in Historical Perspective," *Germans in the Tropics: Essays in German Colonial History*, Contributions in Comparative Colonial Studies 24, Arthur J. Knoll and Lewis H. Gann, eds. (New York: Greenwood, 1987), 151-55.2

5. Rainer Pommerin, *Der Kaiser und Amerika: Die USA in der Politik der Reichsleitung 1890-1917* (Cologne: Böhlau, 1986), 85-86; Zeus A. Salazar, "A Filipino Petition to the Kaiser for German Intervention in Favor of the Philippine Revolution," Zeus A. Salazar, ed., *The Ethnic Dimension: Papers on Philippine Culture, History and Psychology* (Cologne: Caritasverband, 1983), 131-53. The petitioners were José Maria Basa, A. G. Medina, and Doroteo Cortes.

6. Terrell Dean Gottschall, "Germany and the Spanish-American War: A Case Study of Navalism and Imperialism," (Ph.D. diss., Washington State University, 1981); Olli Kaikonnen, Deutschland und die Expansionspolitik der USA in den 90er Jahren des 19. Jahrhunderts: Mit besonderer Berücksichtigung der Einstellung *Deutschlands zur spanisch-amerikanischen Krise, Studia Historica Jyväskyläensia* 20 (Jyväskylä: Jyväskyläan

Yliopisto, 1980); Rolf-Harald Wippich, "'War with Germany is imminent': Deutsch-amerikanisches Säbelgerassel vor Manila 1898," *Vermiedene Kriege: Deeskalation von Konflikten der Großmächte zwischen Krimkrieg und Erstem Weltkrieg, 1865-1914*, Jost Düffler, Martin Kröger, and R.-H. Wippich, eds. (Munich: Oldenbourg, 1997), 513-26; Karl-Heinz Wionzek, ed., *Germany, the Philippines, and the Spanish-American War: Four Accounts by Officers of the Imperial German Navy* (Manila: National Historical Institute, 2000).

7. A. Harding Ganz, "The German Navy in the Far East and Pacific: The Seizure of Kiautschou and After," *Germany in the Pacific and Far East* 115; Gottschall 40-41; Ekkehard Böhm, *Überseehandel und Flottenbau: Hanseatische Kaufmannschaft und deutsche Seerüstung 1879-1902* (Düsseldorf: Bertelsmann Universitätsverlag, 1972), 122-26; Wippich, 516-17.

8. Gottschall, 148.

9. Wippich, 517; Gottschall, 53-56, 58-67, 127-38. For German newspapers' coverage of the Spanish-American War and the Philippine Revolution, see Markus M. Hugo, ed. "'¡Manila tiene que ser nuestra!' La guerra de 1898 en la política y el público del Imperio Alemán," *Los Significados del 98: La sociedad española en la génesis del siglo XX*, Octavio Ruiz-Manjón and Alicia Langa Laorga, eds. (Madrid: Biblioteca Nueva Universidad Complutense, 1999), 179-82; and Portia Liongson Reyes, "Ang Himagsikang Pilipino sa mga Pahayagang Aleman," *Bagong Kasaysayan* 5 (Quezon City, Philippines: BAKAS, 1999), 11-34.

10. PA R 19200: Bülow to Commanding Admiral, Berlin, 1 March 1899; PA R 19204: Bülow to Chief of Staff of Admiralty, Berlin, 7 November 1901.

11. PA R 19474: Diederichs to Commanding Admiral, Manila, 2 August 1898; Gottschall 68; Max L. Tornow, *Die wirtschaftliche Entwickelung der Philippinen* (Berlin: Paetel, 1901), 47.

12. PA R 19200: Krüger to Hohenlohe, Manila, 2 May 1899. Own translation.

13. BA R 901/13065: Krüger to Bülow, Manila, 6 October 1902; See also Reynaldo C. Ileto, "Cholera and the Origins of the American Sanitary Order in the Philippines," Vicente L. Rafael, ed., *Discrepant Histories: Translocal Essays on Filipino Cultures* (Philadelphia, Pa.: Temple University Press, 1995), 51-81.

14. PA R 141706: Krüger to Hohenlohe, Manila, 12 January 1900; BA R 901/13065: Krüger to Bülow, Manila, 6 October 1902.

15. PA R 19205. Krüger to Bülow, Manila, 11 August 1902. Krüger attributed the American officials' actions to racism.

16. PA R 19200: Krüger to Hohenlohe, Manila, 20 March 1899. The destruction of Iloilo infuriated resident Germans particularly because the U.S. gunboat *Petrel* opened fire a day earlier than it had announced in an ultimatum. "The Taking of Iloilo," *Times* (London) 24 March 1899: 4.

17. The United States government, insisting on the legality of its actions, argued that the state of war continued after April 1899—an assertion that, as the German ambassador to Washington pointed out, ran counter to the government line concerning the Philippine-American War, which was to fervently deny that any war was taking place. BA R 901/5001: Hatzfeldt to Bülow, Washington, 28 May 1907.

18. Gottschall notes that Diederichs was "contemptuous of [U.S. General] Merritt's troops. Although well-trained and in excellent physical shape, they lacked discipline and could never stand up to a European army. He derogatorily noted that many carried personal mail tucked into their turned-up shirtsleeves and wore toothbrushes as hat ornaments." Gottschall, 120.

19. PA R 19200: Krüger to Hohenlohe, 3 February 1899. Own translation. The occurrence of these types of incidents is confirmed by Ferdinand Blumentritt. LC, Blumentritt Papers, Folder 7: Blumentritt to Adolf Meyer, Leitmeritz, 14 May 1899.

20. PA R 19200: Krüger to Hohenlohe, Manila, 3 February 1899.

21. "How J. P. Heilbronn First Met Otto Gustav Is Recalled," *Carmelo & Bauermann Supplement, Tribune* (Manila) 9 November 1937: 14.

22. Fritz Rinne, *Zwischen Filipinos und Amerikanern auf Luzon: Skizzen* (Hannover: Jänecke, 1901), 42-43.

According to a German naval officer, a large proportion of the American expeditionary force was of German origin: 10 percent were first generation German immigrants and another 15 percent were sons of German immigrants. Other important immigrant groups represented were Irish (25%), English (10%), and Scandinavians (10%). PA R 19197: Reincke to Commanding Admiral, Manila, 31 October 1898.

23. Rinne, 47.

24. Sackermann had initially requested the presence of a German warship but retracted once it became clear that 200 Philippine troops would be dispatched to Masbate. PA R 19197: Reincke to Commanding Admiral, Manila, 31 October 1898.

25. PA R 19200: Krüger to Hohenlohe, Manila, 2 May 1899. Own translation.

26. "The Philippines," *Times* (London) 24 March 1899: 5.

27. PA R 19463: Sprenger to Hohenlohe, San Sebastian, 3 September 1896; Sprenger to Hohenlohe, San Sebastian, 10 September 1896. BA R 901/33735: note, 7 September 1896.

28. Zeus Salazar, 134.

29. Otto Scheerer, "Alexander Schadenberg, his life and work in the Philippines," *Philippine Journal of Science* 22 (1923), 453.

30. Stefan Rohde-Enslin, "Östlich des Horizonts: Deutsche Philippinenforschung im 19. Jahrhundert," *FDI-Schriften* 7 (Osnabrück: WURF, 1992), 158-59; Harry Sichrovsky, *Der Revolutionär von Leitmeritz: Ferdinand Blumentritt und der philippinische Freiheitskampf* (Vienna: Österreichischer Bundesverlag, 1983), 141-43; LC, Blumentritt Papers, Folder 6: Blumentritt to Meyer, Leitmeritz, 7 August 1898.

31. "Los Sucesos Actuales," *Diario de Manila*, 2 September 1896, and W. E. Retana, "El Catipunan," *El Heraldo de Madrid*, 22. October 1896, *La Revolución Hispano-Filipina en la Prensa: Diario de Manila y Heraldo de Madrid*, ed. Isacio Rodríguez Rodríguez and Jesús Alvarez Fernández, five volumes (Madrid: Agencia Española de Cooperación Internacional, 1998), 1: 84, 391-92; Jonathan Fast and Jim Richardson, *Roots of Dependency: Political and Economic Revolution in 19th Century Philippines* (Quezon City, Philippines: Foundation for Nationalist Studies, 1979), 69. Fressel Papers: Carl Fressel to Wilhelm Fressel, Manila, 14 September, 25 November, and 7 December 1896.

32. Ferdinand Blumentritt, "Deutsche und Philippiner," *Kölnische Zeitung* n.d. [1899]: n. pag.; the possibility that the German fleet raised Spanish morale was especially stressed by American naval officers. "The Philippines," *Times* (London) 29 June 1898: 7.

33. Antonio María Regidor to José María Basa, 1 July 1989, exhibit 141 of John R. M. Taylor, *The Philippine Insurrection against the United States: A Compilation of Documents with Notes and Introduction*, 5 volumes (Pasay City: Eugenio Lopez Foundation, 1971-73) v. 3: 251.

34. According to Diederichs, Spitz was a consummate businessman who was able to strike deals with Filipino troops and the Spanish colonial administration alike. Spitz seems to have sold a large consignment of potatoes, that had been delivered for Manila's German community, to Manila's beleaguered Spanish population. PA R 141706: Diederichs to Commanding Admiral, Manila, 2 August 1898.

35. The letter was published in *La Independencia* of 17 October 1898. PA R 19198: Krüger to Hohenlohe, Manila, 12 January 1899; "Germans are not assisting Tagalos," *New York Herald* 14 January 1899: n.pag.; PA R 19200: Krüger to Hohenlohe, Manila, 25 March 1899. Roder, who managed the pharmacy generally known as Botica Boie, died soon after publication of the letter while on vacation in Germany. Loher, an employee of the Ilang-Ilang distillery A. G. Sibrand Siegert & Co., stayed in the Philippines until his death in the late 1920s. He worked as a botanist in his spare time, and numerous Philippine plants are named after him. *1830-1930 Centennial Memorial Botica Boie* 17, 14. Additional information on Scheerer will be given later in this essay.

36. PA R 19198: Krüger to Hohenlohe, Manila, 12 January 1899. Own translation.

37. LC, Blumentritt Papers, Folder 5: Blumentritt to Adolph Meyer, Leitmeritz, 17 June 1898.

38. LC, Blumentritt Papers, Folder 7: Blumentritt to Adolph Meyer, Leitmeritz, 4 March 1899. For a similar assessment by an unnamed Swiss merchant who visited Blumentritt, see LC, Blumentritt Papers, Folder 8: Blumentritt to Adolph Meyer, Leitmeritz, 10 February 1900.

39. PA R 19200: Rieloff to Hohenlohe, Hong Kong, 16 February 1899; "Germany and the United States," *Times* (London) 13 February 1899: 5.

40. "Germans Are in Sympathy with Aguinaldo," *American* (Manila) 14 January 1899: n. pag.; PA R 19200: Krüger to Hohenlohe, Manila, 22 January 1899.

41. Leon Ma. Guerrero, "The Kaiser and the Philippines," *Bulletin of the American Historical Collection* (Manila) 12 (1984): 10; PA R 19200: Krüger to Hohenlohe, Manila, 5 April 1899.

42. For a discussion of the seizure of the Philippine Revolutionary Papers (formerly known as the "Philippine Insurgent Papers"), see Milagros C. Guerrero, "Luzon at War: Contradictions in Philippine Society, 1898-1902" (Ph.D. diss., University of Michigan, 1977), 28-29.

43. PA R 19205: U.S. Embassy Berlin to Auswärtiges Amt, note verbale, 27 February 1902; Klocke to Sandico, Manila, 4 January 1899. Klocke's letter is also held at the U.S. National Archives. National Archives, College Park, MD, Record Group 350/539/8.

44. The report on this visit is partly printed in Willi Boelcke, *So kam das Meer zu uns: Die preußisch-deutsche Kriegsmarine in Übersee 1882 bis 1914* (Frankfurt am Main: Ullstein, 1981) 277-81.

45. PA R 19205: Klocke to Sandico, Manila, 4 January 1899.

46. PA R 141706: Krüger to Bülow, 17 October 1901; PA Ib Rep. IV Personalia no. 234 vol. 1: Paul Gotthard Klocke, März 1896-Juli 1912. Klocke died in 1912.

47. "Englishmen expelled from the Philippines," *Times* (London) 19 September 1901: 4. The *Times* erroneously interpreted the expulsion as applying to the Philippines as a whole. It is interesting to note that although the British consul was convinced that the testimonials against the British firms involved (Smith, Bell & Co. and Warner Barnes & Co.) had been brought about by water torture, no official complaint was made. Public Record Office, Richmond, Surrey, Foreign Office Records 5/2465: Sinclair to Lansdowne, Manila, 24 September 1901 and Harford to Lansdowne, Manila, 27 December 1901.

48. Rinne, 34, 40.

49. "Prominent citizen passes away," *Mindanao Herald,* 11 January 1913: n.pag.

50. South Bohemian Museum, Ceské Budejovice, Czech Republic, Blumentritt Papers: Scheerer to Blumentritt, Yokohama, 5 June 1902.

51. South Bohemian Museum, Blumentritt Papers: Scheerer to Blumentritt, Yokohama, 5 June 1902; Howard T. Fry, *A History of the Mountain Province* (Quezon City, Philippines: New Day, 1983), 235; Jose N. de Leon III, "A German in the Philippines," *Evening Star* (Manila) 26 April 1989: 4.

52. Fry, 6.

53. MacArthur [January 1901] qtd in Fry, 10.

54. South Bohemian Museum, Blumentritt Papers: Scheerer to Blumentritt, Yokohama, 5 June 1902; Grant K. Goodman, "Filipino Secret Agents, 1896-1910," *Philippine Studies* 46 (1998): 384.

55. University of California, Berkeley, The Bancroft Library, David P. Barrows Papers, BANC MSS C-B 1005, Box 34: Scheerer to Barrows, Yokohama, 28 July 1903.

56. Ruby R. Paredes, "Introduction: The Paradox of Philippine Colonial Democracy," *Philippine Colonial Democracy*, ed. Ruby R. Paredes, Yale University Southeast Asia Studies Monograph Series 32 (New Haven, Conn.: Yale Center for International and Area Studies, 1988), 8.

57. South Bohemian Museum, Blumentritt Papers: Scheerer to Friedrich Blumentritt, Pasay, 30 November 1913. Own translation.

58. Cecilio Lopez, "Rizal and the Beginning of German-Philippine Cultural Relations," *The Joint Enterprise: Philippine-German Cooperation*, Hans R. Stieber, ed. (Manila: Regal; Tübingen: Erdmann,

1967), 36; Marlies Spiecker-Salazar, "German Linguists and Philippine Languages," Philippine Journal of Linguistics 12 (1981): 27.

59. PA R 19200: Krüger to Hohenlohe, Manila, 3 February 1899.

60. PA R 19198: Krüger to Hohenlohe, Manila, 14 March 1899. The board members for Manila were H. Spitz (E. Spitz & Co.), H. Bollhorst (Struckmann & Co.), G. A. Pfützner (Baersen & Co.), Fr. Kammerzell (Germann & Co.), and M. Saelen (Schwenger & Co.).

61. Johann K. von Stechow, "Deutsche auf den Philippinen," *Zeitschrift für Kulturaustausch* 16 (1966): 153; PA R 86257: Timann to Auswärtiges Amt, Manila, 3 January 1923.

Mark Twain's Anti-Imperialist Writings in the "American Century"

JIM ZWICK

In a series of historical fantasies written in 1901, Mark Twain envisioned the creation of an empire where books and libraries were banned, confiscated, and destroyed while history was rewritten to glorify the conquest of foreign lands. Written nearly half a century before George Orwell gave us *1984*, Twain's views were inspired by the creation of an American empire and by the suppression of dissent that occurred during the Philippine-American War. For more than ten years, he opposed the war and imperialism as a vice president and outspoken publicist of the Anti-Imperialist League. From his return to the United States from Europe in 1900 until shortly before his death in 1910, he expressed his opposition to imperialism in numerous essays, stories, and sketches, public and private letters, and interviews and speeches. Mark Twain's involvement with the anti-imperialist movement was one of the longest and most significant political affiliations of his life, and was widely recognized during his lifetime, inspiring editorials and political cartoons from California to London, Bermuda to Canada, and probably further afield. But like the Philippine-American War itself, and turn-of-the-century imperialism more generally, this part of Mark Twain's career is rarely recognized today.

In *Lighting Out for the Territory: Reflections on Mark Twain and American Culture*, Shelley Fisher Fishkin suggests that the way Americans remember Mark Twain often tells us more about present-day Americans than about Twain himself.[1] Hannibal, Missouri, for example, glorifies his "boyhood years" in annual Tom Sawyer Days celebrations without acknowledging its history as a slaveholding community, an element of Twain's experience there that provided the material for his antiracist novels *Adventures of Huckleberry Finn* and *The Tragedy of Pudd'nhead Wilson*. In a town unwilling to address racism past or present, Tom Sawyer's antics are preferred over stories about slavery and racial identity. Americans have a similar national aversion to facing the bloody origins of their "shared history" with the Philippines. Mark Twain's anti-imperialist writings are relatively unknown today because of the nation's inability to deal with that part of its past.[2]

The fact of denial is easy to document. It is present in history texts that typically deal with the fifteen-year Philippine-American War as an insignificant footnote to the three-month "splendid little war" with Spain; in "Spanish-American War" monuments where the dates are given as 1898 to 1902 even though the war with Spain was over by mid-August of 1898; in the constantly repeated "shared history" euphemism that masks the imperial origins of the relationship between the United States and the Philippines; and in what scholars now refer to as the "invisibility" of Filipino Americans, the largest Asian group in the country.

The empire was denied from its start. Advocates of the annexation of the Philippines called themselves "expansionists," not "imperialists," and they derided their opponents for being satisfied with a "little America" while they sought a "greater America."[3] Important events in colonial history were masked with Independence Day symbolism as the establishment of civil rule in 1901, Theodore Roosevelt's declaration that the "insurrection" was over in 1902, and the formal grant of Philippine independence in 1946, all occurred on 4 July. That the war is still most often dated as 1899-1902 is an indication of the success of that early strategy of denial. Made less than a week after the U.S. Senate concluded embarrassing hearings on army atrocities in the Philippines, Roosevelt's 4 July 1902 declaration that the war was over had more symbolic meaning and domestic political influence than anything else. Warfare continued in the northern provinces of the Philippines, but in November of 1902 the U.S. Philippine Commission passed the "Bandolerismo Statute" or "Brigandage Act" which defined all further armed resistance to U.S. rule as banditry.[4] Warfare continued but the war was essentially defined away, and the last holdouts among the Filipino officers on the northern front were hanged as bandits in 1907. Their deaths provided the United States with the opportunity to establish the Philippine Assembly that year; its creation was delayed until "pacification" was complete in the northern islands. While those events were taking place in the north, the United States opened the war's second front against the Muslim Filipinos of the southern Philippines. The Bates Agreement negotiated in 1899 had forestalled warfare with the Muslim Filipinos by promising them autonomy. In early 1903 U.S. troops were ordered to occupy the southern islands. Moro Province was formed under U.S. military rule in September and in March of 1904 the United States unilaterally abrogated the Bates Agreement. Two of the worst massacres of the war occurred in the south in 1906 and 1913, and the U.S. military government of Moro Province was not lifted until December 1913.[5] Mark Twain continued to write about the war until shortly before his death because the war was still going on.

The denial of empire is so pervasive that it often seems overwhelming, but it has been contested throughout the century. The issue of imperialism was kept alive by later annexations, military occupations, and numerous other foreign interventions. Within that debate, Mark Twain's iconic stature in American culture gives his anti-imperialist writings particular importance, and it is clear that all sides understand the significance of attaching his name to a political position. As products of the original debate about imperialism that still retain their political power, Twain's writings provide a good reference for understanding the contours of the public debate about imperialism in the twentieth century. By examining his writings and how they were censored during and after World War I, debated during the Cold

War, and revived from the 1960s onward, we can get a glimpse of how the history of imperialism was suppressed and how Americans became "miseducated" about their country's historic role in the world.[6] The treatment of Twain's writings indicates that the processes through which that history was suppressed were more complex than is usually recognized, involving interactions between broad political contexts, commercial pressures to suppress or to publish dissenting opinions, and choices made by specific individuals and groups. Twain's case undoubtedly includes some unique features, but his are certainly not the only anti-imperialist writings of the period that have been suppressed or ignored. Edgar Lee Masters's anti-imperialist writings—spanning from 1900 to at least the mid-1930s—have never been collected, and those by C. E. S. Wood were excluded from the 1949 edition of his *Collected Poems* and the first general anthology of his writings published in 1997.[7] Also, one of the largest publishers in the United States played a significant role in first suppressing and later reviving Mark Twain's anti-imperialist writings.

During the Spanish-American War, Twain was living in Europe following his round-the-world lecture tour and the writing of *Following the Equator*. Like many others who would later become prominent anti-imperialists, he believed the war of 1898 was fought solely to free Cuba from Spanish oppression. "It is a worthy thing to fight for one's freedom," he wrote to his friend Joseph H. Twichell on 17 June 1898; "it is another sight finer to fight for another man's. And I think this is the first time it has been done."[8] The Treaty of Paris that concluded the war proved to be a bitter disappointment. When Twain returned to the United States in October of 1900, he was asked by reporters about his opposition to imperialism. He had once supported putting "a miniature of the American constitution afloat in the Pacific," he told them. "But I have thought some more, since then, and I have read carefully the Treaty of Paris, and I have seen that we do not intend to free but to subjugate the people of the Philippines." "And so I am an anti-imperialist," he concluded. "I am opposed to having the eagle put its talons on any other land."[9]

During the next few months he made numerous other statements against imperialism in speeches and interviews, and he closed the year with this "Salutation Speech from the Nineteenth Century to the Twentieth":

> I bring you the stately matron named Christendom—returning bedraggled, besmirched and dishonored from pirate raids in Kiaochow, Manchuria, South Africa and the Philippines; with her soul full of meanness, her pocket full of boodle and her mouth full of pious hypocrisies. Give her soap and a towel, but hide the looking glass.[10]

In just two sentences he blasted four prominent manifestations of the imperial surge that was taking place worldwide at the end of the nineteenth century: Germany's seizure of Kiao Chow Bay in China, Russia's occupation of Manchuria, the Boer War in South Africa, and the Philippine-American War. Two weeks later Mark Twain agreed to serve as a vice president of the Anti-Imperialist League of New York.

The Anti-Imperialist League was formed in Boston in November of 1898 when it became clear that the U.S. government was not going to free Puerto Rico, Guam, and the Philippines after the Spanish-American War. Its first appeal for membership proclaimed: "We are in full sympathy with the heroic struggles for liberty of the people in the Spanish Islands, and therefore we protest against depriving them of their rights by an exchange of masters." Frequently quoting the Declaration of Independence and Lincoln's antislavery statements, the League based its appeal against imperialism squarely upon America's democratic and anticolonial traditions. "These principles abandoned," it argued, "a republic exists but in name, and its people lose their rights."[11]

Many of the country's most prominent politicians, businessmen, labor leaders, educators, clergy, social reformers, and literary figures added their support to the movement and local Anti-Imperialist League branches were formed in cities across the country. In October of 1899 a national conference was held in Chicago to form the national American Anti-Imperialist League headquartered in that city. This organization united the various local Leagues under a platform that declared that imperialism was the "paramount issue of the day." The platform urged all League members to work for the defeat of any political candidate who supported imperialism. A remarkable range of people were brought together under that platform. Among the League's officers were many whose names are still widely known today but whose affiliation with the anti-imperialist movement is not often recognized. They include industrialist Andrew Carnegie, American Federation of Labor President Samuel Gompers, philosophers William James and John Dewey, former president Grover Cleveland, urban reformers Jane Addams and Josephine Shaw Lowell, civil rights leaders Moorfield Storey and Oswald Garrison Villard, and one of the leaders of the movement to disfranchise African American voters and establish segregation laws in the South, Benjamin R. Tillman.

While the issue of imperialism divided nearly every contemporary social movement in the United States, opposition to it as "the paramount issue" also brought together people who took opposing positions on other issues. Their reasons for objecting to imperialism were also far from uniform. The League included people who saw imperialism as bad for labor *or* for business, as undermining free trade or protection of national industry. They also held a diverse range of opinions about the peoples of the colonies. Initially believing that the territories annexed in 1898 would eventually become states, some opposed imperialism because they did not want what they believed were racially inferior peoples included in the population of the United States. Others, including Twain's friend, William Dean Howells, opposed annexation of another "race problem" for different reasons. The country was still far from treating African-Americans and Native Americans with justice and they believed it would only do worse overseas. The League's official position, as expressed in its platform, was that "all men, of whatever race or color, are entitled to life, liberty, and the pursuit of happiness," and it led efforts to portray Filipinos in a positive light. The League circulated hundreds of Filipino-authored documents and essays, opposed displays of Filipinos as "primitive peoples" at world's fairs, hosted Filipinos visiting the United States, and facilitated speaking tours for them.[12]

The League's efforts may not have changed the opinions of some of the most racist anti-imperialists, but that group dropped out of the organized anti-imperialist movement after it became clear that the colonies would not become states. Immediately after the Treaty of Paris was ratified, Peace Commissioner Whitelaw

Reid had responded to their concerns by stating, "it is a bugbear that the Filipinos would be citizens of the United States.... The treaty did not make them citizens of the United States at all; and they never will be, unless you neglect your congress." He also urged Americans to "resist the crazy extension of the doctrine that government derives its just powers from the consent of the governed to an extreme never imagined by the men who framed it." Imperialists and racist anti-imperialists were not far apart here. Imperialists used the U.S. military to deny Filipinos their right to self-government while disfranchisement of African-Americans in the South was backed by an increase in racial violence. "The spirit which slaughters brown men in Jolo is the spirit which lynches black men in the South," League President Moorfield Storey observed.[13]

The Anti-Imperialist League launched a massive propaganda campaign against imperialism, publishing anti-imperialist materials in a wide range of formats and making extensive use of the contemporary media. In a 1928 study of the League that focused on its Boston branch, Maria Lanzar-Carpio estimated that it published "a grand total of 1,184,188 printed items in pamphlets, leaflets, broadsides, books, poems, newspapers, cards, circulars and letters." That already sounds like a very extensive publications program, but in 1912 Erving Winslow, the League's national secretary, wrote that "it is certain that over five million documents have been distributed during the history of the League."[14] With the editors of many newspapers and magazines among its officers, the League was also able to gain wide circulation of anti-imperialist essays and speeches through the mainstream press. It also reached substantial audiences through mass meetings held in venues like Faneuil Hall in Boston and Carnegie Hall in New York, and by touring oppositional speakers like Sergeant Andreae and Private Reeves, two returned soldiers who gave stereoscopic "magic lantern" slide presentations about the war under the League's auspices in Chicago, Boston, New York, and Philadelphia.[15]

It was within this massive propaganda campaign against American imperialism that Mark Twain made his most important contributions to the cause. When he returned to the United States in 1900, his fame was rivaled only by the Rough Rider turned vice-presidential candidate Theodore Roosevelt, and he used his fame and his skill as a writer to produce two of the League's most widely circulated publications. His "Salutation Speech" of December 1900 was published in newspapers from coast to coast and printed as a card for national distribution. *The Public*, a Chicago-based weekly, published it along with similar new-century statements by William McKinley, Theodore Roosevelt, and William Jennings Bryan. Although he held no public office, Twain was grouped with the president, his vice president-elect, and their opponent in the recently concluded presidential campaign. "To the Person Sitting in Darkness" also received wide circulation after it was published in the February 1901 issue of the *North American Review*. The Anti-Imperialist League of New York published a pamphlet edition of 125,000 copies—a large edition for those days and the largest ever produced by the Anti-Imperialist League—and the essay was also excerpted and commented upon in newspapers and magazines throughout the country until the middle of the year.[16]

Twain's association with the Anti-Imperialist League influenced many of his later writings and speeches, and was widely known and commented upon during his lifetime. On 3 February 1901, the *Springfield Republican* (Mass.) editorialized that "Mark Twain has suddenly become the most influential anti-imperialist and the most dreaded critic of the sacrosanct person in the White House that the country contains." Twain's audience was as divided over the issue of imperialism as the country at large and not everyone was so enthusiastic about his entrance into the debate. In a letter to Twain written shortly after "To the Person Sitting in Darkness" was published, one of his supporters summed it up well, telling him that "You have hitherto been loved for the friends you have gained, now you are to be loved for the enemies you make."[17] Although Twain published only a fraction of what he wrote about imperialism, he continued to give interviews and make public statements about the conquest of the Philippines until at least November of 1907. The international view of imperialism Twain expressed in his December 1900 "Salutation Speech" also found expression through his diverse organizational involvements. His well-known association with the League led to invitations to serve as an officer of the American Congo Reform Association in 1905 and to chair the organizing committee for a 1906 dinner for Maxim Gorky planned in New York to raise funds for the Russian Revolution.[18]

By the time of his death on 21 April 1910, Twain's involvements in public issues were almost as widely recognized as his career as a popular author. In a memorial article in a May 1910 issue of *The Public*, Daniel Kiefer wrote that many American "pseudo patriots" were willing to criticize atrocities committed by other countries, "but ask him to hear the truth about American outrages in the Philippines, and then you realize what it means to commit an unpardonable sin. Mark Twain did not hesitate to risk all the consequences of this offense. His 'To the Person Sitting in Darkness' brought upon him a shower of abuse from those who make the flag a fetish, but have no sympathy for the principles of which it is but a symbol." In a "Tribute to Mark Twain" published in the prestigious *North American Review*, Andrew Carnegie highlighted his 1902 essay, "A Defence of General Funston": "No man knew Mark Twain who had not seen him aroused by some mean, detestable action which violated his sense of justice. In his wrath he was indeed terrible. One has only to read his condemnation of the capture of Aguinaldo, the Filipino General, to realize this." Numerous other memorial statements and obituaries published after Twain's death also commented upon his writings about the Philippines, and the Anti-Imperialist League mentioned his support of the cause in its publications as late as 1918. The obituary the League published in its annual report for 1910 seems prophetic today: He "employed in the cause of Anti-Imperialism and in behalf of the Filipino those wonderful weapons of satire which were so absolutely at his command, and the members of the League were able to appreciate what is not yet justly understood: that, more than a brilliant humorist, he was a passionate and zealous reformer."[19] What was "not yet justly understood" in 1910 slipped further from public consciousness as both the Philippine-American War and Twain's opposition to it were forgotten in the decades that followed.

By suppressing some of his own writings, Twain participated in the historical silence about the war. But he was also confronted with an exclusive publisher, Harper and Brothers, that refused to publish some of his best polemical writings. In March of 1905, his well-known story "The War Prayer" was rejected by *Harper's Bazaar* as "not quite suited to a woman's magazine." The story is a devastating satire of religious support for war. Amidst patriotic celebrations, a town is preparing to send its young men off to war, and they gather in a church to pray for victory. At the conclusion of the victory prayer, an "aged stranger" enters the church, walks up the aisle and, nudging the minister aside, declares that he has been sent as a messenger from God to show the congregation the full meaning of their prayer and ask them if it is really what they want. He begins:

> O Lord our Father, our young patriots, idols of our hearts, go forth to battle—be Thou near them!... O Lord our God, help us to tear their soldiers to bloody shreds with our shells; help us to cover their smiling fields with the pale forms of their patriot dead;... help us to wring the hearts of their unoffending widows with unavailing grief; help us to turn them out roofless with their little children wandering and unfriended in the wastes of their desolated land...

In this version of the victory prayer, the aged stranger reveals the "unmentioned results" that "follow victory—*must* follow it, cannot help but follow it." The congregation ultimately decides that he "was a lunatic, because there was no sense in what he said." A few days after "The War Prayer" was rejected by *Harper's Bazaar*, Twain wrote to his friend Dan Beard, to whom he had read the story, "I don't think the prayer will be published in my time. None but the dead are permitted to tell the truth." His editor was "responsible to his Company," he explained, "and should not permit laughs which could injure its business."[20]

The following month Harper and Brothers rejected "King Leopold's Soliloquy," Twain's excoriation of the Belgian king's brutal rule of the Congo. Twain wrote to Edmund D. Morel, the head of the English Congo Reform Association, that Harper and Brothers was "doubtful about the commercial wisdom of dipping into Leopold's stinkpot." He added that "They are so situated, by the contract between us, that I cannot make them do right."[21] Because of his exclusive contract with Harper and Brothers, Twain had to obtain their permission before allowing the American Congo Reform Association to publish the essay in pamphlet form. "The War Prayer" remained unpublished until 1923, thirteen years after his death.

Twain's experience with his publisher undoubtedly confirmed his belief that some of his writings were too controversial for publication. "In America—as elsewhere—free speech is confined to the dead," he wrote in his private notebook in 1905. A year later, when he blasted Maj. Gen. Leonard Wood for leading U.S. troops in the massacre of nine hundred Muslim Filipinos—women and children included—he didn't even try to publish his scathing commentary. Marking the manuscript as "not usable yet," he consigned it, like the rejected story "The War Prayer," for publication after his death.

The task of publishing these and other writings was entrusted to Albert Bigelow Paine, Twain's official biographer and first literary executor, who apparently saw his job as that of a censor charged with printing only what he believed would not ruffle the public's image of his subject. In a 1926 letter to an editor at Harper and Brothers, Paine wrote that no one should be allowed to write about Mark Twain for "as long as we can prevent it." Once others were allowed to write about him, he continued, "the Mark Twain that we have 'preserved'—the Mark Twain that we knew, the traditional Mark Twain—will begin to fade and change, and with that process the Harper Mark Twain property will depreciate."[22]

In the volumes of Twain's letters, essays and stories, notebooks, and autobiographical dictations published under Paine's tenure as literary executor, many references to the Philippine-American War and unflattering characterizations of American presidents and soldiers were stricken from the texts, often leaving no indication that the writings were inspired by the war. Paine's judgement and the interests of the "Harper Mark Twain property" did not require consistent removal of all references to the war, however, and the editorial choices Paine made at different times give us a glimpse of the changing attitudes about imperialism from the publication of *Mark Twain: A Biography* in 1912 to his edition of the notebooks in 1935.

Paine's official biography did not mention that Mark Twain was an officer of the Anti-Imperialist League but it did include several discussions of his anti-imperialist writings, including a short chapter on the Philippine-American War. Excerpts from a number of previously unpublished essays, stories, letters, and sketches were also included within the main text or appendices. Of all of Paine's work on Twain, the biography is the most forthright about the latter's anti-imperialist writings and activities. There are some glaring misinterpretations but no obvious signs of censorship.

Paine's two-volume edition of *Mark Twain's Letters* was published in 1917 and it provides the earliest clear example of censorship aimed at preserving the "traditional Mark Twain." Paine silently edited a letter Twain wrote on 24 January 1901, to his Hartford friend and pastor, Rev. Joseph H. Twichell. Fortunately, this letter survives intact in the Beinecke Rare Book and Manuscript Library at Yale University. "I am going to stick close to my desk for a month, now," Twain wrote, "hoping to write a small book, full of playful and good-natured contempt for the lousy McKinley." Twichell knew what to expect from such a book. In a widely reported speech delivered earlier in the month, Twain described President McKinley as the man who sent U.S. troops to the Philippines "to fight with a disgraced musket under a polluted flag." After Paine's editing, the published version of this letter ends with Twain "hoping to write a small book."[23] Period. It seems safe to assume that readers of Mark Twain Letters, like readers of any renowned author's letters, would want to know what that "small book" was about, but "contempt for the lousy McKinley" did not fit Paine's image of "the traditional Mark Twain" that he was in the business of preserving.

Two similarly significant deletions were made in the anti-imperialist essays included in Paine's next volume of Twain's writings, *Europe and Elsewhere*, published in 1923. "The War Prayer" was first published in this volume. But before including "As Regards Patriotism," Paine removed an entire paragraph about the Philippines that discussed the concentration camps established there by the U.S. Army and compared them with Spain's earlier *reconcentrado* policy in Cuba. By eliminating this paragraph, Paine excised all reference to the war in the Philippines, which clearly inspired the essay, and turned it into a generic discussion of patriotism.[24]

In the same volume, Paine edited the concluding section of "To the Person Sitting in Darkness" to remove a discussion of the U.S. Army's khaki uniform, which Twain described as "yellow stuff such as quarantine flags are made of, and which are hoisted to warn the healthy away from unclean disease and repulsive death." William Andrews, who first noted this revision in a 1977 article in the *Markham Review*, argued that Paine removed that section in deference to the army after World War I.[25] This is a plausible explanation, especially because Paine did include Twain's suggestion for changing the U.S. flag in the Philippines to have "the white stripes painted black and the stars replaced by the skull and cross-bones." That this suggestion for the flag was retained is somewhat surprising and is a good example of the inconsistencies in Paine's editing of Twain's writings. Paine also removed Twain's December 1900 speech introducing Winston S. Churchill from his 1923 edition of *Mark Twain's Speeches*. That speech, which was included in the 1910 edition, was a broad critique of imperialism and concluded by referring to England and the United States as "kin in sin" for their imperialist wars in South Africa and the Philippines.

When Paine's edition of *Mark Twain's Autobiography* was published the following year, it included most of Twain's long autobiographical dictations on the massacre of the Muslim Filipinos on Mount Dajo in the southern Philippines. Some nine hundred Muslim Filipinos—men, women and children—were trapped in the volcanic crater and fired upon for four days until all were reported dead (one young girl survived). Twain's comments on the massacre are among his most angry indictments of the conquest of the Philippines. After quoting Gen. Leonard Wood's order to "kill or capture" the Filipinos, Twain comments: "Apparently our little army considered that the 'or' left them authorized to kill *or* capture according to taste, and that their taste had remained what it has been for eight years, in our army out there—the taste of Christian butchers." Paine's editing was restricted to removing several derogatory statements about William McKinley (he was described as "the least masculine of men," among other things) and a long concluding paragraph about the close relationship between Leonard Wood, the commanding officer in charge of the massacre, and Theodore Roosevelt.[26] By 1924, when this book was published, anti-imperialism was experiencing something of a revival in the United States, spurred by growing concern about the country's roles in Haiti, Mexico, Nicaragua, and other parts of Central and South America. Two new anti-imperialist organizations were formed that year, and several influential peace movement organizations were devoting their attention to imperialism. Paine and Harper and Brothers may have seen Twain's critique of the U.S. Army's actions in the Philippines as commercially acceptable in that political climate.[27]

By 1935, when Paine's edition of was released, the situation had changed. The rise of fascism in Europe was leading to increased conformity within the United States, and even the Communist Party disbanded its All-America Anti-Imperialist League in favor of a new united front organization, the League Against War and Fascism. Paine removed all critical references to the war from the notebooks and made other editorial changes that distorted Twain's views. On the book's dust jacket, Paine assured readers that "nothing has been modified, nothing changed. The entries, whatever their unconventionalities and their violences, are as he left them." But, assurances to readers aside, Paine was very selective not only in deciding what entries to publish but also in determining what "unconventionalities" and "violences" he would allow into print. Twain's maxims on free speech provide a good example. They read as follows (text omitted by Paine in italics):

None but the dead have free speech.
None but the dead are permitted to speak truth.
In America—as elsewhere—free speech is confined to the dead.

The minority is always in the right.

When the country is drifting toward Philippine robber–raid henroost raid, do not shirk your duty, do

not fail of loyalty, lest you win and deserve the reproach of being a "patriot."

The majority is always in the wrong.

Whenever you find that you are on the side of the majority, it is time to reform.[28]

This series of maxims was written in early 1905, at about the same time Twain wrote to Dan Beard that "None but the dead are permitted to tell the truth." Their connection with Harper and Brothers' rejection of "The War Prayer" is also evident in the reference to the abuse of patriotism during the Philippine-American War that serves as the central maxim of the series. But Paine removed that passage when he published the notebooks, leaving readers no way to know that they were inspired by Twain's experience as a critic of the war.[29]

In a sense, Paine's censorship of Twain's writings is more insidious than the outright banning of a book. With their illusion of authenticity, Paine's censored versions deceived scholars and general readers alike, successfully preserving "the traditional Mark Twain" and the "Harper Mark Twain property" for several generations. Paine's adulterated versions of Twain's writings are included in Harper and Brothers' multivolume collection of his works—still the cornerstone of many public library collections in the United States—and they have received even wider circulation through later anthologies. Paine's bowdlerized versions of "As Regards Patriotism" and "To the Person Sitting in Darkness," for example, were reprinted in Janet Smith's *Mark Twain on the Damned Human Race* (1962), Charles Neider's *The Complete Essays of Mark Twain* (1963), and Maxwell Geismar's *Mark Twain and the Three R's: Race, Religion, Revolution, and Related Matters* (1973). These later editors were undoubtedly unaware that by relying on Paine's texts they were perpetuating a literary fraud. Smith and Geismar, in particular, were trying to present the critical Mark Twain, but they unintentionally (and carelessly) reproduced censored texts that diluted his views.

Albert Bigelow Paine died in 1937 and Bernard DeVoto became literary executor of Twain's estate. During his tenure, Twain's daughter Clara took up the role of censor. In 1940 DeVoto published an additional volume of autobiographical dictations entitled *Mark Twain in Eruption* that contained several writings dealing tangentially with the war in the Philippines and critical commentary on a number of Twain's contemporaries that Paine probably thought were unfit for publication. But the year before, in 1939, Clara refused to allow publication of *Letters from the Earth*, a collection of Twain's writings on religion and other social commentary. She apparently believed that the views it expressed on religious subjects would tarnish her father's reputation.

Clara's death in 1962 effectively closed the half-century of editorial oversight devoted to preserving the "traditional Mark Twain" and the "Harper Mark Twain property." She willed the Mark Twain Papers to the University of California, the Mark Twain Project was established to publish them, scholars began to have unrestricted access to the papers for the first time, and before the 1960s were over the Project had already released authoritative texts of a number of Twain's previously unpublished anti-imperialist writings.[30] Soon after Clara's death, DeVoto's edition of *Letters from the Earth* was released and portions of it would later become popular antiwar tracts during the war in Vietnam.

Both personal and commercial considerations influenced the decisions made by Paine and Clara Clemens about which of Twain's writings to publish after his death, and the commercial considerations, at least, seem to have been influenced by changes in the political contexts surrounding publication. Paine's removal of the section about the U.S. army's uniform shortly after World War I is the clearest example, but the inclusion of the comments on the Moro Massacre in the mid-1920s and the removal of references to the war in the 1930s were also probably influenced by changing attitudes about the anti-imperialist movement. The overall effect was that Twain's anti-imperialist writings were downplayed, several of his writings were presented without reference to the war, and Twain's association with the Anti-Imperialist League, well-known at the time of his death, could not be documented by scholars such as William Gibson and Philip Foner who published studies of his anti-imperialist writings in the 1940s and 1950s.[31]

Paine's and Clara Clemens's editorial and publishing decisions also set the stage for charges of official censorship of Twain's anti-imperialist writings that were leveled against the United States by critics within the Soviet Union during the Cold War. To Soviet critics, the United States was an imperialist country, and either "reactionary American publishers," "officials," or "editors" were suppressing Mark Twain's anti-imperialist writings to hide that fact. These accusations were first leveled in 1947, and the *New York Times* quoted Bernard DeVoto and Frederick Allen of Harper and Brothers as finding the charges "preposterous."[32] The debate hit its peak from 1959 to 1960 when a series of articles was published in the *Soviet Literary Gazette* that used the widely noted absence of any of Twain's critical writings in Charles Neider's *The Autobiography of Mark Twain* (1959) to level the charges of censorship once again. Neider responded with letters to the Soviet critics, and the debate was carried as front-page news in the *New York Times*. In 1960 the letters were collected and published as a pamphlet entitled *Mark Twain and the Russians* (Hill and Wang), and Neider gave the debate prominent notice in the introduction to his next anthology, *Mark Twain: Life as I Find It*, published in 1961. That volume was a direct response to the charges of censorship. Noting in his introduction that the Soviet Union was publishing a large multivolume edition of Twain's writings that would include many of his critical essays, Neider wrote, "The Russians are proud of their Mark Twain—the anti-American Mark Twain, as they seem to believe he was, and as any of his countrymen know better."[33] To disprove the charges of censorship, Neider's anthology included "A Defence of General Funston," "The Czar's Soliloquy," "King Leopold's Soliloquy," two earlier letters opposing the annexation of Hawaii, several interviews on imperialism, and other critical writings—all reprinted for the first time since their original publications more than fifty years earlier. Janet Smith's collection of Twain's social criticism, *Mark Twain on the Damned Human Race* (Hill and Wang), was published the following year, and in her introduction she also noted the exchange with the Russians. Although *Letters from the Earth* was also published in 1962, its introduction simply related the history of DeVoto's early work on the anthology and Clara Clemens's opposition to its publication.

The highly publicized debate between Soviet and U.S. scholars brought Twain's anti-imperialist writings to a whole new level of meaning. Albert Paine and Clara Clemens were concerned solely with Twain's image and the commercial value of his writings. When Twain's writings became the focus of international debate during the Cold War, they defined the nation as a whole, not just their author. For the United States to appear open and democratic, the anti-imperialist writings that had been ignored for so long had to be reprinted, and 1961 and 1962 (the years of the Bay of Pigs invasion of Cuba, the Cuban Missile Crisis, and the early escalation of U.S. involvement in Vietnam) turned into banner years for Mark Twain's anti-imperialist writings.

Not surprisingly, these writings gained considerable attention later in the decade as opposition to the war in Vietnam became pronounced. The new war in Southeast Asia led to increased attention to both the Philippine-American War and the anti-imperialist movement. Numerous books and articles were published about U.S. imperialism, the Philippine-American War, and the Anti-Imperialist League. While some argued that the war in Vietnam was essentially the same in motive and method as the earlier war of conquest in the Philippines, others argued that there was no comparison. Most notable among the latter was Richard E. Welch's condemnation of the "Vietnam analogy" as "escalating historical parallelism into historical fiction." He wrote that "the Philippine War was essentially the product of a policy of insular imperialism; the Vietnam War, the product of a global crusade against communist expansionism." He discounted comparisons of the movements in opposition to the two wars by noting differences in their trajectories, tactics, and personnel.[34] Those differences were quite natural and to be expected, though. The annexations of 1898 created a dramatic and very unusual split within the country's elite and the anti-imperialist movement could immediately count upon the support of many of the country's leading politicians and some of its wealthiest men and women. People like Mark Twain and Andrew Carnegie did not need to picket the White House because they could walk in through the front door. After the severe repression of antiwar protests during World War I and in the anti-Communist political climate after World War II, elite consensus was restored and dissent on foreign policy issues was marginalized within the United States.[35] In 1899 the Anti-Imperialist League's platform declared that *imperialism* was an "un-American" policy; by the mid-1960s anyone who used the word imperialism was labeled "un-American." Protesters of the 1960s had little direct access to the halls of power until their movement gained enough strength to create a significant split within the elite. Because there were considerable similarities in their ideologies and objectives, as everyone, including Welch, seems to recognize, the two movements should be viewed as part of a continuum of anti-imperialist organizing. This is a common-sense approach that is routinely applied in historical discussions of organizing on women's rights, civil rights, peace, labor, etc., but which is not often applied in studies of anti-imperialists from the 1890s to the 1990s.[36] Efforts to separate the two eras reinforced the marginalization of dissent by denying that people who protested the war in Vietnam could have anything in common with some of the biggest names in American political and cultural history.

At a time when anticommunist sentiments were running strong, and opponents of the war were confronted with slogans like "America: Love It or Leave It," Mark Twain's anti-imperialist writings provided a powerful tool for legitimizing dissent. In 1966 an organization called "Messages for Peace" reprinted an excerpt from "The War Prayer" in a one-third-page advertisement in the *New York Times*.[37] Unauthorized editions of that story were so widely circulated that Harper and Row issued a single-volume illustrated edition in 1968 to meet the new demand. Other short writings were also widely distributed as antiwar leaflets and broadsides. Hal Holbrook, who began performing his legendary one-man show, "Mark Twain Tonight!," in the mid-1950s, revised his program in 1966 to incorporate anti-imperialist materials relevant to the new war in Southeast Asia. "This had an electrifying effect upon the audience in 1966," he recently remembered. "It reminded us that dissent is a tradition of our democracy." Richard D. Fulton recalls that his university's student newspaper reprinted "The War Prayer" as an editorial in 1970 shortly after students were shot by National Guard troops during an antiwar demonstration at Kent State University.[38]

Twain's anti-imperialist writings were similarly used to oppose U.S. military interventions in the 1980s and 1990s. *Nation* columnist Christopher Hitchens contextualized one of his reports of Contra atrocities in Nicaragua by quoting extensively from Twain's comments on the Moro Massacre of 1906.[39] During the Gulf War, "The War Prayer" was reprinted as a pamphlet by a peace movement organization in North Carolina and performed as a play at mass rallies in Connecticut. Popular recording artist Willie Nelson produced a twelve-minute recording with both spoken voices and a new song based on the story that was distributed free of charge by Peace, Inc. of San Francisco. On 18 February 1991, the entire back cover of the progressive weekly newspaper *In These Times* was used to reprint an excerpt from the story, illustrated down the side with dropping bombs.

From the late 1960s to the 1990s, Mark Twain's anti-imperialist writings have been used in a third way, closer to how they were originally presented by the anti-imperialist movement at the beginning of the century. Instead of attempting to control Twain's image or to define the country as a whole, activists have used his anti-imperialist writings to define themselves and to justify their own oppositional positions. "The ordinary epithets cannot be flung at him," the *New York Evening Post* observed in February of 1901. It described him as a "typical and whole-hearted American, who stepped from the pilot-house of a Mississippi steamboat into first a national and then a European fame, and now fearlessly sides with the Filipinos against their American oppressors."[40] That all-American image added power to Twain's anti-imperialist writings at the turn of the century, turned them into a hotly disputed symbol during the height of the Cold War, and seems to offer both popular appeal and credibility to those who use his writings to advance various causes today.

Although some of Twain's anti-imperialist writings have been widely reprinted, they have not always been connected to the earlier war in the Philippines. They have revived Twain as an opponent of wars, but not necessarily as an anti-imperialist. "The War Prayer" is probably the most frequently reprinted and quoted of Twain's anti-imperialist writings, for example, but it has rarely been directly connected to the Philippine-American War. Although both Janet Smith and Maxwell Geismar discussed Twain's anti-imperialist writings elsewhere in their collections of his social criticism, neither of them mentioned the Philippine-American War in relation to "The War Prayer" when they reprinted it in 1962 and 1973. The story was later appended to a 1980 television adaptation of Twain's Civil War memoir, "The Private History of a Campaign that Failed," and in 1995 the Ulster Choral Society of Kingston, New York, presented a musical adaptation by Herbert Haufrecht, *The War*

Prayer Oratorio, as a commentary on the Civil War. The confusion is an understandable product of the denial of empire. The story was written in 1905 and most history texts do not acknowledge that the Philippine-American War continued beyond 1902. There was no clear frame of reference that would help general readers or even many scholars to understand its connection to the war. That connection was buried even further when Paine removed the section on the Philippines before publishing the maxims on free speech that Twain wrote after his publisher rejected the story.

The historical reception of Twain's anti-imperialist writings in the Philippines is beyond the scope of this chapter, and would require a great deal of archival research that has yet to be done,[41] but some observations are worth making to illuminate the point made earlier about both Filipinos and Americans being "miseducated" through the same denial of empire. Most Filipinos are familiar with *Huckleberry Finn* and *Tom Sawyer*, but few are aware that Twain was an outspoken critic of the Philippine-American War. Essays like "To the Person Sitting in Darkness" and "A Defence of General Funston" might seem to be especially relevant to Filipino readers, but books like Huckleberry Finn and Tom Sawyer do not raise uncomfortable issues about the origins of U.S.-Philippines relations.

New attention was focused on Twain's anti-imperialist writings in the Philippines during the centennial activities of 1998. In his Centennial Countdown series in the *Philippine Daily Inquirer* (29 May), Ambeth R. Ocampo highlighted his writings on the war in an article titled "Mark Twain Took Side of Filipinos."[42] It was followed by a 4 July *Philippine Star* editorial on "Fil-American Friendship" that quoted a passage from "To the Person Sitting in Darkness" and proposed that Mark Twain should be honored with "a fitting monument that could serve as the focal point of every annual Fil-American Friendship Day commemoration." That, of course, would represent a break with colonial traditions. It would honor a "shared history" of resistance to imperialism rather than the various stages of imperial conquest, colonial administration, and neocolonial "independence" that made 4 July such a significant date in modern Philippine history. To break with that tradition completely, 30 November might be a more appropriate day to commemorate the anti-imperialist struggle. In a fluke of history, Andres Bonifacio, the founder of the Katipunan, and Mark Twain, one its most outspoken and tenacious American supporters, were both born on that day.

The history of Twain's anti-imperialist writings indicates that we need a more nuanced understanding of the processes through which an imperial ideology became predominant within the United States after the turn of the century. Historians of the anti-imperialist movement, for example, have variously claimed that imperialism became a "dead issue" in the United States after the presidential election of 1900, the official end of the Philippine-American War in 1902, or the demise of the Anti-Imperialist League in 1921.[43] In *America Revised*, a study of history textbooks used in American schools during the nineteenth and twentieth centuries, Frances Fitzgerald notes that accounts of turn-of-the-century imperialism were not fully "revised" until the second half of the century. "With few exceptions, the texts of the first five decades of the century did not propose any radical lines of dissent from United States foreign policy," she writes; "still, none went so far as to call every American military venture an unqualified success or suppress information about domestic opposition to the various government initiatives." That came only in the 1950s when "paranoia reigned" during the Cold War.44

Both the composition of Mark Twain's anti-imperialist writings, which extended well beyond the official end of the Philippine-American War, and their posthumous treatment by editors, publishers, critics, and activists demonstrate that the process was more gradual and complex than these histories suggest. Albert Bigelow Paine's and Clara Clemens's desires to mold Mark Twain's public image interacted with broader political contexts and commercial concerns but were not always bound by them. Their editorial decisions were inconsistent and often idiosyncratic. Clara Clemens's suppression of *Letters from the Earth,* for example, was probably influenced more by her father's earlier belief that those writings were too controversial to publish than any assessment of the religious attitudes prevailing in the United States in 1939 that she might have made herself. There is no evidence that she ever considered the anti-imperialist content of her father's writings in deciding not to allow publication of that volume. The Cold War led to an unquestioning presentation of imperialism in textbooks used in American schools, but it also led to the elevation of Twain's anti-imperialist writings beyond personal concerns to become publicly disputed symbols of the nation as a whole. Published in 1961 and 1962, Charles Neider's *Mark Twain: Life as I Find It* and Janet Smith's *Mark Twain on the Damned Human Race* appeared during what were arguably two of the Cold War's hottest years. Those anthologies debunked Soviet claims of official censorship but they also made some of Twain's anti-imperialist writings widely available for use by activists opposed to the war in Vietnam later in the decade. The posthumous treatment of Twain's anti-imperialist writings demonstrates both the fluidity of the debate about imperialism and the influence of individual initiatives within it. People concerned with overcoming the denial of empire within the United States might find grounds for optimism in that. The denial of empire might be pervasive but it is not immutable, especially now that the end of the Cold War has removed some of the ideological baggage previously attached to the word *imperialism.*

Notes:

1. Shelly Fisher Fishkin, *Lighting Out for the Territory: Reflections on Mark Twain and American Culture* (New York: Oxford University Press, 1996). See especially chapter 1, "The Matter of Hannibal," 13-69.

2. For an early acknowledgment of this, see Whitney T. Perkins, *Denial of Empire: The United States and Its Dependencies* (Leyden: A. W. Sythoff, 1962).

3. See, for example, Arhchibald R. Colquhoun, *Greater America* (New York: Harper and Brothers, 1904). During the Cold War, use of the word imperialism in even academic discussions of U.S. history became so controversial that scholars retreated to the very word the imperialists of the 1890s chose for themselves. See Walter LaFeber, *The New Empire: An Interpretation of American Expansion* (Ithaca: Cornell University Press, 1963), viii.

4. In its report on the effectiveness of the "Bandolerismo Statute" during 1903, the Philippine Commission provided examples of its use that included several cases of political resistance to U.S. rule. See *Fourth Annual Report of the Philippine Commission*, 1903, Part 1 (Washington, D.C.: Government Printing Office, 1904), 34-37.

5. In March of 1906 U.S. troops under Gen. Leonard Wood trapped a large group of Muslim Filipinos in the extinct volcanic crater of Mount Dajo and fired upon them from ships off the coast and from a safe distance in the heights above for four days until all nine hundred were reported dead. In June of 1913 a similar massacre, led by Gen. John J. Pershing, resulted in the deaths of about five hundred Muslim Filipinos at Bud Bagsak. Useful discussions of the later warfare can be found in James H. Blount, *The American Occupation of the Philippines, 1898-1912* (New York: G. P. Putnam's Sons, 1913); Orlino A. Ochosa, *"Bandoleros": Outlawed Guerrillas of the Philippine-American War, 1903-1907* (Quezon City, Philippines: New Day, 1995); and Peter Gordon Gowing, *Mandate in Moroland: The American Government of Muslim Filipinos, 1899-1920* (Quezon City, Philippines: New Day, 1983).

6. I am referring here to Renato Constantino's analysis of American colonial education in the Philippines, "The Miseducation of the Filipino" (N.p., n.d.; reprinted from Weekly Graphic, 8 June 1966), much of which can be usefully applied to Americans themselves to understand how the denial of imperialism has shaped prevailing beliefs and attitudes within the United States.

7. *Collected Poems of Charles Erskine Scott Wood*, ed. Sara Bard Field (New York: Vanguard Press, 1949); *Wood Works: The Life and Writings of Charles Erskine Scott Wood*, ed. Edwin Bingham and Tim Barnes (Corvallis: Oregon State University Press, 1997). Bingham and Barnes defend the exclusion of the anti-imperialist poems by describing them as "hasty, strident, unexceptional attacks on British and American imperialist policies and the verse was jingly and conventional." Still, they represent one of Wood's major political concerns (he was an officer of the Anti-Imperialist League until it dissolved in 1921) and the anthology is incomplete without even a sample of this part of his career. Edgar Lee Masters's most significant anti-imperialist writings include *The Constitution and Our Insular Possessions* (1900); *Maximilian: A Play in Five Acts* (1902); *The New Star Chamber and Other Essays* (1904); *The Blood of the Prophets* (pseud. Dexter Wallace, 1905); *Spoon River Anthology* (1915); *Gettysburg, Manila, Acoma* (1930); and his discussion of them in *Across Spoon River* (1936).

8. Samuel L. Clemens (hereafter SLC) to J. H. Twichell, 17 June 1898, *Mark Twain's Letters*, ed. Albert Bigelow Paine (New York: Harper and Brothers, 1917), 663.

9. "Mark Twain Home, An Anti-Imperialist," in Jim Zwick, ed., *Mark Twain's Weapons of Satire: Anti-Imperialist Writings on the Philippine-American War* (Syracuse: Syracuse University Press, 1992; Philippine edition, Manila: Popular Bookstore, 1994), 5. Unless otherwise noted, all of Mark Twain's writings quoted here are collected in this anthology, and page numbers refer to their appearance there.

10. *New York Herald* (30 December 1900), 7.

11. *Address to the People of the United States* (one-page circular dated 19 November 1898, and signed by Erving Winslow as secretary of the League).

12. "Platform of the American Anti-Imperialist League," in Carl Schurz, *The Policy of Imperialism*, Liberty Tract no. 4 (Chicago: American Anti-Imperialist League, 1899), inside front cover. For more on the League's activities, see Jim Zwick, "The Anti-Imperialist League and the Origins of Filipino-American Oppositional Solidarity," *Amerasia Journal* 24:2 (Summer 1998): 65-85.

13. "President McKinley and Commissioner Reid on the Philippines," *Literary Digest* 18 (25 February 1899): 212, 213; Moorfield Storey, *The Moro Massacre* (Boston: Anti-Imperialist League, 1906).

14. Maria Lanzar-Carpio, "The Anti-Imperialist League, Chapter 12: Propaganda," *Philippine Social Science Review* 5 (October 1933): 264, 263; Erving Winslow, "The Anti-Imperialist League," *The Filipino People* 1 (September 1912): 6. Existing documentation of the publications programs of the various League branches supports Winslow's higher estimate.

15. The content of Andreae and Reeves's presentations is discussed in *The Public* 2 (8 July 1899): 1-2, and (15 July 1899): 2. The League's relationship with them is discussed in Frank Stephens to Herbert Welsh, 23 June 1899, and 1 Dec 1899, and William Lloyd Garrison to Frank Stephens, 29 November 1899, Herbert Welsh Papers, Pennsylvania Historical Society, Philadelphia. Their presentations are discussed within the context of other stereoscopic images produced during the war in Jim Zwick, "The 'Stereoscopic' War of 1899," in Maria Serena I. Diokno, ed., *Voices and Scenes of the Past: The Philippine-American War Retold* (Quezon City, Philippines: Jose W. Diokno Foundation, 1999), 4-5.

16. For a thorough discussion of the prominence of Twain's early anti-imperialist publications, see Jim Zwick, "'Prodigally Endowed with Sympathy for the Cause': Mark Twain's Involvement with the Anti-Imperialist League," *Mark Twain Journal* 32 (Spring 1994): 6-8.

17. Sherman Hand to SLC, 12 February 1901, quoted in Zwick, *Weapons of Satire*, 22.

18. On these other involvements, see Hunt Hawkins, "Mark Twain's Involvement with the Congo Reform Movement: 'A Fury of Generous Indignation.'" *New England Quarterly* (51 June 1978): 147-75; and Louis J. Budd, "Twain, Howells, and the Boston Nihilists," *New England Quarterly* 32 (September 1959): 351-71.

19. Daniel Kiefer, "To the Memory of Mark Twain," *The Public* 13 (13 May 1910): 440; Andrew Carnegie, "Tribute to Mark Twain," North American Review 191 (June 1910): 827; *Report of the Twelfth Annual Meeting of the Anti-Imperialist League* (Boston: Anti-Imperialist League, 1910), 20.

20. "The War Prayer," 159, 160; Elizabeth Jordan to SLC, 22 March 1905, and SLC to Dan Beard, 30 March 1905, quoted in Zwick, *Weapons of Satire*, xxvii.

21. SLC to Edmund Dean Morel, 11 April 1905, quoted in Zwick, *Weapons of Satire*, xxvii.

22. Quoted in Hamlin Hill, *Mark Twain: God's Fool* (New York: Harper and Row, 1973), 268.

23. SLC to J. H. Twichell, 24 January 1901, quoted in Zwick, *Weapons of Satire*, 18; "The American Flag," 14; Paine, Letters, 704.

24. The full text of "As Regards Patriotism" was first published in Frederick Anderson, ed., *A Pen Warmed-up in Hell: Mark Twain in Protest* (New York: Harper and Row, 1972), 28-30. The U.S. military established concentration camps in the Philippines to isolate the Philippine Army from its civilian base of support. Like Spain's *reconcentrado* policy in Cuba, from which it was adapted, it caused tremendous hardship and loss of life among Filipinos. Although most attention has been given to its implementation in Batangas province in 1901-1902, the U.S. military continued to use concentration camps in the northern provinces through at least 1905, several years after the war was supposed to be over. For a contemporary report, see Helen C. Wilson, *Reconcentration in the Philippines and Statistical Table Showing Results of "Benevolent Assimilation"* (Boston: Anti-Imperialist League, 1906).

25. William L. Andrews, "The Politics of Publishing: A Note on the Bowdlerization of Mark Twain," *Markham Review* 7 (Fall 1977): 18-19.

26. "Comments on the Moro Massacre," 171, 177. The complete text of Twain's autobiographical

dictations was first published in Zwick, *Weapons of Satire*, 168-178.

27. The Anti-Imperialist League was disbanded in 1921 after its leaders became convinced that Manuel Quezon and other Filipino politicians no longer wanted independence. See Zwick, "The Anti-Imperialist League and the Origins of Filipino-American Oppositional Solidarity," 79-80. From 1921 onward, many of its leaders turned their attention to other areas of the world and they formed or became officers of the major anti-imperialist organizations created in the 1920s and 1930s. For good discussions of some of the later organizations, see Robert David Johnson, *The Peace Progressives and American Foreign Relations* (Cambridge, Mass.: Harvard University Press, 1995), and chapter 5, "Challenging Economic Imperialism," in Carrie A. Foster, *The Women and the Warriors: The U.S. Section of the Women's International League for Peace and Freedom, 1915-1946* (Syracuse: Syracuse University Press, 1995).

28. The full series of maxims was first published in Zwick, *Weapons of Satire*, 162.

29. Both Albert Bigelow Paine and Dan Beard claimed that Twain suppressed "The War Prayer" himself and never submitted it for publication. Because both of their accounts paraphrase the maxim about free speech included in Twain's letter to Beard, it is possible that these were deliberate denials of the suppression of Twain's anti-imperialist story. See Paine, *Mark Twain: A Biography* (New York: Harper and Brothers, 1912), 1234, and Beard, *Hardly a Man Is Still Alive: The Autobiography of Dan Beard* (New York: Doubleday, Doran and Co., 1939), 343.

30. The Mark Twain Project is now located at The Bancroft Library, University of California, Berkeley.

31. See William M. Gibson, "Mark Twain and Howells: Anti-Imperialists," *New England Quarterly* 20 (December 1947), 466; and Philip S. Foner's *Mark Twain: Social Critic* (New York: International Publishers, 1958), 282-283.

32. "Twain Suppressed, Russian Charges," *New York Times* (28 July 1947). This and other *New York Times* articles mentioned below are available online in Barbara Schmidt's outstanding collection, *Mark Twain in the New York Times*, http://www.twainquotes.com/nytindex.html (12 May 2000).

33. Charles Neider, ed., *Mark Twain: Life as I Find It* (Garden City, N.Y.: Hanover House, 1961), xv. During the Cold War debate, Twain's anti-imperialist writings were also highlighted by the Left within the United States in Samuel Sillen, "Dooley, Twain and Imperialism," *Masses and Mainstream* 1 (December 1948): 6-14, and Foner, *Mark Twain: Social Critic*. Howard Fast's novel, *Silas Timberman* (New York: Blue Heron Press, 1954), is another interesting product of this era. It is the story of a college professor who loses his job and is eventually called before the House Committee on Un-American Activities after using Twain's "The Man That Corrupted Hadleyburg" as the central text of an American literature class. Then still a prominent member of the Communist Party USA, Fast was blacklisted at the time he wrote this book and the Blue Heron Press was a self-publishing venture operated out of his home.

34. Richard E. Welch, Jr., *Response to Imperialism: The United States and the Philippine-American War, 1899-1902* (Chapel Hill, N.C.: University of North Carolina Press, 1979), xiv-xv. For a useful critical review of the literature produced by proponents and opponents of the "Vietnam analogy," see Oscar V. Campomanes, "The New Empire's Forgetful and Forgotten Citizens: Unrepresentability and Unassimilability in Filipino-American Postcolonialities," *Critical Mass* 2 (Spring 1995): 187-189.

35. Dissent was also radicalized but many of the people who participated in the earlier movement were among the officers and supporters of the later organizations. Although it discusses anti-imperialists primarily as peace movement participants, C. Roland Marchand, *The American Peace Movement and Social Reform, 1898-1918* (Princeton, N.J.: Princeton University Press, 1972) remains one of the best general sources on the impact of World War I on this group. A number of more recent studies can be used to study connections between the movements up to the 1980s: Johnson, *Peace Progressives*; Foster, *The Women and the Warriors*; Penny M. Von Eschen, *Race Against Empire: Black Americans and Anticolonialism, 1937-1957*

(Ithaca, N.Y.: Cornell University Press, 1997); Robert David Johnson, *Ernest Gruening and the American Dissenting Tradition* (Cambridge, Mass.: Harvard University Press, 1998); Van Gosse, *Where the Boys Are: Cuba, Cold War America and the Making of a New Left* (London: Verso, 1993); and Van Gosse, "'The North American Front': Central American Solidarity in the Reagan Era," in Mike Davis and Michael Sprinker, eds., *Reshaping the U.S. Left: Popular Struggles in the 1980s* (London: Verso, 1988), 11-50. Some of the continuities in personnel between the Anti-Imperialist League and the later organizations that some of these studies do not discuss are highlighted in Jim Zwick, "Oswald Garrison Villard and American Anti-Imperialism: A Biographical Excursion from 1900 to the 1960s," http://www.boon-docksnet.com/ail/villard.html, in Jim Zwick, ed., *Anti-Imperialism in the United States, 1898-1935*, http://www.boondocksnet.com/ail98-35.html (14 August 1999).

36. Among the few exceptions are Merle Curti, *Peace or War: The American Struggle, 1636-1936* (New York: W. W. Norton, 1936), 182-183, which argues that the League "applied all that they said regarding the Philippines to our imperialism in the Caribbean"; and Julius W. Pratt, *America's Colonial Experiment: How the United States Gained, Governed, and in Part Gave Away a Colonial Empire* (New York: Prentice-Hall, 1950), 312, which notes that in the early 1920s, "though the Anti-Imperialist League might be moribund, there was no lack of anti-imperialists." For a more thorough examination of the Anti-Imperialist League as the founding organization of a distinct anti-imperialist social movement sector, see my "Political Opportunity, Expectations of Success, and Interorganizational Conflict: The Anti-Imperialist Movement, 1898-1921," http://www.boondocksnet.com/ail/socmove.html, in Jim Zwick, ed., *Anti-Imperialism in the United States, 1898-1935*, http://www.boondocksnet.com/ail98-35.html (14 August 1999).

37. *New York Times* (29 May 1966), D7. The organization's executive committee included James Imbrie and Ben Shahn.

38. Hal Holbrook, "Introduction," in Mark Twain, *Speeches* (New York: Oxford University Press, 1996), xxxviii; Richard D. Fulton, "Review: Jim Zwick, ed., *Mark Twain's Weapons of Satire*," *Nineteenth-Century Contexts* 18:1 (1996), 111. See also Maxwell Geismar, *Mark Twain and the Three R's: Race, Religion, Revolution and Related Matters* (Indianapolis: Bobbs-Merrill, 1973), vi, xvii, 103.

39. "Minority Report," *The Nation* 246 (25 June 1988): 887.

40. "Mark Twain on McKinley," *New York Evening Post* (2 February 1901), 6.

41. It is possible, for example, that the Comite Central Filipino might have discussed Twain's anti-imperialist statements of October 1900 in its reports from the United States prior to the presidential election of 1900 or reported on the reception of "To the Person Sitting in Darkness" in early 1901. If any such reports exist, they would likely be in the Philippine Revolutionary Records in the National Library, Manila. Many historians have gone through these, of course, but as far as I know no one has done so looking for commentary on Mark Twain.

42. "Mark Twain Took Side of Filipinos" is collected in Ambeth R. Ocampo, *The Centennial Countdown* (Pasig City, Philippines: Anvil, 1998), 262-264.

43. For examples of these arguments, see Fred H. Harrington, "The Anti-Imperialist Movement in the United States, 1898-1900," *Mississippi Valley Historical Review* 22 (September 1935): 211-230; Richard E. Welch, *Response to Imperialism: The United States and the Philippine-American War, 1899-1902* (Chapel Hill, N.C.: University of North Carolina Press, 1979); and E. Berkeley Tompkins, *Anti-Imperialism in the United States: The Great Debate, 1890-1920* (Philadelphia, Pa.: University of Pennsylvania Press, 1970).

44. Frances Fitzgerald, *America Revised* (Boston: Little, Brown, 1979), 131, 128.

To The Person Sitting In Darkness
[February 1901]

MARK TWAIN

Christmas will dawn in the United States over a people full of hope and aspiration and good cheer. Such a condition means contentment and happiness. The carping grumbler who may here and there go forth will find few to listen to him. The majority will wonder what is the matter with him and pass on.

—New York Tribune, on *Christmas Eve*

From *The Sun*, of New York:

The purpose of this article is not to describe the terrible offences against humanity committed in the name of Politics in some of the most notorious East Side districts. *They could not be described, even verbally.* But it is the intention to let the great mass of more or less careless citizens of this beautiful metropolis of the New World get some conception of the havoc and ruin wrought to man, woman and child in the most densely populated and least known section of the city. Name, date and place can be supplied to those of little faith—or to any man who feels himself aggrieved. It is a plain statement of record and observation, written without license and without garnish.

Imagine, if you can, a section of the city territory completely dominated by one man, without whose permission neither legitimate nor illegitimate business can be conducted; *where illegitimate business is encouraged and legitimate business discouraged*; where the respectable residents have to fasten their doors and windows summer nights and sit in their rooms with asphyxiating air and 100-degree temperature, rather than try to catch the faint whiff of breeze in their natural breathing places, the stoops of their homes; *where naked women dance by night in the streets, and unsexed men prowl like vultures through the darkness on "business"* not only permitted but encouraged by the police; *where the education of infants begins with the knowledge of prostitution* and the training of little girls is training in the arts of Phryne; where *American* girls brought up with the refinements of *American* homes are imported from small towns up-State, Massachusetts, Connecticut and New Jersey, and kept as virtually prisoners as if they were locked up behind jail bars until they have lost all semblance of womanhood; *where small boys are taught to solicit for the women of disorderly houses*; where there is an organized society of young men *whose sole business in life is to corrupt young girls and turn them over to bawdy houses*; where men walking with their wives along the street are openly insulted; *where children that have adult diseases are the chief patrons of the hospitals and dispensaries*; where it is the rule, rather than the exception, that *murder, rape, robbery and theft go unpunished*—in short where the Premium of the most awful forms of Vice is the Profit of the politicians.

The following news from China appeared in The Sun, of New York, on Christmas Eve. The italics are mine:

The Rev. Mr. Ament, of the American Board of Foreign Missions, has returned from a trip which he made for the purpose of collecting indemnities for damages done by Boxers. *Everywhere he went he compelled the Chinese to pay.* He says that all his native Christians are now provided for. He had 700 of them under his charge, and 300 were killed. He has *collected 300 taels for each* of these murders, and has *compelled full payment for all the property belonging to Christians* that was destroyed. He also assessed fines amounting to THIRTEEN TIMES the amount of the indemnity. *This money will be used for the propagation of the Gospel.*

Mr. Ament declares that the compensation he has collected is moderate, when compared with the amount secured by the Catholics, who demand, in addition to money, *head for head.* They collect 500 taels for each murder of a Catholic. In the Wenchiu country, 680 Catholics were killed, and for this the European Catholics here demand 750,000 strings of cash and 680 *heads.*

In the course of a conversation, Mr. Ament referred to the attitude of the missionaries toward the Chinese. He said:

"I deny emphatically that the missionaries are *vindictive*, that they *generally* looted, or that they have done anything *since* the siege that *the circumstances did not demand. I criticise the Americans. The soft hand of the Americans is not as good as the mailed fist of the Germans.* If you deal with the Chinese with a soft hand they will take advantage of it."

The statement that the French Government will return the loot taken by the French soldiers, is the source of the greatest amusement here. The French soldiers were more systematic looters than the Germans, and it is a fact that today *Catholic Christians*, carrying French flags and armed with modern guns, *are looting villages* in the Province of Chili.

By happy luck, we get all these glad tidings on Christmas Eve—just in time to enable us to celebrate the day with proper gaiety and enthusiasm. Our spirits soar, and we find we can even make jokes: Taels I win, Heads you lose.

Our Reverend Ament is the right man in the right place. What we want of our missionaries out there is, not that they shall merely represent in their acts and persons the grace and gentleness and charity and loving kindness of our religion, but that they shall also represent the American spirit. The oldest Americans are the Pawnees. Macallum's History says:

pulá
red
red

putî
white
white

asul
blue
blue

Amin ó ating
bandilà.
Our flag.

Isang águila.
An eagle.

14

From the Painting by Gilbert Stuart.

Iniibig ko ang ngalan ni Washington,
I love the name of Washington,

Iniibig ko rin naman ang aking tinubuang lupà,
I love my country, too,

Iniibig ko ang bandilà, ang mahal na lumang bandilà,
I love the flag, the dear old flag,

Sa ó maguing pulá at puti at itim.
Of red and white and blue.

15

From "The Baldwin Primer" c. 1900

When a white Boxer kills a Pawnee and destroys his property, the other Pawnees do not trouble to seek *him* out, they kill any white person that comes along; also, they make some white village pay deceased's heirs the full cash value of deceased, together with full cash value of the property destroyed; they also make the village pay, in addition, *thirteen times* the value of that property into a fund for the dissemination of the Pawnee religion, which they regard as the best of all religions for the softening and humanizing of the heart of man. It is their idea that it is only fair and right that the innocent should be made to suffer for the guilty, and that it is better that ninety and nine innocent should suffer than that one guilty person should escape.

Our Reverend Ament is justifiably jealous of those enterprising Catholics, who not only get big money for each lost convert, but get "head for head" besides. But he should soothe himself with the reflection that the entirety of their exactions are for their own pockets, whereas he, less selfishly, devotes only 300 taels per head to that service, and gives the whole vast thirteen repetitions of the property-indemnity to the service of propagating the Gospel. His magnanimity has won him the approval of his nation, and will get him a monument. Let him be content with these rewards. We all hold him dear for manfully defending his fellow missionaries from exaggerated charges which were beginning to distress us, but which his testimony has so considerably modified that we can now contemplate them without noticeable pain. For now we know that, even before the siege, the missionaries were not "generally" out looting, and that, "since the siege," they have acted quite handsomely, except when "circumstances" crowded them. I am arranging for the monument. Subscriptions for it can be sent to the American Board; designs for it can be sent to me. Designs must allegorically set forth the Thirteen Reduplications of the Indemnity, and the Object for which they were exacted; as Ornaments, the designs must exhibit 680 Heads, so disposed as to give a pleasing and pretty effect; for the Catholics have done nicely, and are entitled to notice in the monument. Mottoes may be suggested, if any shall be discovered that will satisfactorily cover the ground.

Mr. Ament's financial feat of squeezing a thirteen-fold indemnity out of the pauper peasants to square other people's offenses, thus condemning them and their women and innocent little children to inevitable starvation and lingering death, in order that the blood-money so acquired might be *used for the propagation of the Gospel*," does not flutter my serenity; although the act and the words, taken together, concrete a blasphemy so hideous and so colossal that, without doubt, its mate is not findable in the history of this or of any other age. Yet, if a layman had done that thing and justified it with those words, I should have shuddered, I know. Or, if I had done the thing and said the words myself—however, the thought is unthinkable, irreverent as some imperfectly informed people think me. Sometimes an ordained minister sets out to be blasphemous. When this happens, the layman is out of the running; he stands no chance.

We have Mr. Ament's impassioned assurance that the missionaries are not "vindictive." Let us hope and pray that they will never become so, but will remain in the almost morbidly fair and just and gentle temper which is affording so much satisfaction to their brother and champion to-day.

The following is from the *New York Tribune* of Christmas Eve. It comes from that journal's Tokio correspondent. It has a strange and impudent sound, but the Japanese are but partially civilized as yet. When they become wholly civilized they will not talk so:

> The missionary question, of course, occupies a foremost place in the discussion. It is now felt as essential that the Western Powers take cognizance of the sentiment here, that religious invasions of Oriental countries by powerful Western organizations are tantamount to filibustering expeditions, and should not only be discountenanced, but that stern measures should be adopted for their suppression. The feeling here is that the misionary organizations constitute a constant menace to peaceful international relations.

Shall we? That is, shall we go on conferring our Civilization upon the peoples that sit in darkness, or shall we give those poor things a rest? Shall we bang right ahead in our old-time, loud, pious way, and commit the new century to the game; or shall we sober up and sit down and think it over first? Would it not be prudent to get our Civilization-tools together, and see how much stock is left on hand in the way of Glass Beads and Theology, and Maxim Guns and Hymn Books, and Trade-Gin and Torches of Progress and Enlightenment (patent adjustable ones, good to fire villages with, upon occasion), and balance the books, and arrive at the profit and loss, so that we may intelligently decide whether to continue the business or sell out the property and start a new Civilization Scheme on the proceeds?

Extending the Blessings of Civilization to our Brother who Sits in Darkness has been a good trade and has paid well, on the whole; and there is money in it yet, if carefully worked—but not enough, in my judgment, to make any considerable risk advisable. The People that Sit in Darkness are getting to be too scarce—too scarce and too shy. And such darkness as is now left is really of but an indifferent quality, and not dark enough for the game. The most of those People that Sit in Darkness have been furnished with more light than was good for them or profitable for us. We have been injudicious.

The Blessings-of-Civilization Trust, wisely and cautiously administered, is a Daisy. There is more money in it, more territory, more sovereignty, and other kinds of emolument, than there is in any other game that is played. But Christendom has been playing it badly of late years, and must certainly suffer by it, in my opinion. She has been so eager to get every stake that appeared on the green cloth, that the People who Sit in Darkness have noticed it—they have noticed it, and have begun to show alarm. They have become suspicious of the Blessings of Civilization. More—they have begun to examine them. This is not well. The Blessings of Civilization are all right, and a good commercial property; there could not be a better, in a dim light. In the right kind of a light, and at a proper distance, with the goods a little out of focus, they furnish this desirable exhibit to the Gentlemen who Sit in Darkness:

LOVE,	LAW AND ORDER,
JUSTICE,	LIBERTY,
GENTLENESS,	EQUALITY,
CHRISTIANITY,	HONORABLE DEALING,
PROTECTION TO THE WEAK,	MERCY,
TEMPERANCE,	EDUCATION,
—and so on.	

There. Is it good? Sir, it is pie. It will bring into camp any idiot that sits in darkness anywhere. But not if we adulterate it. It is proper to be emphatic upon that point. This brand is strictly for Export—apparently. *Apparently*. Privately and confidentially, it is nothing of the kind. Privately and confidentially, it is merely an outside cover, gay and pretty and attractive, displaying the special patterns of our Civilization which we reserve for Home Consumption, while *inside* the bale is the Actual Thing that the Customer Sitting in Darkness buys with his blood and tears and land and liberty. That Actual Thing is, indeed, Civilization, but it is only for Export. Is there a difference between the two brands? In some of the details, yes.

We all know that the Business is being ruined. The reason is not far to seek. It is because our Mr. McKinley, and Mr. Chamberlain, and the Kaiser, and the Czar and the French have been exporting the Actual Thing *with the outside cover left off*. This is bad for the Game. It shows that these new players of it are not sufficiently acquainted with it.

It is a distress to look on and note the mismoves, they are so strange and so awkward. Mr. Chamberlain manufactures a war out of materials so inadequate and so fanciful that they make the boxes grieve and the gallery laugh, and he tries hard to persuade himself that it isn't purely a private raid for cash, but has a sort of dim, vague respectability about it somewhere, if he could only find the spot; and that, by and by, he can scour the flag clean again after he has finished dragging it through the mud, and make it shine and flash in the vault of heaven once more as it had shone and flashed there a thousand years in the world's respect until he laid his unfaithful hand upon it. It is bad play—bad. For it exposes the Actual Thing to Them that Sit in Darkness, and they say: "What! Christian against Christian? And only for money? Is *this* a case of magnanimity, forbearance, love, gentleness, mercy, protection of the weak—this strange and over-showy onslaught of an elephant upon a nest of field-mice, on the pretext that the mice had squeaked an insolence at him— conduct which 'no self-respecting government could allow to pass unavenged?' as Mr. Chamberlain said. Was that a good pretext in a small case, when it had not been a good pretext in a large one?—for only recently Russia had affronted the elephant three times and survived alive and unsmitten. Is this Civilization and Progress? Is it something better than we already possess? These harryings and burnings and desert-makings in the Transvaal—is this an improvement on our darkness? Is it, perhaps, possible that there are two kinds of Civilization—one for home consumption and one for the heathen market?"

Then They that Sit in Darkness are troubled, and shake their heads; and they read this extract from a letter of a British private, recounting his exploits in one of Methuen's victories, some days before the affair of Magersfontein, and they are troubled again:

> We tore up the hill and into the intrenchments, and the Boers saw we had them; so they dropped their guns and went down on their knees and put up their hands clasped, and begged for mercy. And we gave it the—*with the long spoon.*

The long spoon is the bayonet. See *Lloyd's Weekly*, London, of those days. The same number—and the same column—contained some quite unconscious satire in the form of shocked and bitter upbraidings of the Boers for their brutalities and inhumanities!

Next, to our heavy damage, the Kaiser went to playing the game without first mastering it. He lost a couple of missionaries in a riot in Shantung, and in his account he made an overcharge for them. China had to pay a hundred thousand dollars apiece for them, in money; twelve miles of territory, containing several millions of inhabitants and worth twenty million dollars; and to build a monument, and also a Christian church; whereas the people of China could have been depended upon to remember the missionaries without the help of these expensive memorials. This was all bad play. Bad, because it would not, and could not, and will not now or ever, deceive the Person Sitting in Darkness. He knows that it was an overcharge. He knows that a missionary is like any other man: he is worth merely what you can supply his place for, and no more. He is useful, but so is a doctor, so is a sheriff, so is an editor; but a just Emperor does not charge war-prices for such. A diligent, intelligent, but obscure missionary, and a diligent, intelligent country editor are worth much, and we know it; but they are not worth the earth. We esteem such an editor, and we are sorry to see him go; but, when he goes, we should consider twelve miles of territory, and a church, and a fortune, over-compensation for his loss. I mean, if he was a Chinese editor, and we had to settle for him. It is no proper figure for an editor or a missionary; one can get shop-worn kings for less. It was bad play on the Kaiser's part. It got this property, true; but it *produced the Chinese revolt*, the indignant uprising of China's traduced patriots, the Boxers. The results have been expensive to Germany, and to the other Disseminators of Progress and the Blessings of Civilization.

The Kaiser's claim was paid, yet it was bad play, for it could not fail to have an evil effect upon Persons Sitting in Darkness in China. They would muse upon the event, and be likely to say: "Civilization is gracious and beautiful, for such is its reputation; but can we afford it? There are rich Chinamen, perhaps they could afford it; but this tax is not laid upon them, it is laid upon the peasants of Shantung; it is they that must pay this mighty sum, and their wages are but four cents a day. Is this a better civilization than ours, and holier and higher and nobler? Is not this rapacity? Is not this extortion? Would Germany charge America two hundred thousand dollars for two missionaries, and shake the mailed fist in her face, and send warships, and send soldiers, and say: 'Seize twelve miles of territory, worth twenty millions of dollars, as additional pay for the missionaries; and make those peasants build a monument to the missionaries, and a costly Christian church to remember them by?' And later would Germany say to her soldiers: 'March through America and slay, *giving no quarter*; make the German face there, as has been our Hun-face here, a terror for a thousand years; march through the Great Republic and slay, slay, slay, carving a road for our offended religion through its heart and bowels?' Would Germany do like this to America, to England, to France, to Russia? Or only to China the helpless imitating the elephant's assault upon the field-mice? Had we better invest in this Civilization— this Civilization which called Napoleon a buccaneer for carrying off Venice's bronze horses, but which steals our ancient astronomical instruments from our walls, and goes looting like common bandits—that is, all the alien soldiers except America's; and (Americans again excepted) storms frightened villages and cables the result to glad journals at home every day: 'Chinese losses, 450 killed; ours, *one officer and two men wounded*. Shall proceed against neighboring village to-morrow, where a *massacre* is reported.' Can we afford Civilization?"

And, next, Russia must go and play the game injudiciously. She affronts England once or twice—with the Person Sitting in Darkness observing and noting; by moral assistance of France and Germany, she robs Japan of her hard-earned spoil, all swimming in Chinese blood—Port Arthur—with the Person again observing and noting; then she seizes Manchuria, raids its villages, and chokes its great river with the swollen corpses of countless massacred peasants—that astonished Person still observing and noting. And perhaps he is saying to himself: "It is yet *another* Civilized Power, with its banner of the Prince of Peace in one hand and its loot-basket and its butcher-knife in the other. Is there no salvation for us but to adopt Civilization and lift ourselves down to its level?"

And by and by comes America, and our Master of the Game plays it badly—plays it as Mr. Chamberlain was playing it in South Africa. It was a mistake to do that; also, it was one which was quite unlooked for in a Master who was playing it so well in Cuba. In Cuba, he was playing the usual and regular *American* game, and it was winning, for there is no way to beat it. The Master, contemplating Cuba, said: "Here is an oppressed and friendless little nation which is willing to fight to be free; we go partners, and put up the strength of seventy million sympathizers and the resources of the United States: play!" Nothing but Europe combined could call that hand: and Europe cannot combine on anything. There, in Cuba, he was following our great traditions in a way which made us very proud of him, and proud of the deep dissatisfaction which his play was provoking in Continental Europe. Moved by a high inspiration, he threw out those stirring words which proclaimed that forcible annexation would be "criminal aggression"; and in that utterance fired another "shot heard round the world." The memory of that fine saying will be outlived by the remembrance of no act of his but one—that he forgot it within the twelvemonth, and its honorable gospel along with it.

For, presently, came the Philippine temptation. It was strong; it was too strong, and he made that bad mistake: he played the European game, the Chamberlain game. It was a pity; it was a great pity, that error; that one grievous error, that irrevocable error. For it was the very place and time to play the American game again. And at no cost. Rich winnings to be gathered in, too; rich and permanent; indestructible; a fortune transmissible forever to the children of the flag. Not land, not money, not dominion—no, something worth many times more than that dross: our share, the spectacle of a nation of long harassed and persecuted slaves set free through our influence; our posterity's share, the golden memory of that fair deed. The game was in our hands. If it had been played according to the American rules, Dewey would have sailed away from Manila as soon as he had destroyed the Spanish fleet—after putting up a sign on shore guaranteeing foreign property and life against damage by the Filipinos, and warning the Powers that interference with the emancipated patriots would be regarded as an act unfriendly to the United States. The Powers cannot combine, in even a bad cause, and the sign would not have been molested.

Dewey could have gone about his affairs elsewhere, and left the competent Filipino army to starve out the little Spanish garrison and send it home, and the Filipino citizens to set up the form of government they might prefer, and deal with the friars and their doubtful acquisitions according to Filipino ideas of fairness and justice—ideas which have since been tested and found to be of as high an order as any that prevail in Europe or America.

But we played the Chamberlain game, and lost the chance to add another Cuba and another honorable deed to our good record.

The more we examine the mistake, the more clearly we perceive that it is going to be bad for the Business. The Person Sitting in Darkness is almost sure to say: "There is something curious about this—curious and unaccountable. There must be two Americas: one that sets the captive free, and one that takes a once-captive's new freedom away from him, and picks a quarrel with him with nothing to found it on; then kills him to get his land."

The truth is, the Person Sitting in Darkness is saying things like that; and for the sake of the Business we must persuade him to look at the Philippine matter in another and healthier way. We must arrange his opinions for him. I believe it can be done; for Mr. Chamberlain has arranged England's opinion of the South

African matter, and done it most cleverly and successfully. He presented the facts—some of the facts—and showed those confiding people what the facts meant. He did it statistically, which is a good way. He used the formula: "Twice 2 are 14, and 2 from 9 leaves 35." Figures are effective; figures will convince the elect.

Now, my plan is a still bolder one than Mr. Chamberlain's, though apparently a copy of it. Let us be franker than Mr. Chamberlain; let us audaciously present the whole of the facts, shirking none, then explain them according to Mr. Chamberlain's formula. This daring truthfulness will astonish and dazzle the Person Sitting in Darkness, and he will take the Explanation down before his mental vision has had time to get back into focus. Let us say to him:

"Our case is simple. On the 1st of May, Dewey destroyed the Spanish fleet. This left the Archipelago in the hands of its proper and rightful owners, the Filipino nation. Their army numbered 30,000 men, and they were competent to whip out or starve out the little Spanish garrison; then the people could set up a government of their own devising. Our traditions required that Dewey should now set up his warning sign, and go away. But the Master of the Game happened to think of another plan—the European plan. He acted upon it. This was, to send out an army—ostensibly to help the native patriots put the finishing touch upon their long and plucky struggle for independence, but really to take their land away from them and keep it. That is, in the interest of Progress and Civilization. The plan developed, stage by stage, and quite satisfactorily. We entered into a military alliance with the trusting Filipinos, and they hemmed in Manila on the land side, and by their valuable help the place, with its garrison of 8,000 or 10,000 Spaniards, was captured—a thing which we could not have accomplished unaided at that time. We got their help by—by ingenuity. We knew they were fighting for their independence, and that they had been at it for two years. We knew they supposed that we also were fighting in their worthy cause—just as we had helped the Cubans fight for Cuban independence—and we allowed them to go on thinking so. *Until Manila was ours and we could get along without them.* Then we showed our hand. Of course, they were surprised—that was natural; surprised and disappointed; disappointed and grieved. To them it looked un-American; uncharacteristic; foreign to our established traditions. And this was natural, too; for we were only playing the American Game in public—in private it was the European. It was neatly done, very neatly, and it bewildered them. They could not understand it; for we had been so friendly—so affectionate, even—with those simple-minded patriots! We, our own selves, had brought back out of exile their leader, their hero, their hope, their Washington—Aguinaldo; brought him in a warship, in high honor, under the sacred shelter and hospitality of the flag; brought him back and restored him to his people, and got their moving and eloquent gratitude for it. Yes, we had been so friendly to them, and had heartened them up in so many ways! We had lent them guns and ammunition; advised with them; exchanged pleasant courtesies with them; placed our sick and wounded in their kindly care; entrusted our Spanish prisoners to their humane and honest hands; fought shoulder to shoulder with them against 'the common enemy' (our own phrase); praised their courage, praised their gallantry, praised their mercifulness, praised their fine and honorable conduct; borrowed their trenches, borrowed strong positions which they had previously captured from the Spaniard; petted them, lied to them—officially proclaiming that our land and naval forces came to give them their freedom and displace the bad Spanish Government—fooled them, used them until we needed them no longer; then derided the sucked orange and threw it away. We kept the positions which we had beguiled them of; by and by, we moved a force forward and overlapped patriot ground—a clever thought, for we needed trouble, and this would produce it. A Filipino soldier, crossing the ground, where no one had a right to forbid him, was shot by our sentry. The badgered patriots resented this with arms, without waiting to know whether Aguinaldo, who was absent, would approve or not. Aguinaldo did not approve; but that availed nothing. What we wanted, in the interest of Progress and Civilization, was the Archipelago, unencumbered by patriots struggling for independence; and War was what we needed. We clinched our opportunity. It is Mr. Chamberlain's case over again—at least in its motive and intention; and we played the game as adroitly as he played it himself."

At this point in our frank statement of fact to the Person Sitting in Darkness, we should throw in a little trade-taffy about the Blessings of Civilization for a change, and for the refreshment of his spirit—then go on with our tale:

"We and the patriots having captured Manila, Spain's ownership of the Archipelago and her sovereignty over it were at an end—obliterated—annihilated— not a rag or shred of either remaining behind. It was then that we conceived the divinely humorous idea of *buying* both of these spectres from Spain! [It is quite safe to confess this to the Person Sitting in Darkness, since neither he nor any other sane person will believe it.] In buying those ghosts for twenty millions, we also contracted to take care of the friars and their accumulations. I think we also agreed to propagate leprosy and smallpox, but as to this there is doubt. But it is not important; persons afflicted with the friars do not mind other diseases.

"With our Treaty ratified, Manila subdued, and our Ghosts secured, we had no further use for Aguinaldo and the owners of the Archipelago. We forced a war, and we have been hunting America's guest and ally through the woods and swamps ever since."

At this point in the tale, it will be well to boast a little of our war-work and our heroisms in the field, so as to make our performance look as fine as England's in South Africa; but I believe it will not be best to emphasize this too much. We must be cautious. Of course, we must read the war-telegrams to the Person, in order to keep up our frankness; but we can throw an air of humorousness over them, and that will modify their grim eloquence a little, and their rather indiscreet exhibitions of gory exultation. Before reading to him the following display heads of the dispatches of November 18, 1900, it will be well to practice on them in private first, so as to get the right tang of lightness and gaiety into them:

"ADMINISTRATION WEARY OF PROTRACTED HOSTILITIES!"
"REAL WAR AHEAD FOR FILIPINO REBELS!"*
"WILL SHOW NO MERCY!"
"KITCHENER'S PLAN ADOPTED!"

* "Rebels" Mumble that funny word—Don't let the Person catch it distincly. [MT]

66

Kitchener knows how to handle disagreeable people who are fighting for their homes and their liberties, and we must let on that we are merely imitating Kitchener, and have no national interest in the matter, further than to get ourselves admired by the Great Family of Nations, in which august company our Master of the Game has bought a place for us in the back row.

Of course, we must not venture to ignore our General MacArthur's reports—oh, why do they keep on printing those embarrassing things?—we must drop them trippingly from the tongue and take the chances:

> During the last ten months our losses have been 268 killed and 750 wounded;
> Filipino loss, *three thousand two hundred and twenty-seven killed*, and 694 wounded.

We must stand ready to grab the Person Sitting in Darkness, for he will swoon away at this confession, saying: "Good God, those 'niggers' spare their wounded, and the Americans massacre theirs!"

We must bring him to, and coax him and coddle him, and assure him that the ways of Providence are best, and that it would not become us to find fault with them; and then, to show him that we are only imitators, not originators, we must read the following passage from the letter of an American soldier-lad in the Philippines to his mother, published in *Public Opinion*, of Decorah, Iowa, describing the finish of a victorious battle:

> "WE NEVER LEFT ONE ALIVE. IF ONE WAS WOUNDED, WE WOULD
> RUN OUR BAYONETS THROUGH HIM."

Having now laid all the historical facts before the Person Sitting in Darkness, we should bring him to again, and explain them to him. We should say to him:

"They look doubtful, but in reality they are not. There have been lies; yes, but they were told in a good cause. We have been treacherous; but that was only in order that real good might come out of apparent evil. True, we have crushed a deceived and confiding people; we have turned against the weak and the friendless who trusted us; we have stamped out a just and intelligent and well-ordered republic; we have stabbed an ally in the back and slapped the face of a guest; we have bought a Shadow from an enemy that hadn't it to sell; we have robbed a trusting friend of his land and his liberty; we have invited our clean young men to shoulder a discredited musket and do bandit's work under a flag which bandits have been accustomed to fear, not to follow; we have debauched America's honor and blackened her face before the world; but each detail was for the best. We know this. The Head of every State and Sovereignty in Christendom and ninety per cent of every legislative body in Christendom, including our Congress and our fifty State Legislatures, are members not only of the church, but also of the Blessings-of-Civilization Trust. This world-girdling accumulation of trained morals, high principles, and justice, cannot do an unright thing, an unfair thing, an ungenerous thing, an unclean thing. It knows what it is about. Give yourself no uneasiness; it is all right."

Now then, that will convince the Person. You will see. It will restore the Business. Also, it will elect the Master of the Game to the vacant place in the Trinity of our national gods; and there on their high thrones the Three will sit, age after age, in the people's sight, each bearing the Emblem of his service: Washington, the Sword of the Liberator; Lincoln, the Slave's Broken Chains; the Master, the Chains Repaired.

It will give the Business a splendid new start. You will see.

Everything is prosperous, now; everything is just as we should wish it. We have got the Archipelago, and we shall never give it up. Also, we have every reason to hope that we shall have an opportunity before very long to slip out of our Congressional contract with Cuba and give her something better in the place of it. It is a rich country, and many of us are already beginning to see that the contract was a sentimental mistake. But now—right now—is the best time to do some profitable rehabilitating work—work that will set us up and make us comfortable, and discourage gossip. We cannot conceal from ourselves that, privately, we are a little troubled about our uniform. It is one of our prides; it is acquainted with honor; it is familiar with great deeds and noble; we love it, we revere it; and so this errand it is on makes us uneasy. And our flag—another pride of ours, our chiefest! We have worshipped it so; and when we have seen it in far lands—glimpsing it unexpectedly in that strange sky, waving its welcome and benediction to us—we have caught our breath, and uncovered our heads, and couldn't speak, for a moment, for the thought of what it was to us and the great ideals it stood for. Indeed, we must do something about these things; we must not have the flag out there, and the uniform. They are not needed there; we can manage in some other way. England manages, as regards the uniform, and so can we. We have to send soldiers—we can't get out of that—but we can disguise them. It is the way England does in South Africa. Even Mr. Chamberlain himself takes pride in England's honorable uniform, and makes the army down there wear an ugly and odious and appropriate disguise, of yellow stuff such as quarantine flags are made of, and which are hoisted to warn the healthy away from unclean disease and repulsive death. This cloth is called khaki. We could adopt it. It is light, comfortable, grotesque, and deceives the enemy, for he cannot conceive of a soldier being concealed in it.

And as for a flag for the Philippine Province, it is easily managed. We can have a special one—our States do it: we can have just our usual flag, with the white stripes painted black and the stars replaced by the skull and cross-bones.

And we do not need that Civil Commission out there. Having no powers, it has to invent them, and that kind of work cannot be effectively done by just anybody; an expert is required. Mr. Croker can be spared. We do not want the United States represented there, but only the Game.

By help of these suggested amendments, Progress and Civilization in that country can have a boom, and it will take in the Persons who are Sitting in Darkness, and we can resume Business at the old stand.

Bencab

Invaders and Resisters
1980
acrylic on paper
102 x 70 cm

A Page From an Officer's Diary
1980
oil on canvas
122 x 244 cm

A Pose After Victory
1972
acrylic on paper
57 x 75 cm

Pit-a-Pit's Metamorphosis
1972
acrylic on paper
56 x 75 cm

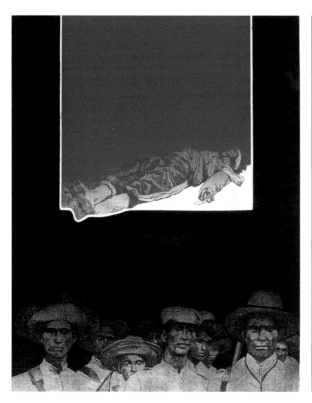

Heroes of The Past II
1976
2-color plate etching
35 x 27.5 cm

Women Waiting
1975
etching/aquatint
23 x 17 cm

Heroes of The Past
1998
charcoal & acrylic on handmade paper
112 x 244 cm

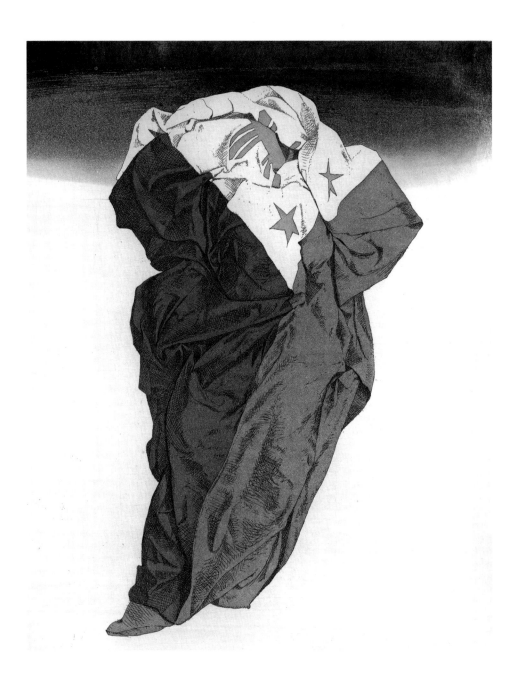

Untitled
1975
etching/aquatint
30 x 25 cm

Antipas Delotavo

Sakuna
(Casualty)
1997
oil on canvas
63.5 x 76.2 cm

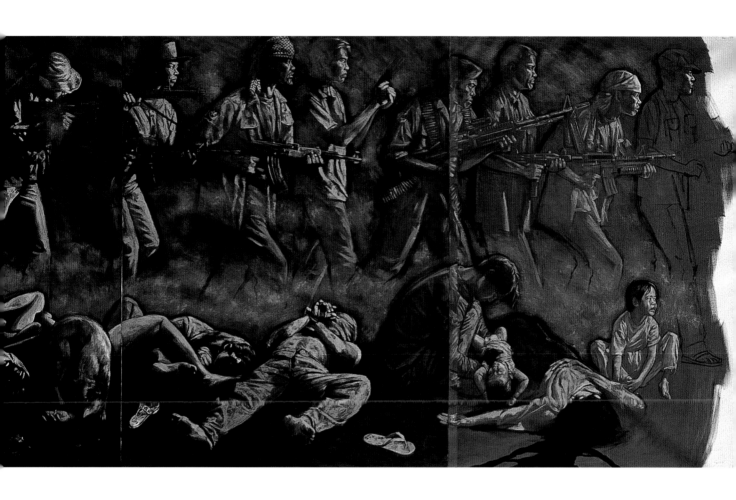

Daantaon (Century)
1998
oil on canvas
5 panels, 95 x 975.36 cm

Itak sa Puso ni Mang Juan
(Dagger at the Heart of Mang Juan)
1976
watercolor on paper
38.1 x 55.88 cm

Brenda Fajardo

Gubat III: Siglo disinuwebe sa panahon ni Sakay at Papa Isio
(Forest III: Nineteenth Century During the Time of Sakay and Papa Isio)
1999
ink and tempera on paper
77 x 112.5 cm
Carlos Cojuangco Collection

Ipinagbili ni Felipe si Mariya kay Samuel
(Felipe sold Maria to Samuel)
1989
ink and tempera on paper
52.5 x 72 cm.

Baraha ng Buhay Pilipino: Ikatlong Lupi ng
Kasaysayan: Paglipat ng Kamay
(Card of Filipino Life: Third Fold In History:
The Change of Hands)
1998
ink and tempera on paper
61 x 47 cm
Singapore Art Museum Collection

Ang Paggahasa sa laman at kaluluwa ni Pilipina
(The Rape of the Flesh and Soul of Pilipina)
1993
ink and tempera on paper
56.5 x 78.5 cm
Carlos Cojuangco Collection

Sa ikatlo and Amerikano, sa ika-apat ang Hapon
(On the third, the Americans: on the fourth, the Japanese)
1999
ink and tempera on paper
54 x 70 cm
Carlos Cojuangco Collection

Photo courtesy Metropolitan Museum of Manila

Ang Tipan ni Ynang Bayan
(Testament of the Motherland)
1998
acrylic on canvas
76 x 91.5 cm
CEMEX Philippines Collection

The Hills Are Still There

RESIL MOJARES

A war never really ends. When the causes for resistance remain, then a war never really ends. It assumes other forms, becomes an illusion of itself, a subversion of what it intends; it is submerged and yet can rise again, find itself once more in the tenacious imagining of a better order of things.

War casts a stark light on society: it brings into sharp relief a political field in which people have to define themselves in relation to each other and the Other. Who and what are threatened by what or whom? On the other hand, war raises not only the threat of loss and destruction but, by unhinging a world, it opens up (as it also closes) possibilities. How and what possibilities are discerned?

In studies of the war against Spain and the United States there has been a tendency to lean toward a simple dichotomy that distinguishes between the response of the elite and that of the masses, ascribing to either one or the other the primary role for the resistance.[1] What is inadequately appreciated is the complex social formation of Philippine society at the turn of the century. A "two-class" model makes for a net too widely spaced it allows a lot of significant data to fall through the sieve. For sure, the model is too cumbersome for the case of Cebu.

On the eve of the war, Cebu province was a socially irregular, unstable, and inchoate landscape. Nineteenth-century economic changes created new social groups, revised old social relations, and primed the appearance of the new social formations. This was most evident in the increasingly differentiated economy and ethnically complex port society of Cebu City. The city was the headquarters of an export-oriented economy, the point for the collecting, processing, and trans-shipping of goods from a hinterland that included not only the island of Cebu but provinces in the Eastern Visayas and Northern Mindanao.

Who were the primary beneficiaries of this order? To begin with, there were the Spaniards who stood at the helm of the colonial government (and, in Cebu, the central figures were the governor and the bishop): They extracted wealth from such assets as land and people as well as from taxes and duties on services, industries, and trade. Yet, Spanish power was more parasitic than dynamic. Outside the Augustinian estates in the Mandaue and Talisay areas, Spaniards were not directly engaged in agricultural production. Spaniards constituted a minuscule portion of the provincial population and they did not own land in the Cebu countryside.[2] Their prominence largely resided in their control of the civil and ecclesiastical bureaucracy.

The most dynamic sector in local society was the foreign merchant houses that presided over the export and import of goods. In the early nineteenth century, these houses had provincial agents that supplied them with the products needed in the markets of Great Britain, the United States, Australia, and Spain. After the opening of the port of Cebu to world trade in 1860, they established permanent offices in Cebu. The American firm of Russell and Sturgis and the English houses of Loney, Kerr & Company, and Smith Bell & Company established control of the trade. They bought agricultural products, supplied credit, accepted funds at interest, had direct access to trade information, operated ships or acted as consignees for shipping lines, and performed insurance and brokerage functions.

On the eve of the war, the Cebuano elite was no longer a homogeneous group.[3] *Principalia* status came from a mix of factors: wealth, public landowners, shopkeepers, doctors, lawyers, pharmacists, as well as artisans, tanners, carpenters, bakers, and seamstresses. Titles of *don* and *doña* were used by people of divergent statuses. A carriage-maker or clerk, who comes from a family that had at one time served in the Spanish administration, may carry such a title. As a social category, then, *principalia* does not quite define the position of persons in the existing power system.

Within the principalia, the important distinction was between those who stood close to the center of the port economy (foreign merchant houses, the highest Spanish officials, and a few Filipino families based in the city) and those who were at its peripheries. The most powerful Cebu families were almost wholly of mestizo stock (Spanish or Chinese), or foreigners, who resided in the city (or headquartered in it), controlled sizeable landholdings, capital, and a network of clients in the hinterland. They had direct links with the foreign merchant houses for which they usually served as agents or *compradores*. In the 1890s, these included the Velosos, Llorentes, Climacos, Osmeñas, and Mejias. These families built up their wealth throughout the nineteenth century, profiting from a symbiotic relationship with both the Spanish administration and the foreign merchant houses. They were almost wholly mestizo in ethnic character— Spanish and Chinese— easily straddling local and global worlds.

At the periphery of the "elite" were a large number of property owners whose holdings were on a much lesser scale than the families earlier mentioned, and who were less aggressive or less favorably positioned to fully exploit the opportunities of the port-oriented economy. Growing educational opportunities (there were 662 students enrolled in the Colegio-Seminario de San Carlos in 1895) and expanding communications raised social expectations.[4] There were cracks and fault lines in the social system: dividing the municipal gentry in the countryside from the aggressive, port-based entrepreneurs; the emerging proletariat and petty bourgeoisie from the Spanish bureaucrats and their allies; and the marginal *indios* from the economically dominant mestizos.

The city population was internally divided by the pressures of a rising cash economy. An occupational census of the city in 1900 shows that 6,014 were employed in trade and transportation and 170 in domestic and personal services as opposed to only 814 city residents involved in agriculture.[5] The city was increasingly populated by people who lived off industry, trade, and the service sectors: wage laborers, skilled craftsmen, market gardeners, domestic servants, hawkers, employees, and professionals. Moreover, the increased circulation of population within the colony in the nineteenth century made for a more diverse, volatile society.

The larger mass of the provincial population, as far as the written records go, was a largely anonymous entity. By the 1890s, however, the shift to commercial agriculture and the export trade had brought large sections of Cebu island into the orbit of the port of Cebu. The rural population was increasingly peasantized and enmeshed in widening networks of social and economic dependency.

Due to the different positions of persons and groups in the social field, they perceived and participated in events differently. Among the elite, the war against Spain was animated by libertarian ideas as well as by the awareness, sharpened by nineteenth-century changes, of the irrelevance of the Spanish presence. The Spanish colonial administration had become excess baggage to a local elite grown confident in their ability to take matters of governance into their own hands.

The war against the United States was fueled by the same sentiments. Nevertheless, it was also a different war. The elite knew that, in the course of the nineteenth century, the Philippines had come within the orbit of a world economy, locked into a dependent relationship with the developed nations of the West (particularly the rising nation of the United States). The elite must have perceived the imbalance in the relationship. Yet, they profited from it, enjoying a prosperity they never experienced before. Collaboration was a stance taken not simply out of self-interested calculations of profit but by the politically demobilizing sense of what, to many, must have seemed the inexorability of historical process. Spain was a country receding into the past, the United States loomed in the future.

On the other hand, there were elements of the elite, more particularly of the lower orders, who participated only peripherally or indirectly in the new prosperity, transcended class-bound interests, and were moved by racial pride and ideas of *liberté*. The most active leaders of the resistance came from this group: socially displaced political agents (Pantaleon del Rosario, Mateo Luga), young students (Andres Jayme, Tomas Alonso), municipal landowners (Jacinto Pacaña, Arcadio Maxilom), and urban bourgeoisie (Alejo Miñoza, Enrique Lorega). They fought a war that, in a sense, was doomed from the very beginning—not only because of the superior martial powers of the United States but because, given the society, Filipinos could not have acted as one.

And what of the now largely anonymous mass of resisters? To say that they simply followed patrons and kinsmen is to deny them political knowledge of the social and economic positions they occupied. The growing intensification in the movement of men and ideas through the countryside in the nineteenth century must have equipped rural dwellers with a sense of membership in an evolving national brotherhood. To this extent, they knowingly participated in what was a national war, first against the Spaniards, and then against the Americans. Yet, their expectations of what the goals of this war were must have been shaped by the economic and cultural positions they occupied in a native society where exploitation wore not only the face of the foreigner but that of fellow Filipinos. Hence, what many of them fought was also a social war, one heavy with the idiom of millenarianism and peasant egalitarianism. This became most visible after the surrender of the republican generals in 1901 when the complexion of the war changed with the spread of the so-called *pulahan* movement.

All these made for a highly asymmetrical war in which who was fighting whom, and for what reasons, was not always clear. Indeed, a war is never simple. In Cebu, complex social tensions played themselves out in a complex way in which Cebuanos fought not only against the Americans but also against each other.

How was the war of resistance structured? A national army waged war against the United States. Provincial troops, as in Cebu, maintained communications with central organs in Luzon, acknowledged the leadership of Aguinaldo, followed orders from higher authorities, adhered to standard commissions and procedures and, in other respects, operated as units of a larger army. In other ways, this national army was a fiction (as much recent scholarship tends to argue). There were groups that operated apart from, as well as against, the Aguinaldo army; the army was often "national" more in form than in substance; the bulk of the population did not actively join in the fighting; and the ideology and motives of the ordinary soldiers who fought within this army may have been different from those of their leaders. Nevertheless, the fact remains that it was a "national" army—albeit inchoate, plagued by contradictions—that embodied the main resistance against the Americans from 1899 to 1901. That it lost the war is to be explained, in large measure, by its failure to become what it claimed to be. This failure was less a matter of strategy and tactics as it was, in the final instance, an outcome of the conditions of social and national formation at the time the war was fought. The resistance was stymied by crosscutting and opposing interests. However, given the society as it was constituted at the time, as well as the shortness of time into which events were collapsed, it could not have been otherwise.[6]

What did it all amount to? The meaning of the Philippine-American War is both diverse and dense. Writ large, America tried to remake Philippine society by implanting "democracy" through a process of guided self-government, popular education, and economic development. It was an enterprise undermined by political cross-purposes, imperial conceit, and parochial naiveté. Contemporary scholarship suggests that the impact of U.S. rule has been less beneficent and more limited than claimed in the past. America embarked on a fresh "adventure" but also worked within the limited (and, often, conservative) parameters of her own culture, which predisposed her to a partnership with the local elite and a simple faith in "popular education" and economic "developmentalism."[7]

On the other hand, the resilience and integrity of Philippine society were underestimated. Filipino response to U.S. rule was mediated by tenacious facts of social structure and historical experience. In the accommodation of American and Filipino conservatisms, much was preserved. The basic problems of poverty and dependency remained and were heightened, the basic social configuration was preserved, and the character of the economy sustained. The United States built on earlier economic accomplishments. The major changes in the economy took place in the nineteenth century, before the U.S. occupation, in the shift from subsistence cultivation to cash cropping. In 1855 the value of goods exported by the Philippines amounted to P5.9 million; P18.9 million in 1875; P36.6 million in 1895. This increased to P69.8 million in 1909, then to P95.9 million in 1913. In 1913 as in

1900, the four principal exports of the archipelago were abaca, copra, tobacco, and sugar. The United States "captured" and presided over a society that, in the nineteenth century, was already increasingly locked into larger worlds.

All these have fostered a tendency in recent scholarship to mitigate the responsibility of the Americans by focusing on the active complicity of local elites and arguing that U.S. occupation had little effect. This tendency must not erase the fact of massive destruction wrought by the American invasion. It must not, at the same time, obscure the fact that the U.S. occupation cleared the ground for the institutionalization of a neocolonial Philippines.

Nothing changed, much was changed. An American military officer, who was stationed in Cebu in 1902, revisited the city in 1911. In 1911, American soldiers were still very much in evidence in Cebu City. Six companies of the Ninth Infantry, under Col. Charles J. Crane, were stationed in Warwick Barracks. The Americans also occupied 12.5 hectares of private land for military reservation and target range purposes, in addition to nineteen houses and rooms in eighth other houses in the city as "officers' quarters." Most of these were located on Colon, Magallanes, and other streets close to the Recollect Plaza (which the Americans renamed Plaza Washington).[8]

The officer saw a changed city.[9] What used to be just two wooden piers in 1902 had become a million-and-a-quarter-peso wharf that could accommodate at the same time five oceangoing vessels as well as a number of small coasters. At the port could now be seen a brand-new customs house and a row of concrete warehouses with foreign names (Castle Bros., McLeod, Stevenson and Company, Ltd.). In the inner city itself were new concrete buildings and thriving British, Chinese, and American commercial establishments. There used to be only three foreign export-import houses in Cebu. Now there were thirteen, in addition to two commercial banks, all of them foreign-owned.

A new waterworks system was in the process of being built and there was talk of building an electric railway within the city. Philippine Railway Company operated a line that extended from Cebu to Danao in the north and Argao in the south, with four trains dispatched daily in either direction from the Cebu station. The city electric plant (Visayan Electric Company) was in the process of being expanded to generate not just night but also day service. The city had a telephone service, an English-language newspaper (Alfred G. Andersen's *The Cebu Chronicle*), two ten-ton ice plants, and several hotels. At the waterfront was a new public market with nearly 300 stalls. A public high school and trade school had just opened; the government had 43,003 students in the whole province. Foreign residents found modern amenities at such social clubs as Club Ingles and United Service Club. Movies were shown with increasing regularity at several cinematografos in the city. At Plaza Washington (now Freedom Park), Cebuanos were taking enthusiastically to the game of baseball.

The visiting American marveled at the changes. The honking of cars had become part of the sounds of the city for, by 1911, livery stable operators had Overlands, Buicks, and Fords for rent. In 1902 it was unsafe for foreigners to walk beyond the inner city, say to Sambag, as insurgents and bandits lurked in the city outskirts. Now, peace-and-order and sanitation conditions had markedly improved. He learned that one could now run up to Danao in an automobile, over a fine road, in forty minutes. It used to be a two-day hike.

The American visitor called on an old friend, Florentino Rallos, the former Cebu presidente. At his house on Colon Street, smaller than the one he occupied in 1901, Rallos reminisced about the past, bitter about how the new politics had left him behind. He had lost a great part of his wealth and now, half-paralyzed, he rarely ventured outside his home. (He died the year after.) He lamented how things had not changed entirely for the better, the young men were leaving the fields, crowding into the towns, seeking work. Asked by the visitor what he thought about what the American occupation had wrought, the old man said: the poor are still poor.

The American wandered back to old Plaza Independencia, looking over the scorched grass toward the fort, and was visited by melancholy over the war he and his friends had fought. Looking landward, he saw once more the barren mountain range of the island and recalled interminable hikes over those burning hills, and the apparent fruitlessness of it all.

It is a different city but the hills are still there.

NOTES:

1. Glenn May, for instance, faults Teodoro Agoncillo and Renato Constantino for the "rigid dichotomy" between masses/resisters and elite/collaborators. In his work on the war in Batangas, however, May commits the same mistake by simply reversing the equation, ascribing to an ill-defined "elite" the primary impetus for the resistance.

2. We have no precise data on the number of Spaniards residing in Cebu in the late nineteenth century. There must have been around thirty Spanish merchants and property owners in Cebu in the 1890s. See Fenner, *Cebu Under the Spanish Flag.*

3. Important work on elite formation in Cebu has been done by Michael Cullinane, "The Changing Nature of the Cebu Urban Elite in the 19th Century," in *Philippine Social History*, ed. A. W. McCoy and Ed. C. de Jesus (Quezon City, Philippines: Ateneo de Manila University Press, 1982), 251-96.

4. For student enrolment, see Fenner, *Cebu Under the Spanish Flag*, 163.

5. *El Pueblo* (9 and 23 May 1900).

6. In what is an otherwise comprehensive analysis of the reasons for the failure of the resistance, Glenn May ("Why the United States Won," 353-77) errs in inadequately defining the social position of his "elites," overstressing clientilism as principle of recruitment and motive for participation, reductively characterizing peasant response to the war as one of "indifference," and in tending toward presentist valuations by not fully taking into account the specificity of nation-formation at the time the war was fought.

7. May (*Social Engineering*, xix) says: "The colony was not a 'laboratory of democracy'; it was, rather, a laboratory for the testing of essentially conservative formulas."

8. USNA, RG 395, entry 2503, box 1, Roster of Troops Serving in the Department of the Visayas (Iloilo, August 1911), no. 4, 9-10; RG 395, entry 2503, box 1, "Warwick Barracks, Cebu. Leases. Fiscal Year 1912."

9. The data in the paragraphs that follow are drawn from USNA, RG 350, entry 2055/18, H. M. Cohen to F. McIntyre, 23 October 1911. Additional details on Cebu in 1910 are from James J. Rafferty, "The Story of Cebu's Progress," *Philippines Monthly* 2 (October 1911), 16-19; Alfred G. Andersen, "Cebu, the Second City in the Philippines," *Philippine Resources* 1 (June 1910), 9-13; Alfred G. Andersen, ed., *Special Boost Edition of the Cebu Chronicle* (Cebu City, Philippines: Cebu Chronicle, 1910).

Body Count: The War and Its Consequences

ALFRREDO NAVARRO SALANGA

4 February[1899]

An American sentry shoots and kills a Filipino soldier trying to cross the San Juan del Monte bridge. The incident ignites the Filipino–American War.

This was no
imagined
dragon—
this bullet
snaking
through
the cold
still air
of San Juan
del Monte.

Deep in its
coiled death
were more
coils,
more deaths
to be sprung
from the brown
coiled souls.

From the brown
coiled throats
of brown men
screaming
brown screams
snaking
through streams

Through rivers
whose banks
long covered
under the
cowls
of friars,

Long braided
by the epaulets
of captains
and governors,

Were on the verge
of uncoiling
themselves
into the sea.

An American Colonial State:
Authority and Structure in Southern Mindanao

PATRICIO ABINALES

INTRODUCTION

Reflecting on his term as a constabulary officer assigned to the Moro Province almost throughout the 1900s, Cornelius Smith described its administration in these terms:

> The government of the Moro Province in my time was practically independent of the Governor General in Manila.... The legislative council... made its own laws which were sent to Manila... for approval. As it developed, this became largely a matter of form. Really, the government of the Philippines and that of the Moro Province constituted a dual authority—the former legislating and controlling the Christian and Pagan tribes in the north, the latter the Mohammedan peoples in the southern islands.[1]

Leonard Wood, first governor of the province also acknowledged that "two homogenous governments under one control" functioned in southern Mindanao, while Mrs. Howard Taft, who accompanied her husband in his tour of Mindanao, similarly noted that the "disorder" there had prompted Americans to "detach them (i.e., the people of the area) from the general organization and place them under a semi-military system with an American army officer of high rank in charge in the dual capacity of Governor and Commanding General of the troops in the Moro Province."[2]

These widely shared observations summed up the American view regarding their "mandate in the Moroland."[3] The emphasis of this commonly held opinion lay on "difference"—the deviation of an area and its people from the rest of the larger colony, and the consequent necessity for the distinct approach to administration. This essay will attempt to ascertain how this distinctiveness came about, by looking at the nature of the "local state structure" that was built and how this "infrastructure" created a different political authority that warranted these comments about its distinctiveness from the rest of the Philippine colony.

With the failure of Spanish colonialism to subjugate southern Mindanao, the incoming Americans faced a number of different choices regarding "Morolandia."

They could have created a colony that was different from the rest of the Philippines based on the information that Spain was never really able to "integrate" the south into its "official" colonial territory. Or, they could have accomplished what the Spaniards originally intended to do albeit in vain, i.e., subjugate the South, and then begin "integrating" the non-Christian groups with the rest of the colony.

I will argue that between 1900 and 1914, the army had to work out an administrative structure that took into consideration the ambiguities of a still-evolving American colonial policy. The Moro Province, the juridical form of which this authority took shape, operated under contradictory premises: presumably a subordinate authority to the colonial center in Manila, it nonetheless functioned as if it were an administration separately governing a territory whose future was not, until 1914, necessarily bound to that of the rest of the colony. When the McKinley policy of "benevolent assimilation" was vaguely defined and Washington was predisposed toward making the Philippines a protectorate, army authorities worked under the assumption that southern Mindanao's intense contrast with that of the rest of the Philippines meant, by necessity, that it had to be treated differently.

As it became clear that the protectorate plans were to give way to political tutelage, with increased Filipino participation toward eventual independence, this assumption and the policies/programs that grew out of it came into contradiction with the Manila-Washington goal. At first, army authorities resisted what they regarded as a "forced integration" of the province from the above, and where resistance waned, sought to extend its character as a "special" (i.e., military-run) area. Eventually, however, the military had to give way to "civilian-ization" and the Moro Province formally became part of the 1930 Philippine Commonwealth. In short, the ambiguous, perhaps even "muddled," character of the colonial state formation in one extremity of the Philippines produced confusing features. On the one hand, and without the army intending it to be, there emerged qualities identified with a functional, vigorous, and self-sustaining local authority. On the other hand, a successful pacification and administration project magnified, instead of diminished, tensions between the "Moroland" and the colonial center in Manila.

THE CREATION OF A "MORO" PROVINCE

The army occupation proceeded with the American recognition that a huge chunk of Mindanao and its population, especially the diverse "indigenous" communities, was only formally part of the colonial territory it bought from Spain.[4] To incorporate a huge area, with parts of it still unexplored and isolated, was quite a problem in itself.[5] Issues of size and impermeability were compounded by the difficulty of reaching out to and controlling a sparse and scattered population. The fact that most of the people lived by the coast and thus could be reached only by a regular and speedy transport system aggravated juridical, administrative and legal problems.[6]

The Americans were similarly aware that, to Spanish colonizers, Mindanao's value as an "unpacified" territory came mainly from serving, together with Guam, as the end-port for penal deportees.[7] Its distance from Manila was only made complicated by the inaccessibility of its interiors. Much of Mindanao was, therefore, imagined as "empty' and "dark," evoking memories of the Western frontier of settlers, cowboys, armies, and carpetbaggers.[8] More important was the knowledge of Spanish failure to subjugate the Muslim groups and the concomitant persistence of Muslim (southern Mindanao) versus Christian (northern Philippines) tensions brought about by Spanish rule and the demands of slave labor in the Southeast Asian trading network.[9] The potential recurrence of active Muslim defiance of Manila with the breakdown of the Spanish colonial order only sustained this perception.

Thus the reputation of the Muslims had been etched in the American mind even before the two groups encountered each other.[10] The task then was not only to establish colonial authority over a large, formidably inaccessible territory but to use that authority over "tribes" unsullied by "any Western civilizing influence" as a means of bringing about their actual integration into the colonial body politic.[11] This wariness notwithstanding, the Americans moved into southern Mindanao aware that the Muslims had been considerably weakened by their wars with the Spanish. The latter's accounts gave Americans strategic knowledge of the extent to which the once powerful Sultanates of Sulu and Maguindanao had weakened, such knowledge being supported subsequently by intelligence reports from the field.[12]

White American bigotry expectedly played a determining role in shaping official and personal perceptions of the Muslims as with the other communities of the Philippines. Despite being aware of the major differences among Muslims, American authorities nevertheless accepted, and even perpetuated, the Spanish colonizers' stereotype of their new subjects: Islamic, barbaric, backward, and led by self-serving strongmen whose powers were based on force.[13] An official consensus was reached to rely on force to ensure Muslim compliance, then to use this force as a way of introducing "American civilization" to these "savages."[14] Some officials did disagree, suggesting that there was more to the Muslims than these racist assertions, and proposing the use and retention of aspects of their "culture" relevant to the civilizing process, even as administrators introduced American policies and perspectives. They were, however, a minority and, while appreciated, hardly made a dent on this official policy.[15]

Accepting that the "non-Christian tribes" were socially and politically backward, the Americans, despite some opposition from within, decided in favor of a new legal system for the entire Province. Leonard Wood succinctly argued the case for a wholesale introduction of laws by pointing out that "the Moros and other savage peoples have no laws—simply a few customs, which are nowhere general, varying from one valley to the next, from one island to another. Such laws as they have been many of them revolting and practically all of them utterly and absolutely undesirable from every standpoint of decency and government." Wood was particularly critical of the Muslims whom he described as a "religious and moral degenerates" who not only had failed to abide by Islamic teachings such that " at the present time there is little or nothing left of them. Those that are left are (concerned) principally with the plurality of wives, the control and protection of concubines and laws regulating property in slaves. In short, nothing has been found worthy of codification or imitation, and little or nothing which does not exist in better from wherever humane, decent and civilized laws are in force."[16]

It was, however, from the same imagined "backwardness" that the Americans proceeded to treat the "non-pagans" differently. Even as no viable code of law could be found, colonial authorities nevertheless defined separately the system of justice for "Moros" and "Pagans" vis-à-vis the Christians. This "double system" caused much consternation among army officers, but until their control was consolidated they had to make do with it.[17] It was not until 1914, when this dual application of colonial laws was repealed, that the army established as unchallenged hegemony all over the Moro Province and hesitantly handed it over to the increasingly Filipino-dominated civil administration in Manila. There was, however, something more than meets the eye with regard to this particular attitude. The perception of Muslim (and other Mindanao "pagan") backwardness evolved against the backdrop of a "broader" racism aimed at northern Christian Filipinos.[18]

Army administrators, sincerely or otherwise, imagined themselves not only as guardians and guides of non-Christian groups but, more important, as their protectors from potential and actual exploitation by lowland Christian Filipinos. Influenced mainly by the ideas of University of Michigan zoologist Dean C. Worcester, they became concerned that non-Christian groups be exploited by Christian caciques and thereby lose not only their pristine savage naivete but control of their resources as well.[19] These apprehensions grew worse as stories of problems caused by Filipino caciques to stabilization efforts spread among the colonizers.[20] Nor were Filipinos regarded by the Americans as capable and worthy of being assigned the role of safe-keeping; for already as early as 1905, American constabulary officials were complaining of corruption and incompetence among the mainly Filipino municipal police.[21] It was not that the Americans had a high regard for the Muslims. On the contrary, they were strongly contemptible of what they observed. Alongside this odium, however, was a kind of paternalism that regarded the Muslims and other groups as people in need of protection, not unlike some of the American Indian tribes at the opening of the Western frontier.

This "fear" of the evils of Filipino caciquism blended well with notions of "savage backwardness" as well as the knowledge of a Christian-Muslim conflict passed on by the departing Spanish to justify the argument that non-Christians needed to be protected while being instructed over a long period on the ABCs of civilization. Moreover, the notion that a principal reason for American occupation was to civilize and train Filipinos in the art of democratic governance further reinforced the above justification. American officials were of the opinion that if Filipinos were to assist in the staffing of the colonial government in southern Mindanao, they would impede rather than hasten the civilization and integration process. That there had yet to evolve a functional civil service, not to mention the persistence of anti-Christian sentiments among the Muslims, strengthened this belief.[22]

What emerged then was a type of colonial "racism" that had a double meaning. While the Americans, in general, regarded the Filipinos as "backward," the same racist attitude was used to protect a perceived "more backward" group within Philippine society from the superior ones. American colonial racism functioned as a shield for non-Christian groups like the Muslims against a Filipino racism believed to be more powerful and sophisticated. It became a case of one racism being used against another.

On 1 June 1903, the Philippine Commission, the highest colonial policy-making body, passed Act No. 787, creating the Moro Province as "the framework, within which transition from military to civilian rule in Moroland would take place wherever and whenever the duly constituted authorities felt it was indicated."[23] An appointive leadership composed of a governor, secretary, treasurer, engineer, and superintendent of schools formed the executive leadership of the province. These officials constituted with powers to create municipalities, raise local revenues, oversee offices like the school system, public works and Moro tribal courts, and enact laws which it deemed necessary for the efficient administration of the province. Finally, the Council was given "a very large measure of discretion in dealing with the Moros and in preserving as far as possible, consistent with the fundamental act, the customs of the Moros, the authority of the *datus*, and a system of justice in which Moros could take part."[24]

The Province was divided into four districts (Davao, Cotabato, Lanao and Zamboanga), each under a district governor with respective district boards. Essentially, the districts duplicated the structure of the higher Provincial authority and more or less exercised the same amount of executive and legislative discretion vis-à-vis their respective areas. The districts, in turn, were subdivided into two types of administrative bodies: the municipalities and tribal wards. The fourteen municipalities were towns with "Christian" majorities, and having more "dense population relative to the rest of the Province."[25] With their "civilized" status, they were patterned like the regular and "pacified" municipalities of Luzon, the Visayas and the northern portion of Mindanao.[26] They were for all intents and purposes, regular municipalities, the only distinction being that they were army-administered. The fifty-one tribal wards were to oversee problems of administrative control specific to the "non-Christian tribes" and to ensure that good relations were cultivated between the American proconsuls and these groups.[27] These wards, together with the tribal courts, were also envisioned to assist provincial authorities in making possible the transition mainly by the Muslim groups from religious (i.e., Islamic) savagery to "Western" civilization.[28]

From its inception, several features already distinguished the Moro Province from others. First, the province was four times larger than any other Philippine counterpart, and even its districts dwarfed in size some of the regular provinces in the north.[29] With the Mountain Province then, the total area that came under army control was over half of the Philippines. This huge expanse, however, contained a sparse population of 395,000 (40,000 Christians, 275,000 Muslims, and 80,000 other non-Christian tribes) spread over 38,888 square miles, a ratio of 10 people per square mile.[30] Large portions were dense hinterland, "near-empty" and unsurveyed. The Americans planned the Moro Province as an administrative body that would open up this unknown territory, thus creating the conditions that eventually allowed people to come in and exploit its resources.

The second important feature of the Moro Province was its administrative makeup, that of being army-administered. After a brief critical review of the British, Dutch, and Spanish experiences, as well as their own "Indian" policies, colonial authorities opted to retain the Spanish classification of "military provinces," infusing aspects of the Dutch system of coopting local leaders into colonially created "tribal" offices.[31] The Province, in the eyes of the Americans, needed time to be pacified before it could join the rest of the "civilian-ized" territories, and for that a transitional period of unstated duration was necessary.[32]

To facilitate administrative stability, the army's Department of Mindanao provided the personnel and administrative functionaries of the Province, partly because they were then the most accessible, and partly because of the American opinion that administration, at the onset, overlapped with stabilizing a perceived volatile area. The army was thus seen as the only institution with the personnel to undertake this dual responsibility.[33]

The significance of all this can hardly be understated. It meant that a large yet empty chunk of the Philippines was to be—even temporarily—insulated from the evolving colonial politics largely played out and determined in Manila. It gave the army (which, as early as 1899, was already at odds with "civilian" administrators) the chance to "play God," unencumbered by "civilian" interference from Manila.

Army officers also saw the opportunity to show the purported superiority of their administrative skills. Those who became provincial overseers had varying reasons for accepting their posts, but commonly shared the desire to prove that the Province could be pacified and administered well. Leonard Wood (1903-1906), Tasker Bliss (1906-1909), and John J. Pershing (1909-1913) were impelled by a determined sense of responsibility and a crusade-like drive to fulfill their racist-paternal role as civilizers of the uncivilized.[34] These men's "credentials" showed zeal and administrative talent:

> (These) three generals one after the other governed the Moro Province. Later each became in turn Army Chief of Staff. Leonard Wood had been entrusted with the military government of Cuba and would return to the Philippines in the 1920s as a governor general. Tasker Bliss had been collector of customs in Cuba and had negotiated the Cuban reciprocity treaty of 1902; during the First World War he would become American military representative on the inter-allied Supreme War Council in Paris, and afterward a member of the American Commission to Negotiate Peace.... After his exploits around Lake Lanao, John Pershing did not remain a captain long. He returned to the (Moro) Province six years later with stars on his shoulders and a senator's daughter by his side.[35]

These officers demanded the same commitment from their subordinates. Wood recommended the hiring of "young Americans" to represent the government in the "remote districts among the half-civilized peoples" in Mindanao; his rigid requirements included their prohibition "from entering into businesses while acting as representatives of the government."[36] Tasker Bliss ordered his officers "to acquire the knowledge and experience necessary for local popular government" and to honestly wield their power over the tribal wards so that "law and order and individual freedom shall be maintained."[37] The reportage on the performance of distinct governors, while at times self-serving, showed strong compliance to their superior's wishes. Capt. John Finley (district governor, Zamboanga) and Lt. Edward Bolton (Davao), for example, received high praises from superiors not only for their accomplishments, but also for their commitment, prompting Leonard Wood to refer to them as a "class of men... anxious to enter the public service in this part of the world and who are well qualified to do so."[38]

This "fine performances" did not imply that patronage features like the use of political and social ties were avoided by these army men. Wood, for example, was appointed on the strength of his connections with Roosevelt who overrode the protests of Wood's rival, Howard Taft. Pershing's promotion was aided by his marriage to Frances Warren, daughter of Sen. Francis Warren, chair of the Senate military affairs committee (then known as the appropriations committee).[39] Wood himself appointed Maj. John Finley, Zamboanga district governor, "because the General knew his (Finley's) brother, a wealthy Washington dentist."[40] Neither were these officers and their commands totally untarnished. Some invariably turned out to be corrupt and ill-trained.... The Constabulary and Scouts themselves were tarnished by moral corruption and subordinates charged with offenses from insubordination to mutiny.[41] Contacts and connections, however, did not undercut the officials' opinion of themselves as exceptional administrators. Wood, Bliss, and Pershing were indeed notorious characters with an arrogant confidence in their abilities to be competent administrators of the new territory.[42] In their minds as well as those of their subordinates, they were most qualified to be governors of the Moro Province.[43]

Their control of all the major positions in the provincial administration was an added edge to their ability to govern. Decision-making processes were centralized, and the implementation of policy was enhanced by the application of army norms all over the administrative structure. There were other colonial institutions which operated in the province, notably the emergent court and educational system, whose administrative hierarchy was Manila-based and accessible to Filipino "participation." But with Americans either heading or dominating these government bureaus, with Filipinos and Muslims occupying very subordinate positions (not to mention their being outnumbered by Americans), these bureaus posed hardly any encumbrance to provincial administration. More important, however, was the unprecedented autonomy given by Manila (and Washington) to the army. Provincial administrators were given the opportunity to work unhampered by "interference" from above, particularly from Filipino leaders who were already being integrated into the colonial state.

The more centralized administration (owing to the government of army personnel as well as the overlapping of the responsibilities of the Army's Department of Mindanao with that of the Province) was therefore complemented by a narrowing of those responsible. What emerged then was a small clique of American army men, insulated from social forces below them and given almost-free rein by its superiors. Its capacity to operate in precision was boosted by a hierarchical structure which overlapped two centralized organizations—the army as well as that of the Province as a special administrative unit. With a mandate based on the premise that southern Mindanao need not conform with the tempo of colonial tutelage all over the Philippines, what appears to emerge from all this is a local authority that had all the remarks of being structurally autonomous. Whether its autonomy and capacities made their mark on how colonial authority was set up in southern Mindanao will be examined in the next section.

PACIFICATION AND STABILITY

Philippine scholars have often overlooked the fact that the army largely succeeded in stamping out opposition to colonial rule in the Province. The numerous accounts of revolts against American authority (especially by the Muslims) notwithstanding, at no time were the Americans ever seriously threatened. Within the short period that it governed the Province, the army was actually able to bring about a fair amount of stability, even in the Muslim regions considered most eruptive. The non-Muslim groups, like the Manobo and Tagacaolo of Davao, presented no problem to the new colonizers. They were not only small in number, they were also more fragmented than the Muslims that it was relatively easier to subjugate them. In Davao, where most of these communities were located, the Americans encountered very little opposition, except for intermittent attacks on officers which, precisely because of their infrequency, tended to be exaggerated.[44]

With the Muslims, the merciless use of firepower and relentless campaigns became the most effective measures to ensure the success of American pacification.[45] In Lanao and Jolo, the army and the newly organized constabulary never let down their attacks on the *cottas* of Lanao *datus*, employing when necessary a "liberal use of ammunition" to achieve "very excellent results against the semi-savages."[46] The result was often brutal, as the "Battles" (more massacres) of Bud Bagsak and Bud Dajo attested.[47] These were not, however, the only factors behind American mastery of the Muslims.[48] Having studied the Spanish colonizers' experience, the army also made vigorous use of "divide-and-rule" tactics to keep opponents off-balance. The tactic worked especially well in areas like Lanao where Muslim *datus* were already at war with each other, and in Cotobato and Jolo where the sultanates had declined so much in power that they were either rendered marginal or were under constant threat from their own lieges.[49] General Wood was so confident of the military firepower and the vulnerability of the Muslims that he announced by the 1907 that "there need to be no apprehension of a general Moro uprising or of concerted action among them."[50]

The Muslims could have unified their forces around the banner of Islam, something which they did against the Spaniards. But they never did. Islam failed to be a rallying symbol against the Americans because the latter—again learning from the Spanish—posthaste declared their hands-off policy toward religion, while passing on the burden of dealing with religious matters to *datus* who cooperated with them.[51] The Americans likewise went out of their way to show the Muslims how under-emphasized religion was in their pacification effort.[52] By this maneuver, the Americans avoided being demonized as anti-Islamic, in contrast to the Spaniards, while undermining Islam's potent unifying capacity by making it an internal matter to be dealt with solely by the Muslims and their leaders. Crucial, too, in the prevention of any unified resistance was the role played by *datus* who opted to cooperate with the Americans and brokered a stable relationship between the colonizers and their people. Parallel to this effort of bringing in the *datus* into the colonial frame, the Americans wisely opened opportunities for their subordinates to become part of the apparatus. A "Moro Constabulary" was created to assist the army which, by 1903, had drawn in as many as 102 Muslims praised for their intense loyalty to their commanders rather than to their "tribes."[53] Once the regular army was scaled down in size, the constabulary and the Philippine Scouts (the forerunner of the Philippine Army) took over, and despite their limited personnel, were still able to keep the Province stable.[54] So confident was the constabulary of its effectiveness that it even emulated what the army did—it cut down its manpower from 800 in 1905 to 657 by 1908—since by then, Muslim opposition had practically ceased and the only inconveniences were caused by criminal bands.[55] By the middle of the first decade of the century, the Province was gradually stabilizing. Lanao was declared pacified in 1906, and the Americans proudly noted that the Lanao *datus* had shifted "from war to agriculture." Cotabato followed suit by 1908, and a year later, the entire Mindanao was declared free of any anti-American resistance from the Muslims.[56] In this last year as governor, General Pershing had transferred even some of the policing duties to the *datus* to certify that "peace (now) prevails in the Moro Province.[57]

WIRING A PROVINCE AND COLLECTING REVENUES

Roads and telegraph line projects became the valuable links that the army set up to widen its net further all over the territory. Early on, the army, obviously concerned with enhancing its mobility during the pacification process, hastily involved itself in setting up these "connective tissues" with over two hundred miles of road carved out of the Davao hinterlands, and a telegraph line that began in Zamboanga and soon extended "through almost the whole western and southern part of Cotobato River Valley—the work of furnishing and setting poles, transporting supplies, and so forth, being done by Moros."[58] The army especially made sure that more important roads connected to, or ended with, the camps.[59] A military road was built around the Lanao area to facilitate the extension of American authority into a turbulent district.[60] However, in more peaceful districts like Davao and Cotobato, signs of road neglect gradually emerged.[61]

A well-paved and enduring road system, however, proved elusive. Army officials and their successors as late as the 1940s were unable to resolve these problems. These natural obstacles made provincial authorities rely on the other connective administrative network—the telegraph and telephone lines which were actually much better in transmitting orders and coordinating troop movements should revolts break out. The over three hundred kilometers of telegraph line "provided speedy communication with the centers of authority and policy-making in Zamboanga, Manila, and Washington. Naval patrols regularly policed the offshore, while doubling up as a troop and supply transports.[62] Logistical problems that were hampered by an inconsistent road system were thus offset by the quickness of these naval patrols to send troops and arms to troubled spots."[63]

What also compensated for a weak infrastructure was the network of army and constabulary outposts that controlled important "choke points" of the province to monitor the movement of and put a necessary check to anti-American Muslim and other groups.[64] They also became launching bases for small but mobile army and constabulary teams to pursue and neutralize "bandit bands" and play reinforcement to the army.[65] The successful wiring of the more important geographic nexus (i.e., coastal and shipping towns, army forts, and agricultural enterprises) did not mean, though, that southern Mindanao had become open and accessible. Large portions of the Province remained unpopulated, and unexplored. As late as 1953, travel through the hinterlands still involved tedious horseback riding and the limited use of mechanical transport given the roads' ever-constant state of disrepair. These resilient geographic and natural obstacles, however, did not undermine the fact that the American's "reach of the state" was far more extensive and successful.

For the first time ever, a different kind of "infrastructure" network linked the more accessible communities of southern Mindanao, one that was based on the predominance of a central power (unlike under the Spanish, where ever-shifting, tenuous, dyadic political alliances and trade exchanges constituted the links), imposing its will through technological and organizational superiority. The Americans were able to dodge the problems the Spaniards encountered where colonial presence and "reach" were assured only through uneasy alliances with Muslim *datus*. With arms, roads, and the telegraph and telephone systems, the latter were replaced, in a way, by modern technology to link most of the Province.

Military and political stabilization inevitably had to be propped up by other facets of administration. Among these, administrative competence—logically the next point worth examining after the issue of stability—was quite remarkable, especially if one keeps in mind that the area governed was unpacified and unexplored. By the mid-1900s, provincial authorities confidently reported that the cost of administering the province was "only 72 percent (that) of the average annual expenditure... in all the other provinces of the Philippines."[66] And it was with some superciliousness that Capt. G. H. Langhorne reported that the 44 percent increase in provincial revenues from 1904 to 1905 outpaced the neighboring country of Sarawak—a feat made remarkable by the fact that the latter antedated the Moro Province.[67] Finally, in 1906, trade in Zamboanga alone had increased so dramatically that the town was listed as the top port town in terms of customs collection.[68]

The provincial authority likewise found out that a combination of repression and enticement resolved the eruptive potential of provincial taxation. After initial resistance from Muslims, a head tax (*cedula*) was regularly collected from different communities with unusual ease and support from even the erstwhile rebellious Muslims.[69] Even as early as 1904, Wood was already claiming that "cedula taxes have been paid the year [1904] *for the first time* in history."[70] The revision of the tax regulation wherein those who collected on behalf of the government would receive 5 percent of the total collected, and those who failed to turn in their collection would not receive their salaries, eventually made tax extraction "acceptable."[71] These measures encouraged *datus* like Cotabato's Piang to value their benefit: with his power over the Maguindanaos, he compelled seven thousand of his people to pay the head tax, the highest collection rate among the districts.[72] By 1907, cedula and other related taxes were bringing in as much as P13,881, indicating "increased participation of the Moro and pagan inhabitants in the financial support of their own Province." The Province, by 1903, was "completely dependent upon its own revenues."[73]

The Moro Exchanges, tightly supervised special markets set up to encourage non-Christian participation in the internal trade by bypassing Chinese and Filipino middlemen, set out to be successful enterprises. The exchanges began as an experiment in Zamboanga, and in due time were replicated in other districts like Davao and Cotabato. They grew dramatically during the early years of the Province, with the Jolo exchange reaching a high of P248,481.36 in 1906.[74] In 1910 these exchanges were replaced by "industrial trading stations" which were essentially similar to their predecessors, except for the closer supervision exercised by an office created specifically to promote and monitor provincial trade.[75] It is interesting to note, however, that while American official protection of the Moro Exchanges was to undermine the control of Chinese middlemen over the internal trading system, there was tacit appreciation of the Chinese presence in towns like Cotobato given their long and stabilizing involvement in the trade with Muslims, as well as the amount of taxes paid to the Province.[76]

Administrative achievements facilitated the introduction of settler-run plantation systems in districts like Davao and Jolo. The Moro Province encouraged settlement of mostly former American soldiers in Davao to spur the production of abaca already begun by some Spanish entrepreneurs in the 1890s. The result was a steady growth of the abaca industry in Davao: from zero in 1900, the industry grew to 42 plantations by 1911, covering 16,410 hectares (from a mere 2,499 hectares in 1902). Hemp production rose from 308 tons (1902) to 8,592 tons (1910) to become the Province's prime export.[77]

In itself, this was an achievement of no small measure given the frontier-like conditions in Davao.[78] A nascent rubber industry was also set up in Davao, while in Cotabato the beginnings of a timber industry were noted; both were spearheaded mainly by small American entrepreneurs.[79] The percentage contribution of Davao abaca to the Philippine total remained in 1915 only at 3.5 percent but dramatically grew to 35 percent in the 1930s. This modest share, however, represented astonishing growth for a district which, a decade ago, had been declared by Manila an impenetrable area.[80] The floundering of the small owner-dominated rubber industry was a setback, but even its stunted growth was enough to keep investors interested.[81] Together with timber, pearl trading, and coconut production, the above commodities became the province's principal exports, generating incomes as high as P3,410,712 in 1910, doubling quickly to P6,468,587 by 1913.[82]

Wood, Bliss, and Pershing pursued policies that altered regulations on such activities as "provincial trade" so that the Province could take advantage of, and participate in, trade outside Manila. A subsidized provincial shipping started fairly well, with Zamboanga becoming a regional port, thereby stimulating a trading network that extended to Borneo. Customs collection in this port town rose, prompting claims that a bountiful trade was well on its way.[83] The goal was to create enough viable trade independent of Manila so as to enhance provincial development and "give the province [the] benefit of customs revenues."[84] While such activities helped the province's income and drew praise from provincial entrepreneurs, it must be noted that these activities were also viewed with apprehension by Manila businessmen who saw the "Moro trade" slipping out of their hands.[85]

Thus, in terms of its capacity to generate revenue, the Moro Province performed fairly well. With the exception of 1909, 1910, and 1912, in which expenses surpassed incomes due to budgetary constraints and Manila's assertion of its fiscal prerogatives, the province's general income was kept well in the black.[86] Tight fiscal management supplemented by innovative promotion of trade and investment boosted this revenue-generating capacity.[87] Constantly reminded of provincial financial dependence on Manila, especially when it came to support for infrastructure, army proconsuls prided themselves on their ability to mitigate this independence through instances of self-funded projects, as illustrated by this detailed report of provincial "improvements." The following statement was but representative of this local conceit:

> The municipalities dependent on the central Government and in the past have
> been given little assistance, but the present policy is to insist that each municipality

shall provide for its own public improvement. The question of improvements has been taken up extensively in Zamboanga, Jolo, Davao and Parang. In Zamboanga notably, the municipal council has during past year appropriated over P20,000 for public improvements such as curbings and markets. In Davao an excellent market has been provided with curbs and gutters and connections made with sewers built by the military authorities. In Parang, the streets have been graded and ditched and a new school house has been built, the municipality bearing half the expense, the Province the other half.[88]

Perhaps the best indication of the extent to which the Moro Province, in a sense, progressed on the revenue side is a comparison of its performance with the rest of the Philippine provinces.

Keeping in mind that before the American Army's arrival, southern Mindanao was virtually untapped by any central authority in Manila, one has to concede that the progress was quite exceptional once the Americans took over. Within eight years, the Province shot up from being last in terms of provincial revenues to having the second highest provincial revenue in the entire colony, surpassing even the two other "major centers" of the colony, Cebu and Iloilo, and superseded only by Manila.[89] A big chunk of provincial revenue was derived from customs and other exactions on the Sulu trade with Southeast Asia, and also from the export of abaca. Jolo and Zamboanga had become, aside from Manila, Iloilo, and Cebu, the main ports of entry for foreign shipping, accounting in 1907, for example, for 27 of the total 125 ships that entered the Philippines.[90] This high revenue profile eventually attracted Manila's attention and became one of the sources of tension between a fairly "rich" province and a colonial center that regarded the centralization of revenues a sine qua non for effective administration.

AUTONOMY

The above "successes" inevitably gave the Province some clout to keep itself relatively outside Manila's control and "interference." As one Muslim scholar notes, "the structure of the Moro Province with its own Governor and Legislative Council provided for a time... a considerable de facto autonomy for Mindanao and Sulu.[91] When provincial gains began to draw the attention of Manila, leading to questions about provincial "indiscretions" and finally demands that it behave like any subordinate province, army authorities succeeded in protecting provincial autonomy. The popular image of Mindanao as a vast, unexplored frontier peopled by savages (some of whom, the Muslims, had once been the scourge of northern communities) was used as a good defensive weapon to keep Manila at bay. Even as annual reports were enthusiastically proclaiming the successful pacification of non-Christian groups, the message was nonetheless "tempered" by constant warnings of the potential for provincial instability that was, expectedly, "the Moro Problem." Army officials continuously insisted that even as the Muslims had been subjugated and accepted colonial authority, they remained a threat to the colonial state and to northern communities.[92]

American mistrust and lack of confidence in Filipinos also figured prominently in this active defense of provincial interests. Army men and American settlers shared a general suspicion regarding the intrusive inquiries of Manila Filipinos.

They believed that the latter's demands that the administration of the province be gradually transferred to civilians and Filipinos were motivated by self-interest, which threatened the integrity of the Province and exposed its wards to harm.[93] Filipinos were also regarded as unable to meet, much more match, the administrative abilities of Americans. Racism was clearly a principal factor here, but instances of incompetence, especially in Christian-Filipino-controlled municipalities also exacerbated American suspicions.[94] Time and again, discussions on "the Moro Problem" were interspersed with apprehensions about the ability of Filipinos to carry on the accomplishments of the Americans, especially in keeping the Muslims under control.[95] These doubts about Filipinos were extended to include even the competence to keep a porous territory intact in a region that bordered the colonial realms of ambitious imperial powers like the British.[96]

Most important of all, what was stressed alongside potential or actual Filipino incompetence was the reality that only the army and the Americans could control the Muslims. In pursuing this point, American proconsuls and their supporters kept reminding their audience (Filipinos and others) of the historical specificity of Mindanao, i.e., its being never integrated into colonial territory before the Americans arrived.[97] These arguments were supplemented by the contention that "civilizing the Moros" demanded an interminable period of time, but demanded an authority respected for its "prowess" by the "warlike" Muslims. It was, therefore, only more vital that the policy of noninterference by Manila, particularly by Filipino politicians, continue.

In 1909 the idea of separating Mindanao was even openly recommended by the provincial leadership when the acting governor, Col. Ralph Hoyt, gave an official imprimatur to the proposal to secede. Warning that local Filipino demand for representation in the new Philippine legislature did not represent the will of the province's majority, Hoyt proposed that Congress disengage Mindanao, Sulu, and Palawan from the rest of the Philippine territory. He proposed that these areas be governed as a new "territory" called the "Mindanao Plantations," where the navy could establish a coal station and American settlers could fully exploit the land and its resources.[98] While his superiors eventually thought this idea too extreme, given the escalating contention over the independence issue, Hoyt still insisted that Filipinos, a minority in the province, keep their "nationalist" agitation to themselves.[99] When not citing "instability" as an excuse for keeping Manila from intruding into provincial affairs, army authorities used the same issue as a reason for Manila to increase its material support to the Moro Province. The colonial center ought not to interfere, but it ought to give more to the Province, relying only on army goodwill and trusting its capacities to keep the "savages" under control. Pershing astutely pursued this line, arguing that despite the subjugation of the Muslims and other "pagans," their allegiance to Manila remained tenuous.[100] Army administrators thus possessed considerable powers to determine the directions of the Province, with little influence from or role for Manila. For instance, they initiated personnel changes like bypassing "older (and nonmilitary) officials for civil posts in favor of young, presumably more able officers," a practice condemned by Manila for its wanton disregard of procedure and, more importantly, for preventing Filipino politicians from filling up provincial posts with their sycophants and supporters.[101]

With the use of these self-defined discretionary powers, offices were also refashioned and the authority and operations of local agencies of the larger colonial bureaucracy circumscribed. In Davao, army district officers unilaterally redefined the "tribal wards" and appointed American settlers as ward leaders, using as pretexts the speeding up of the civilizing process and the integration of tribes like the Manobos and Tagacaolos into the budding plantation system. When functions of "Insular" offices overlapped and conflicted with provincial agencies, army proconsuls demanded (usually successfully) that such "infractions of the law [should be solved] throughout the provincial and district governments," not through Manila.[102]

The Americans were especially protective of their non-Christian "wards" against what they and their wards saw as efforts by Christian Filipinos to encroach into their domain.[103] In fending off these attempts, provincial authorities did not hesitate to enact laws that sought to keep the "tribal wards" insulated from political and administrative changes issuing from the center.[104] Wards were kept away from the courts either by influencing and intervening in appointments to the local courts of first instance. In other instances, the jurisdictional powers of ward courts were expanded by legislative resolution in order to correspondingly limit those of the civil courts.[105] There was a little pride then in Col. Henry Gilhouser's description of his tribal ward powers as being "considerably in excess of the power of the Justice of the Peace."[106]

When necessary, provincial governors opposed Manila by invoking legal arguments, as when Philippine Commission Attorney-General Gregorio Araneta questioned the Legislative Council's power to "modify, amend or repeal Acts of the Philippine Commission in their application to the Moro Province." Provincial authorities responded by citing ambiguities of the law enacted by the by the U.S. Congress. The army legal counsel retorted that "Congress has granted to the Philippine Legislature the power to legislate in matters pertaining to the Islands. Yet *from the fact, it cannot be educed that the Legislature has the power to repeat Acts of Congress applicable to the Islands.*"[107] In citing Congress, provincial proconsuls had cleverly "raised the stakes," forcing Manila to direct its inquiries to a higher body and thus weaken its right to exercise its prerogative as superior body in the province. Where legal arguments proved inadequate, however, provincial authorities invoked culturalist arguments. Wood, Bliss, and their subordinates waxed philosophical in an attempt to explain why the task of uniting the Province's heterogenous population was a "stupendous one and cannot be accomplished in one short generation." In defending the validity of army rule, and in arguing why such a rule was the only one appropriate for civilizing "savages" and why turning over the Province to civil authorities in Manila (coincidentally with growing Filipino presence) retarded the process, Bliss eloquently advances his own interpretation of political Darwinism:

> There are certain evolutional (sic) changes through which society must pass in
> its onward march from barbarism to civilization. One of these stages has always
> been some form of despotism, feudalism, servitude or despotic paternal
> government, and we have every reason to believe that it is not within the
> bounds of possibility for humanity to leap over this transition epoch and pass
> at once from pure savagery to free civilization. If we apply our own system of
> government to these wild peoples we demoralize, we extirpate, and we never
> really civilize. We cannot compress the work of ten centuries into one, and

whatever system we eventually attempt, one founded on nature as a guide is more likely to succeed than by suddenly thrusting upon these people a form of government adapted to a race that has reached a higher plane of civilization.[108]

It helped that in many instances, these governors had allies in the Philippine Commission, the governor general's office, Washington, and most of all, a boisterous American community in Manila. These supporters were especially vital when the excessive use of force during suppression campaigns provided an opportunity for Filipino politicians to demand a stronger Manila involvement in provincial affairs.[109] When Wood, for example, was criticized by the media and his Filipino enemies for the massacre of rebelling Muslims at Bud Dajo, his defenders included Manila-based Americans (official and private) and President Roosevelt himself, fellow Rough Rider and friend.[110] When Filipino politicians questioned the administrative carte blanche given to the army in southern Mindanao, they were smothered by joint responses from American civil and military officials who used the standard argument about the volatility of the "Moro problem" to deflect their critics.[111] As Filipino politicians escalated their demands for a transitional stage to independence, and for Mindanao not to be separated from the Philippines, provincial authorities who regarded these as excuses for intervention or, in certain cases, truly believed that Mindanao had nothing in common with the Philippines and thus could segregate itself from the colony, applauded statements from political figures in Washington who defended their "cause."[112] In 1906 Mindanao "separatism" received support from unlikely politicians such as the populist William Jennings Bryan, who argued that the Philippines could be granted independence, except Mindanao where "the conditions existing... are so different from those existing in the northern islands that the two groups must be dealt with separately."[113] This was energetically backed by the American-owned *Manila Daily Bulletin* which declared:

> The objections to the program (of improving Mindanao by liberalizing land laws) are on the part of the Filipinos, and not of the Moros. The first question that arises is "What business is it of the Filipino anyway?" He never had any control over the Moro people and never had any sort of relations with Mindanao as being in the same class with other islands? If the Moros want to annex themselves to the United States, or to, Borneo, or to the moon, why, what of it?

The editor concluded: "The real objections to the plan are purely political and in no sense industrial or commercial. The inner reason why the Filipinos do not want Mindanao annexed to the United States is because that course might affect the prospects of early independence, and might also diminish the number of offices to be held in the new order of things."[114] When, in 1913, the administrative integration of the Province was just around the corner, army officials continued to fight back, albeit hopelessly, by tapping Washington media to warn of the impending catastrophic consequences of "Filipinization."[115] They were even successful in getting former president Howard Taft to issue a statement deploring the failure of the Jones Bill (the proposed law for Philippine independence) and the Filipinization program to protect non-Christian tribes. Taft's complaint regarding the inability of "the

Filipino educated classes (to show) their capacity for just government as in the treatment of the Moros and non-Christian tribes" was an exact facsimile of the arguments within the Province.[116]

All these were but some of the more important sources of strength of the Moro Province administration. While American officers, in acting like local dynasts, did have much in common with budding Filipino cacique politicians in that their sources of strength emerged from the local and provincial domains, they differed in the extent of autonomy and power they could exercise outside, and in spite of, the larger colonial state structure. Unlike the caciques who needed to establish their powers and raise their ambitions, army proconsuls were content to preserve their "fiefdoms" and deferred only to authorities beyond Manila. The "success" of the Moro Province showed not only army administrative capacity, but the talent of reformists when unhampered by an evolving patronage politics.

A PROBLEM OF PERSONNEL

So distinct were provincial development and its resulting autonomy that it was in fact within the realm of possibility for southern Mindanao to be separated from the Philippines. Yet by 1914, the army relinquished its autonomy and acquiesced to greater central supervision by Manila (especially Filipino politicians increasingly involved in major colonial decision-making processes) without much opposition. This culminated in the formal reclassification of the districts into special provinces under the supervision of the Department of Mindanao and Sulu.[117]

Why did the army eventually lose its control and authority over a province it had managed fairly well? Ironically, the foremost reason is to be found in the character of provincial administration itself. While the military in southern Mindanao was indeed given considerable license by Manila to do what it thought fit to "civilize" the "non-Christians," it also belonged, and was subordinate to, a centralized institution that possessed a dynamic of its own—the United States Army. At the event of American imperial adventure, while the army still had vestiges of what one historian calls "a provincial army," it was already undergoing changes meant to transform it into a modern army.[118] This transformation naturally included the alteration of procedures, one of which was to affect the governance of the Moro Province profoundly: the rotation of personnel.

Army administrators failed to foresee that the routine procedure of shifting personnel, as well as the resignation or retirement of people, would become the Province's bane. As soon as the army began to rotate and reassign its officers and soldiers either back to Manila or to the U.S., the Province began to feel the effects of "personnel loss." Gowing describes some of these turnovers and how they affected the province:

> There was a considerable turnover in the personnel of the Provincial Government. These officers followed Captain Langhorne as Provincial Secretary under General Bliss, two officers and a civilian served in turn as Provincial Engineer, and there were two changes in the office of the Provincial Secretary.... There was an even larger turnover of personnel in the district governments, due to the fact that many of the office-holders were

military officers subject to normal service rotations.... Thus, between 1906 and 1909, the District of Lanao had no less than seven district governors and four secretaries in the same period." All this meant that key officials hardly had time to learn their duties and get to know the people they governed before they were transferred.[119]

The Province's governors and supporters had a frequent litany of complaints. Wood, who did recognize this inherent flaw, complained that, "Civil officers are constantly undergoing a change of personnel, and if there is anything more which should be avoided under conditions such as that existing in the Philippine Islands, it is this constant change of officials."[120] Dean C. Worcester shared Wood's apprehension, noting that the use of army men as provincial officers was a "bad one" since:

No one of them has retained a given office long enough to carry a policy through its logical conclusion and get the results which might thus have been obtained. Frank Carpenter who succeeded Pershing and became the first civilian administrator of the Department of Mindanao himself noted that despite being able administrators, army officials could not fully make an impact on the Province because "just when they were learning enough about their civilian duties and (the) language of their districts," they were reassigned to other posts or positions.[121] Indeed, the lack of a fixed policy, combined with some unnecessary and unjustifiable killing, explain, in my opinion, the fact that the results accomplished have come far short of what might have been expected when one considers the splendid body of men from which the provincial officials have been drawn.[122]

In an attempt to forestall the consequences of this problem, Wood and Bliss sought to extend the tenure of officers, while seeking to train American "civilians" who eventually took over the positions once these officers had return to their mother units. Their effort, however, largely failed as they could not include former army officers to continue as civilian bureaucrats. Most opted for private business, tapping into growing industries like hemp and rubber, while others simply went home. Civilians who replaced army officers proved able administrators, but problems of safety discouraged others from joining the local bureucracy.[123] Pershing, who was bequeathed this responsibility, found his hands tied.[124] His effort to maintain personnel by borrowing from the army ended when the American Congress proscribed temporary assignment of the military to nonmilitary positions and sought to demobilize the army once more for fear of losing control over the situation. The policy of "Filipinization" begun under the administration of Gov. Gen. Cameron Forbes only aggravated matters.[125] Eventually, what sealed the fate of this practice was the transfer of authority over the Province in 1930 from the army to the new Commonwealth government, which promptly created a smaller executive commission to take over the responsibilities of administration.[126]

Consequently, as the Province began to show signs of stabilizing, colonial administration had become, unwittingly, a major problem. The presence and continuity of personnel could not be assured. With army officials leaving and no other Americans volunteering to remain once the army withdrew, the fragility of the Province's structure was exposed. The most likely alternative was the enlargement of "native" participation in provincial affairs, which Pershing did attempt to do.[127] The only problem with this alternative was that there were also no sufficient "native" personnel to take over from the Americans.

The long-term character of American tutelary training of erstwhile "uncivilized" groups like the Muslims basically undermined this option. *Datu* allies and collaborators did assume leadership roles in the province, particularly once the Filipino-dominated Commonwealth government took over the reins of the colonial state.[128]

Yet they were not enough. Leaders could have been found easily in some of the top positions of the Province, but there was still an inadequate supply of personnel to fill a substantial number of positions in the middle and lower echelons of the structure. Despite a barrage of assurances from provincial officials, American civilians remained hesitant to work in Mindanao as the image of the "savage Moros," ironically an analogous message broadcast by the same officials to keep Manila from interfering in provincial affairs, retained its notoriety. Moreover, as Wood noted, Americans who ended up in the Province were more interested in private enterprises. The Moro Province ultimately dashed whatever hopes and plans there were of bringing more "efficient" American bureaucrats to the Province. Provincial officials increasingly discovered that their options were becoming limited.

THE CENTER VS. THE LOCAL AND THE CENTER OVER THE LOCAL

Even as Manila was often kept out of the provincial loop, it was not entirely without means to intrude into local affairs. Subsidies crucial to provincial economic development were the weak points by which Manila sought to reassert control.[129] As Filipinos increasingly dominated the Philippine Commission as well as began to appreciate their powers in the nascent Legislature, financial support for the Moro Province was subjected to more intense scrutiny and control. Provincial officials were forced to fight for every centavo of even sundry expenses.[130] This "inquisitiveness" into provincial financial affairs eased up only after Washington assured Filipino politicians that Mindanao remained part of the Philippines. The Province then reverted to some form of "stability" as army authorities, perhaps resigned to the inevitable, sought to boost provincial fortunes by improving its infrastructure.[131]

When extending or curtailing financial support to fund subsidies (like domestic shipping) or the provincial share of the overall tax revenues, Manila made sure that provinical officials knew who held the purse strings and had the ultimate say on how much allocation the province should receive.[132] By the mid-1900s, official reports were interlaced with warnings as to the implications that increasing financial dependence on Manila could bear on provincial autonomy.[133] The floundering of some of the hitherto prospering local industries, however, weakened the efficacy of these warnings and revealed further the extent to which the Province was inextricably linked to the growing colonial economy centered in, and determined largely by, policies formulated in Manila.[134] By 1912, a Filipino-controlled Philippine Legislature increased the pressure by reminding provincial authorities that it had the power to determine the financial fortunes of the province; the army had no choice but to concede.[135]

The failure of Davao and Zamboanga to become the nexus of provincial trade and industry magnified the financial fragility of the Province. These two districts never did connect with each other economically, frustrating efforts of provincial authorities to instigate these ties to make the provincial economy more self-sustaining. The apathy of Zamboanga merchants toward developing durable trade ties with the relatively isolated American plantations in Davao kept hemp planters outside the provincial trading network. Thus, Davao ended up linking more with Manila than with its neighboring districts, and the provincial economy never really jelled. Those who had hoped that a thriving southern trading network would reinforce provincial autonomy saw their hopes dashed.[136]

These predicaments over personnel and revenues, however, made for a much more profound weakness that had to do with what the Moro Province was turning itself into, as against the transmutation of the "larger" colonial territory, Philippines. Administrative successes had fashioned out, in real terms, a colony within a colony, a state within a state. And the widespread sentiments among army officials of being distinct or even separate from the rest of the Philippines merely "reflected" this reality. The problem, unfortunately, was that the ground on which these concrete accomplishments stood and the corresponding sentiments were nurtured was underpinned by the transitional nature of the Province. Army officials had to face the reality eventually that the Moro Province was a province and not an authority autonomous and insulated from Manila and Washington. They could not continue to regard the province as if it were a separate colony (for personnel problems were already undermining it); they had to concede to a larger scheme that Manila and Washington negotiated.

There was, however, a more fundamental reason for all this, and it had to do with the nature of American colonialism itself. In almost all cases, direct military rule usually anteceded the formal and full establishment of colonial presence. As the colonial process became increasingly "normalized," civilian bureaucrats inevitably replaced army proconsuls for reasons ranging from competition with their military counterparts to division of administrative labor (the army fights, civilians govern).

The United States shared this "colonial habit" with neighboring colonialism, although there was also something distinctly American about it. The desire and the intention to "civilian-ize" had very much to do not only with the intention of benevolent assimiltation to "train" Filipinos in American governance but also with the traditional American wariness of military rule and the popularity of the notion that civilian authority should—for whatever reason—dominate the military.[137] In the Philippines these views meshed well with civilian-army rivalries that began as early as the 1900s. Once "stabilization" was declared to have been attained in the Moro Province, the army lost its raison d'etre for remaining the sole authority there.

As the political and turf battles between Filipino caciques and their American overlords over how a Philippine Commonwealth would look and how "independence" was to be granted became more intense, provincial officials found that they were not entirely insulated from the outcomes of these battles. The debates and impasses over colonial land policy, for example, sent contradictory signals to potential settlers and investors, leading to decisions to defer investments until a clear land policy was enacted. This affected provincial economic targets and performance, prompting both officials and local entrepreneurs continually to demand clarifications from

Manila.[138] Turf battles in Manila also took their toll on some essential, but Manila-dependent, provincial activities. Debates over the qualification of land surveyors, to cite an example, led to the non-legislation of a cadastral survey bill which, in turn, meant that the availability and accessibility of considerable public lands in the province could not be utilized to attract settlers.[139]

Once American colonial policy evolved from "benevolent assimilation" to "tutelary training for independence," the fate of the Province as an autonomous territory was sealed.[140] The weakening of the army, the transfer of its leaders to positions outside of the Province (in cases like Wood and Pershing, back to Washington), and the lack of strong pressure from both indigenous and settler communities, all played out their roles in narrowing provincial options. Ultimately, the setting up of a Philippine Commonwealth as transition to self-rule mortally ended this separate "colonial" dream. The Moro Province and southern Mindanao were to remain formally embedded in the Philippines. The only possible deterrent came from the communities of the Province who could—in alliance with army officials—have gone over Manila's head and appealed for a separate American policy for Mindanao. But while representing what could perhaps be regarded as the epitome of the success of local colonial state-building, these "civil societies" that legitimized and provided "popular support" to the army were handicapped by their very location as well as by their problems and weaknesses.

Conclusion

The preoccupation of most scholars with Manila-centered and Manila-driven politics has blinded them to one inconspicuous detail: that over one-half of the Philippines did not fall under "civilian" authority nor was it classified as a regular province.[141] In the two extremities of the Philippines' official territory, the "Cordillera Central" and the Moro Province, the Army was charged to establish American colonial presence as a prelude to their eventual integration into the larger evolving colonial unit.[142] American racist assumptions blended with a patronizing mission to protect "non-Christian tribes" from the damaging effects of lowland Filipino/cacique politics to justify this transitory arrangement.[143] The administrative grid that was carved out of these "protected" territories was thus not merely American; it was, more precisely, military-American.[144]

From 1900 to 1914, the United States Army was made responsible for establishing order and authority over the southern portion on Mindanao, guided by the assumption that these areas had nothing in common with the rest of the colony.[145] The army was to "open up" the area, pacify the disparate "tribal" groups into administratively manageable communities, educate and lead them to "civilization" (including the art of colonial politics), and eventually integrate "Morolandia" into the colonial territory, the Philippines. To achieve all this, the army was allowed ample latitude by its superiors in Manila and Washington to formulate and implement policies that it saw fit for the Province. Partly because of its rivalry with civilian colonial administrators, and partly because most of its leaders thought of themselves as serious empire-builders, the army succeeded in accomplishing its responsibilities.

The Moro Province was declared "pacified" after a decade of military rule. Whether the ultimate colonial goal of integrating the Province's population into the colony body Philippines was realized under military rule was, however, another thing. From the comments of Smith, Wood, and Taft, it appeared that even as the U.S. Army may have been intended only to create a transitional authority in the Moro Province, the initial lack of clear policy as to whether southern Mindanao was part of or distinct from the rest of the Philippines created opportunities for certain aspects of "state building" to be set in motion, no matter how imperfect and temporal they were. It had its own personnel that exercised considerable autonomy from both their "constituents" and their superiors in Manila; the Province was able to generate enough revenues to be self-sufficient; and its standing was never seriously challenged from below not only because it had superior coercive technology but also because it was legitimate.

The Moro Province thus displayed features of a state-within-a-state. It could even be regarded as an antipode to the increasingly patronage-driven, factious, larger colonial state. This distinctiveness did not escape the eye of its officials, as well as, of the communities within its jurisdiction. For how else could one explain the agitation for separation from the Philippines in the last years of the decade? That the Province never did burgeon into a separate state had to do with two reasons.

On the one hand, it was not able to institute (consciously or unconsciously) the aspects of full-blown, serious state-building process. For instance, no clear outline of the project ever came out of army administrators' minds. The demands to separate Mindanao into a "territory" or to transform it into a "Mindanao plantation" independent of Manila remained mere recommendations with no clear idea as to how to go about implementing them. Even the notion that after the full Filipinization of the colonial state the Americans had to keep the Moro Province a special territory, pending the long duration of training its "non-Christian" inhabitants on the tenets of democratic politics, was never really conceptualized in a programmatic way. They all remained plans, intentions, and rhetoric, and all this had to do with the second reason.

Those aspects of the state-building process mentioned above did get implemented, but only partially. The autonomy of the provincial personnel was temporary, given that their principal official affinity was somewhere else; revenue capacities were, in the end, still subjected to overall colonial regulations on official incomes and expenses; and the legitimacy it derived from the communities it administered was tenuous and transitory.

As long as the general colonial policy was muddled, the local officials of the Moro could continue with their autonomous existence. Once the policy cleared up, however, the Moro Province in the end had to realize that it was, after all, a province, a subordinate organization to a higher colonial body. Yet, the army-run Province left a deep imprint in southern Mindanao. While it succumbed to political and administrative decisions from the outside, it also left a legacy that persisted beyond its administrative life—the preservation of anti-center, specifically anti-Manila and anti-Christian sentiments among its people, the reverberations of which would continue well into the post-colonial period.

NOTES:

1. Cornelius C. Smith, *Don't Settle for Second: The Life and Times of Cornelius C. Smith* (California: Presidio Press, 1977), 92-93. "Corney" Smith was appointed district governor of Davao from 1906 to 1907, then reassigned to the same position in Lanao in 1910.

2. Gen. Leonard Wood, "Report of the Governor of the Moro Province, 1906," in *Report of the Philippine Commission* (RPC), 1906-1907 (Washington, D.C.: General Printing Office (GPO), 1907), 375; and Mrs. William Howard Taft, *Recollection of Full Years* (New York: Dodd, Mead and Co., 1914), 170-171.

3. The phrase is from Peter Gordon Gowing, *Mandate in Moroland: The American Government of Muslim Filipinos, 1899-1920* (Quezon City, Philippines: New Day Publishers, 1983).

4. A major source of this knowledge was, of course, the departing Spanish Jesuits who had a mission in the northern part of Mindanao. See Rev. Pio Pi, S.J., "The Moros of the Philippines," as reprinted in "Department of Mindanao Annual Report, appendix VI," *Annual Report of the War Department* (*ARWD*) (Washington, D.C.: GPO, 1903), 365-378.

5. Hermann Hagedorn, *Leonard Wood: A Biography*, vol. 2 (New York: Kraus Reprint Co., 1969), 3.

6. "Letter of John E. Springer, Attorney of the Moro Province, to the Philippine Commission, October 1, 1904," Exhibit G, RPC, 1904, op. cit., 434-435. One officer noted that Manila was more accessible from the military districts than the districts were to each other. "Report of the 5th District, Philippine Constabulary, June 25, 1904," ibid., 121. In 1904 only one coast guard boat would make two trips covering Malabang, Cotabato, Davao, Banga, Mati, San Ramon Farm, Jolo, Siasi, and back to Zamboanga. See "Annual Report of the Chief of the Bureau of Coast Guard and Transportation for the Fiscal Year ending June 30, 1904," RPC, vol. 8, Part 3, 1904, 133. Other "ships" were mainly engaged in a lot of interception of Chinese and Muslims engaged in stopping "smuggling" in behalf of customs service; all over Zamboanga, Jolo, and Cotabato. "Report of the Coast Guard Cutter, Tablas," 18 July 1904, RPC, vol. 8, Part 3, 182-184.

7. Greg Bankoff, "Deportation and Prison Colony of San Ramon, 1870-1898," *Philippine Studies* 39, 1991: 443-457.

8. Being a veteran of the "Apache" wars was thus an asset, as was the case of Sulu governor Maj. Hugh L. Scott. *RPC*, vol. 11, Part 1, *ARWD*. Fiscal year ended 30 June 30 1904 (Washington, D.C.: GPO, 1905), 12.

9. Compared to the Muslims, the other tribes that populated the southeast portion of Mindanao were "not warlike in the sense that the Moros are warlike," *RGMP*, 1906, op. cit., 419.

10. *Correspondence Relating to the War with Spain, Including the Insurrection in the Philippine Islands and the China Relief Expedition*, 15 April 1898 to 30 July 1902, vol. 2, 1993. Center of Military History, Washington, D.C., 1105-1060. See also Col. Horace P. Hobbs, *Kris and Krag: Adventures among the Moros of the Southern Philippine Islands* (1962, edition of 200 copies) 43; and, Lt. Col. Sydney A. Cloman, *Myself and a Few Moros* (New York: Doubleday, Page and Co., 1923), 6-7, 42-43.

11. "The interior of Mindanao is terra incognito (sic), many parts never having been visited by civilized man, nor is it impossible . . . to visit without great risk any points except those actually occupied by our troops." *Mindanao Herald*, 20 February 1904: 5.

12. See, for example, "Letter of 2nd Lt. Intelligence Office, 10th Co., Philippine Scouts, on Report on Native Tribes, August 31, 1908," and "Report of Oscar J. W. Scott, chaplain, 25th Infantry, U.S. Army, Post of Parang, no date," in Edward Bowditch, "Military Taming of the Moros." Edward Bowditch Papers (ca. 1907-1957). Rare Manuscript Collection, Carl Kroch Library, Cornell University.

13. One headline stated: "Moros are impossible [with] extermination [as the] the only Remedy [to] start a New Race." *Mindanao Herald*, 26 December 1903. See also Russell Roth, *Muddy Glory: America's 'Indian Wars' in the Philippines, 1899-1935* (Massachusetts: The Christopher Publishing

House, 1981), 136 and 151; Vic Hurley, *Swish of the Kris: The Story of the Moros* (New York: E. P. Dutton Co., 1936), 14-15; *History and Description of the Picturesque Philippines* (Ohio: The Croell and Kirkpatrick Co., 1900), 123-130; and novelettes like Chauncey McGovern, *Sarjint Larry an' Frinds* (Manila: The Escolta Press, 1906), 22-50; and Chauncey McGovern, "As the Moro Princess Foretold," *Two Story-Books of the Philippines* (Manila: The Escolta Press, 1907), 231-272.

14. Cogently put by Howard Taft in these terms: "Force seems to be the only method of reaching them in the first instance, and is the only preparation for the beginning of civilized restraints among them," (underscoring mine). *RPC*, vol. 5, *ARWD* (Washington, D.C.: GPO, for Fiscal year ending 30 June 1903), 81.

15. Najeeb Saleeby, *The Moro Problem: An Academic Discussion of the History and Solution of the Problem of the Government of the Moros of the Philippine Islands* (Manila, 1913), 16-31.

16. "*ARWD*, September 1, 1904," in *RPC*, vol. 12, Part 2. Fiscal year ended 30 June 1904-1905 (Washington, D.C.: GPO), 577.

17. Ibid., 585.

18. On facets of American racist attitudes toward Filipinos, see Vicente L. Rafael, "White Love: Surveillance and Nationalist Resistance in the U.S. Colonization of the Philippines," in *Cultures of United States Imperialism.*, eds. Amy Kaplan and Donald E. Pearse (Durham, N.C.: Duke University Press, 1993), 185-218. On the white racist tradition, see Richard Drinnon, *Facing West: The Metaphysics of Indian-Hating and Empire-Building* (New York: New American Library, 1980).

19. Worcester's role in colonial Philippine politics cannot but be underscored... Among the more notable works are Joseph Ralston Hayden, "Biographical Sketch," introduction to Dean C. Worcester, *The Philippines: Past and Present*, vol. 1 (New York: MacMillan, 1930), 3-74; Peter W. Stanley, "'The Voice of Worcester Is the Voice of God': How One American Found Fulfillment in the Philippines," in *Reappraising an Empire: New Perspectives on Philippine-American History*, ed. Peter W. Stanley (Cambridge, Mass.: Harvard University, 1984), 117-141; and Rodney J. Sullivan, *Exemplar of Americanism: The Philippine Career of Dean C. Worcester* (Quezon City, Philippines: New Day Publishers, 1992).

20. Col. J. G. Harbord, U.S. Army, "Report of Officer Commanding 5th District, PC," in *RPC*, vol. 12, Part 3, *ARWD*. Fiscal year ended 30 June 1905, 118-119. On a guarded report on the decline of caciquism, see A. W. Fergusson, "Report of the Executive Secretary, Exhibit no. 2, 1 September 1906," in *RPC*, vol. 7, Part 1. Fiscal year ended 30 June 1906, 143.

21. The same report states: "the municipal police force [of the 5th District, covering the entire Mindanao, including the Moro Province] is among the poorest seen in three years.... There is none in the district which is believed to be worth its cost," ibid., 122.

22. Muslim hostility to the Christian Filipinos dates as far back as the sixteenth century.

23. Philippine Commission Act no. 787. "An Act Providing for the Organization and Government of the Moro Province, June 1, 1903," in "Acts of the Legislative Council of the Moro Province, September 7, 1903 to August 31, 1904" *RGMP*, 1904, Zamboanga, Mindanao, P.I. 1 September 1904: 113-131.

24. "The Government of the Moro Province," in *RPC*, vol. 5, *ARWD* (Washington, D.C.: GPO, 30 June 1903), 78.

25. To Howard Taft, a province was an "area with sufficient people in it to carry on a provincial government, occupied substantially wholly by the Christian members of the Filipino people." See "Statement of the Governor William Howard Taft before the Committee on the Philippines of the U.S. Senate," 1902 (Washington, D.C.: GPO), 5.

26. Legislative Council of the Moro Province. Act No. 35. "An Act to Amend Act No. 82 of the Philippine Commission, entitled, 'The Municipal Code,' as amended in its application to the Moro

Province." Enacted 27 January 1904 and approved on 27 April 1904. Most important of these rights was a limited right to suffrage of all "qualified electors" (i.e., those with money and education).

27. Act No. 39 of the Moro Province's Legislative Council, 19 February 1904.

28. T. H. Bliss, "RGMP, September 10, 1907," in RPC, vol. 7, ARWD, 1907, 1908 (Washington, D.C.: GPO), 393-394.

29. Cotabato was 11,786 square miles; Davao, 9,707 square miles; Zamboanga, 5,591 square miles; Lanao, 3,900 square miles; and Sulu, 1,039 square miles. See "Report of the District Director, 5th District, July 15, 1908," in RPC, vol. 8 Part I, ARWD, 1909 (Washington, D.C.: GPO), 412-423.

30. U.S. Bureau of Census. Census of the Philippine Islands, 1903, vol. 2, 123-127, 400-407. Compare this to the rest of the Philippines which had sixty-seven persons per square mile.

31. "Report of Geo T. Langhorn, Capt. 11th Cavalry to the Government of the Moro Province, August 6, 1904 on his visit to Sarawak, Java and the Federated Malay states," in RPC, vol. 12, Part 2, ARWD, 1905 (Washington, D.C.: GPO), 671-701.

32. Maj. John P. Finley, "The Non-Christians of the Southern Islands of the Philippines—their Self-Government and Industrial Development," speech delivered at the Late Mohonk Conference of Friends of the Indians and other Dependent People. Reprinted in The Filipino People, vol. I, no. 2, November 1912.

33. Not to mention the army's previous role in restoring administrative order in Manila, acting as "the advance agent of American culture and government." John Morgan Gates, Schoolbooks and Krags: The United States Army in the Philippines, 1898-1902 (Westport, Conn.: Greenwood Press, 1973), 70.

34. Gowing described Wood as a "medieval Christian knight fighting the Saracens or the Puritan reformers in Cromwell's England," op. cit., 110 (underscoring mine). Bliss "learned to speak Malay well enough to be understood" perhaps by the datus. Frederick Palmer, Bliss, Pacemaker: The Life and Letters of General Tasker Bliss (New York: Dodd, Mead and Co., 1934), 94.

35. Wayne W. Thompson, "Governors of the Moro Province: Wood, Bliss and Pershing in the Southern Philippines" (Ph.D. diss., University of California, San Diego, 1975), 5.

36. RGMP, 1906, in RPC 1907, op. cit., 50.

37. Bliss, Mindanao Herald, 3 February 1909, op. cit.: 3.

38. RGMP, 1906, op. cit., 356. Bolton, son of an Episcopalian minister, studied mechanical engineering before enlisting in the army, twice, in 1894 and 1897. He rose through the ranks fast, becoming second lieutenant in November 1899 while assigned in Manila. His administrative and technical skills (he was the first to map and survey the Davao-Cotabato boundaries) easily made him a top candidate for Davao district governor. He was promoted to first lieutenant in 1901. Mindanao Herald, 15 June 1906. Maj. Edward Finley was not only known for his governance, he was also respected for "scholarly" investigations. Among Finley's works were The Subanu: Studies of a Sub-Visayan Mountain Folk of Mindanao (William Churchill, co-author), 1913, Washington, D.C., and "The Mohammedan Problem in the Philippines," Journal of Race Development, April 1915. Also admired deeply was Col. Cornelius Smith, who worked on an English version of the Spanish grammar translation of the Maguindanao dialect, while encouraging the Cotabato datus to send their children to public schools. On Smith, his Don't Settle for Second, 92; and on Boyd, see Leonard Wood, op. cit. See also Hugh Lenox Scott (major-general, U.S. Army, retired), Some Memories of a Soldier (New York and London: The Century Company, 1928).

39. Vandiver, op. cit., 332-352.

40. Thompson, op. cit., 7-13; 226-227.

41. Gowing, 171-172.

42. These officers also made it a point to stamp out "corruption" among army personnel. A Pvt. Robert Shroeder, deputy governor of Lumitan subdistrict, Zamboanga, for example, was expelled

from the province for marrying a Muslim woman and accepting the title of "*sub-dato*" given him by new relatives. *Philippines Free Press*, 20 January 1907, 6.

43. Annual Report of General Davis, Department of Mindanao, 1903, op. cit., 39.

44. See, for example, *The Mindanao Herald*, 16 June 1906 (on the killing of Bolton), and 25 August 1906 (on the death of his Tagacaolo "slayer," Mangalayan).

45. Weapons superiority was unquestionably a big factor favoring the Americans. See George Yarrington Coats, *The Philippine Constabulary*, 1901-1927 (Unpublished Ph.D. diss., Ohio State zzzzUniversity, 1968), 361.

46. The Muslims' propensity for fort warfare particularly afforded the Americans an opportunity to display the power of their artillery pieces. See Russell Roth, op. cit., 30-37, 148-154.

47. See also a similar vivid display of brutal American firepower in the "Battle of Bayang," Lanao in Chauncey McGovern, 1906, op. cit.: 100-125. On Jolo, see R. L. Bullard's "Letter to the Adjutant, Infantry Force, Jolo Expedition, November 23, 1903," in Thompson, op. cit.: 55-56. A similar view was expressed by Leonard Wood in his letter to a Frank Steinhard, 26 December 1903.

48. The alliance of Datus Ampuan Agos and Amai-gin-Dalugan in Lanao, for example, failed to work as the Americans persisted in their pursuit against them, even deep into the unexplored interiors of the district. *RGMP*, in *RPC*, Part I, 1907, op. cit.: 385.

49. Harold Hanne Elarth, *Philippine Constabulary*, 84.

50. RGMP, in RPC, 1907, op. cit.: 351 and 384.

51. "Letter of Brig. Gen. Geo Davis to Adjutant-General, October 24, 1901," in ARWD, 1902, op. cit.: 2127; and, Henry Florida Funtecha, *American Military Occupation of the Lake Lanao Region, 1901-1903: A Historical Study* (Marawi City: University Research Center, Mindanao State University (MSU), 1979), 59.

52. Vic Hurley, *Swish of the Kris*, 178-179.

53. Elarth, op. cit., 84. The "Moro Constabulary" original consisted of 17 officers and 353 men, of whom one-third of the latter were Muslims. This unit figured prominently in the *Battle of Bud Bagsak*.

54. The War Department was under intense congressional pressure to demobilize when the Philippine war was becoming more expensive, costing the U.S. over $176 million (or an estimated $1,000 annually per soldier). To cut costs, the constabulary was charged with taking over the army's policing functions in Mindanao. Hurley, 1938, op.cit.: 58-59, 267.

55. See "Report of District Governor, 5th District, Bureau of Constabulary, July 15, 1908," in *RPC*, vol. 8, ARWD, 1908, op.c it.: 416-417.

56. *RGMP*, 1906, op. cit.: 348. See also "Outlaws cleaned out in southern Mindanao," The *Mindanao Herald*, 21 September 1907.

57. *RGMP*, 30 June 1911. Zamboanga: The Mindanao Publishing Co., 24; *Philippines Free Press*, 18 November 1911.

58. Gowing, 1983, *op.cit.*, p.95

59. U.S. Army engineer thus, in 1903, failed to finish a 140mile wagon road from Malabang to Matabing Falls (Camp Vicars, Lanao), ibid, . p.138.

60. By the end of 1902, the army proudly reported "453.8 miles of submarine cable, 66 miles land telegraph line and 98 miles of land telephone line" had connected such areas as Marawai, Iligan, Cotabato town and the port of Zamboanga. Additionally, 50 miles on Cotabato, 23 in Lanao and 10 in Zamboanga were constructed. Appendix III, Headquarters, Department of Mindanao. Report of Maj. Gen. George W. Davis, U.S. Army, Commanding Dvision of the Philipines, June 30, 1903," p. 309.

61. "Problems incident to organizing the Department of Public Works plus limitations of funds resulted in slow progress during the 903-1904 fiscal year. Moreover, an epidemic of rinderpest spread across the Province that year destroying hundreds of work animals. This contributed to the delay in the

construction of public works projects. Road building and repair was confined largely to the vicinity of the principal towns. (In 1904), more was accomplished," Gowing, *op.cit.* pp.138-139.

62. Hurley, 311-313.

63. Gowing, 332.z

64. See the report of Captain Langhorne on the number of trips taken around the Moro Province (four times/month) and other responsibilities of the gunboat *Zamboanga*. *RGMP*, 1905: 5.

65. "Annual Report of Brig. Gen. Henry T. Allen, U.S. Army, Chief Constabulary," in *RPC*, 1904, vol. 8, Part 3: 126.

66. Gowing, 210-211.

67. "*RGMP*, September 22, 1905," in RPC, vol. 10, Part 1, ARWD (Washington, D.C.: GPO, 1905), 327.

68. "Zamboanga, the Banner Port," *Mindanao Herald*, 15 September 1906. Collections in the Zamboanga port totalled P82,240.40 in 1904; P108,719.86 in 1905; and, dramatically increased to P178,818.95 in 1906.

69. Gowing, 60-61.

70. *RGMP*. 1904, op. cit., p. 13.

71. Legislative Council Act No. 39, Sections 15 and 16 "provided that headmen salaried by the province would not receive salaries (ranging from P240 to P1,980 a year) until they turned in collected taxes." See also "Treasurer's report," Mindanao Herald, 17 September 1904: 3.

72. "Report of the Officer Commanding 5th District, Philippine Constabulary," 5 July 1905, RPC, 1906, Part 3, op. cit.: 118.

73. Ibid., 75, 186-7.

74. *RGMP*, op. cit., 1906: 340.

75. Gowing, 228-229.

76. The 3 February 1909 issue of *The Mindanao Herald* listed the following leading merchants in Cotabato: Sui Funero, reputedly the wealthiest of all the Chinese, having been in Cotabato for forty years; Ya Deco, who had controlled the gutta percha trade together with Datu Piang since the Spanish period; Chin Kai, owner of the largest lumber store and agent of the shipping line Compania Maritima. Others mentioned were Messrs. "Chao Sua, Celestino Alonzo (Christianized), Ty Kongco, Cua Consuy, Quipo, Ong Lee, Tan Cacao, Tan Opon, Te Liongco, Lim Peu, Ong Baco, Chu Yuqui, Dy Toco, and Tan Se Tun, described by the *Herald* as "businessmen."

77. Abaca production rose from a mere five hundred piculs a month in 1904 to three thousand piculs a month by 1907. *Mindanao Herald*, 3 March 1907.

78. Lewis E. Gleek, *Americans in the Philippine Frontier* (Manila: Carmelo and Bauermann Inc., 1974). A more substantive study is Hayase, op. cit., 75.

79. Douglas Thompson Kellie Hartley, "American Participation in the Economic Development of Mindanao and Sulu, 1899-1930," (Ph.D. diss., James Cook University of North Queensland, 1983), 38. 44-45.

80. Norman G. Owen, *Prosperity Without Progress: Manila Hemp and Material Life in the Colonial Philippines* (Berkeley, Los Angeles and London: University of California Press, 1984), 80.

81. A long drawn debate on the proper variety of rubber plant likewise added to its stunted growth. See Hartley, op. cit., 44-46.

82. Gowing, 221-222.

83. Custom collections grew from P82,240.40 in 1904, to P108, 719.86 in 1905; and P178,818.96 in 1906. *Mindanao Herald*, September 15, 1906

84. *Mindanao Herald*, 6 July 1907.

85. *Manila Times*, 28 March 1905; *Cablenews-American*, 29 March 1905.

86. *RGMP*, op. cit.: 1906, 349.

87. *RGMP*, 1904: 319-320.

88. "Finances of the Province," *Mindanao Herald*, 15 June 1907.

89. Based on various reports of the governor of the Moro Province.

90. "Report of the Acting Insular Collector of Customs, Exhibit No. 3, August 31, 1907," in *RPC*, vol. 3, *ARWD*, 1907 (Washington, D.C.: GPO, 1908), 83.

91. Datu Michael Mastura, "Administrative Policies towards the Muslims: A Study in Historical Continuity and Trends," in *Muslim-Filipino Experience: A Collection of Essays* (Manila: OCIA Publications, 1984), 71.

92. *RPC*, 1907, op. cit.: 342-343, 355-356; *RGMP*, 1914, op. cit.: 124.

93. *RGMP*, 1904, op. cit.: 21. Peter W. Stanley, 1984, op. cit.: 119.

94. See, for example, *Mindanao Herald*, 15 December 1906.

95. Lanao District Governor Finley to Dapitan Filipinos, ibid.

96. *Mindanao Herald*, June 16, 1906

97. *Mindanao Herald*, 7 July 1906.

98. *Mindanao Herald*, 12 August 1905.

99. Warned Hoyt: "The Moro Province is essentially Moro, 90% of the total population being Moro and non-Christian, and any Filipino *coming within its borders or residing therein should recognize that he must abide by the laws of the Province and rest content to live within its territorial jurisdiction rather by sufferance than by right of heritage*," ibid.: 31 (underscoring mine). This view was later reiterated by Hoyt's successor, Pershing, albeit without the separatist argument. *RGMP*, 1910, op. cit.: 21.

100. *RGMP*, 1916, op. cit., 336. And rightly so. Zamboanga-based ships were trading not only in Manila, but also with Asian ports, from Singapore to Shanghai. Hartley, op. cit., 28.

101. Thompson, op. cit., 82.

102. Gowing, 1983, op. cit., 186.

103. Sometimes to the point of bending colonial laws. The Bagobo leader Datu Asnig was sentenced to 20 years in prison for allowing child sacrifice, but "in view of teh special legislation which vests discretionary powers in (sic) the judge when the accused are non-Christians, the sentence was suspended during (?) good behavior (and) the *datu* returned joyfully to his (new) home... in Digos." *Mindanao Herald*, March 14, 1908.

104. "Law for Moros," *The Mindanao Herald*, Februrary 27, 1904, Vol. I, No. 16, 1-2. *RGMP*, 1904, op. cit., 6-7.

105. *RGMP*, 1904. op. cit., 24. Control of local judicial appointment and limiting appointments to the local Court of First Instance to Americans ensured that the Province was also relatively sanitized from political interference on judicial appointments which was increasingly occuring in Manila. See the different annual reports of the *Official Register of Officers and Employees in the Civil Service of the Philippine Islands, 1903-1910.*

106. Col. Henry Gilhouser, "The Moro Province," op. cit., 52.

107. *Journal of the Philippine Commission*, being a Special Session and the First Session, 28 March 1910 to 19 April 1910 and 17 October 1910 to 3 February 1911, respectively, of the Philippine Legislature (Manila: Bureau of Printing, 1911): 771.

108. Bliss, "The Government of the Moro Province and its Problems," *Mindanao Herald*, 3 February 1909, 4.

109. See, for example, the notes of a traveler as he sought information regarding Mindanao conditions. Carl N. Taylor, *Odyssey of the Islands* (New York: Charles Scribner and Sons, 1936), 18.

110. Thompson, op. cit., 89; *Manila Times*, 5 May 1906; *Mindanao Herald*, 17 March 1906. See also *The Boston Transcript*, May 1906.

111. Thompson, ibid., 139-140.

112. *Manila-American*, 12 August 1906.

113. Philippine Independence speech, 6 June 1906, as reprinted in *Mindanao Herald*, 31 August 1906.

114. *Manila Daily Bulletin*, 27 October 1906.

115. Wood, for example, allowed an American journalist to travel around Mindanao soliciting and writing about anti-Manila sentiments, as well as ridiculing the speeded-up "Filipinization" program of Gov. Francis B. Harrison. See Katherine Mayo, *The Isles of Fear: The Truth about the Philippines* (New York: Harcourt, Brace and Co., 1925), 299-300.

116. As quoted by Gleeck, 157.

117. Philippine Commission Act 2408. "An Act Providing for a Temporary Form of Government for the Territory known as the Department of Mindanao and Sulu, making Applicable thereto, with certain exceptions, the provisions of General Laws now in Force in the Philippine Islands, and for Other Purposes," 23 July 1914.

118. Robert Wooster, *The Military and United States Indian Policy, 1865-1903* (New Haven, Conn.: Yale University Press, 1988), 116.

119. 1983, op. cit., 184.

120. *RGMP*, 1906, 136.

121. Testimoniy of Frank W. Carpenter, House Document 1378. Part III, Sixty-fourth Congress, Second Session, 400-401.

122. Dean C. Worcester. *The Philippines Past and Present*, 1914, Vol. 2. New York: The MacMillan Co., 633.

123. *Mindanao Herald*, 29 February 1908.

124. "Staff Officers going Home," *Mindanao Herald*, 15 June 1907.

125. Thompson, op. cit., p. 190. Pershing managed to delay the Forbes order, when he got the Bovernor to first require complete Moro disarmament.

126. Gowing, 184.

127. Elliot, op. cit., 93-94.

128. Datus Pian and Mandi were eventually appointed successively as representatives of the "Special Provinces" under the Commonwealth.

129. Gowing, 194.

130. See, for example, *Journal of the Philippine Commission*. Second Session (16 October 1911-1 February 1992) and a Special Session (2 February 1912-16 February 1912) (Manila: Bureau of Printing, 1912), 927-943.

131. Gowing, 1983, op. cit., p. 221.

132. *RGMP*, 1910: 7.

133. *Mindanao Herald*, 15 June 1907.

134. *RGMP*, 31 August 1910, 7.

135. *Journal of the Philippine Commission*, 1912: 942-943.

136. *Mindanao Herald*, 6 July 1907.

137. Speech of Milton I. Southard (Democrat, Ohio), *Congressional Record, 45th Congress*, Second Session (Washington, D.C.: GPO, 1878), 963-967.

138. *Cablenews-American*, August 15, 1905; *Manila Town Topics*, August 18, 1905. The issue was again raised in 1906 and 1907. See *Manila Bulletin*, October 27, 1906, and *Mindanao Herald*, June 15, 1905, respectively.

139. Stanley, 1974, op. cit., 169.

140. "The American," 30 March 1905, as reprinted in *Mindanao Herald*, 8 April 1905.

141. The exception is the Austalian scholar, Rodney J. Sullivan, *Exemplar of Americanism*, 150.

142. On the "Gran Cordillera," see Frank Lawrence Jenista. *The White Apos: American Governors on the Cordillera Central* (Quezon City, Philippines: New Day Publishers, 1987), 251-270.

143. Hayden, op. cit., 58-59.

144. On the origins, power and resilience of the colonial administrative grid, see the fascination study of Gerard Anthony Finin,"Regional Consciousness and Administrative Grids: Understanding the role of Planning in the Philippine Gran Cordillera," May 1991. Ph. D. Dissertation, Cornell University.

145. The northern portion of Mindanao island consisted of the "regular" province Misamis. Its "regular-ness" was premised on the preponderance of Visayan-Catholic as well as a more stable Spanish religious and military presence. During the Revolution, Misamisnons formed their own provincial army, swearing allegiance to the Tagalog Republic of Aguinaldo. They fought the Americans, and like many others, surrendered and were coopted into the new colonial order. The Americans, seeing similitudes between these Misamis "elites" and their Visayan and Luzon counterparts, adopted the Spanish classification. Misamis—later on to be subdivided into Bukidnon and Agusan for purposes of electoral districting — thus became one of the regular provinces, as opposed to its southern neighbor, the special Moro Province governed under martial law.

139. Stanley, 1974, op. cit., 169.

Fagen and Other Ghosts:
African-Americans and the Philippine-American War

RENE G. ONTAL

U.S. Army's "Colored" Twenty-Fourth Infantry troopers

Anthony L. Powell Collection

What's wrong with me going to jail for something I believe in? Boys are dying in Vietnam for something they don't believe in.

I met two Black soldiers a while back in an airport. They said: 'Champ, it takes a lot of guts to do what you're doing.' I told them: 'Brothers, you just don't know. If you knew your chances of coming out with no arm or no eye, fighting those people in their own land, fighting Asian brothers, you got to shoot them, they never lynched you, never called you nigger, never put dogs on you, never shot your leaders. You've got to shoot your enemies (they call them) and as soon as you get home you won't be able to find a job. Going to jail for a few years is nothing compared to that.'

— Muhammad Ali on rejecting the draft, 1970[1]

At the height of the Vietnam war, Muhammad Ali's defiance spoke to questions raised by many draft-age African-Americans about fighting for a country in which they were denied their rights and subjected to racial discrimination and violence. They recognized the patterns of oppression carried out by the United States overseas and in domestic society. Thus these young men questioned whether they were willing to help propagate abroad the same policies that beat them down at home. Were they willing to fight and die for a "democracy" that in their reality meant a history of enslavement in its various subtle as well as blatant forms?

Hauntingly, the moral dilemma faced by the young men of Ali's generation was encountered by their forebears during the Philippine-American War at the turn of the century. This essay revisits that confrontation through the saga of David Fagen, an African-American serviceman who was sent to the Philippines to fight for the United States but defected in November 1899 to the nationalist army fighting for Philippine independence. Five months after sailing into Manila, Fagen crossed enemy lines and joined the army of Gen. Emilio Aguinaldo. He was transformed from Private Fagen of the United States Army into a feared guerrilla officer and propagandist. The former buck private commanded hit-and-run sorties against U.S. forces, issued recruitment appeals to his former comrades and attracted front-page notoriety in the American newspapers of the day.[2]

Artist: Kevin Kennedy

During the summer of 1899, Fagen was among six thousand troops in the U.S. Army's "Colored" Regiments ordered as reinforcements to fight in the Philippine archipelago.[3] Their deployment set the stage for a little-known convergence of Filipinos and African-Americans within the setting of colonial war.

In addition to telling the story of one African-American soldier's resolution of a moral dilemma, this essay examines the African-American press and the political commentary regarding the Philippine hostilities. Dispatches from soldiers reporting home to Black-run newspapers and interviews with Black soldiers and Filipino civilians told of the empathic relationships between the soldiers and the civilians, and provided insight into the sociopolitical implications of the first time Black troops were ordered to fight a colonial war in Southeast Asia.[4]

Composite sketch of Private David Fagen, U.S. Army

A STATE OF SIEGE - FAGEN'S AMERICA IN THE 1890s

On 4 June 1898, the twenty-three-year-old Fagen shed a past life as a laborer at a phosphate-processing plant in his hometown of Tampa, Florida, when he enlisted in the Twenty-Fourth Infantry. The Twenty-Fourth was one of four segregated Army regiments formed for African Americans at the close of the Civil War.[5]

After a physical examination where his build and distinguishing marks were carefully noted (5'10", 140 lbs., dark-complexioned, with a curved scar on his chin), Fagen took the oath of allegiance in the presence of his recruiting officer, and scrawled his signature on the dotted line:

> ...and I do solemnly swear (or affirm) that I will bear true faith and allegiance
> to the United States of America, and that I will serve them honestly and
> faithfully against all their enemies whomsoever; and that I will obey the orders

of the President of the United States, and the orders of the officers appointed over me, according to the Rules and Articles of War."[6]

In many aspects, Fagen fit the demographic of the Black enlisted man: single, drawn to military life by the higher-than-average salary as well as the respect and affection showered on Black soldiers by African-American civilians. Lithograph portraits of local men serving in the army were a common feature in Black homes. However, unlike many Black servicemen, Fagen was left without any close kin when his father, a widower, passed away in Tampa shortly before he sailed overseas.[7]

US National Archives

Sharecropping family, 1890s

He donned the uniform at a time of boiling ferment within the segregated ranks. Fagen and his peers came of age during a period in African-American history known as the "Vale of Tears," the most desolate and ruinous years for African-Americans since the end of the Civil War.[8] In their barracks, Black troopers founded organizations such as the Frederick Douglass Memorial Literary Society to assess the state of their besieged communities.[9]

Due to immense changes in political and economic tides (the reunification of white Yankee and Southern business interests) and judicial developments (federal court decisions such as Plessy v. Ferguson in 1896, which upheld segregationist policies in Southern states and cemented second-class status for nonwhites), the Reconstruction agenda for Black equality suffered grievous reversals. As the embers of the Civil War finally cooled, so did hope and progress toward genuine emancipation.[10]

White supremacist militias such as the White Citizens Council and the Ku Klux Klan rode unchallenged in the countryside, spreading an epidemic of lynchings against Black communities. At the peak of the Philippine conflict, between 1899 and 1902, an estimated two thousand Black women, men, and children died from racial attacks in the deep South.[11]

Perhaps the most infamous of these cases was the murder of a Georgia sharecropper named Sam Hose in April 1899. Accused of killing a white landowner and sexually assaulting his wife, the thirty-year-old farm worker was lashed to a tree and burned alive by a cheering mob in Newman, Georgia. An African-American minister named Elijah Strickland was also killed when he tried to intervene.

The Hose and Strickland incident drew international condemnation for its gruesome nature, as well as its morbid epilogue. In unprecedented numbers, white Georgians communed in the atrocity post mortis. When news of the attack spread to nearby Atlanta, the railroad company began scheduling discount excursions to the lynching site, attracting thousands of thrill-seekers from the capital and neighboring communities. Entrepreneurs sold burnt pieces of Hose's bones. His slayers placed one of his fingers in an envelope and gave it to his young son, as an admonishment to "make himself scarce."[12]

The echoes of Hose's and Strickland's deaths spread worldwide, catching the ears of Filipino guerrilla propagandists, and would later reverberate in Fagen's legend.

"'TWEEN THE DEVIL AND THE DEEP SEA"

The Black servicemen themselves were not immune to physical attack. At least twenty-three soldiers, including six Medal of Honor recipients, died in mob assaults during the 1890s.[13]

Soldiers who left their barracks to answer with force were routinely demonized in the mainstream press, portrayed instead as the instigators of the violence.[14] In June of 1898, Fagen's Twenty-Fourth Infantry regiment engaged in running street battles with white volunteer soldiers and sheriffs in his hometown. The week-long race riot was ignited when members of the Twenty-Fourth rescued a Black child from a group of drunken white soldiers, who had been forcing the boy to stand as a target for a marksmanship demonstration.[15]

VIOLENCE OF NEGRO SOLDIERS.

Troopers of the Tenth Cavalry Terrorize a Texarkana Resort—Brought to Bay by Dynamite.

New York Public Library

THE DUALITY OF AFRICAN-AMERICANS

The state of siege gave rise to an identity crisis for Black Americans, depicted by W. E. B. DuBois in his classic work, *The Souls of Black Folk*:

Black troops demonized in the mainstream press

> The Negro is a sort of seventh son, born with a veil, and gifted with second-sight. In this American world, a world which yields him no true self-Consciousness.... One ever feels his two-ness, an American, a Negro; Two souls, two thoughts, two unreconciled strivings.... He simply wishes to make it possible for a man to be both a Negro and an American, without being cursed and spit upon by his fellows, without having the doors of Opportunity closed roughly in his face.[16]

African Methodist Episcopalian (AME) Bishop Henry Turner, a leading Black religious leader, and renowned orator, argued that the two "souls" could never reconcile in white America, and prophesied a bankrupt future for African Americans. From his church pulpit in Atlanta, Bishop Turner advocated a controversial solution: a hejira—the wholesale exodus of southern Blacks to African territories.[17] A former Civil War Army chaplain who had ministered to Black Union troops, Bishop Turner trained his rhetorical sights on Fagen and others who had taken the oath of allegiance.

> The Negro minister of the gospel who would encourage enlistment in the United States army, in the conditions things are now, encourages murder and the shedding of innocent blood for nothing, as the foolish young men do not know what steps they are taking.... Again we say to the colored men, stay out of the United States army. Take no oath to protect any flag that offers no protection to its sable defenders. If we had the voice of seven thunders, we would sound a protest against Negro enlistment till the very ground shook below our feet.[18]

When the sailing orders finally came for the Black troops, they sparked a political firestorm within the Black community. Bishop Turner commanded a key role in the American anti-imperialist struggle, calling the Filipino nationalists "sable patriots" whose fight should be emulated by other people of color.

The U.S. War Department's deployment provoked an outcry among African-Americans across the United States, who pointed out the interconnection between the government's "home treatment" of African-Americans and its foreign policy dealings with dark-skinned people.[19] The moral dilemma of Black troops ushering in the dawn of U.S. imperialism, states historian Willard B. Gatewood, was "the paramount issue of the 1900s" for African-American leaders.[20]

Anti-imperialist leader Bishop Henry Turner

CONCERNED OBSERVERS

A vibrant Black press—over 150 Black-owned weeklies across the nation—also weighed in on the issue. A vocal few, such as the *New York Age* published by Harlem businessman T. Thomas Fortune, rendered a pro-imperialist editorial perspective. Fortune admonished that for the African-American to seem unpatriotic during wartime could only worsen their condition. But newspapers such as the *Indianapolis Recorder* voiced the general sentiment, proclaiming an "ideological" alliance with the Filipinos and howling derisively at government declarations of imminent victory.[21]

The editors often referred to the Philippine natives as "colored cousins," a reflection of how the racial construct of the day sheltered all brown-skinned races as "Colored" or "Negro."[22]

Contrasting the coverage of the February 1899 outbreak of hostilities in San Juan, Manila, by the leading mainstream newspaper and the Black-owned *Indianapolis Recorder* proves instructive. *The New York Times* led the chorus for decisive military action. "The Filipinos have chosen a bloody way to demonstrate their incapacity for self-government... in the insane attack of these people on their liberators... these babes of the jungle from Aguinaldo down... are veritable children.... To commit to their unsteady hands and childish minds political powers... would be to give a dynamite cartridge to a baby for a plaything."[23]

Its 6 February subhead, "American Troops Attacked by Aguinaldo's Forces," betrayed the jingoist tone of the "Grey Lady." A bored Nebraska volunteer named Willie Grayson would later admit to firing the initial salvo.[24]

On the other hand, the *Indianapolis Recorder*, with a circulation of twenty thousand, seethed with moral indignation:

> As long as the impression prevailed in this country that the Filipinos were fighting to throw off the Spanish yoke and seek American annexation, they were called patriots and martyrs, but when they demanded pure and unadulterated independence, they became a set of bloodthirsty barbarians.[25]

Clearly, the nature of African-American opposition to the spreading quagmire was dual and intertwined: it was political, based on a mutual struggle for emancipation, as well as racial, based on an affinity between colored peoples.

Anthony L. Powell Collection

A widely published open letter signed by "the colored community of Boston" declared:

Black troops in the Philippines

> To the colored people of the US:
>
> We, the undersigned, address you at one of the most important points in your history. If there ever was a war of races in this world, the war now going on in the Philippine Islands is precisely that. [26]

The *Helena Reporter* in Helena, Arkansas, appealed to the Black troops in explicitly racial terms.

> Every colored soldier who goes to the Philippine Islands to fight the brave men there who are fighting and dying for their freedom… is fighting to curse the country with color-phobia, lynchings, Jim Crow (train) cars, and everything else that white prejudice can do to blight the darker races… and since the Filipinos belong to the darker human variety, it is the Negro fighting against himself. [27]

THE SOLDIER-JOURNALISTS

On the eve of the Black troops' embarkation for the Philippines, a daunting economic challenge emerged for the Black newspaper publishers. Black soldiers were poised to enter the compelling drama half a world away, but the publishers lacked the funds to sail a reporter to the front. So they came upon a novel solution. The editors prevailed upon their friends in the Black units, especially the noncommissioned officers, to cable dispatches from the front and become de facto correspondents. Many of them eagerly signed on, packing notebooks as well as weapons to the Philippine front.[28]

INTO THE FRAY

Fagen and his Company "I" sailed into Manila on 22 June 1899.[29] Communications from the soldiers soon filled the columns of Black newspapers, spanning a wide breadth of topics.[30]   Some were lighthearted missives. Private Ed Brown of the Twenty-Fourth reflected on his colleagues' enthusiasm for the natives' *tuba* (fermented palm wine), which they referred to as "beno" (wine):

> ...the soldiers are doing well. They would have better health if they would let that beno alone. It is a drink that the Filipinos make. Poco tiempo. Tell my friends that I am just the same as a Filipino.[31]

Others emphasized duty to flag and country over questions of racial solidarity. Sergeant Sadler declared:

> Whether it is right to reduce these people to submission is not a question for the soldier to decide. Our oath of allegiance knows neither race, color, nor nation.[32]

However, the dominant concerns threading through many of the dispatches dealt with the ambivalence the soldiers felt about their mission, their affinity with Filipino civilians, and their unease at the white troops' "home treatment" of the local populace.[33]

Sgt. Patrick Mason of the Twenty-Fourth confessed:

> I have no fighting to do since I've been here and don't care to do any. I feel sorry for these people and all that have come under the control of the US. I don't believe they will be justly dealt by. The first thing in the morning is nigger and the last thing at night is nigger. You are right in your opinions. I must not say much as I am a soldier. The natives are a patient, burden-bearing people.[34]

Mason was killed in action on Corregidor Island weeks after mailing this letter. Another soldier from the Twenty-Fourth Infantry said, "I want to say right here that were it not for the 10 million Black people in the US, God alone knows which side of the subject I would be."[35]

One of the most prolific of the soldier-journalists was Gunnery Sgt. John Galloway. He interviewed Filipino civilians, recording their opinions on independence and relations with Black and white troops, and thus offered us a first glimpse of exported American racism. A physician named Tordorico (sic) Santos replied to his survey:

> Before you arrived, the White troops began to tell us of the inferiority of the American Blacks—of your brutal natures, your cannibal tendencies, how you would rape our señoritas, but the affinity of our complexion between you and me tells, and you exercise your duty much more kindly... in dealing with us. Between you and him, we look upon you as the angel and him as the devil.

Galloway concluded in his report: "I fear that the future of the Filipino is that of the Negro in the South."[36]

David Fagen's company was initially assigned to guard strategic positions around Manila: a vital railway to Dagupan and the city's water pumping station by the Marikina River. The Colored Regiments suffered their first casualties here—not to insurgent gunfire, but the lashings of the monsoon season. On 21 August, ten men from the Twenty-Fourth drowned when their raft capsized in the churning waters of the Marikina.

Fagen's sentry duty ended in November when his "I" company marched into the Luzon interior. During this offensive, Fagen's relationship with his commanders swiftly unraveled.[37] The records remain blurry as to the cause, but it probably did not include incompetence as Fagen had been judged previously of "good character" and "meeting all requirements." Was it a case of a soldier breaking under fire? Or might he have witnessed and objected to "marked severities" against Filipino civilians in the countryside? Whatever the alienating factors, Fagen made a nuisance of himself during the campaign. His official dossier described him as "rowdy" and "bucking" his superiors, landing him "in continual trouble with the Commanding Officer." He had seven convictions for insubordination. A white officer later characterized him as "a good for nothing whelp." The commanders retaliated with physical punishment, and a Black noncommissioned officer observed that he "was made to do all sorts of dirty jobs." The sanctions were such that one trooper later claimed, "I don't blame him for clearing out."[38]

Fagen's predicament perhaps made him ideally receptive to a new phenomenon: recruitment communiqués from guerrilla propagandists that were addressed to the Black soldiers.

His moment of truth came on 17 November. A few days earlier, Fagen and the Twenty-Fourth entered San Isidro, the last known hideout of General Aguinaldo. They found no trace of the Filipino leader, but instead found the streets littered with leaflets and placards, all containing a message to the Black soldiers.

The communiqué bore the hallmarks of the wheelchair-bound Apolinario Mabini, who as Foreign Minister and chief propagandist of the Philippine Revolution had kept abreast of the race problem in the United States. He now referenced the state of the African-American in his appeal:

> To the colored American soldier,
> It is without honor that you shed your precious blood. Your masters have thrown you in the most iniquitous fight with double purpose—to make you the instrument of their ambition, and also your hard work will make the extinction of your race. Your friends, the Filipinos, give you this good warning. You must consider your situation and your history, and take charge that the blood of Sam Hose proclaims vengeance.[39]

On 17 November, "I" Company broke camp, getting ready for its new post, the town of Cabanatuan. Using the confusion of the move as a cover, Fagen gathered as many pistols as he could safely conceal, and calmly walked out of his barracks.[40] He had somehow sent word to the guerrillas a few days before; a saddled horse was waiting for him. Fagen's escape was almost effortless. He mounted up and rode into the jungle, toward the headquarters of the rebels in the densely foliated and volcanic slopes of Mount Arayat, and his new life as an "insurrecto." In the guerrilla base camp, he immediately accepted a first lieutenant's commission in Brigada Lacuña, the feared battalion under the command of Gen. Urbano Lacuña.[41]

Fagen led the way for twenty other Black deserters, at least twelve of whom enlisted for duty with the guerrillas. Historian Anthony Powell calls this "unprecedented in Black military history."[42] Six members of the Ninth Cavalry deserted and joined the Filipinos in Albay province: John Dalrymple, Edmund DuBose, Lewis Russell, Fred Hunter, Grath Shores, and William Victor. The other defectors were valued as marksmanship instructors. White officers would later warn of the added danger involved when confronting guerrillas trained by the Black soldiers.[43]

Fagen would command most of the attention, however. Wasting no time in his new role as insurrecto officer, Fagen fought "like a wildcat" in his first year with the Filipinos. He also issued recruitment appeals to his former comrades to join him in the guerrilla brigades.

On 17 September 1900, General Lacuña recommended him for promotion to Captain. From the citation (translated from the original Spanish):

> In view of the merits of war obtained by the 1st Lieutenant Dewet Pagain (sic), I agree to promote him to a Captaincy. Therefore I direct all authorities, civil and military to recognize him... and to give him all consideration and prominence due him.[44]

Published accounts of his exploits began to appear in the *Manila Times*, an American-owned newspaper, depicting him as a gifted military tactician waylaying American patrols at will and then evading large forces sent in pursuit.[45]

Just days after his promotion, a force under his and General Lacuna's command surrounded a U.S. Army Corps of Engineers unit and captured the highest ranking American prisoner of war; Lt. F. W. Alstaetter. Lacuña would later exchange the West Point graduate for a number of his imprisoned men.[46] Shortly after, Fagen mounted yet another impressive mission. He led over 150 fighters in the seizure of a military supply barge on the Rio de Pampanga. The former laborer from Tampa had become "news fit to print."

"American deserter in the field... recently captured twenty Americans," blared *The New York Times* headline on 9 October 1900.[47]

A former American prisoner in Fagen's custody was responsible for the false promotion to "general." The POW had overheard his Filipino guards affectionately address Fagen as "Heneral," and reported as such to the *Times* reporter.

In the following months, published accounts on the elusive American, accurate and otherwise, proliferated. Another unverified story portrayed him as a cold-blooded executioner of five white American POWs. This allegation was challenged by an ex-prisoner of Fagen, who testified to his fair treatment under his guard. A first-person report also revealed that he had married a local woman.[48]

"THIS WRETCHED MAN"

The media spotlight on Fagen drew the ire of Col. Frederick Funston, the ambitious and publicity-seeking officer from Kansas. A fervent diarist, Funston—soon to gain fame and a second Medal of Honor for his shrewdly planned abduction of Aguinaldo—described the Black guerrilla in his book *Memories of Two Wars: Cuba and Philippines Experiences*: "For months we had known of the presence with the insurgents of this region of an American Negro named David Fagen, a deserter. This wretched man was serving as an officer."[49]

In his memoir entries, Funston proved an eager disciple in the gospel of U.S. expansionism. Earlier in the conflict, the press-friendly colonel blustered to an audience of American reporters: "I will rawhide these bullet-headed Asians until they yell for mercy.... After the war, I want the job of Professor of History in Luzon University, when they build it, and I'll warrant that the new generation of natives will know better than to get in the way of the band-wagon of Anglo-Saxon progress and decency."[50]

No doubt embarrassed by Fagen's activity in his area of operations, Funston was further antagonized when the "wretched man" began taunting him through communiqués:

Fagen "on two occasions had written me impudent and badly-spelled letters. It was well understood that if taken alive by any one of us, he was to stretch a picket rope as soon as a suitable one could be found... he is entitled to the same treatment as a mad dog."

Funston hunted David Fagen all over the provinces of Nueva Ecija and Pampanga. On at least two of these sorties, he traded gunshots with guerrilla elements led by his antagonist. Funston decried one such missed opportunity: "In this fight, I got a fairly good look at the notorious Fagen at a distance of 100 yards, but unfortunately, had already emptied my carbine."[51]

On 23 March 1901, Frederick Funston scored the coup of his dreams. Having obtained Aguinaldo's whereabouts from a tortured courier, Funston led a band of collaborationist "Macabebe"mercenaries to Palanan, Isabela, where he surprised Aguinaldo's guard and finally captured the Philippine president.

US National Archives

Fagen's antagonist: Col. Frederick Funston

Two weeks later, the Filipino leader swore his allegiance to the United States while under house arrest in Malacañang Palace, and ordered his officers to surrender immediately. A general amnesty was declared for those who came down from the hills. On Mount Arayat, Gen. Urbano Lacuña prepared to obey his Supremo but first sat down with Funston in a pre-surrender meeting. According to Funston, his "wily friend" Lacuña's main concern was whether Fagen would be amnestied as well. The American officer replied that, given Fagen's treason and alleged execution of POWs, only his death by hanging would satisfy the U.S. authorities. Lacuña returned to his brigade, and as the evidence would later suggest, began designing an intricate scheme to save his captain's life. Lacuña surrendered his forces in May 1901, but not before releasing Fagen from his command. The renegade American departed his camp with his native wife and several Aeta (Philippine aborigine) guides.[52]

The other Black defectors paid a heavy price for their resistance. Several were court-martialed and sent to Leavenworth Penitentiary for life. Fred Hunter of the Ninth Cavalry was killed while trying to escape. In Albay province, Privates DuBose and Russell were hanged to death before three thousand spectators. U.S. officials charged the soldier-journalist Sergeant Galloway of being "a menace to the islands" and "exceedingly dangerous" for writing of his sympathy with the Filipinos and labeling the war as "immoral." Galloway—a career soldier—was jailed, reduced to private, and forfeited all pension monies when he was discharged without honor.[53]

FUNSTON'S BOUNTY

His hands free of Aguinaldo, Frederick Funston resumed his pursuit of Fagen. He issued a bounty of six hundred dollars for "the head of the American Negro David Fagen, dead or alive." "Wanted" posters in Spanish and English were displayed all over Central Luzon.

Rumors swirled as to the rebel's whereabouts. The *Manila Times* reported an eyewitness sighting of him in a Manila bordello. Others swore he was fighting with Miguel Malvar, a holdout general in Batangas province. Even the *San Francisco Chronicle* added to the confusion: it printed a story about Fagen having made his way back to California, only to be arrested for stealing a bicycle. The "David Fagen" in this instance turned out to be a young petty thief who adopted the rebel's name as a comic tribute. [54]

On the afternoon of 6 December 1901, however, it appeared that Funston's bounty had paid off. Lt. R. C. Corliss, the commanding officer in Bongabong, Nueva Ecija, received a former member of Brigada Lacuña named Anastacio Bartolome. Bartolome, who had become a deer hunter and fisherman, entered the American station bearing a canvas sack. In a sworn affidavit, he claimed that he was fishing in the Umiray river with five companions on the morning of 1 December when Fagen arrived with his native wife and two Negrito friends. Corliss's report describes what happened next:

> "Through fear, and to keep on good terms with Fagan (sic), Anastacio and his party prepared them a meal. Knowing that Fagan was an insurgent, and ladrone (bandit) they secretly arranged to kill him. When the meal was prepared, at about 10 a.m., while all were eating, Anastacio and his party suddenly turned on Fagan and his men with bolos. Fagan was mortally wounded and ran about 100 yards and dropped dead. Both Negritos escaped badly wounded. Fagen's wife ran for the ocean and jumped in and drowned herself. Party then cut Fagan's head off to present here as evidence..." He opened his sack to reveal a badly decomposed head. As further proof, Bartolome submitted among Fagen's personal effects a worn photograph of Urbano Lacuña, his officer's commissions, and a West Point ring he had confiscated from the POW Lieutenant Alstaetter.[55] The US Army could now close the book on Pvt. David Fagen of Tampa, Florida. Funston gloated that the bounty was well-spent, though Bartolome probably lost it all "at the next cockfight."[56]

The *Indianapolis Freeman* offered this eulogy: "Fagen was considered a traitor and died a traitor's death but he was a man prompted by honest motives to help a weaker side,

A DESERTER KILLED

DAVID FAGAN SLAIN AND BE-HEADED BY NATIVE SCOUTS.

Former Member of the Twenty-Fourth (Colored) Infantry Who Turned Traitor for a Commission.

Manila cable: Native scouts from Bengabon, province of Nueva Ecija, have killed the American negro David Fagin, a deserter from the Twenty-fourth (colored) Infantry, who for more than two years has been leading Filipinos against the American troops. The native scouts decapitated their prisoner. The man's head, however, was recognized as that of Fagin's. They also secured his commis-

Fagen's supposed murder was widely reported.

and one with which he felt allied by ties that bind."[57]

Did Fagen die at the hands of a former comrade? Contemporary historians take issue with this version of his demise. In their seminal 1974 account "David Fagen: An Afro-American Rebel in the Philippines, 1899-1901" (*Pacific Historical Review*, 1974), historians Robinson and Schubert pointed out the glaring holes in the army's account. In a war where every dime, nickel, and mule was meticulously accounted for by army quartermasters, there remains no record of a six-hundred-dollar bounty awarded to an Anastacio Bartolome. Furthermore, they discovered several reports of credible sightings of Fagen by army soldiers who knew him, months after his reported assassination. Indeed, Bartolome's testimony was vouched in Army files as the report on "the supposed killing of David Fagen."[58]

Afro-Filipino Beatrice "Aling Edeng" Clarke is searching for her black relatives in the U.S.

Could the account given by the deer hunter have been part of a well-conceived plot involving Lacuña and Bartolome to keep the Black defector alive? Could he have lived a life free from racism and Frederick Funston, long after the cessation of hostilities? Black military historian Anthony Powell contends that Fagen survived well into his sixties. He points to the chronicles of Major Ramsey, a white American officer who fought a guerrilla war against the Japanese Imperial Army during World War II. In his memoirs, Ramsey tells of stumbling into an old "Negro" who said that he had fought in the war at the turn of the century. The man, who had sired many children on this island, embraced Major Ramsey and declared: "I'd volunteer to join but I'm too old to fight... but I'm at peace. I've made my home here, and I'll die among my family, that's what we fight for, ain't it, Major? To live in peace in our home, among our own people."[59]

EPILOGUE

The rest of the Colored Regiments were rotated back to the States in 1902, two years ahead of schedule. Governor-General Taft in Manila had grown increasingly suspicious of the Black soldiers' rapport with the native communities. Indeed, chaplains in the Black units had their hands full officiating marriages between Black servicemen and Filipino women.

Chaplain George Priouleau of the Twenty-Fourth Infantry reported to a Black newspaper:

> My second marriage ceremony was that of a corporal of the 9th and a native
> woman, and before this will reach you, I will perform my third, a member of
> the Black 9th Cavalry.[60]

Over a thousand of the Black soldiers opted to make the islands their home, citing the economic horizons broadened by the lack of racial prejudice. Upon mustering out of the Army, they embarked on second lives all over Luzon as farmers, clerks, small business owners, judges, and agricultural tycoons. William Warmsley was an army surgeon who became a civil court judge and later a successful tobacco farmer in Cagayan de Oro province.[61] Alexander Clarke of the Twenty-Fifth Infantry settled in Cabanatuan, Nueva Ecija, and opened a saloon.[62]

While the retired soldiers themselves for the most part experienced little or no racial discrimination, the same cannot be said of their mixed-race descendants. Between 1899 and 1999, Filipinos learned to call Blacks "niggers."

Courtesy of Ging Ebora

The social engineering of U.S. colonialism—a mandatory schooling system which excluded Black histories, and featured derogatory portrayals of African-Americans in Hollywood films—had altered the racial psyche of Filipinos by the time the Black soldiers' daughters and sons were born. The hierarchy of color, introduced during the Spaniards' reign, was institutionalized under the Americans. Bleaching creams and skin whiteners continue to be top-selling items in present-day Manila and other cities.

"I remember what I went through as a child," Rose Edwards Coleman, daughter of Black soldier James Coleman and his Filipino wife, was quoted to have said in 1974. "They made it miserable for us in school. My kids are spared this because they are light. Those who can pass, do.... I have never been barred from places and money is no problem, but they look down on us here. I can feel it."

From the late 1960s to the early 1970s, Afro-Filipino descendants formed The Colored American Community League of the Philippines, a self-help organization.[63]

Living legacies: Afro-Filipino descendants Evelyn and Ging Ebora

Today, however, some of the Black soldiers' children may yet regenerate the racial affinity that had provided such compelling drama a hundred years ago.

Evelyn Banks Ebora currently resides in Pennsylvania. She is the daughter of William Banks, a gunnery sergeant who decided to make the Philippines his home after his honorable discharge from the army. Ms. Ebora has sought to organize a network of Afro-Filipino descendants of the Black soldiers. She hopes to draw out the commonalities between Filipino and African-Americans in the United States.[64]

Beatrice Clarke, the daughter of Alexander Clarke the saloon proprietor, arrived in San Diego several years ago from Quezon City. She is seventy-four years old. Known as Aling Edeng to her friends, she recalled in a recent interview: "They teased and called me 'Negra' when I was growing up." In her twilight years, she has embarked on a final quest—to make the acquaintance of her African-American relatives in the Boston area, where her father lived with his siblings after migrating from the Caribbean nation of Nevis. In particular, she longs to meet the descendants of her father's favorite sister, Beatrice, after whom he named his daughter.[65]

Living legacies such as Aling Edeng and Evelyn Ebora also preserve the narrative of this convergence of Filipinos and African-Americans in history. Despite the near-erasure of this event from the classrooms and culture, the lessons of an anti-imperialist alliance between African-Americans and Asians—and the saga of one man's leap of faith on behalf of Philippine independence—survive and resonate one hundred years later.

NOTES:

The author wishes to thank Anthony L. Powell for his images and Erna Hernandez for her assistance with the preparation of this manuscript.

1. "The Black Scholar Interviews Muhammad Ali," author unknown, originally published in the Black Scholar periodical, June 1970. From *The Muhammad Ali Reader*, ed. Gerald Early (New York: Rob Weisbach Books, 1998), 83.

2. Michael C. Robinson and Frank N. Schubert, "David Fagen: An Afro-American Rebel in the Philippines, 1899-1901." *Pacific Historical Review* XLIV (February 1975): 68-73. See also "David Fagan (sic), Record of Events, Regimental Returns, Twenty-Fourth Infantry, 28 November 1899," Adjutant General's Office (AGO) File No. 431081, Record Group 94, Military Reference Branch (National Archives, Washington, D.C.).

3. Author's interview with Anthony L. Powell, a scholar of African-American military history, The Presidio, San Francisco, April 1994.

4. Willard B. Gatewood, Jr., *"Smoked Yankees" and the Struggle for Empire: Letters from Negro Soldiers, 1898-1902* (Illinois: University of Illinois Press, 1971), 252-254, 257, 279-290.

5. Robinson and Schubert, "David Fagen," 73.

6. David Fagen Enlistment Papers, 4 June 1898, AGO File No. 431081, National Archives, Record Group 94 , MRB, NA, Washington, D.C..

7. Robinson and Schubert, "David Fagen," 73.

8. Benjamin Brawley, *A Social History of the American Negro* (New York: Macmillan, 1921), 297.

9. Robinson and Schubert, "David Fagen," 71.

10. Willard B. Gatewood, Jr., *Black Americans and the White Man's Burden 1898-1903* (Illinois: University of Illinois Press, 1975), 2-3.

11. Preface by William Loren Katz in George P. Marks III, *The Black Press Views American Imperialism 1898-1900* (New York: Arno Press, 1971), viii.

12. Daniel B. Schirmer, *Republic or Empire: American Resistance to the Philippine War* (Cambridge Mass.: Schenkman Publishing, Co., 1972), 146.

13. Jack Foner, *Blacks and the Military in American History* (New York: Praeger 1974), 10.

14. *New York Times*, 10 January 1899, Microfiche Division, New York Public Library.

15. Gatewood, *Smoked Yankees*, 24.

16. W. E. B. Du Bois, *The Souls of Black Folk* (Illinois: A. C. McClurg, 1931), 3.

17. Gatewood, *Black Americans*, 6.

18. "The Negro Should Not Enter the Army." *Voice of Missions* 7 (1 May 1899). http://www.boondocksnet.com/ailtexts/vom0599.html In Jim Zwick, ed., *Anti-Imperialism in the United States, 1898-1935*, http://www.boondocksnet.com/ail98-35.html (24 Jan 2000).

19. Marks, *The Black Press*, 100.

20. Gatewood, *Black Americans*, 222-23.

21. Marks, *The Black Press*, xvii.

22. "Lucas," *The Seattle Republican*, 19 January 1900, Microfiche Division, Schomburg Center for Research on Black Culture: A brief article about a Manila orphan who was brought to Seattle by an American soldier and eventually adopted by the Redelsheimer family: "As are most of the native Filipinos, this boy shows distinct traces of being an offspring of that race of people known in the United States as Negroes. At school he is exceedingly apt in books and studies, and at home a prince of manliness. His foster parents are much devoted to him and propose to give him a polished education. Should he decide to return to his native land he will be a splendid subject to do missionary work among

the natives for Uncle Sam."

23. Leon Wolff, *Little Brown Brother: America's Forgotten Bid for Empire* (London: Longmans, 1961).

24. *New York Times*, 10 February 1899.

25. *Indianapolis Recorder*, 11 February 1899, from Marks, *The Black Press*, 115.

26. *Omaha Progress*, 3 October 1899, Schomburg Center for Research on Black Culture, MD.

27. *Reporter*, Helena, Arkansas, 1 February 1900, Schomburg Center for Research on Black Culture, MD.

28. Gatewood, *Smoked Yankees*, 16.

29. "Circular Showing the Distribution of Troops of the Line of the U.S. Army, 1 January 1866 to 30 June 1909." War Dept. AGO, 1 July 1909. U.S. Army Military History Institute, Carlisle, Pennsylvania.

30. Gatewood, *Black Americans*, 230.

31. *Indianapolis Recorder*, 9 June 1900 in Gatewood, *Smoked Yankees*, 276.

32. Ibid., 249.

33. Gatewood, *Black Americans*, 230.

34. "Voice from the Grave," *Cleveland Gazette*, 29 September 1900.

35. *The New York Age*, 11 August 1899, in Marks, *The Black Press*, 151.

36. Gatewood, *Smoked Yankees*, 251-255.

37. Gatewood, *Black Americans*, 266-267.

38. Robinson and Schubert, "David Fagen," 74. See also David Fagen information slip (AGO) File No. 431081, Record Group 94, Military Reference Branch, National Archives, Washington, D.C.

39. Rene G. Ontal, "Native Warrior: A Black Man's Embrace of an Asian Revolution," *City Sun* (New York, 31 May-6 June 1995), 10-13. Also *Richmond Planet*, 11 November 1899.

40. Microfiche rolls 249-251 and 258-259 of M665, Returns from Regular Infantry Regiments, June 1821 – December 1916, Military Reference Branch. National Archives, Washington, D.C. (24 November 1899).

41. David Fagen, Record of Events.

42. Author's interview with Anthony L. Powell, a scholar of African-American military history, The Presidio, San Francisco, April 1994.

43. Anthony L. Powell, "Through My Grandfather's Eyes: Ties that Bind: The African-American Soldier in the Filipino War for Liberation, 1899-1902." (1997) http://www.boondocks-net.com/sctexts/powell98a.html In Jim Zwick, ed., Sentenaryo/Centennial: The Philippine Revolution and Philippine-American War. http://www.boondocksnet.com/centennial/ (24 January 2000)

44. David Fagen, Record of Events.

45. Robinson and Schubert, "David Fagen," 75-76.

46. Frederick F. Funston, *Memories of Two Wars* (New York: C. Scribner's Sons, 1914), 376-377.

47. *New York Times*, 10 October 1900.

48. Robinson and Schubert, "David Fagen," 75-77.

49. Funston, Memories, 376.

50. David Howard Bain, *Sitting in Darkness: Americans in the Philippines* (Boston: Houghton Mifflin, 1984).

51. Funston, *Memories*, 376.

52. Ibid., 430-31.

53. Anthony L. Powell, "Through My Grandfather's Eyes," 11.

54. Robinson and Schubert, "David Fagen," 77.

55. David Fagen, Record of Events.

56. Funston, *Memories*, 434.

57. Robinson and Schubert, "David Fagen," 82-83.

58. David Fagen, Record of Events.

59. Author's interview with Anthony L. Powell, April 1994.

60. Gatewood, *Smoked Yankees*, 243, 237.

61. Gatewood, *Black Americans*, 313-14.

62. Beatrice Clarke/*Aling* Edeng interview by Cesar Clemente, Seattle, Washington, 4 June 1996.

63. Era Bell Thompson, "Veterans Who Never Came Home," *Ebony Magazine* XXVII (October 1972), 104-106, 108-115.

64. Author's interview with Ging Ebora, New York, February 1996.

65. Beatrice Clarke/*Aling* Edeng interview by Cesar Clemente, 4 June 1996.

Casualty Figures of the American Soldier and the Other: Post-1898 Allegories of Imperial Nation-Building as "Love and War"

OSCAR V. CAMPOMANES

Across certain parts of the United States, many monuments and memorials stand as mute yet articulate vestiges of the "Spanish-American War of 1898." This war began with Commodore Dewey's victory over Admiral Montojo's armada at Manila Bay in May 1898, and is customarily regarded and uncritically privileged by many American historians as the inaugural event of the United States' "coming out" as a world power.[1] Among these ubiquitous yet widely neglected monuments and memorials to the 1898 war are various incarnations of a life-size piece of sculpture identified by, and inscribed with, the enigmatic name "The Hiker" (see Figure 1).[2]

The sociologist James Loewen forewarns that to regard these Spanish-American War memorials and their inscriptions is to confront a mind-boggling "puzzle." Like many of them, the stately one in front of the State Capitol in Springfield, Illinois, for example, bears the typical descriptive head "Spanish American War Veterans, 1898-1902."[3] At the base of most of these memorials, as Loewen notes, is usually a plaque inscribed with the war's standard symbol: a circle around a Maltese cross, with the descriptive head spanning the circle and four arms of the cross inscribed with "Cuba," "Porto Rico," "Philippine Islands," and "U.S.A." In some monuments, "China" is added in place of "Porto Rico" or the "U.S.A." to adduce the "China Relief Expedition" that was launched from the Philippines in 1900, when the United States intervened, along with the other powers, in the uprisings known as the Boxer Rebellion.[4] But as Loewen pointedly asks, "How did a 100-day war wind up with a five-year time span in its monuments?"

With the Hiker statues, this periodizing or temporal *anomaly* often results in comic and seemingly unaccountable effects for those with some functional knowledge of the key international events of the Spanish-American War and its aftermath. In earlier research, I determined "The Hiker" or "hiking" to be terms coined by the soldiers who fought in the much longer Philippine-American War that followed the three-month Spanish-American War of 1898 (see Figure 3).[5] Philippine war soldiers *specifically* used these terms to describe themselves and their campaigns to root out unyielding Filipino guerrillas from their mountain strongholds or jungle redoubts. Such campaigns typically involved hiking through impenetrable thickets and on dusty/muddy roads for countless miles and several days in heavy rain or under the searing heat of the tropical sun: an image, no doubt, that takes on many self-heroic aspects.[6] Loewen notes that the Spanish-American War monument in Memphis bears this curiously confused and confusing inscription: "The Hiker, Typifying the American Volunteer who fought Spain in Cuba, the Philippines, and Boxer Rebellion." Here, the Philippine Hiker is placed oddly in Cuba where no such "hikings" were necessitated by subsequent political developments in the island. Hence the U.S. occupation did not have to face armed Cuban revolutionary opposition as it did Filipino resistance warfare after Spain's departure from the Philippines. And anyone who recalls that the Boxer Rebellion was directed at the inter-imperial complex of American, British, French, German, Japanese, and Russian interests in Beijing, Loewen adds, is left to "wonder at what Spain was doing in China" in 1900.[7]

O. Campomanes Collection. Photograph by Peter Foulkes

Fig. 1 The Hiker, Pawtucket, Rhode Island (see note 2)

Doubtless, this war is remembered by hegemonic textbook wisdom in the United States as the "splendid little war" (after the eventual Secretary of State John Hay's redoubtable phrase). "It has been a splendid little war; begun with the highest motives; carried on with the magnificent intelligence and spirit favored by that fortune which loves the brave," wrote then Ambassador Hay to then Col. Theodore Roosevelt in July 1898.[8]

It is nonetheless quite telling that even as this little war is remembered as splendid in over three generations of professional and modern U.S. history-writing, considerable anxieties attend or surround its many celebratory recountings. Surveying the extensive contemporary and modern historiography on the Spanish-American War, the historian Louis Pérez found insistent refrains of euphoric national self-celebration (concerning the war's legacies) curiously mixed in with anxiously repetitive tropes of "parody and belittlement."[9] This damning estimate is unsurprising to anyone with a cursory familiarity with the extensive historical literature on this particular war and what its body of texts collectively glosses over. "In reality it was not much more than the two overly glamorized naval victories at Santiago Bay in Cuba in July and at Manila in May [1898]," the critical historian Stuart Creighton Miller would aver by the early 1980s. Early U.S. victories in battles at El Caney and San Juan Hill in Cuba may have made spectacular icons of Gen. Henry Lawton and Col. Theodore Roosevelt. But "the army's only significant land campaign was a disaster" in which the War Department's organizational disarray and Gen. William Shafter's ineptitude as a commander created major embarrassments.[10]

Recalling the state of U.S. readiness for the Spanish-American War, Gen. Hugh L. Scott in *Some Memories of an American Soldier* (1928) admits that he and fellow officers "knew" to themselves that "our army was organized for peace, not war." Indeed, a candid and solidly researched account by the scholar Allan R. Millett reads General Hugh's 1928 "admission" as a polite way of saying that the United States War Department and the Armed Forces were not in any decent shape then to enforce the nation's emergent imperial will and desires. According to this authoritative account, both the U.S. War Department and the Armed Forces actually assumed and evolved a twin strategy. "The major weapons to free Cuba would be the United States Navy and the Cuban Revolutionary Army."[11] For the early campaign in the Philippines, the U.S. Navy under Dewey similarly sought a *de facto* alliance with the Filipino Revolutionary Army led by Gen. Emilio Aguinaldo, and nurtured this alliance carefully, at least until President William McKinley could hastily dispatch three waves of a Philippine expeditionary and occupation force consisting of U.S. Army volunteers and regulars between June and August 1898. (These troops were eventually instructed to displace and limit the Filipino government's own territorial claims and military victories, creating the tensions between the anti-Spanish "allies" that ultimately resulted in open war by February 1899.) This common strategy for Cuba and the Philippines was based on the actual unpreparedness of the U.S. Army in war footing and significant congressional opposition against increasing the less than 80,000 (1898) strength of Army regulars to meet the 100,000-man force projected by planners as necessary to enforce American political will. It also depended heavily, for much of the "little" war, on the almost chimeric strength of the U.S. naval fleets, themselves sorely in need of modern upgrading.[12]

O. Campomanes Collection. Photograph by Peter Foulkes

Fig. 2 Maltese Cross mounted in front of The Hiker, Woonsocket, Rhode Island (see note 4)

Quite apart from the brevity of hostilities between the United States and Spain, what in effect made this war splendid and little for the United States is the fact, often glossed over, of the already preexisting *revolutionary* situations on the Cuban and Philippine fronts. All the hard work, bloodletting, and the laborious years of armed struggle of Cuban and Filipino "insurrectionists" (and their supporters among their native populations) had practically and effectively withered Spanish power at the point when the United States came in with its "rescue" missions.[13]

It certainly remains, as the critical historian Richard van Alstyne once so aptly put it, that the Spanish-American War of 1898 was "a little war with big consequences."[14] Among these, the least considered and most actively minimized by what Gareth Stedman Jones once called "State Department" historiography is the longer, more costly, and more *consequential* imperial war to which "the war with Spain" ultimately led. The radical historian Howard Zinn had noted long ago "the odd imbalance of treatment in our usual history courses, where the war with Spain, a brief but victorious military romp—a splendid little war as some called it—is the central event in the foreign policy in that period and the taking of the Philippines a shadowy anti-climax."[15] As with the public monuments and their aporetic allegories, U.S. historical textbook wisdom awkwardly shoehorns and absorbs the eventual and indisputably more eventful war of conquest and resistance in the Philippines (1899-1910s) into the Spanish-American War of 1898. This categorical displacement of one war by another produces a number of effects and performs certain political functions that build upon one another in a tautological chain of causations.

What Zinn laments as an "odd imbalance" is no "accident," as the war with Spain and the Philippine conquest themselves would be predominantly construed in mainstream U.S. history-writing until recent times. This imbalancing is a continuously anxious exercise that actively plays curious tricks on the very stakes that drive the enterprise of writing history or memorializing it through other means: remembering and knowing.[16] In actively reproducing the Spanish-American War as a hegemonic category of historical analysis and public memory in narratives of U.S. empire- and nation-building, mainstream historiography shares with public war memorials the tendency to speak to two *imperialist* imperatives. One, to sustain the contemporary fiction of a "splendid little war" and to uphold the legitimacy of resulting U.S. territorial and sovereignty claims over what others have called its "inadvertent island empire," subsequent acts and genres of remembrance in the United States are held to the task of ceaselessly renewing the active contemporary dismissal of the Cuban and Filipino nationalist revolutions against Spain (climactically, 1895-1898, for Cubans; and 1896-1898, for Filipinos). Two, and relatedly, standard or official U.S. historical accounts and the conventional designation "Spanish-American War" are called upon to posit and insistently reproduce contemporary perceptions of this international crisis as solely a matter between two empires—one in its emergence (the United States), the other in its decline (Spain).

A "HIKER."

Fig. 3 The Hiker in graphic image, illustration that accompanied the "stories of Filipino warfare" published in the *Chicago Record, 1899-1900* (see note 5)

The odd chronological displacement of the Philippine-American War by the Spanish-American War in and through the memorial inscriptions on existing national monuments, therefore, does not really constitute much of a mystery or a puzzle. As Loewen himself unsurprisingly points out,

> The answer to this puzzle points to one of America's least happy foreign adventures—our war with the Philippines. Except for the curious dates on our Spanish-American war memorials, this war lies almost forgotten on our landscape. Hostilities began on February 4, 1899 and may be said to have ended by the early summer of 1902. Hence the "1898-1902."[17]

This temporal elision of the war in the Philippines is as chronotopic as it is symbolic. Indeed, as Loewen finds out, "Words that appear *on the wall behind* the Spanish-American War monument in Springfield" contain the only possible clues to the periodizing puzzle that is certain to confront anyone possessing some memory of the splendid little war and regarding such *monumental* displacements: "the Philippine Insurrection."[18] Loewen observes that the official and historical "terminology" to designate the bigger and unsplendid Philippine war as the "Philippine Insurrection" requires radical reconsideration, if not overhaul.[19]

1

To say that American memories of the Philippine-American War (and the U.S.

neocolonization of the Philippines that it entailed) have a vestigial and sedimentary quality about them is perhaps to reiterate a fact that is by now unsurprising. This is plainly indicated by what remains, and by what is artifactually documentary of that war's recurrently neglected events and episodes. These oddly situated and fragmented artifacts or vestiges point to the possibility that perhaps the Philippine-American War never truly ended. Hyperbolic as it may sound, a "war" over its actively repressed memory and legacies continued to be waged and rages—an "other war" whose desired stake is precisely to set the terms for their critical recuperation or continued containment in U.S. historical or popular consciousness.[20] Waiting to be re-read or re-framed, these partial artifacts and vestiges of the Philippine-American War testify to this war as a war made other by the U.S. war with Spain and to an even more other war as its continuing ramification in the present.

In this essay, I wish to suggest that in the first decade of the twentieth century itself, when the actual Philippine-American War just as precipitously ebbed in importance to the American public as it precipitately arose after the war with Spain, this other war was already being fought and staked out with perhaps more anxiety and determination on the continent than in the actual Philippine battlefields. The weapons with which this other war was waged had effects as lethal as those inflicted by the ordnance being deployed in the Philippines (the quick-loading Krag-Jorgensen, dum-dum bullets, naval cannonade, the so-called infernal machines)—and the metaphorical ammunition or troop supply for it was at least as inexhaustible *as* the body and military supplies for the actual war could become tenuously low or be cut off at any point.[21]

To appreciate the ultimately irrepressible significance of the Philippine-American War that might, in part, help to account for its active containment in official and popular memory and the cultural or historiographic skirmishes waged around it in the United States, one has only to consider its scope and scale in comparison to the Spanish-American War. For "an enterprise so modestly begun," the military historians David Kohler and James Wensyel note, the Philippine war eventually saw a total deployment of 126,000 American officers and men. "Four times as many soldiers served in this undeclared war in the Pacific as had been sent to the Caribbean during the Spanish-American War" and logged 2800 engagements. These U.S. Army historians cite a scrupulous and much-cited U.S. Army body count of 4234 killed and 2818 wounded on the American side by 1902, but do not note that no systematic information has yet been compiled for American casualties as the Philippine war decentralized and moved to regions in the South. As do other historians who are aware that statistics were deliberately not kept for Filipino casualties and losses, Kohler and Wensyel enumerate the conventionalized figures of 16,000 casualties for the Filipino army, from an estimated 1898 strength of 20,000 to 30,000—which apparently is by itself a case of undercounting—and civilian or noncombatant deaths of 200,000 "from famine, pestilence, or the unfortunate happenstance of being too close to the fighting." I have seen a more consensual figure of 250,000 Filipino deaths but those who cite it do not explain the basis for their common agreement. Indeed estimates have ranged from a low one hundred thousand to a high of one million, which at its worst would have meant the depopulation, by one-sixth, of the turn-of-the-century Philippines. No disputes arise over the total war cost to the U.S. Treasury of $600 million, and at least $8 billion more in veterans' pensions over the succeeding years.[22]

The Philippine-American War also bears sustained critical reconsideration for the acute ways it posed the history and the then-uncertain vectors of American national and imperialist expansionism. Perhaps no other war, except for the Civil War over a generation before it, and the Vietnam War six decades later, would divide the nation as widely and critically as that in the Philippines did. The most conspicuous expression of the radical national crisis that it provoked was the major constitutional debacle that the ensuing question of Philippine annexation inescapably heightened.

This constitutional crisis was quickly anticipated before the war and was given deadly precision by the war's extended duration and immediate political consequences. A dominant position taken in these sharply divided debates was most baldly exemplified by the imperialist senator Henry Cabot Lodge who thundered to a U.S. Senate in executive session debate over the Treaty of Paris on 24 January 1899 that "I believe that the power of the United States in *any territory or possession outside of the States themselves* is absolute." But Lodge was merely adumbrating similar positions in several debates that had commenced in Congress in late 1898 and were to be maintained in increasingly shrill tones by expansionist politicians and opinion leaders throughout the subsequent eruption and unfolding of the war with Filipinos.[23] Such debates were jumpstarted by a resolution filed by the Missouri senator George C. Vest in early December 1898 (in anticipation of the treaty then in negotiation) that the federal government was not empowered by the U.S. Constitution "to acquire *territory* to be held and government permanently as *colonies*."[24]

Specifically, these debates turned upon the novel constitutional implications of the prospective U.S. annexation of the "Philippine Islands." Philippine annexation, through a peace treaty with Spain, was feared or anticipated by concerned citizens, writers, and politicians to pose a major political crisis that could prove unexampled in the history of the nation and might result in the United States becoming a mere clone of European imperialist nation-states and their extensive colonial systems. The anxieties surrounding this constitutional crisis over "imperialism," brought to the surface by the envisioned new expansions beyond the nation's continental borders, were what other subsequently proposed congressional resolutions (such as Vest's) had sought to address, with mixed success and with results that to this day strike a few critical students as largely unresolved.[25] But with nothing less than the veracity and integrity of that founding document of the national polity, the U.S. Constitution, as the center of contention (and widely considered in jeopardy because of the possible extension of its sovereignty and reach beyond the nation's settled continental frontiers), Senator Lodge himself would backtrack a bit from his claim of "absolute power" over "outside possessions" and assert the Constitution's *selective* application or exception (at least, its "anti-slavery" clause) to these areas and their populations after eventual annexation.[26]

It is against the backdrop of these contemporary divisions, subdivisions, and quicksilver political realignments stemming from the prospects and duration of a Philippine-American War that one can speak of the contemporary existence and postcontemporary extensions of an "other (Philippine-American) war." Two important stakes must be marked here for this critical narrative of an other war to emerge. First, the constitutional crisis that shaped up and intensified also cleaved to an undeniable tenuousness of U.S. sovereignty claims over the Philippines from the perspective of international law, a crisis of legitimacy which the Treaty of Paris did not resolve and, in fact, clearly foregrounded.[27] Second, the unpreparedness of the U.S. Army and War Department in war footing itself became an issue, sharpened by the grim turns that the Philippine war was taking and would take within the two years after this war was repeatedly declared by campaigning U.S. generals to be a quick and easy one for the U.S. armed forces.[28] As army and war atrocities mounted and the increasingly genocidal tenor of the war became quickly evident, two problems became endemic: troop discipline breakdown and sagging national morale, especially as the Filipinos resorted to guerrilla warfare by November 1899, after losing in set piece and conventional battles in which they suffered from decisive disadvantages.

With mounting criticism of the war's conduct abroad and from a rising anti-imperialist or citizen opposition among important sectors of the American public and intelligentsia, patriotic appeals and appeals for fresh troops would be ceaselessly made by the McKinley government and imperialist writers. It is within this context that one can begin to reconsider the relentless efforts of U.S. authorities to dismiss the cause of the Filipino revolutionaries, Filipino appeals for U.S. withdrawal from the Philippines, neutrality or, at worst, limited protection from other powers interested in annexing the Philippines into their own dominions. It was in this context that American representations of Filipino "racial incapacity for representative government," "Filipino savagery," and "Aguinaldo's despotism" began to be massively produced, to escalate and intensify, to circulate widely, and to have decisive political effects both in the United States and in the realm of international relations.

In turning to the extensive archival trove that remains from this U.S. *cultural politics* (as an other war), one cannot but be struck by its aspect of massive proliferation and nearly obsessive self-reproduction in the continent during the period co-extending with the Philippine-American War of conquest and resistance. Taken together, the texts produced during this period represent a formidable cultural armory that elaborated a kind of imperialist violence and aggression distinct from, and yet related to, the savagery of the U.S. conduct of war in the islands. Scores of early motion pictures, thousands upon thousands of photographs, countless graphics or cartoons, reams of journalistic prose, tomes of instant ethnographies and colonial reports, and major world's fairs exhibits (1901-1909) subjected Filipinos and the Philippines to a process of *racialization* and *alteritism* that worked to extend the imperative of conquest and military victory into the arena of U.S. popular culture and cultural production.[29]

These forms of cultural production unquestionably belonged to the same order of conquest and imperialism as the very wars and the advocacy work directed by expansionist politicians and military men. But what accounted for their power was precisely their status as independent and highly contingent initiatives through which the U.S. culture industry could intervene in the larger debates over empire-building and national consolidation. Filmmakers, photographers, graphic artists, anthropologists, journalists, and other cultural producers wielded and borrowed from the language of turn-of-the-century visual culture and the technologies of mass media or communication to supplement and elaborate the work otherwise performed by a clunky war machinery that could not accomplish on its own the "pacification" of both an agitated American public and intransigent Filipino resistance.

This "other war" as cultural politics, or this culture war, revolved around a set of elusive but obsessive questions and came under the rubric of what was then called "The Philippine Question" or "The Philippine Problem." One question it foregrounded was that of American national identity or purpose in light of imperial expansion, which now needed to be clarified or elaborated precisely through interested advocacy and the test of public discourse, under challenge as it was by Filipinos and before the eyes of the world. Another involved the vaunted supremacy of American political culture (*civilization* and *self-government* were the contemporary keywords) which now needed to be ritualistically affirmed and against which Filipino *primitivism* (or as coded then, *native savagery* and *tribalism*, etc.) were ranged as its salient Other and contestant. But as I go on to argue below, this culture war also implied and inadvertently foregrounded a war with and within what was doubly posited as an American national "Self" and other-self.[30]

These contested concepts were far from empty or abstract and the war waged over them was far from contained within or limited to an airtight ensemble of U.S. referents and protagonists. Even if the referents were actively excised or not explicit, the concepts or constructs deployed had very *specific* targets against which the heft of the resulting cultural armory was precisely weighed. For example, *primitivism*, when deployed by these cultural texts was not simply a racial denigration of Filipinos but a reinflection of the recalcitrance or conduct of Filipino guerrilla activity as a mode of "uncivilized warfare." In this case, the *reference* or orientation of the political deployment of the concept testifies, implicitly, to an unmarked other: the undesirable persistence, for U.S. authorities, of Filipino guerrilla resistance itself.

Civilization and *self-government* were, to be sure, two of the most contested keywords with regard to the political aspirations of Filipinos during this period. A developmentalist language suffuses this other war's cultural archive, setting the terms for the wholesale denigration of Filipino desires for self-determination and independence on racialist and cultural-determinist grounds. It is a language that, as the critic Vicente Rafael has aptly described, "envisions an essential continuity between the individual's possession of its body—its ability to rein in its impulses and consolidate its boundaries— and a people's control over the workings and the borders of its body politic."[31] But again, while in this case it is a language raucously spoken in the United States in explicit reference to the "primitive" Aguinaldo's "tribal" peoples, the widespread use of this language could also be marking or referring implicitly to the crisis pervading that conjuncture in the history of U.S. nation-building as a result of imperialist expansion.

Selfhood or *self-government* here, I argue, would be syntactical encodings of a war or a struggle deep in the heart of a nation poised to see its borders break down as it expands imperially beyond the continent just as it still confronts the "other" problem of assimilating many racial or ethnic others into its body politic: emancipated blacks, assertive white women, vanishing Indians, and millions of Europe's "unwashed" non-Anglo immigrants.[32] In the end and in this light, imperialist expansion actually sharpened the problem of assimilating subjects and territories that are also being defined, by nature, to be racially or historically unassimilable (or only partly assimilable) into a nation whose borders are simultaneously expanding and requiring contraction. Because imperialist expansion dangerously distended the borders of the nation to include "other" territories and peoples, such borders themselves now needed to be secured or redrawn. It is this anxiety-ridden paradox that the other/culture war symptomatized as well as addressed. And if "war is politics by other means," and the politics at stake was national consolidation at the very moment of imperial expansion, then this other war actually faced the larger mandate of making imperial-national expansion (and consolidation) as much a micropolitics as a macropolitical one. These questions were to be as much an individual concern for the ordinary citizen as a common experience for the entire nation being reimagined—or whose borders needed to be redrawn—at the very cusp of empire-building "abroad."

Ultimately, an examination of the other war would enable us to think of "casualty figures" beyond actual body counts and the brute reality of war atrocities and violence. For this other war produced a form of violence very difficult to appreciate, even now with the hindsight afforded by the passage of a hundred years: precisely, it makes of the actual war an *other* itself. In so aestheticizing it (for to make something other is to reduce it to an aesthetic grid), the actual war is brought back to the continent but now shorn and cleansed of its mess, many costs, and savage malevolence. And a major "casualty figure" of this other war and war with the Filipino other, I argue, is the figure most directly tasked to prosecute it for the imperially expanding but paradoxically endangered nation (whose unconditional support he must now sustain, and whose "love" he must "win" or deserve): the American soldier.

2

In *Fallen Soldiers: Reshaping the Memory of the World Wars*, the historian George Mosse tracks the genesis, many lives, and rhetorical compulsions of a symbolic discourse emerging out of postrevolutionary and early nineteenth-century Europe and peaking during World War I (and it is a discourse equally true of the now-passing "American Century" and now extensive war résumé of the United States). Calling this symbolic discourse "The Myth of the War Experience," Mosse notes that it revolves around a figure who simultaneously or alternately elicits admiration and revulsion, respect and dishonor, veneration and abasement from the very imagined communities or entire nations he is imputed with the power to symbolize and represent. Mosse designates this pivotal figure and constitutive element of this myth and the modern war experience the "citizen-soldier," or the soldier as citizen.[33]

Developed in over two centuries by an array of influential (and some obscure) European statesmen, intellectuals and philosophers, poets and visual artists, and by countless soldiers and war veterans themselves, this myth linked the war experience as "organized mass death" to post-Enlightenment narratives of ethical formation; that is, it linked the fighting soldier or army to modern citizenship and the ideological and territorial imperatives of the imperial nation-state.[34] Post-revolutionary France and post-Napoleonic Germany, in appealing to, and compelling, male citizens to fight for no other motives than "freedom" and the "Fatherland," became (for Mosse) the inaugural and fertile grounds for the formation of this myth; that is, in fighting on behalf of beleaguered Germany or expansionist France, or yet again in the grisly trench warfare of the "Great War" much later, ordinary male citizens as brave and manly soldiers were also privileged as "representatives of the local or national community" and gained entry into these nations' pantheon of heroes.[35]

But this nationally "representative" charge of the soldier that evolves in the West is not as unproblematic or easily imputed as it sounds. To hold these fermenting developments in the historical understanding of the citizen-soldier (and his focal place in the libidinal economy of nationalism) together with an appreciation of the curious work performed by Loewen's American war memorials is to get a sense of a haunting paradox. Benedict Anderson has pointed to the special power that the "cenotaphs and tombs of Unknown Soldiers" possess, for example, and observes that their claim on people's attention is vertebrated with conflicting demands. They are able to solicit "public ceremonial reverence" only because they do not purport to identify or contain the actual remains of soldiers. Although *emptied* of empirical referents (they refer to every one and no particular soldier), these tombs are "nonetheless saturated with ghostly *national* imaginings."[36]

Gen. Douglas MacArthur's 1962 Address to the U.S. Military Academy, as Anderson quotes him, performs similar operations: in this famous speech, he conjures the American soldier in the paradoxical yet simultaneous terms of ethereal absence and corporeal presence. For MacArthur, "a million ghosts in olive drab, in brown khaki, in blue and grey, would rise from their white crosses, thundering those magic words: Duty, honour, country" if the soldier's sacrifices are not recognized by the American public. Claimed by the future as the herald of American ideals, he is also made to "belong" to the present, to the American people, and to the past or a long line of accomplishments by martial forebears. The uniform colors invoked in this speech symbolize the two world wars, the Spanish-American War, and the Civil War in a kind of temporal regress.[37]

We can actually track back, beyond MacArthur, to another hortatory speech made at Canton, Ohio against the backdrop of the extending period of the Philippine-American War in 1903 to get a better sense of the power and appeal evoked by these compulsive exhortations. Perhaps no one has more plainly made these double moves of celebrating the American soldier while reducing him to anonymity than then Secretary of War Elihu Root who intoned:

> When the war with Spain was over, the 250,000 men who had been raised for that war *disappeared as quietly* to their homes, never thinking for a moment of exercising the slightest influence upon the political life of the country. *That this is so unnoticed*, and causes so little surprise among our people, is the highest testimony to the abiding confidence of the people in the soldiers of the American army. They have their faults, but their faults are small and their virtues are great; and they are justly the pride of the American people from whom they come, and to whom, when their duty is done, they return.[38]

Root, in this speech, renders up the American soldier as a paradoxically self-limited and limiting figure. The citizen-soldier is subjected to the abstractive demands of nationalist symbolisms, and inadvertently exposed as vulnerable to disavowal by the very nation whence he springs and whose "love" he must elicit.

Appeals like MacArthur's and Root's perform this work by resituating the American soldier in a line of affinity and a range of relationships to underscore to whom he belongs and who belongs to him as the fulcrum of common national patriotism. The American soldier is made to constitute "a center of power that help[s to] define who are the outsiders and insiders in American culture" over the course of the generations.[39]

An element of transhistoricism thus subtends the relationship between the soldier and the nation. Root underscores this for the American soldier and his audience in an 1899 speech extolling the soldiers who were being sent to fight the war of conquest in the Philippines: "On every field from the day when along the stone walls that line the Cambridge road, the men of Concord and Acton each made his own disappearing gun carriage to the day when the flag floated over the citadel of Manila, the American soldier has answered loyally to every call of duty." Apart from situating the citizen-soldier within a valorized genealogy, Root's exhortation here is twofold: to the American people, in Root's concluding words, to "be faithful and fair to them [who] maintain the honor of the flag and the integrity of American sovereignty"; and to the male youth of the nation to renew the sacrifices of their predecessors that they may be so remembered in the present and the future.[40]

In what remains of this essay, I address these paradoxical images of the American soldier and the demands upon him to become *both* a victorious hero and a casualty *figure*, especially in relation to the Philippine-American War and his onerous task of consolidating imperial nationality and nationhood across temporal, spatial, and social barriers through his war work. Following Root and Mosse in a sense, I argue that more than the cenotaphs, tombs, and monuments themselves, it is really the *figure* of the American citizen-soldier that carries the charge of national symbolism and kinship. Memorialized by the monuments, the figure of the American soldier becomes the spirit of his people, but in ways that produce tenuous connections and contradictory effects. Anderson himself suggests that the monuments steep the soldier in anonymity and abstraction and inspire his eternal life and momentary deaths (and so do, equally, the hortatory speeches). As a specially burdened citizen, he risks potential neglect even as he also becomes the common sign in which an imperially expanding nation is exhorted to recognize itself. Here I wish to emphasize the constitutive weight and impossibility of the soldier's burden which, when coupled with the brute realities of war violence that he must face, must mean that his morale and resolve are ever fragile resources that require constant replenishment.

Indeed, "the theater of war," to borrow a fatally felicitous military phrase, involves more than playing the part of the unquestioning patriot. Every citizen *and* soldier must face the grim reality of violence and the imminence of death, grief, and loss that war occasions. How, then, can a nation (an imperial nation, in this case) create or sustain the force for its fighters and supporters to face such objectively daunting odds?[41] Such appeals as Root's or MacArthur's do not and cannot always suffice, especially when the war being fought is actually or potentially unjustifiable, and doubt and dissent arise from critical members of the imagined nation or from those who inhabit its margins and contest its claims.[42] It is in being mindful of the anxious lack or insufficiency of imperialist verbal and monumental exhortations that we turn to the other war and the ways in which its cultural work both extended and supplemented national empire-building, politics, and actual war work abroad.

3

In this final section, I wish to indicate something of the *political* work and aspirations of the many cultural texts that were deployed in the other war. If anything, these texts are shot through with vestigial casualty figures of the American soldier and of this other/culture war that was fought on the continent. Here I endeavor to expand the notion of the war monument, as Loewen and Anderson have used it, into a *complex* of representational genres and texts that would include contemporary U.S. mass communication and visual culture products.[43] In this case, I focus on early American cinema productions or "moving pictures," as they were called then at the very moment of film's inception as a form. At the heart of my remaining discussion is a close reading of a 16-mm film in three parts, titled *The American Soldier in Love and War* (hereafter cited as *ASLW*). Photographed by the filmmaker G. W. Bitzer on 9 July 1903, it was released for public exhibition by the American Mutoscope and Biograph Co. (AMB) in October 1903 and redistributed in 1905.[44]

Very little was known about *ASLW* when I began my own research on it and on other "Spanish-American War" films at the Library of Congress in the early 1990s. The film archivist Paul Spehr found it to be among the first "long entertainment" releases of the AMB, although perhaps it is more properly classified as a "story film"; that is, one that has a protonarrative structure before "narrative cinema" emerges with filmmakers like D. W. Griffith after 1907-1908. Film historian Charles Musser provided a generic one-paragraph discussion and reproduced some studio stills of the film in the first number of his multivolume work on early American cinema; but Musser's contextualization of this film in his chapter on the Spanish-American War and the birth of U.S. cinema predictably ignored the significance of the film's recovery as a *Spanish-American War* text and took that classification for granted, an historical elision about which I make a critical point below.[45]

Unsurprisingly, an earlier descriptive digest of the film by the famous archeologist of early American cinema Kemp Niver bore similarly indicative lacunae. While Niver renders the film's cinematic action in the deadpan and proximate ways that were true for the other films in the research guide that he compiled, some intriguing traces of the *trajectory* of Niver's heroic recovery project on the first-generation film prints—of which this particular early American film was a part—led me to an initial speculation that Niver misclassified the film and left out important details about its "story" and productive orientations.[46] Niver identifies the "Spanish-American War" as the unifying theme for the prints, a description that made me suspect that something was left out. He also presents them as a *separable* unit, hence, his serial numbering and the self-contained synopses he provides for each print. But from his three-part description alone, an organic conception of the film emerges, no matter how dimly.[47]

The American Soldier in Love and War, no. 1 [32 ft.]: A woman is sitting at a table with her head on her arms in a set of a living room. She moves when a man in military uniform comes into the room from behind a curtain. He walks towards her and begins to comfort her. The film ends as the man in military uniform is embracing the woman.

The American Soldier in Love and War, no. 2 [31 ft]: A painted backdrop depicts a jungle. From camera right, a man in the uniform of a Spanish-American War soldier enters. He acts as if he is wounded or exhausted and falls to the ground. Two actors, a man and woman dressed as natives, enter from camera left. The male native immediately sets upon the fallen American soldier and attempts to kill him. There is a scuffle. The woman begs for the life of the soldier as the film ends.

The American Soldier in Love and War, no. 3 [27 ft]: This was filmed from the point of view of a theater audience. The set and surroundings convey the impression of a jungle or a desert island, with heavy foliage and an ocean nearby. The only onstage piece of equipment is a doorway to a hut. A white man in an Army uniform with a large bandage around his head is sitting in front of the hut. Standing alongside, facing the camera, is an actor made up to resemble a large black woman. She is fanning the man with a palm fan. Another native is holding a bowl from which the wounded soldier is eating. The next action shows a man with a beard and pith helmet arriving accompanied by a white woman wearing a large picture hat. The woman rushes into the arms of the soldier. After much embracing, the soldier indicates that the black woman had saved his life, and the picture closes with the white woman removing her necklace and handing it to the other woman.

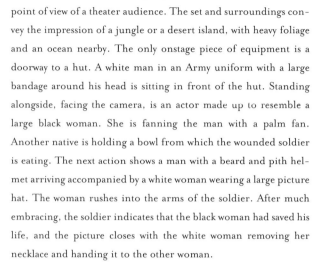

No. 2418 5.
Title The American
Soldier in Love and War
Length 55 ft.

On viewing the prints themselves, one discovers that they actually form a continuous "plot" or an organic series of actions that depict the American soldier's heroism and predicament. Elaborated in three shots and scenes, this film retains the same characters and sutures the themes of separation, conflict, reconciliation, and reunion that mark the hero's displacements. Indeed, the company that produced the film advertised and marketed it as one unit while indicating its tripartite design: in 1903, the year of its making and first release, and again in 1905, long after the war to which it specifically alludes was considered over[48].

2418 The American Soldier in Love and War [161 feet]

These three scenes are to be used in connection with two war views, to make a complete story in one film for projection. The first scene shows the young American officer parting with his sweetheart and starting for the Philippines. The second shows the regiment leaving its post to embark on the transport—then comes a fight in the brush, then the wounding of the young officer; his capture and rescue by a Filipino girl, and finally his meeting the sweetheart and her father in the Filipino hut, where he has been nursed back to life.

Significant textual riddles about the film would result if the 1903 description is contrasted with that of 1905, information from the company's surviving photo catalogs, and Niver's 1967/1985 digest.[49] What is vaguely described in the 1903/5 announcements as the departure of the soldier's regiment for the

Philippines (preceding the "scuffle with the male native" in the second scene) does not survive with the extant version and must now be considered lost. And while the 1905 blurb essentially retains the 1903 description, it drops the original specification of inserting "two" war views for the more general "war views": a cue to exhibitors to make variable kinds of inserts from already available and extensive newsreel footage on the Philippine- or the Spanish-American war.

Charles Musser identifies such "two war views" to be an actuality film of troops marching off to war at Governor's Island, "Fifteenth Infantry, USA" (the full title is actually "Fifteenth Infantry Off for Cuba"), and "Warfare Practice" which he calls "a realistically staged battle footage."[50] It is curious that Musser, usually a scrupulous researcher, should lop off that important part of the title for one insert, "... off for Cuba." Like Niver, Musser glosses over the specifically Philippine-American War reference or content of the film. This is evident in his unconsidered acceptance of the film's prior classification by Niver and others as a Spanish-American War text. But it is puzzling that Musser would also excise the reference to Cuba in the full title for the insert which would have made the misclassification consistent. I suggest that these are not incidental forms of omission or inconsistencies but a function of how American film and cultural historians, in their acts of mediating or relaying cultural texts of the "Spanish-American War," also fall prey to this term's tendency to make the Philippine-American War a shadowy other and minor historical episode: an effect completely at odds with the artifactual remains of the film in question, whether in the form of fragmentary prints or contemporary exhibition cues.

Even in its fragmentary state, this film recharges the American soldier with iconic powers in ways that recall, if exceed, Anderson's and Loewen's monuments.[51] The film functions as an allegory on the nobility of American national purpose against the "brutality" of Spanish oppression in Cuba and Filipino guerrilla resistance. Although the contextual referents here consist of the two *distinct* wars with Spain and the Filipinos, the suggested insertion of the "Fifteenth Infantry Off for Cuba" footage after the parting scene in *ASLW* No. 1 between the white soldier (who is specifically leaving for the Philippine war) and his "sweetheart" (who fears for his fate in such a far-away land), should signal their patent conflation in the spectator's gaze. Spain, itself a white nation, may have been imaged in contemporary cultural forms as a "brute" but only at the risk of effacing the intrication of the "brutality" of the primitive with race and color (as in the film's scuffle scene between the white hero and the "Filipino" in blackface, where race and color are

Fig. 4 G. W. Bitzer, *The American Soldier in Love and War* (scenes #2 and #3), 1903/1905. Stills from the Museum of Modern Art, New York. Against the painted backdrop of a tropical (Philippine) jungle, a mortally wounded American soldier finds himself in a brutal life-and-death struggle with his club-wielding Filipino "primitive"

coded as signs of the Filipino's primitive brutality).[52] If anything, this transposition of "primitive brutality" onto any Other only illustrates what Mariana Torgovnick has called the "generalized notion of the primitive" that subtends Western discourses of empire/nation-building and selfhood.[53]

Yet that Niver substituted the war with Spain for the film's Philippine context is

semantically strategic. It is a move guaranteed by the film's own incongruous representation of troops headed for Cuba as no different from those sent to fight the Filipino rebels. The meaning of nation as empire (and of the soldier as both its icon and envoy) was certainly pulled between the short and glorious war with Spain and the long and gruesome war against Filipinos that followed it. What should be denoted here is the difference between fighting a war of conquest against a struggling people and fighting a "war of liberation" for Cubans against oppressive Spanish colonists. The war in the Philippines would be rhetorically rendered with the same "nobility of purpose" as the war in Cuba, but this semantic extension became untenable as anti-imperialist critics and Filipino publicists emphasized the emergent contradiction in their critiques.[54]

Conflated or reckoned together, these two wars enfold between them the valor and villainy, celebration and neglect, symbolism and anonymity, that shape the soldier's half-life as a national emblem.[55] It is within the semantic field bordered by such *extreme* valuations of the work performed by the soldier that the film performs its own mediations. In plotting the American soldier's various dislocations and their meanings, the film distributes certain kinds of labor among the various characters even as it typifies their characteristics.

For example, the white soldier-hero is courageous and stoic and the white heroine is inconsolable in her grief during the parting in *ASLW* No. 1. The soldier's seriousness of purpose and his efforts to allay the heroine's fears are emphatically signified by the actor's dignified comportment. The many hugs and kisses, and the interminable good-bye exchanged between the lovers illustrate, through "acting by indication"—in the absence of sound, the convention of screen acting at the time[56]—these contrastive actions/reactions of the hero and the heroine. By sharper contrast, the Filipino male "primitive" is depicted as a treacherous brute and "the Filipino girl" comes off as a clear subordinate and his hesitant accomplice during his savage attack against the American soldier in *ASLW* No. 2. This idea of treachery is simultaneously inflected by a shadowy form of cowardice on the Filipino's part—a metaphorical reference to ideas in circulation in U.S. public discourse that Filipino guerrilla resistance was a mark, precisely, of uncivilized warfare and "cowardly" conduct—when he enters from camera-left in *stealth* after the soldier falls, wounded. Here the Filipino's simian features are suggested through makeup and his "black skin" is indicated by his "underclothes," as if to ensure that color was the most visible and phenotypical sign of Filipino primitivism.

The female primitive, "a large black woman" and thus hardly girlish in visage, hovers to the left as the soldier grapples with the club-wielding Filipino warrior. She is *flung* to a kneeling position beside the disabled hero to beg for his life after she grips the male primitive's stone club from behind, suggesting the primal and brute force of the Filipino—an allusion to and a rearticulation of the Pocahontas-Capt. John Smith "culture story," specially for the ways in which it could engender (in the multiple senses of the term) the Filipino-American colonial encounter.[57] That the "Native American" romance is retold at the same time as an "Africanized" post-Reconstruction scenario designates the "Filipino" as a foreign presence made familiar and a familiar image made alien in the complicated contexts of American colonial conquests and domestic racial crises. Strikingly, the intransigence of the Filipino as the new other abroad is here refigured into subordination while the subjugation of "the colored races at home" hints at and renews the idea of their racial intractability or unassimilability as emancipated or adopted citizens of the nation.

The opposition between the first two scenes and their characters in itself makes it plain who between the races at war possess the "civil" virtues and the "primitive" traits but also divides the labor in terms of gender between the men who do the fighting and the women who support, nurture, and grieve for them. *ASLW* No. 3 curiously presses the female primitive/s into the role of "slaves" of affection as well. In this scene we see the "Filipino girl" or Pocahontas who saved the soldier's life providing him relief from the tropical heat with a palm fan, off-center. On camera-right, another Filipino woman from nowhere is shown sitting by the soldier's side, nursing him back to vitality and feeding him from a bowl.

The most astonishing twist to this film, apart from the heroine violating the division between home and alien terrain (one would wish to know how and why she ended up in the jungle), is the entry of the heroine's father—"the man with a beard and a pith helmet"—into the scene of the action. This insertion of the father's presence signals another abstractive and distributive currency that the film energizes with regard to the soldier, war, and empire-/nation-building. In thus framing the costs and risks of war (*ASLW* No. 2) between personal sacrifice (*ASLW* No. 1) and familial support (*ASLW* No. 3), the film structures war and its relation to national purpose as at once a family affair and a personal romance, or indeed as a "dark" form of *family romance*. It not only cues people to translate the disruption, by colonial war, of their personal lives and loves (and their possible losses) into multiple investments; it also transvalues them as viable "individual" gains writ large as "national" goals. More significantly, in this case it asks viewers to imagine both an expanded and a sharply delimited structure of kinship, in which colonized Filipinos are imagined or represented as simultaneously assimilable and excludable, dependent upon the "place" within the familial/national structure that could be allowed them at all. Although seemingly a marginal figure, "the man with a beard and a pith helmet" is identified by the 1903 blurb for the film as the heroine's father, which makes him a different center for the hero's affective relations and now marginal others.

I suggest that the old man stands for the soldier's paternal double, the nation in its age and wisdom, the Father that rules, the empire-builder. He registers as a benign or "benevolent" presence in *ASLW* No. 3, and takes to the primitive woman on camera-left after his daughter gives her necklace to the other in gratitude. If he is the other half of the empire/nation for whom the soldier is a surrogate fighter, he also holds the power to recognize and embrace the hero as his son "in law" and to take the "colonizable" others into his fold where they take up specific roles. The daughter signals to the female primitive/s this adoptive gesture of the family/nation with the necklace with which, I argue, she also signifies and shares her own form of "bondage." In *ASLW* No. 3, we see a quick but almost imperceptible division of scenic space into *center* and *margin*: the white characters in the middle and the two female primitives on camera-right and -left. What fate awaits the male primitive who is *written out* of the picture at this juncture is implied as the female primitive is obviously and almost inexplicably split into two incarnations: one "dressed to resemble a large black woman" (from *ASLW* No. 2), which suggests a maternal role for her; another (who emerges out of the "Filipino hut" in *ASLW* No. 3) who looks young, comely, and servile. The containment or subjugation of the primitive is thus partly achieved by its projection to the plane of desire and the feminine, or indeed, of the other as desirably feminized/feminine.[58]

The borders of nation are henceforth redrawn in the paired structuring patterns of race and gender, but what one may call the "erotics of empire,"[59] in these respects, are played out by inadvertence. This is perhaps the highest level upon which the film performs its semantic labor but with risks for representations of the soldier as the fulcrum of national consensus and his relationship with kin as the core for empire and nation. If representing the war for nation as a personal romance and a family affair abstracts war of its grim underside of violence or death, it also poses the paradox of "love" for adopted others when colonizing them.[60] The primitive is not only a "real" Other but also a trait, a "primitive corporeal virility" that white men and soldiers in these moments of empire seek to recuperate for a nation that is imaged to have "overcivilized" itself.[61] Thus the scuffle scene, in which the white soldier grapples with the primitive, simultaneously reduces the latter into a measure of one's (and a nation's) progress and a sign of repressed or lost origins. This implies a conception of self, history, "assimilation" (now far from "benevolent"), and nation in which the masculine primitive is not only an exteriorized other but also an actively repressible instinct. Banished to the nether regions of personal and national subjectivity by the demanding process of "civilization" and *"self-government,"* the primitive is now to be sought in nether regions abroad where it presumably resides undisturbed.[62]

The crisis of a nation, uncertain over the integrity of its body politic at this time, is thereby allegorized through the crises of masculinity and civilization that are here acknowledged. This national crisis is occasioned by imperially expansionist love and war, where seeking and doing battle with one's "primitive" might offer the ritualistic revival of the ideal of self-government but also force one to confront its untold risks, costs, and deficits. *War* becomes the site in which to recover and test the limits of national vigor and manhood, and earn the love and recognition of nation, kin, and colonial subjects. But in encountering the primitive within and without the nation's borders, the soldier must also face the "transcendental homelessness" that the quest of "going primitive" entails.[63] The soldier is to be *separated* from loved ones to be eventually reunited/reconciled with them even as this happy pattern might be revised by injury, death, and war's contingencies. Dead or surviving, the American soldier must inevitably witness the various doubles and settings for his quest falling away to make him stand in anonymity and solitude as the nation incarnate in graphic images and monuments. Abstracted as such, he is to "expatiate" [ex- out; *spatiari*, walk, roam; enlarge] the borders of empire and nation even as he is perpetually expatriated, either to be claimed or disowned, recognized or neglected.

CODA

The Philippine (American) war soldier as Hiker appears in monumental and graphic image as a solitary figure, his rifle slung over a shoulder or embraced in one arm, as if it were both a burden needing to be borne and a weapon of conquest requiring secure possession. Rife with allegorical resonance, this image of the soldier was a much contested iconic staple of the Philippine-American (culture) war on the continent. Imperialist politicians and cultural producers would repeatedly invoke the cant of "bearing the white man's burden" in arguing for Philippine conquest and annexation; but the burden of the citizen-soldier in turning ideological cant into bloody reality was simply unredeemable. The Hiker's gun, at ready, symbolized his presumptive readiness to kill or be killed by the other, in the process and in the name of conducting the nation's imperial errands abroad. And "killed a million" the Hikers did.[64] But while we know that only several thousands of them were killed in a war whose memory remains partial and actively suppressed, an other war nonetheless litters the national memorial and cultural landscapes with these soldiers' uncountable casualty figures and their artifactual *remains*.

NOTES:

Research for this essay, and for the larger project from which it is excised, was enabled by generous support from the Smithsonian Institution. For their precious counsel as my Smithsonian fellowship advisers, I am deeply grateful to Gary Kulik and Charles McGovern; for their keen commentaries on a roughly expanded presentation of this essay, my thanks also go to the members of the Tuesday Colloquium of the National Museum of American History during my fellowship year. Thanks to Jim Roane of the N.M.A.H. Library Branch and Paul Spehr of the Library of Congress, for their research assistance; and to Rey Ileto, Wigan Salazar, Eric Reyes, and Jody Blanco for their comments.

1. In the parodic words of the diplomatic historian Thomas Bailey, "Dewey staged [the] memorable coming out party [of U.S. imperialism] at Manila Bay on May Day [1898]." In a comprehensive critique of the voluminous U.S. 1898 war historiography produced over the past century, the historian Louis Pérez Jr. sardonically notes that it is otherwise "a wholly fortuitous event," the sinking of the U.S. battleship Maine in Havana harbor in February 1898, "to which is attributed the cause of a war that altered the course of U.S. history." Bailey, "America's Emergence as World Power: the Myth and the Verity," in Alexander DeConde and Armin Rappaport, eds., *Essays Diplomatic and Undiplomatic of Thomas A. Bailey* (New York: Appleton-Century-Crofts, 1969), 8; Pérez, *The War of 1898: The United States and Cuba in History and Historiography* (Chapel Hill, N.C.: University of North Carolina Press, 1998), 59.

2. "The Hiker" monument erected in Pawtucket, R.I., "To Perpetuate the Memory of All Who with Unfailing Loyalty Defended on Land and Sea the Nation's Honor in the War with Spain,

Phillipine [sic] Insurrection and China Relief Expedition [1898-1902]." In Rhode Island, where research for this essay first began, several Hikers were mounted at various times and in strategically central sites of cities and towns. For example, one was erected in "The City of Woonsocket to Her Sons Who on Land and Sea Defended the Nation's Honor in the War with Spain and the Philippine Insurrection, 1898-1902." Yet another Hiker, bluish from exposure to the elements and bird shit, also stands rarely appreciated at the Kennedy Square in the capital city of Providence. I am grateful to the self-admitted history hobbyist Mr. Peter Foulkes for first alerting me to the existence of these monuments while we were researching together in the early 1990s at the American Antiquarian Society in Worcester, Massachusetts. Mr. Foulkes then believed that many such monuments might have been erected in many small American towns, probably from the same foundry cast that he speculated was made by some commissioned sculptor/artist for a New York foundry, "[sic] Williams, Inc." in 1904 or even earlier. A Woonsocket Hiker photodocument provided this author by Mr. Foulkes bears that foundry's stamp and this inscription: "The Hiker, copyrighted by Allen G. Newman, Sc. 1904." This cast was apparently being used as late as 1922 to make more copies. Another photodocument of the Pawtucket R.I. Hiker supplied by Mr. Foulkes bears this date of installation and also confirms Newman's identity as one possible sculptor in an inscription on the left side of the statue's base.

3. Loewen, "Springfield: A Lost Memory that Might Have Prevented a War," mss. It has recently been published as a chapter in Loewen, *Lies Across America: What Our History Sites Get Wrong* (New York: New Press, 1999), 136-144. I had no access to the published version by the final rewriting of my essay, but I am grateful to Professor Loewen for the authorization to cite from the manuscript that he sent me when we first exchanged rough drafts in 1997 and for the updated bibliographic information on his work. Personal communication, 14 July 1999.

4. A legible variation of this standard presentation is an actual, although miniaturized, Maltese cross mounted in front of the base of the Woonsocket, R.I. Hiker in addition to the usual plaque (see Figure 2). Two circles are actually etched within and at the center of the cross, whose top arm bears "U.S.A." and bottom arm bears "Cuba" in large caps while "Philippine Islands" and "Porto Rico," respectively, are borne on the right and left arms in smaller caps. At the center of the inset circle is the word "UNITED" framed by "ARMY" at the top and "NAVY" at the bottom. Within the circumference formed by the inner and outer circles is the inscription "SPANISH WAR VETERANS 1898-1902." Encoded in this artifact is an emergent narrative of imperial U.S. nation-building after 1898, an allegory that would seem to be too obvious to admit of extended exegesis here but whose constitutive elements should at least be sketched. The privileged placement of the U.S. as the nation invested with the task of uniting or encompassing the various major sites of its territorial expansion is only counterpointed by the strategic placement of Cuba as the centrally symbolic space of that expansion's vaunted aims of liberation and benevolence for others groaning under the weight of old world Spanish imperialist oppression. The U.S. Army and Navy are cast as the twin instrumentalities for the work of making this expanded Union a simultaneously imaginable and accomplished end. The displacements of the "Philippine Islands" and "Porto Rico" to the framing margins of this new Union signal their actual and subsequent colonizations as extraneous to the typicality of U.S. rescue and liberative work in Cuba which, through the Platt Amendment, was presumably made a nominally independent nation after North America's "Spanish War" and interventions there (cf. the rhetorical formulation [North America's] "Vietnam War," which has the same effect of writing out Vietnamese national self-determination several decades later like the American excision here of any memory of the Cuban Revolution after 1898). Loewen notes a similarly incipient imperial allegory in the inscription for the Dover, N.H. Hiker which narrates that Americans fought "*to succor the weak and oppressed against foreign tyranny and to give Cuba and the Philippines a place among the free peoples of the earth*" (quote in italics is the exact

phraseology on the monument). Although it is debatable if the Spanish-American War in Cuba began "with a tinge of anti-imperialist sentiment" and made Cubans truly "free," Loewen quite acutely notes that in the Philippine-American War, the U.S. was indisputably *"the foreign tyranny"* (emphasis supplied). Loewen, "Springfield" mss.

5. "The Hiker," illustration from John McCutcheon, *The Chicago Record's Stories of Filipino Warfare* (Reprinted from the *Chicago Record*, 1900)—a copy of this rare compilation of Philippine-American War correspondence is in the Edward Everett Ayer Collection at the Newberry Library in Chicago. I am grateful to the archivists John Aubrey and Michael Kaplan for their research assistance during my tenure there as a Library fellow.

6. For a typical and vivid example of contemporary usage, see the 21 November 1900 letter of the soldier Peter Lewis to his brother Alexander Lewis, published in H. R. Kells, comp., *Foot Soldier in an Occupation Force: Letters of Peter Lewis, 1898-1902* (Manila: Linguistics Office, De La Salle University, 1999), 89-90. Referring to a typical campaign, he writes in his unedited English: "We had a pretty hard time of it on that 'hike' most of the time we were up to our waists in mud you see we had to go through Rice fields, the Rice fields are always soft the Rice grows in mud and water, and we had to plow through them, as it happened we did not come across any amount of Insurgents, but I held a Filipino up and took his Bolo away from him, I have the Bolo now, the Bolo is a heavy knife that is most used by the Filipinoes, they use it to cut Bamboo with. We started out on that 'hike' we got orders to take away all arms and Boloes that we find on Natives, so I captured this one."

7. Draft update in Loewen, personal communication, 14 July 1899. This reference in the update is footnoted, according to Loewen, in *Lies Across America*, 465. Results from Loewen's further research also indicate that at least fifty Hikers dot the national memorial landscape, installed in various sites through the advocacy work of the National Association of Spanish War Veterans. One sculptor, Theodora Ruggles Kitson, is determined to be responsible for slightly over a half of these monuments with the rest by other sculptors including, presumably, Newman for the Rhode Island ones. Loewen cautions however that this is a rough, not a definitive, count.

8. Hay, "the last to congratulate" Roosevelt on "the brilliant campaign" (a specific reference to Roosevelt's celebrated heroics and antics in the Battle of San Juan), shared his hopes that the war was "now to be concluded with that fine good nature which is, after all, the fine distinguishing trait of the American character. That a war should take place anywhere and they not profit by it." Letterbook (no. 1), John Hay Papers, John Hay Library, Brown University, Providence, R.I.

9. Pérez, "The Meaning of the Maine: Causation and the Historiography of the Spanish-American War," *Pacific Historical Review* 58 (August 1989), 292-322; slightly revised and recently republished as Chapter 3 of Pérez, *The War of 1898*, 57-80. Relatedly, Amy Kaplan offers an exhaustive reading of Roosevelt's and other spectacularized accounts of the Battle of San Juan as accounts that rewrite the otherwise "parodic" aspects of this battle through strategies of "belittlement" directed at its "others." In her account, masculinist and racialized representations of the battle actually stage a tableau of imperial-national hierarchization that erases the heroism of participating African American ("colored") troops and repositions the black population within the national body politic while placing Cubans (and Filipinos) in the realm of the "unassimilable" and beyond the pale of representative (or self-government). See "Black and Blue on San Juan Hill," in Amy Kaplan and Donald Pease, eds. *Cultures of United States Imperialism* (Durham, N.C.: Duke University Press, 1993), 219-236.

10. *"Benevolent Assimilation:" The American Conquest of the Philippines, 1899-1903* (New Haven, Conn.: Yale University Press, 1982), 12.

11. *The General: Robert L. Bullard and Officership in the United States Army, 1881-1918* (Westport, Conn.: Greenwood Press, 1975), 91. In the same account where he had little trouble accepting the conceit of

a splendid little war, H. Wayne Morgan himself figured as one of the earliest and few modern American historians to concede the fact of "the questionable ability of the American army to enforce [American] demands" and resulting territorial or war claims. *McKinley and His America* (Syracuse: Syracuse University Press, 1963), 397.

12. The figure of "less than 80,000" is estimated by the military historians David R. Kohler and James Wensyel in their equally candid account, "Our First Southeast Asian War," *American History Illustrated* (January/February 1990), 21. Millett, *The General*, 112, specifies an "authorized wartime strength" of 65,000 by 1898 for the regular army, a figure from which the Senate would not budge, even by the time more troops were required and projected for the "Philippine Insurrection." More, the final draft of the Army Reorganization Act of 1899, according to Millett, mandated a review by 1901 "for possible reduction" of that force, and the War Department was only authorized to raise another 35,000 volunteers for a separate 100,000-man force projected to complete the subsequent Philippine conquest and occupation.

13. How the U.S. war machinery could not match the heightening jingoistic bluster of imperialist rhetoric (during and immediately after the Spanish-American War) and was not in shape to enforce eventual U.S. jurisdictional claims over the "new possessions" was evidenced in the fact that the initial priorities of U.S. military planners were largely "defensive." On the fear that the Spanish Navy would "panic the American public or upset the American naval effort" by laying siege to Atlantic Seaboard harbor facilities, the War Department spent much of its share of the March 1898 $50 million war appropriation by Congress on coastal defense. The disorganization of the War Department and the army, inversely equalled by their clunky bureaucratic procedures, along with the twin strategy described above (Millett calls this a "manpower policy compromise" between the War Department and congressional opponents concerned to preserve the state identities of the regiments to be raised) entailed a "major cost." Although 20 percent of career army officers were already assigned to state regiments to aid in the efficient mustering and preparation of troops, the deluge of 250,000 State volunteers who responded to McKinley's call for war service simply strained the regular army's troop supply and preparation system to the breaking point and resulted in chaotic and badly supplied training camp conditions. Consequently, as Stuart Creighton Miller notes, "tropical diseases struck down many more Americans than did Spanish bullets." Millett qualifies that, in fact, there were "more dead Americans *at home* than Spanish bullets and tropical diseases killed *outside* the United States" (emphasis supplied). The account here is drawn entirely from Millett, *The General*, 91–93; see also Miller, *"Benevolent Assimilation,"* 12. Graham A. Cosmas, *An Army for Empire: The United States Army and the Spanish-American War* (College Station: Texas A & M University Press, 1998 [1971]) is a sedate and classic account of the "modernization" and professionalization of the army as having its beginnings in late-nineteenth century internal-institutional reform but is unable to revise the picture that such changes did not come decisively until after the debacle of 1898 and precisely during and after the even more exacting war in the Philippines.

14. Van Alstyne, *The Rising American Empire* (New York: Oxford University Press, 1960), 165. One big consequence of this war for U.S. nationalist and establishment historians was that it delivered to the United States what Paris Treaty chief U.S. negotiator William Day euphorically called "a goodly estate indeed." Through the much-contested 1898 Treaty of Paris with Spain (the negotiations for which actively excluded and refused to recognize the rights of belligerency of both Cuban and Filipino revolutionists), the United States would lay claim to the last remnants of the Spanish Empire as its "new possessions." The Philippines, Cuba, Puerto Rico, and Guam would be militarily occupied for varying periods and assigned variable forms of neocolonial status within a now imperially expanded "union" or nation. And relying on the flurry of the expansionist zeitgeist in July 1898 and the political momentum

unleashed by postwar public euphoria, the United States furtively took Hawai'i. McKinley quickly signed the resolution for its annexation, capping nearly a decade of national hesitance on the continent and earnest lobbying by American settlers in the islands toward that end (since the illegal 1893 coup against Queen Lilieukalani's government by renegade U.S. planter interests and consular/missionary/settler elements). Loewen clarifies that we have yet to account for the incorporation, after the Paris treaty, of former Spanish colonies in Africa such as Rio de Oro (Western Sahara), Spanish Guinea, and about three other small territories outside of Africa. Personal communication, 14 July 1999.

15. Introduction to Daniel Boone Schirmer, *Republic or Empire: American Resistance to the Philippine War* (Cambridge: Shenkman Publishing, 1972), vii. Gareth Stedman Jones, "The Specificity of U.S. Imperialism," *New Left Review* 60 (March-April 1970), 61. Stedman Jones's parodic label is an oblique reference to the inordinate influence of George Kennan's realist school on U.S. "international relations" historiography, an influence most directly embodied in the long-standing predominance of Kennan's *American Diplomacy, 1900-1950* (Chicago: University of Chicago Press, 1951) and Kennan's own association with the U.S. State Department.

16. By "knowing," in particular, I mean to highlight here the highly mediated and politicized forms of U.S. knowledge production on the Philippines and the history of U.S. involvements there. For example, a famous journalist—whose problematic historical account of Philippine-American colonial relations was released and won the Pulitzer Prize after the People Power Revolution of 1986 that overthrew Marcos sparked renewed U.S. public interest in that part of the globe—has had to admit: "Most Americans may have forgotten, perhaps never even knew, that the Philippines had been a U.S. possession." Stanley Karnow, *In Our Image: America's Empire in the Philippines* (New York: Random House, 1989), 3. For excellent critiques of this book and its reproduction of a similarly configured and anxiety-ridden body of U.S. specialist scholarship on the Philippines, see Michael Salman, "In Our Orientalist Imagination: Historiography and the Culture of Colonialism in the United States," *Radical History Review* 50 (Spring 1991), 221-232; and Reynaldo Ileto, *Knowing America's Colony: A Hundred Years from the Philippine War* (Manoa: Center for Philippine Studies Occasional Papers Series no. 13, 1999 [1997 John A. Burns Lectures]), 41-65.

17. "Springfield: A Lost Memory," mss. For the duration of the war beyond the termination date of 4 July 1902 declared by President Theodore Roosevelt which many historians take uncritically as valid, a careful reading of Russell Roth's *Muddy Glory: America's Indian War in the Philippines, 1899-1935* (West Hanover, Mass.: Christopher Publishing, 1981) is extremely suggestive. It is impossible to regard the subsequent wars against the "Moros," *ladrones, tulisanes* and new *katipunans* as well as the coalitional or antagonistic politics that unfolded with colonial or recalcitrant native "parliamentarians" as separate from the so-called "pacification" effort. See also Reynaldo Ileto, *Pasyon and Revolution, 1840-1910* (Quezon City, Philippines: Ateneo de Manila University Press, 1979); Ileto, "Orators in the Crowd: Independence Politics, 1910-1914," in Peter Stanley, ed. *Reappraising an Empire: New Perspectives on Philippine-American History* (Cambridge: Harvard University Press, 1984), 85-114; and Jim Zwick, "The Anti-Imperialist League and the Origins of Filipino-American Oppositional Solidarity," *Amerasia Journal* Centennial Commemorative Issue, Part 1 24:2 (1998), 65-85.

18. By "chronotopic," I mean that the temporal and spatial displacements of the Philippine-American War fuse to induce highly selective and artifactually misleading forms of remembering both the time and the place of, and those who fought during, this other war; or better yet: the temporal displacement takes a spatial form while the spatial expression itself displaces the markers of temporality or chronology.

19. In an act of recognition as rare as it is bound to be hotly disputed by other American scholars, Loewen asserts: "This term suggests that the United States held legitimate power in the Philippines, against which some Filipinos rebelled. Nothing of the sort took place. The Filipino independence

movement was exercising control over most of the nation, except Manila, when the United States attacked. This was a war, not an insurrection by a subordinate faction..." Loewen, "Springfield: A Lost Memory," mss. Among the earliest in the Vietnam War-era critical historiography to make and elaborate a similar point is Luzviminda Francisco, "The First Vietnam: The U.S.-Philippines War of 1899," *Bulletin of Concerned Asian Scholars* 5 (1973), 2-16, see n1. This categorical displacement has practical consequences for serious research (as I myself can attest to in my own). Loewen observes that the army's Web site includes the Spanish-American War and pointedly excludes the Philippine War in its list of "major wars." Yet "it lists eleven different campaigns under "Philippine Insurrection, [and] only three under Spanish-American War." Loewen, "Springfield: A Lost Memory," mss. The Library of Congress classification of the "Philippine Insurrection," which has played tricks on beginning researchers, has recently been changed to "Philippine-American War," on similarly reasoned argument and advocacy of concerned scholars and Filipino American community groups. We do not know what this transformation portends or promises in terms of stimulating and sustaining research on the war in the Philippines but it is now a much welcomed step.

20. One thinks here of recent resurgences, centering on the very monuments or popular icons memorializing the "Spanish-American War" such as the Balangiga Bells controversy or the Dewey Memorial in Union Square in San Francisco. With the Dewey Memorial controversy in 1997, the 90-foot-tall granite column "honoring the victor of the Battle of Manila Bay in 1898" struck protesting Bay Area Filipino American community groups as celebrating a battle "that set the stage for a United States occupation of the Philippine Islands and a war of resistance" barely remembered in popular or textbook knowledge. With sympathizers, they asked for a plaque at the base of the Memorial to put into historical perspective the popularly unacknowledged implications of the Battle of Manila Bay and to provide a more candid appraisal of Philippine-American relations. "What's missing is the aftermath: Filipinos rejected their transfer from one colonial power, Spain, to another. Battles broke out, and Dewey's ships soon were lobbing shells into Filipino-dug trenches." Loewen documents a similar controversy involving Filipino American community advocacy for a similar plaque for a monument in Minnesota, a plaque which community cultural activists and their sympathizers took upon themselves to install, pending negotiations about long-term revision of the existing inscriptions. John King, "Filipinos Want Full Story Told on Dewey Memorial," *San Francisco Chronicle*, 31 March 1997, A13-A14. Loewen, draft update, 14 July 1999.

21. Within four months of the outbreak of the war with the Filipino army in February 1899, the U.S. already confronted a shortage of troops as it became evident that the war would be longer and far more drawn out than the confident predictions of a speedy end to the "insurrection" made by Maj. Gen. Elwell Otis. Stuart C. Miller and a few other historians note that 50 percent of the 30,000-strong invasion and occupation troops sent to the Philippines were state volunteers whose terms were ending that summer after the formal exchange of treaties between Spain and the United States on 11 April 1899 determined their discharge and repatriation within six months of that date. Miller notes that some state governors were already demanding the return of their state volunteer regiments, and agitation for their return from parents and in public meetings was swirling in such states as Minnesota, Oregon, Washington, Tennessee, Nebraska, and South Dakota. One outspoken Populist governor, according to Miller, "warned McKinley that keeping the volunteers any longer would be as 'unconstitutional as the war itself.'" Indeed, Miller further notes, only an estimated 7 to 10 percent of the Philippine war volunteers decided to reenlist, on $500-bonus inducements. Miller, *Benevolent Assimilation*, 78-80.

22. Kohler and Wensyel, "Our First Southeast Asian War," 20. I am indebted to Jim Zwick for the important qualification on uncounted casualties for the war as it extended to other Philippine regions and as continued but now highly localized Filipino guerrilla resistance began to be officially reported by

the U.S. military and civil government records as "banditry" or "brigandage" by or after 1901. For a contemporary accounting based on a study of government records, that produces the figure of $600 million war cost (a figure that dwarfs the Spanish-American War initial appropriation of $50 million), see Edward Atkinson, *The Cost of War and Warfare from 1898 to 1902* (Brookline, Mass.: n.p., 1902).

23. *Congressional Record* (55th Congress, 3rd session), 958.

24. *Congressional Record* (55th Congress, 3rd session), 20; emphasis supplied.

25. We are only beginning to understand how the interventions and adjudication of the U.S. Supreme Court in these debates through the so-called "Insular Cases" worked to create several "resolutions:" a) they mollified these widespread public anxieties and enabled the legal expressions of American neo-imperialism; b) they produced the anomalous forms of simultaneous annexations and disincorporations of the Philippines and Puerto Rico as "territories" and their people as differentially located "subjects" of the Union; c) and they continued containing, through 1922, the many ramifications of the rulings themselves in terms of the "constitutional" exercise of U.S. global power and the question of citizenship and naturalization concerning the inhabitants of domains imperialized by that power. See the excellent and exhaustive studies of the Puerto Rican legal scholars Efren Rivera Ramos and Edilberto Roman. Ramos, "The Legal Construction of American Colonialism: The Insular Cases (1901-1922)," *Revista Juridica* (Universidad de Puerto Rico Law School Journal) 65: 2, 225-328; Roman, "The Alien-Citizen Paradox and Other Consequences of U.S. Colonialism," *Florida State University Law Review* 26 (Fall 1998), 1-47. I am grateful to Professors Ramos, Roman, and Leti Volpp for our exchanges on these questions.

26. Only "the limitation placed upon such *outside* possessions by the thirteenth amendment" posed the "single exception" to this absolute power, the senator qualified. Lodge here specifically referred to Section 1 of Article XIII of the U.S. Constitution which formally codified the abolition of slavery on 18 December 1865 and provided that "Neither slavery nor involuntary servitude, except as a punishment for crime whereof the party shall have been duly convicted, shall exist within the United States, *or any place subject to their jurisdiction*" (emphasis supplied). Senator Vest's assertion that no sanction could be had from its Constitution for the U.S. "to acquire *territory* to be held and government permanently as *colonies*" was one that was increasingly being made at this critical juncture by a heterogeneity of voices, groups, and interests loosely ranged under an "anti-imperialist" position and by a vocal and recently established Anti-Imperialist League.

27. (The treaty's ratification by the Senate in February 1899 by a close margin of one vote was notably timed with the outbreak of the Philippine-American War.) In the apt words of the "anti-imperialist" Stanford University President David Starr Jordan: "Even the most headlong of our people admit that we stand in the presence of a real crisis, while, so far as we can see, there is no hand at the helm....By the fortunes of war the capital of the Philippine Islands fell, last May, into the hands of our navy. The city of Manila we have held, and by dint of bulldog diplomacy, our final treaty of peace has assigned to us the four hundred or fourteen hundred islands of the whole archipelago. To these we have as yet no real title. We can get none till the actual owners have been consulted. We have a legal title, of course, but no moral title and no actual possession. We have only purchased Spain's quit claim deed to property she could not hold, and which she cannot transfer." "The Question of the Philippines" [Address Delivered before the Graduate Club of Leland Stanford Junior University, 14 February 1899] (Palo Alto, Ca.: J. J. Valentine, 1899), 5.

28. Unchecked U.S. army atrocities and the scorched-earth tactics adopted by certain generals against Filipinos—combatants and noncombatant alike—would result in military press censorship and embarassing congressional hearings (in which the errant officers were given a slap on the wrists) by 1902. The selection of testimonies before Sen. Henry Cabot Lodge's Senate Committee on the

Philippines in Henry Graff, ed., *American Imperialism and the Philippine Insurrection* (Boston: Little, Brown and Co., 1969) is a good place for any beginning researcher to start.

29. A critical study of Filipino "racialization" during this period that promises to qualify a great deal of the largely dissatisfying studies that exist is Nerissa Balce-Cortes's Ph.D. dissertation-in-progress, "Disciplining the Natives: Imperialism, Culture and Representations of the 'Filipino' After 1898," Ethnic Studies, University of California, Berkeley. "Alteritism" is a neologism invented by the literary critic Sara Suleri-Goodyear to refer to the obsessive and limiting binarist logic of selfhood and otherness that substructures both the constitution of imperial will/discourse and the colonial studies that fixate upon it as the object of critique. See *The Rhetoric of English India* (Chicago: University of Chicago Press, 1992), especially 1.

30. "Otherness" or alterity is a concept no longer in need of theoretical exposition here, given its now commonplace character in cultural critique, although a provocative deconstruction of its highly problematic deployments in colonial studies is found in Suleri, *The Rhetoric of English India*; it is a still useful critical conception that I hope to demonstrate operationally in the analysis that follows.

31. Vicente Rafael, "White Love: Discipline and Surveillance in the United States Colonization of the Philippines" (paper read at the Dartmouth Conference on the *Cultures of U.S. Imperialism*, Dartmouth College, NH, 22-24 November 1991), 5; it is significantly revised and now published as "White Love: Surveillance and Nationalist Resistance in the U.S. Colonization of the Philippines" in Kaplan and Pease, eds., *Cultures of U.S. Imperialism*, 185-218.

32. A tandem reading of the following groundbreaking accounts of this conjunction between nation-building and imperial expansion at this time can indicate something of the intractable anxieties in the general culture over the possible disintegration of U.S. national identity, as it had been constituted up to that point, by the (im)possible inclusion or assimilation of alien others and non-Anglos: Matthew Jacobson, *Special Sorrows: The Diasporic Imagination of Irish, Polish, and Jewish Immigrants in the United States* (Cambridge: Harvard University Press, 1995), especially Chs. 4 and 5; Gail Bederman, *Manliness and Civilization: A Cultural History of Gender and Race in the United States, 1880-1917* (Chicago: University of Chicago Press, 1995), 77-215; Louise Newman, *White Women's Rights: The Racial Origins of Feminism in the United States* (New York: Oxford University Press, 1999), 3-85, 116-131; and Kristin Hoganson, *Fighting For American Manhood: How Gender Politics Provoked the Spanish-American and Philippine-American Wars* (New Haven, Conn.: Yale University Press, 1998), 107-199.

33. Mosse, *Fallen Soldiers: Reshaping the Memory of the World Wars* (New York: Oxford University Press, 1990), 19. I was encouraged to reflect upon the recency of the allegorical relationship between nation and citizen-soldier in the context of generating commentary for a conference panel, "Contested Bodies and Battlegrounds: Fighting over American Manhood in Europe, Haiti, and the Philippines." The panel was organized by Kristin Hoganson for the 1997 American Studies Association Annual Meeting and chaired by Robert Rydell.

34. Ibid., 3. Mosse notes that with the French Revolution and the German Wars of Liberation, soldiers in Europe acquired a *respectability* that military service in the name of King or God could not accord their predecessors. (If anything, Christic or chivalric iconography of courage, self-sacrifice, and redemption was itself absorbed into and redeployed in this new valorization of the soldier as citizen.)

35. Ibid., 19 and 22.

36. *Imagined Communities: Reflections on the Origin and Spread of Nationalism* (London & New York: Verso, 1983), 17.

37. Ibid., n2.

38. Root, *The Military and Colonial Policy of the United States* (Cambridge: Harvard University Press, 1916), 18-19.

39. Edward T. Linenthal, *Sacred Ground: Americans and Their Battlegrounds* (Urbana: University of Illinois Press, 1993), 216.

40. Root, *Military and Colonial Policy* , 13. Anderson prefers to call this "transhistoricism" to nationalist narrative "intrahistorical," concerned as he is to mark where religion and nationalism actually part in their rhetorical or hortatory labor (when they are not otherwise conjoined or homologous in their claims); that is, although nationalist appeals around the American soldier in this case are saturated with Christic (McArthur's "white crosses") or religious tropes—or as Linenthal would put it, "acts of folk-reverence" that are demanded of the American people for their soldiers as "sainted heroes"—it remains the case that the best that the citizen-soldier can hope for is a niche six feet deep (perhaps, even an unmarked grave) and he is not guaranteed a place in heaven as religion's divinely mandated warriors would be: the citizen-soldier becomes a casualty figure, as it were, of the nation's secularism and modernity. See Anderson, "The Goodness of Nations," in *Spectre of Comparisons: Nationalism, Southeast Asia and the World* (London: Verso Press, 1998), 360-368; and Linenthal, *Sacred Ground*, 138.

41. Here lies the appeal of nations as imagined communities "because regardless of the actual inequality and exploitation that may prevail in each, the nation is always conceived as a deep, horizontal comradeship," as Anderson has classically written. This powerful affinity is equalled only by religious faith in its capacity to make "so many millions of people, not so much to kill, as to willingly die for such limited imaginings." Anderson, *Imagined Communities,* 16.

42. Root's 1899 speech, for example, contained a veiled barb against the emergent anti-imperialist critique launched by a motley group of concerned citizens as early as mid- to late 1898: "I protest in the name of the American soldier against all those who, believing because they wish to believe, without opportunity for explanation or contradiction, circulate and print the idle stories which fly through the air from malicious tongues, impugning the honor of the true and noble Americans who are protecting the honor of our flag."

43. As will become quickly evident, the curious forms of "history-writing," of which the war monument was the supplementary obverse (both the monumental inscriptions deciphered by Loewen and "transhistoricism" flagged by Anderson as incipient allegories of empire-building and nationalism), also have their own analogues to the cultural texts, or at least the cinematic texts, that I examine here.

44. Copyright nos. H33641, H33642, H33643, 21 July 1903, American Mutoscope & Biograph. Co., Paper Print Collection, Library of Congress. The combined length of the surviving footage is ninety feet and runs, on projection, for a brisk three minutes. See Paul Spehr, "Filmmaking at the American Mutoscope and Biograph Co, 1900-1906," Roger Holman, Ed. *Cinema 1900-06* (Brussels: Fédération Internationale des Archives du Film, 1982), 325, for the first launching date of the film; and 322-327, for a brief account of Bitzer's early filmography for the AMB (also known as the Biograph) from 1900 to 1906. See also American Mutoscope and Biograph Co. (AMB), Bulletin no. 55, 27 November 1905, in *Biograph Bulletins*, 1896-1908, comp. Kemp Niver and ed. Bebe Bergsten (Los Angeles: Locare Research Group, 1971), 213, for the 1905 redistribution date.

45. Spehr, "Filmmaking at the American Mutoscope and Biograph Co.," 325; Musser, *The Emergence of Cinema: The American Screen to 1907* (New York: Charles Scribner's Sons, 1990) [vol. 1 of the History of the American Cinema Series, ed. Charles Harpole], 342-343. Subsequently, I found out that Peter Davis's parodic videodocumentary on the Philippine Question and the Philippine-American War, *This Bloody Blundering Business* (1975), also used the surviving footage, setting it to parlor music (as was the exhibition custom of the time) and providing mock inter-titles to fill in the lacunae of the extant prints. Understandably, Davis does not cite documentation of the provenance and does not note the generic classification of this film.

46. Niver has been rightly celebrated for converting the nearly three thousand early films into negatives

from the paper prints in which they were originally submitted to the Library of Congress for copyright purposes until 1912 and for reconstructing their production history from rare sources such as publicity catalogs/bulletins, early trade publications, and production logs. His epic and painstaking effort involved a dedicated staff that rephotographed the prints frame by frame for over a decade, later viewing and annotating them for production credits, casting, location and date of production, and alternate versions/titles. Paul Spehr, "Foreword," vii, and Niver, "Preface," ix-x, in Kemp Niver, *Early Motion Pictures* ed. Bebe Bergsten (Washington, D.C.: The Library of Congress, 1967; rep. 1985).

47. Description from Niver, *Early Motion Pictures*, 7.

48. American Mutoscope and Biograph Co. (AMB), Bulletin no. 9, 29 August 1903 and Bulletin no. 55, 27 November 1905, in Biograph Bulletins, 1896-1908 , 90 and 230.

49. One AMB photo catalog [n.d.] breaks down the stipulated length of 161 feet of the release print into 55 feet for No. 1, 47 feet for No. 2, and 53 feet for No. 3. This photo catalog and the 1905 announcement for the film list specific production numbers and codes for its three scenes: 2418 —"Garzatori," 2419—"Garzatura," and 2420—"Garzava," respectively. See *Biograph Photo Catalog*, vol. 5, Reel 2, *Motion Picture Catalogs by American Producers and Distributors*, 1894-1908 (Microfilm Edition), Motion Picture and Television Reading Room, Library of Congress; and AMB, Bulletin No. 55, 27 November 1905, in Niver and Bergsten, *Biograph Bulletins*, 213. The film's internal and advertised structures may also have constituted a copyrighting stratagem, given the widespread piracies and litigious patent wars among producers that characterize the early period of American film and technological invention. David Levy states that the AMB developed "notoriously erratic copyright practices" in its early years. See "Re-constructed Newsreels, Re-enactments and the American Narrative Film," in Holman, ed. *Cinema 1900-06*, 249. Indeed, Niver lists three separate copyright numbers for each scene of the film even as they all carry the same copyright date. On the "patent wars" and resulting litigation and their precipitant effects on early film form, technological innovations, and early film as intellectual property, see André Gaudreault, "The Infringement of Copyright Laws and its Effects (1900-1906)," 114-122, and Janet Staiger, "Combination and Litigation: Structure of U.S. Film Distribution, 1896-1917," especially 189-191, in Thomas Elsaesser, ed. *Early Cinema: Space, Frame, Narrative* (London: British Film Institute, 1990).

50. *The Emergence of Cinema*, 342. These specified inserts even exceed the three main parts in length: "No. 1575, Fifteenth Infantry Off for Cuba" (the full title) was listed for 73 feet in the AMB Picture Catalogue of November 1902, 183, Box A-47, "The Biograph Co.," MPTV Reading Room, Library of Congress. "Warfare Practice" (No. 516) was titled "Skirmish Fight" and listed for 180 feet, in the AMB Photo Catalog (n.d.) vol. 2, Reel 2, *Motion Picture Catalogs*, n.p.

51. As will be obvious, my reading of the filmic inscriptions of the American soldier here is also considerably oriented by Amy Kaplan's suggestive essay on primitivism, the crisis and construction of masculinity, and the reconstruction of American nationhood through imperial expansion in "Romancing the Empire: The Embodiment of American Masculinity in the Popular Historical Novel of the 1890s," *American Literary History* 3 (December 1990), 659-690.

52. See Michael Hunt, *Ideology and U.S. Foreign Policy* (New Haven, Conn.: Yale University Press, 1987), 65, for an 1898 cartoon that depicts Spain as a simianized and treacherous foe who tramples a miniaturized American flag while stepping on a fresh grave whose tombstone reads: "Maine soldiers murdered by Spain." This brute is shown wielding a knife that drips with the blood of the three American soldiers in the cartoon whose "mutilated" corpses are strewn about him.

53. *Gone Primitive* (Chicago: University of Chicago Press, 1990), 22, 276.

54. A thumbnail discussion of the anti-imperialist Americans is in Stuart Creighton Miller, *Benevolent Assimilation*, 104-128 although accounts of this sort are considerably elaborated and refined in

work such as Willard Gatewood, *Black Americans and the White Man's Burden* (Urbana, Ill.: University of Illinois Press, 1975) which widens the debates on the Philippine Question that are normally limited by historians to the elite imperialist and anti-imperialist sectors. See also the texts cited in n32, this essay. Jim Zwick's much awaited manuscript on U.S. anti-imperialism, "The Anti-Imperialist League and the Development of a Foreign Policy Opposition, 1898-1921," promises to radically overturn a great deal of our received wisdom on the much maligned and much misunderstood Anti-Imperialist League and their assiduous commitments to Philippine "independence." For a typical example of Filipino efforts abroad to dispute American claims on the Philippines, see Felipe Agoncillo, *To the American People* (Paris: Imprimerie Chaix, 1900).

55. The dispute over the war atrocities of the U.S. armed forces in the Philippine-American War continues without let-up (and especially in the analogical context of the Vietnam War) in the work of the few scholars who work on the subject. See the vituperative debate that ensued after Brian Linn criticized Stuart Creighton Miller's thoughtful account of the war and its impact on national opinion, *Benevolent Assimilation*, as "one of the severest attacks on the U.S. Army ever published." Linn, "Stuart C. Miller and the American Soldier" *PILIPINAS* 7 (Fall 1986), 45-52; S. Miller, "Response," Ibid., 53-66; Linn, "Reply [to Miller's Response]," Ibid., 67-69; Miller, "Rejoinder," Ibid., 71-73; John Gates, letter to the Editor, and Miller's reply, *PILIPINAS* 9 (Fall 1987), 79-82. Miller is condemned for amplifying the anti-imperialist critique and such earlier accounts as Leon Wolff, *Little Brown Brother* (Garden City, N.J.: Doubleday, 1961), which take an unblinking look at the excesses committed in this war of conquest. For works that stop short of completely exonerating the U.S. Army, see Glenn May, *Battle for Batangas: A Philippine Province at War* (New Haven, Conn.: Yale University Press, 1991), John Gates, *Schoolbooks and Krags: The U.S. Army in the Philippines* (Westport, Conn.: Greenwood, 1973) and Linn's *The U.S. Army and Counterinsurgency in the Philippine War, 1899-1902* (Chapel Hill, N.C.: University of North Carolina Press, 1989).

56. Musser, *Emergence of Cinema*, 3, 5, 36, and 211.

57. For a sense of the striking homologies between the multiple permutations of the Pocahontas story and its reiteration in interested presentations like this film, see Frances Mossiker, *Pocahontas: The Life and the Legend* (New York: Albert Knopf, 1976), 15ff, 37ff, 61-71.

58. Kaplan, "Romancing the Empire," 665-667, 671-675.

59. See Kaplan, "Romancing the Empire," for how empire's relationships with eros are elaborated in the rescue and performative narratives of the best-selling American historical romances at the turn of the century, leaving readers awash in the heady atmosphere of imperial adventurism or inviting them to refigure the imaginative exploration of remote regions as also the invigoration of atrophied bodies.

60. A close dissection of the rhetorical relationship between the American war of conquest in the Philippines and American claims of "Benevolent Assimilation" is in Rafael, "White Love."

61. Kaplan, 664. As Kaplan notes, this contemporary crisis of masculinity (bewailed as cultural "effeminacy" caused by "overcivilization" or industrial overproduction) was less a social pathology than a frame for discussing the current questions of overproduction, national culture, and "social atrophy" that came with the closing of the frontier, the swift urbanization, the massive immigration from non-Northern Europe, the breakdown of Anglo-Saxonism as a basis for national identity, and the consequent social/racial conflicts that guaranteed expansionism and the redrawing of national boundaries. For example, no less than the revitalization of American manufacturing and industry by the search for global markets was staked in the idea of "national muscle-flexing" (the phrase is from Kaplan).

62. For the deployment of this language by American imperialist ideologues and cultural producers in the face of the multiple crises of the 1890s and their resulting recourse to a programmatic primitivism and anti-modernity, see T. Jackson Lears' classic *No Place of Grace: Antimodernism and the Transformation of American Culture, 1880-1920* (New York: Pantheon, 1981). For a historically specific account of the

recurrence of this cultural tendency in American political culture and among key nineteenth-century political figures, see Ronald Takaki, *Iron Cages: Race and Culture in Nineteenth-Century America* (Seattle: University of Washington Press, 1979). Primitivism, if we can call this tendency thus, recurs as a "Western" response to the endemic crises of developmentalist modernization and constitutes a feature of its cultural logic of modernism. See Torgovnick, Gone Primitive.

63. Torgovnick establishes the equivalence of these phrases in *Gone Primitive*, 185-188. As she argues, "Going primitive is trying to go home to a place that feels comfortable and balanced... (p. 185) 'Going home' involves only an individual journey—actual or imaginative—to join with a 'universal' mankind in the primitive. There can be homelessness then." (p. 188).

64. Mark Twain, "Thirty Thousand Killed a Million," reprinted in *Atlantic Monthly* (April 1992), 62.

U.S. Racism and Intervention in the Third World, Past and Present

DANIEL B. SCHIRMER

ORIGINS

White supremacy at home has been a support to U.S. military intervention in the Third World, and, conversely, such intervention has been a stimulus to domestic racism. This double-barreled tendency in U.S. politics was first observed and laid before the public more than a century ago by the Anti-Imperialist League. A small number of lawyers and other professionals, representatives of business and reform, white and male, met in a downtown Boston office in November of 1898 to form this organization. The founders chose to call it "anti-imperialist" because they opposed President McKinley's plans to annex the Philippines as a U.S. colony by force of arms. They believed this policy to be contrary to our country's best democratic traditions.

By February of 1899, McKinley's plans had turned into a full-fledged war of conquest, the Philippine-American War. The Anti-Imperialist League, in turn, initiated a broad and massive movement, bringing trade unions, farm organizations, and many others into alignment with its cause. The Boston organization expanded nationally, with chapters in major cities and more than a hundred thousand members—Democrats, Republicans, independents, and socialists.

AGAINST IMPERIALISM AND MONOPOLY

An important reason for the sharp and sudden growth of their organization was the fact that anti-imperialist leaders connected U.S. imperialism with the burgeoning influence of big business. Industrial and financial corporations were becoming dominant in U.S. society at just this time. The anti-imperialists said imperialism was the foreign policy of the newly powerful trusts and monopolies. By defending the annexation of the Philippines as a requisite to U.S. commercial expansion, President McKinley himself lent credence to this position. By linking imperialism with monopoly, the anti-imperialists drew upon a great reservoir of public support, for the displacement of many small entrepreneurs by a few giant corporations in the economic life of our country had aroused hostility in key segments of the population. Middle-class and professional people felt diminished and threatened by the power of the great corporations, and many became leaders of the anti-imperialist movement throughout the country.

In the 1890s, great strikes against the Pullman Corporation and Carnegie Steel had made manifest the hostility of organized labor. When, at an early anti-imperialist meeting, George McNeill, the Boston trade union leader who was nationally known as the father of the eight-hour day, declared that monopoly and imperialism were one and the same thing, he was the first to put this key teaching on public record.

Farmers in great numbers were antagonistic to the corporations that, as they saw it, charged high prices for manufactured goods and gave them low prices for agricultural products. It was a political representative of the farmers of the South and West, the Democrat William Jennings Bryan, who became the outstanding political figure connected with the anti-imperialist movement, giving it voice as he ran for president in 1900.

Perhaps the clearest expression of the connections being made at the time can be found in the name chosen for an African-American anti-imperialist organization. Formed in 1899 and headed by William T. Scott of Cairo, Illinois, the National Negro Anti-Expansion, Anti-Imperialist, Anti-Trust and Anti-Lynching League had a national slate of officers drawn from major cities from New York to Seattle. Clifford H. Plummer, a Boston lawyer, served on its executive committee.

ABOLITIONIST ROOTS

The anti-monopoly position of the anti-imperialists helps to account for the rapid growth of the movement. It does not explain why this movement started first of all in Boston and got its most effective leadership from that city. The reason for this primacy springs especially from the following circumstances: in the nineteenth century, the city of Boston had been a leading center (if not *the* leading center) of the abolitionist movement, and the majority of the Boston anti-imperialist leaders had cut their political teeth in the antislavery struggle. When the U.S. government moved to conquer and colonize the Filipinos, a people of color on the other side of the globe, these former abolitionists rebelled. Why should they allow Washington to enslave a dark-skinned nation abroad when they had given the best years of their lives to the struggle against black slavery at home? The Boston anti-imperialists identified U.S. imperialism with the white supremacy and racism they had opposed in their youth. Some may have felt their personal integrity demanded that they take up the fight again, in these new terms. A glance at the lives of three outstanding Boston anti-imperialists will tell the story.

F. B. Sanborn was a writer and teacher who lived in Concord. As a young man, he had given aid to John Brown and gathered rifles for Harper's Ferry. Called to Washington after Brown's death by a congressional investigation, he refused to appear. When two federal agents came to take him down to Washington, Sanborn's friends and neighbors surrounded his home and refused to let them take him. Sanborn wrote for the *Springfield Republican* (Mass.), which had achieved national circulation as a result of its previous support for the Union cause, and his column regularly brought the views of the anti-imperialist movement to many readers.

Moorfield Storey, a prominent Boston lawyer who was president of the American Bar Association in 1894, later became president of the Anti-Imperialist League. In his formative years he had been personal secretary to the outstanding abolitionist senator from Massachusetts, Charles Sumner; many years later he was a founder of the National Association for the Advancement of Colored People (NAACP).

A Unitarian minister, Thomas Wentworth Higginson, was an active speaker and writer for the anti-imperialist cause. In his younger days he had led a raid on a Boston jail to free the fugitive slave Anthony Burns. The raid was unsuccessful, but it earned Higginson a saber slash on his cheek that marked him for the rest of his days. He led a black regiment in the Civil War, when the Confederates threatened white officers in such a capacity with hanging on the spot if captured.

Personalities such as these did not hesitate to challenge the slavocracy when it controlled the federal government and contravened what they saw as democratic principle; nor did they shrink from such a challenge when corporate power took over and, in their eyes, similarly ruled. They formed the core of Boston anti-imperialism. But the strength of the anti-imperialist movement in Boston came from other sources as well. Boston blacks in large numbers opposed imperialism, identifying their own cause with that of the Filipinos, and an African-American minister of that city, the Reverend W. H. Scott, was elected to the leadership of the Anti-Imperialist League. Boston's Irish working people, remembering Ireland's experience with the British Empire, brought Democratic support to the movement, as the Yankee abolitionists brought Republican. Women in Boston were active anti-imperialists, though none were elected to the league's Boston leadership during its first few years. Protestant and Jewish religious leaders gave support. Catholic clergy were helpful elsewhere but not in Boston.

All of these forces combined to make Boston the initial and outstanding center of anti-imperialism in the United States.

It must be noted that not all anti-imperialists were opposed to racism. Some, especially in the ranks of Southern Democrats, based their opposition to McKinley's policies of conquest and colonization on racist sentiments. They did not want the U.S. government to enter into a colonial relationship with the Filipinos because they considered them to be inferior people of color.

THE RACIST WAR

Boston leaders of the Anti-Imperialist League denounced the U.S. war against the Philippines as racist through and through. Evidently, this condemnation was well justified. At the highest levels of policy the war was placed in a racist context from the very beginning, thus giving it ideological as well as economic sanction. A spokesman for the U.S. empire-builders proclaimed very clearly that it was the duty of the United States as a white Anglo-Saxon nation to uplift and civilize the Filipinos, who were seen as a colored and inferior race. President McKinley himself gave utterance to such views.

Moreover, the U.S. military conducted the war in a markedly racist and genocidal manner. The U.S. public learned this from soldiers' letters written home and published in the press. About four months after the war began, at the end of May 1899, the Anti-Imperialist League published a collection of these letters.[1] Some told of action at Caloocan, a suburb of Manila. "Caloocan was supposed to contain seventeen thousand inhabitants," wrote Captain Elliott of a Kansas regiment. "The Twentieth Kansas swept through it, and now Caloocan contains not one living native. Of the buildings, the battered walls of the great church and dismal prison alone remain." A Kansas private wrote: "With my own hand set fire to over fifty homes of Filipinos after the victory at Caloocan. Women and children were wounded by our fire." Still another Kansan told that his company took four prisoners at Caloocan and asked an officer what to do. "He said, you know the orders and four natives fell dead." "With an enemy like this to fight," a private in the Utah Battery wrote, "it is not surprising that the boys should adopt 'no quarter' as a motto, and fill the blacks full of lead before finding out whether they are friends or enemies." A volunteer from the state of Washington wrote: "Our fighting blood was up and we all wanted to kill 'niggers.' This shooting human beings beats rabbit hunting all to pieces."

A soldier of the First Idaho Regiment testified that officers encouraged racist attitudes among the rank and file. "It kept leaking down from sources above," he wrote, "that the Filipinos were 'niggers,' no better than Indians, and were to be treated as such."

RACISM AT HOME
Boston anti-imperialists believed that racist military intervention in the Philippines was linked to—and stimulated—racism in the United States, and they drove the point home on many occasions.

In December of 1898, President McKinley made a trip to Atlanta, Georgia, and participated in a civic parade from which officials in charge had excluded black quarrymen and stone masons. White members of the Atlanta Federation of Trades had withdrawn from the parade in protest, and the anti-imperialist *Springfield Republican* thought McKinley should have done so as well. But the Washington correspondent for the *Boston Evening Transcript* explained that those who were close to him said the president was as "fully convinced of the need for white supremacy" as his Southern hosts.[2]

In the course of the Philippine war a wave of lynchings swept the South and there were violent attempts on the part of whites to keep blacks from voting and participating in government. During the election campaign of 1900, there were bloody attacks against blacks in New Orleans, Akron, and New York City. On April 23, 1899, a particularly atrocious lynching took place in a town near Atlanta. Sam Hose, a black farmhand, was accused of killing his white employer in a dispute over wages. Hose was chained to a tree and horribly mutilated before oil was poured over him and he was burned to death. More than a thousand whites were on the scene, and after it was over Hose's remains were cut up and sold—a small piece of bone for twenty-five cents and "a bit of liver crisply cooked for ten."[3] When news of the lynching reached Atlanta, the press reported that four thousand whites took special trains. Arriving late, they brought home souvenirs.

In Boston, headquarters of the anti-imperialist movement, there was a sharp reaction to this event. Boston blacks held a meeting of protest at which W. H. Lewis, a young African-American lawyer and member of the Cambridge City Council, spoke with indignation: "What a spectacle America is exhibiting today. Columbia stands offering liberty to Cubans with one hand, ramming liberty down the throat of the Filipinos with another, but with both feet planted upon the neck of the negro."[4] Thomas Wentworth Higginson presided at another protest rally, and on

25 April the *Springfield Republican* asked a telling question: "Is the contempt we have shown for the rights and protests of the natives of the Philippines... the killing of them by the thousands and the looting of their homes... calculated to increase the southern white's regard for the negro as a fellow-being of like feelings and claims to life and liberty as himself?"

The imposition of colonial rule on the Philippines entailed a hard-fought war that lasted officially for more than three years, unofficially for longer still. It stimulated massive disaffection at home, as reflected in the six million votes the Democratic Bryan got as an anti-imperialist presidential candidate in 1900, losing to McKinley, the Republican empire-builder, who got a million more. Never able to gain widespread, uncritical support for its imperial policy, the U.S. governing elite turned from the practice of outright colonial rule to that of informal empire: a policy of securing dominant influence in nominally independent countries by suborning and supporting the native elite. This remains the case today.

THE REAGAN AND BUSH YEARS

The people of the United States currently face other conditions that show striking similarities to those of one hundred years ago. No one can deny that, now as then, the country is dominated by huge industrial and financial corporations. These corporations pour massive funds into election campaigns to influence candidates, as they started to do in McKinley's time.

At the beginning of the century, President McKinley carried out military interventions in Cuba, Puerto Rico, and the Philippines with U.S. corporate interests in mind. In the closing years of the last century, presidents Reagan and Bush intervened in the Third World three times: in Grenada in 1983, Panama in 1989, and the Persian Gulf in 1991. Certain results of these interventions may provide a clue to their purposes.

The U.S. invasion of Grenada (population 110,000) smashed a government of Marxist tendencies that was pro-labor, pro-social reform, and friendly to Castro. Thirteen months later, a conservative government, friendly to Reagan, was elected with the help of CIA funds. I saw other results of the invasion during a visit there in 1991: two industrial zones, one in operation, the other under construction, where U.S. corporations could build plants to take advantage of cheap Grenadian labor (and export U.S. jobs in the process).

Grenada is a tiny island of no strategic significance to the Pentagon. But Panama until recently was the seat of the U.S. Southern Command, an institution that facilitated U.S. military control over Central and South America. For years Washington supported Manuel Noriega, a brutal Panamanian dictator and alleged drug-runner, as a means of protecting the Southern Command's military bases. In 1988, when domestic opposition threatened Noriega's rule, Washington finally broke with him. He in turn declared that the Southern Command and its bases would have to go. A U.S. invasion resulted in a new Panamanian government inaugurated under U.S. protection on a U.S. military base. But the U.S bases and the Southern Command were withdrawn in 1999 in accordance with a U.S.-Panamanian treaty signed in 1978 during the Carter presidency.

While the 1991 Gulf War was a coalition effort, it was primarily the U.S. military that drove Saddam Hussein (another brutal dictator Washington supported for years) out of Kuwait and reinstalled the Kuwaiti royal family. The Kuwaiti royal family is reactionary and corrupt but accessible to U.S. oil corporations. Saddam's defeat in Kuwait removed his threat to Saudi Arabia, the U.S. corporations' main satellite in their control of Mideast oil. In this way the Gulf War preserved the dominance of U.S. wealth in this lucrative field of investment.

RACISM AND INTERVENTION

U.S. anti-imperialists at the turn of the century charged that U.S. military intervention in the Philippines had a racist character and stimulated racism at home. These attributes seem to hold true of U.S. military intervention in the Third World today.

In the invasions of Grenada and Panama, the government of the white superpower flagrantly and illegally violated the sovereignty of two small countries overwhelmingly inhabited by peoples of color. In Grenada, the greatest military power on earth— white—crushed the government of one of the world's smallest nations—black. There it was all over quickly, since an unpopular domestic coup had rendered the government of Grenada ineffective and disoriented its people. In the invasion of Panama, the U.S. military carried out an aerial bombardment of a densely populated, black working-class neighborhood in the vicinity of Noriega's command headquarters. Many civilians were killed and their bodies bulldozed into mass graves before they could be counted. While the Pentagon insists that a total of only 202 civilians died as a result of the invasion, independent sources place the figure at many times that number. After this victory, the Bush administration, as if to underline its contempt for the people of Panama and international law, kidnapped Noriega in 1989 and brought him to the United States for trial as a drug-runner, thus robbing Panamanians of their sovereign right to pass judgment on the misdeeds of their head of state, had they so wished.

In the Gulf War, the military forces led by the United States killed thousands and thousands of Iraqis, people of color, and today many Iraqi children still suffer and die as a result of sanctions imposed due to the war. But consider the attitude of a leader of the white establishment in the United States to the question of the war and its casualties. On 19 January 1992, U.S. Rep. Stephen Solarz had an opinion piece in *The New York Times* defending the Gulf War against its critics. "The opponents of the war told us that we would be hopelessly bogged down in a desert war with massive American casualties," he wrote. "Yet we won in six weeks with fewer than 150 American fatalities." Solarz, the Democratic leader, boasted of the small number of U.S. casualties in total disregard of the thousands of deaths the war brought to those of darker skin. Such an ethnocentric attitude can only be described as racist and indicates the character of the war itself. Solarz was defeated for reelection in 1992 when his district was changed to include large numbers of Hispanic voters.

FROM BAGHDAD TO LOS ANGELES

Was there a correlation between more recent U.S. government-promoted violence against peoples of color in the Third World and domestic racism, as the early anti-imperialists believed? What has happened in this regard in the United States as its government intervened in Grenada, Panama, and the Gulf?

Not long after the conclusion of the Gulf War, Arthur Fletcher, chairman of the

U.S. Commission on Civil Rights, gave a significant interview reported in the *Boston Globe* of 1 May 1991. He told the press that racism was pervasive in the United States and had become worse in recent years. "In my 40 years in civil rights," he said, "I don't think I've seen it any more tenuous than it is right now…. Just about every major institution in the country is being impacted by negative attitudes with respect to race and gender." (Fletcher coupled sex discrimination with racism. This linkage may have seemed evident to many who saw white male legislators harassing a black woman, Anita Hill, during the Clarence Thomas Supreme Court nomination.)

The Gulf War was mounted in a period of recession. And in Fletcher's view, the economic difficulties that led to unemployment were partially responsible for the current growth of racism. It is probable that the overbearing and unbridled militarism the U.S. government displayed in Third World countries was also a factor. A Boston civil rights leader evidently believed that the explosion of hate and bigotry had such roots. In the summer of 1991, a Nazi swastika was painted on Plymouth Rock. In discussing this episode with a reporter from the *Boston Globe* (25 August 1991), Louis Elisa, president of the Boston branch of the NAACP, said he thought a rise in "militarism" prompted by the Gulf War had contributed to a mentality that seeks victories over victims. "It sounds like a war against Iraq, but it's a war against difference," said Elisa. "It brings out the worst in people that have the worst in them."

At the end of the Gulf War, the U.S. Air Force mercilessly slaughtered Iraqi troops who were running from the field of battle in full retreat. Not long after this, television stations across the country played the videotape of white police officers in Los Angeles viciously beating a single black motorist, Rodney King, lying prone on the ground. These two images had an undeniable bond. The one reflected the other.

Around 1900, white racism provided the ideological rationale for the U.S. war in the Philippines. But for more than forty years, anti-Communism supplied the main arguments for U.S. military intervention in the Third World, as in Korea and Vietnam (though the element of racism was not absent, either, with the enemy called "gooks" in both cases, for example).

Given the collapse of the Soviet Union, the Pentagon was compelled to conjure up new targets to justify the maintenance of U.S. military supremacy, with its huge public expense, its profitable defense contracts, its jobs and promotions for the army, navy, and air force. The Pentagon found these new threats in what it called "regional conflicts." A Pentagon document leaked to *The New York Times* in February 1992 revealed that these hypothetical conflicts include an Iraqi invasion of Kuwait and Saudi Arabia; a North Korean attack on South Korea; simultaneous assaults by Iraq and North Korea; coups involving U.S. citizens or vital interests (such as bases) in Panama and the Philippines; an attack on Lithuania by Russia; and the emergence of a new and aggressive superpower by the year 2001. Of this list of seven possible future conflicts, five involved countries of the Third World.[5]

The Pentagon thus saw the United States in the 1990s as the global policeman of the Third World. That is to say, the United States, the white superpower, was to maintain military dominance over the peoples of color of the Third World. The racism of the Pentagon vision was implicit. But this vision not only reflected racism, it served to encourage it, thus providing its own support.

During the Reagan and Bush administrations, from 1981 to 1992, our national government followed a policy of military supremacy, the better to intervene in the Third World. During those years a sharpening of racist sentiment could be observed.

THE CLINTON YEARS

JOSEPH ILETO

In Southern California on 10 August 1999, Buford Furrow, an official of the Aryan Nation, a white supremacist group, shot and killed Joseph Ileto, a Filipino postal worker.

Just before this incident, Furrow had opened fire on children and workers in a Jewish Community Center, injuring several there. The next day, Furrow turned himself in to authorities and gave out a statement defending his behavior. He had opened fire at the Jewish Community Center "as a wake-up call for Americans to kill Jews." He had killed Joseph Ileto, the postal worker, because as a "non-white" and federal employee, he was a "target of opportunity."

Furrow's "wake-up call" to kill Jews and "non-whites" is in direct line with the warning Private Willie Grayson of the 54th Nebraska regiment gave his fellow soldiers as he fired the shots on 4 February 1899 that began the Philippine-American War: "Line up, fellows, the 'niggers' are here all through these yards." A little over one hundred years ago, the U.S. government began a war of conquest in the Philippines under the banner of White Anglo-Saxon Protestantism. Furrow and his kind evidently hope the United States will one day be riven, like the Kosovo of the '90s, by genocidal conflict: a religious war against non-Christians, and a racial war against "non-whites."

Beside that of Buford Furrow, Clinton's two terms saw other acts of racist violence. Horrible was the murder of the African-American James Byrd in 1998, dragged to dismemberment and death over rough back-country roads in Texas.

CLINTON'S VIOLENT INTERVENTIONS IN THE THIRD WORLD

President Bush's military intervention in the Third World and his promotion of U.S. military supremacy seemed to create a public atmosphere conducive to racist acts of violence. President Clinton carried on these Bush policies with similar results.

Clinton continued the war Bush waged against Saddam Hussein because the latter challenged U.S. corporate control of Middle East oil. Clinton kept in place the economic embargo against Iraq, causing civilian deaths, especially those of children. He used the U.S. Air Force to bomb Iraq, as did Bush.

In October 1998 Clinton air-bombed two nations of color, Sudan and Afghanistan, illegally and in a terrorist manner, in retaliation for the bombing of U.S. embassies in Kenya and Tanzania allegedly by Muslim terrorists.

Clinton led the NATO air war against the Serbian government to stop the oppression of the Albanian population of Kosovo. Here there were many civilian casualties, and the problem of ethnic violence still festers. The people of Serbia are white, but the practice of violent reprisal was the same.

In his last months in office, Clinton turned again to military measures. He proposed a $1.3 billion program of U.S. military aid to the government of Colombia. For forty years this government has been fighting a left-wing guerrilla movement entangled with the drug trade. President Clinton said the aid was necessary to stop the flow of drugs from Colombia to the United States. In contrast, Senator Leahy of Vermont declared the money would go to a war of counterinsurgency masquerading as a war against drugs. As Clinton proposed military aid the Colombian army was busy removing members of the U'wa tribe of Colombian Indians from ancestral lands on which a transnational corporation, Occidental Petroleum, planned to drill for oil.

Buford Burrow's murder of Joseph Ileto and the dragging death of Richard Byrd are only two of many racist atrocities that took place during the two administrations of President Clinton. It is hard to believe that violence used by the U.S. military against the peoples of color in Iraq, Sudan, Afghanistan, and the Caucasians of Serbia did not embolden U.S. white supremacists to inflict similar violence upon Asian-Americans, African-Americans, and other minorities here in the United States.

ENHANCING U.S. MILITARY SUPREMACY

Clinton maintained the huge U.S. military machine (including a large nuclear arsenal) that had served to assert U.S. military superiority over the rival superpower, the Soviet Union. In his two terms he revived and strengthened the military alliances and foreign military deployments that had served the same purpose.

In Europe under Clinton's leadership, Poland, Hungary, and the Czech Republic were added to NATO, bringing it to former Soviet borders and providing new markets for U.S. defense industries. The U.S.-led NATO intervention in Kosovo asserted U.S. military supremacy in Europe in an absolute and unprecedented fashion.

EMPHASIS ON ASIA: A NEW WAR ALLIANCE WITH JAPAN

Perhaps the Clinton administration's foremost achievement in strengthening the forward position of the U.S. military was in the Asia-Pacific region, particularly in relation to Japan. U.S. troops and bases in that country had supported U.S. military interventions in Korea, Vietnam and the Middle East. And Clinton insisted that the 59,000 U.S. troops and many bases in Okinawa and mainland Japan be maintained there indefinitely. Even more significant was his revision of the U.S.-Japanese Cold War military alliance. This had pledged the U.S. military to support Japan against possible Soviet aggression. The revised alliance committed the Japanese military to give support to the U.S. military in peace and in possible U.S. wars of intervention in Asia and the Middle East.

Clinton's Secretary of Defense was a Republican, William J. Cohen, formerly a Senator from Maine. On Asian matters Clinton appeared to work very closely with Cohen, his link to the Pentagon. It was Secretary Cohen who stepped forward in July 1998 to announce that the 37,000 U.S. troops in South Korea would remain in place, even if Korea was unified, their use for possible intervention to be expanded from Korea to the entire Asia-Pacific region.

Clinton's Asian military buildup, however, represented a top-heavy achievement, strong in the political and military elite of the countries concerned, but weak down below. There was (and still is) considerable popular resistance to the U.S. military in the Philippines, Japan, and South Korea.

In a October 1998 C-SPAN broadcast, Secretary Cohen spoke before a conference, held in Pittsburgh, of the CEOs of *Fortune* magazine's top 500 corporations. Explaining why the Clinton administration continued a military buildup even though the Soviet Union was no more, he told them, "Business follows the flag...

you provide the investment; we provide the security."

Cohen's words, presumably representing the views of the Pentagon, echoed the teachings of Admiral A. T. Mahan, the main military ideologist of nascent U.S. imperialism at the time of the Philippine-American War. They also helped explain U.S.-Philippine relations in the Clinton years. In 1991 the Philippine Senate had refused to renew the U.S. bases in that country. Early in his first term Clinton had tried to revive the U.S. military presence there. Finally in 1999 he succeeded when a more conservative Philippine Senate, elected in 1998, voted for the Visiting Forces Agreement. This gave the Pentagon the right to hold large-scale military exercises in the Philippines, which have since taken place. Meanwhile at the same time, in the decade of the '90s, U.S. corporate investment in the Philippines grew by $20 billion, making the United States the Philippines' largest foreign investor.

Global Supremacy for the U.S. Corporate Elite

During Clinton's two administrations, U.S. corporations moved to strengthen their already dominant position in the world economy. In this endeavor they received the full support of the president. Mr. Clinton also heightened the preeminent position of the U.S. military. In the Clinton years it seemed that the United States reached the very apogee of world supremacy. That supremacy Charles Emory Smith—a Republican publicist and close adviser of President William McKinley during the latter's war against the Philippine independence movement—envisioned in 1895. Smith gave lectures before Boston and New York bankers and industrialists where he outlined a program for the United States to achieve what he called "unchallenged primacy" among the nations of the earth. This included establishing military and commercial strongholds in the islands of the Caribbean and the Pacific, and winning both global financial and industrial supremacy. The first goal was achieved by the U.S. in wars against Spain and the Philippines (with the Philippines and Guam won as colonies in the Pacific; in the Caribbean, Puerto Rico a colony and Cuba a protectorate). A start toward the second was made in 1900 when J. P. Morgan granted England's request to finance the Boer War. A little more than a century later, after being on the winning side in two world wars and a cold war, the U.S. has unquestionably achieved global supremacy.

The people of the Philippines were the first to resist the encroachments of U.S. corporate imperialism in foreign lands. One hundred years later, in August 1999, a Committee for Human Rights in the Philippines based in Oakland, California, issued a statement acutely critical of what had become an imperial superpower of global dimensions. The statement eloquently condemned the glaring racist violence with which Buford Furrow murdered Joseph Ileto, the Filipino postal worker. With equal eloquence it condemned the fertile ground from which springs such horrific violence. This is the institutional racism, the police harassment and brutality, the diminished economic opportunity and other forms of "low profile" violence that are part of the daily life of poor people of color in today's United States. As for the effect of the Clinton superpower on the world at large this statement went to the heart of the matter: "Beyond its borders the U.S. government violently suppresses those who do not conform to its 'new world order.' Through direct military intervention in Iraq and Yugoslavia, the ominously escalating 'low intensity warfare' in Colombia, the U.S. military comeback via the highly unpopular 'Visiting Forces Agreement' in the Philippines and countless other military interventions, violence is what maintains the United States as a global superpower for big business."

President George W. Bush
"That Election Was Stolen"

Bobby L. Rush is a Democratic member of the House of Representatives from Illinois. An African-American, he is also secretary of the 37-member Congressional Black Caucus. On 14 February 2001 in celebration of Black History month, he spoke on the floor of Congress about the November 2000 presidential elections: "...in the opinion of a significant number of American citizens, and I would say indeed of the majority of black American citizens that election was stolen from the rightful owner." The Congressional Black Caucus believed it was the violation of African-American voting rights in the state of Florida that was the cause of this injustice. When the Florida vote was announced, Bush led by 1,784, less than 1/2 of 1 percent, automatically necessitating a machine recount. The National Association for the Advancment of Colored People (NAACP) and Jesse Jackson spoke out, protesting that the narrow Bush victory was the result of the illegal suppression of the African-American vote in the state.

The NAACP Hearing

After the election, on December 11 the NAACP held hearings in Florida on the vote in that state presided over by the NAACP president (and former Congressional Black Caucus chairman) Kweisi Mfume. Testimony at this hearing revealed many violations of black voting rights, from voters being denied the right to vote because they "were not on the rolls" (even though some had their voter registration cards as well as identification showing their names and addresses) to being asked to provide both photo ID and current voter registration card even though the law does not require that voters present both.

Two poll workers testified that "headquarters" had instructed them that they should apply "qualification" procedures very strictly and if there was the slightest doubt to deny the request to vote. They were also told to refrain from giving out any written verification of the refused voters' requests, including affidavits. This was illegal; the law required that any voter whose attempt is challenged be given an affidavit of challenge signed under oath by the poll worker.

Fortifying the testimony at the hearing, the increase in black-voter turnout convinced the NAACP that Gore would have won Florida if so many black votes had not been recorded by malfunctioning, old machinery as non-votes. U.S. Representative Corrine Brown, a leader of the Congressional Black Caucus from Jacksonville, told the press 16,000 of the 27,000 ballots left uncounted in Duval County were from black precincts. Such malfunctioning voting machinery was prevalent in black and poor voting precincts throughout the state—with similar results.

Gore Disregards the Violation of Black Voting Rights

Gore, who had nearly 100 percent support from African-American voters in Florida, and his colleagues in the Democratic leadership turned a blind eye to what appeared to be a massive violation of black voting rights and made nothing of it in their postelection struggle for the Florida vote. Of explosive political and moral impact, this was the issue that posed the heaviest threat to the Bush claim of victory; the Democrats never took it up. Instead they chose to engage Bush in an overwhelmingly legalistic battle for voter recount, almost devoid of any but rudimentary partisan content. Reverend Al Sharpton, the prominent African-American civil rights leader of New York City, described the Democrats' behavior at this decisive moment in the sharpest terms: "The Democratic Party betrayed us in Florida by not raising the voting rights matter."[6]

The Supreme Court and Congress Decide for Bush

On December 12, 2000, by a vote of 5 to 4 the U.S. Supreme Court overruled the Florida Supreme Court decision of December 8 allowing continued manual recount across the state. With this decision the Supreme Court, in effect, ratified the election of a presidential candidate whose victory came as a result of violations of the voting rights of Florida's black minority. It was a racist decision, compounding the injustices of the Florida voting process.

One last chance remained to challenge the Florida vote. This would occur when the votes of the Electoral College were to be ratified by a joint session of the U.S. Congress. The Congressional Black Caucus had written a formal objection to Florida's Electoral College votes to be presented to this joint session before their ratification. Brief and factual, it summarized the violations that had nullified the votes of thousands of African-Americans in that state.

To have an objection to the Electoral College vote recognized by the joint session of Congress it had to be signed by one member of the House and one of the Senate. Try as they might the Congressional Black Caucus could not get a single member of the Senate to sign their objection. Democrats joined Republicans in refusing to allow representatives of the African-American minority to present their legitimate grievances with the Florida vote to the joint session of Congress. Both parties displayed "bi-partisanship" and "national unity"—at the expense of the blacks—putting the culminating racist stamp on the Bush election campaign.

As it ended in Florida, the Bush election campaign was one in which government officials, both Republican and Democrat, local, state, and national, either caused or condoned the nullification of thousands of African-American votes. From the Florida election process to the Supreme Court decision to the gag rule at the joint session of Congress—the election of Bush was one of the most significant assertions of white supremacy our country has seen since the pre-Civil War days of slave-owner's power.

"Corporate Power in Overdrive"

The Republican Party has been the favored party of corporate wealth since the days of McKinley. With an arrogance swollen by its election victory, the new Republican administration immediately began a conservative onslaught against U.S. policy, both domestic and foreign. The violation of the rights of the country's black minority opened the door to this wholesale attack on the well-being of the country's majority, irrespective of skin color.

With insolent speed Bush dropped his campaign mask of compassion to reveal a conservatism that was aggressive and militant. On the campaign trail Bush had promised a measure to reduce carbon dioxide emissions, a factor in global warming. After a White House conference with Vice President Cheney, like himself a former Texas oil industry executive, the president withdrew his pledge, saying it would be bad for business. Before the vote, Bush had promised "to leave no child behind." In the White House he reduced grants for training physcians for childrens' hospitals by $35 million. He made similar cuts in funding for day care and for programs to combat child abuse and neglect. He has also proposed further measures adverse to labor, women's rights, the environment and the conservation of national parks and reservations... and a tax cut, beneficial to the minority of great wealth.

In his first months in office Bush has taken the same harsh conservative line in foreign policy. He moved easily and quickly from the violation of African-American voting rights to a renewed and heightened bombing of Iraq, on military targets nearer the capital city Baghdad than had been the case under Clinton.

The new administration's first big foreign policy problem has revolved around U.S. relations with China. There is a split in our country's ruling circles on the question of China. Much of corporate finance and industry favors the peaceful and profitable penetration of the huge China market. On the other hand the Pentagon, the defense industries, and the ultra-right Republicans favor a policy of military confrontation. Under Clinton the first interests seemed to have the upper hand. Under Bush so far the second set of interests seems to have the edge. Bush enthusiastically pushes a national missile defense to contain China, an issue Clinton postponed. He has cancelled Clinton's policy of engagement with North Korea, China's ally, and increased U.S. support for Taiwan's military buildup in the face of China's opposition. Most significantly he has pledged to intervene with military force on Taiwan's side, should there be an armed conflict between China and Taiwan (an issue on which previous administrations had pursued a studied ambiguity). He and his administration have since vociferously backed away from this pledge, signifying the internal struggle taking place on China policy.

One of Bush's early appointments was that of Richard L. Armitage as Undersecretary of State. In the summer of 1999, at a time of tension between China and Taiwan, Armitage, then serving as foreign policy advisor to presidential candidate Bush, said in an interview to an Australian paper, "Australia must stand ready to give military support to the United States if Washington goes to war with China over Taiwan."7 Later in the interview Armitage backed away from this declaration as did President Bush after making a similar prediction. An episode in his past career may suggest Armitage's attitude towards dealing with Third World peoples of color. He was chief of the U.S. team that tried unsuccessfully to negotiate a renewal of the U.S. bases in the Philippines. A leading negotiator for the Philippine side later wrote that Armitage's arrogance was a key factor in turning the Philippine Senate against base renewal.

There is a two-sided Republican policy, first appearing in the days of McKinley, that the new Bush regime seems to exemplify and renew: a combination of disregard for the rights of the African-American minority in this country, with hostility to Third World peoples of color. The Bush regime, representing the white superpower, shows active but varying degrees of hostility towards China, North Korea, Iraq, and Iran. As if to mitigate the public relations effect of this sharp, white/non-white dichotomy, the new administration has appointed two well-respected U.S. individuals of color to foremost foreign policy positions: Colin Powell as Secretary of State, and Condoleeza Rice as national security advisor. Whatever their individual inclinations, however, it is more than likely these two will be affected by the strong hold the Pentagon and the ultra-right appear to have on President Bush's foreign policy. Colin Powell, for example, shortly after his appointment to office, called for a continuation of President Clinton's policy of engagement with North Korea, only to be overruled by President Bush.

The New York Times of March 18, 2001 carried an opinion editorial piece by Robert B. Reich, former labor secretary, entitled "Corporate Power in Overdrive." In this Reich summed up the meaning of the first weeks of the Bush regime: "There's no longer any countervailing power in Washington. Business is in complete control of the machinery of government. The House, the Senate and the White House are all run by business-friendly Republicans who are deeply indebted to American business for their electoral victories." Reich's vision of the future: "At some point—perhaps as soon as the 2002 midterm elections, surely no later than the next presidential election—the public will be aghast at what is happening. The backlash against business may be thunderous." In the United States today democracy (with a small "d") badly needs a popular awakening of the sort Robert Reich foresees.

Many thanks to Madge Kho of the Boston Friends of the Filipino People for providing me with important reference material

NOTES:

1. *Soldiers Letters* (Boston: The Anti-Imperialist League, 1899).

2. *Boston Evening Transcript*, Dec. 24, 1898.

3. *Springfield Daily Republican,* April 27, 1899.

4. Lewis's statement appeared in the *Boston Evening Transcript* on 25 April 1899; the word "Negro" was not generally capitalized until later.

5. Patrick Tyler, "Pentagon Imagines New Enemies to Fight in Post-Cold War Era," *The New York Times,* Feb. 7, 1992.

6. Scott Sherman, "He Has a Dream—the Grand Ambition of the Reverend Al Sharpton," *Nation,* April 16, 2001.

7. As quoted in *The New York Times,* Dec. 23, 1999.

The Miseducation of the Filipino

RENATO CONSTANTINO

Education is a vital weapon of a people striving for economic emancipation, political independence, and cultural renascence. We are such a people. Philippine education, therefore, must produce Filipinos who are aware of their country's problems, who understand the basic solution to these problems, and who care enough and have courage enough to work and sacrifice for their country's salvation.

NATIONALISM IN EDUCATION

In recent years, in various sectors of our society, there have been nationalist stirrings which were crystallized and articulated by the late Claro M. Recto. There were jealous demands for the recognition of Philippine sovereignty on the bases question. There were appeals for the correction of the iniquitous economic relations between the Philippines and the United States. For a time, Filipino businessmen and industrialists rallied around the banner of the Filipino First policy, and various scholars and economists proposed economic emancipation as an immediate goal for our nation. In the field of art, there have been signs of a new appreciation of our own culture. Indeed, there has been much nationalist activity in many areas of endeavor, but we have yet to hear of a well-organized campaign on the part of our educational leaders for nationalism in education.

Although most of our educators are engaged in a lively debate on techniques and tools for improved instruction, not one major educational leader has come out for a truly nationalist education. Of course, some pedagogical experts have written on some aspects of nationalism in education. However, no comprehensive educational program has been advanced as a corollary to the programs of political and economic emancipation. This is a tragic situation because the nationalist movement is crippled at the outset by a citizenry that is ignorant of our basic ills and is apathetic to our national welfare.

NEW PERSPECTIVES

Some of our economic and political leaders have gained a new perception of our relations with the United States as a result of their second look at Philippine-American relations since the turn of the century. The reaction which has emerged as economic and political nationalism is an attempt on their part to revise the iniquities of the past and to complete the movement started by our revolutionary leaders of 1896. The majority of our educational leaders, however, continue to trace their direct lineal descent to the first soldier-teachers of the American invasion army. They seem oblivious of the fact that the educational system and the philosophy of which they are the proud inheritors were valid only within the framework of American colonialism. The educational system introduced by the Americans had to correspond, and was designed to correspond, to the economic and political reality of American conquest.

CAPTURING MINDS

The most effective means of subjugating a people is to capture their minds. Military victory does not necessarily signify conquest. As long as feelings of resistance remain in the hearts of the vanquished, no conqueror is secure. This is best illustrated by the occupation of the Philippines by the Japanese militarists during the Second World War. Despite the terroristic regime imposed by the Japanese warlords, the Filipinos were never conquered. Hatred for the Japanese was engendered by their oppressive techniques which in turn were intensified by the stubborn resistance of the Filipino people. Japanese propagandists and psychological warfare experts, however, saw the necessity of winning the minds of the people. Had the Japanese stayed a little longer, Filipino children who were being schooled under the auspices of the new dispensation would have grown into strong pillars of the Greater East-Asia Co-Prosperity Sphere. Their minds would have been conditioned to suit the policies of the Japanese imperialists.

The molding of men's minds is the best means of conquest. Education, therefore, serves as a weapon in wars of colonial conquest. This singular fact was well appreciated by the American military commander in the Philippines during the Filipino-American war. According to the census of 1903:

> General Otis urged and furthered the reopening of schools, himself selecting and ordering the textbooks. Many officers, among them chaplains, were detailed as superintendents of schools, and many enlisted men, as teachers.

The American military authorities had a job to do. They had to employ all means to pacify a people whose hopes for independence were being frustrated by the presence of another conqueror. The primary reason for the rapid introduction, on a large scale, of the American public school system in the Philippines was the conviction of the military leaders that no measure could so quickly promote the pacification of the islands as education. Gen. Arthur McArthur, in recommending a large appropriation for school purposes, said:

> This appropriation is recommended primarily and exclusively as an adjunct to military operations calculated to pacify the people and to procure and expedite the restoration of tranquility throughout the archipelago.

BEGINNINGS OF COLONIAL EDUCATION

Thus, from its inception, the educational system of the Philippines was a means of pacifying a people who were defending their newly won freedom from an invader who had posed as an ally. The education of the Filipino under American sovereignty was an instrument of colonial policy. The Filipino had to be educated as a good colonial. Young minds had to be shaped to conform to American ideas. Indigenous Filipino ideals were slowly eroded in order to remove the last vestiges of resistance. Education served to attract the people to the new masters and at the same time to dilute their nationalism which had just succeeded in overthrowing a foreign power. The introduction of the American educational system was a subtle means of defeating a triumphant nationalism. As Charles Burke Elliott said in his book, *The Philippines*:

> To most Americans it seemed absurd to propose that any other language than English should be used in schools over which their flag floated. But in the schools of India and other British dependencies and colonies and, generally, in all colonies, it was and still is customary to use the vernacular in the elementary schools, and the immediate adoption of English in the Philippine schools subjected America to the charge of forcing the language of the conquerors upon a defenseless people.
>
> Of course such a system of education as the Americans contemplated could be successful only under the direction of American teachers, as the Filipino teachers who had been trained in Spanish methods were ignorant of the English language.
>
> Arrangements were promptly made for enlisting a small army of teachers in the United States. At first they came in companies, but soon in battalions. The transport *Thomas* was fitted up for their accommodation and in July, 1901, it sailed from San Francisco with six hundred teachers—a second army of occupation— surely the most remarkable cargo ever carried to an Oriental colony.

THE AMERICAN VICE-GOVERNOR

The importance of education as a colonial tool was never underestimated by the Americans. This may be clearly seen in the provision of the Jones Act which granted the Filipinos more autonomy. Although the government services were Filipinized, although the Filipinos were being prepared for self-government, the department of education was never entrusted to any Filipino. Americans always headed this department. This was assured by Article 23 of the Jones Act which provided:

> That there shall be appointed by the President, by and with the advice and consent of the Senate of the United States, a vice-governor of the Philippine Islands, who shall have all the powers of the governor-general in the case of a vacancy or temporary removal, resignation or disability of the governor-general, or in case of his temporary absence; and the said vice-governor shall be the head of the executive department known as the Department of Public Instruction, which shall include the bureau of education and the bureau of health, and he may be assigned such other executive duties as the governor-general may designate.

Up to 1935, therefore, the head of this department was an American. And when a Filipino took over under the Commonwealth, a new generation of "Filipino-Americans" had already been produced. There was no longer any need for American overseers in this field because a captive generation had already come of age, thinking and acting like little Americans.

This does not mean, however, that nothing that was taught was of any value. We became literate in English to a certain extent. We were able to produce more men and women who could read and write. We became more conversant with the outside world, especially the American world. A more widespread education such as the Americans desired would have been a real blessing had their educational program not been the handmaiden of their colonial policy. Unfortunately for us, the success of education as a colonial weapon was complete and permanent. In exchange for a smattering of English, we yielded our souls. The stories of George Washington and Abraham Lincoln made us forget our own nationalism. The American view of our history turned our heroes into brigands in our own eyes, and distorted our vision of our future. The surrender of the Katipuneros was nothing compared to this final surrender, this leveling down of our last defenses. Dr. Chester Hunt characterizes this surrender well in these words:

> The programme of cultural assimilation combined with a fairly rapid yielding
> of control resulted in the fairly general acceptance of American culture as the
> goal of Filipino society with the corollary that individual Americans were
> given a status of respect.

This, in a nutshell, was (and to a great extent still is) the happy result of early educational policy because, within the framework of American and Filipino goals and interests, the schools guided us toward action and thought which could forward American interest.

GOALS OF AMERICAN EDUCATION

The education system established by the Americans could not have been for the sole purpose of saving the Filipinos from illiteracy and ignorance. Given the economic and political purposes of American occupation, education had to be consistent with these broad purposes of American colonial policy. The Filipinos had to be trained as citizens of an American colony. The Benevolent Assimilation Proclamation of President McKinley on 21 December 1898, at a time when Filipino forces were in control of the country except Manila, betrays the intention of the colonizers. Judge Blount in his book, *The American Occupation of the Philippines*, properly comments:

> Clearly, from the Filipino point of view, the United States was now determined
> "to spare them from the dangers of premature independence," using such
> force as might be necessary for the accomplishment of that pious purpose.

Despite the noble aims announced by the American authorities that the Philippines was theirs to protect and to guide, the fact remained that these people were a conquered nation whose national life had to be woven into the pattern of American dominance. Philippine education was shaped by the overriding factor of preserving and expanding American control. To achieve this, all separatist tendencies were discouraged. Nay, they had to be condemned as subversive. With this as the pervasive factor in the grand design of conquering a people, the pattern of education, consciously or unconsciously, fostered and established certain attitudes on the part of the governed. These attitudes conformed to the purposes of American occupation.

AN UPROOTED RACE

The first and perhaps the master stroke in the plan to use education as an instrument of colonial policy was the decision to use English as the medium of instruction. English became the wedge that separated the Filipinos from their past and later was to separate educated Filipinos from the masses of their countrymen. English introduced the Filipinos to a strange, new world. With American textbooks, Filipinos started learning not only a new language but also a new way of life, alien to their traditions and yet a caricature of their model. This was the beginning of their education. At the same time, it was the beginning of their miseducation, for they learned no longer as Filipinos but as colonials. The ideal colonial was the carbon copy of his conqueror, the conformist follower of the new dispensation. He had to forget his past and unlearn the nationalist virtues in order to live peacefully, if not comfortably, under the colonial order. The new Filipino generation learned of the lives of American heroes, sang American songs, and dreamt of snow and Santa Claus. The nationalist resistance leaders exemplified by Sakay were regarded as brigands and outlaws. The lives of Philippine heroes were taught but their nationalist teachings were glossed over. Spain was the villain, America was the savior. To this day, our histories still gloss over the atrocities committed by American occupation troops such as the water cure and the reconcentration camps. Truly, a genuinely Filipino education could not have been devised within the new framework, for to draw from the wellsprings of the Filipino ethos would only have led to a distinct Philippine identity with interests at variance with those of the ruling power.

Thus, the Filipino past which had already been quite obliterated by three centuries of Spanish tyranny did not enjoy a revival under American colonialism. On the contrary, the history of our ancestors was taken up as if they were strange and foreign peoples who settled on these shores, with whom we had the most tenuous of ties. We read about them as if we were tourists in a foreign land.

ECONOMIC ATTITUDES

Control of the economic life of a colony is basic to colonial control. Some imperial nations do it harshly but the United States could be cited for the subtlety and uniqueness of its approach. For example, free trade was offered as a generous gift of American altruism. Concomitantly, the educational policy had to support this view and to soften the effects of the slowly tightening noose around the necks of the Filipinos. As a matter of fact, from the first schooldays under the soldier-teachers to the present, Philippine history books have portrayed America as a benevolent nation which came here only to save us from Spain and to spread amongst us the boons of liberty and

Photograph by Angel V. Shaw

Zamboanga City, 1988

democracy. The almost complete lack of understanding at present of those economic motivations and of the presence of American interests in the Philippines are the most eloquent testimony to the success of the education for colonials which we have undergone. What economic attitudes were fostered by American education?

It is interesting to note that during the times that the school attempts to inculcate an appreciation of things Philippine, the picture that is presented for the child's admiration is an idealized picture of a rural Philippines, as pretty and as unreal as an Amorsolo painting with its carabao, its smiling healthy farmer, the winsome barrio lass in the bright clean patadyong, and the sweet little nipa hut. That is the portrait of the Filipino that our education leaves in the minds of the young and it hurts the country in two ways.

First, it strengthens the belief (and we see this in adults) that the Philippines is essentially meant to be an agricultural country and we cannot and should not change that. The result is an apathy toward industrialization. It is an idea they have not met in school. There is, further, a fear born out of that clear stereotype of this country as an agricultural heaven, that industrialization is not good for us, that our national environment is not suited for an industrial economy, and that it will only bring social evils which will destroy the idyllic farm life.

Second, this idealized picture of farm life never emphasizes the poverty, the disease, the cultural vacuum, the sheer boredom, the superstition and ignorance of backward farm communities. Those who pursue higher education think of the farms as quaint places, good for an occasional vacation. Their life is rooted in the big towns and cities and there is no interest in revamping rural life because there is no understanding of its economic problems. Interest is limited to artesian wells and handicraft projects. Present efforts to uplift the conditions of the rural masses merely attack the peripheral problems without admitting the urgent need for basic agrarian reform.

With American education, the Filipinos were not only learning a new language; they were not only forgetting their own language; they were starting to become a new type of American. American ways were slowly being adopted. Our consumption habits were molded by the influx of what came in duty-free. The pastoral economy was extolled because this conformed with the colonial economy that was being fostered. Our books extolled the Western nations as peopled by superior beings because they were capable of manufacturing things that we never thought we were capable of producing. We were pleased with the fact that our raw material exports could pay for the American consumption goods that we had to import. Now we are used to these types of goods, and it is a habit we find hard to break, to the detriment of our own economy. We never thought that we too could industrialize because in school we were taught that we were primarily an agricultural country by geographical location and by the innate potentials of our people. We were one with our fellow Asians in believing that we were not cut out for an industrialized economy. That is why before the war, we looked down upon goods made in Japan despite the fact that Japan was already producing commodities on a par with the West. We could never believe that Japan, an Asian country, could attain the same superiority as America, Germany, or England. And yet, it was "made-in-Japan" airplanes, battleships, and armaments that dislodged the Americans and the British from their positions of dominance during the Second World War. This is the same attitude that has put us out of step with our Asian neighbors who have already realized that colonialism has to be extirpated from their lives if they want to be free, prosperous, and happy.

TRANSPLANTATION OF POLITICAL INSTITUTIONS

American education in effect transplanted American political institutions and ideas to the Philippines. Sen. Claro M. Recto, in his last major address at the University of the Philippines, explained the reason for this. Speaking of political parties, he said:

> It is to be deplored that our major political parties were born and nurtured before we had attained the status of a free democracy. The result was that they have come to be caricatures of their foreign model with its known characteristics— patronage, division of spoils, political bossism, partisan treatment of vital national issues. I say caricatures because of their chronic shortsightedness respecting those ultimate objectives the attainment of which was essential to a true and lasting national independence. All throughout the period of American colonization, they allowed themselves to become more and more the tools of colonial rule and less and less the interpreters of the people's will and ideals. Through their complacency, the new colonizer was able to fashion, in exchange for sufferance of oratorical plaints for independence, and for patronage, rank, and sinecure, a regime of his own choosing, for his own aims, and in his own self-interest.

The Americans were confronted with the dilemma of transplanting their political institutions and yet luring the Filipino into a state of captivity. It was understandable for American authorities to think that democracy could only mean the American type of democracy, and thus they foisted on the Filipinos the institutions that were valid for their own people. Indigenous institutions which could have led to the evolution of native democratic ideas and institutions were disregarded. No wonder, we, too, look with hostility upon countries who try to develop their own political institutions according to the needs of their people without being bound by Western political procedures. We have been made to believe in certain political doctrines as absolute and the same for all peoples. An example of this is the belief in freedom of the press. Here the consensus is that we cannot nationalize the press because it would be depriving foreigners of the exercise of freedom of the press. This may be valid for strong countries like the United States where there is no threat of foreign domination, but certainly this is dangerous for an emergent nation like the Philippines where foreign control has yet to be weakened.

EDSA Event,
by Bencab
1986

RE-EXAMINATION DEMANDED

The new demands for economic emancipation and the assertion of our political sovereignty leave our educators no choice but to reexamine their philosophy, their values, and their general approach to the making of the Filipino who will institute, support, and preserve the nationalist aims. To persist in the continuance of a system which was born under the exigencies of colonial rule, to be timid in the face of traditional opposition would only result in the evolution of an anomalous educational system which lags behind the urgent economic and political changes that the nation is experiencing. What then are the nationalist tasks for Philippine education?

Education must be seen not as an acquisition of information but as the making of man so that he may function most effectively and usefully within his own society. Therefore, education cannot be divorced from the society of a definite country at a definite time. It is a fallacy to think that educational goals should be the same everywhere and that therefore what goes into the making of a well-educated American is the same as what should go into the making of the well-educated Filipino. This would be true only if the two societies were at the same political, cultural, and economic levels and had the same political, cultural, and economic goals.

But what has happened in this country? Not only do we imitate Western education, we have patterned our education after that of the most technologically advanced Western nation. The gap between the two societies is very large. In fact, they are two entirely different societies with different goals.

ADOPTION OF WESTERN VALUES

Economically, the United States is an industrial nation. It is a fully developed nation, economically speaking. Our country has a colonial economy with a tiny industrial base. In other words, we are backward and underdeveloped. Politically, the United States is not only master of its own house; its control and influence extends to many other countries all over the world. The Philippines has only lately emerged from formal colonial status and must still complete its political and economic independence.

Culturally, the United States has a vigorously and distinctively American culture. It is a nation whose cultural institutions have developed freely, indigenously, without control or direction from foreign sources, whose ties to its cultural past are clear and proudly celebrated because no foreign power has imposed upon its people a wholesale inferiority complex, because no foreign culture has been superimposed upon it destroying, distorting its own past and alienating the people from their own cultural heritage.

Marlboro Country,
by Bencab
1975

What are the characteristics of American education today which spring from its economic, political, and cultural status? What should be the characteristics of our own education as dictated by our own economic, political, and cultural conditions? To contrast both is to realize how inimical to our best interests and progress is our adoption of some of the basic characteristics and values of American education.

By virtue of its world leadership and economic interests in many parts of the world, the United States has an internationalist orientation based securely on a well-grounded, longheld nationalistic viewpoint. American education has no urgent need to stress the development of American nationalism in its young people. Economically, politically, culturally, the United States is master of its own house. American education, therefore, understandably lays little emphasis on the kind of nationalism we Filipinos need. Instead, it stresses inter-nationalism and underplays nationalism. This sentiment is noble and good but when it is inculcated in a people who have either forgotten nationalism or never imbibed it, it can cause untold harm. The emphasis on world brotherhood, on friendship for other nations, without the firm foundation of nationalism which would give our people the feeling of pride in our own products and vigilance over our natural resources, has had very harmful results. Chief among these is the transformation of our national virtue of hospitality into a stupid vice which hurts us and makes us the willing dupes of predatory foreigners.

UN-FILIPINO FILIPINOS

Thus we complacently allow aliens to gain control of our economy. We are even proud of those who amass wealth in our country, publishing laudatory articles about their financial success. We love to hear foreigners call our country a paradise on earth, and we never stop to think that it is a paradise only for them but not for millions of our countrymen. When some of our more intellectually emancipated countrymen spearhead moves for nationalism, for nationalism of this or that endeavor, do the majority of Filipinos support such moves? No, there is apathy because there is no nationalism in our hearts which will spur us to protect and help our own countrymen first. Worse, some Filipinos even worry about the sensibilities of foreigners lest they think ill of us for supposedly discriminating against them. Worst of all, many Filipinos will even oppose nationalistic legislation either because they have become the willing servants of foreign interests or because, in their distorted view, we Filipinos cannot progress without the help of foreign capital and foreign entrepreneurs.

In this part of the world, we are well nigh unique in our generally non-nationalistic outlook. What is the source of this shameful characteristic of ours? One important source is surely the schools. There is little emphasis on nationalism. Patriotism has been taught us, yes, but in general terms of love of country, respect for the flag, appreciation of the beauty of our countryside, and other similarly innocuous manifestations of our nationality.

The pathetic result of this failure of Philippine education is a citizenry amazingly naïve and trusting in its relations with foreigners, devoid of the capacity to feel indignation even in the face of insults to the nation, ready to acquiesce and even to help aliens in the despoliation of our natural wealth. Why are the great majority of our people so complaisant about alien economic control? Much of the blame must be laid at the door of colonial education. Colonial education has not provided us with a realistic attitude toward other nations, especially Spain and the United States. The emphasis in our study of history has been on the great gifts that our conquerors have bestowed upon us. A mask of benevolence was used to hide the cruelties and deceit of early American occupation. The noble sentiments expressed by McKinley were emphasized rather than the ulterior motives of conquest. The myth of friendship and special relations is even now continually invoked to camouflage the continuing iniquities in our relationship. Nurtured in this kind of education, the Filipino mind has come to regard centuries of colonial status as a grace from above rather than as a scourge. Is it any wonder then that having regained our independence we have forgotten how to defend it? Is it any wonder that when leaders like Claro M. Recto try to teach us how to be free, the great majority of the people find it difficult to grasp those nationalistic principles that are the staple food of other Asian minds? The American architects of our colonial education really labored shrewdly and well.

THE LANGUAGE PROBLEM

The most vital problem that has plagued Philippine education has been the question of language. Today, experiments are still going on to find out whether it would be more effective to use the native language. This is indeed ridiculous since an individual cannot be more at home in any other language than his own. In every sovereign country, the use of its own language in education is so natural no one thinks it could be otherwise. But here, so great has been our disorientation caused by our colonial education that the use of our own language is a controversial issue, with more Filipinos against than in favor! Again, as in the economic field Filipinos believe they cannot survive without America, so in education we believe no education can be true education unless it is based on proficiency in English.

Rizal foresaw the tragic effects of a colonial education when, speaking through Simoun, he said:

You ask for equal rights, the Hispanization of your customs, and you don't see that what you are begging for is suicide, the destruction of your nationality, the annihilation of your fatherland, the consecration of tyranny! What will you be in the future? A people without character, a nation without liberty—everything you have will be borrowed, even your very defects!…. What are you going to do with Castilian, the few of you who will speak it? Kill off your own originality, subordinate your thoughts to other brains, and instead of freeing yourselves, make yourselves slaves indeed! Nine-tenths of those of you who pretend to be enlightened are renegades to your country! He among you who talks that language neglects his own in such a way that he neither writes it nor understands it, and how many have I not seen who pretend not to know a single word of it!

It is indeed unfortunate that teaching in the native language is given up to second grade only, and the question of whether beyond this it should be English or Pilipino is still unsettled. Many of our educational experts have written on the language problem, but there is an apparent timidity on the part of these experts to come out openly for the urgent need of discarding the foreign language as the medium of instruction in spite of remarkable results shown by the use of the native language. Yet, the deleterious effects of using English as the medium of instruction are many and serious. What Rizal said about Spanish has been proven to be equally true of English.

BARRIER DEMOCRACY

Under the system maintained by Spain in the Philippines, educational opportunities were so limited that learning became the possession of a chosen few. This enlightened group was called the *ilustrados*. They constituted the elite. Most of them came from the wealthy class because this was the only class that could afford to send its sons abroad to pursue higher learning. Learning, therefore, became a badge of privilege. There was a wide gap between the *ilustrados* and the masses. Of course, many of the *ilustrados* led the Propaganda Movement, but they were mostly reformers who wanted reforms within the framework of Spanish colonialism. In a way, they were also captives of Spanish education. Many of them were the first to capitulate to the Americans, and the first leaders of the Filipinos during the early years of the American regime came from this class. Later they were supplanted by the products of American education.

One of the ostensible reasons for imposing English as the medium of instruction was the fact that English was the language of democracy, that through this tongue the Filipinos would imbibe the American way of life which makes no distinction between rich and poor and which gives everyone equal opportunities. Under this thesis, the existence of an *ilustrado* class would not long endure because all Filipinos would be enlightened and educated. There would be no privileged class. In the long run, however, English perpetuated the existence of the *ilustrados*—American *ilustrados* who, like their counterparts, were strong supporters of the way of life of the new motherland.

Now we have a small group of men who can articulate their thoughts in English, a wider group that can read and speak in fairly comprehensible English and a great mass that hardly expresses itself in this language. All of these groups are hardly articulate in their native tongues because of the neglect of our native dialects, if not the deliberate attempts to prevent their growth.

The result is a leadership that fails to understand the needs of the masses because it is a leadership that can communicate with the masses only in general and vague terms. This is the one reason why political leadership remains in a vacuum. This is the reason why issues are never fully discussed. This is the reason orators with the best inflections, demagogues who rant and rave, are the ones that flourish in the political arena. English has become a status symbol, while the native tongues are looked down upon. English has given rise to a bifurcated society of fairly educated men and the masses who are easily swayed by them. A clear evidence of the failure of English education is the fact that politicians address the masses in their dialects. Lacking mastery of the dialect, the politicians merely deal in generalities.

Because of their lack of command of English, the masses have gotten used to only half-understanding what is said to them in English. They appreciate the sounds without knowing the sense. This is a barrier to democracy. People don't even think it is their duty to know, or that they are capable of understanding national problems. Because of the language barrier, therefore, they are content to leave everything to their leaders. This is one of the root causes of their apathy, their regionalism or parochialism. Thus, English which was supposedly envisioned as the language of democracy is in our country a barrier to the full flowering of democracy.

In 1924 the eminent scholar Najib Saleeby wrote on the language of education in the Philippines. He deplored the attempt to impose English as the medium of instruction. Saleeby, who was an expert in the Malayo-Polynesian languages, showed that Tagalog, Visayan, Ilocano, and other Philippine dialects belong to the same linguistic tree. He said:

> The relation the Tagalog holds to the Bisaya or to the Sulu is very much like or closer than that of the Spanish to the Italian. An educated Tagalog from Batangas and an educated Bisayan from Cebu can learn to understand each other in a short space of time and without much effort. A Cebu student living in Manila can acquire practical use and good understanding of Tagalog in less than three months. The relation between Tagalog and Malay is very much the same as that of Spanish and French.

This was said forty-two years ago when Tagalog movies, periodicals, and radio programs had not yet attained the popularity they enjoy today all over the country.

Saleeby further states:

> Empirically neither the Spanish nor the English could be a suitable medium for public instruction in the Philippine Islands. It does not seem possible that either of them can become the common or national language of the Archipelago. Three centuries of Spanish rule and education failed to check use of the vernacular. A very small minority of Filipinos could speak Spanish in 1898, but the great mass of the people could neither use nor understand it. Twenty-five years of intensive English education has produced no radical change. More people at present speak English than Spanish, but the great majority hold on to the local dialect. The Spanish policy might be practically justified on colonial and financial grounds, but the American policy cannot be

so defended. It should receive popular free choice, or give proof of its practicability by showing actual and satisfactory results. The people have as yet had no occasion to declare their free will, and the present policy must be judged on its own merits and on conclusive evidence.... But teaching English broadcast and enforcing its official use is one thing, and its adoption as the basis of education and as the sole medium of public instruction is a completely different matter. This point cannot be fully grasped or comprehended without special attention and experience in colonial education and administration. Such policy is exalted and ambitious to an extreme degree. It aims at something unknown before in human affairs. It is attempting to do what ancient Persia, Rome, Alexander the Great and Napoleon failed to accomplish. It aims at nothing less than the obliteration of the tribal differences of the Filipinos, the substitution of English for the vernacular dialects as a home tongue, and making English the national, common language of the Archipelago.

This is more true today. Very few college students can speak except in mixed English and the dialect. Our Congress has compounded their confusion by a completely unwarranted imposition of twenty-four units of Spanish.

IMPEDIMENTS TO THOUGHT

A foreign language is an impediment to instruction. Instead of learning directly through the native tongue, a child has first to master a foreign tongue, memorize its vocabulary, get accustomed to its sounds, intonations, accents, just to discard the language later when he is out of school. This does not mean that foreign languages should not be taught. Foreign languages should be taught and can be taught more easily after one has mastered one's own tongue.

Even if the Americans were motivated by the sincere desire to unify the country by means of a common tongue, the abject results of instruction in English through the six decades of American education should have awakened our educators to the fact that the learning process has been disrupted by the imposition of a foreign language. From 1935 when the Institute of National Language was organized, very feeble attempts have been made to abandon the use of English as a medium of instruction. Our educators seem constantly to avoid the subject of language, in spite of the clear evidence of rampant ignorance among the products of the present educational system. This has resulted in the denial of education to a vast number of children who after the primary grades no longer continue schooling. In spite of the fact that the national language today is understood all over the country, no one is brave enough to advocate its use as the medium of instruction. There is the constant argument that new expenditures, new efforts in the publication of new textbooks will be required. There are arguments about the dearth of materials in the national language, but these are feeble arguments that merely disguise the basic opposition of our educational leaders to the use of what is native. Thus, the products of the Philippine educational system, barring very few exceptions, are Filipinos who do not have a mastery of their native tongue because of the deliberate neglect of those responsible for the education of the citizens of the nation.

A foreign tongue as a medium of instruction constitutes an impediment to learning and to thinking because a student first has to master new sounds, new inflections, and new sentence constructions. His innermost thoughts find difficulty of expression, and lack of expression in turn prevents the further development of thought. Thus we find in our society a deplorable lack of serious thinking among great sections of the population. We half understand books and periodicals written in English. We find it an ordeal to communicate with each other through a foreign medium, and yet we have so neglected our native language that we find ourselves at a loss in expressing ourselves in this language.

Language is a tool of the thinking process. Through language, thought develops, and the development of thought leads to the further development of language. But when a language becomes a barrier to thought, the thinking process is impeded or retarded and we have the resultant cultural stagnation. Creative thinking, analytic thinking, abstract thinking are not fostered because the foreign language makes the student prone to memorization. Because of the mechanical process of learning, he is able to get only a general idea but not a deeper understanding. So, the tendency of students is to study in order to be able to answer correctly and to pass the examinations and thereby earn the required credits. Independent thinking is smothered because the language of learning ceases to be the language of communication outside the classroom. A student is mainly concerned with the acquisition of information. He is seldom able to utilize this information for deepening his understanding of his society's problems.

Our Institute of National Language is practically neglected. It should be one of the main pillars of an independent country. Our educators are wary about proposing the immediate adoption of the national language as the medium of instruction because of what they consider as opposition of other language groups. This is indicative of our colonial mentality. Our educators do not see any opposition to the use of a foreign language but fear opposition to the use of the national language just because it is based on one of the main dialects. The fact that one can be understood in any part of the Philippines through the national language, the fact that periodicals in the national language and local movies have a mass following all over the islands, shows that, given the right support, the national language would take its proper place.

Language is the main problem, therefore. Experience has shown that children who are taught in their native tongue learn more easily and better than those taught in English. Records of the Bureau of Public Schools will support this. But mere teaching of the national language is not enough. There are other areas that demand immediate attention.

Philippine history must be rewritten from the point of view of the Filipino. Our economic problems must be presented in the light of nationalism and independence. These are only some of the problems that confront a nationalist approach to education. Government leadership and supervision are essential. Our educators need the support of legislators in this regard. In this connection, the private sector also has to be strictly supervised.

THE PRIVATE SECTOR

Before the Second World War, products of the Philippine public school system looked down upon their counterparts in the private schools. It is generally accepted that graduates of the public schools at that time were superior to the products of the private institutions in point of learning. There were exclusive private institutions but these were reserved for the well-to-do. These schools did not necessarily reflect superiority of instruction. But they reflected superiority of social status.

Among students of the public schools, there was still some manifestation of concern for national problems. Vestiges of the nationalistic tradition of our revolution remained in the consciousness of those parents who had been caught in the mainstream of the rebellion, and these were passed on to the young. On the other hand, apathy to national problems was marked among the more affluent private school students whose families had readily accepted American rule.

Today, public schools are looked down upon. Only the poor send their children to these schools. Those who can afford it, or those who have social pretensions, send their children to private institutions. The result has been a boom in private education, a boom that unfortunately has seen the proliferation of diploma mills. Two concomitant tendencies went with this trend. First was the commercialization of education. A lowering of standards resulted because of the inadequate facilities of the public schools and the commercialization in the private sector. It is a well known fact that classes in many private schools are packed and teachers are overloaded in order to maximize profits. Second, some private schools which are owned and operated by foreigners and whose social science courses are handled by aliens flourished. While foreigners may not be anti-Filipino, they definitely cannot be nationalistic in orientation. They think as foreigners and as private interest. Thus, the proliferation of private schools and the simultaneous deterioration of public schools have resulted not only in lower standards but also in a definitely un-Filipino education.

Some years ago, there was a move to grant curricular freedom to certain qualified private institutions as well as wider leeway for self-regulation. This was a retrograde step. It is true that this move was in answer to charges that state supervision would enhance regimentation. But in a country that is just awakening to nationalist endeavors, it is the duty of a nationalist administration to see to it that the molding of minds is safely channeled along nationalist lines. The autonomy of private institutions may be used to subvert nationalist sentiments, especially when ownership of schools and handling of social sciences are not yet Filipinized. Autonomy of private institutions would only dilute nationalist sentiments either by foreign subversion or by commercialization.

OTHER EDUCATIONAL MEDIA

While the basic defect in the educational system has been responsible for the lack of nationalist ideals, there are other media and facilities that negate whatever gains are made in some sectors of the educational field. The almost unilateral source of news, films, and other cultural materials tends to distort our perspective. American films and comics, American press services, fellowships in America, have all contributed to the almost total Americanization of our attitudes. A distinct Filipino culture cannot prevail if an avalanche of cultural materials from the West suffocates our relatively puny efforts in this direction.

NEEDED: FILIPINOS

The education of the Filipino must be a Filipino education. It must be based on the needs of the nation and the goals of the nation. The object is not merely to produce men and women who can read and write or who can add and subtract. The primary object is to produce a citizenry that appreciates, and is conscious of, nationhood and the national goals for the betterment of the community, and not an anarchic mass of people who know how to take care of themselves only. Our students hear of Rizal and Bonifacio but are their teachings related to our present problems or do they merely learn of anecdotes and incidents that prove interesting to the child's imagination?

We have learned to use American criteria for our problems and we look at our prehistory and our past with the eyes of a visitor. A lot of information is learned but attitudes are not developed. The proper regard for things Philippine, the selfish concern over the national fate—these are not at all imbedded in the consciousness of students. Children and adolescents go to school to get a certificate or diploma. They try to learn facts but the patriotic attitude is not acquired because of too much emphasis on forms.

What should be the basic objective of education in the Philippines? Is it merely to produce men and women who can read and write? If this is the only purpose, then education is directionless. Education should first of all assure national survival. No amount of economic and political policy can be successful if the educational program does not imbue prospective citizens with the proper attitudes that will ensure the implementation of these goals and policies. Philippine educational policies should be geared to the making of Filipinos. These policies should see to it that schools produce men and women with minds and attitudes that are attuned to the needs of the country.

Under previous colonial regimes, education saw to it that the Filipino mind was subservient to that of the master. The foreign overlords were esteemed. We were not taught to view them objectively, seeing their virtues as well as their faults. This led our citizens to form a distorted opinion of the foreign masters and also of themselves. The function of education now is to correct this distortion. We must now think of ourselves, of our salvation, of our time. And unless we prepare the minds of the young for this endeavor, we shall always be a pathetic people with no definite goals and no assurance of preservation.

From Colonizer to Liberator:
How U.S. Colonialism Succeeded in Reinventing Itself After the Pacific War

BIENVENIDO LUMBERA

The Treaty of Paris of 1898 launched the United States of America as an imperialist power when it acquired the Philippines from Spain at the cost of twenty million dollars. Filipino playwright Aurelio Tolentino, in his 1902 allegorical play *Kahapon, Ngayon at Bukas* (*Yesterday, Today and Tomorrow*), which was suppressed on the very night it opened, satirizes the new colonizer of the Filipinos through the characters Bagongsibol and Malaynatin whose names describe the United States as "a new sprout" and its colonial administrators as "who knows what they are up to." Another character, purportedly Chinese but actually referring to the United States, was called Haringbata, a "new-born monarch."

Having been born in 1932, I have lived through the political and cultural processes that saw U.S. colonialism assume a new aspect as liberator in the years often summed up in the Filipino phrase "noong liberation" which roughly translates into "in the days of Liberation" or "shortly after the end of the war." Having thus witnessed and experienced U.S. colonialism, I may claim what here might seem purely personal observations to have a certain objective validity, as they have been checked against available historical accounts, policies promulgated, and narratives by key personalities of the times.

In 1934 the U.S. Senate legislated the Philippine colony into a Commonwealth, setting a transition period of ten years that was to culminate in independence in 1946. The law that created the Commonwealth was the fruit of a twenty-eight-year legal campaign waged by various patriotic politicians representing remnants of the leadership of the short-lived republic. The Pacific War broke out in 1941, and Filipinos spent three years of the transition period under the Japanese imperial forces which had driven out the Americans under Gen. Douglas MacArthur. The populace resisted Japanese efforts to win them over, and a nationwide guerrilla movement plied them with news about developments in the United States' efforts to recover from its military setbacks. In a dramatic radio address on 20 October 1944, MacArthur announced, "People of the Philippines, I have returned!"

The reoccupation of the Philippines signaled by MacArthur's words was greeted by the Filipinos with rejoicing, and the return of the colonizing forces was seen as "liberation" rather than a return to captivity. Such reaction has been interpreted as the articulation of the Filipinos' innate tendency to prize gratitude in their relationship with people who have done them a good turn, in effect naturalizing, and thereby sanctioning, what was in truth a reaction induced by historical and sociopolitical processes.

The perception that MacArthur's forces were liberators was easy enough to understand in 1945, given the agony Filipinos had had to endure under the Japanese. That it persisted beyond the end of the Pacific War and into the 1960s is an anomaly that calls for analysis. Such an analysis might start with the interlocking forces that created the "miracle" which transformed the colonial power into a liberator of the very people it had colonized in 1898.

Conquest and Resistance by Bencab 1999

Although it lasted for only a brief period, the Japanese occupation in the minds of those who lived in fear, hunger and instability was three almost interminable years, "three years without God," as the title of a Tagalog movie was to recall the time many years later. I was nine years old and in the third grade at the Lipa Elementary School when the war broke out. The schoolyear 1941–1942 was barely halfway through, and for a school child who could not see beyond tomorrow, the sudden ending of classes turned the days ahead into a blur that clarified itself only as I moved from one day to the next.

"Evacuate" was a new English word, and for children of my age who were town residents, it simply meant spending time in a barrio not too far away from town, while adults were sizing up the situation and waiting for the safe time to go back to town, there to try to resume normal lives of civilians under wartime conditions. Hiking through coconut groves, eating ripe guavas off trees that seemed to grow just about anywhere, bathing in brookwater while mothers and aunts with their tin flatbasins did the weekly laundry—without a schoolbell to mark the hours of a schoolboy's day, life flowed lazily and aimlessly on.

In the final days of the war, "evacuate" had been absorbed into Tagalog, and the adopted word "bakwit" carried sinister overtones of flight from imminent danger and grim visions of capture, rape, and death in the hands of retreating, defeat-crazed Japanese troops. I was turning thirteen at this time, and an atmosphere of doom hung over our household at dusk when the adult males had hied off to sleep in the forest to avoid capture should the Japanese decide to raid the village. It was on one such occasion that I resolved in my heart, as I lay on my mat listening and waiting for the tramp-tramp of Japanese boots, that should I find myself an adult in another war, I would rather be a soldier fighting in the battlefront than a civilian at home ever in mortal dread of enemy soldiers who might swoop down at the most unexpected hours.

Extreme economic hardship was imposed by the war on a people that depended for their subsistence on agricultural production which hardly yielded any surplus. The Japanese army, when it occupied the country, did not have an abundant supply line that would keep its troops fed. Instead it found itself competing with the local populace for rice that was only enough to feed Filipinos. As a result, there was never enough rice in the market, and government rationing of the staple grain was a feature of the economy of the time which has stuck in the public memory. Crushed corn or chopped cassava was mixed with rice to make the family supply last until the next ration. All kinds of rice substitutes were discovered and invented, such as unaccustomed root crops, fruits, and legumes.

Knowing that the populace was generally sympathetic to their enemy, the Japanese resorted to political repression which took many forms. Incarceration, torture and execution were commonplace penalties for men and women suspected of guerrilla activity. Many times people were killed because they had been unable to explain themselves to soldiers who did not understand the native languages. Takeover of private property, such as homes and vehicles, by the Japanese army was common, and Filipinos fearing for their lives and limbs usually allowed it to go unchallenged lest they be accused of political resistance.

For forty years prior to the Japanese invasion, Filipinos had been acculturated as Westerners by American popular culture. Movies, magazines, comic books, phonograph records, and even candy bars from the United States freely inundated Philippine society, introducing Filipinos to American customs, food, fashion, and entertainment. The war cut off the flow of culture items from America and the resulting deprivation intensified the fervor of waiting for the return of the Americans. Then the Americans did come back in 1945, and memories of "liberation" later would always include "Babe Ruth," chewing gum, and cigarettes made from aromatic Virginia tobacco.

The first American GIs I ever saw were splashing about in the nude in the stream that cut across the center of the town of Rosario, Batangas. We were evacuees who came into town from the barrio where we had sought refuge after marching out of our village in Lipa in a caravan. During the last days of the Japanese occupation, noncombatants in town and barrio had been intimidated by known sympathizers of the Japanese who told them that "only Filipinos made of gold" would live to see returning Americans. And so on the morning of our first day in Rosario, I was with a group of teenage boys who wanted to take a look at the American soldiers in town to be able to savor the sensation of being "golden." And at this stream, where the women of households bathed the children and washed the laundry, there was this crowd of soldiers brazenly exposing themselves to the townspeople who were presumably grateful that they were seeing their first "liberators."

Getting to look at the naked bathers was understandably a magical moment for us who had survived the war. If the adults among the onlookers did not feel violated by such a blatant disregard for the townspeople's sense of modesty, that was a measure of their readiness to overlook any cultural slight by soldiers whose very physical presence affirmed that indeed they had been turned to gold.

In the final days of American colonial rule, before independence was granted in 1946, Gen. Douglas MacArthur wielded tremendous influence in shaping the "special relations" between the United States and the Philippines. Not quite happy with the performance of Sergio Osmeña who took over as head of the Commonwealth government following the death of President Manuel Quezon, MacArthur did not bother to conceal his preference for another leader. Osmeña was aging and slow to act at a time when postwar conditions called for decisiveness. Therefore, MacArthur picked his friend Manuel Roxas, who was young and brilliant and indebted to the general. Although Washington had earlier laid down the policy of prosecuting Filipino government officials who had aided the enemy during the Japanese occupation, MacArthur chose to judge for himself who in the elite leadership in the Philippines were to be prosecuted as collaborators. Consequently, he decided to pardon Roxas, wiping clean the taint of collaborationism that would bar the young politician from the leadership of the government the

Americans were readying for the Filipinos as they prepared to give up the colony.[1]

With Roxas exonerated without the say-so of any court, collaboration ceased to be a major issue in the 1945 elections. MacArthur's pardon was in effect an endorsement by the American hero of the moment, and Roxas rode on it to victory over Osmeña. The general's pardon paid off for the United States as subsequent events were to prove. Roxas would pay back MacArthur and the country the general represented by the fervor and enthusiasm with which he rallied the electorate to vote "yes" in the plebiscite that gave American citizens the right to exploit the natural resources of the country, a right that the Philippine Constitution had originally reserved for Filipinos. In his inaugural address as president of the Republic of the Philippines, Roxas proved to be a grateful client of U.S. benevolence when he said: "Our safest course, and I believe it true for the rest of the world as well, is in the glistening wake of America whose sure advance with mighty prow breaks for smaller craft the waves of fear." A military officer by the name of Commodore Julius C. Edelstein of the U.S. Navy was Roxas's speech writer.[2] Knowing this, one could be pardoned the suspicion that the president's extravagant rhetoric was in all likelihood put in his mouth by an American.

Two military units organized to respond to exigencies arising from the war gave substance to the image of savior and protector clinging to "G.I. Joe." These were the PCAU (Philippine Civil Affairs Unit) and the CIC (Counter-Intelligence Corps). The PCAU functioned as a relief agency that extended help, in the form of foodstuffs and medicine, to war victims ravaged by hunger and disease. The Commonwealth government of Osmeña had yet to fully organize itself to respond to the economic crisis in the cities and towns of postwar Philippines, and it was the PCAU that took up the slack. Municipal employees and teachers had to be paid their salaries as the bureaucracy and the school system were being revived. The PCAU paid out salaries and created temporary jobs for laborers to get the economy going. If one is interested in seeking out the roots of the dependency that would eventually stand out as a feature of the Philippine position in its relationship to the United States, the PCAU might very well be the institution which fostered such a mentality.

If the PCAU was the relief agency, the CIC was the unit that saw to security matters. As its title announced, it was the body tasked with ascertaining the political acceptability of those recommended by the Commonwealth president for positions in the provincial and municipal governments in the bureaucracy that was being rebuilt. It had jurisdiction over prisoners charged with the crime of collaboration, so it was in direct touch with powerful members of the Philippine elite, among them Roxas himself, Jose P. Laurel, Claro M. Recto, Jorge Vargas, Benigno Aquino Sr., and Sergio Osmeña Jr. Needless to say, the CIC was an all-powerful unit of the U.S. army in the days when the Commonwealth government was just beginning to get up on its feet amid the ruins of war. Any politician who would continue to pursue his ambitions would have to be in the good graces of the United States military in charge of this body. As in the case of the PCAU, the CIC might be seen as the original paradigm of the mechanism for American intervention in Philippine political and military matters, and its influence during the period of its existence in the U.S. Army could account for the habitual deference Filipino officials would manifest even in our time when they discuss matters of state with representatives of the United States.

The Bell Trade Relations Act, which provided for free trade relations between the United States and the Philippines, and the Tydings Rehabilitation Act which set aside $620 million to defray the cost of rebuilding infrastructure destroyed by the war, might be regarded in retrospect as grand political gestures that further cemented "special relations" between the exiting colonizers and the people who underwent tutelage under them. Unexamined, the two Acts of the U.S. Congress could be seen as generous pieces of legislation meant to benefit the Filipinos, and this was how the members of the elite who championed "parity rights" for Americans perceived it or made it appear when they exhorted the voters to sanction amending the Constitution. In truth the two pieces of legislation were locked together through the intervention of the then U.S. High Commissioner Paul V. McNutt who foresaw stiff opposition to the "parity" provision in the Bell Trade Relations Act. McNutt, who did not believe in independence for the Philippines, was responsible for tying the implementation of the Tydings Rehabilitation Act to the approval of the Bell Trade Relations Act.

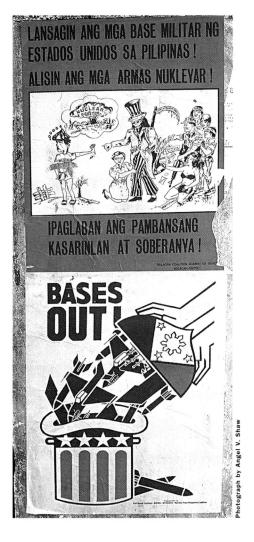

Photograph by Angel V. Shaw

The pattern of American political maneuvering was to be pursued in subsequent cases of Philippine-American relations. When the administration of President Elpidio Quirino proved itself unable to suppress the Communist insurgency spearheaded by the Hukbalahap rebellion, the American ambassador and the chief U.S. military adviser intervened directly and got the Filipino president to appoint Ramon Magsaysay as secretary of national defense. It was therefore two Americans, Myron Cowen and Leland Hobbs, who began the process of putting down the rebellion that was considered a threat to U.S. hegemony in Southeast Asia and the Pacific.[3]

As soon as Magsaysay had been installed in the Department of National Defense, the Central Intelligence Agency (CIA) moved in, detailing operative Edward Lansdale as military adviser attached to the Joint U.S. Military Advisory Group (JUSMAG)

Malolos, 1988

in Manila. Lansdale met with Magsaysay and the stage was set for America's most elaborate and, as subsequent events were to prove, most effective political drama on the theme of "special relations." A counter-insurgency expert, Lansdale steered the defense secretary toward cleaning up and revitalizing the Philippine Army, waging psycho-warfare against the Huks, weaning peasant support away from the Huks, and through an ambitious re-settlement program, providing farms in Mindanao for Huk surrenderees.

In 1950 the morale of the army was high and with improved intelligence work the military succeeded in capturing the top leaders of the Hukbalahap movement and of the Partido Komunista ng Pilipinas. This was a climactic moment in the career of the young defense secretary, and with expert image-building under the guidance again of Lansdale, Magsaysay was on his way to achieving the status of a living hero. In 1953

Magsaysay ran against Elpidio Quirino who was seeking a second term as president and won a landslide victory that gave him 69 percent of the total number of votes cast. Like Roxas before him, Magsaysay proved himself to be a grateful client of the United States as shown by his steadfast pro-American stance in the ideological standoff between that country and the Soviet Union. When the United States was lining up its allies to plan collective defense for Southeast Asia after the fall of Dien Bien Phu to the communist Viet Minh, Magsaysay was unequivocal in his support for the United States and its diplomatic confrontations with Communism all over the world. Dead before he could complete his term as president, Magsaysay during his incumbency sought to project himself as a Filipino patriot who found no incompatibility between being loyal to his people and country and being beholden to the United States. Perhaps, among the populace that loved him, it was the image of Magsaysay that crystallized the illusion that the Filipino could remain a patriot even as he continued to cater to the political and economic impositions of the Americans.

In high school, the teacher who taught us world history was a devout Catholic. One day in 1947 when the class was assigned to report on "current events," someone came with a clipping on the victories of the Red Army in Mainland China. Our teacher told about the heroism of Catholics in China who stood up to their communist captors and refused to deny their religion. The class was then challenged to stand up for the faith should Chinese Communists take over the Philippines and line up Filipinos against the wall, ask who among them were Catholics. The sobering challenge was to remain in my mind even up to the time I was a college senior in the University of Santo Tomas.

It was not always the case that the Filipino leadership had been manipulated into making concessions to the former colonial master. It was also true that security needs drove Filipino leaders to seek shelter beneath the wings of the American eagle. The Cold War cornered the Philippines into taking the side of the United States in the confrontation between the Communist bloc and the so-called free world. The Chinese Revolution was advancing inexorably in Mainland China, and the fear was that with so many Chinese residents in the Philippines, it would be an easy matter for Mao Zedong's forces to take over the country if they so willed. Within the Philippines itself, the Hukbalahap rebellion was spreading beyond Central Luzon, and a corrupt bureaucracy was fast alienating from the government the majority of the citizenry with no access to wealth and power. Confounding the country's instability, anticolonial wars in Indonesia and Vietnam were thrusting out the Dutch and the French. Indeed, all around the Philippines, the old world seemed to be falling apart, and the newly installed republic had barely begun to take firm footing. When the Korean War broke out and Chinese troops intervened to help the North Koreans fight back the Americans, the People's Republic of China became even more fearsome as a potential invader.

Breaking the advance of the Hukbalahap movement and giving the country respite from the shooting war was Defense Secretary Magsaysay's claim to preeminence as a leader. But that achievement was not enough to put to rest the fears of the oligarchy, for they themselves did not think that military suppression had killed off dissent in the Philippine countryside. In the United States, Sen. Joseph McCarthy was whipping up hysteria over the "virus" of Communism that he feared had infected American society. In the Philippines, a similar frenzy had spurred lawmakers to set up a counterpart of McCarthy's House Un-American Activities Committee (HUAC).

This was the Committee on Anti-Filipino Activities (CAFA), and its investigations were aimed at intellectuals who might pursue the left path of the dead and jailed membership of the Hukbalahap and of the Partido Komunista ng Pilipinas.

In 1957 an Anti-Subversion Act was passed by Congress and it succeeded in planting enough fear among university intellectuals to keep them quiet. The following year the University of the Philippines sponsored a conference of young writers and when the participants were asked to pass a resolution protesting "military interference in intellectual affairs," they failed to act on the issue. Indeed, the youth had been cowed by the military surveillance visited upon such outspoken journalists as Renato Constantino, I. P. Soliongco, and Hernando Abaya.

Intellectual suppression was abetted by one's religious affiliation. The hierarchy of the Roman Catholic Church was especially vigilant in the 1950s about possible Communist infiltration of the media. In Manila the newspaper *The Sentinel* was set up to counter views and information deemed contrary to Church teaching, and it had a captive audience in the student population of Catholic schools all over the country. Foreign missionary priests expelled from China were hosted by religious groups, and their tales of martyrdom and steadfast faith further raised fears among Filipino faithful about the possibility of Communist rule in the Philippines.

The image of the CIC as protector asserted itself vis-à-vis the United States' efforts to keep the Philippines within its circle of allies in its propaganda war against the Soviet Union and its satellites. As a military unit that screened potential government officials immediately after the war, the CIC wielded influence laced with fear among Filipino politicians and bureaucrats who aspired to a career in government. It did not matter that these Filipinos had been dedicated to the service of the Commonwealth. What mattered was that they professed loyalty to the United States before the CIC and ingratiated themselves to the military officials in the said body, and survived the investigations.

One looks back to the prevalent paranoia over Communism in the two decades following the Pacific War and finds in it the root of the general passiveness to the politics of "special relations." Nationalism in those two decades was often suspect as but a step away from anti-Americanism and communistic leaning, and in such a situation the safer alternative was to seem neutral when it was not prudent to be simply cynical.

After I graduated as a literature major from the University of Santo Tomas, my one consuming dream was to go to the United States for further studies. In 1956 my opportunity came when I was designated alternate candidate for a Fulbright travel grant. Fortunately, some misfortune kept the lucky grantee from leaving, and so I found myself in Indiana University enrolled in the comparative literature program. The first phone call I made when I got to the campus in Bloomington was to the bus depot to inquire which Greyhound bus would take me to Fairmount, Indiana, where James Dean had been buried after his fatal car accident. We were a trio of writing friends in Manila who actually believed that the young American actor "expressed" us and our world in the

Follow the lead of Adrienne Ames and send the men in the camps the cigarette that's Definitely **MILDER** and **BETTER-TASTING**

The Lopez Memorial Museum Collection

From *Sunday Tribune Magazine*, 14 December 1941

Philippines. The three of us, separately and together, had followed Rebel Without a Cause *and* East of Eden *from one moviehouse to another, braving bedbugs and piss-smell in third-run, double-feature theaters, until we could recite to one another chunks of dialogue from the two films. But no Greyhound bus passed through the town of Fairmount, so it was with much regret that I had to give up my pilgrimage.*

"Popular Images of America" was the title of a conference in Honolulu, Hawaii, where a paper on the images of America as culled from Tagalog stories published in the weekly *Liwayway* was read by the sociologist Laura Samson in 1976. Samson noted that in the period between 1946 and 1961, the reader could chart a shift in the image of America. In the early part of the period, America was perceived as friend, ally, and liberator, but from 1961 onward, the stories began to reflect the sentiments of nationalist activists. In the 1946 stories, the return of the Americans was much awaited and their eventual return was greeted with joy. In 1951 the stories continued to recall the return of the Americans, but this time America was seen as a place where Filipinos could obtain a liberating education. By 1966, the positive image of America was being viewed through more realistic eyes, with allusions to colonial mentality and the alienating effect of American education on Filipino professionals. By 1971, the depiction of America had begun to reflect a certain degree of politicization among the writers.

The presence of America in the consciousness of Filipinos born after the Pacific War was a creation of the media and the various genres of popular culture they purveyed. Commercial television came in 1953, and the shows it brought into Filipino households came mainly from the United States. Print in the form of glossy magazines and fashion and mail-order catalogues was an early carrier of American culture, followed in the second decade of American occupation by film, which immediately enjoyed popular patronage. It was television, however, that firmly established America in the minds of Filipino youth.

In 1960 an American resident opened a television station and hosted a live children's program. Bob Stewart was a daily presence on Channel 7 and children in his show addressed him as "Uncle Bob." Surrounded by children and dispensing goodies, Stewart might be said to have reinforced the image of America as a dependable dispenser of goodies for underdeveloped countries ever in need of aid. Another American institution on television was the Jesuit Fr. James B. Reuter who introduced many pioneer Filipino practitioners of the craft to drama production for television. Father Reuter's audiences and students included theater lovers from exclusive Catholic schools, for he was also famous as the director of well-publicized productions of Broadway musicals and religious dramas.

Radio introduced Joan Page to Filipino audiences as a pert American girl who was to endear herself to listeners as a comedian. Her heavily accented Tagalog gave the impression that she was trying heroically to fit into Filipino society. She was to graduate to film in 1952 when she starred as the leading lady of a popular movie idol in a comic role as an American woman whose marriage to a Filipino country boy brings mayhem to a provincial village. Titled *Ang Asawa Kong Amerikana (My American Wife)*, the movie was to win an award for its script in the Asian Film Festival.

At a time when a written screenplay was a rarity in the Philippine movie industry, an American by the name of Rolf Bayer found a special niche in Tagalog films.

Lamberto V. Avellana was a highly esteemed director, so when he employed Bayer as scriptwriter, the American shared in the acclaim that greeted the films *Anak Dalita* (*The Ruins*, 1956) and *Badjao* (1957). Bayer did not write in Tagalog (his scripts were translated), but he succeeded in ensconcing himself in the industry because of the narrative skill and thematic thrust of his scripts.

Fr. John Delaney, S.J., was not a media man, but his presence in the pulpit as an American commanded attention. He was chaplain of the Catholic chapel in the University of the Philippines and his speeches and sermons made him a public figure who wielded much influence among university intellectuals. He was a staunch anti-communist and his campaign for the right of religious student organizations to field candidates at student elections was part of a campaign to counteract the spread of secularism and positivist philosophy on campus.

The late 1940s and the 1950s were years of unrelenting Americanization in Philippine society. Music played over the radio was mainly popular music from the recording industry in the United States, bringing to Filipino homes the voices and messages of such singers as Jo Stafford, Perry Como, Bing Crosby, Frank Sinatra, Nat King Cole, Doris Day, and Elvis Presley. The sentiments and values communicated by the songs were those of Middle America which merged with the sentiments and values of native Filipino music. Increasingly, native traditional songs were marginalized by American popular music which enjoyed the status of being in English and, therefore, prestigious. Filipino singers enjoyed much popularity when they sang American songs in renditions almost identical with "the original." Perceived as complimentary in this period were such titles bestowed on Filipino musicians as "Perry Como of the Philippines" or "the Filipina Jo Stafford."

Hollywood stars and the fantasies they inspired inhabited the consciousness of Filipino moviegoers. As in popular music, it was not unusual for the promotion of local movie stars to highlight similarities in looks and talent between Filipino actors and actresses and famous Hollywood personalities.

In Manila, it must be noted, the best and plushiest moviehouses were reserved exclusively for the exhibition of American movies, with only two first-run theaters showing Tagalog films. Thus exposed to more American movies than local ones, young Filipinos took for role models such popular and charismatic American stars as John Wayne, Errol Flynn, Tyrone Power, Audrey Hepburn, Grace Kelly, Doris Day, Sandra Dee, and in later times, James Dean and Marlon Brando. The movie genres that took hold were swashbuckling action-adventure films and cowboy-Indian westerns. These forms were held in higher esteem than the local film melodramas which were consigned by college-educated audiences to the level of low-life entertainment fit only for ignorant and gullible women and children.

The culture that enshrined Americans as saviors and protectors in the imagination of Filipino moviegoers grew out of the "gratitude" implied in postwar films which featured G.I. Joe as lover and fighter. In 1946 alone, eight such movies produced by the revived local film industry reached theaters even as war debris had only begun to be cleared. *So Long, America* had what in retrospect was a prophetic subtitle, *I'll Be Seeing You, Everywhere*. *Victory Joe* was a title based on the popular greeting addressed by children to American soldiers walking down the street. The movie gave prominent billing to unknown Art Cantrell who played an American soldier whose charms almost wrecked the relationship between a young woman and her Filipino sweetheart. Within the same year, *Honeymoon*, a sequel to *Victory Joe*, was released and it had a role again for Cantrell. A romantic comedy played on the theme of the American soldier who is parted from his Filipino girlfriend under the title *Hanggang Pier* (*No Farther than the Pier*). The title was derived from a popular derisive expression thrown at the native girl left crying at the pier by her American lover.

Other films were movies glorifying the heroism of Filipino guerrillas who fought side by side with American soldiers in the final showdown with the Japanese. *Death March* was advertised as "a historic portrayal of the most thrilling episode in a people's struggle for freedom and democracy amidst a reign of terror and oppression." *The Voice of Freedom* told about men and women whose clandestine radio broadcast made waiting for the return of MacArthur such a hazardous activity during the Japanese occupation. *Maynila* and *Intramuros* recalled the hand-to-hand fighting and the Japanese massacre of civilians that made the retaking of the capital city in 1945 such a bloody campaign.

A study on "national identity formation in a Philippine public elementary school" conducted in 1982-1983 by a doctoral student may serve as a gauge of the ravages visited on the sensibility of young Filipinos by U.S. cultural domination. Published in 1989 as *The Limits of Educational Change* (Quezon City: University of the Philippines Press), the study by Maria Luisa Canieso-Doronila exposed the colonial character of the Philippine educational system that had only served to make young Filipinos want to be, first, American, and second, Japanese. To be Filipino was only a third choice.

After a year at Indiana University, driven by a perception that contemporary Tagalog poetry was not at par with the poetry that had been turned out in Europe early in the twentieth century, I began writing what I presumptuously thought would be "modern" Tagalog poetry. In my final year on campus, I got approval for a dissertation topic which would take me on an exploration of the history and aesthetics of English writing by Indian fictionists. It was 1960, and a young writer had just arrived in Bloomington from the Philippines where a resurgent nationalism was directing the minds of the young to things Philippine. He asked me when he found out what I was going to write on: "Why not write on a Philippine topic?" I was flabbergasted. I had not until then thought it important to relate my intellectual work to the culture of my native land.

Dr. Doronila's book was an eye-opener for those who would accept what nationalist activists were saying, only when confronted with findings on the educational system supported by scientific methodology and incontrovertible data. *The Limits of Educational Change* gives educators, sociologists, political science experts, and various social reformers ground to stand on when they demand an overhaul of our educational system. Now we can be certain that it was not only history and the horrors of war visited on the Filipino people, nor the manipulatory politics played by American officials and their Filipino proteges, nor the nightmares induced by Cold War propaganda by the CIA, nor cultural representations that tended to perpetuate stereotype images of the American liberator, that gave long life to the ideological distortions of "special relations." The educational system that was set up by U.S. colonialism at the opening of the century had set the ideological foundation for the present system running our schools.[4] It is a continuing mechanism that to this day ensures long life for images and attitudes that Philippine history in the past ninety-nine years has implanted in the consciousness of the Filipino.

NOTES:

1. Renato Constantino's reading of the post-Pacific War history of the Philippines in *The Continuing Past* (Chapter VII, "The Politics of Liberation"; Manila: Renato Constantino, 1971, 1998) has provided the framework for organizing my own hindsight about political figures and events of the period. Much light was shed by the infectious liveliness and cogency of Constantino's account on my then teenager's perception of Philippine society of that time, and a footnote can only faintly acknowledge my indebtedness to him.

2. Ibid., 197.

3. Ibid., 234.

4. Elsewhere, I have treated this topic in the essay "Ang Sentenaryo ng Imperyalismong US sa Pilipinas: Sanhi at Bunga ng Mahabang Pagkaalipin" ("The Centenary of US Imperialism in the Philippines: Cause and Effect of Prolonged Subjection"), published in *Philippine Social Science Review* (special issue, January-December 1999).

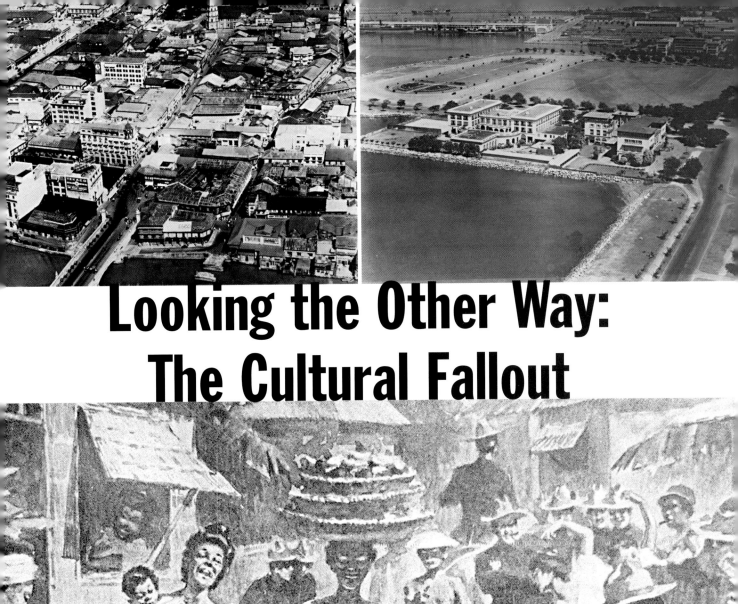

Looking the Other Way:
The Cultural Fallout

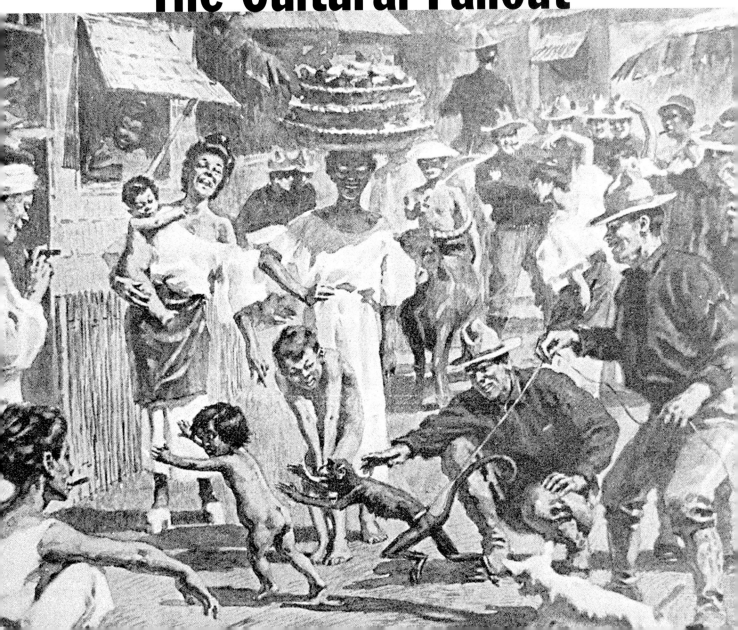

ALFRREDO NAVARRO SALANGA
5 February [1899]

*Gen. Emilio Aguinaldo issues a proclamation announcing a state of war between the
Philippines and the United States as American forces attack San Juan del Monte and succeed
in capturing the reservoir.*

Find no
symbol in
the capture
of the reservoir:
water can
do no sculpting.

The laws
of physics
tell us
that water
takes the shape
of its
every container.

The North
Americans have
captured nothing
but a vessel
of water,
nothing that
our sun
will find difficult
to empty
with its rage.

Do not weep
over water,
remain dry
as bones,
dry as
scorched earth,

Earth that
breaks open
to swallow
its economies.

We will
swallow them
—whole
and be
the reservoir
of their pulp,
their watered
dreams
of empire.

Baguio Between Two Wars:
The Creation and Destruction of a Summer Capital

ERLYN RUTH E. ALCANTARA

PROLOGUE

At the turn of the century, Baguio in the Philippine province of Benguet in northern Luzon was a small Ibaloy[1] hamlet, a vast meadow and grazing land for large cattle herds that far "outnumbered people."[2] In 1901, as the Philippine-American War raged in the lowlands, Americans began building a mountain road into Baguio, blasting their way into the Bued River canyon. Only five years later, insular officials would speak of Baguio as "the American Simla in the Far East." In 1913 Baguio's contrived cultural landscape acquired all the key features of a classic hill station: Western architectural forms, sprawling golf courses, athletic fields, a formal market-place and nearby gardens for temperate fruits, vegetables, and flowers.[3]

The creation of Baguio defied simple classification, given the singular nature of its historical generation: its unique political and cultural role, particularly during the first three decades of American rule, has set it apart from other colonial towns in the Philippines. Its controlled development, however, fit into a much larger colonial scheme. At the height of the Philippine-American War, a military cantonment in the highlands was essential to the recuperation of convalescent and fatigued troops. Moreover, from the point of view of American military strategists, Baguio's location in the Benguet mountains could be used to advantage in the event of a lowland revolt.

One vital factor made Baguio's location exceptionally appealing to the new colonists: its proximity to the Benguet gold mines. At the height of the Benguet gold rush in the 1930s, Baguio's cultural landscape changed dramatically as it became the hub of the mining community.

In summary, the Americans created in Baguio a popular mountain haven that eventually became known as the Philippine summer capital. The Americans may have built Baguio but they also destroyed it. In March 1945, American fighter planes demolished the city with napalm and bombs.

This is the story of the creation and destruction of a city.

BAGUIO AS GRASSLAND

Bágyu (*bágiw*), as used by Ibaloys as well as Ifugaos, refers to a waterweed, a submerged slimy water plant with floating leaves that grew along the streams and damp cover.[4] With the entire watery bottom between Guisad Valley and La Trinidad practically covered with *bágyu*,

US National Archives

An Ibaloy Settlement, July 1900. In the 1800s, the vast Baguio meadow was grazing land for large herds of cattle, horses and carabaos. At the time this composite photograph was taken, there were about twenty houses in *Kafagway* (Ibaloy name for present-day downtown Baguio). As the townsite developed, many Ibaloy families moved to the outskirts for their sources of livelihood.

the word could have been used to identify the place, and caught on with repeated use.

At the time of Spanish conquest, what is now called downtown Baguio was a grassy clearing with scattered pine stands, giant tree ferns, and luxuriant tangles of damp tropical vegetation. From the gently rolling hills, several streams meandered toward the basin of the valley. The largest of these streams was Minac Creek. In later years, it was tapped as the source of Burnham Lake.

In the late 1700s, herds of cattle, carabaos, and horses accumulated through the gold trade grazed across the meadow and rolling hills of present-day Kisad area, Happy Homes, Campo Sioco, Santo Tomas, and Camp John Hay. Toward the late 1800s, Kafagway (from the Ibaloy word *paway*, referring to an area of high grass) alluded to the grassy valley now known as Burnham Park and part of the central business district. Kafagway was one of the thirty-one rancherias into which the entire province of Benguet was divided. Kafagway was a small rancheria of about twenty houses.

GOLD: A MAGNET TO THE IMPERIALISTS' HEARTS

Like the Spanish colonists before them, the Americans also suffered from "a disease of the heart which [could] only be cured by gold."[5] Months before the McKinley government even formulated an official Philippine policy, Benguet already figured prominently in the minds of American officials. No other place in the archipelago shared that distinction. United States peace commissioners, negotiating the terms of the Treaty of Paris in August 1898, received a report on the archipelago's geological and mineral resources. This report, which read "like a mining stock prospectus,"[6] contained copious information on the Benguet gold fields.

In its evolution of a Philippine policy, America's commercial stake in China was a vital factor. When substantial American interests in the Chinese market came under serious threat in the fall of 1897, the United States urgently needed to secure an additional footing in the Orient. The acquisition of the Hawaiian Islands, Wake, Guam, and the Philippines suited an expansive plan to build a system of stations for coal, cable, and naval ports to maintain an integrated trade route that would support America's overriding ambition: to enter the China market and dominate it. In the larger picture, therefore, the Philippines emerged as the crucial stepping stone. American officials began to view the archipelago as "an American Hongkong," a commercial entrepôt to the coveted China market and a center of military power in Asia.[7]

In its bid for supremacy over its economic rivals, the United States joined the scramble of leading European powers to divide what is now called The Third World into colonies and spheres of influence.[8] As the United States looked overseas for new foreign markets, investment opportunities, and raw materials, the colonies of imperial Spain presented themselves as suitable acquisitions. The United States declared war on Spain with the proclaimed intention of aiding Cuban nationalists who had risen in revolt against the Spanish colonial masters. In May 1898, less than two weeks into the Spanish-American War, the American navy bombarded the Spanish armada at Manila Bay. Immediately after the celebrated naval victory, the Treasury Department at Washington began working on a "Report on the Financial and Industrial Conditions of the Philippine Islands." Less than a month later, by arrangement between the secretary of war and the Department of the Interior, a geologist of the U.S. Geological Survey joined the military expedition to the Philippines to conduct an extensive reconnaissance. Shortly thereafter, geologists produced a mineral map of the archipelago, revealing distinct prospects for a profitable mining industry, particularly in Benguet.

American Historical Collection

Baguio before the Burnham Plan, 1905. View of what later became the Abanao-Camp Allen area. Toward the middle is the first Municipal Building, on the same site where City Hall stands today. The barn-like structure at the left was the sanitarium barracks that became a horse stable after a new hospital opened on another site in 1908.

When the war with Spain pushed across the Pacific, the Philippine frontier with its hostile natives and its fabled wealth offered enterprising Americans the same "heady mix of risks and riches."[9] Hundreds of soldiers participated in the relentless pursuit of Gen. Emilio Aguinaldo in the mountain fastness of northern Luzon. Enduring the rugged terrain and rough living conditions, many of these young, adventurous soldiers were sustained by the lure of gold through the dreary war years.[10] Cavalry boys of Nebraska, Arkansas, and Idaho, and those who had panned gold in the Klondike or in the leavings of strikes in California, went their own ways to explore Luzon's mountain of gold. American volunteer soldiers began prospecting in Benguet, "having waited doggedly through long months for the right moment to strike."[11] Most of these soldiers fought in the Philippine arena of the Spanish-American War. Some of them had joined the 1899 expedition to the Benguet mountains.

Early in 1900, even under wartime conditions, Commanding Gen. Elwell Otis commissioned a twenty-man task force on a special mission to northern Luzon to plot mining concessions that had been granted by the Spanish government and were now being revoked by the new colonial rulers.

Provided with initial estimates of Benguet's mineral and geological resources, the Philippine Commission awaited detailed assessments and declared that "if those figures are even in part true,"[12] then unquestionably Benguet would soon be "one of the greatest mining regions known."[13]

Indeed it was. A vast field of gold-producing ore lay practically in the entire central range of Benguet, including the eastern belt and the district of Kayapa (now a part of Nueva Vizcaya). Benguet's mountains cradled the richest Philippine lodes so coveted by the Spanish colonists since the sixteenth century.

After 1898, when the Philippines became the chief prize of the Spanish-American War, these gold mines were the prime share of the war booty.

ENTRY OF AMERICAN COLONIAL FORCES

One of the first aims of the Philippine Commission in 1900 was to select a site for a hill station. Tasked to investigate the conditions for a health and recreation resort in the highlands, two members of the Philippine Commission under the direction of Secretary of War Elihu Root embarked on an exploratory trip to Benguet. Commissioners Luke E. Wright and Dean C. Worcester organized an expedition to Benguet in July 1900, taking with them two doctors, two naval officers, and Horace L. Higgins, president of the Manila and Dagupan Railway Company, as well as a cavalry troop escort. The visit to Baguio only validated recommendations earlier made by the Spanish Benguet Commission. There was no doubt in the minds of the Worcester-Wright Committee that Baguio was indeed an ideal site for a highland resort.

For the new colonists, a mountain resort would be highly beneficial to the military personnel and civil officials who needed to regain strength and vigor in cooler regions. With a temperature almost twenty degrees (Fahrenheit) lower than Manila, Baguio was, literally, a breath of fresh air: like a balm, the cool, pine-scented breezes soothed weary Americans unaccustomed to Manila's tropical heat. Convinced that this mountain haven offered great opportunity for recuperation and renewal of strength, Taft wrote on 15 November 1903:

> In connection with the subject of health, reference should be made to the province of Benguet and to Baguio, the capital of that province... If there can be brought within twelve hours' travel of Manila a place with a climate not unlike that of the Adirondacks, or of Wyoming in summer, it will add greatly to the possibility of living in Manila for ten months of the year without risk. It will take away the necessity for long vacations spent in America; will reduce the number who go invalided home, and will be a saving to the insular government of many thousands of dollars a year. It will lengthen the period during which the American soldiers who are stationed here may remain without injury to their health and will thus reduce largely the expense of transportation of troops between the islands and the United States.[14]

While Baguio presented excellent potential for a hill station and health resort, its location was also ideal for other key purposes. From a military viewpoint, Baguio could have served as an American heartland in case of a lowland rebellion.[15]

GENESIS OF AN AMERICAN HILL STATION

Insular officials had to move promptly as American mining prospectors in Benguet had their own plans. In November 1900, the first civil government in the Philippines was established in Benguet primarily to pre-empt the move of mining prospectors to take over the political organization of the province. Many American mining prospectors, some with experience in the 1897–98 Klondike gold rush, were prepared to control Benguet in the American mining camps' tradition of self-government.[16] Thus, even before the establishment of a civil government in the country, the Philippine Commission passed Act No. 48 creating a local government in the nineteen townships of Benguet.

For lowland Filipinos, 1901 was a year of destruction and utter savagery as the American infantry waged a relentless offensive against Filipino revolutionaries. American troop arrivals swelled progressively, reaching 120,000 by July 1902.[17] In central and southern Luzon as well as in the Visayan islands, American troops swept over entire populations, exterminated tens of thousands of noncombatants and wiped out hundreds more by pestilence in concentration camps. In Batangas alone, over a hundred thousand died following Maj. Gen. J. Franklin Bell's orders to raze villages and ruthlessly garrison the entire population.[18] (General Bell would later be exalted in Baguio and immortalized after a picturesque amphitheater at Camp John Hay was named in his honor.)

For the new colonial government, 1901 was a year of creation and new conquests. In January, as the United States Army geared for a full-scale military campaign in the lowlands, the insular government ordered the immediate construction of a road into Baguio. By the middle of the year, a road work gang under the direction of American foremen began blasting their way into the Bued River canyon. Having set their sights on the Benguet gold mines and on creating an American enclave in the mountains that later became Baguio City, the new colonists persisted against all odds in building the road that they envisaged would become the bed of an electric railway.

Opening a road into Benguet ushered in numerous changes in the lives of people not just in Baguio but in the entire northern Luzon Cordillera region. Essentially, it eased the creation of an American hill station, ultimately remaking the small rancheria of Kafagway into the country's summer capital. In the larger scheme of things, opening a road effectively integrated Benguet and the greater region in the American colonial experience.

Within two years, there was little visible progress in the road construction. During the first six months, it became quite obvious that Capt. Charles Mead, the road's first engineer, had grossly underestimated the time and costs of construction. Mead had expended the entire appropriation by July 1901 but the road barely reached the foothills. The Philippine Commission released new funding, and another huge sum a year later. New appropriations exceeded the original estimate of $75,000 but the Commission remained confident that "the accruing benefits warranted the expenditure."[19] Besides, the plans for Baguio could not be abandoned so easily. In February 1903, the Philippine Commission delineated 14,000 acres (5,668 hectares) as town site reservation.

The exceedingly high and still rising costs of building the Benguet Road did not escape the critics of government. By the summer of 1903, protests against the huge expense on the road construction snowballed into an opposition to the plans for Baguio. Scathing condemnation of the costs of the mountain road splashed across Manila newspapers' front pages such that each appropriation was "greeted with storms of abuse."[20] In a larger sense, the extravagance put the entire hill station enterprise in a new light. The Filipino press, in particular, became sharply critical not just of the road costs but also of the proposed mountain resort that they believed would benefit only the American colonial elite and a few wealthy Filipinos. Building such a hill station, the press said, also meant enabling "American imperial control to be maintained in their country for an indefinite but certainly prolonged period of time."[21]

Although faced with the prospect of abandoning the idea of a mountain resort, the Philippine Commission forged ahead. Asserting its colonial authority, it responded to its critics and drafted a resolution on 1 June 1903 designating Baguio as the official summer capital of the archipelago.

In August 1903, less than a month after the passage of the Commission resolution, Maj. Lyman W. V. Kennon took charge of the Benguet Road construction. Kennon, a major in the regular army and a colonel in the U.S. Volunteers who served as regimental commander of the 34th Volunteer Infantry deployed to the Ilocos during the Philippine-American War, succeeded where his predecessors failed miserably. Like a good soldier, according to Governor-General Forbes, the major took his orders to complete the road "literally and unquestionably, ramming it through regardless of expense, or even of human life."

By the time the road opened to wagon traffic in 1905, construction costs had reached $1.9 million for the total length of twenty-eight miles (forty-five kilometers). At current prices the 1905 costs would be $32.6 million[22] or a staggering P1.24 billion.

The error in the choice of a route into Baguio was "abundantly demonstrated"[23] in the years following the opening of Benguet Road. Every storm season invariably brought landslides, requiring large work gangs to keep the road open. With each passing year, repair costs swelled beyond anyone's estimates. The combined effect of the Commission's shortsighted haste and the road builders' "woeful ignorance"[24] of the topography of the region cost millions and almost spelled the end of Baguio. In the long term, fundamental flaws in the selection of a route would require exorbitant maintenance costs. These costs continue to drain government coffers to this day.

THE CREATION OF A SUMMER CAPITAL

Having spent nearly two million dollars on Benguet Road, the Commission spurned any further expenditure toward the development of Baguio. It became an embarrassment for the government that after it had spent vast amounts of money for the road, the supposed summer resort recently opened up had only the government sanitarium of a few beds and about three or four roughly built houses as accommodations. Without the funds to develop Baguio into the intended summer capital, this "made the Benguet Road seem like the city avenue which ran into a street, the street into a lane, the lane into a cow path, the cow path into a squirrel track and the squirrel track up a tree, for while one could get to Baguio, there was very little there after one arrived."[25] By the summer of 1905, Baguio was

> only half a success… the journey up is still slow and carries enough discomfort to make it a hardship for weak or tired people and half the people who go up there don't like it, probably… because there is nothing to do, no society, no games, no drives, no men folk about and no very good place to stay.[26]

Pressed for an alternative, W. Cameron Forbes, then secretary of commerce and police, proposed the holding of a sale of lots within the vicinity of the urban reservation. In 1906 private lots presented at the first public auction sold briskly. Of 128 lots, ninety-one were sold mostly to Westerners and affluent Filipinos while remaining lots were sold in a subsequent sale in Manila.

Applying a city plan designed by the renowned architect Daniel H. Burnham, the government delineated sites for parks, public buildings, government cottages, structures for religious institutions, and residential areas. On a fine tract of land reserved for a military post began the construction of temporary barracks and cottages for the commanding general and officers.

During a trip to the country to open the Philippine Assembly in 1907, Secretary of War William Howard Taft visited Baguio. Upon his return to the United States, he enthusiastically reported that "the Benguet Road means eventually a railroad will be constructed into Baguio and possibly through Suyoc [in the mineral region of Southern Lepanto]..."[27]

A construction trend at Baguio went into full swing in 1908, beginning with a large sanitarium, a group of school buildings, constabulary school and headquarters, and a public market. To encourage other Americans and rich Filipinos to follow his example, Forbes built two handsome structures in Baguio: the governor general's residence which he called Mansion House, and Topside, his elegant private residence. Frequently spending his own money to get his plans off the ground, he provided initial funds for the Baguio Country Club, ordered the construction of a polo field near the club's grounds and went out of his way to manufacture enthusiasm in building homes in the country's summer capital.

By 1913, Baguio had the amenities of a typical twentieth-century American city: Camp John Hay operated as a rest and recreation center for the U.S. Army; Baguio Country Club became the center of Baguio's American community; the Government Center, a large administrative structure, hosted the insular government's summer excursions; Teachers' Camp had new permanent cottages and larger mess halls for the summer assemblies of teachers; Hotel Pines and other inns offered sufficient tourist accommodations; there was a modern hospital, a school, and other amenities. During Manila's hot summer months, the colonial officialdom moved its offices to Baguio, a practice terminated by the Harrison government in 1914.

CAMP JOHN HAY: ONE OF AMERICA'S MOST BEAUTIFUL ARMY POSTS

In October 1903, President Theodore Roosevelt signed a presidential order setting aside 535 acres (216.85 hectares or one-twenty-fifth of the Baguio reservation) for the U.S. army reservation. Given the name Camp John Hay,[28] the army post began with a hospital, a few cottages for officers of the two Igorot companies of the 12th Battalion, Philippine Scouts, and barracks for recuperating enlisted men. As commanding general of the Philippine Department from 1909 to 1914, Gen. J. F. Bell sought funds for the camp's development. Baguio was his mountain playground and Camp John Hay became his favorite project. General Bell's landscape design changed the former pasture's sprawling terrain: a road network was laid out, several buildings and camp utilities were built, and the beginnings of recreational facilities constructed. In succeeding years, military officials continued to build more cottages, sports and entertainment facilities for the U.S. army and navy personnel in the Philippines.

From the beginning and throughout much of its existence, Camp John Hay was an American turf. It had its own life. While there were no outright restrictions to civilian entry, Baguio residents rarely wandered into the camp save for a few tourists with private vehicles going on a city tour. In the 1960s, Camp John Hay was designated as a recreation center of the 24th Air Depot of the U.S. Air Force in the Philippines, and some of its facilities such as restaurants, the library, and the Main Club's bingo games drew a significant civilian crowd. Since gate passes were required at the time, having one became a status symbol. Many applied for gate passes specifically for the bingo games which for several years were the favorite social gathering of the middle class. To the city's social elite, two events were unsurpassed for grandiose reception: the Ambassador's New Year's Reception and the Commander's Ball, both being highly formal affairs inside the camp. For the general public, "Open House" on 4 July (Fil-Am Friendship Day) or 12 June (Independence Day) was a real treat. It meant not only gate pass-free entrance but also the chance to line up at the Base Exchange for that rare opportunity to buy, at discounted prices, "delicious" Washington apples, Hershey's chocolates, and other American goodies. The long queues on such occasions had become a "tradition," certainly to the embarassment of other Baguio residents.

Over the years, the scope of the military reservation expanded, and when Camp John Hay was finally turned over to the Philippine government in July 1991, its area covered 1,672 acres (677 hectares or about one-eighth of Baguio's land area).

CONQUERING THE BENGUET GOLD MINES

Baguio's proximity to the Benguet gold district proved extremely valuable and further enhanced its merits as a hill station. With the opening of Benguet Road and its maintenance throughout the year, investors felt assured of the safe transport of machinery to their locations. From that point on, Americans shifted from the stage of mining prospects to the era of mines and mining corporations.[29] Thus began the development of an extremely promising mining district. Within the first decade of American rule and barely two years following the opening of the wagon road, a number of gold mines started developing lodes, thereby shaping Baguio's future as a mining center.

With the exception of small workings by Igorots using traditional technology that yielded "small handfuls of gold and small amounts of copper,"[30] the mineral resources of Benguet were largely unexplored. The prospects thus became even more favorable. Unlike the slow and archaic Igorot mining techniques, the Americans introduced new amalgamation methods and soon applied the highly efficient cyanidation method. Notwithstanding the crude machinery available during the early 1900s, early American miners secured the greatest possible value from the ore body and produced gold in quantities that Igorot miners could not have understood nor found necessary to extract at any one time. The Igorots, after all, mined only enough to trade for their immediate needs, did not accumulate any surplus, and kept the gold more securely in the earth than in their houses. This ethos, however, had no place in the American capitalist system.

As early as 1903, the provincial office processed three hundred claims filed by American prospectors who "had flocked to stake claims" on the gold and copper mines in southern Benguet.[31] Benguet Consolidated Mining Co. (Benguetcorp today), the pioneer mining company in the Baguio Mineral District registered officially in November 1903 but actual operated in the Antamok area and eventually expanded its operations to Balatoc and Acupan, Itogon.

In 1906 there were 544 mining claims in Benguet, 105 of which had been located only that year. Other companies opened ground working operations and began developing lodes in the mining district. Such a momentum in the mining industry impressed Gov.William F. Pack of Benguet and in 1906 he reported being entirely convinced that "an astonishing source of wealth"[32] awaited the United States government through the gold that the mountains of Benguet would yield. This notwithstanding, the Benguet mines needed enormous capital for exploration. In the end, few adventurers and prospectors struck it rich; those that survived were companies able to raise enough resources to maintain annual assessment work and to support systematic development necessary to transform a prospect into a mine.[33]

By 1933, the production of the Benguet gold mines constituted 95 percent of the country's total industry output. In 1940, before World War II loomed in the horizon, the mines produced 1.09 million grams of gold valued at $37 million, an amount equivalent to $615 million in 1999.

As the Benguet mines' boom town, Baguio changed rapidly in the 1930s: more businesses opened to serve the thriving industry, new and reinforced concrete buildings were constructed and streets widened to accommodate increased traffic. Baguio's population tripled due to the employment opportunities at the mines and in new commercial establishments. From a total of 5,464 in 1918, the population swelled to 24,117 in 1938.[34] Lowlanders and highlanders flocked to the city to work as miners, laborers, or merchants. More foreigners who opened hotels or inns, restaurants, and supply stores settled in the city; among them were British and other European nationals, East Indians, Fukien Chinese and Cantonese. Baguio, the once tranquil summer resort, became a melting pot animated by the variety of players in the gold rush scene.

Downtown Baguio, 1923. View of the town center from 200 feet above the ground showing Session Road, part of Burnham Lake, the market, City Hall and the new Central School built that year.

DECLINE OF TRADITIONAL IBALOY SYSTEMS

As in other traditional societies, subsistence agriculture enabled the Ibaloys to produce their food requirements. Root crop cultivation in the *uma* (swidden farms) yielded *camote* (sweet potatoes), *gabi* (taro), and *ube* (yam). As cattle became the base of the Ibaloy economic system, gradually replacing gold mining and trading, estancias (grazing land) emerged as a new type of landed property. By the turn of the nineteenth century, land use options other than lode mines, uma, and estancias evolved. Irrigated rice terracing in Benguet developed as an alternative mode of subsistence agriculture. Serving rice, especially during ritual public feasts, became a measure of prestige for the Ibaloys. In Baguio, rice cultivation was successful in low-lying areas such as Loakan, Muyot, and Camp 7.

Traditional land ownership involved a sharing system between the *baknang*[35] and their kin that guaranteed mutual responsibility for the land, the produce, and the animals. New property laws under the American regime required land registration and became the requisite to legal ownership. Save for some *baknang* families, many failed to comply and therefore most of their holdings and vast communal areas were declared as public land. This breakdown in the ritual and custom law that dictated land ownership, transfer, lease, and inheritance undermined and ultimately eroded the subsistence economy. The American market system and the social infrastructure that made this new system work, namely the legal system, not only superseded a self-reliant economy but also "replaced the body of customary law[s] that once governed access to different land types and labor resources."[36]

New colonial policies reshaped Baguio Ibaloy society as these eroded the base of the village economy: the *baknang* lost their land, their gold mines, and control over land use. Additionally, when the American land tenure system challenged traditional land use practices, many Ibaloy families moved to the outskirts for their sources of livelihood.[37] As the insular government declared pasture lands as forest reserves and parks, the number of cattle heads decreased progressively. Eventually, some Ibaloys began selling lots to non-Ibaloys. Other cattle owners moved their herds to nearby plateaus. Cattle raising soon became a small backyard venture while the baknang's large herds moved to the peripheries or to as far south as Ansagan and Tuba, while others retreated to Kayapa, Sagubo, then San Gabriel.[38] The cattle enterprise eventually declined in southern Benguet.

Without the gold trade that "supported his cattle, created and maintained his status, the whole traditional system of the *baknang* slowly collapsed."[39] With the superimposition of the American political system on traditional society, the role of the baknang as the bridge between the economic system, the ritual system, and political organization disintegrated.[40] Not long after, a new class, mostly Americans and a handful of affluent Filipinos, replaced the local elite.

Baguio Ibaloy society was profoundly shaken by the changes brought about by the development of corporate mines and the growth of the new townsite. On the one hand, the Americans conquered yet another traditional society. On the other, they introduced institutions like the new churches, hospitals, and a public school system, as well as new pastimes such as baseball, poker, booze, and movies. Health services for ailing Ibaloys and educational opportunities for the youth (including those from the lower class) ranked high among the new order's immediately perceivable benefits. Although a totally alien phenomenon for primitive societies, the schools became accepted as places for self-improvement. The schools for Igorot children, built within the first decade of American rule, were the Bua School for Girls, the Industrial School for Boys, and Easter School. Nevertheless, complementary systems of modern education, religious conversion, health services, and increased trade gradually subverted traditional Igorot society, changing it irreversibly before the first three decades of the American era drew to a close.

UCCP Baguio Diamond Jubilee Program

April 1945. View of the heavily bombed areas showing Burnham Park at the upper left. At mid-left are the remnants of Hotel City Lunch (now Sunshine Supermarket) and towards the middle are the Cold Store used as a Japanese garrison (now Bayanihan Hotel) and Baguio Theater (now Juliana Apartments).

MIGRANT POPULATION GROWS

After the completion of Kennon Road, a good number of its workers chose to remain and sought jobs in the newly opened township. Many of its Chinese and Japanese workers, some of whom were farmers, stayed on and ventured into vegetable gardening or provided much of the skilled labor during the period. Ifugao and Kankana-ey workers sent for their families and established communities along the road at Twin Peaks and Camps 3 and 4. When the road opened to vehicular traffic, ascendants of the present-day Chinese community came up for jobs, went into the retail trade, and later put up bakeries and restaurants. In the first decade of development, large work gangs were required for road-building and soil-moving work for building Burnham Park, the market, and the military reservation. The first large groups of highlanders—Ibaloy, Kankana-ey, Kalanguya, I'uwak, and Ifugao—and lowlanders from La Union and Pangasinan came to Baguio.

With the construction of government buildings, public utilities, and parks, the city's migrant population grew rapidly. More people from the lowlands and the Cordillera provinces came for wage labor and office jobs or to engage in trade. Wave upon wave, migrants arrived with their families to settle permanently. The opening of Kennon Road, followed by Naguilian and Halsema roads, ushered in continuous migration into the city, making it one of the most ethnically diverse cities in the country. By the 1930s, the Ibaloys had become a minority comprising less than ten percent of the population.

JAPANESE IMPERIAL ARMY ATTACKS U.S. MILITARY IN THE PHILIPPINES

Baguio's location, though ideal in most respects, also attracted its own ruin. With Camp John Hay in its midst, Baguio drew the first attack by the Japanese Imperial Army. When Japanese forces bombed Pearl Harbor on 7 December 1941, many Baguio residents saw it as a signal for an all-out war. Only five hours later, this perception was affirmed as eighteen planes flew over Baguio in three perfect V formations and dropped seventy-two 550-pound (250 kilograms) bombs on Camp John Hay. Intended targets of the bombs dropped on the Officers' Mess and other officers' cottages were American pilots who,

Above left:
Downtown Baguio,
April 1945. Session
Road was practically
leveled to the ground.
Only the Roman
Catholic Cathedral
(right), stood largely
intact as a recogniza-
ble landmark in the
area, its grounds,
jammed with refugees
in makeshift shelters,
had also been bombed
earlier.

Above right:
The Ides of March,
1945. Another view of
the Roman Catholic
Cathedral, mid-right.
At mid-left is Burnham
Park. Decades later,
many Filipino and
American survivors
still find it difficult to
understand why the
U.S. Army Air Corps
bombed so many
civilian-occupied
buildings in
March 1945.

the Japanese believed, were vacationing there from Clark Field. This attack on Baguio signaled the beginning of World War II in the Pacific.

On 27 December 1941, both the Philippine and American flags at City Hall were taken down and the Japanese flag was hoisted: Baguio officially became an occupied city. Later that same morning three truckloads of Japanese soldiers entered the city and by nightfall, an entire battalion of the Ninth Infantry had arrived, ushering in the city's forty-month occupation.

Toward the last quarter of 1944, Japan sought to secure the sea lanes around the Philippine Islands as these were crucial to its supply of oil, rubber, and rice from other parts of Southeast Asia. Chosen to plot the defense was Gen. Tomoyuki Yamashita, Japan's best field commander, who had recently been pulled out of Manchuria. Yamashita moved his troops from Leyte to the mountains east of Manila and positioned them in northern Luzon, knowing Manila's open flat land was virtually indefensible. He picked Baguio as his headquarters, aware that its natural defenses would work to his advantage.[41]

U.S. Army Air Corps Bombs Baguio

The presence of Yamashita's headquarters in Baguio made the city an obvious target of the U.S. Army Air Corps. On 7 January 1945, coinciding with the naval bombardment of Poro Point in San Fernando, La Union, American gunships raided Baguio and bombed Camp Holmes in La Trinidad.

Three days later, a massive invasion convoy of the U.S. Sixth Army, the Seventh Fleet, and hundreds of Air Corps fighters and bombers packed Lingayen Gulf. This calculated show of force was the largest military thrust of the Pacific War, with the entire convoy totalling 818 vessels. The thundering sound of distant gunfire echoed across Baguio.[42]

In other parts of the country, Americans demolished Japanese air units and quashed the imperial navy in Leyte. The Japanese started to retreat. After the commander of Japan's air unit escaped to Taiwan, only General Yamashita's 14th Area Army remained in the islands. Meanwhile, reinforcements from the south poured into Luzon. Running out of targets, the U.S. Air Command and the Marine Squadrons zeroed in on General Yamashita, the supreme commander of the Japanese forces in the Philippines. More than a slogan, "Let's get Yamashita" became a frame of mind and a military mission.

Eager to become a separate service, the U.S. Army Air Corps was searching for

US National Archives, photograph by K. R. Fall

opportunities to demonstrate its capability to support ground operations. Before its major offensive, Fifth Air Force planes in 910 sorties dropped 933 tons of bombs and 1,185 gallons of napalm in Baguio between 4 and 10 March. The "Liberators" (B24s), A20s, B25s, P38s and often, single dive bombers, battered the city in successive air raids.[43] Townspeople fled to the outskirts with their belongings in pushcarts or carried in bundles. In seven days of steady bombing, Baguio turned to rubble: buildings collapsed into heaps of broken concrete, ashes lay where wooden houses used to stand, and pine groves were reduced to stumps.

But the worst was not over.

After 9:00 a.m. on 15 March 1945, four squadrons of eighteen B-24s in perfect V-formations approached Baguio from the south and, as they drew near the city, formed into a single file and discharged bombs methodically: two squadrons swept through the areas south to north and the other two squadrons southwest to northeast. Other planes from the Fifth Air Force and the 13th Air Force followed through. This time, many of the bombs were thousand pounders (455 kilograms). On that day alone, 170 planes raided Baguio in only two hundred square patterns, an unusually dense and deadly mode that later became known as "carpet bombing."[44]

After the Japanese Navy took over Baguio General Hospital, the few blocks that remained intact were the Roman Catholic institutions—from the Cathedral at the top of Session Road to St. Louis School and the adjoining Notre Dame Hospital. Refugees, many of whom had fallen ill from dysentery, jammed the compound. In spite of the earlier bombing of a convent and a temporary hospital, everyone, including American refugees, had faith that the Cathedral and the huge red crosses on other buildings could be "talismans to charm away warheads."[45] It seemed highly unlikely, even unthinkable, that American aircraft equipped with the remarkable Norden bombsight would ever hit a hospital that had roofs painted with huge red crosses. But it happened: two bombs directly hit Notre Dame Hospital, killing eleven persons including five Americans. One of them was E. J. Halsema, city mayor from 1920 to 1937.[46]

When the flames died and the black pall finally lifted, the survivors could not believe how the U.S. Army Air Corps bombed so many civilian-occupied buildings. Slowly, the shell-shocked refugees surfaced from shelters to retrieve pitiful remnants of their possessions and to pick up any remaining threads of their existence.

On 26 April 1945 the Americans seized control of the ruined city.

On 3 September 1945 General Yamashita and other Japanese officials signed the

Above left:
A virtual wasteland, April 1945. At mid-right is the market building whose stone walls survived the bombardment. Towards the middle are the remnants of the Baguio Theater and the United Church of Christ in the Philippines.

Above right:
Surveying the debris, April 1945. American infantrymen survey damaged buildings in the downtown area. Only chimneys and skeletons of concrete buildings remained standing while wooden structures were reduced to ashes.

BAGUIO 1999

Elevated View of Session Road

Hills in the background are now densely populated residential areas. From left to right: Mirador Hill, Quezon Hill, Camp Allen, Hilltop, Pinsao and Quirino Hill

Document of Surrender during official ceremonies held at the United States high commissioner's residence at Camp John Hay. General Yamashita surrendered his sword to Maj. Gen. Edmond H. Leavey, special representative of the commanding general of the American Forces, Western Pacific (AFWESPAC). The ceremony signaled the end of World War II in the Philippines.

After the bombings, Baguio showed no trace of its past grandeur as the country's summer capital. It was a virtual wasteland. Few concrete buildings remained standing, wooden houses were reduced to ashes, the streets and parks were wrecked, almost all familiar landmarks had been demolished, and public utility systems laid waste.

In the arena of World War II, the colonial creation became the ideal demolition target: aerial bombardment of the popular summer capital not only demonstrated American air force capability and overall military strength at the time, but also attained the desired effect of staging the United States as the dominant world power in the Pacific.

EPILOGUE

After World War II, urbanization changed Baguio's cultural landscape even if visible continuities of its colonial past lived on. The Baguio Country Club has remained the playground of the fashionable class although its membership now comprises mostly the Filipino elite and a few expatriates. Brent School, founded in 1909, has always been a prestigious school for Americans in the Philippines. In the 1920s, as the Benguet gold industry developed, the school's boarding students were mainly children of American executives in the mines. In the 1950s, Brent School's enrollment consisted largely of dependents of U.S. air force and navy personnel stationed at Camp John Hay or Clark Air Base. After the turnover of American miltary bases to the Philippine government in 1991, the school's enrollment dropped significantly but it has also gained new enrollees from wealthy Manila-based families, a few expatriates, and Baguio's upper class. Camp John Hay, now under private management, is being developed into a world-class resort with an exclusive golf club, country log homes, manors, suites, and other Western-style facilities designed primarily for the upscale market. Fashionable quarters of Baguio continue to be the enclaves of the elite.

Though not explicit in Burnham's essentially functional city plan, inherent social distinctions in the fundamental design have been carried over to the present. True, the Burnham Plan adhered closely to the natural contours of the Baguio plateau to tap the proposed city's "unique monumental possibilities."[47] It carefully delineated primary spaces for government buildings, the commercial district, an ecclesiastical center, a school for American children, an executive mansion, the army post, a navy reservation, a clubhouse, and two major public parks for Filipinos of "moderate means."[48] But at the outset the city plan also segregated areas of poor Filipino dwellings from the homes of the wealthy class.[49] For decades, places like the Baguio Country Club, Camp John Hay, Brent School, the Army-Navy Club, the Mansion House, South Drive, and Outlook Drive, though not specifically off limits to poor Filipinos, were perceived as exclusive and inaccessible. Today, Campo Filipino and neighboring areas are the most populous sections of the city while the South Drive-Topside area is still considered one of the private districts for the rich.

Baguio's parks and hiking grounds, built before or around the 1920s, were probably the most pleasant and only recreational spaces of their kind in the country. Today, those recreation places built in the early American period are still the obvious choices as tourist haunts. In the 1980s, when vendors and mass tourism invariably invaded the public parks, Camp John Hay became the city's favorite playground and the only remaining forested park.

Fewer traces of the hill station archetype remain recognizable as the city's still growing resident population[50] continues to irretrievably change the Baguio landscape and ecosystem. Rapid population expansion, overbuilding and serious environmental problems continue to impinge on the city's infrastructure, including its water, waste disposal, electrical, and road systems.

Sadly, the continuous decline in the area's distinctive indigenous cultural expression has become irreversible.

In spite of the abovementioned concerns, Baguio has assumed new functions. Its key role in the region's banking, education, trade and communications has created a highly diversified local economy, thrusting the city into the role of a major urban center. No longer merely the exclusive playground of the colonial elite and fashionable Filipino society, Baguio now serves a more serious function, that of the Northern Luzon Cordillera's regional capital.

NOTES:

1. Indigenous peoples of southern Benguet; also called Benguet Igorot ("Igorot" is a collective term used for peoples of the northern Luzon Cordillera, which literally means "people of the mountains.")

2. Bienvenido P. Tapang, "Innovation and Economic Change: A Case History of the Ibaloy Cattle Enterprise in Benguet," (thesis for the Graduate School of Economics Education, Center for Research and Communication, Manila, 1982), 93.

3. Robert R. Reed, *City of Pines: The Origins of Baguio as a Colonial Hill Station and Regional Capital* (Baguio City, Philippines: A-Seven Publishing, 1999), xii.

4. Otto Scheerer, "On Baguio's Past," *German Travellers on the Cordillera*, ed. W. H. Scott (Manila: Filipiniana Book Guild, 1975), 176.

5. William Henry Scott, *Discovery of the Igorots* (Quezon City, Philippines: New Day Publishers, 1974), 9.

6. James H. Blount, *American Occupation of the Philippines, 1898-1912* (New York: The Knickerbocker Press, 1913), reprinted as Book 24, Filipiniana Reprint Series, ed. Renato Constantino (Manila: Cacho Hermanos, 1991), 48.

7. Thomas J. McCormick, "The Philippines Were Insular Stepping Stones to the Chinese Pot of Gold," *American Imperialism in 1898: The Quest for National Fulfillment*, ed. Richard Miller (New York: John Wiley and Sons, 1970), 129, 133; Daniel B. Schirmer, *Republic or Empire: American Resistance to the Philippine War* (Cambridge, Mass.: Schenkman Publishing Co., 1972), 66-67; Bonifacio Salamanca, *The Filipino Reaction to American Rule, 1901-1913* (Quezon City, Philippines: New Day Publishers, 1984), 1; John Morgan Gates, *Schoolbooks and Krags: The U.S. Army in the Philippines* (Westport, Conn.: Greenwood Press, 1973), 4-7.

8. Daniel B. Schirmer and Stephen Rosskamm Shalom, eds., *The Philippines Reader* (Boston: South End Press, 1987), 5-6.

9. Ed. C. de Jesus, *Benguet Consolidated, Inc.: 1903-1978, A Brief History* (August 1978), 13.

10. Salvador P. Lopez, *Isles of Gold: A History of Mining in the Philippines* (New York: Oxford University Press,1992), 49.

11. Ibid.

12. Report of the Philippine Commission, 1900-1903 (Washington, D.C.: Government Printing Office, 1904), 87. Hereinafter referred to as RPC.

13. RPC, 1908, 347.

14. Dean C. Worcester, *The Philippines Past and Present* (New York: Macmillan, 1914), 367.

15. Rodney J. Sullivan, *Exemplar of Americanism: The Philippine Career of Dean C. Worcester* (Quezon City, Philippines: New Day Publishers, 1992), 146-147.

16. Howard T. Fry, *A History of the Mountain Province* (Quezon City, Philippines: New Day Publishers, 1983), 8-9.

17. Renato Constantino, "The Origin of a Myth," in Blount, *American Occupation of the Philippines*, 127.

18. Luzviminda Francisco, "The Philippine-American War," in Schirmer and Shalom, eds. *The Philippines Reader*.

19. RPC, 1900-03, 627.

20. Forbes, *Philippine Islands*, 570.

21. Fry, 91.

22. Computed using the *New York Times* cost-of-living calculator.

23. Forbes, *Philippine Islands*, 569.

24. Reed, 85.

25. Worcester, *Philippines Past and Present*, 373.

26. Forbes, *Notes on Early Baguio History*, 14.

27. Fry, 75.

28. U.S. Secretary of State John Milton Hay in October 1898 advised American peace commissioners, then negotiating the Treaty of Paris with Spain, that the entire Philippine archipelago should be ceded to the United States. Hay was secretary of state from 1898-1905. The army post in Baguio was named in his honor after his death in 1905.

29. RPC, 1909, 64.

30. RPC, 1906, 69.

31. Felix Keesing and Marie Keesing, *Taming the Philippine Headhunters* (Stanford, Ca.: Stanford University Press, 1932), 163.

32. RPC, 1906 part I, 200.

33. Cable News American Yearly Review Number, 1911, 73.

34. Cordillera Consultative Committee, "The Nature of Urban Land Problem in Baguio," *Dakami Ya Nan Dagami* (Baguio City, 1985), 118.

35. Wealthy, prestigious, and powerful.

36. Bienvenido P. Tapang, "Face/Off: Reflections of the Ibaloy in Historical Texts on the Baguio Mineral District," paper presented during the Regional Seminar-Workshop on Cordillera Historiography, Mountain Lodge, Baguio City, 6 August 1999, 12-13.

37. Interview with Bernard C. Okubo, 9 May 1997, Baguio City.

38. Anavic Bagamaspad and Zenaida Pawid, *A People's History of Benguet Province* (Baguio City: Baguio Printing and Publishing, 1985), 234.

39. June Prill-Brett, "Baguio: A Multi-Ethnic City and the Development of the Ibaloy as an Ethnic Minority," (Cordillera Studies Center Working Paper 15, September 1990), 20.

40. Tapang, "Innovation and Economic Change, " 145.

41. James J. Halsema, *E. J. Halsema, Colonial Engineer: A Biography* (Quezon City, Philippines: New Day Publishers, 1982), 310.

42. Ibid., 314.

43. Ibid., 315.

44. Halsema, 320; Fry, 205.

45. Halsema, 319.

46. E. J. Halsema left a singular mark on the physical landscape of Baguio and in the minds of the city's American and Filipino residents. Essentially, he gave substance to the Burnham Plan and designed the hydroelectric plants, street system, sewage, and other public utilities that Baguio still largely relies upon. In the Northern Luzon Cordillera region, he is best remembered for the Baguio-Bontoc Road which he built as concurrent Bureau of Public Works (BPW) district engineer. Baguio continues to benefit from Halsema's legacy as a competent administrator and city engineer.

47. Daniel H. Burnham and Pierce Anderson, "Report on the Proposed Plan of the City of Baguio," (typsescript) Chicago, 3 October 1905: 5-6.

48. Reed, 102.

49. Daniel H. Burnham, "Notes on the Preliminary Plan for Baguio," (typsescript) Chicago, 27 June 1905: 3-4.

50. Baguio's resident population in 1998 was 260,000. In addition, the city also has a semi-permanent student community and a floating population of occasional laborers that exceeds 125,000. See Reed, xxvi.

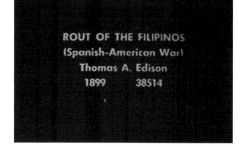

Imperialist Fictions:
The Filipino in the Imperialist Imaginary

NICK DEOCAMPO

In 1899 the film studio of American inventor Thomas Alva Edison began to produce a series of films that depicted the Philippine-American War.[1] These newsreels, many of them lasting no more than a minute each, brought the U.S. colonization of the Philippine Islands to vivid life onscreen. They drew large audiences to American theaters with their portrayal of American troops routing Filipino soldiers in battlefields. The immense popularity of these films and similar ones made about the Spanish-American War in Cuba marked a major turning point in the emergence of American cinema. To contemporary audiences, the films offer valuable opportunities for regarding the ways in which history is encoded by cinema.

Although there were other studios that made films about the Philippine-American War[2], the Edison Manufacturing Company's "newsreels" provide the most problematic accounts today of the almost forgotten war. While the films remain visually valuable, one cannot help but ask how actual historical events were subsumed into filmic fantasies by such an agent of illusion as cinema. In the Edison films, historical narratives yielded to imperialist fiction as cinema became a tool of America's desire to colonize faraway islands such as the Philippines.

It is interesting to see how these films present problems for contemporary viewers in terms of racial representation, narrative, ideological discourse, and notions of entertainment. These questions will be raised as cinema's role in creating an imperialist "imaginary" is studied in relation to the Filipino subject which became an object of America's cinematic fantasy.

CINEMA AND AMERICAN COLONIZATION

Cinema came to the Philippines at a time when Filipinos had set ablaze the fires of revolution against their Spanish rulers. The crisis between the two peoples had not yet been settled when another war was sparked between the natives and the Americans. While the fight against Spain was resolved by the Treaty of Paris, under whose terms the U.S. Government purchased the Philippine Islands for $20 million, the Filipinos' war against the Americans officially lasted another three years. But even after the guns of war had been stilled, the battle to colonize the Filipinos continued on other fronts. It was during this time of U.S. political adventurism that cinema began to flourish in the Philippines.

Introduced in 1897 by Spanish business entrepreneurs, cinema enjoyed phenomenal acceptance, particularly among low- and middle-class Filipinos. It took almost a decade for it to stabilize its hold on the native population when the American government finally took firm control of the affairs of the new colony. The popularity of cinema in the United States, and subsequently in its colony, the Philippines, came at an opportune time, when the American people had become optimistic about their role in the emerging world order. With the dawning of a new century, Americans prided themselves on being the world's new political and economic power.

America's going to war had a lot to do with the triumph of cinema over theater as the new century's most popular entertainment form. The outbreak of the Spanish-American War in 1898 offered a good opportunity for the new technical invention to establish itself as the medium that brought the urgency and vividness of the war to the American people's consciousness. During those early days, the moving pictures, no matter how crude, brought a sense of realism that was unparalleled by the more traditional communication media such as print and theater. The war footage, when shown in theater houses, captivated millions of viewers as reel after reel unraveled the adventures of American soldiers conquering foreign territories and vanquishing strange enemies.

Viewed amidst the safety and nearness of moviehouses so close to their homes, war stories provided fodder for the cinematic apparatus to produce a steady stream of films that not only affirmed America's war efforts but also provided entertainment to millions. The tremendous patronage of films about the bombing of the U.S. battleship *Maine* at a harbor in Havana, Cuba awakened America to the importance of films in rallying support for the controversial war that it was waging against Spain. When the United States went a step further by conquering former Spanish territories like the Philippines, cinema was once more deployed to stir up mass support for America's imperialist efforts.

When Commodore George Dewey won in a naval encounter against the decrepit Spanish armada on 1 May 1898, his naval victory was celebrated on the American moviescreen. Films like *Battle of Manila Bay* became box-office hits. Like the newspapers that screamed banner headlines about the war, these films served as "visual newspapers."[3] They contained visual accounts that fed the American public's curiosity about such current events. The films also swelled the American people's patriotic pride with their accounts of the country's triumph onscreen. As early American cinema scholar Charles Musser noted: "(M)otion picture showmen evoked powerful patriotic sentiments in their audiences, revealing the new medium's ideological and propagandistic force."[4]

Interestingly, it was the "faked" newsreels rather than the actualities, or films taken in actual battle scenes, that were widely cheered. "Faked" newsreels, also known as "reenactments," were about battles or events that happened abroad but were shot in America's backlot studios. *Battle of Manila Bay* was one example. It was filmed on the rooftop of Vitagraph Studio's headquarters in New York City using cardboard ships and an overturned table filled with water. Producers J. Stuart Blacton and Albert E. Smith shot the 33-second film.

Smith recalled later how the film was made:

> At this time street vendors in New York City were selling sturdy photographs of ships of the American and Spanish fleets. We bought a set of each and we cut out the battleships. On a table, topside down, we placed one of artist Blacton's large canvas-covered frames and filled it up with water an inch deep. In order to stand the cut-outs in the water, we nailed them to a length of wood about an inch square. In this way a little 'shelf' was provided behind each ship and on this shelf we placed pinches of gunpower—three pinches for each ship —not too many, we felt, for a major sea engagement of this sort.[5]

Although these films may appear crude to present-day audiences, the large number of "faked" newsreels produced at the turn of the century, particularly of the war efforts waged by America, proved the popularity of this genre. Audiences loved the films because they stirred them to express their patriotic fervor collectively and in public. As a favored subject, war helped to establish the size and influence of early cinema. In these toddling narratives, Filipinos became entangled with America's myth-making enterprise. For their debut in cinema, Filipinos were portrayed as "the enemy" defeated by heroic American soldiers. The Filipinos' genuine struggle for freedom was turned into a diegetic material for war narratives. As cinema and imperialism fanned each other, the Philippines became prized both as a conquered territory and as an object of cinematic fancy.

IMPERIALIST FICTIONS

Thomas Alva Edison was among the first producers to make films about the conquest of the Philippines. From his pioneering invention, a peep-show machine that allowed the viewer to see a loop film inside a viewing machine for a nickel, his studio developed a camera called the Kinetoscope and a projecting machine called the Kinetograph. Also widely known as a canny entrepreneur, Edison established the Edison Manufacturing Company which steadily produced films for a growing market.

Encouraged by the popularity of war pictures, Edison even gave the Kinetograph a martial name, the "Wargraph." Among the films that made reference to the battle being fought in the Philippines, an actuality called *Troop Ships for the Philippines* was one of the first to be made. It was shot on 25 May 1898.

The outbreak of the Philippine-American War in 1899 made the "Wargraph" more productive. Six of the newsreels made by the Edison studio were shot as reenactments at the West Orange studio in New Jersey. The films released in June 1899 were *Filipinos Retreat from Trenches* (c. 5 June 1899), *U.S. Troops and Red Cross in the Trenches Before Caloocan, P.I.* (c. 5 June 1899), *Advance of Kansas Volunteers at Caloocan* (c. 5 June 1899), *Capture of Trenches at Candaba* (c. 10 June 1899), *Rout of the Filipinos* (c. 10 June 1899), and *Col. Funstan Swimming the Baglag River* (sic)/ *Col. Funston Swimming the Bagbag River* (c. 23 September 1899). Made at a time when cinema had yet to establish its filmic conventions (genres like the documentary had yet to be invented), these films contained the tension of fact and fiction within their filmic makeup. While they contained history in their narrative, they also spoke the language of war.

Three of them will be discussed here: *Advance of Kansas Volunteers at Caloocan*, *Rout of the Filipinos*, and *Col. Funstan Swimming the Baglag River* (sic) / *Col. Funston Swimming the Bagbag River*. An analysis of them will help establish the complicit role cinema played in America's empire building. Short descriptions will be followed by a detailed analysis of the texts and their significations.

In *Advance of Kansas Volunteers at Caloocan*, the Filipino soldiers are lined up before the camera in firing-squad fashion. They begin firing as they advance towards the camera. While they are doing so, a cloud of smoke enshrouds them from sight. Suddenly, a phalanx of American soldiers springs from the direction of the camera and assaults the now retreating Filipinos. Prominently displayed is the American flag which is being held by a soldier seen at center frame. (In contrast, the Filipino flag at the extreme side in the distant background can hardly be deciphered.) As an emotional highlight of the film, the American flag bearer is shot and falls to the ground. The American officer, brandishing his sword, picks up the fallen flag, lifts it high up, and waves it patriotically. At this time, American soldiers rejoice over the defeat of their foes who are nowhere to be found onscreen. In their moment of triumph, American soldiers take command of the screen space.

Remarkably, the two other films share the same conquest narrative contained in similar cinematic codes. In *Rout of the Filipinos*, thick foliage hides a group of crouching soldiers. From offscreen left they enter with rifles pointed and fire at unseen enemies in an obvious movement of defeat. A man with a hat and a sword manages their exit to offscreen right while a dark flag is being waved from the distance.

After a lull, an advancing American troop drives away its retreating enemies completely off-screen, outside the very margins of the screen. An American soldier then waves his hat, followed by a few others, signaling their triumph. Once more, the American flag is unfurled in the center of the screen.

The third film, *Col. Funstan Swimming the Baglag River* (sic)/*Col. Funston Swimming the Bagbag River*, appears to be the longest among the three, running for a hundred feet compared to, say, *Advance of Kansas Volunteers at Caloocan*, which runs only seventy-five feet.

Through the familiar foliage is now seen a river. In the foreground, a group of American soldiers stands on a raft. An officer (presumably the character Colonel Funston) undresses and starts to swim across the river. From the other side of the river, in the background and peeping through the bushes, are Filipino soldiers aiming their rifles at their white enemies. Shooting commences as the colonel jumps into the water. The raft then moves toward the other bank as the Americans provide the colonel cover from enemy fire. Unmindful of the cross-fire, Colonel Funston reaches the other bank and continues to frolic in the water. The Filipinos retreat.

When the raft carrying the Americans reaches the opposite bank, Colonel Funston moves to the left margin of the frame. He puts on his uniform as his soldiers wave their hats again as a sign of victory. The U.S. flag, of course, is unfurled once more. On the other hand, the Filipinos are once again chased out to the farthermost margins on the left side of the frame. They reappear and hover over the outline of the hill (like Indians in later-day Hollywood cowboy movies) as they scuttle away to offscreen right, never to be seen again.

Colonel Funston can be seen riding a white horse which appears from nowhere. His soldiers disembark from their raft and march up a hilly embankment as the Filipinos can no longer be found. Obviously, the Americans have conquered another territory.

A close analysis of the three films reveals that they clearly articulate an unmistakable discourse on what was then a raging issue: imperialism. Anything to support the imperialist war was reified onscreen. Abstract notions such as racial discrimination, colonialism, bigotry, and "other-ness" appear in no uncertain terms as they take material form in the narrative construction, point of view, spatial composition, screen action and direction, and other visual codes. Since many of these coded messages suggesting an affirmation of America's power to subjugate other people recur in several films, a form of visual language may be deemed in place. These coded signs, articulated through frequent screening for America's viewing millions, spoke in a visual language that even illiterate migrants could comprehend.

The visual tropes, although they may have been unwittingly deployed by the producers at the Edison studio, recur all too frequently so that one cannot miss the deliberate intention to construct subjects that would be supportive of war. The subliminal effects of these works have deeper consequences on the ideological formation of their viewers, particularly in the way they saw the world and their relation to it. A critical analysis of the films offers the chance to see how the films work in awakening the patriotic sentiments of the American people.

In the "reenactments," Edison's studio fabricated scenes which, even if based on factual events, were nonetheless manipulated. Shot in New Jersey, the film shows thick foliage which is supposed to suggest the tropics. Most surprising of all, Filipino guerrillas are represented onscreen by African-Americans wearing loose white shirts and pants that vaguely resemble the uniforms worn by native *revolucionarios*. All of them carry rifles rather than bolos or machetes which were the more numerous native weaponry. The flag, which is supposed to represent the Filipino banner, is non-defined and always gets lost among bushes or in the distant background. On the other hand, the American flag is always unfurled in the foreground and distinctly at center frame, the favored site for the triumphant Americans.

The events that happen within the short running time, usually not exceeding forty-five seconds, favor the triumph of American soldiers. From the titles alone, one can see a biased slant which describes either the Filipinos as defeated or the Americans as winners: *Advance of Kansas Volunteers at Caloocan*, *Rout of the Filipinos*, and *Filipinos Retreat from Trenches*, to cite three titles. All the films depict scenes that bolster the American public's confidence about winning the war.

The optimism of the titles is aptly supported by the movement of characters within the frame. As all films were shot with a one-camera setup, the camera allows one to see within seconds how Americans triumphed over native soldiers. This is done by literally and completely obliterating the Filipinos from the camera's frame, hence, from sight. This constitutes what appears to be the Edison studio's recurring visual trope: film space as metaphor for a contested territorial space.

This strong predilection for the narrative allows actual personages to "become" fictional characters. They can be regarded as protagonists or antagonists. Their conflicts are resolved with the protagonists' (read: American) triumph over their foes (read: Filipino). As war "reenactments," the Edison films become cloaked in fiction rather than facts.

Textually, space is a deeply significant element of the films. Understanding how space is deployed to create meaning leads to a crucial understanding of the films. Space here refers both to the pro-filmic action and to the space in the frame. The use of onscreen/offscreen space as a site of triumph and defeat, the use of background/foreground as another site of conquest, the crucial use of left/right margins of the frame for the refuge of the defeated, and the significance of the center frame as a hallowed place for the victor—all these point to the calculated encoding that the Edison studio invested in these works, again wittingly or not. Besides the use of space, the Edison studio dressed the Filipino soldiers in white uniforms that made obvious the fact that the Filipinos were played by African-Americans. On the other hand, the Americans, dressed in black cavalry uniforms, stand out because of their white skin. Their gestures are also encoded, as when a soldier waves his hat in circles to mean victory. The hat may be displaced by a sword, or by a flag, as in the case of the officer who picks up the flag after its bearer is felled by a bullet and waves it to signify success.

All these examples show the ideological encoding of these films. Meant to stir up the patriotic zeal of the American public, the showing of these films to millions became a political necessity to support the colonialist adventure.

THE "I" OF THE "EYE": UNMASKING THE IMPERIAL GAZE

There is something in the way the Edison films were shot that makes contemporary audiences uneasy about suspending their disbelief. It is disturbing that the films contain a point of view which serves as surrogate identity for the one who made them. In unmasking this point of view, one realizes that these films have the power to persuade an audience to be sympathetic to the war effort by subjecting them to the camera's imperial gaze.

One film articulates this point. In *Advance of Kansas Volunteers at Caloocan*, a troop of Filipinos is lined up before the camera. Revealing this troop through the camera's "eye" entails the act of "looking" at the cinematic object through the "gaze" cast by the camera. While one is made to believe that a "Filipino" troop is being looked at, it is hard to determine the identity of the onlooker. Who is looking at the Filipino troop? What is the reason for the look? Why is the look directed at the Filipinos? How is the look sustained, given the impossible situation that what the look sees is combat? While it is evident that what is visible to the eyes of the onlooker is the image of the enemy, what is left unseen, meaning the source of the look, remains a mystery. But not for long. Precisely from the direction of the camera where the look emanates springs a phalanx of American soldiers. With their appearance coming from the fixed gaze of the camera, they break the spell of the look and finally reveal the identity of the onlooker. It is the look of the American troop as it is crouched behind the camera. The "look" and the American troop are revealed to be one and the same. From the privileged view of the camera, the Filipinos are reduced to the position of an "other," an enemy trapped by the cinematic gaze. While holding on to the "look," the almighty camera expresses power. As Filipinos line up before the camera, they appear vulnerable, as though facing easy slaughter. The power of the unblinking look remains uncontested till the end. Filipinos start withering away from the hail of bullets that dart from the direction of the murderous look cast by the camera.

The implied invincibility with which the camera is imbued is another disturbing feature of the film. Despite the gunfire repeatedly produced by Filipinos toward the camera, it remains an unharmed participant in the bloody massacre. It is invincible! Superman may trace his lineage to this film. Identifying themselves with the camera's gaze, the American soldiers survive the volley of fire.

The primal function of the camera—to see the world the way the filmmaker wants his audience to see it—greatly informs our understanding of the way early American films were made. Films caught up in efforts to make war acceptable to American moviegoers made use of the capacity of the camera to reify the imperialist agenda. The powerful gaze cast by the camera proved persuasive in convincing millions of American moviegoers to see the war as its supporters did.

These films contain images of the Filipino. How he is represented is evidenced by the way he has been imagined. The Filipino is begotten first through the act of "looking." The camera casts its "gaze" and what it sees are Filipinos displayed in front of the camera as "enemies." The camera first casts the "look" and the "look" turns murderous as American soldiers spring from the direction of the camera to launch an attack that will annihilate the Filipinos.

Through the imagination with which the film image is constructed, the Filipino loses all virtues of his complex reality as he is reduced to one-dimensional fiction. In the imperialist imagination, the Filipino is constructed merely as "the enemy." The Filipino, as imagined, is he who gets killed, defeated, and literally pushed out of the screen in order to erase his presence and therefore mark his "absence." The Filipino, while present as "enemy" onscreen, actually ends up "absent" from history.

His absence is marked in two ways, in the substitution of Filipinos with African-Americans onscreen and in his actual erasure when he is dislodged by the appearance of American soldiers. There is not even a trace of his dead body to occupy a space in the frame. None of his remains are left as evidence of America's crime of racial genocide. Emptied of the Filipino dead, the scene is left with triumphant Americans celebrating their victorious presence. American soldiers colonize the screen.

Sadly, the substitution of Filipinos with African-Americans onscreen makes Filipinos unable to even claim their defeat as their own. Their replacement by another people of color robs them of a chance to feel the tragedy of war fully. Robbed of their own defeat, they are unable to grieve their own loss. How then can they feel real anger? Their presence is only indicated; their actual sorrow is denied. The fiction of war is effective in eliding war's true tragedies and the substitution of the enemy proves effective in deadening grief.

In the eyes of the imperialist, all colored peoples share the same color, and that can be anything except white. So the fiction continues. Blacks can be red Indians or brown tropical islanders. In the eyes of the black-and-white camera in the hands of white people, all colored people have the color of the enemy.

Complicity in the act of looking does not spare even present-day viewers. The camera maintains its imperial gaze as we in the present time look in horror (or maybe in amusement?) at the genocide that happens onscreen. We in the audience see the murder through the point of view of the same camera that first saw the crime a century before. The present is caught in a complicit relation to the act of murder that happened in the past, through the gaze. The gaze that proves fatal in annihilating the Filipino troop remains vital evidence of the crime.

The Filipino viewing the film today is implicated in the act of murder as he sees his own representation massacred onscreen through the point of view offered by his colonizer's gaze. He sees his own massacre the way his killer wants him to see it. By his look, framed within the camera's look, a look that belongs to the colonizer, a look that kills, he now commits the crime of killing. His look is now tangled with the look of his enemy that makes an enemy of himself. With his look, he kills his own image. He participates in the crime. The Filipino as murderer of his own! No matter how much he protests the look as not his own, his implication lies in the very act of looking. Looking becomes his crime. He would wish he did not look at all. But there is no innocent look. He cannot escape the look once the look stares back at him from the screen and from his distant past.

Who then is the "I" of the "Eye"? What constitutes his identity? What power relations govern him and what he looks at? How does one define the act of looking? Does the Filipino trapped a century ago in the image of the "enemy," through the "look" cast by his own enemy, have a chance to liberate himself from the colonial "gaze"? If a "look" can be enslaving, can it be also liberating? It appears that the Filipino's redemption lies in his own consciousness.

Unmasking the identity behind the "look" affords one an understanding of the tangled relations caught up in the simple act of looking.

THE IMPERIALIST IMAGINARY

There is a distinct process by which the Filipino was represented in the early American films. His representation is very much tied up with the imaginary that constructed his identity. This investigation of the complex act of representation is indebted to Luiz Costa Lima's concepts of representation as contained in his book, *Control of the Imaginary: Reason and Imagination in Modern Times*.[6]

Costa Lima's concept of the imaginary as that which "annihilates things and thematizes them as absent" helps to clarify a lot of issues related to the representation of Filipinos in early cinematic works. It helps to address questions like: Why are Filipinos absent from the screen—either they are substituted with African-Americans or they totally disappear at the end of the shot? How is an imperialist fiction formed? What forces help to construct an imperialist imaginary?

In the world of 1899, an actual war erupted between Filipino and American soldiers. This real event was known and information about its progress was relayed outside the arena of battle through the transmission of messages made in symbolic signs, i.e., news dispatches as relayed by telegraph. Films played a more symbolic role when they started to depict the stories relayed through the wires or heard from the war front. The moving pictures seen on celluloid offered such a strong resemblance to reality that on many occasions audiences who got to see them were convinced that what they saw onscreen were real.

In the case of Edison's newsreels, the reenacted scenes from the war front became symbolic representations of actual battles fought by American soldiers. By imitating real events, the Edison studio provided the necessary fiction to sustain the war. Of interest in the fiction that is produced is the imaginary that causes its production. Unable to hide its true nature, the imaginary becomes revealed as "imperialist" as Americans literally occupy the screen space and turn Filipinos into an absent presence. The Filipino appears in the film's unfolding as the product of the imperialist "imaginary," imagined by his conqueror. This happens when Filipinos appear on film as a function of representation, only to become absent when fiction is shaped by ideology.

The imperialist imaginary, caught between mimesis and fiction, reveals the erasure of "real" Filipinos either as they are replaced by "imagined" ones, or worse, by their very absence. The imaginary annihilates the actual object it represents. Absence takes the place of the real. In the case of Filipinos replaced by African-Americans, imagination bestows on the replacement the tantalizing trait of verisimilitude which makes it possible for the imitation to resemble, even if vaguely, the reality that has been erased.

Thus the Filipinos are present in the film while being absent. The African-Americans, pretending to be "Filipinos," could only reveal their fakeness and in doing so point to that which is absent from the screen: Filipinos as themselves. Filipinos are seen onscreen only as signified, as imagined. They do not exist as they are. Their absent presence fulfills a function in the creation of the imperialist fiction: Filipinos as enemies. As they are vanquished through the defeat of their surrogate presence in the form of the African-Americans, the imperialist imaginary becomes fulfilled: American soldiers colonize the screen and declare their triumph.

THE GHOSTS OF WAR

As war spelled big business for the movie industry, film became an opportune medium to replicate America's imperialist ideology. The language of the market found an ally in the language of cinema that spoke of war. Because the war footage itself internalized within its very construction the spirit of war, films shown onscreen became extensions of war fought in battlefields, no matter how distorted reality became in the celluloid dream.

The deployment of cinema, with its persuasive use of visual symbols, helped perpetuate America's colonialist agenda to expand its territories (not only geographically but also politically and economically) long after the guns of war had been silenced. Understandably, the imperialist policies that vanquished the Filipinos' right to self-rule went beyond conventional warfare. It seeped into the symbolic medium of film, among the many other forms of conquest such as those imposed in culture, politics, and the economy.

Vestiges of the war spread throughout America's vast entertainment empire. It was not only films that contained elements of war. Even the way films were promoted internalized the values of imperialism, colonization, discrimination, bigotry, and racism. Directly related to film promotion were film catalogues which, while serving to promote the sale of films, also contained in their program notes and synopses ways in which Americans demeaned Filipinos. While racial misrepresentations of Filipinos were evident, synopses contained in catalogues affirmed and aggravated colonial supremacy.

Film catalogues printed in the early days of cinema were replete with degrading remarks about Filipinos. One example is to be found in Siegmund Lubin's catalogue containing the following synopsis for *Philippino War Dance* (1903):

> We are interested in the Philippine Islands and its unruly inhabitants, and this film in particular will give an idea of how these semi-savages prepare for war. In their scaty costime they go through numerous antics, brandishing their deadly spears and uttering unnatural sounds, dancing all the while. These half-civilized men represent the following of the notorious Aguinaldo, the chief of the revolutionists, but who will finally be subdued by the brave American soldier boys now in the Philippine Islands. You want this film, as a star of all war films.[7]

The above quotation reveals the promoter's blatant derision of the film's subject, the Filipinos (peculiarly spelled "Philippinos"). While expressing American "interest" in their newly acquired territory, it describes the native inhabitants in demeaning terms: "semi-savages"; "unruly inhabitants"; "half civilized"; who wear "scanty costume"; go through "numerous antics"; brandish "deadly spears"; and utter "unnatural sounds."

The revolutionary leader, Gen. Emilio Aguinaldo, is described as "notorious" while the American soldier boys who captured him are "brave." The film, incidentally, was promoted as "a star of all war films," indicating that it elicited great interest. It appeared as if, in 1903, what crudely started as war reenactments in the early Edison studio now found their fitting equivalent in reality with this film.

Other forms of entertainment supported American imperialism. Stage plays containing the theme of Philippine conquest were produced. When Admiral George Dewey took possession of the Philippines, a melodrama in four acts, titled *Dewey, Hero of Manila*, was mounted. Musical compositions that took the form of popular songs, marches, operas, and coon songs sung by traveling minstrels were likewise inspired by the war. For example, there were two versions of "Battle of Manila Bay," a serio-comic song and a number for a brass band.

Illustrated magic lantern and stereopticon slide shows also depicted the colonized Philippines. In one catalogue printed by Sears and Roebuck, a slide show called "A

Company of Ingorrote (sic) Spearmen" once again betrayed colonial supremacy: "If these people were more enlightened and educated, they would realize how foolish it is to oppose our army with such primitive weapons." Even naval shows and state fairs depicted scenes of the Philippine-American War and its aftermath.

All these forms of entertainment appealed to a popular audience. The films, stereopticon slides, magic lanterns, stage plays, operas, musical compositions, fairs, naval shows, and the like fed the curiosity and fancy of a general viewing public, euphoric over being regarded as the world's new superpower. Many of these entertainment forms served their purpose in days gone by, but even today films continue to exercise their popularity. American films have matured from the early, "primitive" stage at the turn of the century to become the twentieth-century's most popular entertainment form. Today, Hollywood movies have become a global monopoly. As they enter the new millennium, American films will attain new heights by assuming varied expressions using the new media technology.

In the Philippines, where America first found stories to help assure initial box-office success, the movies have been embraced as the preeminent cultural form The natives did not take long to internalize the medium that had been an instrument of their own colonization. In fact, cinema in its most popular expression also became an instrument for exploiting and even demeaning other Filipinos by those in control of the film apparatus.

In Manila, where cinema enjoyed phenomenal success, film became an instrument of commercial exploitation in the hands of local businessmen. Tagalog cinema came to symbolize the native form of imperialism with regard to the aspects of native life it tried to capture onscreen. For example, the way the Muslims of southern Philippines are treated in the imaginary of Tagalog cinema shows how cinema continues to replicate the colonizing power of the past. Other sectors of society have been treated the same way: women exploited in sex films, poor people portrayed as agents of crime, ethnic communities like the Chinese as "outsiders," prostitutes as evil temptations, homosexuals as perverse, among others. The colonizing look has been owned by the colonized themselves, and the gaze that once proved fatal is now trained dangerously on the natives themselves.

The history of cinema and its power to colonize with the gaze is a long one. That history has its roots in war, imperialism, and capitalism. It is important for present-day Filipinos to realize that while the war that spurred cinema into becoming a popular medium may have ended, cinema continues to be haunted by vestiges of war. Given the way cinema exercises control over the imaginary of filmmakers and the way audiences mindlessly devour "film entertainment," the vestiges of war have hardly been laid to rest.

The war, it seems, had not only the power to kill but also to resurrect ghosts.

NOTES:

1. The Philippine-American War was the subject of several newsreels produced in 1899 until around 1903 by the Edison Manufacturing Studio. As they were however annotated as "The Spanish-American War," the films' nomenclature dates and labels later posed problems. While it was the "Spanish-American War" that happened in 1898, the dates 1899 or 1903 found in the Edison newsreels ought to have been properly described as "The Philippine-American War." Stereopticons and lantern slides produced at almost the same time were more accurate in identifying their subject. The use of "Spanish-American War" to label the films that depict scenes from the "Philippine-American War" shows the insignificance given to this almost forgotten war, an event considered by many American historians as merely a Filipino insurrection.

2. Other American film studios that made films about the Philippine-American War included the American Mutoscope and Bioscope Co., Lubin, and Vitagraph.

3. Charles Musser, *The Emergence of Cinema: The American Screen to 1907* (Berkeley: University of California Press, 1990), 225.

4. Ibid., 225.

5. Albert E. Smith, with Phil A. Koury. Two Reels and a Crank (Garden City, N.J.: Doubleday, 1952), 66-67.

6. Luiz Costa Lima, *Control of the Imaginary: Reason and Imagination in Modern Times* (Minneapolis: University of Minnesota Press, 1988), ix.

For Costa Lima, there are three important elements in the understanding of the way the world becomes represented, for example, aesthetically, as in works of fiction. These triadic elements are mimesis, imaginary, and fiction. Recognizing that there is a natural world out there that exists independently of the symbolic act of representation, the mode of learning about the world that also leads to the human process of socialization itself is made through—first and foremost, according to Costa Lima—the act of mimesis. Mimesis helps human beings to internalize social values which in turn help sustain human lifeways. The act of mimesis presupposes identification or similarity. Oftentimes associated with imitation that allows a subject to merely copy external traits of its model, mimesis differs from imitation as it presumes a network of psycho-social meanings which links the subject to its modeling element, say, of the physical world. Defying conventional wisdom of mimesis as identification, Costa Lima argues that "the real path of mimesis... supposes not copy but difference." Remarkably, Costa Lima's argument that "imitation is a product of difference" appears convincing when one realizes that no matter how close a copy an imitation may be to the original, it will always maintain its distinct identity as a copy. Imitation leaves its telltale signs on the copied object that betrays its own fakeness. The product of mimesis, on the other hand, is fiction. As one imitates, fiction is produced as a copy of the original. Costa Lima defines fiction as "a type of territoriality configured through signs." A fiction is governed by rules that, Costa Lima declares, are normally not conscious. The author of fiction conjures an imitation of a real object, person, or event, and tries through evocation of signs to copy that which is original. Signs are vested with meanings and it is with the use of signs that fiction is configured by virtue of fiction being a system of meaningful signification.

Between mimesis and fiction is the imaginary. The imaginary is one of the two ways by which the world is thematized. According to Costa Lima, "while the other form, the perceptual, locates things as present, the imaginary annihilates them, thematizing them as absent." It is the element of absence that distinctly marks the imaginary. (As Costa Lima writes, "I perceive what surrounds me, but I can imagine only what is absent.")

7. Description as found in *Lubin's Films* (Complete Catalogue), January 1903.

Food and War

DOREEN G. FERNANDEZ

What food has to do with war is immediately obvious. Wars are food-driven, since food supplies must be gathered and stored; meals must be prepared for troops must be fed, and hungry soldiers have been known to leave; leaders must distribute and control food; the food of war must be in convenient and accessible form. Food can also be a weapon, as when it is banned or kept from circulation (blockaded, embargoed), or when it is destroyed (burned, spoiled) and made unavailable.

What happens to food after the war is not so easily read, since that which war leaves behind is not always immediately visible. Rusted equipment, ruined houses, lists of casualties, new systems of transportation and marketing are visible to the naked eye. Yet food is the battlefield on which culture and consciousness clash and conquer. After the fray, food stays on the land quietly and invisibly, takes root in home and custom, seeps into the soil, and grows into the lifestyle.

The galleon trade between Manila and Mexico (1565-1815) brought in not only colonial silver and soldiers, friars and faith-practices, but food products and a food culture. The 300-some years under Spain were a continuing cultural war that left clear food-marks on Philippine culture.

With American troops at the turn of the century came not only Philippine-American interactions (later, lastingly, in language, education, trade, government), but food and ways of eating it, and eventually a burgeoning popular culture and lifestyle.

In a country where "*Kumain ka na?*" ("Have you eaten?") is a standard greeting and concern, food is a vital field of study—even only as vestige of war, as index of struggle.

THE SPANISH LEGACY (*LA HERENCIA ESPAÑOLA*)

In the Spanish colonial era, while the native Filipinos ate their rice, fish, and vegetables, the Spaniards not only brought in their bread, meats, olive oil, and seasonings, but also new foods (mostly from Mexico) that had not been here before. Among these were vegetables like corn, *sayote/chayote*, peanuts, tomatoes, *singkamas/jicama*, and sweet potatoes; fruits like guavas (*bayabas*, the Mexican *guayaba*), camachile (*cuauhmochitl*), chico (*chico sapote*), *atis* (the Aztec *ahate*), and many more. Left on the soil, on this they fed, grew, and adjusted, to become the particular vegetables and fruits that they are now, special to Philippine soil, climate, locations, and current usage.

Even more clearly artifacts, and with wider impact, are dishes, the names of which identify their origin: *embutido, menudo, relleno, paella, mechado, cocido, champurrado*. At first they were probably made almost entirely of ingredients from Spain and Mexico, since the Philippines did not have the olive oil, *pimientos morrones, pimenton, chorizos*, and wines for their making. Eventually, adaptations were made and the dishes became indigenized—still traceable to their Spanish originals, but using local ingredients and tuned to the Filipino taste.

The current *paella*, for example, is roughly based on the original from Valencia, a field-cooked dish that contained vegetables and available meat (a passing rabbit, a chicken). In the Philippines, however, it holds everything considered high-class and Spanish: seafood, ham, fowl, *chorizos*, vegetables, spices, in reckless abandon.

The reason for that is the less visible vestige of the power struggle with the colonizer: the elite position of Spanish cuisine. Because of the imported ingredients, this was less attainable, rarer; thus better, more "high-class," and therefore food for feasting and the elite. Because it was the food of the friar and the conquistador, it was desirable, a mark of social ascendance. The humbler fare of peasants and fishermen—rice, fish, and vegetables, now pronounced by dietitians one of the healthiest diets in the world—was ordinary, "low-class," for everyday consumption and not for special people or occasions.

Christmas feasting, which before Christianity came in was harvest feasting, used to be rice—(the staple food, the basic bounty) based: hundreds of varieties of *puto, suman, bibingka*, and the like. After Spanish domination, it came to require apples, oranges, walnuts, chestnuts, sugar-glazed ham, Edam ball cheese, *ensaimadas* (sugared brioches), and hot, thick chocolate. Today the poor still have the rice dishes; the middle class may have those and chicken and fruits; the elite have all of the above, plus *pavo embuchado, capon rellenado, tocino del cielo, torta del rey, abrillantados*, and other such luxurious vestiges of Spanish culture.

In advertisements, in cooking literature, in memoirs of Christmases past, the Spanish dishes emerge the victors, and the Filipino dishes the forgotten foot-soldiers of the cultural war. Two decades ago Filipinos would never have thought of serving guests native food; they gave them the best Spanish-colonial dishes or took them to Spanish restaurants, of which, as a result, we have the best in Asia.

Many of these dishes came to be promoted in status, to ranks beyond their origins. The field dish *paella*, for example, is now cooked only after all the expensive ingredients are gathered, and served at feasts or to honored guests. The weekend *cocido*, for which ingredients are available in every Spanish kitchen, is now a special family-reunion or Christmas dish, although it does have a great Filipino addition, the relish of eggplants or squash mashed in garlic and vinegar. *Champurrado*, Filipinized by the addition of flaked tuyo or tapang usa, is a special breakfast dish. *Bacalao*, the dried codfish served to sailors and the populace as part of penitential Lenten fasting, is now a luxury, since both the dried fish and the olive oil must be imported. Philippine cod is, alas, seasonal and fresh, and will not do.

From the 300-year experience with Spain, therefore, which includes both feasts and battles, what we find left on the battlegrounds are food products, dishes, ways of cooking and serving, and especially an attitude. Spanish food is "class" and for the elite and

MORE THAN EVER

Wars Are Fought With Food

The Philippines is blessed, indeed, by the peace and plenty now obtaining... but in the event of any calamity our population—military and civilian alike—have in NATIONAL FOODS one of the best sources of what it takes to maintain the people well fed and contented!

SARDINAS ESTILO FRANCES

The Lopez Memorial Museum Collection

special occasions. Filipino food is for every day, for the masses, for marketplaces, for the home (elite or not), and for Filipino-style feasting (rural festivals, barrio fiestas). Even though contemporary chefs modify, reinvent, and serve it at diplomatic and formal dinners, really important occasions (e.g., state dinners) generally feature continental or antebellum (mostly Spanish) cuisine, with a token native dish or two.

From *Sunday Tribune Magazine*, 31 October 1941.

THE "SPAM CULTURE"

American food, first brought in for the soldiers of the Philippine-American War (called an insurrection in U.S. military annals), is also here to stay, heavy with cholesterol and protein, sodium and fats. Consider the new comparison: the native rice-fish-vegetable diet versus the bread, butter, and canned food brought in as soldiers' rations in the Philippine-American War, then as commercial products in the free trade of the 1920s and 1930s, and again as military supplies in World War II.

Spam, for example, is a cultural phenomenon. The world champions in Spam patronage are said to be Hawaii and Guam, with the Philippines running a close third. For Hawaii and Guam, the reason is clear: both had and have large American bases. Spam, a canned luncheon meat, is convenient food for (American) armies. For the Philippines, the connection is less clear. Yes, there were American bases then, but the stronger motive is the colonial mentality: what the Americans brought in was great, modern, definitely to be patronized and emulated.

Today it is not only Spam (despite its high fat, cholesterol, and sodium content) that is desirable. Just as coveted are other canned foods like corned beef, corned beef hash, Vienna sausages, sardines, salmon, pork and beans. They are not only canned (*de lata*); they are American, therefore modern, also rarer and more expensive than native provender. Many have experienced visiting a provincial home and being offered the best the family has: the sole chicken in the yard, sacrificed to make *adobo* or *tinola*; but more especially, canned corned beef or Spam, *de lata* being a luxury worthy of serving as the coin of hospitality.

The attitude of adulation extends to almost all other American food (fried chicken, hamburgers). Filipinos have been taught through the educational system (home economics classes) kitchen hygiene and sanitation (dishcloths, cleanser, and garbage disposal), American cooking equipment (ranges, ovens) and cooking products and processes (pies, cakes, punches; pressure-cooking and freezing). Students trained by American teachers during American rule and returning government scholars trained in the United States in turn furthered the Americanization of food culture. This can be seen in the fact that today many modern homes have gleaming chrome-and-tile kitchens, as well as "dirty kitchens" where native food is cooked on charcoal and wood fires, in the old way.

The above education, and that coming informally and effectively from popular culture—cookbooks, magazines, movies—encouraged an acceptance and commitment to American food ideals, to food convenient (precooked, plasti-packed, frozen), portable (chip packs, sandwiches), and fast. The "modern" lifestyle has won over such traditional culinary ways as the patient fattening of chickens and pigs; long, slow boiling or steaming over rock salt; dicing and chopping, sun-drying and marinating; the rhythm and logic of *guisa*/sautéeing (garlic, onion, tomato; shrimp, then pork, in a certain pace and order).

Pangtawid-gutom, food "to bridge hungers," or traditional snacks (*puto, bibingka, dinuguan, arroz caldo, pansit*) has lost out to chips, gum, candies, sandwiches, doughnuts, et al., because of convenience and portability, as well as media appeal. In print and TV advertisements, native food is practically invisible (except in barrio fiesta settings); the foreign is in, both adopted (served as the Americans serve it) and adapted, for example, Spam *paksiw* (cooked in vinegar), corned beef *adobado* (marinated in vinegar and garlic and fried crisp), salmon *guisado* (sautéed with tomatoes and onions).

Drinking sessions in barrio and town may start with *tuba* and *lambanog*, but now more frequently are dominated by bottled beer, gin, and whiskey, sometimes with bottled soft drinks as mixers. The preferred *pulutan* (food to "pick up") to go with them, however, are not chips and nuts, but *buro't mustasa, kinilaw, sinugba*, and the rarer manta ray, sea urchin, or goat head.

Clinical nutritionist Sanirose S. Orbeta has said that the old rural, traditional diet pattern of rice (high carbohydrate/fiber), fish (low protein), and vegetables is healthy and suited to Filipino lifeways. The pace and distribution of meals depend on occupation: farmers have dawn breakfasts; fishermen, depending on whether they fish at night or in the day, might have it later or even earlier. Farmers may have their lunches taken to the field; fishermen may literally catch it along the way. The Western breakfast, lunch, and dinner, generally in the morning, at noon, and in the evening, require that the person adjust to the meal, rather than the meal to person and occupation.

The urban Filipino now often opts for the high-cholesterol ham-and-eggs, bread-and-butter breakfast, and a mixture of rural and urban, native and foreign food for the other two meals. Lately, however, the Filipino breakfast (quick, hearty fuel for the worker) of *tapsilog* (*tapa*, leftover rice fried with garlic, eggs) and its brethren (*longsilog*, *tosilog*) has been rediscovered for home, restaurant, or breakfast stall.

The urban/Western pattern, Orbeta asserts, is often less healthy, and parts of it may be unhealthy for the Filipino. Many Filipinos are lactose-intolerant, lacking an enzyme for the digestion of milk, so that the milk-rich American diet, so attractively portrayed in print and broadcast media, actually causes upset stomachs in some Filipinos.

The Filipino athletes who have made poor showings in the Asian Games and the Olympics were mostly suffering from diarrhea and strained digestive systems, because the milk, steaks, and chops (harder on the digestion than fish and seafood) had discomfited their stomachs and weakened them. Proof of this are the three gold-medalled boxers of the 1996 Asian Games, whom Orbeta had personally put through a native training diet of rice, fish, and vegetables, teaching them when and how to eat. "You mean we can eat our *adobong kangkong*?" they marveled. "How come we are hitting harder?" The traditional Filipino strength had come from the rural, traditional diet.

The colonial mentality—a vestige of colonization—extends even to the manufacture or source of the food. Many housewives (before the withdrawal of the American bases) used to drive to Clark Field to buy "PX goods" either with privilege cards or at the stalls in Angeles, Pampanga selling run-offs (or stolen goods) from the base. But why, when Kraft mayonnaise and Anchor butter had long been available in the supermarkets? Because, the shoppers felt, the goods at Clark Air Base were "made in the U.S.A." and thus superior; a local franchise would not produce anything as good.

Drives to "Buy Filipino" are started again and again, to save the local food industry. However, even now that Spam luncheon meat and Libby's corned beef are prohibitively expensive, the supermarkets supply other imported substitutes: corned beef from Argentina, Australia, Brazil, etc., and the famous Ma-Ling luncheon meat from China, that is brought into the markets of Zamboanga (the barter trade zone, so-called, although mostly stocked with smuggled goods) in such quantities that it has caused official government alarm.

The food from the Philippine-American War, extended and supplemented by education (textbooks, home economics classes) and popular media (radio, TV, film, magazines), was embedded and enshrined by the colonial mentality, and is now among the most visible facets of Filipino food culture. It is not, as Spanish food was, considered elite and high-class, but it is hygienic, practical, and "modern," fit for the new generation.

THE JAPANESE OCCUPATION

Survival food was the legacy of the Japanese occupation (1942-1945), not Japanese food, which was not available to the native population. The increasingly severe food shortages and the breakdown of food distribution and marketing systems caused much suffering, but were met with hardiness and ingenuity.

Rice, which was not being planted then, became rarer and more expensive, and what was available was stretched with the addition of corn, taro, sweet potatoes, and cassava. Even rice salvaged from a sunken ship, blackened and tasting of mildew, was sold and consumed. Tubers—*kamote, kamoteng-kahoy, gabi*—were in great use and demand, made into many kinds of food, some of which had originally used flour (*kakanin*, cakes). One mother in Negros Occidental made noodles from the skins of cassava roots. Some used rice flour for bread, which had to be eaten immediately because it hardened when cold.

Eating became an obsession among the hungry populace, and all manner of street food was sold: *binatog* (corn kernels boiled until puffed and soft; eaten with grated coconut), boiled bananas, peanuts, young corn. Since the deep-sea fishing boats went out of operation, small fishes from ponds, rivers, and lakes were salted, dried in the sun, roasted crisp, and eaten—flesh, head, spine, tail and all.

Food was hoarded and stored, and techniques were found to make it last (pick out worms and weevils; dry the rice in the sun). Vegetables were planted in home plots, with nary a stem, leaf, or root thrown away. One piece of dried fish was used to flavor as many as twenty potfuls of vegetables. Coffee grounds were boiled many times till color and flavor disappeared. When it was gone, *salabat* (ginger tea) replaced it. Cakes were made of coconut *sapal* flour; soup or *sinigang*, of the leaves and stems of the formerly spurned water lily. An ingenious invention was *castaniyog*: a piece of mature coconut roasted on coals and said to taste like *castañas* (chestnuts).

When the Americans returned ("Liberation" in 1945), the dreamed-of, prewar food came back too. By this time it had become both icon of the good times and metaphor for peace and prosperity.

Children reveled in Hershey bars, after three years of coconut candies cooked in *panocha*. The American chocolate bar addiction is still deeply imprinted in yesterday's children, who are today's adults. Their parents luxuriated in Coca-Cola and whiskey, Portola sardines and S&W pink salmon and, again, the luncheon meat that came with K-rations—a reinforcement of the "Spam culture."

The actual survival food of those years is no longer around, but its successors thrive in the hard times of economic crises: rice extended with corn; barbecue not only of pork and chicken flesh, but also of chicken feet, blood, combs, intestines (carefully cleaned and neatly threaded on thin sticks, and irreverently called "IUD"), and pigs' ears; vegetables planted in backyard plots, recycled tin cans and plastic automotive oil containers; day-old male chicks, formerly thrown away by poultry farms, reinvented as *pulutan*. It is especially the attitude that remains, however: the thrift, inventiveness, flexibility, and hardiness that enable survival in the wars of everyday.

FOOD TODAY

Elders today worry that the young have been so influenced by the "Spam culture" (read: foreign, imported, "modern," adopted/adapted) that when they grow up, they will hardly remember the goodness of traditional food, and when they have charge of households, will not consider it worth their time to prepare. They can and will reach for cans, packs, boxes, frozen food, precooked food, TV dinners, fast food, and perhaps astronaut-type food to suit their speeding lifestyles. Even traditional Filipino food, which has not disappeared from their palates, now comes in packs, mixes, instant forms, frozen or precooked.

Will they ever know, their elders ask, how it is to prepare communally for a fiesta? Grandparents, aunts, and parents planning, inviting, polishing silver, cleaning house, and cooking family specialties, helped by troupes of relatives and tenants dicing, chopping, slicing, cooking in vats, cleaning and spit-roasting pigs, and taking home packets of *pabaon* for those who could not come to the feast? Will they experience the joy of pouring not only money but personal time and skill into a family feast? They may remember with nostalgia hometown feasts and mothers' and grandmothers' cooking, but will they have the time and the will to do it for their children and grandchildren?

Will they realize that meals at home, lean or luxurious, planned and prepared by mothers and aunts; shared with parents, siblings, and members of the extended family; scrounged out of hardship in times of war or economic crises; reflecting tradition, foreign inputs, and custom, are what shaped them and their values? Will they someday see that food and meals are the location of the battle of values?

AND SO, AFTER THE WARS...

Food native and foreign (Indian, Chinese, Spanish-Mexican, American, and now global) have thus met, competed, merged, changed and been changed in the interaction within, through, and after wars. These encounters have affected the design of meals, the patterns of consumption, the dietary habits of current and future generations, and their principles of taste and pleasure. The encounters have had impact on the food lexicon even of the vernacular languages, which now include such terms as *lumpia, pansit, lomi*; *merienda, postre, pica-pica*; sandwich, snack, microwave; pizza, taco, and *tempura*.

Individual dishes are cultural encounters in microcosm, for example, the Mexican corn-based, husk-wrapped *tamal* that transformed into the Filipino rice-based, banana leaf-wrapped *tamales/tamalos*.

The meal—rural, urban; traditional, adaptive; regional, national, global—must be seen as a microcosm of national rituals. In them time and custom sculpt the rituals of national identity.

The wars—with the Spaniards, the Americans, the Japanese—were and still are being fought on the battlefield of culture. Alongside them occur more peaceful encounters (immigration, travel, overseas employment, trade) that exert food influence as well. Food is a cultural artifact and weapon, as well as the field of war on which clash consciousness and values.

Cakes and pies versus *puto* and *sapin-sapin*. Beer, whiskey, and Coke versus *salabat, buko*, and *lambanog*. *Sinigang* and *paksiw* versus *salpicao* and *paella*, hot dogs, and hamburgers. The homegrown rural versus the imported urban. Tradition and its slow, deliberate, healthy ways versus modernity, considered new, trendy, progressive, "class," with-it, "*in na in*."

This war from below has not ended and it has not been completely won by the foreign invaders. The indigenous survives and retains strength. The native warriors stand in some danger, however, and could possibly have been vanquished, except for the fact that they are sturdy and have staying power (homegrown, thus available, affordable, and accessible, and also enshrined in memory). Even today's most sophisticated, well-traveled urbanites still nurture longings for *patis, bagoong, tinapa, tuyo, sinigang, kinilaw*. None of the native dishes have been wiped out by the foreign. They just compete for the food budget and for TV time.

Food as vestige of war is weapon and battlefield, cause and effect, microcosm and metaphor. In it history and struggle are coiled and recorded. Through it conflict becomes consciousness. In it can be read values and identity. Through it, clearly, insight and reconciliation may be achieved.

GLOSSARY

Legend: Fil. = Filipino; Mex. = Mexican, Span. = Spanish

Abrillantados	(Span.) sweets in spun sugar
Adobado	(Fil.; Span.) 1. cooked adobo style, i.e. with vinegar; 2. A dish of meat stewed in wine
Adobo	(Fil.) 1. a stew of chicken, pork, or pork/chicken cooked in vinegar, garlic, bay leaf, and peppercorns 2. seafood or vegetables cooked in the same way
Adobong kangkong	(Fil.) swamp cabbage cooked in vinegar and garlic
Arroz caldo	(Span.) literally a rice soup with chicken or tripe, a dish of Chinese origin
Atis, ahate	(Fil.; Mex.) sugar apple, sweetsop
Bacalao	(Span.) codfish, especially dried salted cod
Bagoong	(Fil.) salted, fermented small shrimps or fish, used as a sauce, dipping sauce or relish
Bayabas/guayaba	(Fil.; Mex.) guava
Bibingka	(Fil.) rice cake, sometimes with cottage cheese and salted eggs, usually served with grated coconut
Binatog	(Fil.) a dish of corn kernels boiled till puffed and soft then served with grated coconut
Buko	(Fil.) young coconut
Buro't mustasa	(Fil.) fish fermented in rice, served wrapped in a fresh mustard leaf
Camachile/ Cuauhmochitl	(Fil.; Mex.) Madras thorn fruit
Camote/kamote	(Fil.) sweet potato
Capon rellenado	(Span.) stuffed capon
Castañas	(Span.) chestnuts
Castaniyog	(Fil.) composite of "castañas" and "niyog" (coconut), a wartime food of coconut meat roasted to taste like chestnuts
Champurrado	(Fil., Mex.) rice cooked with chocolate
Chico/Chico sapote	(Fil.; Mex.) Naseberry, marmalade plum
Chocolate	(Span.) chocolate; a hot chocolate drink
Chorizo	(Span.) pork sausage
Cocido	(Span.) a stew of mixed meats (beef, chicken, pork), ham, sausages and mixed vegetables
De lata	(Span.) canned, from the can
Dinuguan	(Fil.) a stew of blood and variety meats
Embutido	(Span.) minced pork roll
Ensaimada	(Span.) a brioche-like roll, buttered and sprinkled with cheese
Gabi	(Fil.) taro root
Guisa, Guisado	(Span.) to sauté; sautéed
Kakanin	(Fil.) snacks, often rice cakes
Kamote	(Fil.) sweet potato
Kamoteng kahoy	(Fil.) cassava root
Kinilaw	(Fil.) fish or seafood briefly marinated in vinegar or citrus, seasoned with ginger, pepper and onions, between raw and cooked
Kumain ka na?	(Fil.) Have you eaten?
In na in	(Fil. colloquial) current, in vogue
Lambanog	(Fil.) distilled coconut liquor
Lechon	(Span., Fil.) spit-roasted pig
Longsilog	(Fil.) a coinage derived from *longaniza, sinangag itlog*; thus a breakfast of sausages, fried rice, and eggs
Mechado	(Span.) a beef roll with a pork lardoon
Menudo	(Span.) originally a dish of variety meats and potatoes; adapted in the Philippines into one of cubed meats, potatoes and carrots
Merienda cena	(Span.) a meal between merienda (tea) and cena (supper), heavier than one and lighter than the other
Paella	(Span.) a dish of rice, meats or seafood, vegetables, sausages, typically flavored with saffron

Pabaon	(Fil.) a food packet to take home from a feast
Paksiw	(Fil.) a dish cooked in vinegar and garlic, e.g. fish; the process of cooking in vinegar and garlic
Pancit, pansit	(Fil.) a dish of noodles seasoned with meat, seafood, or vegetables; a dish of Chinese origin
Pangtawid-gutom	(Fil.) food taken in between regular meals, literally "to bridge hungers"
Panocha	(Fil., Mex.) raw brown unrefined sugar, sometimes molded in a coconut shell
Patis	(Fil.) a thin brown sauce made from salted, fermented fish, used for dipping, flavoring and cooking
Pavo embuchado	(Span.) stuffed turkey
Pimenton	(Span.) paprika
Pimientos morrones	(Span.) red capsicum peppers
Postre	(Span.) dessert
Pica-pica	(Span.) finger food; cocktail food
Pulutan	(Fil.) food to go with drinks, literally meaning that which is "picked up with the fingers"
Puto	(Fil.) steamed rice cake
Relleno	(Span.) stuffed; also used to refer to dishes like bangus (milkfish) relleno, stuffed chicken, stuffed eggplant, etc.
Salabat	(Fil.) ginger tea
Salpicao	(Fil.) short for salpicado, a dish of fried tenderloin tips with garlic
Sapal	(Fil.) coconut meal; what is left after the milk has been squeezed out
Sapin-sapin	(Fil.) a rice dessert or snack in soft, sometimes multicolored layers
Sayote/chayote	(Fil./Mex.) Mirliton pear
Singkamas/Jicama	(Fil./Mex.) yam bean
Sinigang	(Fil.) a stew of fish, seafood or meat with vegetables, in a broth soured with tamarind or other sour fruits or leaves
Sinugba	(Fil.) fish or meat grilled on coals
Suman	(Fil.) any of many cakes/snacks of sticky rice cooked with coconut milk
Tapa/tapang usa	(Fil.) dried beef, pork or game; tapang usa is dried venison
Tapsilog	(Fil.) a breakfast of tapa (dried meat), sinangag (garlic-fried rice) and itlog (eggs), the name contracted from its elements
Tamal/tamales	(Mex.; Fil.) in Mexico, a dish of corn meal steamed in corn husks; in the Philippines, ground ric flavored with meats and eggs, steamed in banana leaf packs
Tinapa	(Fil.) smoked fish
Tinola	(Fil.) chicken stew with green papaya and pepper leaves
Tocino del cielo	(Span.) literally "Heaven's bacon"; actually tiny, sweet milk-egg custards in syrup
Torta del Rey	(Span.) a multi-layered Spanish torte
Tosilog	(Fil.) a breakfast of tosino (cured meat), sinangag (garlic-fried rice) and itlog (egg)
Tuba	(Fil.) coconut toddy
Tuyo	(Fil.) dried, salted fish

REFERENCES

Alegre, Edilberto N. *Inumang Pinoy*. Pasig City, Philippines: Anvil Publishing, Inc., 1992.

———. *Pinoy Forever: Essays on Culture and Language*. Pasig City, Philippines: Anvil Publishing, Inc., 1993.

———. *Pinoy na Pinoy: Essays on National Culture*. Pasig City, Philippines: Anvil Publishing, Inc., 1994.

———. and Doreen G. Fernandez. *Kinilaw: A Philippine Cuisine of Freshness*. Makati City, Philippines: Bookmark, Inc., 1991.

Enriquez, Milagros S. *Kasaysayan ng Kaluto ng Bayan*. Manila: Legacy Publishing and Communications Corp., 1993.

Fernandez, Doreen G. "Colonizing the Cuisine," and "The Flavors of Mexico in Philippine Food and Culture." *Tikim: Essays on Philippine Food and Culture*. Pasig City, Philippines: Anvil Publishing, Inc., 1994. 220-230; 183-200.

Fruits of the Philippines. Makati City, Philippines: Bookmark, Inc., 1997.

———. "An Internment Camp Cookbook" and "Surviving Off the Land." *The Japanese Occupation*, vol. 7 of *Kasaysayan: The Story of the Filipino People*. Manila: Asia Publishing Company Limited, 1998. 90-91; 202-203.

———. "The Nineteenth Century Filipino Table." *The World of 1896*. Manila: Bookmark, Inc., 1998. *Palayok: Philippine Food through History, on Site and in the Pot*. Manila: Bookmark, Inc., 2000.

———. "Street Food, Fastfood." *Up from the Ashes*, vol. 8 of *Kasaysayan: The Story of the Filipino People*. Manila: Asia Publishing Company Limited, 1998. 36-37.

Fernandez, Doreen G. and Edilberto N. Alegre. *Sarap: Essays on Philippine Food*. Manila: Mr. & Ms. Publishing Company, Inc, 1988.

Fernando, Gilda Cordero. *Philippine Food and Life*. Pasig City, Philippines: Anvil Publishing, Inc., 1992.

Leynes, Soledad H. "Survival Meals," and Felice P. Sta. Maria, "The Turn-of-the-Century Kitchen," in *The Culinary Culture of the Philippines*. Gilda Cordero Fernando, ed. Manila: Bancom Audiovision Corporation and GCF Books, 1976. 188-195; 60-65.

English Is Your Mother Tongue/
Ang Ingles Ay ang Tongue ng Ina Mo

ERIC GAMALINDA

Commodore George Dewey, the hero of the Battle of Manila Bay, had this to say about the Philippines: "The Philippines were to us a terra incognita. No ship of our service had been there for years. When, after my appointment as commander of the Asiatic Squadron, I sought information on the subject in Washington, I found that the latest official report relative to the Philippines on file in the office of naval intelligence bore the date of 1876."[1]

More than a century later, the age of the Internet may have made information on the Philippines more readily available, but it remains a fact that most Americans know no more about their former colony than Dewey did in 1898. Few Americans are aware of the history of the United States in the Philippines, a history that was kept secret from their own people for many reasons. This history was also largely unknown to many Filipinos who grew up during and after the Second World War— grew up, that is, with the belief that the United States was a savior twice over, saving them first from the Spanish and later from the Japanese.

The image of savior and redeemer was something the United States exploited with the precision and efficiency of a professional publicity agent from 1899, when it invaded the archipelago. Since then, there have been two major deities in the pantheon of the Filipino psyche: God and America.

Those of us who grew up in Manila in the 1960s and 1970s know this only too well. We learned English the moment we were ready for school—around the age of five, if not earlier, when we learned it at home. We were taught that A was for Apple and we learned to sing America the Beautiful and we were aware that in December there was snow and Santa Claus came down our chimneys, even if we had none. We watched *I Love Lucy* and *Flash Gordon* and listened to Top 40 radio and watched Hollywood movies and read all the great Anglo-Saxon authors and knew all the fifty states (well, some of us did). And most important, most of us had some next of kin in the United States, whose *balikbayan* boxes regularly arrived like manna from heaven.

How strange to discover that in the United States people would ask questions like "Where did you learn to speak English?" and "Do Filipinos live in trees?" How disappointing to learn that while we knew everything about America—knew possibly more about America than the average American did—the average American knew next to nothing about us. The effect may be something like praying for a hundred years to God, and finding out that God never really knew we existed.

But that's the way it is, and that is indicative of the one-way traffic of commerce and information that has existed between the United States and the Philippines since 1899. And this relationship applies to the way we use the English language, and the way English is used upon us. To understand that, we have to go back to 1901, three years after the wakening American Empire defeated Spain. The United States was about to embark on one of its most ambitious missions: to transform the inhabitants of the 7,100 islands of the Philippines into an English-speaking people. That year, a shipload of teachers on the *SS Thomas* sailed from San Francisco to the Philippines. These "Thomasites," as they called themselves, were selected from the best universities in the United States. Their task was to give basic education to as many Filipinos as possible, and to teach them to speak in the language of the civilized world, meaning English.

The 1901 log of the *Thomas*, a souvenir publication printed on board by the Thomasites, said: "Our nation has found herself confronted by a great problem dealing with a people who neither know nor understand the underlying principles of our civilization, yet who, for our mutual happiness and liberty, must be brought into accord with us. Between them and us is a chasm which must be bridged by a common knowledge and sympathy; fellowship must be made possible."[2]

The chasm they spoke of meant many things. They were coming into a territory in an era in which the balance of power in Asia had just tilted in favor of the United States. But this power did not come peacefully. Two years earlier, the race to exploit the Orient, in particular the great market that was China, intensified political and economic rivalries among Great Britain on one hand, and France, Germany, Russia, and Japan on the other. Russian and German competition was jeopardizing Great Britain's trade centers in Asia. France was no help: Britain was disputing its control over African territories. Germany was becoming more blatant about its ambition to dominate the region. Only the United States remained as Britain's possible ally, and for a now evident reason: the United States, only a generation after the Civil War and the last Indian wars, was becoming aware of its future role as the world's next great power.

In *Philippine American Literary Relations, 1898-1941*, Lucila Hosillos wrote, "Since the Civil War and the Reconstruction, national developments in the United States had been directed by the industrial revolution in the capitalistic economy. Technology and economic progress had complicated the democratic ideals of independence, equality, individual rights, and social welfare. By the end of the nineteenth century, capitalistic development had engendered the feeling of power and its philosophy of force and political recognition of racial superiority on one hand and the spirit of humanitarianism and the concept of 'manifest destiny' on the other."[3]

Manila was a strategic base from which to conduct America's commerce with China. This motive becomes clear when we recall that as soon as the Spanish-American War broke out in 1898, the United States sent Commodore Dewey to the Philippines, purportedly to aid the Filipinos who were then fighting a war of independence against the Spanish government there. After it defeated Spain, the

United States decided to colonize the archipelago, "largely in an eclectic effort to construct a system of coaling, cable, and naval stations for an integrated trade route which could help realize America's overriding ambition in the Pacific—the penetration and ultimate domination of the fabled China market."[4]

Commodore Dewey recalled: "Hitherto the United States had been considered a second-class power, whose foreign policy was an unimportant factor beyond the three-mile limit of the American hemisphere."[5]

Although the United States anticipated some recalcitrance from Filipinos, it never imagined the acrimony of the independence movement that the Filipinos would carry over from their war with Spain. The Philippine-American War was one of the bloodiest and costliest wars in American history. But because of the temper of the times, the invasion of the Philippines would initially find overwhelming support among the American public.

"The fact is that the atmosphere of the late nineteenth century was so thoroughly permeated with racist thought (reinforced by Darwinism) that few men managed to escape it," wrote Christopher Lasch in *The Anti-Imperialist as Racist*. "The idea that certain cultures and races were naturally inferior to others was almost universally held by educated, middle-class, respectable Americans—in other words, by the dominant majority."[6]

Why did the Filipinos continue to oppose an obviously unbeatable enemy? In a letter written on 31 August 1900 to Gen. J. F. Bell of the American cavalry, Apolinario Mabini, reputed to be the theorist of the Philippine Revolution, wrote: "The Filipinos know only too well that by force, they can expect nothing from the United States. They fight to show the United States that they possess sufficient culture to know their rights even when there is a pretense to hide them by means of clever sophisms."

American victory over the Philippine Republic—just over three months old when the war began—was all that the United States needed to become a global empire at the turn of the twentieth century. Later, the United States strengthened colonial ties to make sure the Philippines remained dependent in many ways. In 1946 the United States would finally grant independence, but would also make sure the colonial ties would be tightened with the passage of several acts that guaranteed economic subservience. The United States passed the Philippine Rehabilitation Act only on the condition that the Philippines would accept the Bell Trade Act, which ensured the unrestricted flow of American goods to the Philippines and granted "parity" rights allowing U.S. citizens equal rights to exploit Philippine natural resources. Manila, being the second most devastated city in the world after the Second World War, had no choice but to accept the terms. The Military Assistance Pact gave the United States, through military aid, control over the military forces of the Philippines. Furthermore, the Military Bases Act allowed the United States free use of twenty-three base sites. This act expired in 1992 and today has been replaced by the Visiting Forces Agreement. Signed in February 1998, the VFA was opposed by many individuals and organizations, among them the Catholic Bishops' Conference of the Philippines, which said that "the VFA was signed without public consultation." Among the VFA's provisions are the following: "Philippine authorities' waiver of primary right to exercise jurisdiction when requested by U.S. authorities" and "unhampered and unrestricted movement of (American) vessels and aircrafts."

The United States also strengthened colonial ties through the idea of tutelage. Ignoring the fact that the constitution of the Philippine Republic of 1898 was patterned after those of France and America, the United States had to convince its public—and the Filipinos themselves—that Filipinos were inept in the art of self-government. In order to justify its invasion of an independent republic, the United States had to create not only its own image as redeemer, but of the Filipinos as a people in need of redemption.

That redemption came in the form of public education, and education was to be conducted in English. Philippine governor general of 1932 Theodore Roosevelt, the son and namesake of the former president, reported in *Colonial Policies of the United States*: "English was adopted as the basic language, and rightly so, for the Philippines were not like Puerto Rico, which had already a single language that had been used for years. What was necessary in the Philippines, if there were to be a united people, was a single language, at least for official use. Spanish was reasonably widely spoken when we took them, but it had not reached the back country or the smaller towns to any great extent. Probably because of the logic of this action there never has been the resistance to English encountered in Puerto Rico."

The imposition of English was not as simple as that. It involved a calculated program to discredit Spanish and the existing native languages, to convince the Filipinos of their inferiority and therefore their need for upliftment, and to glorify the material and intellectual progress the English language promised.

One proof of the Filipinos' inferiority was the alleged fact that they had not been able to produce a national literature. "The languages have produced little or nothing which can claim to be literature in the sense of elegant and artistic writing," wrote Frank R. Blake in *American Anthropologist* in 1911. "The literature of the Philippine languages is literature only in the broader sense of written speech."[7]

This was not entirely true, as Governor General Roosevelt would assert in later, less unenlightened times. He would say: "The average individual has an entirely wrong impression of the Filipinos. He thinks of them as savages. They are not savages any more than the citizens of the United States are savages. Even before the Spaniards came they had their own civilization. They in no fashion resembled the Indians of America. They had a literature and a written language. What is more, this was recognized by the people who came in contact with them. La Perouse, the French explorer, said in 1787 that the Filipinos were 'in no way inferior' to the people of Europe."[8]

La Perouse was not the only one to make that observation. As early as the seventeenth century, missionary grammarians already recognized the maturity of Filipino (Tagalog) poetics. In 1744 the friar Juan Francisco de San Antonio wrote in his *Cronicas*: "The natives are fond of verses and representations. They are indefatigable where verses are concerned, and will act them out as they read them. When they write, they heighten their style with so many rhetorical phrases, metaphors, and pictures, that many who think themselves poets would be glad to do as much; and yet this is only in prose. For when it comes to poesy, he who would understand it must be very learned in their language even among his compatriots."

Moreover, many epics were written in the native languages, some of which were already translated into Spanish by the late nineteenth century. Among these were the Ilokano epic *Lam-ang*, first recorded in 1889; the Bicolano *Ibalon*, first recorded in W. R. Retana's *Archivo del Bibliofilo* in Madrid in 1895; the Bagobo *Tuwaang*, discovered by E. Arsenio Manuel in 1956; the Ifugao *Hudhud* and *Alim*; *Hinilawod*, the epic of the Sulod people of Panay; the Maguindanao *Indarapatra and*

Sulayman; the Tausug *Parang Sabil*; the *Bantugan* of the Maranaw, and the *Baybayan* of Bukidnon. In a 1962 study, Manuel found thirteen epics from pagan Filipinos, two from Christians, and four from Moslems.

But there would be more proofs of the Filipinos' supposed intellectual inferiority. One was the fact that after three centuries under Spain, Filipinos allegedly never produced any significant literature in Spanish. Again this was not true. It ignored the reality of censorship, the fact that Spanish friars deliberately withheld the language from the Filipinos, believing that knowledge of the language would incite Filipinos to rebel against ecclesiastical control.

Harley Harris Bartlett, in a study called "Vernacular Literature in the Philippines," published in *Michigan Alumnus Quarterly Review* in 1936, wrote: "Nothing could be printed without permission, and permission was seldom granted, except for a religious book of which it could be certified by the censor *aparece que nada contiene contrario a la fe*. All too prevalent among the clerics was the attitude of the Franciscan friar, Miguel Lucio Bustamante, who, writing in Tagalog, told Filipinos that they ought not to understand Spanish, for the moment they could speak Spanish they would become enemies of the King and God. They ought to learn only to say their prayers and to spend the rest of their time on their carabaos."

The clergy's paranoia was not unfounded. By the late nineteenth century, the Philippines was opened to international trade, creating a new Filipino middle class who sent their children to be educated in Europe. This new generation of Filipinos brought home radical ideas and created what is now referred to as *El Siglo Oro*, the golden age of Hispanic Filipino literature. Among the writers of this age were José Rizal, José Burgos, Marcelo del Pilar, Graciano López Jaena, and other intellectuals of the Reform Movement.

Only later would the American regime take advantage of Rizal's anti-clerical works to cut Filipinos from their Spanish past. But to curtail the infestation of nationalist ideas, and because most anticolonial literature was still being written in Spanish, the United States passed the Sedition Law on 4 November 1901, limiting writing in that language and imposing the death penalty or prolonged imprisonment on anyone who spoke, wrote, or published "scurrilous libels" against the American colonial government. The unintended effect here was it stimulated writing in the Philippine languages, led by the growing lingua franca that was Tagalog, which were not understood by the censors, and which they had already decided was not worthy of producing "artistic writing." But by censoring the use of Spanish, the United States made sure anything written in it would remain inaccessible and, therefore, nonexistent.

"The ability to read means little in a society where people had nothing to read worthy of being called literature," wrote James Le Roy in *The Americans in the Philippines* in 1914. "It was felt that the Philippines had not produced a body of writings which would serve to either acquaint its people with world movements and thought or to bring to them a rich native culture."9

It was all very clear: The fact that Spanish never became the common language despite three centuries of Spanish rule, that no significant literature in Spanish was ever produced by the Filipinos, and their native languages were not sophisticated enough to produce art, were all proofs that the Filipinos were backward and incapable of self-rule, and that colonization was justified, and necessary. By having them go through the pains of learning a new language, the United States reinforced the mentor-pupil relationship, reinforced also its superiority over what Rudyard Kipling described in his famous poem as America's "new-caught sullen peoples, half-devil and half-child."

Filipino writer Nick Joaquin described it this way in 1957 in the *Sunday Times Magazine*: "A people that had got as far as Baudelaire in one language was being returned to the ABC's of another and taught to read 'Humpty-Dumpty' and 'The Little Red Hen' instead of Cervantes, Calderon de la Barca, Lope de Vega, and Ruben Dario."[10]

The terms used to refer to Filipinos in several reports and letters from that period reveal what the current attitude was: they were "savages," "injuns," "niggers," and "gooks." By proving beyond doubt that Filipinos were inferior, President McKinley's divine mission to carry out the United States' "manifest destiny" in the Pacific was now justified.

"The political and economic background of Philippine American relations colored the Filipino image in the United States," wrote Hosillos. "Biased reportage and partisan writing, playing up the defects of the Filipino character and ignoring Filipino achievements, distorted the Filipino image. Organized business interests, both in the United States and in the Philippines, lauded works distorting the Filipino image as part of the campaign for racial prejudice and anti-independence."

English, naturally, would pluck the Filipinos out of their backwardness and keep them attuned to the progress made possible by Anglo-Saxon knowledge and traditions. Popular education was something the Filipinos never had under Spain, and was therefore an effective way to further demonize the vanquished colonizers. In 1900 the director of education made English the official language "with the intention of making it the common language of the people, the medium of expression on the street and in the home, as well as in the classroom, in the school shop, and on the school playground."

Bienvenido Lumbera and Cynthia Nograles Lumbera, editors of *Philippine Literature: A History and Anthology*, wrote: "Through English, the flow of cultural influence was facilitated and an immediate gain for the colonizers as the progressive deterioration of resistance to American colonial control. English opened the floodgates of colonial values through the conduits of textbooks originally intended for American children; books and magazines beamed at an American audience that familiarized Filipinos with the blessings of economic affluence in a capitalist country; phonograph records that infected young Filipinos with the same concerns and priorities as American teenagers; and films that vividly recreated for the Filipino audiences life in the U.S., feeding the minds of the young with bogus images of a just and altruistic government and its wondrously happy and contented citizens."

Historian Renato Constantino, in an essay called "The Miseducation of the Filipino," reprinted in this book said: "The Filipinos became avid consumers of American products and the Philippines, a fertile ground for American investment." But there was something else that English achieved in the Philippines. He wrote: "English became the wedge that separated the Filipinos from their past at the same time that it helped to further separate educated Filipinos from the masses."[11]

In other words, English became a mark of social standing. The more proficient one was in it, the more education one was presumed to have had. This perception was important in controlling the islands. When the United States organized the

Philippine Assembly shortly after the Philippine-American War, it restricted voting to Filipinos whose incomes were above a certain level and who had had considerable American education. Historically, this is nothing new. The policy is similar to the one adopted when the original thirteen United States were integrated, whereby only people of property were allowed to participate in democracy.

By doing this, the United States ensured that members of the native lawmaking body would come from wealthy Filipinos who would protect their own businesses as well as those of the United States. These native lawmakers would be kept under the tutelage of the United States, a relationship that ensured that only the United States would decide if and when the Filipinos were smart enough for self-rule.

Richard E. Welch, Jr. wrote in *Response to Imperialism*: "If American administrators sought to promote 'progress' in the islands, they often fell victim to the occupational disease of the pedagogue who would dominate as well as instruct and who remains reluctant to declare his pupil equipped for the freedom of graduation. Tutelage can have a crippling effect, and apprenticeship too long continued can promote a sense of psychological as well as economic dependence."[12]

Today in the Philippines, English is the official language of the media, government, business, and higher education. English is a status symbol, an indication of being civilized. The perception that English is a sign of progress and education and the native languages a sign of backwardness has been so successfully instilled in Filipinos that even today many Filipinos are ashamed to be caught speaking their language. In everyday life, from shopping to government and business transactions, a Filipino must speak English if he or she is to be taken seriously. This bias is reinforced even in the United States, with accent discrimination. In the American mass media, for instance, a person with an accent is often portrayed as stupid, no matter how articulate he may be in another language. An interesting exception has been pointed out to me, however: this form of discrimination does not generally apply to people with British or French accents.

"Colonial subjugation for more than three hundred years during which the Filipinos were kept ignorant and made to believe that they belonged to an inferior race produced a cultural neurosis which admitted the superiority of the conqueror," observed Hosillos. "The trend toward growth and progress attainable only through Westernization and the American outlook encouraged imitation in almost all phases of life. The ability to speak, read, and write in English became an enviable achievement of the 'modern' Filipino; it became the key to one's success in life."

This idea of success became more apparent to students during the first two decades of the American regime. They were young, modern people who witnessed the gradual demise of Filipino literature in Spanish, a demise occasioned by dwindling audiences. At the same time, American education created an increasing English readership. From this milieu—the transition of the Philippines from one language to another—a new branch of Philippine literature would emerge: the literature of the American colonial people.

Philippine literature in English began as an extension of the tutelage relationship between the United States and the Philippines. In the case of literature, it was literally so: in the first decade the United States established the University of the Philippines, and patterned it after Harvard. Training here was rigorous and graduating from it would soon rival the distinction of graduating from the universities founded by the Spaniards in the seventeenth and eighteenth centuries. In 1910 the University of the Philippines published its *College Folio*, the first scholarly journal in English to be published in the country. It was a landmark of sorts, because through the efforts of Dean and Harriet Fansler of the English Department, Filipinos for the first time were encouraged to write beyond imitations of the standard reading texts of Longfellow, Irving, Holmes, Arnold, Eliot, and even Shakespeare.

By 1915, the American-owned *Philippines Free Press*, which had published only Americans, was receiving so many poetry submissions from Filipinos that it gave in, but not without first commenting: "The *Free Press* is not much in favor of encouraging the young Filipino to verse, for he seems to take to it like a duck to water, and with much less reason."

It can be said that Philippine literature in English began when Filipinos writing in English began writing about themselves. Teachers like T. Inglis Moore were responsible for weaning Filipino writers from the early Romantic models. In 1930 he wrote: "The Filipino... has to learn not only to write with English but to write against it. He has to write English without becoming an Englishman or American. This difficult task is necessary not because Filipino English is better than English, but because a Filipino literature must remain Filipino if it intends to be literature."

Many Filipino poets followed his advice. The nationalism created by the literature of the Reform Movement would still echo under the new colonial regime, and not surprisingly, once Filipino poets began writing "Filipino English," many of them wrote about their dual identity.

A poem by Trinidad Tarrosa Subido, written in 1940, summed up the angst of the age:

> They took away the language of my blood,
> Giving me one "more widely understood."
> Now Lips can never
> Never with the Soul-of-Me commune:
> Alas, how can I interpret my Mood?
> They took away the language of my blood.

Similarly, Rafael Zulueta y da Costa, in his famous poem "Like the Molave" (1940), questioned the alleged paucity of Filipino culture and took inspiration from an American literary rebel, Walt Whitman:

> My American friend says:
> Show me one great Filipino speech to make your people listen through centuries;
> Show me one great Filipino song rich with the soul of your seven thousand isles;
> Show me one great Filipino dream, forever sword and shield—
> Friend, our silences are long but we also have our speeches . . .
> Speeches short before the firing squad, and yet of love.[13]

The issue of language and identity would become more prominent in the 1960s, the period of renewed nationalism in the Philippines. The sentiment would become stronger among Tagalog writers, who continued to write in the dialect despite the disadvantage posed by English media and education. Alejandro Abadilla, in his book *Tanagabadilla* (1965) wrote:

Ang poesiyang Ingles
Pilipino'y huwad,
Lagi nang maisip
Paintelektuwad!

English poetry
By Filipinos is a fakery,
Always in deep thought,
In intellectoilet pose![14]

Whether it was fake intellectualism or not, soon a number of Filipinos would eventually study in the United States, or settle there. In 1905 Philippine American government scholars, known as *pensionados*, published in Berkeley *The Filipino Students' Magazine* which carried poems in English and Spanish. We can also say this was the beginning of Filipino-American literature; later, after several waves of immigration from the Philippines to the United States, these two branches of Filipino literature in English would develop their own literary histories, with sometimes interweaving and sometimes conflicting intersections.

Two Filipinos who received considerable recognition during the early years of Filipino-American literature were José Garcia Villa and Carlos Bulosan. No two writers could be more different from each another.

In the Philippines, Villa was lionized because he represented the break from morality and tradition that Filipino poets had long wanted to achieve. The combination of Hispanic Catholicism and American Protestanism left no room for the moral and artistic experiments of Villa, who was suspended from the University of the Philippines for using sexually graphic language in his poetry.

Settling in New York City's Greenwich Village at age 21, he was lauded by poets like Marianne Moore, Mark van Doren, e.e. cummings, and Edith Sitwell, who wrote, in her introduction to Villa's *Selected Poems and New*, "The best of these poems are amongst the most beautiful written in our time." Villa received several of the country's major national awards and fellowships, and loved to portray himself as a global artiste:

The country that is my country
Is not of this hemisphere, nor any
Other: is neither west nor east:
Nor is it on the north or south:
I reject the littleness of the compass.
Is not the Philippines:
Nor America: nor Spain...
I disclaim
Nations, tribes, peoples, flags:
I disclaim the Filipino.[15]

Bulosan, an icon of Filipino-American literature, was born in 1911 and immigrated when he was eighteen. A self-taught writer, he worked in farms on the West Coast and helped organize farm labor. While he is more remembered for his fiction, particularly his classic *America Is in the Heart*, he also wrote poetry and became a champion of

Filipino immigrant workers living in harsh conditions in the United States. Interestingly enough, his works never really caught on in the Philippines, where his portrayal of farm life and racial prejudice ran against the still commonly held image of America as a wealthy, happy utopia:

> You did not give America to me, and never will.
> America is in the hearts of people that live in it.
> But it is worth the coming, the sacrifice, the idealism.[16]

Both these writers broke ground, because after them it became clear that the United States offered unlimited opportunities for publication. In 1958 Filipino writer N.V.M. Gonzalez wrote in the *Free Press* that "some genius... might make a name for himself in the United States." This obsession pervades Philippine letters to this day. While opportunities for publication and prizes and professorships have grown in the Philippines, publication in the United States is still the desirable goal. A writer in the Philippines is not "made" until he has been published in the United States. At the same time, a more international readership seems to be the only alternative for a writer with a dwindling audience in his own home.

Today, the Filipino writer in English seems to be facing the same fate as the Filipino writer in Spanish did a hundred years ago. With ever increasing nationalism in the Philippines, the Tagalog-based national language, Filipino, is gaining more ground as the official medium of education and government communications. Increasingly, too, the mass media use Filipino. The death of Philippine literature in English had been predicted since the 1960s. In a symposium conducted by the United States Information Service in 1954, writer Gregorio Brillantes said that "the outlook for Philippine writing in the 1960s was less bright than it had been in the 1940s." But in the same symposium poet and novelist Nick Joaquin gave a less pessimistic prediction. "There are many young writers, he said, and they are doing something to the English language: it is no longer simple English; not the English of America or England, but their English. These young writers, said Mr. Joaquin, will continue to write."[17]

Why then do Filipinos continue to write in English? In the 1960s and 1970s English was a burning political issue, and many writers were compelled to do some soul searching. Can English truly express what I think and feel? Am I a traitor to my country for writing in English?

A poet and former *pensionado*, Francisco Arcellana, wrote: "There is something uncommon in the not enviable situation of the Filipino writer in English and this is the insuperable problems of language. The life from which he draws substance is lived in a language different from the language he uses. He is therefore twice removed: by the language and by the work of art. But the writer doesn't choose his language—no more than he chooses to write. It is surely an accident that the Filipino writer in English writes in English, a historical mistake."[18]

A curious mutation of this "historical mistake" was the increasing popularity, beginning in the late 1950s, of Taglish, the urban-centered, media-fueled, hip young lingo that merged Tagalog and English. Poet Rolando Tinio was perhaps the first to use the language in poetry, creating poems like "Valediction sa Hillcrest," written in Iowa in 1958:

Pagkacollect ng Railway Express sa aking things
(Deretso na iyon sa barko while I take the plane),
Inakyat kong muli ang N-311 at dahil dead of winter,
Nakatopcoat at galoshes akong
Nag-right turn sa N wing ng mahabang dilim...[19]

After the Railway Express collected my things
(They're heading straight to the boat while I take the plane)
I took the N-311 once more and since it was dead of winter,
I was wearing my topcoat and galoshes
As I made a right turn to the N wing in the lengthy darkness...[20]

Although Tinio disavowed Taglish poetry after a while, he maintained the freedom of the poet to write in any language he wanted: "There seems very little in our national literatures which can be solved in terms of programs. The Tagalog writer will write in Tagalog for those who wish to read in Tagalog. The Spanish writer will write in Spanish for those who wish to read in Spanish. And, for as long as there are readers in English, the best thing for the Filipino writer in English is to write in English. If tomorrow, I suddenly decided to read nothing but Tagalog poems, perhaps even to write Tagalog poems—well, isn't that nice? Perhaps I will, and perhaps I won't, but whatever I choose to do is certainly nobody else's business."[21]

Even today the issue of language and identity continues to be discussed in the Philippines. In an issue of the *Asian Pacific American Journal* in 1998, novelist and poet José Dalisay said: "Among the writers I know here in Manila, the issue of whether to write in English has ceased to be an issue—if it ever truly was; you write in the language you know, and through which you can do more knowing; otherwise, quite simply, you can't and you don't."[22]

Clearly, one legacy of the imposition of English in the Philippines is a continuing identity crisis among Filipino writers, a crisis that was not even present during the Spanish era. If the dire predictions do come true, however, and Philippine literature in English dies a natural death, there is evidently another center in which this literature will continue. A new generation of Filipinos and Filipino Americans is being published in the United States, a trend that seemed to have hit its stride shortly after Filipinos overthrew Ferdinand Marcos in 1986. It has been noted that political interest fueled interest in Philippine literature at the beginning of this century, and it still does today.

Whether the United States will accept the literature of its former pupil is a different matter altogether. In a seminar on British literature in Cambridge, England, in 1989, the critic George Steiner said that the most exciting British literature was coming from its former colonies. Will America look to its former colony and give its literature the same honor? Possibly, but in doing so the United States will also eventually have to confront the truth about 1899: even today, there is no official acknowledgment that the Philippine-American War was a war of aggression. The economic relationship that motivated the United States to colonize is still largely in place. Filipinos, by virtue of their unceasing poverty and political instability, are still seen as the backward children that they were a hundred years ago, the infantiles who could not produce literature, in Spanish, English or their native languages, because of what Arthur Riggs, in an essay called "Filipino Literature and Drama" published in *Overland Monthly* in 1905, blamed on "a lack of hard, common sense, analytic powers, power of synthesis or grasp of principles."[23] By using these same constructs applied a hundred years ago, it is easy to justify why such a people still need to be continually uplifted and civilized.

And Filipino literature in English—will it suffer the same fate as Filipino Hispanic literature? A decade ago, this seemed likely. But today, when the centers of literature are no longer geographically predictable, and the Internet continues to create new readerships throughout the world, it may just be possible that this literature will survive for a while. But one thing is certain. At the close of the first century of the American Empire, it is obvious that the United States has achieved its goal: to transform Filipinos, or at least a great majority of them, into an English-speaking nation.

NOTES:

1. George Dewey, *The Autobiography of George Dewey* (New York: Charles Scribner's Sons, 1913), 156.

2. Ronald P. Gleason, ed., *The Log of the Thomas*. Publisher not specified, 1901, 11.

3. Lucila Hosillos, *Philippine American Literary Relations, 1898-1941* (Quezon City: University of the Philippines Press, 1969), 27.

4. Thomas J. McCormick, "Insular Possessions for the China Market," *American Imperialism and Anti-Imperialism.* (New York: Thomas Y. Crowell Company, 1973), 64.

5. Dewey, 219.

6. Christopher Lasch, "The Anti-Imperialist as Racist," *American Imperialism and Anti-Imperialism* (New York: Thomas Y. Crowell Company, 1973), 117.

7. Hosillos, *Philippine American Literary Relations 1898-1941*, 107.

8. Theodore Roosevelt, *Colonial Policies of the United States.* (New York: Doubleday, Doran & Company, Inc., 1937), 134.

9. Hosillos, *Philippine American Literary Relations 1898-1941*, 40.

10. Ibid, 44.

11. Renato Constantino, *The Filipino in the Philippines and Other Essays.* Quezon City: Malaya Books, 1966.

12. Richard E. Welch, Jr., *Response to Imperialism.* University of North Carolina Press, 1979.

13. Excerpts of Tarrosa Subido and Zulueta y da Costa from Gemino H. Abad and Edna Z. Manlapaz, eds., *Man of Earth.* Quezon City: Ateneo de Manila University Press, 1989.

14. Translation by B. Lumbera in Antonio Manuud, ed., *Brown Heritage* (Quezon City: Ateneo de Manila University Press, 1967) 357.

15. José Garcia Villa, *Selected Poems and New* (New York: McDowell, Obolensky, 1958.)

16. *Man of Earth*.

17. Manuud, 794.

18. Ibid, 607.

19. Bienvenido Lumbera, Cynthia Nograles Lumbera, eds., *Philippine Literature: A History and Anthology* (Manila: National Bookstore, 1982), 368.

20. Translation by Gamalinda.

21. Manuud, 619.

22. *Asian Pacific American Journal* (New York: Asian American Writers Workshop, 1998.)

23. Hosillos, *Philippine American Literary Relations 1898-1941*, 107.

Baguio Graffiti

SANTIAGO BOSE

Mad Alley Gang
(neighbor hoods)
with plant mascot
1961

And I have no doubt when the morning papers of May 1st, 1898, flashed with the news "ADMIRAL
DEWEY SINKS SQUADRON IN MANILA BAY" many an American breakfast was interrupted with
a search for the Atlas or "Mary where-is-your-geography?" And many a cup of coffee grew cold while
the head of the house's finger traced the shore line of Cuba in vain effort to locate Manila Bay. And so
knowing neither inhabitants or islands, they as Pres. McKinley said, "fell into our laps and there was nothing
for us to do but take the islands, educate the Filipinos, and uplift, civilize and christianize them..."
—Edith Ebeale, Palm Tree & Pine, 1927[1]

And so, according to the simple-minded reasoning of Edith Ebeale, the entire
colonizing imperative of the United States in the Philippines was justifiable for the
simple reason that it was improper for an entire nation to escape the knowledge of
the everyday American.

Somehow, however, knowledge of what really made the Philippines and the
Filipinos "tick" always managed to evade the colonizers. This is a tale about the failure
of colonizing influences to seal over certain cultural practices and beliefs.

My own story starts in the city of Baguio, an American army base in northern
Luzon. My memories of my childhood days are threaded with contradictions and
events that don't fit into a "standard" account of growing up either in the "East" or the
"West," wherever those poles might lie. The images and stories I have been engaged in

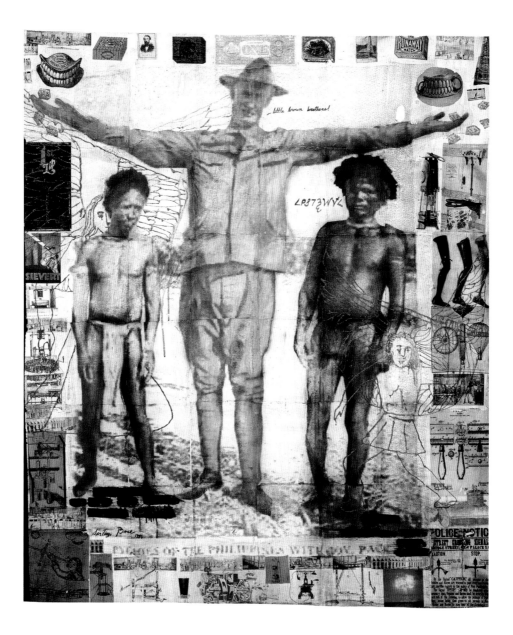

Free Trade
1998
177.8 x 152.4 cm
Mixed media
on canvas

creating since that time all bear witness to the gamut of influences that were part of everyday life while growing up in that hill station, amidst a climate, a topography and a sociological mix not often associated with the traditional Filipino experience.

But let me begin at one of the many possible beginnings, for while this is a tale about Baguio, it is also in part a tale about all of us who have spent time in that fascinating, compelling, and frustrating place. It is also, therefore, a story about the origins of my art, and if I seem to linger on my tale of this small city, it is because very few critical accounts of my art take time to bear witness to the importance of this context. So, as the old boy scout song says, "Back to Baguio..."

Americans stationed in the Philippines soon discovered that there was more than a simple price to pay for the enforced occupation of this small piece of colonial paradise. Foreign individuals who visited the islands describe in many accounts and documents the tropical heat in ways that make it seem like a claustrophobic, suffocating hell.

The interminable difference of living in "an-Other" state of awareness made men's minds exaggerate the physical discomforts so that the psychological discomforts of colonialism seemed less intrusive. Administrators from Washington and the U.S. army brought with them amenities of the civilized world. Aside from their guns and cannons, they brought the comforts of life to which they had been accustomed in the States. This new environment, however, had a perverse way of turning comfort into torment: the thick blue shirts and pants must have been agony for America servicemen fighting the hellish heat in the Philippine lowlands.

In the words of Maj. L. W. Kennon, officer-in-charge of the 10th Infantry:

Welcome to Baguio
1997
mixed media
121.92 x 121.92 cm

There are hotter places than the lowlands of the Philippines hotter places than Manila—but there is none where there is such a never-ending, boundless continuity of heat, day in day out, week after week, month after month, throughout the whole cycle of the year—none which insidiously saps the vitality and relaxes the springs of energy native to men from colder climates. Our troops suffered from the effects of it and search was made for some cool spot in the islands where convalescing invalids could regain strength and vigor.[2]

The inventive U.S. War Department soon found other, more lucrative ways of dealing with the "hellish" tropical heat. In 1899 Dean C. Worcester, the U.S. secretary of interior until 1912, was surprised to be informed by a young aide of Colonel Duval, who was in charge of the garrison in La Trinidad, a town near Baguio, that some "Negro" soldiers who were stationed there complained of the cold all the time and asked for spare blankets. He wrote: "We were literally dumbfounded when within a space of a hundred yards we suddenly left the tropics behind us and came out into a wonderful region of pine parks."[3]

This chance discovery of the existence of a temperate zone close to the searing plains of the lowlands marked the beginning of Baguio. The city was planned by the famous Chicago architect Daniel Burnham who, enchanted by the prospect of reproducing an example of "civilized" perfection in the middle of a "savage" overseas outpost, offered his services free. But for the Philippine Commission to realize its dream of a highland enclave, it was first necessary to construct the Benguet Road, a challenging enterprise that would link the summer resort with central Luzon and Manila.

The construction of the Benguet Road offered a steady income to all the unemployed of the Philippines. Representatives of forty-six nations went to work on that road, including, surprisingly, North American Indians, Hawaiians, Mexicans, Peruvians, Chileans, Hindus, Chinese, Japanese, Russians, Germans, Irish, English, French, and Swedes: a road gang of expatriates, refugees, exiles, and émigrés all working together to create an imperialist vision through a land that was not their own.[4]

The input of other "outsiders," however, had long been established in this region.

Centuries before the United States attempted to establish this small capital of First World "civilization" using the labor of others who had been dispossessed by similar colonial influences elsewhere, Baguio had been an important crossroads for tribal and traditional culture, a traditional gateway from the lowlands to Northern Luzon and the Cordilleras.

Indigenous tribes abound in the highlands. The south-ernmost tribal people of the Cordilleras, the Ibaloys, were spread out in small villages in southern Benguet. The Kankana-ey tribes had bigger settlements in the North. Baguio was also an enclave for tobacco smugglers evading the Spanish sentry posts along the coastline. The cultures of these tribes proved to be as impervious to the influences of U.S. imperialism as they had been to the Spanish who had been lured to the highlands in search of gold, silver, and copper which were abundant in these mountains. It is these indigenous influences which have remained an important "lower heart beat" to my work over three decades of practice.

Rainy Day Man
1977
etching on recycled
paper and pine pulp
25.4 x 23.5 cm

To a large extent, the tribal villagers in the Cordillera mountains remain committed to the traditional structures and beliefs of village life. The village elders have been vigilant in maintaining traditional values despite the influences of modernity. Many villagers are still engaged in the making of traditional crafts to fulfill the demands of the tourist market. To this day, the rich and diverse cultural wealth of these tribal peoples is evident in the souvenir items, primitive artifacts, weaving, wooden sculptures, tin smithing, and pottery that fill Baguio's markets. Such examples are more than curios, however. Beyond the tourist brochures, tribal peoples still observe and hold sacred their traditional rituals and beliefs. These differences had intrigued me even as a child watching them come down to Baguio every weekend to sell their produce, to barter, and to socialize in the city market. They would sit on the fringes of the market in their colorful attire surrounded by their entire families. Naively, I would imagine that there was no end to their noble life in the mountains.

The small city of Baguio steadily grew into "the summer capital of the Philippines." During the summer, the seat of government was transferred to the city and its population would swell to fifty thousand with the arrival of civil servants and their families, and the exodus of rich Manileños who owned vacation houses there. By then, it had all the amenities of a small city: an enviable road network, an airport, water systems, electricity, schools, and a hospital.

My earliest imaginings, then, were caught between naive dreams of a pristine traditional past and the reality of a small regional city burgeoning with the equally exotic trappings of modernity.

BAGUIO BOY

I was born in this hill station fifty years after it was built by the Americans for their soldiers fighting in the Philippine-American War. The Americans planned the city as a concrete embodiment of U.S. ideology, a kind of civic shrine where the citizens would profess greater allegiance to the American lifestyle of "elsewhere" than to the communities, villages, and townships that lay beyond the boundaries of the town plan.

My parents were civil servants from the smaller northern town of Abra; mother was a teacher and my father a policeman. Each was lured to Baguio after World War II. During the war, my father was a prisoner of the Japanese Imperial Army in Baguio but despite that experience, he came to like the city and moved back there after the war to look for work. He became a policeman and later studied law part-time. My mother opened a shop in the city market selling tribal crafts and souvenirs she bought from the indigenous tribal peoples in the region.

Song for Manong
1988
mixed media

My earliest memories of "home" include the indigenous woodworkers who would come in from the regions with their wood carvings and handicraft items for my mother's shop. Some of the woodcarvers would prepare their work outside my aunt's house in the family compound. I still remember the rich smell of mountain timber and the exoticism of the mountain people who would stay for short periods.

My aunt's husband, uncle Bert, was a well-to-do Filipino (*balikbayan*) farmer from Delano, California, who had struck it rich as a contractor in the asparagus fields in that state. He returned to the Philippines after the war and established the first gas station in Baguio. He owned a flashy two-tone brown 1949 Chevy and counted piles of money behind the cash register all day. That is my most vivid memory of him. Despite his commercial ambitions, he retained the superstitions of his youth. He patronized a young faith healer named Maestro and his band of followers, who would come on weekends to perform their faith healing in my uncle's sprawling house. This cult of *espiritistas* would pull out aching teeth, soothe sick patients, and entertain the neighborhood with trances and gossip about departed souls and saints, spirits and heroes. They would also hold processions and mass trances in the neighborhood, and be ridiculed by non-believers who subscribed to the less imaginative ideals of modern suburban life. Bedecked with fascinating amulets and chanting in a language I had never heard before, these indigenous mendicants, and their beliefs and practices, had powerful, seductive influences on me. Their amulets and images, and the magic that surrounds my memories of those days continue to play an important role in the images I create.

I guess growing up in Baguio offered a particular point of view that was very different from that imbibed in other regions of the Philippines. To begin with, a topography of five thousand feet above sea level generates different perspectives of seeing. Secondly, the Catholic Church in Baguio is not at the core of social life the way it is in many parts of the country. This had a somewhat liberalizing effect on people that was augmented by the PX (post exchange) flavor that flowed from Camp John Hay, the U.S. recreational facility which was the center of Baguio's social life before its turnover to the Philippines in July 1990.

Beyond our magical suburban communities, the U.S. military "rest and recreational camp" was an inviting sight. With a special pass, a holder and his guest could have access to the sprawling complex and its services. I recall trips to the base with my relatives for bingo games where we hoped to win the elusive "U.S.-made" oven, refrigerator, or the latest-model vacuum cleaner. Particular incidents are etched indelibly in my memory: in the middle of a long black-out game my uncle got so carried away that he yelled "Bingo!" Everybody was quiet, and then relieved when it was announced that he had made a mistake. We felt very embarrassed as we walked toward the parking lot afterward.

The U.S. base gave us our first taste of "America" via chocolates and bubblegum. It was to John Hay we went to play mini golf or to take our ugly blind dates and enjoy the live music, or to have a real steak at Main Club. It was in its library that I read all the Hardy Boys mystery books and books about art and painting. Its radio station AFRTN introduced me to rock 'n' roll through the Beatles. My friends and I started to grow our hair and pleaded with our parents to buy electric guitars and drums for our band. Being seen playing golf or drinking something expensive in John Hay was a measure of class and success in those days. *Mad* magazine was a big influence on our humor and the base moviehouse updated us on Hollywood. We took great pains to emulate the heroes of the silver screen, and in the process earned the ridicule of the adults. Invited to a party at Main Club, I remember spraying beer on my hair so I could have my hero Bob Dylan's locks, but the effect was disastrous; my hair looked more like a broom that had undergone shock-treatment. When I showed up at the party, I was almost thrown out by bodyguards of a politician's daughter.

Although the hedonistic offerings of the army base seemed inexhaustible at first, their seductive power did not take long to fade. My romance with Camp John Hay came to an abrupt end before my high school graduation, when my friends and I were harassed and verbally abused by American MPs and guard dogs for keeping our car fog lights on as we approached the sentry post. This incident brought home to us the fact that, to the Americans, we were outsiders, we didn't count. No matter how many American appliances we owned, and how well we could mimic the songs broadcast on American airwaves and how closely we mimicked the postures and phrases of the Americans, we would always be little brown interlopers, never anything more than second-class.

It took time and distance for me to sort out these contrasting experiences and emotions and make hybrid sense of them all. In the mid-1960s I left my childhood haunts for the larger city of Manila. My early works began to be motivated by the sense of "difference" and an accompanying sense that this difference was not something to be ashamed of but in fact to be celebrated. My interest in Phlilippine history—particularly Spanish Catholic iconography and Mexican colonial history—has provided a store of visual language for my art, which can be used to analyze who we might be and where we might be going.

At the University of the Philippines during the 1960s, revolution was changing the times. A deeper understanding of Philippine nationalism and the aspects of Fil-Am relations, our prolonged economic domination by the United States, the Vietnam War, the clash between modernism and the traditional, presented me with structures through which to think about the marginalization we had experienced as a nation, and which each of us had personally experienced. The U.P. was a valuable experience in reeducating myself. Having gained glimpses of what it meant to be Filipino, I began to question why I would sing "White Christmas" in the sweltering heat of Manila.

My education and the political ferment of those times also provided me with the means to reevaluate the influences of my childhood in Baguio. The more I thought about it, the more I realized that Camp John Hay and the entire municipal layout and

To the Person Sitting in Darkness
1998
mixed media
121.9 x 243.8 cm

planning of Baguio was a glossy and efficient success story only on the surface. Immediately beneath all this cut-and-dried order was a layer of willful chaos and a subversive mindset that refused to be brought under colonial control. The colonizers refused to see the invisible culture that informed and inspired the minds of the Filipino. The *amoks*, the bandits for nationalism, the cult religions, and Rizal: all these represent an embodiment of the Filipino psyche. These enclaves of alternative thinking have long offered a kind of passive resistance to the successive influences of foreign cultures.

Since the halcyon days of my youth, Baguio has undergone at least as much transformation as I have. As the population grew and the city expanded, our old haunts in the woods were gradually bulldozed to make way for the incoming hordes. In the 1960s the city-elected local officials attempted to cope with the the growing population's incessant demands for jobs. In the late 1970s, "progress" was equated with big business, export processing zones, tourism by the busload, megamalls, and a proliferation of diploma-mill universities. With progress, the population quadrupled and subdivisions were developed to fill the acute need for housing. Slum areas mushroomed as a result of the lack of cheap housing. Overnight, tourist spots and public lands were invaded by tin structures.

Today, the expansive, inspiring views I used to enjoy on my hikes around the outskirts of the city are obstructed by tin roofs and shanties, and overlaid with a thin, gray veil of pollution. The city's basic services are strained to their limits. Water supply is poor, sanitation is bad, and the main roads are clogged with traffic. Half a million people now crowd a city that was built for fifty thousand. John Hay Air Base is gone, closed for renovation by a consortium headed by technocrats and politicians. At one point, they even considered turning the area into a Disneyland. They have promised to make the former recreational base a "world-class" tourist center, with five-star hotels, malls, and the kinds of restaurants that deliver the same fare everywhere. Houses will be offered for sale. This "world-class" dream for the already overburdened city includes golf courses that place a further strain on the already scarce water supply. "World-class," of course, means "expensive," and thus not affordable by the local residents.

The last time I took a walk there, only a crumbling concrete statue of Liberty was still standing amidst the debris as a reminder of the former U.S. base. There is little doubt that, like Camp John Hay, the "world-class" tourist destination being planned for Baguio will be prepared on a foundation of ordered perfection. But, like the ordered military structure, there is little doubt that this commercial venture will not prove watertight. Underneath the foundations the wellsprings of Filipino beliefs still trickle invisibly.

Just as in the past the rich undercurrent of Filipino folklore and community practices welled up and seeped into all attempts to eradicate local culture, there is hope that such infuences will pervade into the twenty-first century.

In my art, I draw from such observations and research into aspects of the spirit of insurrection that has long characterized Filipino culture. My art is a means whereby I can gradually work toward reinstating the importance of indigenous traditions in establishing a contemporary world view, cosmology, and in developing contemporary cultural symbols.

I remember, when I was young, drawing at the back of calendars in my mother's store, unaware that the indigenous artifacts that surrounded me would eventually prepare me to understand "other" cultural practices. There have been other influences, other places since. Later travels in the United States, and subsequent research into the lives of Filipino immigrant workers would confirm my faith in the sustaining power of Filipino traditional beliefs. But my childhood experiences in landlocked Baguio, growing up in a hillside city caught between tradition and the inexorable movement of change gave me a cultural education and a bedrock of experience that has inspired me throughout my artistic career.

NOTES:

1. Sylvia Mayuga, *Ermita Magazine*, vol.1 no. 6, July 1975, 17.

2. Maj. L. W. Kennon, "Report on the Construction of the Benguet Road," *Who's Who Among the Pioneers and Builders and Contributors of Baguio and Mt. Province Progress* (Baguio City, Philippines: Ayson-Gutierrez Press, 1951), 17.

3. Dean C. Worcester, Member of the First Philippine Commission, *Who's Who Among the Pioneers*, 7.

4. L. W. Kennon, 17-20.

Genara Banzon

"...Pilipinas kong minumutya ... lupain ng ginto't bulaklak... aking adhika makita kang sakdal laya..."

—from "Bayan Ko," nationalist song

This is dedicated to all who have fought for justice, freedom and peace for the Philippines—for humankind through-out the years—in and outside of the country, around the globe—in all dimensions—soldiers, writers, artists, children—the common "tao," and finally: especially unsung women...

KKK: KATARUNGAN, KALAYAAN, KAPAYAPAAN

*"Though Filipino nationalists initially allied with the U.S. in the hope that a country born
of revolution would honor, Commodore Dewey's conquest of Spain quickly escalated to a
war that would last until 1902 leaving as many as half a million Filipinos dead as well as
a legacy and conflict between Filipino nationalists and American colonists."*

The heroes and heroines of whom our ancestors sang since the Neolithic or perhaps even from the Paleolithic in their epics and narratives during death dirges were generally "culture heroes." They were outstanding personages, semi-human beings, but in the context of the village of the tribe or group. They were paragons of love for the home lot, the piece of land which they and their forefathers had tilled from time without number, and which they call "our place." These were generally persons who exemplified their highest degree of love of parents, of forebears whose bones lie in the hallow resting place, of home in its wider meaning, as the place where you were born, bred, socialized, excelled in games and exercises- demanding strength of limbs and fleetness of mind.

—Francisco Demetrio, S. J., in his *Myths and Symbols Philippines*

PAGMULAT/AWAKENING

I learned and enjoyed entertaining our relatives and friends by showing the bullet hole marks that show through a couple of my father's books and the termite eaten housepots—evidences that the Japanese occupation was real.

There is this one story my father rarely told—and told with much difficulty—of seeing a young boy eating his dead mother's corpse with his bare hands, he was alone and hungry in the forest. My father would always say: War was terrible—as he tried to hold back his tears.

I don't stay long… I run out—this is the only time I see my father cry.

AMEN! - KULAM

To this consciousness, for which the Other World of spirits and ancestors is both place and the state of being, are the living bound in seamless reality. It is the source of the primordial strength with which Filipino Christianity, split-level as it is, continues to sway the nation and its leadership.

To enter again, unconditioned by conversion, into that ancient world Christianity has presumed to speak for, is to touch presences and states of mind with the purity and power we grope for.

Alwin Reamillo

HUMAYO KAYO

(Go Forth)

AT MAGPARAMI

(And Multiply)

Lumayo Kayo at Magparami/
Go Forth and Multiply
**A para site specific installation with
found and fabricated objects/painted
banner exhibited at the Fremantle Cold
Storage Building, Western Australia on
Monday, Feast of the Pentecost,
24 May 1999**

View From the Diaspora

ALFRREDO NAVARRO SALANGA
10 February [1899]

A fierce battle is waged between Filipino and American forces in Caloocan.

They have
run out
of masks
to wear.

Now their
real tongues
must out
to be cut
in half.

(Cut as
cleanly as
the spine
of palms)

We who have
worn but one
face only
do not bother.

(Masks do not
weigh us
down)

Our tongues
have spoken
one truth only.

(Our faces
were open
as ripe
coconuts)

Now the war
we fight is
over what
their tongues
meant.

The battle
all the more
fierce
for their
having worn
masks
to table.

16 February [1899]

Apolinario Mabini writes to Galicano Apacible in Hong Kong informing him of the outbreak of the war and blaming the Americans for starting the hostilities.

Their gods
in Washington
willed it
long before

Just like
the overlords
of Mexico

They must
have imagined
a bridge
was what
our islands
afforded
them.

A bridge
to the East,
a place
to feed
their tired
sea horses
of steel
and coal.

What good
will come
of this?

Some knowledge,
perhaps,
to pass on

To our
children:

Do not
step on
bridges
built by
white men's
words —
they are
as brittle
as firewood,
they are
to be
burned.

Above:
*The Pure Products
Go Crazy*
video still
1998
single channel video
installation
video projection size
7.62 x 0.16 cm

Right:
snapshot of ear
from the artist's
collection

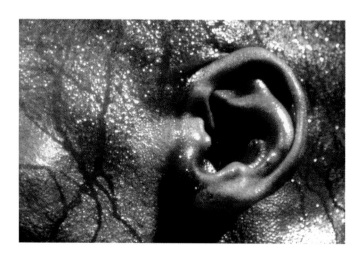

Quod Nomen Mihi Est?
Excerpts From a Conversation With Satan

PAUL PFEIFFER

#I

I was ten years old the first time I was possessed by the devil. It happened in the small city of Dumaguete on the island of Negros in the Philippines, where I was attending sixth grade at one of the oldest American missionary schools in Asia. One night I was jolted from my sleep in the wee hours of the morning by a terrifying feeling. I woke to find my room and my body completely out of proportion. My head and hands felt too big for my body. My heart was racing. And as I looked around the room my sense of space was becoming monstrous and strange: my vision felt decentered, like I was floating outside of myself; everything around me was small and far away, like I was looking through the wrong end of a telescope. Or maybe the room was looking at me. It was full of a presence that penetrated me with a gaze that seemed to come from every direction at once. I jumped out of bed, ran out of the house, and stll, barefoot and in my shorts, began walking instinctively in the direction of sunrise. I didn't stop or turn around until the sky began to glow a dull blue and the birds announced the coming dawn.

At the time of this encounter, if anyone had asked the question "What scares you?" I would have answered with a series of movie titles: *Jaws, Helter Skelter, The Amityville Horror, The Exorcist.* The last two of these, *The Amityville Horror* and *The Exorcist*, entail scenarios of demonic possession in enclosed domestic spaces, and both scared me so much that I never dared to watch them. But that didn't stop me from thinking about them with a kind of morbid fascination, to the point that I practically reinvented the scenes over in my head. So when I woke up that night in the Philippines, I recognized my altered state of consciousness as a sign that the devil had entered me and I was possessed. After that incident I became afraid of my room and of sleeping in the dark, quiet heat of the tropical night. For what seemed like a long time afterward I dreaded the moment when all the lights in the house would go off and I would be left alone, lying awake in my room with the devil waiting for me to drift off to sleep.

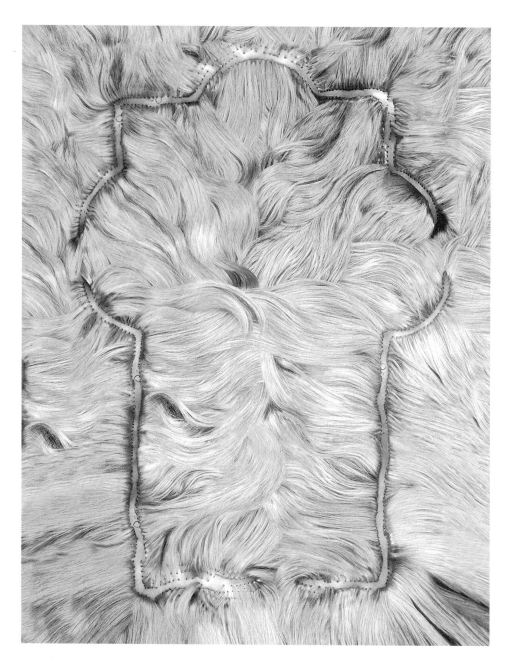

Leviathan
1998
digital c-print
122 x 152.5 cm

#2

There is a book that brings me back to the scene of childhood terror: the novella *Heart of Darkness* by Joseph Conrad. Set in the late 1800s, at the height of the industrial revolution, *Heart of Darkness* follows the trail of Marlow, a young seaman, up the Congo River where he has been sent by a mining interest called The Company to survey the expanding imperial domain of King Leopold of Belgium. More specifically, he has been sent to look for the enigmatic Kurtz, a Company agent who has cut off contact with the home office, and whose activities in the farthest reaches of the African jungle are now a matter of suspicion and doubt. The novel could be read as a fictionalized travelogue: a geographic and historical account of the events and landscape during the heyday of European colonial expansion. Yet, as Marlow goes deeper and deeper into the African continent his journey becomes as much psychological as geographic. He reaches his final destination at the end of the book to discover he has come full circle, facing not a dark secret about the jungle but a dark truth about himself and the values of his society.

The plot is surely familiar to all by now, if not through Conrad's book, then through the various Hollywood remakes that have come since: from Orson Welles's adaptation for radio, through Francis Ford Coppola's *Apocalypse Now*, to his wife Eleanore's subsequent exposé on the making of her husband's epic, to Nicolas Roeg's telenovela starring John Malkovich as Kurtz and Iman as his jungle bride. More broadly speaking, *Heart of Darkness* exemplifies a narrative structure shared by every journey into the unknown, a pattern that extends from Oedipus to *Star Wars*, from Medusa and the Sphinx to *Aliens*, from Homer's *Odyssey* to Pigafetta's journals, *Nanook of the North*, *South Pacific*, *Lost Horizons*, *Jungle Fever*. Many have sought to understand the endurance of this pattern. There is much to support the theory that the hero's journey is the very spark and engine of the narrative drive itself. Nor is the jungle setting of *Heart of Darkness* particularly new. The homes and bodies of black people, of women, and the poor have always been the preferred site for the hero's transgressions.

Yet two things distinguish Conrad's version of the plot, the first being that it takes place just as the foundations are being laid for the economic order we live in today. Contemporaneous with the Philippine-American War and with the annexation of Cuba, Guam, Hawaii, the Philippines, Puerto Rico, and Samoa as new U.S.-controlled territories, Marlow's journey up the Congo—and by extension, up all the Congos of the world—is the precise journey into nature that makes global capitalism possible. The second thing that distinguishes *Heart of Darkness* is its psychological depth. Written just as Sigmund Freud was laying the groundwork for the nascent science of psychoanalysis, *Heart of Darkness* is full of descriptive clues and literary symptoms that provide a window into the perceptions and phantasms of the colonial imagination. The novella stands as a rare case study of the Western psyche at the dawn of the modern era. Marlow himself narrates: "It would be interesting for science to watch the mental changes of individuals, on the spot. I felt I was becoming scientifically interesting."

And what characterizes this psychological profile? As we follow Marlow upriver, we find his perception of the jungle becoming increasingly paranoid. He says, "I had... judged the jungle of both banks quite impenetrable—and yet eyes were in it, eyes that had seen us." Throughout the story the feeling of eyes watching from the trees grows stronger, until it seems it is not just animals or people watching but something much bigger, maybe the jungle itself. "The inner truth is hidden—luckily, luckily. but I felt it all the same; I felt often its mysterious stillness watching me at my monkey trick...."

Toward the end of the journey, Marlow's boat is enveloped by a dense white fog. As it descends, the crew is filled with fear because suddenly they are robbed of their power of sight—that primary, if paranoid, sense perception that has kept them centered on their tenuous course upriver, and has protected them from running aground on the shallow banks. More disturbingly, without the benefit of a panoramic view it becomes virtually impossible to judge depth and distance with any accuracy, much less to maintain a safe distance from the threatening presence in the trees. In this moment of sensory overload the jungle rushes in, becomes suffocating and tactile, seeps into the very pores of their skin. Marlow recounts, "Our eyes were of no more

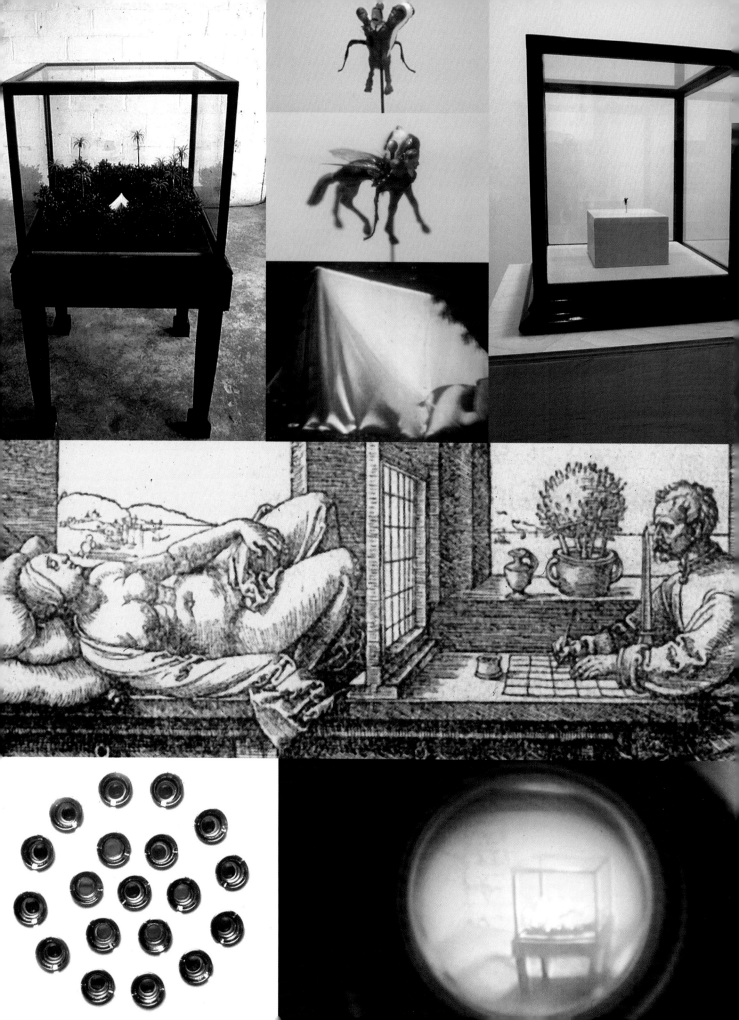

use to us than if we had been buried miles deep in a heap of cotton wool. And it felt like it too—choking, warm, stifling."

This is an identity crisis in the deepest sense: a face-to-face encounter with an other, where the boundary between subject and object, self and other, narrator and story, Marlow and the jungle seems to blur and disappear. It is a moment rich with visual resonance: imagine a mode of perception so paranoid that visual reality seems to fall apart and ceases to make sense. In such moments, distinctions between inside and outside, nationality, religion, and language lose their power to explain. For an artist, this is the moment of truth.

#3

In a scene from the 1972 blaxploitation thriller *Across 110th Street*, a mafia don stands at the window of his Central Park South apartment, looks out across the trees, and says to his son-in-law, "What do you see?" The heir apparent answers, "Central Park." To which the don replies, "Central Park, *si*. But there is also no-man's land that separates us from the blacks in Harlem." In October 1998, as I was preparing to mount an exhibit at the newly opened gallery The Project on West 126th Street, I thought about this scene and about what it would mean to have denizens of the downtown art world going uptown in search of new art. Of course, New York's bohemians and investors have always looked to the more exotic parts of town for novel thrills and new ideas. At this moment it is too late to buy up property above the park. Disney is opening a mall right down the street.

The central piece in the exhibit was conceived as an extension of the downtown patron's journey uptown into the Heart of Harlem. The viewer would come out of the subway on 125th, walk one block north and two blocks west until you arrived at the gallery. Once inside, you would go downstairs into the basement and through a dark hallway to find a wood, and glass, display case, a replica made from a 1911 photograph in the archives of the American Museum of Natural History. Inside the case was a little diorama of a jungle scene, and in the middle of the jungle was a little white tent. The contextual details of the scene were left purposely minimal. The historical setting was specific. It could have been any jungle in the world, but it definitely had to be somewhere in the tropics. And the tent would indicate that wherever this was, there was somebody there who was not at home in the terrain.

Moving into a second room, the viewer would then find a large, floor-to-ceiling movie screen, onto which was projected a life-size image of a tent against a leafy background. If you were to move back and forth between the room with the projection screen and the room with the jungle diorama, you would realize that you were looking at a live-feed video signal coming from inside the glass case. This was made possible by a tiny surveillance camera hidden in the trees and pointed at the tent. If you looked hard enough, you could even see the peering eyes of other viewers looking at the diorama, caught on camera and projected as giants among the trees. Going upstairs again, you would then find an arrangement of peepholes set into the wall in a dark corner of the main gallery space. Looking into the peepholes, you would see another live-feed image of the room downstairs with the diorama you had just left. If there were people downstairs, you could observe a fly's-eye view of the viewers peering at the little tent in the little jungle of the diorama.

The title of the piece is *Perspective Study (After Jeremy Bentham)*. Jeremy Bentham was

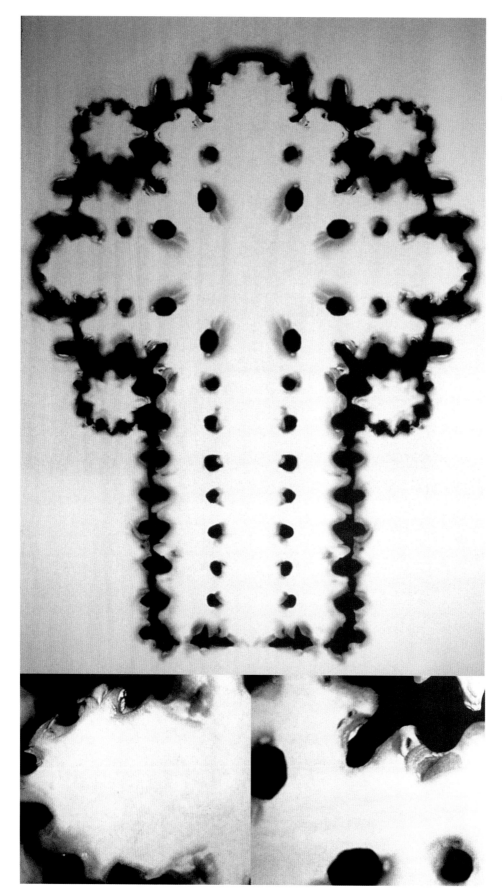

Above:
*Vitruvian Figure
[After Pavia Cathedral]*
1998
digital blueprint
91.5 x 183 cm

Below: Details

the architect of the Panopticon, the pioneering eighteenth-century prison design that would become the template for the modern penitentiary, among other things. The central principal of the Panopticon is total visual access to the inmate's every move. The guard is positioned at the center of a multileveled rotunda; the prisoners' cells are spaced evenly along the inside perimeter. The front of each cell is made of metal bars so that the captive is in plain view at all times. The inmates cannot see each other, only the guard tower. The observer in the tower at the center sees all. As for the "Perspective Study" that makes up the rest of the title, it is a reference to a famous etching by Albrecht Dürer, the sixteenth-century artist and proto-naturalist. The etching shows the artist in his studio surveying the world (a female model) through the newly invented technology of the Cartesian grid. In the *Perspective Study (After Jeremy Bentham)* in Harlem, the viewer is enveloped and positioned within a web of shifting perspectival lines—a network of ocular relationships, of seeing and being seen. There is no singular "meaning" to the work. It merely functions as a three-dimensional schematic diagram for one's consideration. One may note, however, that there is an implied obverse relationship between the Panopticon and Marlow's jungle. The suggestion is this: that the man who sees and controls all must also be the most paranoid man alive.

#4

The mechanics of perception and the formation of identity have always been intimate bedfellows. In Vitruvius' *Ten Books on Architecture*, the oldest surviving treatise on the Western building tradition, the ordering of space through strict laws of proportion was not just about making a shapely building, it was a projection of an imagined accord between individual bodies, social relations, and the natural universe. And in the Renaissance, as many studies have shown, the discovery of linear one-point perspective and Cartesian space was pivotal in laying the foundations of modern science. In 1936 Walter Benjamin made the link explicit in the context of Marx's theory of class struggle when he wrote, "During long periods of history, the mode of human sense perception changes with humanity's entire mode of existence."

The matter of human sense perception becomes a question of faith in the 1973 horror classic *The Exorcist*. In the movie a modern family unit in the nation's capital struggles to come to terms with a rather severe identity crisis on the part of their daughter Regan. Regan develops a series of bizarre and baffling symptoms: she flies off her bed as though propelled by some unseen force; she speaks in a voice that is not her own; she pees on the rug in the middle of a cocktail party and announces to the guests, "You're all going to die up there"; she stabs her face and genitals with a crucifix, shouting to anyone who will listen, "Let Jesus fuck you"; her head spins 360 degrees on her neck in defiance of the fundamental laws of human anatomy. After all else fails to cure the child, a priest named Father Karras is brought in and he attempts to discover the identity of the demon by engaging him in conversation. Father Karras asks, "*Quod nomen mihi est?*" (Who are you?), to which the devil replies, "*La plume de ma tante*," (the tail feathers of my aunt). Sheer nonsense.

So who is the devil? If we follow Regan and her family closely through the movie, some interesting clues emerge. Before the demon even makes his appearance, we find that Regan has already been possessed on two different counts: first by Hollywood,

and second by medicine. In an early scene, Regan's mother, played by Ellen Burstyn, prepares to tuck her daughter into bed and finds her asleep with the lights on. Sticking out from under her pillow is a Hollywood fan magazine. The mother picks it up, at which point we discover that she is, in fact, a famous movie actress, because there before us is her face on the cover of the magazine. Alongside her we also find Regan's smiling face, suggesting that by default she has become a part of the film industry, her life permeated by her mother's onscreen personality and career.

Later on in the movie, as Regan starts to become "sick," she is taken to the hospital and there is subjected to a series of grueling and invasive medical tests. She is strapped to a metal bed under fluorescent lights, surveilled via closed-circuit TV, injected with dyes, brain scanned and X-rayed, and tapped for spinal fluids. The hospital scenes are in fact some of the most graphic in the movie. In one particularly terrifying scene, Regan is strapped to an operating table and an intravenous needle is inserted into her neck, sending blood spurting out in spasms. The needle is then taped down and used to pass a long plastic tube through her neck and deep into her body.

What are we to make of such images? Are we to see a link between the media, the medical establishment, and the forces of evil? Does it even make sense to think about technology in religious terms? From the earliest days of this century, new technologies—from the movie camera to the microscope—have been the source of deep feelings of ambivalence, promising transcendence to a new level of human consciousness while at the same time representing a Pandora's box leading to self-destruction. But the human propensity for both good and evil is nothing new. Questions of ethics predate the advent of genetic engineering, just as the idea of community predates the interactive CD-ROM and the Internet. If anything, the invention of powerful new technologies merely increases the stakes, multiplies the costs, and heightens the impact of established values and morals on our daily lives. As Donna Haraway puts it, "It means there has been a deepening of how we turn ourselves, and other organisms, into instruments for our own end." Like a guilty wish or an unconscious desire, technology is already deep inside us. The more we deny and repress its existence, the more it grows, and grows against us, until it returns as an alien being from another dimension. This, to me, is what remains compelling about the movie *The Exorcist*: the vision of an evil doubly terrifying because there is no possibility of shutting it out or running away; no escape because it is inside us; without recourse, even, to any distinction between it and ourselves.

Above left:
Memento Mori
installation view
1998
wood, glass, metal,
linen, plastic, enamel
Box size 30.48 x
40.64 x 15.24 cm

Right: Detail

#5

The new diaspora is not about us, it's about Michael Jordan. To see him soar through the air, a sparkling, shiny creature traveling at the speed of light, landing in every First, Second, and Third World city all at once, is to understand you play a minor role in a very big game. He has visited more of our extended families than we could ever dream of doing. His reach defines the meaning of community in the television age. In the Philippines, voter turnout for nationwide local elections in 1996 reached a record low during the airing of game six of the NBA playoffs (the Bulls won). When Jordan announced his retirement in January 1999, his life and times were the top story in the daily news of your hometown.

It is no coincidence that black is the color of his skin, the color that fills the television screen in your living room. Darkness has always been used to express the depths and farthest frontier of the knowable universe. Like the scientist-turned-insect in the sci-fi classic *The Fly*, Jordan is an experiment in human evolution: an exceptional talent repackaged and distributed by Turner Sports and David Stern; grafted with sixteen million parts Nike, five million parts Bijan Cologne, five million parts Gatorade, four million parts MCI WorldCom, and two million parts Rayovac Battery.

Editha Bensi, a working-class homemaker and mother of five from the Central Visayan island of Cebu, is another face of the new diaspora. A vial of her blood appeared alongside three others on the cover of *The New York Times Magazine* on 26 April 1998. Her family's blood is a genetic gold mine: for generations the mutant gene considered to be the cause of cleft lip and palate disease has been running through their veins. Editha Bensi's DNA is now part of the Human Genome Diversity Project, a detailed road map of disease genes that promises to provide an operating schematic for mankind—a detailed picture of who we are and how we work.

For her services she is given a plastic washtub, a beach ball and a thermos, a fast-food lunch, and candy and cookies for the children. On the agreement she signs with the project, the stated reason why she is not paid in cash is that "...money is a means of coercion, and compliance cannot be truly informed and voluntary if it is purchased." When the doctors come to take blood samples from Editha Bensi's children, they struggle to free themselves from the doctors' grip and run away. Mrs. Bensi explains that they are fighters, that they have had to be because they are different. And when Operation Smile arrives with the opportunity for corrective facial surgery, Editha Bensi flatly refuses. The doctors and her husband attempt to

persuade her, and she snaps, "You said it didn't matter how I look." So why did she agree to give blood to the geneticists? For the good of medical science? For the benefit of future generations? When she is asked, her answer is clear and simple: "Because they wanted it," she says, "because they asked."

On 4 February 1999, about a year after his arrival in New York City from Guinea, Africa, Vietnam, Singapore, and Thailand, Amadou Diallo, an unarmed twenty-two-year-old, was killed at the entryway to his apartment in the Bronx by four plainclothes policemen. They said it was a mistake, that they were suffering from Marlow's jungle disease: they panicked in the face of an illusory threat they thought to be real. A child of the diaspora, Amadou Diallo was, after all, W.W.B. when they shot him—Walking While Black. There is no mistaking the message written in a shower of forty-one bullets from four semiautomatic handguns in nine seconds. The letter of the law has always been written in black ink on white paper. And the message is this: In the richest city of the richest nation in the world, we will do anything and stop at nothing to protect our interests and the lifestyle to which we have become accustomed.

On 126th Street in Harlem, just down the street from The Project, there is an Episcopal church which flies the African liberation flag above its steps. The meaning is clear if you turn your head to the police precinct across the street. The new diaspora is not about crossing national borders, biracial babies, or dual citizenship. There is no such thing as being in between two cultures, half and half, or the best of both worlds. It is a battle between good and evil, a question of morality, a matter of faith. A dense white fog is descending. Space and time are becoming monstrous and strange. The devil already lives behind our eyes, his name is branded on our flesh, he is built into the structure of our DNA. He is standing just outside the door. It doesn't matter if we let him in. He is already traveling in the blood through our veins.

References:

Benjamin, Walter. "Art in the Age of Mechanical Reproduction." *Illuminations*. New York: Schoken Books, 1969.

Conrad, Joseph. *Heart of Darkness*. New York: Bantam, 1981. (The novella was serially published in *Blackwood's* magazine in 1899 and not seriously reviewed until its reprinting in 1902 in a hard-cover volume of Conrad's stories called *Youth*.)

Goodeve, Thyrza Nichols and Donna Jeanne Haraway. *How Like a Leaf: An Interview with Thyrza Nichols Goodeve*. New York: Routledge, 1999.

AMERICAN FRIEN

Above:
American Friend
mixed media drawing
1984
101.6 x 152.4 cm

Left:
Defining Moments
two of a six-part
b+w photo ensemble
1992
each photo 50.8 x 40.64 cm

290

Kindred Distance

YONG SOON MIN

... to brush history against the grain[1]

The more a thing is torn, the more places it can connect.[2]

I was a Cold War baby, conceived during the Korean War and born several months before its end. The Korean War, the first of many Cold War conflicts that the United States would perpetrate, proved to be a significant early event in the progress of U.S. global hegemony that has defined the second half of the twentieth century. More than just a coincidence of dates, the war's residual effects have shaped and informed my life and my art work. It is seemingly assimilated into the very core of my subjecthood.

In 1953, near the close of the war and two months before I was born, my father emigrated to the United States. An American officer named Elliot, whom my father served as a translator, helped him gain a scholarship to attend college. The rest of the family—my mother, my brother, and myself—would not be reunited with him for seven years due to the restriction on emigration imposed by U.S. puppet president Syngman Rhee (Korea's version of Ferdinand Marcos). It was not until Rhee was overthrown by a popular uprising in April of 1960 (much like that of the Philippines' "people power" that overthrew Marcos)[3] which I witnessed as a seven-year-old in the streets of Seoul, that our family was finally able to leave South Korea and reunite.

This personal and political story of my family's background has been told in some of my artwork such as *American Friend*, *Back of the Bus*, *Talking Herstory*, and *deCOLONIZATION* with the aid of family photos.

I seem to have made the adjustment to the new life in the States more quickly and easily than the rest of my family. I also demonstrated a greater attachment to the past in terms of my self-designation as the keeper of the family photo album. I knew its contents intimately and often conjured elaborate stories for the many heroes and heroines depicted. At some point I realized that our family's story paradoxically speaks volumes about photographs that are missing. All of the existing images in our family's first album were from the time after the war and, for the most part, post

immigration. The first time I saw my parents' wedding picture was at my aunt and uncle's house soon after their immigration from South Korea in 1968. I was startled to see such a large formal portrait of my parents in traditional wedding costume— an image I had never seen in our own album.

When asked about the missing photo, my parents pointed out that it was one of the many casualties of the Korean War. With the swift and deep penetration of the North Korean forces into the South in the early months of the war, residents of Seoul had to evacuate with little advance notice. My parents, with my older infant brother and sister in tow (before my birth), left behind almost all of the family belongings which were later destroyed in the U.S. bombing raids over Seoul. When pressed, my parents have periodically spoken of some of the hardships that they, like countless other war refugees, endured. After only a week together, my father left my mother behind in the countryside while he fled farther south since the risk of being captured by North Korean forces close to enemy lines was greater for a male of fighting age, which he was. My mother remembers taking refuge in empty houses in the countryside during the brutal winter months, and constantly scavenging for food. She has often spoken of her affinity for the movie, *Dr. Zhivago*, especially of the winter scenes the family spent in refuge. She recounts collecting rice stalks in the frozen fields and husking them by hand in order to obtain some kernel of rice for food. Her frail three-year-old daughter, Byoung Hi, perished in the second year of the war and was buried in an unmarked grave by the roadside. There are no images of her, only my parents' recollections, to preserve the memory of an older sister I have never known.

Like the missing photos in our family album, the Korean War, and the Philippine-American War before it, largely missing from most accounts of U. S. history that I was taught in my formal education here. When I think back on that education, I draw a blank in terms of information about the Korean War or much else that validated my Korean heritage or experience. For instance, my favorite part of a

Above left:
deCOLONIZATION
mixed media
installation
1984

Above right:
Talking Herstory
lithography collé
1992
76.2 x 55.85 cm

world history course in middle school was coloring maps of changing nation-states but I don't recall ever coloring maps of Korea or the Philippines. What I now know about the Korean War I had to seek out for myself as an adult. Fortunately, in the mid-1980s, I joined a national organization based in the United States called Young Koreans United (YKU), which aligned itself with the Democracy and Reunification movements in South Korea. The YKU was started by a student leader of the Kwangju uprising who fled capture and persecution in South Korea for his role in this watershed event. He became the first South Korean to attain official political refugee status in the United States. The uprising in Kwangju, a prominent city of a southern province in South Korea, was a mass mobilization to protest and defy the claim to power of Chun Doo Hwan, a military general who became the president soon after this event. He ordered his shock troops to brutally crush the uprising, resulting in hundreds of deaths. This event became the catalyst for the rebirth of the democracy movement in the 1980s which eventually led to the first civilian government in the 1990s. YKU, which disbanded in the early 1990s gave me an unparalleled education on the radical history of Korea, from a Marxist perspective that foregrounded ongoing struggles for social and political equality and justice.

The fiftieth anniversary of the outbreak of the Korean War was marked on 25 June 2000. The war erupted five years after Korea's liberation from thirty-five years of Japanese colonial rule, and three years after the Soviet Union and the United States installed separate, hostile governments on either side of the 38th parallel. Although over three million Koreans and nearly thirty-five thousand American soldiers died in the war, the Korean War has been called the *Forgotten War*, the *War Before Vietnam*, and even *a Police Action* by Truman, the U.S. president who led the country into war. He initially underestimated the military preparedness of North Korea and the utter disarray of U.S. Pacific forces in the aftermath of the defeat of Japan. By 1952, however, the United States waged a devastating air campaign as part of its "scorched-earth" policy to not only cut communication routes and supply lines but also to exhaust the population by relentless bombing. Just about everything in North and central Korea was completely leveled. Napalm was, to use Winston Churchill's phrase, "splashed" over the Korean people and landscape.

Unlike the Vietnam War a little over a decade later, there has been little attempt to commemorate or come to terms with this war. (The national Korean War memorial located in The Mall in Washington, D.C. was established in 1995, thirteen years after the national Vietnam War memorial.) And, although the Korean War left an enduring visible vestige, a fault line of ongoing division and unresolved hostility— the DMZ, where part of the thirty-five thousand U.S. troops stationed in South Korea stand on ever-ready alert with South Korean troops—it hardly registers in the "hearts and minds" of Americans, to mimic the government-speak made popular during the Vietnam War.

In 1954, a year after the Korean War ended in an armistice, the first major conference of the five leading world states since 1945 was held in Geneva. Korea was its focus in the first two months, the main issues being elections and the withdrawal of foreign troops. The North proposed nationwide elections and the simultaneous and proportionate pullout of all foreign forces before the elections. The United States and South Korea proposed that elections be held only in North Korea, under Southern law and under U.N. auspices. The North came to negotiate, but the conference ended

Bridge of No Return
mixed media
installation
1997
2.44 x 7.32 x 1.54 m

in a deadlock, with no movement toward the reunification of Korea.

An event which occurred at the end of the Korean War served as the point of departure for a spatial exploration of the multiple locations of division and displacement. *Bridge of No Return*, the title of a mixed-media sculpture done in 1997, is the name of an actual bridge that stands near the 38th parallel. After the war, it was used to allow prisoners of war one irreversible crossing before the borders were sealed. The bridge still stands today, heavily guarded on both the North and South Korean sides of the DMZ. To me this bridge has come to epitomize the absurd yet undeniable reality of divisions—geopolitical, ideological, cultural, et al.—which render border crossing hazardous, even an oxymoron.

The sculpture consists of a room-sized eight-foot-high curved wall made of mesh wire fencing and based on the yin-yang-like 'S' form. This work uses magnetically attached text, clocks, and images of flowers to symbolically convey the intertwined relationship of the North and South Koreas, akin to the polarized forces of attraction and repulsion of a magnetic field. The curved-wall structure creates three physical spaces: the two façades which are traversed one side at a time and an embedded third space that exists in the narrow gap between the two wall surfaces. The two outside surfaces are randomly covered on the top on one side and on the bottom on the other with small magnet pieces that contain words or phrases such as "half full," "half empty," or "tick," "tock" that denote in some cases binary pairs and in others, words such as "always already," "interstitial" that convey concepts of discursive positionality. Along the midpoint of each side, photographic images of flowers, one side pink, the other light blue, line the wall with magnetic pieces of text adhering the images to the metal screen wall. The two sides constitute one twenty-four-hour day: the blue North Korean side begins at midnight and ends at noon; the pink South Korean side starts at noon and finishes at midnight. Each flower panel contains a second hand of a clock, spinning to suggest both the visible passage of time as well as the persistant mutability of location—that of a compass continually marking its variable positions. On the backsides of the banal pink and blue flower images are full color images of "official" images that North and South Koreas project about themselves in government and tourism promoting publications. These contesting and contrasting images face each other within the narrow gap of the third space that is visible only at close range.

Meanings are generated as much by the symbolic realm of the overarching structure and its attendant materials as by the profusion of language and representations cast within an aggressive narrative drive. In her catalog essay about the function of words in

Far left:
Bridge of No Return detail

Left:
Bridge of No Return detail

DMZ XING
entrance
wood structure,
mixed media
installation
1994
243.84 cm diameter

Right: Detail

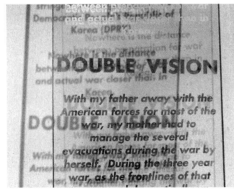

the work, Elaine H. Kim comments, "(A)t times Min's text undercuts the images; at other times, the words speak besides, although not necessarily about, the visual material. The words themselves are like discreet magnets, hidden forces holding up the double-sided images."4

Another artwork, *DMZ XING*, 1994, focuses on the parallels and intersections between the histories and the legacies of the Korean and Vietnam wars, the two Cold Wars that the United States lost. The double entendre of the title of this work alludes to this cultural, historical, and political "xing" or crossing as well as the negating or destructive effect of the DMZ that afflicted both Vietnam and Korea. I began work on *DMZ XING* by interviewing a number of Southeast Asian refugee families (Hmong, Laotian, Vietnamese, Amerasian, and Cambodian) who were serviced by the Connecticut Federation of Refugee Assistance Association. What began as an oral history project to gain a better understanding of this often marginalized sector of Asian America eventually took shape as a public installation which integrated their stories within a broader context of the history of the Vietnam War and its relationship to the Korean War and my stories as a Korean-American.

DMZ XING consists of a sixteen-inch-diameter rotunda that is to be entered. The interior contains a centrally placed octagonal column of mirror which functions like an all-seeing and reflecting panopticon. Along the edge of the circle stand sixteen tall glass panels etched with texts alternating between refugee family stories which also incorporate color photos taken from the interview sessions, historical information about the wars and the immigrant experience, and my own narratives. A centered mirror column and the outlying curve of glass panels are linked by six channels cut into the wood floor which project intense red light. The light flickers on and off, suggesting that all who enter this zone are put in a heightened sense of alarm and readiness. The length of the channels is gradated so that, as one reaches the end of the circular narrative, the sense of heightened tension subsides.

The Vietnam War was never officially declared while the Korean War was never officially resolved. In the case of Vietnam, the same Geneva conference in 1954 established accords in which the United States opposed the indigenous liberation/communist movement. Although the Vietminh forces under Ho Chi Minh won a decisive victory over the French at Dien Bien Phu, the world leaders at this conference persuaded Ho Chi Minh to accept a temporary partition of Vietnam at the 17th parallel with elections to reunify the country in two years. The South under Ngo Dinh Diem, with U.S. backing and enormous financial aid, denounced the Geneva accords and refused to participate in the reunification elections. The division of Vietnam hardened, leading up to the war. This echoed U.S. actions in Korea since 1945, the date of Korea's liberation from thirty-five years of Japanese colonial rule. At this point the United States supported the anticommunist forces in the South, thwarting all efforts to conduct nationwide elections which would have assured leadership by the communist forces under Kim Il Sung. This turn of events precipitated the Korean War.

During the 1950s, the United States supported the corrupt and autocratic rulers in both South Korea and South Vietnam (and later Marcos in the Philippines) as part of a foreign policy informed by the Cold War notion of a domino theory in which the spread of communism had to be held in check at any cost lest one country's fall to communism lead to another's. With this ideological smokescreen, the United States refused to accept indigenous developments of national liberation movements.

Another harrowing parallel to the horror and scale of the atrocities of the well-documented 1968 My Lai massacre during the Vietnam War were the recent revelations of war crimes committed during the Korean War. On 30 September 1999, the Pentagon declared that it would launch a full-scale investigation into allegations that U.S. infantrymen massacred several hundred South Korean civilians during the opening weeks of the Korean War. This abrupt about-face comes after years of stonewalling attempts to shed light on claims made by Korean survivors and victims' relatives as well as U.S. veterans. South Korean civilian refugees, most of them women and children and old men were pinned under a railroad tunnel in a hamlet named No Gun Ri where they were fired upon by U.S. troops. The captain of the regiment, who is said to have given the orders to open fire, is reported by infantryman Eugene Hasselman to have said, "Let's get rid of all of them." Hasselman goes on to say, "We didn't know if they were North or South Korean.... We were there only a couple of days and we didn't know them from a load of coal." (*Los Angeles Times*, 1 October 1999). Bruce Cummings, a noted American historian and author of *The Origins of the Korean War*, predicts that this case will lead to information about other similar incidents in the Korean War.

Another equally obscured atrocity committed by the U.S. troops occurred during the Philippine-American War. In March 1906, troops under Gen. Leonard Wood's command trapped a large group of Muslim Filipinos, mostly women and children,

Far right:
Geography of Desire
**entrance, site-specific
collaborative room
installation with
Allan deSouza and
Luis H. Francia,
mixed media
1993**

Right: Main Doorway

in the extinct volcanic crater of Mount Dajo [in Muslim Mindanao] and fired upon them from ships off the coast as well as from a safe distance in the heights above, for four days until all 900 were reported dead. A similar massacre at Bud Bagsak in June of 1913, led by Gen. John J. Pershing, resulted in the deaths of about five hundred Muslim Filipinos.

While the much-heralded New World Order of global capitalism has arguably blunted Cold War ideology, the vestiges of the Korean War retain a remarkable resiliency. Wars end but hostilities have an immeasurable half-life affecting subsequent generations not directly involved in the wars. My story of an inextricable personal/political connection to this chapter in Korean history is common to many of the current Korean generation. The trauma of the Korean War lives on in the establishment of separate countries, Democratic People's Republic of Korea (DPRK) in the north and Republic of Korea (ROK) in the south, tens of thousands of divided families, orphaned children, an entire generation raised under oppressive authoritarian military rule, and the diaspora of Koreans, mostly to the United States.

The lure of the "American Dream" is another enduring vestige of the war and U.S. global domination. That the American Dream affects Koreans and Filipinos alike was the basis for a collaborative installation (with Allan deSouza and Luis H. Francia) presented at the Fourth Baguio International Art Festival in 1993. The piece, titled *Geography of Desire*, consisted of a red schoolhouse called a "School of Desire." All who ducked to enter the lowered threshold saw a blackened interior stenciled in gold transnational corporate logos. Numerous lessons and critiques of desire were offered, such as the lines written in chalk on a blackened wall from Luis H. Francia's influential essay, "Memories of Overdevelopment"; "Black Market: Comprador Catalog," an opiate-like collection of seductive fashion advertisements lifted from pages of glossy U.S. magazines; another book entitled "Dream," a book which begins with images from the Los Angeles riots and is followed by pages which are progressively burnt; and a wall-panel reproduction of a historical image depicting

a schoolmarm teaching barefoot Filipino children an updated lingua franca of the "ABC's of New World Order" (such as AIC [advanced capitalist countries], IMF [International Monetary Fund] and NIC [newly industrialized countries]).

For many Korean Americans, the L.A. riots of 1992 sorely tested their "American Dream" of materialism, mobility and modernity.[5] Since the dramatic economic transformation of South Korea in the 1980s, the lure of America has been based on more than strictly economic aspirations—as was the case with my parents seeking an alternative to the bleak reality of a war-torn Korea of the 1950s.

In July of 1998, I visited the DPRK as part of a small invited delegation of Korean American feminists. Having made several trips in the past to the borders of North Korea, from the Chinese side in the north and from the South Korean border at the DMZ, I considered it a momentous occasion to actually set foot in this remote territory that is difficult to access for U.S. citizens such as myself and is off-limits to South Korean citizens. I found myself constantly trying to decipher and gauge from things and events large and small my sense of similarity to and difference from my fellow Koreans in the north. All the while, I struggled against an encroaching sense of intense alienation and disorientation. Indeed, fifty years of division have created another "bridge of no return."

The Korean War and its legacy is an inheritance that is at once a burden, emboldening me at the same time with a sense of responsibility to keep this history vital in seeking and creating new connections and possibilities. Especially when "everyone except Koreans and Korean Americans, it seems, would just as soon forget."[6]

In grappling with the history of the Korean War in my work, I attempt to excavate "counter-memories" and "counter-histories," sites of residual histories where division and difference, demilitarized desire, and decolonized body politic animate the imagination. I wish to activate history in order to better understand and change the present by placing it in a new relationship with the past. My engagement with history is political not only because it is shaped by present politics but also because the dissemination of new histories is a political action with historicized consequences. Knowledge is produced about the past, not simply recovered. History is powerful because knowledge about the past helps to construct knowledge in and for the present—and knowledge, as we know, is power. The Korean War, then, represents a history of the present.

MY BODY LIES

OVER THE OCEAN

MY BODY LIES OVER THE SEA

MY BODY LIES OVER THE DMZ

OH BRING BACK MY BODY TO ME

BRING BACK, BRING BACK, OH BRING BACK MY BODY

TO ME.[7]

NOTES

1. Walter Benjamin, "Thesis on the Philosophy of History," *Illuminations* (New York: Schocken Books, 1968), 257.

2. Meredith Stricker, "Island," *Looking for Home: Women Writing about Exile*, eds. Keenan and Lloyd (Milkweed Editions, 1990), 273.

3. Syngman Rhee's presidency (1948-60) is toppled by a massive protest which erupted on 19 April when tens of thousands of college and high school students march toward the South Korean presidential palace to protest rigged elections and government corruption. Demonstrations spread across the country when police fire upon and kill 130 students. One of the students killed is a medical student who boarded in our Seoul house. Within one week, Rhee is deposed and given exile in Hawaii.

4. Elaine H. Kim, "On Yong Soon Min's Bridge of No Return," *Yong Soon Min* (exhibition catalog, Krannert Museum and Temple Gallery, 1997): 7.

5. Concepts derived from: Nancy Ablemann and John Lie, *Blue Dreams: Korean Americans and the Los Angeles Riots* (Cambridge, Mass.: Harvard University Press, 1995).

6. Kim, "On Yong Soon Min's Bridge of No Return," 5.

7. Excerpt of text in "Defining Moments," a six-part black-and-white photo series from 1992. The text is etched on the glass cover which overlays the first image, my silhouetted body. This work was made in response to the Los Angeles riots of 1992, called Sa-i-gu by Koreans, which literally translates as 4-2-9, 29 April, the first day of the riots that resulted in the mass burning and looting of businesses, mostly those owned by Korean Americans. This work chronicles the often uncanny conjunctions between formative events in my personal history and those of major historical events for Koreans and Korean Americans such as Sa-i-gu, which also happens to be the date of my birth, as well as the end of the Korean War which, as mentioned earlier, corresponds to my birth year, and so on. Blending historic documentary images with that of my face branded with the words *DMZ* and *Heartland*, and creating visual linkages of personal and political histories onto the body, is to suggest the notion of an embodied, intimately claimed and possessed knowledge and understanding, in this case, of history.

With parents just before Vietnam was divided in half, 1952

Photograph courtesy of Nguyen Qui Duc

The Hairy Hand

NGUYEN QUI DUC

There's a joke I like to tell: Why is there never a coup d'etat in the United States? Because in the United States, there isn't an American embassy.

I still am surprised that so many people to whom I tell this joke do not appreciate it. It is as though they have forgotten all about the stories of American involvement in the affairs of Iran, Iraq, Panama, Chile, and a host of other nations around the world. I should clarify that those who do not find poignancy in the joke tend to be American-born, usually people from a younger generation seemingly afflicted with the common American disregard for history, however recent.

Among the friends who do break into knowing laughter upon hearing the joke, many are from other countries: foreigners who have come to live in America following a period of turmoil in their homeland. I hear in their laughter an instant recognition of the truth inherent in the flip side of the joke's punch line. Where there is an American embassy, if not a coup d'etat, there would be attempts at influencing state, economic, social, military, and cultural affairs. Such attempts may be a normal part of foreign diplomacy for any nation, and they may often wear benevolent monikers. But, like the French's "mission civilisatrice" of the nineteenth and early twentieth centuries, American "democratization" and "development" efforts overseas bear the distinct imprint of imperialistic intents.

In the case of the Americans, there is perhaps a genuine, at times self-righteous, desire to "help" others. But that could only be said about the attitude of the average well-meaning citizen. The intents and motives pursued by policy makers cannot always be so benign.

I laughed hard when I first heard the joke about the United States embassy. Perhaps we Vietnamese have developed a perverse sense of humor, having had to deal with overwhelming foreign powers for so long in our history. From the days of our legendary founding as a state two thousand years ago, we'd always had China as a powerful and aggressive neighbor. Chinese emperors considered Vietnam as a vassal state, and conquered or dominated us for a thousand years. Generations of Vietnamese followed their own warlords and emperors to drive out the "northern invader." Between 1850, when the first French boats arrived on our coast, to 1954 when tattered soldiers and officers went back to France in defeat, the Vietnamese had known another invader. In the 1960s and 1970s, the southern half of our nation allied with America, while the other half fought its soldiers and suffered through its bombing. In the postwar period, Vietnam, isolated from the world because of its presence in Cambodia, relied on an overbearing and weakening Moscow. Our nation has had over a millennium of adverse dealing with foreign powers.

Laughing at your own terrible fate is often the best way to deal with it. And so, we laugh at such jokes that remind us of how powerless we can sometimes be.

I suspect it's the distance, both in time and space, between where I now live and my old homeland that allows me to appreciate the joke without becoming angry. The anger has long faded away, replaced perhaps by a sense of resignation, of recognition of the futility in it all. And sadly, too, a sense of loss. Loss of opportunities, of faith, and of a desire to do anything about this American attitude.

What will I do in the face of American aggression? The old homeland has gone through so many wars. Three million men, women, and children have died. Others have been left physically maimed, psychologically bruised. No one knows how many Vietnamese disappeared during the years of bombing and warfare. So many of us have had to fight from so many different sides, and so many of us have had to suffer for so very long. So many are suffering still. I cannot think of much good that can come from being angry. Unlike the adolescent attitude one sees in America, the Vietnamese way to deal with anger is often to internalize it.

It seems that for every Vietnamese the best solution is to not dwell on past American aggression. Not that the Vietnamese had the luxury to do so. Immediately after the war with Americans, Vietnam plunged into a period of extreme poverty. And barely four years after the last American helicopters left Vietnamese skies, Vietnamese tanks were heard going off to the battlefield again. Men of my age and younger donned their weapons and knapsacks and went to Cambodia, to fight another devastating war with the Khmer Rouge that lasted until 1989. Others were sent to the northern border, to yet another war with our giant neighbor, the Chinese.

Stunned by its defeat in Vietnam, America obsesses. From the end of the war in 1975 until today, America has spent enormous time licking its wounds, searching for the missing-in-actions, searching for an explanation of its ordeal in a small Southeast Asian nation. Thinkers and writers in America talk endlessly of a loss of innocence during and after the war. And still America persists in getting involved in Somalia, Panama, Grenada, Bosnia, and everywhere else, it seems.

I've always assumed it's the Buddhist upbringing that allows us Vietnamese to accept suffering as an undeniable, unavoidable part of life. During my first visit back to Vietnam in 1989, veterans of the American war kept asking me, why worry about the past? To paraphrase them: "War is a constant condition for the Vietnamese. Our forefathers fought the Chinese to maintain independence. Our fathers fought the French to maintain independence. We fought the Americans to maintain independence. Now the Americans soldiers have left. We don't need to worry about them. We need to rebuild our families, raise our children, move on with our lives."

And with the difficult postwar conditions, one can't afford to harbor too much thought of resistance against the newest form of American aggression, namely the economic kind.

A visit to Vietnam these days always surprises the American visitor. Many have wondered how the Vietnamese can welcome them with such genuine smiles and warmth. Where is the rancor that surely resides in the hearts of a people who suffered so much during the years of American involvement in Vietnam? What of the terrified peasants, blindfolded and kneeling under gunpoint? What of the babies deformed by Agent Orange? What of the bombs, the burned-out villages, and the countless families torn apart in the years of war?

I try to explain over and again about all the wars the Vietnamese have endured. Before and after the war with the Americans. I try to explain about the Vietnamese' submission to fate, and the practical nature that demands that one move on from life's difficulties. The Vietnamese simply don't have the time to deal with past difficulties. Current problems are weighty enough. And then I'll revert to that sense of futility. What good is it now to hold rancor against the Americans for what was done thirty years ago?

Many in Vietnam, Vietcong and Communist veterans, still speak proudly of the years of struggle to resist American aggression, defeating an enemy far superior in raw forces. Meanwhile, many Vietnamese overseas, southerners allied with the Saigon regimes of the 1960s and 1970s, lament their fate: abandoned by their American allies, imprisoned by the victorious communists of the North, driven from their birthplace, becoming part of the dispossessed and powerless class in America, forever living with the guilt and shame of having lost a war.

The luxury of being angry, of constantly revisiting the past, does not belong to the Vietnamese. At least to those of a certain generation, to those whose lives have been ironically turned entirely upside down partly because of the American involvement in Vietnam. Sadness is what remains, but anger has long ago faded away.

I was born in Dalat, a small and hilly town in the highlands of Vietnam, some five years after America became actively concerned with our country. Even before then, as far back as 1945, after President Roosevelt's death, Harry Truman opened the way for the French reconquest of Vietnam. By 1954, following the French defeat, America was installing its own man, Ngo Dinh Diem, in the southern half of the country, while the communist leader Ho Chi Minh asserted control over the north. Fighting broke out immediately after the Geneva conference which divided our nation, and by then American men in uniforms were already getting to know the lay of the land.

I was a year short of draft age when the war ended in Vietnam in 1975. Naturally, my view of America and the Americans was influenced by the circumstances of my birth. Our family was part of the South: we didn't believe in Communism, and we espoused the notions of democracy—as portrayed and heralded by Americans.

In their small and hilly town in the highlands of Vietnam, my parents struggled with the changing circumstances of our country. Born into families from the intellectual class, they didn't believe in wars, and they didn't believe in military solutions, especially those involving Americans. They preferred public to military service. My father came to the United States in the 1950s and 1960s to study public administration. He and my mother believed in educational and cultural exchange programs between the United States and Vietnam. They became involved in the Vietnamese-American Friendship Association, helping to administer scholarship and education projects, and they welcomed to our home those Americans who came to Vietnam as teachers and social workers.

Dancing much of my youth, I was not taught to view American soldiers as the saviors of the southern republic. Upon their return from visits in the United States, my parents talked of the technical, educational, and cultural aspects of American society. But on American military might, they were silent. I ended up not thinking of Americans as heroes, or as a terrible enemy. I was perhaps too young, perhaps too sheltered, and had not come into contact with people whose lives had been altered by the American presence.

In my teen years, after we'd moved to a coastal town in central Vietnam, I began to hear other stories as my sources of influence went beyond my parents and their circle of friends. In the late 1960s, Danang was a magnet for people from northern provinces seeking to avoid the battles escalating in their villages. Danang also allowed them the opportunities that came as the town blossomed in part due to the presence of nearby American bases. Military trucks and bars appeared, and teachers began to run laundry services washing tons of army fatigues, while merchants peddled television sets and T-shirts and cooking oil stolen from American supply centers.

Those were times when I met people whose views would change what I'd learned earlier. Countless times uncles and aunts and teachers and older friends explained the war in terms of a conflict between world powers, and we Vietnamese were mere victims. I could detect anger in their voices, but it was the sadness and resignation that soon took over, and the explications were delivered in a matter-of-fact tone.

"It's because we have this long coastline," someone would say, and explain that between the Russians and the Americans there was a lot of desire to control the sea lanes off our coast. These types of explanations would come to me in simple terms, and were not accompanied by ideological name-calling. No such words as hegemony, colonialism, and imperialism.

I don't remember being too confused about the war that was intensifying in the countryside. And perhaps I shouldn't expect that my teenage friends and I would be quite capable of worrying too much about hegemony, colonialism, and imperialism. We did our homework, wrote the secretive notes to the girls we were infatuated with, and hung out like boys all over the world, exchanging old hobbies for new ones every few months. At night we'd sit in fear when the enemy sent his rockets into our town, but somehow we managed to get up in the morning, have breakfast, go to school, and sit in class dealing quite coherently with the teachers' questions.

Things were happening, however, that put doubts into our minds. We were growing into our mid-teens, and we were discovering new things.

We discovered fun things. Like American rock 'n' roll, Jimi Hendrix, and the Creedence Clearwater Revival. Fashionable sweatshirts imprinted with the names and mottos of American universities. We began to wear long hair, and the peace sign in chains around our necks, because that's what young Americans were doing on campuses in America. To be sure, we weren't harboring antiwar thoughts, for our elders and our government taught us otherwise. But it was cool, and rebellious in a window-dressing kind of way.

And then here and there we were discovering things that weren't fun. Like the incident I witnessed when an American army truck ran over a young Vietnamese boy on his bicycle, and casually left the scene of the accident. Or the time an American soldier in a passing truck reached down to grab the conical hat of a girl riding home from school on a scooter. Within seconds, the girl's bike had gone into a spin and she was lying dead on the asphalt as the truck sped away.

And then there were more terrible things we heard about, such as the My Lai massacre, and the stories about GIs burning our villages and raping young girls. These were the things that confused us. How can the same country produce both the cool hippies and the brute soldiers? The confusion soon gave way to a measure of anger. But unlike the youths of Saigon, we didn't take to the streets. In the coastal town in conservative central Vietnam, we didn't dare defy the authorities. We were terrified of the special paramilitary forces that would descend upon us, throw us in jail, or send us to the battlefields. We were left in the odd position of emulating American youngsters and their hippies' ways, and at the same time harboring hateful and disdainful attitudes about the soldiers that had come to our country. We barely understood that either way we were caught up in forces of American export, as opposing as they were.

Later, while working in Europe in the mid-1980s, I met an old classmate. In a café in Paris, we spoke of our past. Vo Chau Quang, who had been stuck in Vietnam after the war ended and spent many difficult years under Communism, said to me: "If I'd been a bit older then, and a little more thoughtful, I would have joined the Vietcong."

I agreed, knowing that his statement was one that could have branded us as traitors to our families and our nation.

Some years ago, upon one of my return visits to Vietnam, I went to a beach village just outside Danang. I had stopped there for a rest on a motorcycle journey, and as I sat in the thatch hut that served as a roadside café, I thought to myself, I would have joined the Vietcong had I grown up in this village during the war.

The village was just on the other side of the river separating me from my old hometown. In that rural and peaceful setting, I suddenly remembered that during the 1970s, endless American military convoys had been through here, kicking up dust and sand and noise on the highway, sending old farmers and young children and cows and chickens rushing into the fields.

It still escapes me how it is that so many obvious things weren't obvious to me when I was growing up in Vietnam. In that café in Paris, Quang talked about the amount of American weapons that had gone into the Vietcong's hands.

"Do you think they cared?" he asked, referring to the Americans conducting the war. Guns were American products, Quang maintained. That they got lost or sold into enemies' hands didn't matter. More guns would need to be produced, employment secured for thousands of Americans, and American gun-makers were making money. That was all that mattered.

Quang concluded for me that it wasn't so much a question of war and ideology. To produce goods that would be consumed was the idea. It didn't matter that the products were warplanes and arms and rockets. It's the working of imperialism, Quang said in the end.

It was, I believe, the first time I heard the word imperialism applied to Americans by a Vietnamese who was not a communist. I knew Quang had no illusion about Communism, and in that conversation at the café, he spoke a great deal about the failings and abuses of the system. That he referred to America's policies as "imperialism" was to me a novelty.

During the war years, communist propaganda was forbidden and intercepted by the South Vietnamese government. But somehow, in Danang, I came to hear or read the Communists' line about "the struggle to fight American imperialists." Neither my friends nor I believed the line.

De quoc My, Imperialist America, was the communist name for the United States. Sometimes people in the South repeated the name as a joke, a way to dismiss it as mere Communist propaganda. It was used so much by the propaganda machine that it became a word without meaning. Still, as meaningless as it was, the word was banned in the South. *America was our ally, there to help us protect our sovereignty and democratic way of life. The other side, the Vietcong and North Vietnam, were the Communists.* Their words must be dismissed. And so, all through my teen years, I never believed that America was an imperialist force. Because the Communists said it, it wasn't true.

The way I heard and began learning about American imperialist motives was through a different metaphor. In those days, people spoke of *Ban Tay Long La*, or The Hairy Hand. This was a reference to the American hand, which had a way of getting into Vietnamese affairs and influencing their outcomes.

Whenever my friends and I could occasionally distract ourselves from our youthful doings, we'd read newspapers and books and listen to conversations that had references to The Hairy Hand.

The Hairy Hand killed or had President Ngo Dinh Diem killed, and gave power to the military men of South Vietnam. The Hairy Hand exposed the corruption amongst members of the government cabinet and the Congress of the Republic of South Vietnam. The Hairy Hand *allowed* for such corruption, using, for example, Air America, the CIA-run airline, to support high-ranking government officials and their drugs operations. And thus, *controlling* such influential people. The Hairy Hand permitted certain battles to be lost or won, to test the public mood, or to influence U.S. Congress. It got to a point where, whenever anything happened, you could jokingly say, The Hairy Hand gave the green light.

I was too young to be completely angered about the power of The Hairy Hand. I remember absorbing the sighs and frustration of older relatives, friends, and acquaintances. And I know now that even then I was beginning to succumb to the notion of resignation that we were a backward, powerless nation caught between the war of influence between the two superpowers, the United States and the Soviet Union (and its recalcitrant ally, China). Vietnam was caught between two foreign ideologies and "empires."

I was then learning the songs of Trinh Cong Son, who in the late 1960s and early 1970s conveyed to us that it was futile to think in terms of Communism and anti-Communism. All we should care about was the destruction of Vietnamese lives. In the end, choosing to view things in terms of the suffering of all Vietnamese was the only choice left. It was the philosophical and humane side, while choosing Communism or Nationalism or any other ideology was merely to choose a war that was killing us. Trinh Cong Son did not, like the Communists, write songs about the heroic and patriotic soldiers. He wrote about the dead soldier and the dead civilian. The dead Vietnamese.

Trinh Cong Son's songs replaced American rock 'n' roll songs. They carried the same youthful energy, but they weren't angry, raging songs. They were sorrowful laments and they suited our fatalistic temperament. His songs were banned by the government because they no longer portrayed the enemies as enemies. The enemies were our brothers, and those who brought destruction to our people were the real enemies. An entire generation of Southern Vietnamese became sad old people, no longer capable of supporting the war. We were no longer capable of anger. We were just sad, and amazingly we didn't think of American imperialism.

I think that sadness stayed with me until the end of the war. Living with relatives horrified by the thought of living under Communism, I followed them and escaped out of Vietnam in April of 1975. There was chaos in the streets of most towns and cities in Vietnam. Airports and boat docks were overrun with refugees. And communist tanks were at the edge of town. I left behind my father, who had been lost in prison under Communism for nearly ten years by then, and my mother, stuck in central Vietnam. A sister was also left behind with other relatives in Saigon.

I came to America as a refugee, and the sadness in me intensified from the separation from the homeland and my family.

In the years since, many American friends have often asked about the circumstances of my presence in America. I'd explain about the war, its bloody legacy, and the family ordeal. I have wondered, but cannot explain, how I haven't ever answered these questions with the kind of anger others have infused in their explanations.

For some years after arriving in America, I held jobs with social service agencies assisting refugees from Vietnam and other countries. One of my colleagues, Michael Huynh, headed a community-based agency and once organized a benefit dinner for Amerasians, part of the sad legacy of the war. In a speech that night, he asked the audience, "How dare you ask me why I am here—when at any one time during the war, there were tens of thousands of American soldiers in my homeland?"

It was a defiant question that must have raised questions in the minds of those present about the fifty-eight thousand lives America lost during the war. Somehow, Michael's forceful words prevented any retort. No matter how one feels about the fifty-eight thousand American lives that had been lost during the war, there was so much truth in Michael's question that silence was the only appropriate answer.

Joey Ayala, the leader of the Filipino folk group Bagong Lumad, asked the same question at a San Francisco concert some years back, and the answer he gave, accompanied by a chuckle of irony, was simple. Yet there was no mistaking the anger in his voice. What goes around comes around, he said. If there are many Cubans and Filipinos and Koreans walking around the streets of San Francisco today, it's because Americans were in Cuba and the Philippines and Korea in the past.

As simple as that, and as truthful. Nothing was said about what Americans were doing in Cuba and the Philippines and Korea, and Vietnam. But Joey Ayala and my friend Michael no longer need to spell out the doings of The Hairy Hand.

I am left these days with the occasional need to explain the punch line of the U.S. embassy joke. But then, if it needed explaining, it would be almost futile. Americans have an inordinate ability to forget, to not know. Those who do care would debate with me. The history lessons seem not to be learned.

I have become selective in telling the joke now. You either get it or you don't. It scares me that I must sometimes explain the joke.

I debate with myself whether I am avoiding my responsibilities by merely laughing at the fate of my people. I question the reason I don't feel the anger that will make me repeat over and over again what I personally know of America involvement in my homeland. Anger wasn't going to give me my youth back. Or my father, or the dead.

Anger wasn't going to give me back my hometown and my country. There were worries, too, about my mother left behind in a repressive and vindictive Communist society. And all the boat people who were landing on Southeast Asian shores, or perished at sea in the early 1980s and later. I went to work in a refugee camp in Indonesia, but still wondered, as I do today, whether I should allow myself to live with my sense of futility and of loss.

I know I am capable of anger. There was the time, just five or six years ago, when I shared a ride with a young American on the way from the Hanoi airport into town. He was barely in his mid-twenties, and most probably had an MBA, and carried himself with the air of someone from a comfortable background. He had been posted to Vietnam by some American business concern, during the years in which American firms were allowed to explore opportunities but were not yet able to conduct business for America still held a trade embargo against its former enemy.

The young man and I were chatting in the car driven by his chauffeur, when he suddenly said, "This damn music is driving me crazy." It was some old Vietnamese song the chauffeur was listening to on the car stereo system. The young American then reached for the stereo, ejected the cassette tape from it, and with untempered anger, threw the tape on the floor.

I was shocked, and angry. I don't know why I didn't say anything about it to the young businessman. Out of politeness, perhaps, for he had offered me the ride. Perhaps the years in America hadn't taken away from me the Vietnamese custom and need to avoid a confrontation. Or maybe it was just the simple desire not to have an unpleasant argument with the man for the rest of the journey.

I do not know whether the man detected my annoyance. For the rest of the journey, he carried on with his views about my homeland, the business opportunities, the excitement of living there through the period of changes Vietnam was undergoing. The young man said nothing about the power he held as an American in a Vietnam just emerging out of impoverished postwar years.

I turned mostly away, looking at the peaceful green fields rolling by. I listened to the eager words of the man, but thought of the driver in the front seat. He was old, easily the age of the young man's father. He probably had fought in the wars against both the French and the Americans.

He, too, maintained his silence. He had gone through so much in his life, I thought. What could the incident with the tape and the music mean to him? In the time he'd been working for the young American, how much more abuse had he been subjected to, and simply ignored? Perhaps he had ignored it for fear of losing a good income. Perhaps he didn't care to hold angry feelings. Perhaps he had had enough of difficult times in his life and now valued peace above all.

I knew I was angry, but didn't do anything, either. After a while, the young man ceased to be merely an arrogant American. He became a symbol of American imperialism and somehow I knew I did not need to mess about with him. There would be bigger battles.

Since my encounter with the young American, numerous other occasions have occurred to make me feel a wave of anger. Such as the times in the late 1990s when I heard about the abuses of Vietnamese workers in the Nike factories in North Vietnam. Or the U.S. ambassador to Vietnam speaking of human rights as something that would come only after market reforms. Or the demands made by Washington on Vietnam vis-à-vis American soldiers declared missing-in-action since the war, past debts, and bilateral trade. Even the Coca-Cola signs and Hard Rock Cafés on the streets of Ho Chi Minh City, Hanoi, or other towns and cities.

It is embarrassing to admit that I haven't quite found a satisfactory course of action with the anger I have often felt when reminded of America's imperialistic bent. An article here and there, an essay, and countless conversations with friends and colleagues, especially those from the Third World who know well the doings of The Hairy Hand. Other than that, I haven't found any solutions. And I am not even sure that there are any.

Violence and terrorism isn't an obvious or a simple choice. And I believe enough in democracy to have voted, and occasionally write a letter to a newspaper, or to a member of Congress. But I have lived long enough in America to know that such actions could never make that much of a dent in the foreign policies of the United States, and I have developed a healthy distrust of politicians in my years in America.

I also believe it isn't purely foreign policies one must be concerned with. It is also how the United States and its leaders, for all the lofty check-and-balance and democratic systems, lull its citizens into continued belief in America's righteous ways. It is about keeping its people happy with their life in America while the leaders invent all types of pretexts to get involved, influence, and dominate other nations' political, social, and economic affairs.

I think of the times every once in a while, mostly during fund-raising seasons, when America's public radio stations air specials about secret CIA maneuvers in Central America, Africa, Asia, and elsewhere in the world. In such moments, I hear an amplification of the otherwise feeble and ineffectual voices of criticism of the government, of Congress, of America's foreign policies, the media and other official institutions. The phones on the pledge lines ring, and I hear in them the excitement and anger of people who believe they are participating in democracy, raising their voices against whoever they think is running America. They donate a sum of money to keep the public television and radio stations functioning. And then they simply resume their lives. Such lives include a silencing of oneself, a complicity in pursuit of one's notions of happiness. The consumption of goods, of succumbing to advertising, and ultimately ensuring the survival of mammoth corporations, which I suspect will in turn dictate who will survive or not in the White House and at the Capitol, and what foreign policies they are to adopt.

Such policies will be translated into action by The Hairy Hand inhabiting countless American embassies around the world. It will be trade agreements, or arms shipments, a green or red light for assassination and corruption. It will be war, and killing and destruction. It will all be in the name of democracy, couched in words acceptable or least offensive to a public already bent on forgetting history.

Those of us who have lived through the results of such policies will feel anger. We will almost certainly suffer. We will sometimes review our initial assessment and judgment of America. Will we all finally revert to acceptance or resignation, or will we chose a more active path? Or will our sad wisdom simply make us acknowledge it all with a joke, witty and bittersweet, about the possibilities of an American embassy and its subversive ways?

Notes From the Other Cartography

GUILLERMO GOMEZ-PEÑA

The following collage includes excerpts of Gomez-Peña's books Warrior for Gringostroika *(Greywolf Press),* New World Border *(City Lights), and* Dangerous Border Crossers *(Routledge Press). The selection of these texts was made by the editors in consultation with the author. Portions of these texts were performed on 26 February 1999 at the Joseph Papp Public Theater in a cultural event called "Elegant Chaos: The Philippine–Mexican Collision." Agnes Magtoto, Filipino performance artist, took part in the performance and is responsible for the Tagalog translations in this collage.*

Dear Reader:

Rather than establishing an obvious connection between the Filipino diaspora to the United States and the Chicano/Mexicano border experience, I have chosen to include in this book certain performative texts in which these links are implicit: from our shared Spanish colonial history, to our permanent condition of Imperial subjects and consumers of U.S. corporate culture; the Philippines and Mexico have had parallel developments.

Furthermore, once in the United States, whether as labor or political orphans, Filipino-Americans and Mexican-Americans have been treated as second-class citizens, taking on similar menial jobs and sharing the same or equivalent living spaces and barrios. We have been employed and cast as fruit pickers, sweatshop workers, nannies, waiters, chefs, gang members, Hollywood extras, and exotic musicians and dancers. Our languages—Spanish and Pilipino—and identities have been similarly criminalized. Because of all this, our political struggles as so-called "U.S. minorities" are intertwined in many ways. The job of my generation of Chicano performance artists has been to shed some light in the darkest zones of the Mexicano immigrant experience; to build conceptual bridges between the mythical "homeland" and our new hybrid nation; and ultimately to reverse the gaze and make our new Anglo audiences experience, if only for the duration of a performance, what does it mean to be "the brown Other." In my performance cartography, Mexico, as the Philippines, is a "central" culture and Anglos are nomadic minorities in search of identity, clarity, and citizenship. Many Filipino artists of my generation are embarked in parallel projects. *Comenzamos pues....*

I.

I left Mexico City in 1978. It has been almost twenty years now of traveling from South to North and back; from city to city; from country to country; from English to Spanish, and vice versa; from myth to social reality and back to the origins (by now mythical as well), retracing the footprints of my biological family and revisiting my many overlapping communities: i.e, the diasporic Mexicans, the deterritorialized citizens of everywhere and nowhere, the inhabitants of the so called "margins" and the crevasses, *los vatos intersticiales*; the hybrids, exiles, cultural, and sexual renegades. It is precisely a partially conscious attempt to trace back the footprints of these peoples and communities that propels my uncontrollable desire to move. And this objective separates my personal road movie from the American genre, which is largely about finding yourself on the road. *Aclaro:* I don't wish to find myself. I assume whole-heartedly my fluid condition of loss, my multiple and incomplete identities, and I celebrate them....

II. ON LANGUAGE AS MY PASSPORT

Lights. I step on the map of my America. I walk from Puerto Rico to Florida, and then across Texas and the southwest back into Mexico, the Philippines while speaking... then up the coast to New York. I meet with Filipino performance artist Bing Magtoto on the stage of the Public Theater.

Ilaw. Nakaapak ako sa mapa ng aking Amerika. Maglalakad ako mula Puerto Rico patungong Florida tatawirin ang Texas at ang southwest pabalik sa Pilipinas habang binibigkas:

I speak therefore I continue to be	
language, my passport to your country	*Ako ay nagsasalita, samakatuwid ako ay nananatili*
language, my journey to your arms	*wika, pasaporte ko sa iyong bansa*
language, my most effective weapon	*wika, aking paglalakbay patungo sa iyong kandungan*
language, my two-way ticket to the past	*wika, aking pinakamabisang sandata*
language, my abracadabra	*wika, aking balikan bilyete sa kasaysayan*
a memory per line	*wika, aking abrakadabra*
a thread of life per sentence	*isang ala-ala bawa't linya*
ten dollars a poem	*hibla ng buhay sa bawat pangungusap*
a memory per line	*sampung dolyares bawat tula*
postcard included	*isang ala-ala bawa't linya*
life in Gringolandia,	*kasama na rin ang postcard*
a cheesy TV talk show	*buhay sa Gringolandia*
	isang TV talk show na puno ng kabaduyan

III.

The great experience of migration and nomadism in the 1990s is by no means "marginal." As our continents collide and overlap culturally, nomadism and immigration have become central experiences of millennial postmodernity. Why? Whether we like it or not, the much touted "globalization" and the ongoing migration of the South to the North, and of the East to the West, are redefining everything: geopolitical borders (and therefore nation-states), language (the currency of the linguas francas), identity (national and personal), political activism, pop culture and art. And my colleagues and I have been sailing these troubled waters in hopes of one day in the immediate future finding the coastline .

Is there really a coastline? Have we arrived? In these troubled waters, the ships of Filipinos and Mexicans often intersect, but we bypass one another without noticing it.

IV. Prerecorded Spanish Lesson #227

(Two voices. Spanish is purposely mispronounced to sound like a stereotypical tourist in Tijuana)
Dear Friends:
The following Spanish/Pilipino lesson is directed to all the American people who are still having problems communicating with monolingual Latinos/Filipinos. Please repeat after me:

— Maria, tienes tus papeles en orden?
— *Maria, ayos na ba ang iyong mga papeles?*
— Mary, are you fully documented?

— Puedo verlos ahora mismo por favor?
— *Maaari ko bang makita?*
— Can you show me now proof of residence or citizenship?

— Tu tienes muchos hijos?
— *Marami ka bang anak?*
— Do you have many children?

— Tienes donde dejarlos mientras trabajas?
— *Meyron ka bang pag-iiwanan habang ikaw ay nagtatrabaho?*
— Do you have a place to leave them while you come to work?

— Estas a dieta?
— *Ikaw ba ay negdyedyeta?*
— Are you on a diet?

— La comida del refrigerador no es parra tuya.
— *Ang pagkain sa refrigerator ay hindi para say iyo.*
— The food in the fridge is not for you.

(With men, one has to be a bit tougher)
— Panchou, irriega el jardin.
— *Kiko, diligan mo na ang hardin.*
— Frank, water the garden.

— No seas tan flojo, amigo.
— *Huwag kang tatamad-tamad, kaibigan.*

— Don't be so lazy, my friend.

— Tienes aliento alcoholico.
— *Amoy alak ka.*
— You stink of alcohol.

— No me veas asi tan directo.
— *Huwag mo akong titigan ng ganyan.*
— Don't you look at me so directly.

— Yo voy a hablarle a la policia si no cambias.
— *Kung hindi ka magtitino, tatawag ako ng pulis.*
— If you don't behave, I am going to have to call the police.

Now, if Panchou has finished his job, and you are feeling restless, or adventurous, you may tell him:

— *Amorrcito, ven a mi cuarto y enséñame tus misterios.*
— *Mahal, halika sa kuwarto at ipakita mo sa akin ang iyong tinatagong misteryo.*

If you repeat these phrases as often as possible to yourself and any Latino/Filipino you encounter, you won't have communication problems anymore. For information on other Spanish lessons/Pilipino lessons about food, politics, identity, and sex, please call (name of guest organization).

V.
I truly believe that people in the United States know more Spanish than they think they do or than they are willing to accept. And I wish to prove my point with a poem right now!

LECCIÓN DE GEOGRAFIA FINISECULAR EN ESPAÑOL
(didactic voice/school teacher)

Dear Perplexed Audience Member,
repeat with me out loud:
Mexico es California
Filipinas es Nueva York
Marruecos es Madrid
Pakistan es Londres
Argelia es Paris
Cambodia es San Francisco
Turquia es Frankfurt
Puerto Rico es Nueva York
Centroamerica es Los Angeles
Honduras es New Orleans
Argentina es Paris
Beijing es San Francisco

and suddenly you're homeless
you've lost your land again
your present dilemma is

to wander
in a transient geography de locos

VI.

Home? The Bay area is my temporary point of departure and return, since that's where my most recent "physical home" is located. The physical home, la casa, is the place where my computer, my books, videos, and archives happen to be. It is also the place where I rehearse before going back to my other home, the "conceptual home," the road, la jornada, my personal Bermuda triangle. My Mexican home, my little family house located in a nineteenth-century working-class neighborhood in Mexico City, the capital of the continental crisis, is quite mythical to me. It is the place to which I go back in search of political enegy, tender memories, maternal love, good food, and yes, occasionally to perform. Where is home? What does home mean?

VII. FREEFALLING TOWARD A BORDERLESS FUTURE

I see
I see
I see a whole generation
free falling toward a borderless future
incredible mixtures beyond sci-fi:
cholo-punks, cyber-Mayans
Irish concheros, Benetton Zapatistas,
Gringofarians, Buttho rappers, Hopi rockers...
I see them all
wandering around
a continent without a name,
the forgotten paisanos
howling corridos in Fresno & Amarillo
the Mixteco pilgrims heading North toward British Columbia
the Australian surfers waiting for the big wave at Valparaiso
the polyglot Papagos waiting for the sign to return
the Salvadorans coming North to forget
the New Yorkers going South to remember
the stubborn Europeans in search of the last island
Zumpango, Cozumel, Martinique
I see them all
wandering around
a continent without a name
el TJ transvestite translating Nuyorican versos in Univision
the howling L.A. junkie bashing NAFTA with a bullhorn
El Warrior for Gringoistroika scolding the First World on MTV

Cholo warriors pointing their camcorders at the cops
AIDS warriors reminding us all of the true priorities in life
Lacandonian shamans exorcising multinationals at dawn
yuppie tribes paralyzed by guilt & fear
grunge rockeros on the edge of a cliff
all passing through Califas
enroute to other selves
& other geographies
(I speak in tongues)
standing on the map of my political desires
I toast to a borderless future
with...
our Alaskan hair
our Canadian head
our U.S. torso
our Mexican genitalia
our Central American cojones
our Caribbean vulva
our South American legs
our Patagonian feet
our Antarctic nails
jumping borders at ease
jumping borders with pleasure
amen, hey man

Pappy's House: History, Pop Culture, and the Reevaluation of a Filipino-American "Sixty-cents" in Guam
VICENTE M. DIAZ

PREFACE: FROM A LONG LINE OF DIAZES[1]

Hilario Diaz was an *indio* from Iba, Zambales. He hung out with the big boys because as an *herbolario*, he possessed folk knowledge that impressed the *ilustrados*, and had practical applications for the nationalist march against the imperialists. Hilario's son, Vicente, extended the lineage as a highly decorated freemason and through advanced *cartillas*. And then Vicente's eyes met those of Bibiana Valero, a fellow educator and staunch mestiza, who mandated that Vicente first convert to Catholicism and renounce his affiliation with the Church's sworn enemy. From his decision, and her satisfaction, came Ramon, the first son, who received a law degree from the University of Santo Tomas and a commission in the Philippine Army just before the Japanese invasion and occupation. A survivor of Bataan (because he ate his *monggo* beans, as our version of child psychology would have it), Ramon left the Philippines in 1949 in search not simply of the legendary American dream but of a site to build a career that had been interrupted and shaped by war, and also for a place to raise his young family. In Guam Ramon discovered an island similar enough in climate and culture to the Philippines, and far enough from a domestic situation that had, according to his wife, Josefina, become too much like a battle zone. His move to America, or rather where "America's Day Begins," as Guam is popularly known, was a salvage operation for Ramon's upstart family. So too was *Pappy*'s eventual naturalization as an American "sixty-cents," as he punned, ambivalently, his new status as an American "citizen."

Besides the injunction to finish one's *monggo* beans, among Pappy's most solid convictions is the maxim "Blood runs thicker than water." I have inherited this tenet, but it has been mediated by my upbringing in postwar Guam, intellectual training, and most recently, fatherhood of my own. I would like now to trumpet a new generation of Diazes but with a qualifier: blood may run thicker than water, but the flow that counts is neither genetic nor racial, but narratological in constitution.

This essay takes stock of my stock, especially as it circulates through *indio* and mestizo displacment in Filipino, Spanish, and American acts of remembering, and as

mediated in filial stress and tension in post–World War II Guam.[2] Here I yearn not merely for a spot in what Vicente Rafael calls the "differentially articulated locations of Filipino-ness," but for a more culturally appropriate, and culturally appropriated, way to engage the perimeters of that highly local and well-entrenched battleground called one's *familia*.[3] My approach will be personal, familial, one aim of which would be to illustrate just one moment in the ambivalent character of colonial discourse.[4]

**Left to right:
Lolo Vicente Diaz,
Lolo Vicente and Lola
Bibiana and Familia,
Judge Diaz, Superior
Court of Guam**

PAPPY'S HOUSE

Years ago, while Pappy was still on the bench, I chanced upon a friend, a cop, who asked about his welfare. My friend had been detailed several times to monitor Pappy's house in the Kaiser subdivision in Dededo, on account of an escaped convict. Now he had an opportunity to address a curiosity: "Your house must be really nice in the inside, huh?" His question alluded to the incongruity of a prominent judge living in a rather rundown, low-cost tract home. It was like, "What's up with your house, man?" I confessed that the house was the same in the inside as it was on the outside, but he didn't believe me, and he left still convinced that the exterior of the house was a ruse to downplay in public what he thought was in fact the material wealth and prosperity of a prominent citizen.

In fact the inside was not only as *magulo* (messy) as the outside, it was worse: bubbled ceilings, stained carpetry, pocked linoleum. In our *comedor* (dining room) sat rickety chairs and a table whose susan had become too lazy to swivel due to piles of books, legal pads, and bills. By the time Pappy and Mammy moved next to Marilen and Pascual, the house brimmed with fifty years of things from ten children and more grandchildren. In the final days, Pappy's House was like a tomb, sighed Mammy: dark and cooped up. But if it be likened to a tomb, let it be the famous one on the eve of redemption, for the house also carried half a century of the woman's crosses to bear it all.

Half a century earlier, Mammy and Pappy had moved to Guam. In the mid-1960s they finally settled in Kaiser, Dededo, which was then one of Guam's first public housing subdivisions, built specifically to accommodate residents who had lost their homes to Supertyphoon Karen ("the Killer") of 1962, and more importantly, the first government-funded, all-concrete, no-nonsense, typhoon-proof homes. This important moment in Guam's postwar history of urban development also coincided with the influx of Filipinos, and later, Micronesians, in search of the proverbial pie in America's "westernmost" territory. But for the majority of the Filipinos, Kaiser Dededo would be renamed "Tagalu land" or "Little Manila," despite the fact that the hordes were neither exclusively Tagalog nor from Manila.[5]

But Kaiser Cement and Steel represented more than security and calm during subsequent typhoons, the real causes for bubbled ceilings and stained carpets.[6] It also concretized Pappy's determination to be a good provider. Eventually, the surrounding overgrowth bespoke Pappy's epic struggle to convert a barren sea of *cascajo* (crushed coral or limestone) into a green lawn, another unsuccessful emulation of American (or was it prewar Filipino?) suburbia in Guam. If anything, Pappy's yardwork only paved the way for the bush's return with a vengeance: planting seedlings (never fun) gave way to futile cycles of weeding and mowing. Yard maintenance, like housework inside with ten children, escalated quickly into a full-scale war to keep nature at bay. And though he fought valiantly, often armed with pumps of pesticides, Pappy, like modernity displaced in the tropics, lost most of the skirmishes.

But Pappy's concern with exteriority was not restricted to the surface appearance of the house. He also sought to regulate our public image. Like nature, we resisted things like *camisetas* (T-shirts) that were supposed to absorb our perspiration; or globs of pomade, later Brylcream, designed to hold our indio (read: *magulo*) hair. In the postwar interethnic tension that was mounting on Guam too, we would learn to quickly control, if not disguise, our Pinoy accents as well. In this milieu an unmarked (now marked) "standard American English" canon would make great strides in washing out vestiges of linguistic and cultural difference and carving out

Kaiser, Dededo, 1967

for itself, with ambivalent and even eager assistance from Chamorros, Filipinos, Micronesians, and other Asians, the privileged position as the lingua franca.

Left to right:
Battling outside the
court; with Mammy

Pappy's gaze penetrated the surface, too. He was infamous for speaking his mind, the accent notwithstanding. All had to "mark" his words (never "minced"). This was especially true when it came to morality, of which there were only two kinds: right and wrong. Carlitos would inherit, and contest, Pappy's moral mathematics thus: "There are three kinds of people in the world: those who can count and those who can't!"

OF RIFFS AND RIFTS

Kaiser Dededo was Pappy's "jackpot," as he once put it to me. For me, though, the house (now) is simply rundown. And like my Lolo Hilario (Pappy's Pappy's Pappy) at the end of last century, a century later I too am feeling a bit up*routed*.[7] In a day when rap music snags all the pop music awards, a "house" is not just a home but a coming together of people who are cool, with whom you prefer to "hang," as the hip-hop brand of twenty-first-century pop culture puts it. In need of a more "down home" (visceral) theory and method, I sample rap's riffs to address the colonial legacy of my rifts, and my desire to proceed with a difference.

Hip hop, cousin to "rap," originated in Black street culture in New York and later, in California '*hoods* (neighborhoods) like Crenshaw, Compton, and Carson City (Tony's way of pronouncing the Spanish word for underwear).[8] Hip-hop has also become *down* (acceptable) among Filipino and other Pacific Islanders whose own hoods, like the John and Maryann Carr-hood in Fullerton, rank among the fastest-growing communities in California. Of course hip-hop and rap have roots in jazz and blues, with roots of their own in the legacies of African slaves in the Americas. But in this cross-cultural mix I contend that the relationship between Pappy, pop, former slaves, and displaced indios such as Chamorros and Filipinos have deeper implications than are understood by trendy scholarly traffic in pop culture. *Know what I mean*? Let me ground some of these stakes, or routes, by returning tactically to my roots.

PAPPY [PAPI]

"Pappy" is the patriarch of Todos Los Diazes. In an argument with Marilen not long ago, Pappy was adamant about men's natural status as heads of families and societies, that women should be subservient. Len countered that even Pappy didn't raise her like that. I got into it too, and interrogated him about where he got this so-called natural law. His answer was "from Mama," Lola Bibiana, the matriarch by all accounts. My pointing out the peculiar notion of patriarchy-derived-from-matriarchy met with Pappy's pointing out the inferiority of my American education.[9]

Nonetheless, the word *Pappy* is one of those terms whose universal variation is slim enough that the objects they signify appear to be natural, like the idea of patriarchy as a natural law. The striking phonetic similarities among Europe's "Papa," the Middle East's "Aba," Oceania's "Apa," and Chamorro "Tata" tempt us to conclude that their signified, the English "Father," like patriarchy, is indeed rooted in nature. Or if not in nature, then in the divine. Allow me to digress tactically on another onomatopoetic word with equally mythic reach and dwelling power: Pappy's *pedo*. Pedo is what Todos Los Diazes "throw" (e.g., "quien tiran el pedo?" Who "threw" the fart?, or, in Tagalog, "*ai, bastus!*" Hey, you gross filthy person!), which our in-laws across the States decry as "fart," which Chamorros in the House might perform as *do'du*, and for which Tony would need to change his Carson City. Of course, there is no law, natural or divine, requiring that words for the odoriferous miasma be uniform in sound. For example, in the Micronesian island of Pohnpei (homeland of Lolo Miguel), the appropriate term is *seng*, which explains why our Pohnpeian relations giggle at the late Karen Carpenter's pop tune that goes:

> Seng
> Seng a Song
> Seng out Loud
> Seng out Strong!

Speaking of *anima*, Todos Los Diazes will not forget the time in our lives when we laughed at, nay, rejoiced in, Carl's successful bids to fart at will. How the release of gas entrapped in his cancerous colon, cause of great agony, could be music to our ears. Two years after his death, memories of Carl's effort to heal our bodies with laughter become sacred; their dwelling power, recontextualized and now culturally syncopated, remixed, so to speak, can also be regarded as a sort of post-natural folk remedy. Go on, try it, with my Pohnpeian tongue, and seng the Carpenter song again. Seng out loud. Seng out strong. And continue the verse that follows, but with memories of your special person's last(ing) days with us:

> Seng of Good Things Not Bad
> Seng of Happy, Not Sad.
> (Join me, won't you? La La La La La...)

The digression is the point: terms like "Pappy," and like his pedos for that matter, have 1) an interestingly wide circulation in time and space, and 2) have original meanings that can be remade, and remade in the interest of tapping sources of authority, or even deflecting their reach. With these pedo-principles in hand, let us return to the American deep South for a particular brand of pop culture to illustrate the additional value, and deeper mess, of "Pappy's House."

[PAPI]

The term *Pappy* is common in the American south, but with a twang, as [Paa-PEE]. To me, Paapee conjures two interrelated images: Colonel Sanders and old black men fishing the Missouri River (Maribel and Tom's hood) as escaped slaves. But between the two images of white and black Paapees is an unevenly experienced history of slavery and race relations that still manages to produce the term Paapee as the name of the father for both black and white folks alike.

How a single term of endearment for "the father" can be embraced by black and white folk alike is an interesting question.[10] But how to account for the presence of the term in our tropical neck of the woods? The answer lies in the intertwining of racialized, gendered, and sexualized histories of European imperialism and native responses thereto, and how these transactions are shaped by, and in turn further shape, notions of parental authority. In our case, the one two punch of Spanish and American rule, and our embrace of key terms like "padre" and "Papa" and "Daddy" would produce hybrids like "Pappy." It is in these political processes

Mammy and Pappy

of creolization that we can better understand what Chamorros in the House call *Kostumbren Chamorro*: Chamorro customs and practices, couched heavily in Spanish Catholicism, whose own arrival in the Marianas was actually a hybrid form of "Mexican" and "Filipino" mixtures, which were historical and cultural hybridities themselves. And like Filipino or Mexican "culture," Chamorro *Kostumbre* also reactivates older native values and principles such as *taimamahlao*. Like *walang hiya*, to be labeled *taimamahlao* is to be reproached big time: to be accused of having "no shame." In Guam, to be called *taimamahlao* is to be likened to an *Amerikanu*. Whatever the added (or subtracted) value, terms like *mamahlao* reveal indigenous histories of unequal relations of power and authority, later recharged through Euro-American colonization and native responses thereto. *Bueno*. But how are these hybridities here linked to those there, in the American deep South? Consider first the southern "Paapee" in relation to the southern "Maamee."

PAPPI AND MAMMY

Like Paapee, the term Maamee is used by blacks and whites alike. And like Paapee, there are pop images for Maamee as well. Recall Colonel Sanders, the quintessential

Southern gentleman. We might imagine him in his younger days to have been a dashing officer, quick to defend, even to death, the honor of his woman, the southern belle, the debutante. I imagine southern Paapees as former Confederate soldiers. It is in the name of women, children, money, and nation, that men go to war, and in this context it is the Civil War's contest between rebels defending the honor and the economy of the south against Yankees defending the integrity of a northern-conceived (and female-engendered) nation.

But if to the white South the image of the father is Colonel Sanders, I concur with Barbara Christian that the white image of the mother is not a white woman but the ubiquitous black momma best imaged in Aunt Jemima of the pancake-and-syrup fame.[11] It is this particular Maamee, whose apron and bandanna symbolize domestication and labor, who attends exclusively to the domestic needs of the white estate. According to Christian, the recurring figure of the nurturing, caring Black Mammy is what enabled the narrativization of such archetypical white identities as chivalrous southern gentlemen and debutante belles, and their epic romance and tragedy set in the deep South.[12] Christian argues that in both the literary and social texts of the region, Aunt Jemima shouldered the brutal actualities of life, for "in the mythology of the South," she writes, "men did not fight duels or protect the honor of a woman who was busy cooking, scrubbing floors, or minding children, since the exclusive performance of this kind of work precluded the intrigue necessary to be a person as ornament." In marking the inextricability between racialized and gendered images of self and other

Guam Newsletter, U.S. Navy, Vol. 4, No. 1, July 1912

"More Like His Dad Everyday"

here, Christian also illustrates the deep links between popular culture and histories of colonization. But you might still ask, unconvinced, what the interconnections are between those Paapees and Maamees, and ours. Let's ask the children.

PICANINNIES ONE AND ALL

In the South and beyond, the term *picaninny* referred initially to children of slaves, and later became the metonymic reduction of all blacks in the belief of their natural inferiority and infantility. White authority, in terms of benevolent parenthood, is at stake here. Though these sentiments are not exclusive to the deep South, nor to the United States, it is useful to trace the term and its actions here for a moment.

After the Civil War, and as an integral component of its national reconstruction, the United States began to lay claim on the globe. The end of the nineteenth century, America believed, was its destiny's crossroads: it had survived political and economic collapse and was witnessing tremendous technological advancement and social upheaval, particularly through the perceived hordes of uncouth immigrants from both sides of the continent. America also believed that it had reached some limits, like land and wilderness, whose transformation was the stuff of progress, whose taming was the mark of its genius. At this time, America's *homies* (peers) *barkada* (mates), like Germany, France and Britain, had already been taking over the 'hood, as Spain had for three hundred years, except that Spain now couldn't *hang* (keep up). And so in 1898 America evicts Spain with stolen rap riffs like *Cuba Libre!* but in ways that exempted Cuban insurgents, and later, Filipino *insurrectos*, from their own presumed national destinies. But what does all this have to do with picaninnies, and picaninnies with us? *Todos*. When the United States beat Spain and snatched Cuba and Puerto Rico over there, and Filipinas and the Marianas over here, American publications would run cartoons that consistently depicted their peoples —us! —as little black children, as picaninnies.

Interestingly enough, the term picaninny, once thought to be the province of the deep South but now elevated to national and international assertions of American supremacy, turns out to be what else but the anglicized contraction of the Spanish term *pequeño niño*![13] And what is pequeño niño but an earlier strategic articulation of the Spanish *imperio*'s own racialized pecking order, beginning, at the top, with *peninsulares* followed by displaced *criollos*, then by even more confused mestizos whose vexed indio heritage is always either debased or ennobled in colonial or postcolonial versions of domination.

For Spain, colonial regulation of money, gender, race, sexuality, language and identity took place within, among other institutions and practices, the *Patronato Real*, a bureaucratic apparatus which for many reasons failed to ensure the integrity of the monarchy's will across the Atlantic and the Pacific. According to Vicente Rafael, the Patronato Real was modeled on the idea of a "patron-client" relationship between God and the king, which was replicated below, between the king and his surrogates, and the surrogates' surrogates dispersed throughout the far-flung empire.[14] Rooted in the idea of the benevolent law of God the Father, the term *patron* also shaped the identity of His principal client/offspring, the king, that sought to regenerate itself through the downward and outward flow of royal patronage system. Transposed across cultures, this Spanish brand of paternalism produced the idea that Spaniards **The children**

were white parents to indios figured as dark children, or pequeños niños, or their Anglo-American cousins, the picaninnies, in need of proper guidance and upbringing. But the critique of postcolonialism also shows us that the power of colonialism is more magulo than unidirectional or monolithic. That colonial discourse also insinuates itself in indigenous discourses of power and vice-versa so that its power and effects become epic in their multiple modes of regeneration. With this particular genealogy, it should also become our legacy to contend with the Man (or Woman) in our house, however we define that house.

PAPPIES IN THE HOUSE

In a summer seminar on the legacies of the Spanish, Philippine, Cuban, and American War of 1898 organized and conducted by Virginia Dominguez and Jane Desmond at the University of Iowa's Obermann Center for Advanced Studies, I was presented with an *ethno-op* (ethnographic opportunity) to ask other historically and culturally informed pequeños niños from Cuba, Philippines, Hawaii, Puerto Rico, and Kansas, about "Pappy." Pappy, I discovered, was not one. His Houses, many. At least for us heirs to ongoing histories of Euro-American colonialism (and who is not?). My sheepish question, "Who is Pappy?" elicited specific names, including, for the men, their own. One answer was a corrective: "not who is Pappy, but what is Pappy?" Not surprisingly, I discovered that Pappy had multiple and deep meanings that ran the gamut from a term of deep affection for one's father or one's son, to a term for an acquaintance ("Hola Pappy!"), to cat calls ("Hoooy Papppppy!"), to steamy talk between hot lovers ("Oooh pappppeeee"). In this unscientific survey, Pappy was alternately a figure of authority, a helpless boy, a stud, a spoiled brat, a lover. One informant, a woman, replied: "Me. I'm Pappy."

Though Pappy is intensely personal, he is also inside everyone of us in a way that makes him an intensely collective, public, historical artifact precisely through his meanderings. Moreover, Pappy's historical and cultural multiplicity is just one example of the multiple meanings that have been made of figures and terms of imperial authority, whose structures consist as much in the gaze of authority as in the festive and, at times, irreverent and subversive play of meaning-remaking by diverse peoples subject to that authority. And if that is the case, at least as claimed by those who celebrate or lament the condition of globalization at the cusp of the next century, the question becomes not who is Pappy but, as first raised by my friend the cop: "What's up with *your* house?"

Fred Morgan, *Philadelphia Inquirer*, 1898

"Uncle Sam's Newly Caught Anthropoids"

Photographs courtesy of the Diaz family. Reproduced by William Hernandez.

NOTES

1. This subtitle and the genealogies within it are inspired by Cherrie Moraga's "A Long Line of Vendidas," in *Loving in the War Years* (Boston: South End Press,1983). This essay is dedicated to Tina and Nicole, and especially little Gabriella, who demands that the subject of this essay be grounded.

2. Guam is an "unincorporated territory" of the United States, a euphemism that obfuscates its actual status as a colony of the United States. A former Spanish colony that was treated as an offshore province of the Philippine command, Guam was seized by the United States at the outbreak of the misnamed Spanish-American War in 1898 and held as a possession since. The indigenous people of Guam (and the surrounding Mariana Islands) are called "Chamorros" and are said to have settled these islands from Southeast Asia beginning about four thousand years ago. Like all Oceanic languages, the Chamorro language belongs to the Austronesian group.

3. I remain indebted to Vicente Rafael's analyses of and relentless skirmishes with nationalist discourses in their multiple forms. The quote is from his analyses of affect and nationalism in "'Your Grief Is Our Gossip': Overseas Filipinos and Other Spectral Presences," *CSST Working Paper 111*, University of Michigan, October 1996. On the broader condition of Filipino colonial and postcolonial displacement, see Vicente Rafael, ed. *Discrepant Histories: Translocal Essays on Filipino Cultures* (Philadelphia, Pa.: Temple University Press, 1995), and Yen Le Espiritu's "The Intersection of Race, Ethnicity, and Class: The Multiple Identities of Second-Generation Filipinos," *Identities*, 1:2, 1-25. The names mentioned in this essay are either siblings, in-laws, and extended family members who comprise what we affectionately refer to as "Todos Los Diazes," now living in Guam, across the fifty states, in places like Australia and probably the Middle East, as *balikbayans* or OCWs (Filipino overseas contract workers), as critically distinguished in Rafael 1996.

4. Bhabha's notion of the ambivalence of colonial discourse first published in Homi Bhabha. "Of Mimicry and Man: The Ambivalence of Colonial Discourse."*October*, 28, 1984: 125-133.

5. Of the total population of Guam in 1996 (156, 302), the Filipino population comprised 23 percent and is the second largest ethnic group, next to the indigenous Chamorros (42%). Other major groups are "Caucasians" (14%) which include white American and other Europeans, "Other" (13%), which includes East Asians like Japanese, Chinese, Taiwanese, Koreans, etc., and finally, "Micronesians" (7%), which refers to islanders from the surrounding island nation states (the Republic of the Marshall Islands, the Republic of Palau, and the Federated States of Micronesia) which entered into "free association" with the United States in the 1980s and 1990s, and whose terms provided unrestricted travel and residence between these islands and American territories and states like Guam and Hawaii. Population estimates are from Ron Stade's *Pacific Passages: World Culture and Local Politics in Guam*. (Stockholm: University of Stockholm, 1998), v.

These demographics are a cause for alarm among many Chamorros, who only since the 1980s as an "ethnic" group dropped below 50 percent of the total population. Depending on who you talk to, the Chamorros are either "a minority in our own homeland" or are "the biggest ethnic group" in the island, a significant gap in description and perception that captures (and fuels) the growing sense of social tension within a society that is widely and uncritically categorized as "American." In this social set-up, pun intended, Filipinos are often stigmatized as leading the charge of aliens in the process of dispossessing Chamorros of their land and jobs, in spite of (or perhaps precisely for) the long history that Chamorros and people from the Philippines have maintained since Spanish times. For a sense of the asymmetrical relations between Filipinos and Chamorros within the asymmetrical relations of Spanish and American colonialism, see Diaz, Vicente M. 1995. "Bye Bye Ms. American Pie: Chamorros and Filipinos and the

American Dream," *Isla: Journal of Micronesian Studies* 3:1 (Rainy Season): 147-160. For a productive, if provocative, treatment of the construction of cultural and ethnic identity in Guam, see Stade above.

6. For the social expenses of Kaiser Cement and Steel in California, see Mike Davis's *City of Quartz: Excavating the Future in Los Angeles* (New York: Vintage Press, 1992).

7. For a general critique of the routedness of culture and the culture of travel, see James Clifford's *Routes: Travel and Translation in the Late Twentieth Century* (Cambridge: Harvard University Press, 1997). From the Pacific, see Teresia Teaiwa's "Yaqona/Yagoqu: Routes and Roots of a Displaced Native" *UTS Review* (forthcoming), and "Loosing the Native," (Paper presented at the Eleventh Conference of the Pacific History Association, Hilo, Hawai'i, July 1996).

8. For cultural histories see essays in *Microphone Friends: Youth Music and Youth Culture*, eds., Andrew Ross and Tricia Rose (New York: Routledge Press, 1994).

9. My American education in the disciplines of history, anthropology, and political theory has also fed me a steady stream of tenets and axioms like the notion that precontact island societies were "matrilineal" in kinship and social structure, in which an individual's identity and resources are reckoned through "the mother's" (and not the father's) lineage. David Schneider's critical cautions notwith-standing, notions such as "matrilineality" continue to serve as deep markers not only of the exotic, but as determinants of native authenticity: where patriarchy and patrilineage, especially as introduced by Western imperialism, take root, authentic local culture disappears. Among other things, this essay is part of an ongoing bid to trouble the recovery of purity, but especially purity and innocence through valorized ideas of matrilineage or matriarchy. See David Schneider. *American Kinship: A Cultural Account.* (Chicago: University of Chicago Press, 1980. On Schneider on kinship in Oceania, see David Schneider. "Conclusions," in Mac Marshall, ed. *Siblingship in Oceania* (Ann Arbor: University of Michigan Press, 1981), 389-404. For a recent assessment of kinship in Micronesia, see Mac Marshall's "'Partial Connections': Kinship and Social Organization in Micronesia," in Kiste, Robert C. and Mac Marshall. 1999. *American Anthropology in Micronesia* (Honolulu: University of Hawai'i Press), 107-143.

10. One answer is found in the way a particular postbellum African-American discourse of racial "uplift" appropriated and replicated a social order that upheld white paternalism. See Kevin Gaines, *Uplifting the Race: Black Politics and Culture in the United States Since the Turn of the Century* (Chapel Hill, N.C.: University of North Carolina Press, 1995). On the other hand, see M. M. Manring's wide-ranging and insightful analyses of the durability of the figure of Aunt Jemima in the making of authority for black and white folks in *Slave in a Box: The Strange Career of Aunt Jemima* (University of Virginia, 1997).

11. *Black Feminist Criticism* (New York: Pergamon Press, 1985).

12. Manring's, *Slave in a Box*, above.

13. I thank Kelvin Velez-Santiago for pointing this out.

14. The foregoing draws from Vicente Rafael's *Contracting Colonialism: Translation and Christian Conversion in Tagalog Society under Early Spanish Rule* (Durham, N.C: Duke University Press, 1993).

Emilio Ganot

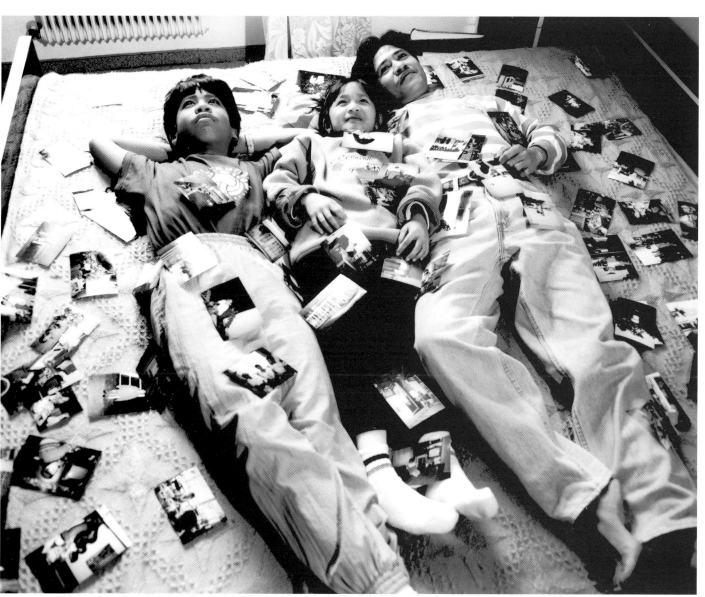

"HOME IS WHERE YOU ARE"
KARL, CANDY & KENNEDY

SALZBURG, 1995
GANOT

"HOME IS WHERE YOU ARE"
GELINE

SALZBURG, 1995

"HOME IS WHERE YOU ARE"
LUCIA

SALZBURG, 1995
GANOT

"HOME IS WHERE YOU ARE"
BANYAGA

SALZBURG, 1995
GANOT

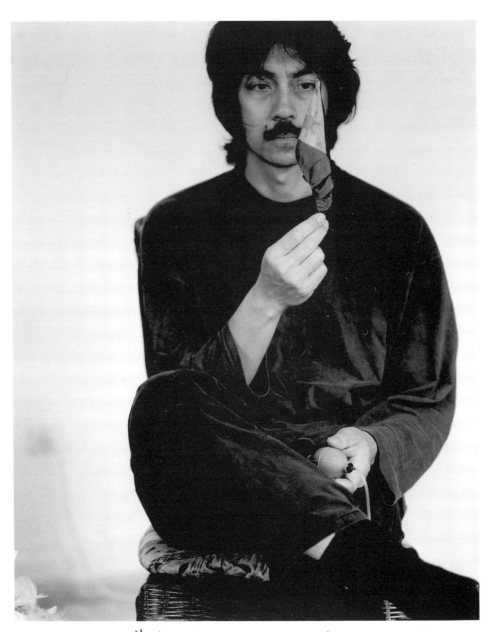

" HOME IS WHERE YOU ARE "
SELF-PORTRAIT

SALZBURG, 1995
GANOT

Scenes From the Play, *Dogeaters*

JESSICA HAGEDORN

Author's Notes

"Dogeater" is a pejorative term for the Filipino, which, according to my late Lola Tecla and other good sources, was coined by American soldiers during the Philippine-American War. *Dogeaters* became the painful title for my novel, which was published in 1990 and nominated for a National Book Award. It has since been translated into several languages and is happily still in print.

In 1997 I was persuaded by dramaturge Greg Gunter and director Michael Greif to adapt the novel into a play. We developed the script with a core group of actors (which included Alec Mapa, Jojo Gonzalez, Seth Gilliam, and Ching Valdes Aran) in several workshop settings, most notably at the Sundance Theatre Lab in Sundance, Utah. The play premiered at the La Jolla Playhouse in the fall of 1998. Michael Greif directed, Loy Arcenas designed the set, John Woo designed the media, Brandon Barone designed the costumes, lighting was by Ken Posner, and the soundtrack was created by Mark Bennett. An extraordinary cast of fifteen actors, many of them Filipino and Filipino American, brought *Dogeaters* to life. A successful New York production was presented by producer George C. Wolfe at the Joseph Papp Public Theatre in the 2000-2001 season. Director Michael Greif was once again on board, along with dramaturge Shirley Fishman, media designer John Woo, sound desginers Mark Bennett and Michael Creason, and costume designer Brandin Barone. This time, the set was designed by David Gallo and the lighting was by Michael Chybowski. Along with veterans from the Sundance workshop and La Jolla production, the remarkable New York cast featured Arthur Acuña, Hill Harper, Raul Arañas, Rona Figueroa, Kate Rigg, Eileen Rivera, Ralph Peña, Mia Katigbak, Jonathan Lopez, Christine Jugueta, Christopher Donohue and Philippine film star Joel Torre. The play's critical and popular reception, plus this amazing ensemble of actors, made the New York production a deeply rewarding and memorable experience.

The play shifts back and forth between two time frames 1959 and 1982. Like the novel, it tells a many-layered story of urban Philippines as seen through the eyes of its disparate and often desperate characters—from a privileged mestiza schoolgirl named Rio, who dreams of one day becoming a writer, to Joey, a junkie hustler from Tondo born from the union between a prostitute and an African-American soldier; from Andres, an Ermita drag queen who reinvents himself as "Pearl of the Orient," to Daisy Avila, an unhappy beauty queen who is the daughter of the doomed Sen. Domingo Avila; from a manipulative, weepy, and powerful First Lady named Imelda, to the praying woman named Leonor and her tormented torturer of a husband, Gen. Nicasio Ledesma.

The play was, and continues to be, a profound and visceral experience for me and especially for the Filipino actors involved in the production. The scenes excerpted here will hopefully give the reader a sense of the vast terrain and epic scope of *Dogeaters*. Humor and spiritual faith are key to survival in the often harsh and unforgiving landscape of both the play and the novel. Radio melodramas, corny jingles, bittersweet *kundiman*, class conflicts, rock 'n' roll music, and Hollywood movies all figure prominently in the story. Gossip, a.k.a. *tsismis*, provides ambience and narrative links.

The time: 1959 and 1982. The setting: primarily Manila, with a side trip to the Cordilleras toward the end of Act Two. America looms large. Family and tribal ties run deep.

ACT ONE, Scene Seven
GIRL TALK

TITLE PROJECTION: "Girl Talk"
(CORA CAMACHO'S TV talk show, featuring guest IMELDA MARCOS.)

CORA:

Alam ninyo, Madame, there are rumors circulating—
IMELDA:
There are always rumors circulating. (Theme Music/Transition)
CORA:
We are talking with our very, very special guest, the First Lady. Madame, there have been suggestions made that perhaps the best way to deal with the Daisy Avila scandal is to take away her title and crown. Give it to the runner-up...
IMELDA:
I wasn't aware there was a scandal. Are we talking about Senator Avila's daughter?
CORA:
(*puzzled*) Why, yes, M'am. Our new "Miss Philippines."
IMELDA:
A beautiful girl. *Talagang* "native beauty."
CORA:
Yes, M'am.
IMELDA:
You know, Cora, it's about time we Filipinos honor our own type of beauty. Like Miss Avila, for example. *Di ba?* In the past, we were always choosing 'yung mga mestiza types. Light skin, pointy noses. Tall... like me. *Pero ngayon*, we have Daisy Avila. Another type of beauty! Dark. Eloquent, like her father. Bookish, like her mother. Mysterious. (*beat*) She can't sing, she can't dance, but no matter. I hear she's really...

What was it Daisy did for the talent segment of the contest?

CORA:

Well, M'am. I thought you were there.

IMELDA:

Of course I was there. I never said I wasn't.

CORA:

I'm sorry, Madame. (*Imelda gives Cora a withering smile.*) If you... ah, remember... Miss Avila recited a long poem in Filipino and a short poem in English.

IMELDA:

Of course. She did a wonderful job. Wonderful! And I applaud our forward-thinking judges. Don't you, Cora? There's room *talaga* for all of us.

CORA:

Exactly. Anyway, about this scandal—

IMELDA:

I don't speak ill of my detractors, Cora. You know me. I'm a bona fide romantic. I believe in the positive elements of all human beings. I'm a proud Filipina—emotional, through and through. (*weeping softly*) Next to God and my husband, my country comes first. That's just the way I am—old-fashioned. When I was chosen "Miss Manila," I felt honored. I'm blessed to be beautiful. And why not? Beauty is a gift from God. But you know, Cora, these are different times. Hard times. Modern times. And we must be just. If Miss Avila wants to turn her back on her country, then that's her business.

CORA:

Do you think Senator Avila had anything to do with Daisy's decision to denounce the beauty contest?

IMELDA:

Certainly not.

CORA:

There are rumors circulating.

IMELDA:

There are always rumors circulating. This country runs on *tsismis*. And if I may quote from our good Senator Avila's prize-winning collection of essays, *The Suffering Filipino*: "*Tsismis* is a fact of life in Pilipino culture." Do you agree, Cora?

CORA:

I haven't read—

IMELDA:

Oh, you must! I'll have a copy sent to you immediately. Whatever our little disagreements with the good senator are, the President and I are big fans of his writing.

CORA:

But didn't you ban his books?

IMELDA:

(*sweetly*) Me? Of course not.

CORA:

Of course, I didn't mean you personally, Madame—

IMELDA:

I hope not.

CORA:

We seem to be running out of time. About these rumors—

IMELDA:

What rumors?

CORA:

That Daisy Avila is involved with the NPA—

IMELDA:

N. (*beat*) P. (*beat*) A. (*beat*) Ha! New People's Army, *daw*. "Nice People Around." You know, Cora. This is the kind of dirty *tsismis* that gives me goosebumps.

CORA:

Well, Madame, I—

IMELDA.

There are people. There are people. There are people... with such a... negative agenda, *talaga*. Their mission in life is to destroy what is so beautiful and true about our country. It breaks my heart—(*takes out handkerchief and dabs her eyes*)—and the President's, too, Cora—to listen to this... negativity. That's what the communist insurgents want, *di ba*? *Tsismis* to fly! Rumors to go around and around, breaking us down. (*sobbing in anguish*) Daisy Avila... has shamed me personally... and insulted our beloved country... Negative! Nervous! Zero! Breakdown! (Camera zooms in for a close-up of Cora Camacho looking alarmed.)

CORA:

And now... a word from our sponsor. (*Light change as they break TV transmission*)

Tsismis # 1

VOICE 1:

HOY, BRUJA! KUMUSTA? ANO ba? Long time no hear! What's the latest *balita*? Sit down, let's make *tsismis*. You want Sarsi or TruCola? Diet Coke, or Nescafe?

VOICE 2:

Dios ko 'day, it's too hot for coffee...

VOICE 1:

Aba bruja, what's the latest on Daisy Avila?

VOICE 2:

Naku! First she broke down crying and denounced the beauty pageant—

VOICE 1:

On "live" TV, pa!

VOICE 2:

Tapus, Daisy has *bangungot*—sleeping sickness, *daw*! PLUS she's having an affair *daw* with that NPA guy—*sino ba iyon*?

VOICE 1:

SANTOS. Santos Tirador.

VOICE 2:

Is he cute, *ba*?

VOICE 1:

Darling, Communists are always cute.

VOICE 2:

According to one of the maids in her house, Daisy Avila's *buntis*—

VOICE 1:

Buntis! Ay! What kind of a beauty queen is that, *ba*? Falling in love with communists, throwing away her crown—Crying-crying

VOICE 1 & 2:

Sleeping-sleeping

ACT ONE, Scene Nine
DAISY AVILA'S BEDROOM

TITLE PROJECTION:
"LOVE LETTERS EPISODE 275"
Manila, 1982

(*Theme music from radio soap opera. Sounds of a woman softly sobbing.*)
PONCIANO:

Please, Magdalena. Don't—

MAGDALENA:

Ponciano, what are we going to do? Rosalinda's our only child.

PONCIANO:

She's determined to go.

MAGDALENA:

(*sobbing harder*) To Manila? *Dios ko*! How can she do this, all by herself? We have no money, no way to help her... Ay Ponciano... please. I beg you, talk to her—

PONCIANO:

I've tried, Magdalena. (*sound of approaching footsteps*) Ay! Who's there?
[SENATOR AVILA enters, murmuring: Daisy... Daisy...]

ROSALINDA:

It's only me, Papa. (*beat*) Mama! Dear Mama. Are those tears I see, flowing from your eyes? What's wrong? (*AVILA turns down radio*)

* * *

(*Interior, Daisy Avila's bedroom. DAISY tosses and turns in her sleep. Senator Domingo AVILA enters.*)

AVILA:

(*gets coffee, approaches bed*) *Putang ina*. WAKE UP. I don't like this. Not at all, not at all. (*beat*) Daisy, I'm talking to you. You think it's your fault. Everything that happens to this country is somehow personally connected—I can't bear to see you like this. Goddammit, wake up! (*Daisy whimpers. The Senator goes to touch her, then stops himself.*) Your wise mother advised me not to wake you so abruptly. Let sleeping dogs lie. *Ay, anak.* "Miss Universe," "Miss World," "Miss Globe," "Miss—" Look at you... Daisy, Daisy. (*He shakes Daisy lightly. She struggles to open her eyes .*)

DAISY:

Santos. Is that you?

AVILA:

It's Papa.

DAISY:

Leave me alone. (*starts to drift off. Senator Avila forces her to sit back up in bed and shakes her again*) You're hurting me.

AVILA:

I'm sorry. I just don't want you falling asleep again.

DAISY:

Everything hurts.

AVILA:

Here. (*pours her a cup of coffee*) Strong and bitter, the way you like it. (*Daisy sips a little, then sinks back into the pillows.*) Don't shut your eyes. Come, get up. Off the bed.

DAISY:

No. (*Closing her eyes*) It's better if I sleep. (*He forces her to stand up and slowly walks her around the room.*)

AVILA:

You've been sleeping too much. Who's Santos? (*Daisy is silent.*) Were you referring to Santos Tirador?

DAISY:

Maybe.

AVILA:

Don't be coy with me, Daisy. He's a wanted man. If General Ledesma ever gets a hold of him—

DAISY:

General Goon. General Doom. General *Gago*. (*giggling*)

AVILA:

I wouldn't laugh about it, if I were you. He's your uncle.

DAISY:

(*contemptuous*) Maybe he's your bastard cousin, but he's not my fucking uncle. Is it Monday or Tuesday, *Biyernes o Sabado*?

AVILA:

Friday. It's Friday. How did you meet Santos? Did your cousin Clarita introduce you? You realize it isn't beneath him to exploit you—

DAISY.

By accident.

AVILA:

By accident? You met one of the most wanted members of the NPA by accident?

DAISY:

That's right. I met him at… a party. My "post-coronation" ball at Malacañang Palace. Don't you remember? He asked me to dance. We did the boogaloo, the hustle, the cha-cha—

AVILA:

Goddammit, Daisy.

DAISY:

(*sarcastic*) Don't worry. I've confronted Santos about our good name and all that.

He's a big fan of yours too, you know. (*beat*) Where's Mama? (*bitter*) I've disappointed and humiliated her by winning a stupid beauty contest. She wouldn't come to my coronation. She won't even come near my room. I just wanted to be frivolous for one goddamn moment... was that so awful? And where's Aurora?

AVILA:

Your mother's at work. Your sister's visiting your grandparents.

DAISY:

Liar! Mama doesn't teach on Fridays. And you sent Aurora away on purpose. (*softens*) Have I humiliated and disappointed you too? The press hounding me, the ugly rumors—

AVILA:

No.

DAISY:

You're a bad liar, Papa.

AVILA:

How bad?

DAISY:

Bad. You should learn how to lie better. Ask the President to teach you. (*beat*) How long have I been asleep?

AVILA:

168 hours.

DAISY:

I feel awful. (*starts to cry*) Make it stop. Once I start, I can't stop. A flood of tears. (*weeping*) Papa, please. My eyes feel like they're bleeding. Make the tears go away. Say something!

AVILA:

I can't.

DAISY:

Come on, Papa. Aren't you the great orator, the poet of politicians, the noble statesman? Remember when the family of nine was massacred by the military in Nueva Ecija. Little children, Papa. Two, three, four years old! Limbs hacked off, females raped and raped and raped and raped... The army went looking for "suspected communist insurgents" and got the wrong house. And remember when they took my classmate Rodel away? "Business as usual," Papa. Will I ever see Rodel again? I doubt it. Come on, you've got answers—

AVILA:

Daisy, please—

DAISY:

—I need an answer. What do I do? Which do I choose—lipstick, the rosary, or a gun? (*delirious*) Perhaps all of the above. Perhaps.

AVILA:

Forgive me.

DAISY:

Don't bore me with self pity. There's nothing to forgive.

AVILA:

Be careful. They're watching you.

DAISY:

Of course they are. They're watching you, too. God, let me sleep.

AVILA:

Rizal wrote: "The sleep had lasted for centuries. One day the thunderbolt struck, and in striking, infused life…" He was referring to our young nation, of course—

DAISY:

So what? Rizal can't help us now.

AVILA:

Don't despair, Daisy. There are many good people fighting back.

DAISY:

Like who… *you*? I see you out there at rallies and demonstrations, marching with your pious nuns and priests. Polite and orderly and… pathetic!

AVILA:

Don't do this to yourself. If I've failed you—

DAISY:

I'm scared shitless—

AVILA:

Your language has gotten so crude and democratic. I can't get used to it.

DAISY:

Scared shitless, Papa. Scared shitless and alone.

(*Senator AVILA takes his daughter's hand, in an attempt to comfort her. NESTOR and BARBARA appear at the microphone. Lights fade down as Nestor and Barbara lipsynch to the Platters' "Twilight Time."*)

ACT ONE, Scene Eleven
GOLF

TITLE PROJECTION:

The Monte Vista Golf & Country Club
Makati, Manila

(*The sound of a golf ball being hit. Lights up on Sen. Domingo AVILA, poised in a golf swing.*)

RIO:

Later that afternoon.

BARBARA:

The Monte Vista Golf & Country Club. With Senator Avila are army chief of staff Gen. Nicasio Ledesma; Ledesma's twenty-eight-year old protegé, Lt. Pepe Carreon; and tycoon Severo Alacran, dubbed "the king of coconuts." He's Boomboom's father, the richest man in the Philippines, richer than the President.

(*ROMEO ROSALES, Alacran's "personal waiter," hovers close by to attend to Alacran's needs. It is very bright and hot; everyone is sweating profusely.*)

ALACRAN:

Nice shot, Doming.

LEDESMA:

Very nice.

AVILA:

Ha. Probably landed in one of those damn man-made swamps of yours.

ALACRAN:

(*pleased*) How do you like my tricky golf course? Pretty challenging, *di ba*? Designed to drive the Japs crazy. "As good as, if not better than, Pebble Beach," according to *Golf Digest* and *Esquire*.

AVILA:

(*amused*) Daw.

ALACRAN:

Daw? I'm not joking, Doming. Don't you have last month's issue of *Esquire*?

AVILA:

Sorry. I don't subscribe.

LEDESMA:

Too busy making stirring speeches, I suppose.

AVILA:

(*smiling*) You might say that, Nicasio.

ALACRAN:

(*smoothly*) Well then, I'll have copies of both articles xeroxed for you. And if your ball truly landed in a swamp, we'll just have to send one of our "ditch boys" or maybe my waiter, Romeo here (*gestures*), to dive in there and retrieve it. (*beat*) And how is that lovely daughter of yours?

LEDESMA:

Our delicate beauty queen.

AVILA:

Daisy's fine, thank you.

ALACRAN:

I'm relieved to hear that.

LEDESMA:

(*crosses himself*) Me, too.

AVILA:

Are you? (*beat*) Things are running smoothly at your infamous Camp Meditation, I suppose?

LEDESMA:

Smoothly.

AVILA:

And everything's running just as smoothly at your "V.I.P." interrogation lounge?

LEDESMA:

I don't know what you're talking about.

AVILA:

We Filipinos are so witty, *di ba*? With our fondness for clever acronyms. "V.I.P.," I believe, stands for *Very Important Prisoners*.

CARREON:

Putang ina.

ALACRAN:

There's been a lot of troubling *tsismis* about your daughter recently—

LEDESMA:

Yes, very.

AVILA:

What sort of *tsismis*?

ALACRAN:

Political stuff. Your daughter's been accused of associating with NPA types. Can't be good for you, Doming—

AVILA:

What do you mean, Severo?

ALACRAN:

There you go, calling me Severo. How long have we known each other? Since right after the war... over thirty years... and you're still the only close associate who insists on calling me Severo. (*beat*) My friends call me Chuchi.

AVILA:

I'm aware of that.

ALACRAN:

Do you feel a certain hostility toward me?

AVILA:

Not at all. We're all here playing golf, aren't we? Partaking of your wit and gracious hospitality. I'm enjoying myself. As far as our fondness in this country for nicknames, I've come to believe it serves to infantilize us in the eyes of the world. How can I take you seriously if I run around freely addressing you as Chuchi or Baby... or General Nicky? (*The men all share a hearty laugh, except for Carreon.*)

CARREON:

Putang ina, talaga. I don't get it.

ALACRAN:

And you probably never will, young man. Senator Avila's right, of course. This country will never progress, if we keep acting like playful children.

AVILA:

Don't misinterpret me. One of the beautiful contradictions of our culture is this ability we have to laugh things off—

ALACRAN:

Yes, I know. I've read your latest editorial, "*Fatalism is fatal.*" We Filipinos are a complex nation of cynics, descendants of warring tribes which were baptized and colonized to death by Spaniards and Americans, a nation—"

AVILA:

(*interrupting*)—Betrayed and then united only by our hunger for glamor and Hollywood dreams.

LEDESMA:

(*groaning*) Oh, Doming, please. Get off your nationalist soapbox.

ALACRAN:

You paint such a negative image of our young nation, Domingo. There! You see? I've called you by your formal name.

AVILA:

I appreciate it.

ALACRAN:

Good, good. I'm sincerely sorry your books are now banned by our government. Even the President's lost his sense of humor—

AVILA:

You haven't.

ALACRAN:

I'm a sophisticated man, Domingo.

CARREON:

(*to Avila*) I've read your stuff, and I don't like it.

AVILA:

You're entitled to your opinion.

CARREON:

It's anti-Filipino, if you ask me.

AVILA:

I'm glad you read, at least.

CARREON:

The students are circulating your work illegally—

AVILA:

I don't mind.

CARREON:

It's against the law!

LEDESMA:

Okay, Pepe. Shut up and play.

CARREON:

I think I'll pass.

LEDESMA:

Nonsense. It's your turn. Play.

CARREON:

What's the point? I'm doing so badly.

LEDESMA:

Don't be an idiot. You've got to learn sometime.
(*Carreon swings at his ball and misses.*)

CARREON:

Putang ina.

ALACRAN:

Coño. It's the heat that's gotten to you. ROMEO! (*Romeo dabs Alacran's face gently with a towel.*) Don't worry, Carreon. Anytime you want, private lessons with our golf pros can be arranged.

LEDESMA:

Fuck that. Pepe's had all the lessons he needs. (*to Carreon*) Just hit the damn ball!

AVILA:

(*to Ledesma*) Really, Nicasio. Let's not get carried away.

LEDESMA:

(*realizing he's overstepped his bounds*) Chuchi, I didn't mean to—

343

ALACRAN:

Not at all.

LEDESMA:

I apologize—

(*With a strange smile, Alacran holds up his hand to stop the general from saying anymore*)

AVILA:

Perhaps it's this young man who could use an apology.

LEDESMA:

(*furious*) What?

AVILA:

Lieutenant Carreon. (*beat*) Your protegé.

LEDESMA:

(*to Avila*) Be careful what you say, cousin.

(*It's Severo Alacran's turn to take a long, beautiful swing. Everyone stops to watch, impressed. Alacran is pleased with himself.*)

CARREON:

(*startled by something he sees*) Putang ina!

(*The men peer in the direction Carreon is pointing.*)

ALACRAN:

(*mocking*) Was it a ghost or a beautiful woman, Carreon?

CARREON:

(*terrified*) A snake. A cobra. A small one, female probably, but a cobra just the same. Her hood's expanded, she's excited—

ALACRAN:

Sounds rather delicious and obscene. (*addresses ROMEO*) *Sige* Romeo, go get *Mang Berto*... (*Romeo exits*) My master snake-catcher will take care of it, gentlemen. (*to Carreon*) Do reptiles unnerve you, Carreon?

CARREON:

No. I was caught by surprise, that's all.

AVILA:

(*to Alacran*) You don't seem surprised. About the presence of so many poisonous snakes on your luxury golf course, I mean. *Tsismis* has it that you purposely don't exterminate them, to scare the Japs away—

ALACRAN:

Really, Domingo. Are you accusing me of being—what do the Americans call it—a racist? If you open your eyes and look around, you'll see how many Japanese guests and members are enjoying the club's... (*Romeo brings Alacran a drink*) *como se dice*? Amenities.

CARREON:

Too many damn Japs, if you ask me.

ALACRAN:

Well, no one did. And you're much too young to know anything about the war—

CARREON:

Yes, but my father—

ALACRAN:

I know your father. Fuck him. I survived the goddamn war with the Japs, and my first wife was tortured and killed. And so were my father and my younger brothers. My mother and I were the only ones who made it, and believe me—we made it with a vengeance. Don't bore me, Carreon. All the men here, even the lowliest caddy, have terrible dreams about the war. That's nothing special. (*beat*) You're a typical Filipino. You'll never be successful in business, because you take everything personally.

LEDESMA:

Are you saying all Filipinos are doomed to fail?

ALACRAN:

No. (*gestures toward Carreon*) Just him. (*Men share a laugh*)

CARREON:

I'm a soldier, not a businessman.

ALACRAN:

Then, *gago ka talaga*. The same thing applies to soldiers. (*to Avila and Ledesma*) In my old age, I'm hardly surprised by anything—least of all, snakes. We live in a jungle, after all.

LEDESMA:

Really, Chuchi. This is Manila. Not the rain forests of Mindanao—

ALACRAN:

Ay, Nicky. Your literalness never ceases to amaze me.

AVILA:

He's a military man.

CARREON:

What the fuck is that supposed to mean?

LEDESMA:

Pepe—

CARREON:

I'm sick of these insults! (*to Ledesma*) Why did you insist I join you today for this fucking... charade?

LEDESMA:

(*to Carreon*) Do I have to shoot you to shut you up?

ALACRAN:

Gentlemen, please. Perhaps it's time to head back to the clubhouse. We can all cool off and have a drink. Drinks and merienda to soothe the savage beast. (*Romeo exits*) Big night tonight, *di ba*? Madame's film festival and we're all expected.

AVILA:

I don't think she'll be expecting me.

CARREON:

(*to Ledesma*) I wasn't invited.

(*Mang Berto, brandishing a small sack, enters.*)

ALACRAN;

Ahh, success.

(*The dead snake is pulled out to show everyone; Carreon visibly recoils at the sight. The snake is put back into the sack. Mang Berto exits.*)

AVILA:

Very impressive.

ALACRAN:

He's a *mangkukulam*, you know. A shaman and healer. (*beat*) I've got my money, my religion, my Ivy League education, my father confessor, my high-strung wife, my pampered debutante of a daughter, my angry son, my movies, my soft drinks, my country club, my loyal servants, my obsequious staff, my private army, my coconut plantation, my mistress—

LEDESMA:

Mistresseses—

ALACRAN:

"sss," my Western physicians, my ninety-year-old mother, and above all, Mang Berto, my formidable—

AVILA:

—witch doctor.

ALACRAN:

Exactly. (*pulls out a tiny leather pouch hanging from a chain around his neck*) See this? Mang Berto's *anting-anting*. Dried baby octopus, garlic flowers, god knows what else...

AVILA:

I guess we all need something.

ALACRAN:

Exactly. It can't hurt to get your own *anting-anting*, gentlemen. (*to Ledesma*) To drive away evil spirits.

LEDESMA:

Exactly.

ALACRAN:

(*to Avila*) I'll ask Mang Berto to make a special *anting-anting* for you, Domingo.

AVILA:

No, thanks. I've already got one.

LEDESMA:

Do you?

AVILA:

You know I do, cousin. (*beat*) I have you.

Five Poems

LUIS H. FRANCIA

FOUR POEMS FROM *THE MANONG* * *CHRONICLES*

A Manong Meditates

Experience, that clever leveller, with
Its greedy mouth, ate the walls
One by one behind which I had hid.

I fall and know my
Place among the faceless
Know the numbness of my race

Often have I stood naked upon
An imaginary peak, surrounded
By decay, and felt, though I was
Brown, the overpowering sense
Of negritude,

Desolation, my keeper
Hostility, my bread.

But still as light as time was
Heavy, still moving in me, a
Voice small but musical
Singing and singing those green notes
As when I was a boy

Under a bright rainwashed
Sky of jasmine
Watching the earth daily turn

Into grace, watching the good
Things of every season hurling
Themselves against the dark, as
Stones at an overwhelming sea
That skipped long and along

Making of the waters one vast symphony

Where now is that boy's innocence
My exile's faith, nuclear
Large but in shards of beauty
In shapes of an apocalypse?
Where in a white world can
This grain of unhusked rice spin?

Must I always think of war
The raw element of it, the blood
The blows to the psyche?

* *manong*= older brother; old timer

America Is in the Heart
by Bencab
1987

But the song, however faint, hums
Along, and I resist, resurrect that
Boy's tune to catalogue in wonder
The beauty of our darkness

Our odors, our foods
Our violent tempers and gentle manners

Our delicate bones, our
Millennial colonial contradictions
The humanity of the subjugated but undefeated

These are the thoughts of a brown man
Indomitable in the season of aridity.

Blue in the Face

I can tell you I am a man
Of some weight and a certain
Past, a brown man

Until I am blue in the face

And I can tell you what I am
Not, not black nor red
Not yellow and not certainly
White

I can tell you all this is true
Until I am blue in the face

I can tell you
Only the moon speaks to me
Only the sun listens

I can tell you
Until I am blue in the face

Only pigeons coo over me
Rats whisper in my ear

Telling me to sing even more
I, a St. Francis manqué
My miracle
Is this, that I can
Turn blue in the face
While remaining brown

That I have survived
Cities running through
Corridas of my life
Seeing in me only
The red flag of race

I tell you all this and I am blue in the face

I can tell you I have hurtled
Through circuses of towns under
The big beautiful American
Tent, defying the whistles, the desire to see

This body in a shotgun marriage with dirt

With my panoply of flips, somersaults,
And heaven-blessed twists
No net below

An aerialist of uncommon grace

I can do this, a fly Filipino
From fly bar to fly bar as

My face turns blue

And you with your looking glass
Oh say can't you see
This man of certain weight
A certain past

A speck from the
Cold ground below and in
The Eye of Indifference above

This daily miracle
Of contradicting gravity
This brown man turning
Without wings until
Blue in the face

A Manong Complains, as the Star-Spangled Banner Is Played

Forget this corrupt, this routine
Hymn, where's the god in it?
The life I'm in escapes all
Melody, the dream curdled, damnation
In my heart
So with the cutting up
Inside, by the blades of common
Wisdom, by the munificence of
Men baptized in mayhem

So with the rat that struts in
His public chamber

So with the shouts that go
Up in the halls of stout menace

Padre, my spirit has been
Sterilized, my slate clean, my text
Jittery with purpose but
Unhallowed by spark.
Padre, I demand my god to be dark,
Squat, thick-lipped, bright with
Garlicky speech and
Full-fledged erection,
To infect my tongue with divine
Blasphemy that I can charm hibiscus
from my
Dead lover's hair far away and

Hear once again earth beneath me sing
Of how for sixty winters
In Californ' and Oregon
In the vales of Washington
I made love to her, made her
Hear me patiently and mother me
A lover forlorn,
She who can and does take all:
Seed, sorrow, the song of lament
And murderous thought

When my dark god comes
When the sea spills out of the sky
I'll be on a mountain of skulls
Of those who christianized me
Who english'd me
Who split my speech and fed me
The foul meat of false promise

When the deluge comes I will
See your white faces
A grin of horror before you
Go under
And I'll sail by in my bamboo ark

Dropping jasmine petals in
Your wake
Two by two
Two by two

Walls

I know about laws
How well they set up walls

Do's in a small room
Don'ts in a labyrinth of huge halls

I know about
Official trust
How they apportion it
Like chunks of bad
Meat for the hungry

I know all about the smooth
Wall in the law
Difficult to see

But I keep bumping
Against it

How it hides what's true
By telling me I'm a
Swell fella
Filipino brother
(no you're no bother at all)
But it's the other way
Around

I know its surfaces
Very well

How when you try to
Climb it you
Find you've
Fallen farther

Than before

AGATONA OF ARINGAY, HENRY OF PHILADELPHIA

I

In Havana his orphan's grief
Had found rhum.
By Manila they had become chums
As he pondered the varieties of
Water the islands held.

His iris was green, and he
Was Irish and young
When for war
This forlorn four-leaf lover in the clover
Crossed an ocean a long time ago
Seeking the rebel assimilable.

Sent north to the Ilokos
To shoot the damn *insurrectos*
What *Lolo* found instead was *Lola*.
Battle enough.

Upcountry perhaps the
Only gun he fired was in bed.
He almost didn't live to talk about it.
She did.

Such were the perils of love.
This schoolmistress of strict sense
Riding him as she rode her horse
Found in his new tongue
The pleasures of masculine speech.

Whoa, Henry of Philly said, I thought
You would be my filly.
Monsieur, she replied, I may be a
Jeune fils and you can take me
But never for a fool.

And remember, my fine Philadelphia
Fellow, putting her hand on his gun,
Trust in God but
Never forsake your revolver.

Comprende, Señor mi amor?
A dumbfounded *si* issued forth.
To the world, her pupil brown
Looked to have bowed before
His emerald eye, looked to have
Dropped her books to

Set up house, but this
Green text she took to school
Polishing his life's syntax
The rough grammar of a Yankee soul.

Henry of Philadelphia
Devoured her country as
Hungrily as she devoured him.
In a mimesis of stars

He and Agatona
Formed a miniconstellation
Of girls, Alice and Josephine,
Fair of cheek but
Filipino to the bone.

Every season wet or dry
Henry grew tropical
a lizard in thatch,
Conjugal in his taste for green
Mango and *bagoong*,
Basi and pork rind.

Agatona swayed to Iberian
Fandangos, to Ilokano love songs, though
She grew puzzled at swing,
Exclaiming, what is this thing?

Oh Henry of Philadelphia,
You who rumbled in
Cuba and Cagayan
Did you in
Your wildest dreams imagine
A lizard life or wife?

Did you on the torrid plains of
Luzon, or in the Visayan jungles
Aim your rifle or worse to
Civilize an Indio Bravo?
Were you, civilizer, civilized?
When you shared Agatona's bed
Did you think yourself
Master of the land?

Oh Agatona of Aringay,
Mi abuela, *aking lola*, did you dream in
Chinese, in Spanish confess,
Murmuring love in English and Ilokano?
Did you see the tall West
Entering your doors?
Was your ache that of an archipelago?
In your head was there the buzz
Of the native dead?
Did their voices linger on in the courtyard
And garden of your Aringay house?
When Henry uttered sweet nothings,
Did you hear echoes of war?

II

This late February morning
The past melts,
A blink in the world's eye.
Yet I will not discard it
This war of long time ago
For all the dead and the living both
Bless and curse my blood.

The sun shines at its
Fiercest and brightest.

My grandson's love for them
Raises my sight
But this war of long time ago
   I cannot not remember
Not while I espy my invisibles
Nor while this earth cleaves
   To my feet

In the wild stretch of ocean, on
The unruly voyage between two
Shores, where shall I place my belonging?
What degree longitude will determine
The heart's spin, what latitude to lay
My head in?

A sea of questions breaks upon me.

Not while a country of no history spurns
Lives lost, of a million
Brown men and women
Alive but for the greed
   for their ancestral ground

Look up, urges Lolo
Look up, advises Lola

High over my path gleams

The host of a sun raised by
An invisible shaman. Far above the

Not while this heart rages
And my mouth tastes the
Metal of hard lament

Nor while this hand continues to write
And memory marks me,
Mirror and amanuensis.

Isle of Manhattan
(Look up look up!
They cry)
How suspended between
East and West

February 4, 1999

Lolo = Grandfather	*bagoong* = shrimp paste
Lola = Grandmother	*basi* = palm wine
Ilokano = a Philippine language	*mi abuela* = my grandmother
Insurrectos = rebels	*aking* = my

Dust Memories

DIONISIO VELASCO

PLAYWRIGHT'S NOTE:

Dust Memories was originally conceived as a one-act play. The piece was developed with performance poetry in mind. Thus it was first staged with one player/actor alternately performing the two monologues. It was subsequently performed with two actors in a staged reading for the Ma-Yi Theater group.

Churning surf rock guitar music. Lights up on bare college dorm room, the only furniture a chair and two tall stacks of books on top of which is a Super-8 movie projector. At rear stage on the wall is a wrinkled white bedsheet which serves as a makeshift projection screen. A Filipino-American student, twenty-one years old, wearing a rumpled, untucked light blue Oxford shirt, chino pants and back-flipped baseball cap, remembers a road trip he once made to Agbayani Village in central California to visit the elderly men who live there: retired Filipino migrant farmworkers. Propelled by the music, Fil-Am jump-starts into the monologue.

FIL-AM: White line highway, black tar shimmering, verdant valley, cow peniteniary, straight down California Interstate 5 from San Francisco past Fresno. Into the heart of the San Joaquin Valley, four cars filled with Filipino-American students from Berkeley and San Francisco State University, about two dozen of us, plowing into Delano, California, rolling into history. Doing eighty down I-5, 100 degrees outside and dry, no wind. The road cuts straight through, on one side desolate scattered brush and dust, on the other fertile green farm fields. Whooooo-oooooo-woooooo, careening down that freeway, four cars with the windows open wide 'cause we're young and brown and we wanna know who we are.

> *Reverie music drones, ambient noise. Fil-Am mimes a farmer walking a carabao through a rice field.*
> Carabao caravan tromping in the mud,
> Carabao caravan knowledge in the blood.
> Tromp tromp, tromp tromp.
> Carabao caravan rolling down the highway.
> *As in a reverie.*

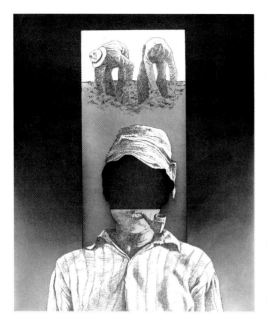

Pinoy Worker Abroad
by Bencab
1975

FIL-AM: I'm five. The sun is strong. Our land is wide. Gently, father flips the rope across the carabao's back. The two of them plod slowly across the field, the plow blade cleaving the rich soil as they move. Father teaches me that our carabao is family to us. I see him cooing in the carabao's ear, whispering to it like a lover. I see him caress the carabao's nape, bloodied by the yoke, caked with dried mud. I see the heat rising from the carabao's back, flaring my father's nostrils as he moves with the carabao.

Exuberant, naive and scampering about the stage, Fil-Am unloads Super-8 camera equipment and sets up the tripod.

The first film footage that I ever shot in my life was at Agbayani Village in Delano, California. The *manongs*—or oldtimers, like they're fond of calling themselves—live here in the middle of nowhere. They're brown Filipinos like us. *Manong* Frankie, *Manong* Berto, *Manong* Allos, their names roll off the tongue like the sweat that poured from the faces of the farmworkers. We've come to record their oral histories.

I go around in their neatly cramped rooms and take their images on Super-8 film. Meanwhile the other Filipino-American students dart about, in and out of different rooms, trying to interrogate the *manongs*, getting their stories down with cassette tape recorders. It never occurs to me until later—much much later perhaps, when I already have a more firm grasp on the technical side of filmmaking—it never occurs to me that their voices and their images may not *match*, may not be in sync.

Manong sad
Manong strong
Manong eager to sing us your songs
Manong anxious for us to know who we are.

I set up a shot with my movie camera. Wide shot: a group of *manong* at the dining hall table. They all sit there facing the camera, posing stock still as if I'm taking a photograph. Um excuse me, this is a movie camera. I'm making a moving image, a moving *document*. *Po. Po* is a sign of respect. Ha! Who am I to laugh? This is the first time that I've ever used a movie camera. But for me the important thing is the truth, and getting it down on film. So then I have the film processed.

He flicks on projector and sits in front of screen to view his footage. On the screen we see a grainy black and white film image, poorly defined. He approaches screen, touching it, addressing it.

I've failed: the faces are dark, all you see is a collective silhouette, forms without detail or a definite shape. I look at this and it tells me nothing. I see nothing.

He slaps his forehead with the palm of his hand, as if he's forgotten something.

There's this hole in my head. A *maya* bird must have pecked a hole there. Memories fly out—and there's no net to hold them. I try to remember. I try to re-member an ancient self…. *Taga-ilog ako.* I'm from the river… the river people. Tagalog. What of this river that runs in my veins?

Melancholy flute music. Fil-Am walks off right. Onscreen we see film images of **manong** *in close-up, talking, their lips moving, but we do not hear their words. Flute music segues into steamship foghorn, as film images continue.*

Manong *enters wearing a three-piece suit and a straw hat, clutching to his breast a* **bayong** *that holds all his belongings. He steps up on a chair and looks left and right at his new surroundings. He begins his monologue in halting English with a thick provincial accent.*

MANONG: I arrive in America on 16 June 1929 aboard the steamship *President Madison*. I'm sixteen years old. I've promised my father that I will continue my education in America. My education in America… like the one I had in grade school in Ternate. Oh those bright-eyed, brown-haired American teachers who we all fell in love with. They teach us to read English, they teach us to write English, they teach us to speak English. From George Washington we learn truth; from Thomas Jefferson we learn democracy; from Abraham Lincoln freedom.
I arrive in America aboard the steamship *President Madison*.

He jumps off chair. Wide-eyed, wistful.

Ama, I want to continue to learn in America. I want to fall in love with brown-haired American teachers. I want to become president of the greatest nation in the world.

Takes off vest and places it in **bayong**. *He mimes the movements of row farming. The tone of his monologue shifts from a monotone rhythmic cadence to one of seething anger. Flings farming tool to the ground, cursing in Ilokano dialect.*

I never did get that American education. Instead I pick prunes in Gilroy, harvest onion flowers in Coyote, pick tomatoes, lettuce, I learn to cut asparagus and top sugar beets. Up at four in the morning, out in the field by five. Morning chill. Soft sunlight. Promised land. All day long we bend and stoop, bend and stoop, ten hours a day bending, stooping and hauling, bowing to the earth until dusk. Break your back, knees ache, arms ache, legs ache. Carabao caravan tromp tromp tromp. Itchy dust and sweat. Choking with dust, eyes burning with dust, bending and stooping, bowing to the earth until dusk. Four score and seven years ago our forefathers brought forth this… *ukinam*!

He trails off in his emotionless recitation of Lincoln's Gettysburg Address.
Sound fx: oncoming train. He sizes up train, preparing to jump; he leaps.

We ride freight trains between jobs in the fields, sleeping in boxcars and dreaming of home. Loco-motive, loco-motive, loco-motive. Riding the rails from one labor camp to the next, breathing the cold night air, drinking wine with hoboes, howling at the moon, ah-ooooooooo, landscapes blurring, farm fields receding, bright cities approaching, remembering the hills of home and the sound of our language...

Lost in reverie, he hums a kundiman.

I run across the fields at night to join the other men gathered around the nipa hut. We lift the grass roof onto our shoulders. Then we place the rafters on long bamboo posts. We have our house on our shoulders. We're stripped to the waist, our cotton trousers rolled up to the thighs. Women come with earthen jars, hauling drinking water, pausing in the clear moonlight to watch us with secret joy. Together we march through the field, carrying the family house to a new village... Locomotive. Loco-motive. But can you carry a home on your back when you cross an ocean to another land, a strange country. *Nay? Tay?* Rosa...

Now singing the kundiman, manong *walks off right.* Kundiman *music up. Images of* manongs *again appear on screen. Fil-Am walks in and sits on chair looking at images on screen.*

FIL-AM: *Lola* shows me a sepia photograph of a young Filipino woman standing next to a small boy. *Lola, sino ba siya?* Who is she? *Naku,* says *Lola,* you forgot already. You don't remember your *yaya?* She used to look after you before you went to the States.

I dream. That I'm walking next to a woman, along a narrow winding ridge, on the steps of a mountain rice terrace. Slowly we walk along the ridge. She's brown. Smooth brown skin and fully pregnant. But she's old already, as ancient as the rice terraces, her hair long and white, lines etched above her forehead and around her eyes, but her eyes, her eyes are young, radiant and black. She holds her round belly gently as we walk and we are silent and calm. I don't see myself in the dream, yet I am the seer who dreams her like this, already ancient, forever young.

He turns off movie projector and faces audience.

Growing up in America I never learn to speak Tagalog. But I *understand* it—that's what all the Flips in America say, I don't speak but I can understand it. When our parents address us they speak to us in English; they converse with *each other* in Tagalog. Tagalog becomes lodged in my subconscious, but never a part of my speech. Incredibly, my own language is strange to my tongue, removed, yet somehow so *familiar.*

So in college I major in English.

When I hang out with other Filipino students, they speak Tagalog in lively discussions. I look around at their faces, out of it. I'm breathless trying to keep up with them.

Soon I'm alone.

Turns on projector and moves toward screen, then faces audience. Images on screen: snapshots of Filipino immigrants in America.

Gook: Webster's definition—a native usually belonging to a brown or yellow race. Etymology, "origin unknown." American soldiers referred to Filipino people as "goo-goo" or "gook" during the Philippine-American War. That's what they called the Vietnamese: Gook. Fucking gooks. Kill the fucking gooks. You know, like those Oliver Stone movies. Good ole Ollie Stone making all these Oscar-winning Vietnam movies, but he shoots them in the Philippines. How many people out there know that the Philippine-American War was the first Vietnam? The first American war of conquest.

Goo-goo, gook. In Spanish *gago* is one who stutters. In Tagalog *gago* is stuttering, or a fool, a stupid person. In English *gaga* is crazy, infatuated. *Gaga. Gago.* Crazy, stuttering fool. Gaga-goo-goo. Baby talk. Goo-goo, gook.

Manong Felix speaks about the oldtimer *Pinoys* who were ashamed of younger Filipinos who spoke Filipino dialects in public. (*Parodies* Manong *Felix's voice*) People might want to know what you are saying. These younger Filipinos they speak Ilokano or Tagalog in restaurants. But we oldtimers, when we are in the public we are talking in English, regardless of how bad we talk. So people won't say, "Hey, you are in America now, why don't you talk English. You don't like this country you go back where you belong."

Mother, were you protecting us from insults and ridicule when you chose not to speak to us in Tagalog? Did you want us to become good little English-speaking coconut Americans? Mother, my head may be confused but my blood knows its course.

Parodies his mother's voice.

Becos I dont know to you
Becos you dont talk back to your parents
Becos why dont you ask your pader
BECOS I DONT KNOW TO YOU

Walks off right. Dancehall music. Manong enters complete in a three-piece suit and hat: slick dude. Dances with imaginary "blondie" much taller than he. Plays to movie screen.

MANONG: Maybe in one month I can save five dollars, the next month maybe seven dollars: soon I have enough for a suit. The best tailor is from McIntosh of Hollywood. He comes to our camp in the farm. That's my trademark—McIntosh. We dress up—me and my best partner, Fermin—to go dancing with blondie in the taxi dance hall. Fermin is just too quiet. It's all he likes to think about is his *Pinay* sweetheart he left back in the island of Cebu. He's just too quiet, that Fermin, and too timid to the American girl. But he always accompany me anyway to the dancehall every weekend. You buy a roll of tickets. Each ticket costs ten cents and for every minute dancing with blondie you pay one ticket. In ten minutes no more tickets, so I buy more and more tickets. Blondie is too tall to me, but I don't care. Fermin just like to watch, and sometimes he goes home himself early.

A mob of white men come, hundreds, many high school boys. Outside the dance hall they shout, "Keep your hands off our women!" "Go home, brown goo-goo monkeys!" They're jealous becos we dance with American women. They shoot their guns in the air, but the police make them leave. Later in the night the mob come to our camp. They break the windows. Burn the bunkhouse. The Pinoys run from the fire, and the white men catch them, kick them, beat them, smash them with clubs. We all run into the fields to wait and hide. "Goo-goo monkey! Go home!" Finally it's quiet. *'Tang ina, mga puti. Tarantado talaga sila.* The few of us return to our bunkhouse, still afraid. I open the door to the closet and find my partner Fermin there trying to hide. But he's dead already. The bullet shot him straight to the heart. Just like that.

Music. Takes off hat, squats and delivers eulogy to Fermin in Ilokano, then cursing obscenely through his teeth. Walks off right. Film images: group of brown pinoys *on beach surrounding a lone blondie in bathing suit. Fil-Am enters, caresses screen.*

FIL-AM: The *manong* are grateful for our visit.

When we leave Agbayani Village, they ask me and the other students, How come you visit us only now?

Will you visit us again?

When will you show us your movie?

Manong Felix told me about the time when Filipinos were not allowed to associate with white women. It would get kind of lonely. At night in the bunkhouse they would sing their favorite songs and ask each other to dance.

He alternates between Manong's voice and Fil-Am's voice, dancing with himself.

MANONG: Do you know how to dance, boy?

FIL-AM: Who me? No!

MANONG: It's very easy, you just follow my steps.

FIL-AM: Can we please sit down?!

MANONG: Oh no no, I spent my whole day's earnings on these dance tickets. We're going to dance all night.

They dance as one. Takes off hat, switches on projector. Left profile to audience. Film image: manong *and rooster. Music up:* Stardust Memories. *He bows in profile with hat off, his shadow bowing to the* manong *onscreen. Curtain.*

FIRST SHOT IN
FILIPINO-AMERICAN WAR
HERE, AT 9:00 O'CLOCK IN THE
EVENING OF FEBRUARY 4TH,
1899, PRIVATE WILLIAM GRAYSON
OF THE FIRST NEBRASKA
VOLUNTEERS FIRED THE SHOT
THAT STARTED THE FILIPINO-
AMERICAN WAR.

1941

WW2
STAR WAR

The Past Meets the Present

ALFRREDO NAVARRO SALANGA

20 February [1899]

The American forces capture the town of Manduriao in Iloilo after a heroic resistance by Filipino troops under the command of Gen. Martin Delgado.

The North
never had
monopoly
of heroes.

All of
our islands
are equally
blessed.

Northern
or southern
moon — both
have the
same blankets
to show.

The same
sky opens
itself as
one face
to all
who look
up to it
in prayer
and supplication.

All smoke
rises in
the same
direction
and we
are all
capable
of the same
sacrifice.

The men
of Manduriao
will have
the same
heaven.

Parricides, Bastards, and Counterrevolution: Reflections on the Philippine Centennial

VICENTE L. RAFAEL

The task of this essay is to address the celebrations surrounding the Philippine Centennial. My interest lies in inquiring after the triumphalist tenor and progressivist narrative that have characterized official commemorations, calling attention to the historical contradictions that are constitutive of, yet are excluded from or cannot be accounted by, such celebrations. I then ask about the possibility for alternative modes of marking the historicity of the Philippine Revolution and its counterrevolutionary aftermath among Filipinos in the Philippines and Filipino Americans in the United States today. We might begin by asking the following questions: One, what exactly is the event or series of events that the Centennial is commemorating? Two, how is it that these events have come to take on such importance in the history of the Philippines? And three, to whom have such events become so important, and why?

At the outset, the answers to these questions seem obvious. One, the Centennial commemorates the birth of the Philippine nation beginning with the revolution of August 1896 and culminating in the declaration of independence on 12 June 1898. Two, that such events draw their significance from the fact that they mark the end of Spanish colonial rule and the beginning of Filipino nationhood; they therefore have made it possible for Ilocanos, Cebuanos, Tagalogs, Muslims, Igorots, Bicolanos, and even Chinese mestizos to take on a common identity: as "Filipinos" over and above their local identities. More recently, the commemoration of the events of 1896-1898 have been used to assert an underlying "Filipino-ness" connecting overseas Filipinos all over the world. And three, the Centennial matters most to all those who have a stake in the Philippines and in being "Filipino," since without 1896-1898, there would be no Filipino people as such, no nation, no "us," but only a disparate collection of ethnolinguistic groups.[1]

The Centennial as it has been officially constructed is meant to remind us of this essential unity amid our diversity. It bases this unity on the notion of a common history of revolution and independence that begins at the end of Spanish colonial rule and continues through the American colonial regime, the Japanese military occupation, all the way to the present. The years 1896-1898 then signify a radical break with the Spanish past, followed by the unfolding of a straight path into a future to which our present, whoever and wherever we are, irrevocably belongs.

These are in some ways odd notions. By locating the origins of the Filipino nation in revolution, they assert that the nation is founded on catastrophe: the violent struggle to wrench free of colonial control. How can revolution in all its disorderliness serve as a basis for order? How can the mass mobilization and displacement of men and women, the bloody exchanges between enemies, and the production of death characteristic of war come to be commemorated as the beginning of a stable identity, a peaceful nation, and the improvement of life in the country? How is it possible for terror to lie at the basis of sovereignty? The historian Reynaldo Ileto has written that unlike other Southeast Asian countries, the Philippines never had a classical precolonial civilization that it could look back to: no Angkor Wat or Borubudur, no great seaport like Malacca or Prambanan.[2] At the most, Muslim principalities existed that had considerable commerce with parts of island and mainland Southeast Asia and China, but no classical civilizations or extensive empires celebrated in *hikayats* or other epical forms. Indeed, the first monumental architecture in the Philippines was the Catholic church built by Chinese and *indio* workmen for the benefit of Spanish colonial missionaries and their converts.

In the face of this absence of a classical precolonial order that could be invoked as a symbol of national unity, the Philippine nation-state has instead looked to the Revolution of 1896 and the revolutionary government of 1898 for the origins of nationhood. Unable to find in the precolonial past a suitable source for establishing the archaic and therefore timeless stretch of the Filipino nation, nationalist historiography has instead looked to the moment of rupture from Spanish colonialism as the ground zero of its historical becoming. Such an assumption has remarkable implications. It means that the Filipino nation did not emerge as the return of a glorious past that had been repressed by an alien invasion. Instead, it was precisely the coming of outside forces that allowed for its genesis. Put in the starkest terms: without colonialism, there would have been nothing to break from. For this reason, there would not have been a revolution, and therefore no revolutionary government, and no Filipino people. Filipino nationalism strangely enough owes its emergence to the very thing it sought to reject. It is not too far-fetched to say that colonialism was the forebearer of nationalism in the Philippines. At the same time, nationalism has sought to do two rather contradictory things: it has sought to acknowledge its historical debt to colonialism—to Spanish Catholicism, for example—even as it has tried to disavow such connections. When Centennial celebrations such as those sponsored by the Philippine state under President Fidel Ramos and his successor, Joseph Estrada, commemorate the revolution and the revolutionary government, it is also implicitly and with absolutely no irony celebrating the colonialism that made these possible.[3]

How can this be? Isn't the Centennial, according to various pronouncements by public officials, community leaders, and designated academics, about the celebration of one hundred years of Philippine independence? Isn't it supposed to remind us that we have been a free and sovereign people even in the face of repeated attempts at colonization by other alien forces? And that what joins us together as Filipinos is precisely this history of struggle against those alien forces that would impose their will on us, exploiting our labor, if not our goodwill? Indeed, even if we have not been politically free these last hundred years, have we not always sought freedom, whether through armed resistance, immigration, or legislative battles? This desire for independence that is now a century old—isn't this what makes us Filipinos whoever and wherever we are, joining us in spirit even if our bodies and body politic remain captive to imperialist avatars such as the World Bank, the International Monetary Fund, American and Japanese multinational corporations, Arab or Singaporean employers, or the structures of racism, sexism, homophobia, and so forth? If so, then how is it possible to think of Filipino nationalism, one that is grounded in the desire for freedom now a century old, to be at the same time indebted to the legacy of colonialism, the very system of unfreedom that it has set itself against?[4] What is this revolution and the revolutionary government that we celebrate that is also at the same time the seizure—in the double sense of cessation and appropriation—of colonial structures and colonial logics? Is it also the case that what we celebrate is the counter-revolution that shadowed and eventually came to overwhelm the revolution in the form of the revolutionary government and the American colonial regime which followed it?

To understand this weird relationship between revolution and counterrevolution, and between nationalism and colonialism, it is necessary to return to the questions I posed at the beginning of this essay. The answers which I originally gave and which seemed so obvious are in fact only partially true. In the first place, they give us the impression that the history of Filipino nationhood occurred as one continuous process, progressing from the death of the old Spanish colonial regime and the birth of the new Filipino nation, maturing through the twentieth century to the point where we now have Filipinos in charge of their own destiny in the Philippines, and Filipinos capable of participating as full citizens in the United States. One sees this particular kind of story being told in such disparate places as the parades at Luneta on Independence Day, to the exhibit of Filipinos in Hawaii at the Bishop Museum.[5] It is a predictable and conventional story of a people once oppressed coming into their own and triumphing over adversity, achieving recognition from and equality with those who had formerly been above them, while at the same time maintaining what is distinctive about them, their "cultural heritage." Yet, it is precisely in its smooth predictability that this story is suspect. Some things have been left out. What might these be?

First, there is the complicated political history of the revolution itself. Despite the various arguments in the historiography of the revolution, we can be reasonably clear about the trajectory of certain events. Late-nineteenth-century Filipino nationalism began as a politics of assimilation among an emergent and overwhelmingly male, racially mixed bourgeoisie who were the direct beneficiaries of a long process of agricultural commercialization, on the one hand, and reforms in higher education, on the other, throughout the nineteenth century. They organized mostly in Spain where it was possible to speak out without fear of imprisonment and death, seeking reforms that would grant Filipinos equal rights with Spaniards and mitigate the undue influence of the Spanish friar orders on the colony. We also know that this politics of assimilation floundered, though it never disappeared, existing side by side (and often within the same person) with a politics of separation seeking to extricate the Philippines from Spain. Led by members of the petit bourgeois—small merchants, government clerks, school teachers, and provincial elites—this separatist movement could at the same time draw on the support of the lower classes. However, the possibility of broadening what began as a political revolution aimed at replacing Spanish authorities, into a social revolution that would radically alter social relations of property and propriety, was quickly compromised and repressed.[6]

As early as March 1897, barely eight months into the revolution, elections were held in Tejeros in Cavite, the site of the most stunning revolutionary successes. Called by Emilio Aguinaldo and his Magdalo faction, the elections were meant to subsume the secret society that had started the revolution, the Katipunan, into a revolutionary government that would coordinate and centralize the revolutionary forces. Scholars concur that these elections were most likely rigged, designed to marginalize Andres Bonifacio, then acknowledged as the Supremo and the "father" of the revolution, in favor of a local provincial leader who had been Bonifacio's follower, who had in fact been initiated into the Katipunan secret society by the Supremo himself, none other than Emilio Aguinaldo. When Bonifacio refused to accept this lower place given to him, he proceeded to conspire and plan a coup against the newly formed government. Humiliated by those who he thought should have been beholden to him, Bonifacio began to plot his revenge. Getting wind of this conspiracy, Aguinaldo ordered the arrest of Bonifacio, but not before Aguinaldo's followers started a rumor campaign against Bonifacio. They spread rumors that the Supremo was a heretic, that he was an agent of the Spanish friars and a spy of the Spanish government, that he was a thief who had stolen the Katipunan's funds, and that he had designs of installing himself as King of the Tagalogs, turning the country into an absolutist monarchy. That Bonifacio was, in short, a counterrevolutionary.

Tried in the court of public opinion, Bonifacio would in time be found guilty in the court of Aguinaldo's revolutionary government. Along with his brother Procopio, Bonifacio was arrested and, after a mock trial, executed in May of 1897 just as Spanish reinforcements were beginning to press on to Cavite. His wife, Gregoria de Jesus, was tied to a tree and sexually molested by soldiers who had arrested the brothers; later on, when she sought to find her husband, she was lied to so that she wandered about the mountains of Cavite vainly searching for his remains until, as she says in her memoirs, her feet became a bloody mess and her clothes were so filthy she could barely take them off and then had to burn them. The bodies of the Bonifacios were never found and to this day, no one is certain where exactly they died. Hence there is not even a proper grave to mark their death. Their controversial deaths, which partisans of Bonifacio have called murders and those of Aguinaldo have referred to as a necessity, arguably mark the beginning of the end of the revolution.[7]

The history of the revolution thus begins with the circulation and transmission of a message within the Tagalog regions. The message had come down from the first generation of nationalists like José Rizal and Marcelo H. del Pilar, traveled between the Philippines and Spain to people like Bonifacio and Aguinaldo, and after 1897 spread to non-Tagalog regions. As we read through the literature of the nationalist movement, this message in effect was about *la Patria*, in this case Mother Spain and the Spanish fathers, especially the friars who refused to listen to the demands of those below, their Filipino "sons and daughters." Instead of the solicitous attention that parents were supposed to give their children, nationalist writers criticized colonial authorities for responding to the pleas of their colonized subjects with the violent language of mockery, racial epithets, arrests, torture, exile, and executions. *La Madre Patria* and *los padres españoles* were thus guilty of abusing *los hijos y las hijas de las Filipinas*. In response, the latter formed secret societies loosely modeled on Masonic lodges from Europe, giving them such provocative names as Revolucion, Solidaridad and Nilad, where they began to plot and conspire, crafting a different kind of message to send back to the colonial fathers. It would be a message that would seek to match the force of Spanish response, hence a message of separation and revenge.

As if assuming the roles of nationalist protagonists in José Rizal's great novels, *Noli me tangere* (1887) and *El Filibusterismo* (1891),[8] Filipino nationalists came to see themselves as deprived of la Patria's care and affection, driven to secrecy, hiding and exile, condemned without a future by los padres and the colonial state. Again taking their lead from Rizal's short-lived La Liga Filipina or Filipino League, which was meant to organize prominent Filipinos into lodges that would serve as sites for preparing them for independence, los hijos y las hijas de Filipinas formed the Katipunan, which of course is the shortened version of the name of the revolutionary organization, Kataastaasan Kagalanggalangan Katipunan ng mga Anak ng Bayan, that is, the Most Noble and Respected Union of the Sons and Daughters of the Country. And as sons and daughters of the country, they sought to recruit other members through secret meetings and to arm themselves against the colonial fathers, first by devising secret codes in Tagalog to elude surveillance, then by fashioning weapons out of bamboo and arranging without much success to buy arms from Japan. Pledging to fight to the death, Katipuneros also steeled themselves to kill before they were killed.

In this sense, we can think of Bonifacio the "Supremo" as the first son of the Katipunan. He became the "father" of the revolution by virtue of his willingness to kill Spanish fathers. His name, like that of other Katipuneros, became associated among Spaniards with nothing short of parricide. Small wonder then that Spanish accounts of the revolution invariably accuse Filipinos of showing the most unpardonable ingratitude.[9] Spaniards became hysterical when they discovered the paraphernalia of the Katipunan secret society which included, among other things, a masonic-like apron that depicted two hands, one clutching the dismembered head of a bearded Spaniard, the other the bloody knife that had cut that head apart.[10] Spanish hysteria fed further rumors that the Katipunan had been planning a race war designed to annihilate all the Europeans in the colony. How could they turn against those that had brought them civilization and led them to the light of Christian salvation, Spanish writers wondered. How could they be so ungrateful as to strike the very hand that fed them and cared for them? How could native sons and daughters dare to usurp the place of the Spanish father, cutting his head and seeking to separate themselves from the mother?

For indeed the revolution was conceived in the writings of both Spaniards and Filipinos in the most intimate of terms: as a family romance gone awry. To the Spaniards, Filipinos were ungrateful children whose demands for separation meant only one thing: the murder of all Spaniards. The Filipinos, as evidenced in nationalist writings from Rizal's novels to the Katipunan newspaper *Kalayaan*, thought of themselves as once loyal sons and daughters who were no longer able to bear the neglect, the insults, and the violence of the father and so were forced to rise and kill him. By so doing, they, or at least the sons, could in turn seek to father a new nation. In giving up their desire for Mother Spain, they also conjured a new mother, *Inang Bayan* or Mother Philippines, of which they were both its sons and its fathers. And they did so only by repudiating, to the point of killing, those who had long claimed primacy over the country's paternity. Having embarked on parricide, Filipino sons subsequently found themselves by March 1897 turning on those who claimed to be the new fathers, beginning with the "father" of the revolution himself.

Revolution in the Philippines was thus conceptualized by both Spaniards and Filipinos in terms of a language of family romance. Ingratitude led to neglect, neglect to abuse, and abuse to phantasms of revenge culminating in parricide. Revolution meant turning against one's colonial parents, la Patria itself. Parricide in turn triggered a chain of other violations: electoral fraud, attempted coups, murder, sexual harassment, then more parricide. Brought on by the crime of colonial conquest, revolution brings with it a series of other crimes characterized by the spiral of violence and the multiplication of death. For to live amid a revolutionary era is also to live out recurring moments of terror and to live with the omnipresence of death. Pitched battles and then guerrilla warfare, as the memoirs of revolutionary leaders make clear, led to a harvest of corpses. War begot disruption and disease, food shortages, and starvation. In a time of revolution, death seemed to be everywhere, always ready to appear. As such it appeared out of place—dead bodies floating on the river, hanging from trees, strewn on the roadside. Such sights undoubtedly incited terror and fed further the desire for revenge, making for even more violence and more death.

When Aguinaldo sought to replace the Katipunan with a revolutionary government, he was trying to establish a state apparatus that would perhaps limit the movement of the revolution and control its excesses. In a way he was seeking to recolonize the revolutionary nation where social hierarchy, beginning with the relationship between colonial parents and colonized children, between fathers and sons, and between elites and non-elites had become unstuck and destabilized. A revolutionary government would seek to restore order and hierarchy, but this time under the regime of local elites with Aguinaldo as its head. By doing so, he could claim, as all heads of state do, a monopoly over the use of violence. He could thereby give death a place. As head of state, Aguinaldo could vest himself and his followers with the power to distinguish between acceptable and unacceptable deaths. As such, he could establish himself as the new principle of legitimacy, the "father," as it were, of the Republic.

But doing so meant launching what would amount to a counterrevolution. Bonifacio was widely regarded by Filipinos even in his time as the father of the revolution, for it was he who sought to usurp the place of the colonial fathers. But to the Spaniards he was, like Rizal, the symbol of indio ingratitude and thus an illegitimate offspring: the bastard son of la Patria. The Katipuneros, on the other hand, called Bonifacio the Supremo and saw in him the chief agency of revenge. These two views of Bonifacio do not so much cancel each other out as complement and complete each other. To establish himself as the new source of legitimacy, which is to say the new source of law that would regulate death and redirect the economy of violence, Bonifacio first had to break the law and kill the fathers of colonialism. His ingratitude was his weapon, and only because he was condemned to be a bastard could he think of cutting himself off from the colonial family.

Aguinaldo followed suit, but with a difference. For unlike Bonifacio, Aguinaldo did not harbor a deep dislike for Spanish friars, and from his position as a local official within the colonial bureaucracy—a *gobernadorcillo*, or little governor as he was called—was more anxious to negotiate an arrangement with the Spaniards that would leave him and those of his class relatively secure in their positions of local power. A good deal of evidence exists to suggest that Aguinaldo was always more eager to cut a deal with the colonial authorities than to get rid of them.[11] This may partly explain why he was willing to put Bonifacio to death. Aguinaldo thus broke the law of the law-breaker himself, thereby founding the putative legitimacy of the revolutionary state and the republican government on a series of illegitimate acts. Thus, the profound contradictions at the bottom of nationalist history. Colonialism begets its own death in the form of revolution; revolution in turn sets the stage for counter-revolution, which is the return of colonialism by other means. Just as parricide, symbolic and otherwise, lies at the origins of nationalist fatherhood, criminality lies at the root of law, while the legitimacy of powerful figures, the new fathers, is produced by a series of what appeared to be illegitimate acts from the perspective of colonial morality.

Centennial commemorations with their drive toward progressive and unified narratives cannot even begin to acknowledge, much less account for, these contradictions. The dialectic of colonialism and nationalism, revolution and counter-revolution, criminality and the law appears to be unthinkable within the context of officially sanctioned celebrations. Instead, there is a tendency to suppress these contradictions and to marginalize their implications for the present. Moreover, the very history of this suppression remains concealed in official celebrations. In these official narratives the revolution becomes an evolution: the inevitable progression from the old to the new, whereby the growth from political immaturity to sovereign maturity is inexorably laid out in the events of 1896-1898. It is an evolutionary development that marches on despite obstacles, including the Philippine-American War of 1899-1902, and the U.S. colonial regime that followed in its wake.

This evolutionary understanding of revolution raises a question that remains largely unasked in many of the Centennial events: what is the place of the United States and of American colonialism in the narratives of the revolution? Again, Ileto provides us important clues. He argues that American colonizers and Filipino ilustrados propagated the notion, made commonplace in history textbooks of the early twentieth century, that "the revolution (was) the originary event of modern Philippine history." Directed against Spain, here understood as feudal and unenlightened, the revolution was "propelled by liberal... ideals of the ilustrados. It led to the formation of a short-lived state (in Malolos) with such modern trappings as a constitution, a congress, a judiciary, and armed forces." Hence could the Philippine revolution be understood in terms of Western history: as the repetition of European and American revolutions in "an oriental setting" and the emergence of the "world spirit" by way of the modern nation-state.[12] The eventfulness of the revolution—its disruptiveness, contradictions, and radical potential—was thus domesticated in these American colonial accounts. It came to be regarded as the belated arrival of developments already witnessed in the West that would presumably lead to the same end: the rise of a modern state. And that state was precisely the gift that American benevolence provided the Filipinos.

Of course, what is repressed in these accounts is the fact of a protracted and brutal war between Filipinos and Americans which began in 1899, ending officially in 1902 but unofficially continuing until 1912. As Ileto points out, American accounts often depict the revolutionary government and the Malolos Republic as abject failures while remaining silent on the major cause of that failure: the outbreak of the war and the eventual defeat of Filipino forces. Invasion, torture, reconcentration, deportation, and murder were all characteristic of American colonialism at its inception, reminding us of the illegitimacy of its origins in the Philippines. But it is precisely that illegitimacy that is subsequently covered up and repressed in and through the re-narrativization of the revolution.

Again Ileto: "In order for American intervention to be emplotted as a liberating event, it was necessary for the revolution to be presented as a beginning, certainly, but ultimately a failure. Colonial textbooks put the formal end of the revolution as late 1898, when the United States acquired the Philippines from Spain. There follows an ominous silence about the resistance to U.S. occupation....In colonial textbooks, the revolution ends where America takes up the cudgels of modernization. The revolution becomes just a prelude to the development of nationalist and democratic consciousness during American colonial rule."[13]

The American narrative learned by generations of Filipinos in colonial-era public and private schools and perpetuated in the post-Independence era depicted the "real" revolution in terms of the political overthrow of Spain, now characterized in evolutionary terms as "backward" and "feudal." Gone are the highly charged metaphors of family, love, betrayal, ingratitude, and revenge so common in the Castilian-language discourse of Filipino nationalism and in Spanish accounts. Instead of mothers and fathers and sons and daughters, the new narrative turns on such tropes as "tutelage," "maturity," "race," and "development." American narratives and their Filipino ilustrado renderings saw the revolution as the overthrow of a feudal Spanish regime instigated by the most enlightened and Westernized Filipinos and then completed by the even more enlightened Americans.

Perversely enough, Americans came to be situated by this colonial-national narrative as the true heirs of the revolution which faltered in the hands of elite Filipinos. Caretakers of a revolution that, after all, was no more than a repetition of their own, Americans proceeded to act as the executors, as it were, of the revolutionary legacy. They moved quickly to co-opt revolutionary leaders into the colonial bureaucracy, the colonial judiciary and legislature, and the colonial military as early as 1899 and through 1907. Equally important, they also regulated the forms of nationalist expression. While they proscribed the more militant manifestations of nationalist sentiments—moving, for example, to ban certain kinds of Tagalog plays deemed seditious because of their revolutionary content and symbolism, or to ban the public display of the Philippine flag from 1907 to 1913—they also allowed, and even encouraged, the more conservative forms of nationalism among prominent ilustrados. It was through American sponsorship, for example, that Rizal Day celebrations were regularized and policed, and that the hero's monument at Luneta Park was erected in 1912. It was also under the Americans that the historical rehabilitation of

Bonifacio and other revolutionary figures began, carried out by ilustrado bureaucrat-scholar-journalists like Manuel Artigas y Cuerva and Epifanio de los Santos. In time, the conventional outlines of the historiography of the revolution, characterized mainly by hagiographic accounts of heroes and the omission of Filipino resistance beyond 1898, were laid out by Teodoro M. Kalaw in the 1920s and Gregorio Zaide in the 1930s.

Under American colonialism then, the revolution is given a place. While it terminates Spanish rule, it finds its fulfillment in the coming of the Americans. It is a revolution therefore, whose ends are realized by the modernizing efforts of nation-building under a colonial state. Revolutionary nationalism, which begins with a desire for a kind of utopic modernity, climaxes in this narrative in colonial containment and mass collaboration. It thus terminates "naturally" in counter-revolution, bringing with it the restoration of social hierarchy. Officially sanctioned centennial commemorations thus share in and perpetuate this colonial narrative about the ends of revolution. Given their conservative leanings and administrative bent toward ordering the memory of disorder and disruption, these narratives work to secure the state as the terminus of all political action and aspiration. Such commemorations of the revolution are thus fundamentally antirevolutionary and never fail to use the talk of independence and the history of freedom to conceal this fact.[14]

I want to conclude these reflections on the Centennial with a note on possible alternatives to official commemorations. Are there such things? Can the memorialization of a revolutionary event ever become what it seeks to remember? Or is the recollection of revolution like the remembering of the dead, an act of mourning whereby we consolidate and replace our memories of the departed while he or she was alive with an image? How and when does commemoration become a radical act that sometimes spills into radical social action? Can the memory of violence become so compelling as to lead to more violence?

The history of Philippine social movements suggests as much. As various scholars have shown,[15] popular commemorations of important events such as the revolution or the executions of Rizal and Bonifacio throughout the first half of the twentieth century have often roused expectations, mobilizing peasant armies into militant opposition and striking fear in the colonial state and Filipino elites, who often enough responded with violence. In the post-independence period, academic debates in the Philippines sought to repoliticize the legacy of the revolution, stressing its popular and anticolonial nature. Scholars of this period consciously broke away from their ilustrado precursors, their fathers, as it were, as they launched their own revolutionary revision of nationalist history as a people's war. Such revisions were picked up by the generation of the 1960s and infused with a Marxist-Maoist vocabulary of struggle and opposition. Since then, the question of the revolution has been a contentious one: both the State and its opponents, especially those identified with the National Democratic Front and the Communist Party of the Philippines, have claimed to be the heirs of the revolution, the soldiers fighting what has come to be known in contemporary nationalist rhetoric as the "unfinished revolution." The notion of the "unfinished revolution" underlines the gap between the political and social legacies of the events from 1896 to 1902, reminding us of the disjunction between the egalitarian promise of the anti-colonial struggles and the actual intensification of socio-economic inequalities that have come in their wake.

Finally, overseas Filipinos have in their own ways appropriated the legacy of the revolution, commemorating its centennial in various and sometimes unexpected ways. Among Filipino-Americans, for example, such commemorations range from the banal to the inspired. While there are the usual parades, beauty contests, and embassy-sponsored exhibits of photographs and memorabilia, there have also been attempts to counter American amnesia about the Philippine-American War. The Filipino-American community in Minnesota, for instance, successfully campaigned to install a plaque on the walls of the state capitol beside that of an American veterans group. While the latter celebrated the war as a great victory against Filipino "insurrectos" and referred to Aguinaldo as "chief" of the Tagalogs, the Filipino plaque subtly corrected "insurrection" into "war" between two sovereign states, and redesignated Aguinaldo as "president" rather than some Indian headman.[16]

More recently in New York City, a coalition of Filipino-American, Puerto Rican, and Cuban-American writers and artists held a round of poetry readings and exhibits aimed at what the organizers called the "dis-commemoration" of the Treaty of Paris that resulted in "handing over the spoils of the Spanish-American to the United States."[17] Running through the list of participants as these appeared on the Internet, I was struck by the wild variety of their works, evoking the languages of nationalism while gesturing toward some other region of identification yet to be disclosed. They author such books as *My Sad Republic* and *Screaming Monkies*, curate art exhibits titled "Memories of Overdevelopment," edit magazines like *Bamboo Girl* written "for and by but not exclusive to loud and smart young women of color, especially those of Asian mutt descent." They identify themselves to an unknown and anonymous public as "queer," "transgendered," or "bisexual," who work in writers' collectives and practice using the *balisong*, teach design and poetry, direct videos, perform as DJs in raves, and stage one-woman performances as well as elaborate variety shows called "PNCs" (or Pilipino Cultural Nights), live in large metropolitan cities like New York, Los Angeles, and San Francisco, and fashion intricate Web sites that accommodate a bewildering variety of voices.

They would seem to be far removed from the "first" Filipinos, the generation of Rizal, Bonifacio, and Aguinaldo. And yet I would argue that such Filipino-American artists, writers, and activists much like their compatriots in the Philippines, are as much "heirs" to the revolution as, for example, the followers of José Ma. Sison's Communist Party holed up in the Netherlands and directing an armed struggle from a distance. Here, to "inherit" a revolution need not mean owning it, as if "revolution" were something that could be fixed into a tradition and bundled into a stable thing, then deeded like property to succeeding generations. Rather, it means coming to be traversed by the force of certain unsettled questions and unknowable futures that disrupt existing social arrangements. As such, overseas Filipinos in general and Filipino-Americans in particular come to share in the predicaments of Filipino-ness with which all of us who claim to be Filipinos of some sort are infected. They are, like Rizal, Bonifacio, and their generation, possessed by the ghosts of colonialism even as they seek to come to terms with its effects. As with Rizal and company, they feel the intensity of their dislocation whether at home or abroad, and seek to make that sense of alienation the basis for their engagement with the world. Similarly, they share with the first generation of nationalists a keen fascination with new technologies of expression that allow them to speak past the language of convention and received identities.[18]

The latter is of crucial significance, for it allows them to stand in a different relationship to the past, particularly that of their parents and grandparents, who are in many ways their most palpable connection to a certain Philippines. Filipino-Americans are set apart from Filipinos in the Philippines not only by their geographical and socioeconomic situation. "Filipino-American," to begin with, is a social formation inconceivable before the twentieth century. Where the historical dialectic of revolution and counterrevolution informs the conflictual foundations of Filipinoness and the Philippine nation-state, "Filipino-American" by contrast is a post-revolutionary category. It does not emerge as a consequence of the political revolution of 1896-1898 but as an effect of American imperialism and the social revolutions that have swept the United States from the 1930s to the 1990s by way of labor union organizing, the civil rights movements, and the struggle for women's, gay and lesbian rights. Although a good number were involved in the anti-Marcos struggles and worked in coalition with the National Democratic Front in the 1970s and 1980s, Filipino Americans nonetheless have remained physically and linguistically rooted in the United States, and unlike nationalist exiles, are not inclined to relocate to the Philippines. Allied as they may be with Philippine social movements or holding on to nostalgic memories of Philippine culture, Filipino-Americans are at the same time haunted by assimilationist anxieties. On the one hand, they are racialized in the United States as nonwhite or are equally problematic as "Asian-Americans," so that their American-ness is constantly under question. On the other hand, they are attached to the political and symbolic economies of the United States such that their "Filipino-ness" remains of dubious authenticity to Filipinos in the Philippines.[19]

Given their fundamental ambivalence toward the nation-states of their ancestry as well as that of their residence, one might argue that Filipino-Americans have something in common with the earlier generation of nationalists. Like the ilustrado nationalists of the nineteenth century who were never quite fully at home either in the Philippine colony or in the metropolitan capital, they find themselves arriving but never quite resting on a "Filipino" identity imbedded in, but constantly at odds with, other identities. This sense of intense dislocation does not, of course, make for a revolutionary condition. But neither is it co-optable into counterrevolutionary narratives. For that reason, it furnishes a location from where to generate alternatives to official commemorations of the Centennial that seek to freeze and commodify the revolution into a set of still images and predictable narratives. Rather than a national identity, Filipino American writers and artists (and, quite possibly, all overseas Filipino migrants) convey the sense of constant departures and arrivals, of movement both physical and imaginary that evades the demands of the nation-state for fixity. While they do not conspire to overthrow states and aspire to acts of parricide, they nonetheless produce the conditions for different retellings and revisionings of these histories. Rather than represent the revolution and so, like the state, set aside the force of its claims, they embody its contradictory effects. They know themselves to be bastards of both the Philippine and American nation-states, and see in this irony not a source of shame but a site for connections. They make us think then of what it means to come before the revolution and its counterrevolutionary aftermath in both senses of the word: to be both pre- and postrevolutionary and pre- and post-counter-revolutionary, to be, that is, a kind of Filipino brought back and led forward to the non-foundational foundations of the nation-state.

NOTES:

1. The orthodoxy regarding the Centennial can be seen in various presidential pronouncements, embassy press releases, and coffee-table books that have appeared in Manila and other parts of the world. But the most powerful purveyors of this official construction of the Centennial have been Philippine newspapers written for and by national elites and those who aspire to their ranks. See, for example, the coverage of Centennial events and speeches published in the January to June 1998 issues of the *Philippine Daily Inquirer* which comes pretty close to being the country's newspaper of record (though its circulation is a relatively small 300,000 in a nation of close to seventy million people, a reflection of the enormous social and economic disparities in the country, if there ever was one).

2. Reynaldo C. Ileto, *Filipinos and their Revolution: Event, Discourse, and Historiography* (Quezon City: Ateneo de Manila University Press, 1998), 241. See also William Henry Scott, *Prehispanic Source Materials for the Study of Philippine History* (Quezon City: New Day Press, 1984).

3. In this regard, we can recall the lavish welcome laid out by the Ramos administration for the visiting Spanish monarch King Juan Carlos in 1997 that culminated in the opening of the Centennial theme park (the construction of which, Ramos critics allege, was ridden with massive corruption) on the grounds of the former U.S. military base, Clark Field. For a discussion of the ironic constitution of the "Philippines" and "Filipinos," see the Introduction of Vicente L. Rafael, *White Love and Other Events in Filipino History* (Durham, N.C.: Duke University Press, 2000).

4. Such colonial legacies would include, for example, the colonial state, both Spanish and American, whose basic structures are still visible and palpable in the workings of the present-day Philippine government agencies. The entire judicial apparatus of the Philippines is modeled on the American system, with one telling exception, the absence of a jury system, which effectively places judicial procedure in the hands of judges and lawyers who historically have not been beyond graft and corruption. The continued persistence of a hierarchy of language, a direct legacy of the Spanish, then American colonial period which privileges the colonial language—Spanish and, since the turn of the century, English—as the language of rule and learning, as well as protest and resistance—while situating vernacular languages below, a linguistic order which in important ways mirrors enduring class divisions in the country: this, too, is the ghost of colonialism that continues to haunt nationalism. Indeed, what could be more ironic than protesting against such a linguistic hierarchy in the very terms of that hierarchy, as evidenced, for example, in the writings of middle-class nationalists ranging from University of the Philippines professors to the leaders of the National Democratic Front? Finally, the enduring power of what I have referred to elsewhere as a mestizo cultural hegemony is yet another example of the ways in which nationalism in the Philippines is profoundly implicated in the very colonial thing it seeks to repudiate. For a sustained discussion of the relationship between linguistic hierarchy and social divisions in Philippines, see Rafael, *White Love and Other Events in Filipino History*, chapters 4, 6, 7, and 8. For a discussion of the origins of linguistic hierarchy, see Vicente L. Rafael, *Contracting Colonialism: Translation and Christian Conversion in Tagalog Society Under Early Spanish Rule* (Durham, N.C.: Duke University Press, 1993).

But this dilemma is not very different from the situation of other Third World nationalisms, fatally wedded to their colonial histories even as they seek to escape and transform them. There were for example, the Sukarno and Suharto regimes in neighboring Indonesia which sought to refine techniques of power first introduced by the Dutch. In the 1960s, Frantz Fanon wrote extensively on the pitfalls of nationalism and the dangers they present to those who would seek emancipation from colonial overlords in *The Wretched of the Earth*, trans. Constance Farrington (New York: Grove Press, 1963).

More recently, Benedict Anderson probed into the contradictions of nationalism and its dialectical relationship to colonialism in *Imagined Communities: Reflections on the Origins and Spread of Nationalism* (London: Verso, 1983); and in a Philippine context, "Cacique Democracy in the Philippines: Origins and Dreams," in Vicente L. Rafael, ed., *Discrepant Histories: Translocal Essays on Filipino Cultures* (Philadelphia, Pa.: Temple University Press, 1995), 3-50.

We can thus think of nationalism as the essentially inconclusive and ongoing project to deal with the legacy, which is to say, the gift that is also the curse of colonialism. This is what constitutes the modernity of nationalism, especially in Third World contexts: that, whereas it appeared initially as the uncanny undoing of colonialism's power, reflecting upon colonial rule and thereby redoubling colonialism's founding violence and illegitimacy, nationalism also succeeds (in all senses of that word) colonialism by assuming its logics and conserving its structures. All of its logics and structures? Certainly not. Revolution seeks to do away with oppressive structures, and in the Philippine case to do away with class and gender divisions. But this revolutionary moment, almost from its inception, had always, ironically, cohabited with its counterrevolutionary other, a cohabitation that is the subject of the rest of this essay. Philippine nationalism is a history of double hauntings, possessed simultaneously by nationalism's emancipatory promise and its conservative tendencies. It is small wonder that the figure of José Rizal, at once revolutionary and reactionary, dominates the landscape of the Filipino historical imagination.

5. For a description of the 12 June 1998 Independence parade at the Luneta in Manila, see Reynaldo Ileto, ibid., 239-241. The Bishop Museum exhibit bears the instructive title of "Filipino Americans of Hawaii: A Celebration of Courage, Service and Achievement" (2 October 1998-28 February 1999) organized by the Bishop Museum and the Philippine Centennial Committee-Hawaii with funding from the State of Hawaii and several other large corporate sponsors from Sprint to the Bank of Hawaii as well as the ILWU Local 142. One can imagine the historical floats heading down Roxas Boulevard to head directly across the Pacific and land comfortably and neatly on the grounds of the Bishop Museum in Honolulu and then proceed into Golden Gate Park and thence to Chicago and New York and Madrid and back again to Manila without so much as a pause. Such is the utterly nonironic understanding of Philippine history professed by the organizers of the Centennial celebrations.

6. The literature on the history of nationalism and the beginnings of the revolutionary movement is large and, as one might expect, uneven. The locus classicus of the early period of nationalism is John Schumacher, S.J., *The Propaganda Movement, 1880-1895* (Manila: Solidaridad Publishing House, 1973). For a more recent examination of the social history of the nineteenth century that contributed directly to the emergence of nationalist consciousness, see Jonathan Fast and Jim Richardson, *Roots of Dependency: Political and Economic Revolution in the Philippines in the 19th Century* (Quezon City, Philippines: Foundation for Nationalist Studies, 1979).

7. The most important studies of this first phase of the revolution and the beginnings of counter-revolution include Teodoro Agoncillo, *The Revolt of the Masses* (Quezon City: University of the Philippines Press, 1956), and most recently the problematic and somewhat sloppy detective work of Glenn A. May, *Inventing a Hero* (Madison: Center for South and Southeast Asian Studies, University of Wisconsin, 1996). See also the very useful writings of the historian-journalist Ambeth Ocampo, *Bonifacio's Bolo* (Pasig: Anvil Publishing, 1995), and *The Centennial Countdown* (Pasig: Anvil Publishing,

1998). There are also several published memoirs of revolutionary leaders that are important for reconstructing the events of the times. The more substantial of these include Santiago Alvarez, *The Katipunan and the Revolution: Memoirs of a General*, trans. Paula Carolina S. Malay (Quezon City: Ateneo de Manila University Press, 1992); Carlos Ronquillo, *Ilang Talata tungkol sa Paghihimagsik (Revolucion), 1896-1897*; ed. Isagani Medina (Quezon City: University of the Phillippines Press, 1996); Artemio Ricarte, *Memoirs of Artemio Ricarte*, ed. Armando J. Malay (Manila: National Heroes Commission, 1963); and Apolinario Mabini, *La Revolución Filipina*, 2 vols. (Manila: National Historical Institute, 1961). Finally, see also Carlos Quirino, ed., *The Minutes of the Katipunan* (Manila: National Heroes Commission, 1964).

8. The former first published in Berlin in 1887; the latter, in Ghent in 1891. It is remarkable indeed how the plots of both novels, along with vignettes about the re-encoding of Tagalog for secret and future purposes, and the language of sentiment used to articulate political aspirations in the book, found their way repeated and amplified by other nationalist writings, including and especially those that appeared in the Katipunan newspaper *Kalayaan* in 1896.

9. The more significant and symptomatic of such Spanish accounts include those of Manuel Sastron, *La Insurreción en Filipinas y Guerra Hispano-Americana en el Archipelago* (Madrid: Imprenta de la Sucesora de M. Minuesa de los Rios, 1901); José M. del Castillo y Jimenez, *El Katipunan o el Filibusterismo en Filipinas* (Madrid: Imprenta del Asilo de Huerfanos del S.C. de Jesus, 1897); Juan Caro y Mora, *La Situación del Pais*, 2da edición (Manila: Imprenta del Pais, 1897); and the report of Olegario Diaz, of the Guardia Civil, in W. E. Retana, ed. *Archivo del Bibliofilo Filipino*, 5 vols. (Madrid: 1892), vol. 3, 332-360.

10. See Caro y Mora.

11. See for example the essays of Ocampo, op. cit.

12. Ileto, 241.

13. Ileto, 242.

14. Here it is worth noting how recently Filipinos started commemorating 12 June as their date of independence. Until 1962, Independence Day was celebrated on 4 July, the date assigned by the United States legislature as early as the 1930s, first in the Hare-Hawes-Cutting Bill, then in the Tydings-McDuffie Act which created the Philippine Commonwealth and provided a timetable for the granting of independence within ten years of its enactment. In 1946, amid the awful devastation of the war and the growing Huk rebellion in Central Luzon, 4 July was set aside as the date for the transfer of state power from the United States to the newly elected Republic of the Philippines. As the historian Ambeth Ocampo points out, it was President Diosdado Macapagal who ordered the change in 1962 from 4 July to 12 June. He did so for political reasons of his own. The United States Congress had delayed the passage of a war damage assistance bill for $73 million set aside for the Philippines. To register his displeasure and capitalize on growing anti-American sentiments, Macapagal moved the date for the commemoration of independence. The arbitrariness of this change is further underlined by the fact that Macapagal himself was uncertain at first as to what the new date should be. He had considered 21 January, marking the opening of the Malolos Congress in 1899, or 23 January marking the ratification of the independence proclamation of 12 June. Finally, upon the advice of the Philippine Historical Association, he settled on 12 June. Having decided on the new date, Macapagal then hastened to assure President John F. Kennedy that he meant no disrespect to the United States, but that his decision was in fact an act of homage to American history. Just as the thirteen American colonies had declared their independence on 4 July 1776 which was not to be recognized by England until 3 September 1783, so the Filipinos declared 12 June as the "true birthday of an independent Filipino nation" when Aguinaldo proclaimed independence from Spain, though this was not recognized until 4 July 1946 by the Americans. Macapagal then represented what he did not as an act of defiance but as a matter of paying tribute to the United States. The calendrical revision of Philippine independence was at the same time a reiteration

of the Philippines' "special relations" with its former colonial master. And what was commemorated was not the reality of independence itself, which as I have argued above continues to remain elusive, but its rhetorical performance. Only three years before the climb to power of Ferdinand and Imelda Marcos and the liberalization of the U.S. immigration laws that would make possible the flow of new, mostly middle-class Filipino immigrants to America, the celebration of Philippine independence on 12 June was fraught with the sharpest of ironies and the deepest of historical amnesias. See Ambeth Ocampo's utterly subversive essays on these matters in *The Centennial Countdown* (Pasig City, Philippines: Anvil Publishing Co., 1998), 295-301.

15. See, for example, the differently inflected work of David Sturtevant, *Popular Uprisings in the Philippines* (Ithaca, N.Y.: Cornell University Press, 1976); Reynaldo Ileto, *Pasyon and Revolution* (Quezon City: Ateneo de Manila University Press, 1979); Milagros Guerrero, "Luzon at War," (unpublished Ph.D. diss., University of Michigan, 1977); John Schumacher, S.J., *Revolutionary Clergy* (Quezon City: Ateneo de Manila University, 1986); and Benedict Kerkvliet, *The Huk Rebellion* (Berkeley: University of California Pres, 1977).

16. I owe this information to Michael Cullinane.

17. "Diss-Commemorating the Treaty of Paris", The Asian-American Writers' Workshop, New York City, 3 December 1998. This information was downloaded from the listserv Filipinoarts-L@home.ease.lsoft.com moderated by Allan Bennamer, 1 December 1998.

18. For a discussion of the nationalist ilustrado fascination with technologies of communication, especially the technology of the Castilian language, see Vicente L. Rafael, "Translation and Revenge: Castilian and the Origins of Nationalism in the Philippines," in Doris Sommer, ed., *The Places of History: Regionalism Revisited in Latin America* (Durham, N.C.: Duke University Press, 1999), 214-235. For the penetrating and suggestive study of the workings of nationalism as a technology for the transmission of the powers of transmission and its subsequent blockage in the context of Indonesia, see James T. Siegel, *Fetish, Recognition, Revolution* (Princeton, N.J.: Princeton University Press, 1997).

19. For a fuller discussion of the ambivalent connotations of "Filipino American," see Vicente L. Rafael, "'Your Grief is Our Gossip': Overseas Filipinos and Other Spectral Presences," in *Public Culture*, vol. 9, no. 2, winter 1997: 267-291. For very useful backgrounds to the historical predicaments that define Filipino American-ness, see Yen Le Espiritu, *Filipino American Lives* (Philadelphia, Pa.: Temple University Press, 1995), 1-36; and Lisa Lowe, *Immigrant Acts: On Asian-American Cultural Politics* (Durham, N.C.: Duke University Press, 1996), 1-36.

Manuel Ocampo
Heridas de la Lengua
1991, oil on canvas
180.34 x 154.94 cm
Collection of Tony Shafrazi, New York

An Open Wound: Colonial Melancholia and Contemporary Filipino/American Texts

SARITA E. SEE

Because when you see the scars on her hands and you feel them, you feel where the skin has healed over a wound like that, you just get this sensation that nothing can hurt you. I mean, it's not even that—but that you can bear the pain...

—*Nailed*, Angel Velasco Shaw

Pangit ako! (I'm ugly!)

—*Flipzoids*, Ralph Peña

Images of bodily injury suffuse recent Filipino/American[1] art and cultural production, graphic depictions often attended by hurtful humor and a rhetoric of pain. Consider the work of artist Manuel Ocampo, videomaker Angel Velasco Shaw, and playwright Ralph Peña. Ocampo's oil paintings trade on a gorgeous, grotesque corporeality—torn bellies, spilling hearts, and headless, defecating corpses. In the experimental video *Nailed*, Shaw documents the self-inflicted crucifixion of Lucy Reyes, a faith healer in the Philippines who annually dons a yellow buttercup wig and crown of thorns before having her hands and feet partially nailed to a cross. Set in the "hostile landscape" of southern California, Peña's play *Flipzoids* centers on an alienated, multigenerational trio of Filipino/Americans whose playful banter inflicts pain upon themselves and one another.[2] Binding these otherwise wildly divergent texts is a dramatic pattern of wounds that is rooted in a traumatic history of colonial violence and loss. These visual and rhetorical representations of injury form a belligerent response to the numbing effects of imperial forgetting.[3] Ironically, however, the violence depicted in Filipino/American art and cultural production inevitably turns inward. These are portraits of self-mutilation. Yet the representation and rhetoric of pain are oddly stubborn, defiant, and even celebratory. Here, the representation of the body is inextricably linked to the desecration of that very same body.

To make sense of this pattern of self-injury and injury, I juxtapose these texts first with Sigmund Freud's writings on melancholia and then with Reynaldo Ileto's examination of the *pasyon* narrative in mass movements in the Philippines. In his 1917 essay "Mourning and Melancholia," Freud offers a fascinating, if open-ended, explanation for the phenomenon of melancholia, a prolonged and severe form of depression. I take up Freud's intriguing claim that the "complex of melancholia behaves like an open wound" (174).[4] Freud's analogy links physical trauma with psychic trauma and forms the basis for the theorization of what I call colonial melancholia.[5] To complement and complicate this negative, rather reactive portrait of colonized subjectivity, I turn to Ileto's writings on the cultural and political significance of Christ's crucifixion in late nineteenth-century and early twentieth-century Philippines. In *Pasyon and Revolution: Popular Movements in the Philippines, 1840-1910,* Ileto focuses on the shifting meanings of Christ's crucifixion and underscores the potentially revolutionary significance of the pasyon as a complex source of inspiration for anticolonial, anticlerical resistance movements. I argue that, as a theatrical performance of self-injury, the pasyon has continued to evolve as a powerful source of cultural expression and political engagement in contemporary Filipino/American art.

COLONIAL MELANCHOLIA: A HISTORY OF LOST HISTORIES

In "Mourning and Melancholia," Freud compares the common experience of mourning with the pathological condition of melancholia. Both mourner and melancholic have suffered from a profound loss. But melancholia differs from mourning in two important ways: first, the unconscious nature of melancholic loss; and secondly, the drastic drop in the melancholic's self-esteem.

According to Freud, while a grieving person can name the lost object, it is not clear what exactly the melancholic has lost. The melancholic does not know—cannot consciously perceive—what has been lost, even though he or she experiences the loss. How can one mourn properly if one cannot even name what has been lost? As it turns out, the ability to mourn is inextricably bound up with language. Successful mourning entails naming the lost object, thereby processing and recovering from bereavement. In a colonial regime, though, language itself constitutes the lost object. The attempted destruction of native languages and the imposition of a singular, dominant language mark the catastrophic foundation of a colony—what Ocampo calls *Heridas de la Lengua (Wounds of the Tongue)*. Deprived of the ability to speak, the colonized subject cannot name loss and, therefore, cannot mourn. The colonized subject attempts to mourn the loss of language   but necessarily fails. In other words, the colonial subject paradoxically mourns the loss of the ability to mourn. The history of the colonized   turns out to be structurally melancholic, a history of lost histories.

Bereft of language, the colonized subject has nothing left but the body to articulate loss, hence the prevalence of fragmented, damaged bodies in Filipino/American art. If the vocalization of pain occurs at all—as in the slaughtering of a pig in Angel Velasco Shaw's *Nailed*—it is through inarticulate sounds, such as screaming, that take the place of language. Significantly, in his painting *Heridas de la Lengua*, Ocampo pointedly uses Spanish, the language of the colonizer, in the title, which also appears in capital letters within the painting. Ocampo puns on the linguistic and bodily wounds to the *lengua*—meaning both "language" and "tongue." Ironically, the Spanish language provides the double entendre that enables the representation of lingua-somatic violence committed against the colonized. Ocampo's use of Spanish symbolizes a kind of double violence: not only does his use of Spanish symbolize the attempted suppression of native languages, it underscores the desperate position of the colonized subject who must articulate his or her pain in the language of the colonizer.[7] Because such articulation must occur in Spanish, the attempt at expressing pain reinscribes the power of the colonizer and repeats the violence done to the native *lengua*. Thus, Ocampo's use of a Spanish title symbolizes the vicious circle in which the very articulation of colonial loss repeats the scene of colonial violence.[8] Ocampo's painting does not merely repeat the violence, however. In *Heridas*, this violence is amplified to the point of absurdity. The bodily injuries are not limited to the excision of the tongue but extend to the amputation of the head and limbs. The violence of colonization deprives the colonized subject of both head and tongue, of both subjectivity and language.

Melancholia departs from mourning in a second, significant way. There is a drastic drop in the subject's self-esteem, a drop that is absent in mourning: "In grief the world becomes poor and empty; in melancholia it is the ego itself" (Freud 167). Indeed, melancholics are known for their constant, public self-berating and "delusional belittling." In short, the ego learns to treat itself as an object. All the former ambivalence toward the lost object is redirected at the ego itself. No longer the lost object but the ego is the target of extreme hostility, what Judith Butler has called "unowned aggression." There is "something profoundly unchosen" about this destructive rage, which inhabits within yet does not belong to the colonized subject.[8] Unsurprisingly, what makes melancholia so dangerous is this self-destructive impulse. Fundamentally, melancholia describes the management—or mismanagement— of unowned aggression. This radical not-belonging also may be called "dis-enfranchised grief," inextricable from the dispossession of land, language, and autonomy at the core of the colonial enterprise.[10] In colonial melancholia, the original dispossession of land and autonomy translates into dispossessed rage and grief. Thus, the tragedy of colonial melancholia arises not merely from the loss of an object but from the theft of an object. This is a layered theft: not merely losing an object, or losing the right to own that object, but losing the right to own that loss.

CULTURE OF COM/PLAINT

And yet the melancholic's "delusional belittling" exhibits traces of social protest. All of the melancholic's hostile attention to the self radically diminishes the ego, but oddly enough, melancholics tend to display this routine self-abasement in rather public ways: "The patient represents his ego to us as worthless, incapable of any effort and morally despicable; he reproaches himself, vilifies himself and expects to be cast out and chastised. He abases himself before everyone and commiserates his own relatives for being connected with someone so unworthy" (Freud 167). If melancholics are so ashamed of their failures and deficiencies, the constant exhibition of these faults doesn't make sense at first. What motivates this theatrical self-exposure? Freud notes that these incessant "complaints" about the self are really "plaints in the legal sense of the word" (169). All the complaints about oneself actually apply to someone else. The self-reproach is indexical: it points at something or someone else. As Freud puts it, this is an "attitude of revolt" (170). Ironically, of course, the plaint consistently misses its target. The colonized subject's legitimate plaint and "attitude of revolt" against the colonizer misses the target (the colonizer) and is redirected and transformed into complaint about the self. In other words, instead of aiming at the injustices of the external world, the melancholic diverts this rage against the self. The melancholic does not hide but rather displays this unceasing self-flagellation because the "complaints" are fundamentally accusatory, not self-accusatory. Melancholia is a way of replaying, remembering, and representing loss,

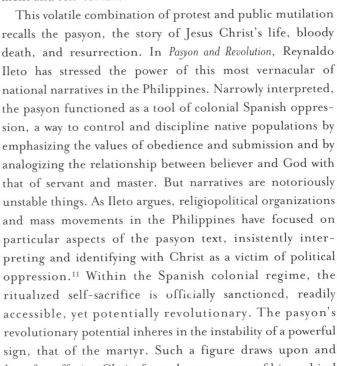

but at an extraordinary cost, that of unceasing self-punishment and self-torture.

This volatile combination of protest and public mutilation recalls the pasyon, the story of Jesus Christ's life, bloody death, and resurrection. In *Pasyon and Revolution*, Reynaldo Ileto has stressed the power of this most vernacular of national narratives in the Philippines. Narrowly interpreted, the pasyon functioned as a tool of colonial Spanish oppression, a way to control and discipline native populations by emphasizing the values of obedience and submission and by analogizing the relationship between believer and God with that of servant and master. But narratives are notoriously unstable things. As Ileto argues, religiopolitical organizations and mass movements in the Philippines have focused on particular aspects of the pasyon text, insistently interpreting and identifying with Christ as a victim of political oppression.[11] Within the Spanish colonial regime, the ritualized self-sacrifice is officially sanctioned, readily accessible, yet potentially revolutionary. The pasyon's revolutionary potential inheres in the instability of a powerful sign, that of the martyr. Such a figure draws upon and

Manuel Ocampo
Senakulo
1989
acrylic on
canvas and wood
177.8 x 121.92

converts the symbolic value of a suffering Christ from the acceptance of hierarchical relationships, i.e., between God and man and between colonizer and colonized, to the acceptance of the pain that necessarily accompanies an anticolonial struggle for a greater, communal good.[12]

This combination of self-degradation and protest has survived Spanish colonization and the violent transition to American rule. Indeed, the presence of "passional culture," a term used by a scholar of Spanish penitential rites, is all too evident in contemporary Filipino/American art.[13] The sheer physicality and theatricality of Filipino/American art are inescapable. Colonial melancholia is played out literally through the body, through violent images of bodily fragmentation. Here, the melancholic's failure to hit the target—the confusion of (anticolonial) plaint with (self-injurious) complaint—has a cultural, political significance that is tied to the colonial relationship between the Philippines and Spain. In the Filipino/American context, however, the struggle for cultural and political expression is additionally shaped by the burden of massive forgetting: the almost complete erasure of the Philippine-American War and America's imperial legacy from the United States' national imaginary. In other words, imperial forgetting enacts a kind of psychic violence. Unsurprisingly, in Ocampo's, Shaw's, and Peña's texts, psychic injury coincides with physical injury. These artists attempt to represent colonial loss and violence in their work and, more significantly, to engage with the very terms of cultural representation in the United States, which continue to reinscribe a politics of imperial forgetting. Filipino/American art insists on an intimate connection between psyche and soma or, more specifically, between psychic trauma and physical injury. Thus, in the most literal sense, there is something psychosomatic about the violence and contestation that define colonial melancholia.

WOUNDS OF THE TONGUE

Manuel Ocampo's paintings are explicit variations on the pasyon, which is used repeatedly as a symbol of colonial violence. As I suggested in the introduction above, Ocampo's use of Spanish text illustrates the primacy of language as a site of traumatic violence and melancholic loss. In the following close readings of Ocampo's *Heridas de la Lengua*, though, I address the physicality of these portraits of decapitated, amputated figures and the physicality of colonial violence. Significantly, the figure in *Heridas*, *Senakulo*, *Regalo de Sacrificio*, and other pasyon portraits is male. As such, *Heridas* lends itself to the model of castration as the primary, if problematic, way to theorize colonized subjectivities. Below, I first outline the uses and limitations of using castration as an interpretive model. I then turn to melancholia as an alternative model that more fully accounts for Ocampo's disturbing combination of violence and self-mutilation and that allows more fluid delineations of colonized subjectivities.

Manuel Ocampo
Regalo de Sacrificio
1990
acrylic on canvas
182.88 x 121.92 cm
Collection of
Georganne Deen,
Los Angeles

It is almost banal, but still necessary to address the castration anxiety that pervades the depiction of beheading in *Heridas*. *Heridas* works as a powerful portrayal of colonial castration. Yet it simultaneously resonates with, and appeals to, a male chauvinist nationalism. How so? Recall Freud's classic scene of castration, which underwrites his conception of fetishism. Once upon a time, the little boy is horrified by the sight of his naked mother's—not breast, not pubic hair, but—vagina, otherwise known as the missing penis. In this clearly misogynist formulation, the boy (never a girl) learns his first, rather traumatic lesson about sexual difference. Happily, of course, his penis assures him that he is on the right side of difference. Unhappily ever after, however, he is haunted by the threat of castration. In other words, the boy's castration anxiety derives from a visual threat to his sense of bodily integrity. As the feminist narratologist Mieke Bal puts it, "one gender's wholeness must be safeguarded by the other's fragmentation."[14]

In the colonial context, one nation's integrity is safeguarded through the dismemberment of another nation. In *Heridas* a beheaded male figure represents the scene of colonial castration. Oblivious or defiant, the figure sits upright and stubbornly clutches a knife. Someone else, let us say the colonizer, beheaded and amputated the man. The centered, bleeding heart turns and faces us, a frontal attitude that discomfits us even as it fascinates us. Like it or not, the viewer is forced to participate in the colonizing gaze. In other words, we are compelled to gaze at the castration that secures our own sense of wholeness. Viewed as a scene of castration, *Heridas* offers a powerful representation of colonial subjugation that engages and troubles the colonizing gaze.

Yet the interpretive model of colonial castration reveals some of the limitations of Ocampo's representations of colonial violence. The power of *Heridas* relies on a very particular (straight, male) subjectivity that passes itself off as normative, even universal. Within the framework of colonial castration, Ocampo's selection of male figures has disturbing repercussions for the theorization of colonized subjectivities because the problematic representation of woman as lack in Freudian castration parallels the absence of woman as colonized subject in Ocampo's paintings.[15] The Philippine nation is figured as masculine, a disturbing conflation between man and humanity. According to the fetishism model, women count as incomplete subjects at best. In Ocampo's paintings, women do not enter as colonial subjects and anticolonial nationalism seems to be a male prerogative.[16]

This conclusion is a bit too hasty, though, and the dismissal of Ocampo's work as chauvinist is peremptory. What happens if one reverses the relationship between (Freudian) theory and (Ocampo) text? Instead of assuming that the castration model reveals the limitations of Ocampo's paintings, how might one read *Heridas* such that it begins to reveal the inadequacies—no pun intended—of the castration model? How might *Heridas* mark the limits of Freudian castration?

Consider a melancholic reading of *Heridas*. Glance again at the decapitated head and severed limb. If a painting can be taken as a composite of visual signs, the head, hands, and feet are two obvious indications of pointing and looking.[17] They direct our attention to things within or without the painting. But in *Heridas* both head and leg have been lopped off. Hence, the eyes that would gaze back at us that would accuse the colonizer—are missing in this grotesque, visual narration of violence committed against the colonized. Similarly, the finger that would accuse is missing in *Regalo de Sacrificio* (*Gift of Sacrifice*). In this scene of self-amputation, the left hand is missing while the right hand grips a knife, angled precisely at the point of amputation. Symbolized by the missing left hand, the plaint—the legitimate protest against colonialism—is markedly, violently absent. Instead of posing a threat against an external enemy, the right hand clutching the knife turns inward as the direction and target of rage change. Thus, the plaint against the colonizer becomes an act of self-injury.

Take a second look at the bleeding heart in *Heridas*. At first glance, the arced strokes resemble blood spraying out of the chest. But upon closer inspection, one notices that the brush strokes move in the opposite direction of what one would expect from blood.[18] They begin outside, on the margins of the painting, and move in toward the chest. Instead of spurting blood, the curved lines look like the blurred, frozen movements of something stabbing at the torso. What's more, the curving streaks are gray, not red. The wound to the chest simply is not as literal and as gory as the bright red amputated limbs. The chest injuries occur at another level altogether, daubed onto the seated figure as a second layer of paint and meaning. Supposing that *Heridas* is a self-portrait, the artist's brush itself becomes a self-mutilating dagger. *Heridas* contains a layered representation of colonial melancholia wherein the distinction between self-injury, subject-formation, and political expression is difficult to detect.

MELANCHOLIC LAUGHTER

Yet should we always take Ocampo's paintings so seriously? What happens when we allow the interjection of humor in our third and final reading of *Heridas*? Though disturbingly pathetic, the beheaded figure's stubbornness may also strike us as absurd, ludicrous, and even funny. His head and leg are sliced off, and still he clutches a knife! What does this fellow think he is doing? Doesn't he know when to give up? He resembles a chicken running around with its head cut off, and even the spouting blood looks cartoonish. It is horrifying to watch. Yet we want to laugh a little even though we know it is tragic.

The open wounds of *Heridas* turn out to be jokes in which Ocampo is poking fun at himself. This self-mocking, perhaps melancholic, laughter is a powerful, if extremely unpredictable, source of pleasure. While such laughter risks trivializing the violence that underpins colonial rage, the laughter clearly functions as a defense mechanism, a way to survive the ravages of grief. Moreover, in poking fun at himself, Ocampo calls upon a community to do something other than tear others and self apart, instead to explode in laughter, to fall apart laughing. However ephemerally, the communal act heals even as it causes pain to both the group and the individual. Melancholic laughter functions as aural evidence within a community that daily contends with a history of colonial loss and the forces of imperial amnesia and postcolonial absence. *Heridas* exploits the melancholic tension between individual complaint and collective plaint, shifting and converting the symbolic value of images of injury from that of martyrdom and suffering to that of communal laughter and healing. Ocampo's pasyon paintings are prototypical examples of colonial melancholia in Filipino/American art, wherein the representation of bodily injury is simultaneously an expression of social protest, self-denigration, self-mockery, and communal regeneration.

THE "WIDE OPEN" EYE AND THE CUTTING STYLE OF *NAILED*

Like Ocampo, Filipino/American videomaker Angel Velasco Shaw engages and critiques the colonizing gaze in her 1992 experimental documentary *Nailed*. *Nailed* is a remarkably dense onslaught of sound and scene, in which Shaw weaves performance art and personal narration with live footage from her year-long stay in the Philippines. Here, too, the act of self-affirmation is invariably, paradoxically self-injurious while the act of self-injury turns out to be self-affirmative. After all, the fifty-minute video centers on a woman's reenactment of Christ's crucifixion. But while Ocampo's paintings offer melancholic laughter as a source of communal healing, Shaw's intense identification with Lucy Reyes's suffering posits a substantially different kind of colonial melancholia that mobilizes a complex politics of nostalgia and that foregrounds the gendering of colonized subjectivity. Out of the mélange of images and events that make up *Nailed*, I analyze three distinct sections that precede or interrupt the depiction of Lucy Reyes's crucifixion: the opening dream-montage; the juxtaposition of an infant's baptism with the slaying of a pig; and, finally, a performance piece by artist-writer Jessica Hagedorn.

Belying the title's promise of pain, *Nailed* opens with a tranquil montage of Philippine sky and beach imagery. Over these stereotypical images of a tropical Eden, Shaw narrates a disquieting dream about battling angels, one of which falls to earth and explodes into fragments: "When he hit the ground, his body shattered into a lot of different parts, but one portion of his face remained intact. It quickly solidified into the ground. His eye was wide open. And a golden tear formed....That was a dream I had one night." Shaw's narration transforms landscape into dreamscape.

The images of sun-drenched beaches and tumbling blue waves lose some of their tourist, escapist appeal and instead become highly personal and somehow numbing. Shaw's tone is personal, intimate, and yet detached, befitting the word-image of the fallen angel's cracked head, staring eye, and single tear. From the very beginning of

Nailed, Filipina/American subject-formation is associated with deformity and fragmentation.[19] Only two things keep this partial subject "intact." The golden tear symptomatizes the presence of nostalgia, a special kind of colonial melancholia that vacillates between wistful longing and tempered rage.[20] The "wide open" eye potentially registers the horrors of colonization or perhaps gazes longingly at the landscape impossibly designated as home. In the form of a video camera, of course, this "wide open" eye functions as a recording device of past and present injuries.

After this opening dream-montage, two interwoven events frame the pending appearance of Reyes: an infant's christening and the slaughtering of a pig. Like much of *Nailed*, this twelve-minute section is filled with jarring jump cuts and unlikely couplings of images. A series of jump cuts begins with benign portraits of Shaw's baby goddaughter at her baptism. Her still floppy head nestled in her mother's arms, the newborn yawns at the camera documenting the communal affirmation of her identity. Abruptly, her christening is relentlessly intercut with much too close, lingering shots of a live pig being staked and gutted in preparation for a feast presumably held after the naming ceremony. Its life and horrifying death are recorded and resurrected on screen. One of the last images of the pig is implicitly Christlike, its decapitated head hanging on the side of a tree. Basically, Shaw chronicles a pig's *pasyon*.

According to *Nailed*'s editing logic, the tortured animal's awful shrieks mark the child's naming and inclusion within a specific community. From several angles and at close range, we witness the first cutting of the pig as a wooden stake is driven through its abdomen. The pig's shrill death scream holds at a single sustained pitch, pausing only for quick, sharp gasps before continuing to cry. Head shots of the baby and then of the pig form tightly paired edits, spliced together by the intolerable scream. In one of these paired edits, the baby's blurry, limp head floats sideways in the foreground, her body cut off by the edge of the screen. In the next frame, the pig writhes in pain, the camera focused on its moving mouth and unblinking eyes. The pig is stabbed, drained of its blood, disemboweled, roasted, carved, and then methodically chopped up into neat little squares. The animal gradually disintegrates while the oblivious infant is gently rocked and cradled in her relatives' arms.

Angel Velasco Shaw, Scenes from *Nailed*, "Reverence"

On the one hand, the child's baptism provides the occasion for the affirmation of the communal self, and the celebratory feast reinforces kinship ties and strengthens group identity. On the other hand, Shaw's attention to the pig's pain foregrounds the cost of such communion and foreshadows *Nailed*'s main event, Reyes's crucifixion. According to this sequence of images, self-affirmation coincides with extreme pain and physical mutilation. In other words, Filipina/American subject-formation is here associated with a paradoxically self-affirming desire for disjointedness and fragmentation that colonial castration cannot account for.

Yet, while the central event of *Nailed* remains the exhibition of a woman's pain, the video is emphatically "autoethnographic," a combination of ethnography and autobiography.[21] *Nailed* is an explicitly autobiographical video that contains elegiac elements. As the closing credits roll, we read that the documentary is dedicated to the "spirit" of Shaw's dead father. At the same time, *Nailed* identifies itself both with and against traditional ethnography by foregrounding questions of authority and spectacle. The narrator's perspective is plainly subjective, unlike ethnography's tradition of neutral objectivity (which of course usually turns out be a veiled subjectivity). If *Nailed* functions as a portrait of another woman, it is simultaneously a self-portrait, constantly shifting and playing with the subject and object of observation. The videomaker herself appears in several scenes, accentuating the fictitiousness of documentary objectivity and explicitly inscribing herself into a text that foregrounds the ambivalence of postcolonial identity. For example, Shaw strolls down a bustling Manila sidewalk dressed in a traditional Spanish Filipino *saya* and reading excerpts from a Mark Twain essay on American imperialism—an incongruous melding of past and present that typifies the postcolonial aesthetics of *Nailed*. In another example of autoethnographic technique, an actress (Jessica Hagedorn) sits with her back to the camera as she watches *Nailed* on a small television. Effectively, we look over the actress's shoulder as we watch her watching a penitent flagellate himself. In *Nailed*, looking at someone else entails looking at oneself. Or, more accurately, looking at someone else always entails looking at oneself looking at someone else. *Nailed* affords the viewer a space for critical self-reflection. It offers a mode of looking that keeps the masterful, colonizing gaze in check.

Perhaps this is why the first images of Reyes are rather ordinary, almost easy to miss. The faith healer is plainly dressed, calmly talking amongst her followers, quiet images that the viewer almost misses since they are intercut with the more dramatic splicing of the pig's pasyon and the infant's baptism. Narrating her first meeting with Reyes, Shaw recalls Reyes's explanation of her motives for the annual crucifixion, that she had had a vision of the Santo Niño when she was eighteen years old. According to Reyes, the Santo Niño told her that she had a "calling" that involved annual crucifixion. Shaw says, "And that was kind of a hard story to hear, even if it was in translation, from this woman who was so sweet. I mean, she had the face of a cherub." Of course, *Nailed* is a visual narration of what was a "hard story to hear." Using another technique typically found in autoethnographic film and video, the narrator speaks in first-person voice-over throughout the video. Shaw's tone is personal, intimate, and at times self-enclosed, making us feel as if we were eavesdropping on an internal conversation as she repeats phrases like "I'm not part of this trance" and "routines that are rituals." Already, we feel anxious or even guilty about hearing and seeing something to which we are not usually privy.

Despite what she claims, however, the narrator does sound like she is in a trance. Shaw's first-person voice-over is an aural reenactment of Reyes's trance-like performance on the cross. Because Reyes is figured as a messenger of God, apparently possessed by the Santo Niño, Catherine Russell's study of ethnographic films of possession rituals seems relevant. Russell notes:

> The actual experience of possession remains outside the limits of visual knowledge and constitutes a subtle form of ethnographic resistance: films of possession cannot, in the end, represent the "other reality" of the other's subjectivity. Possession is itself a form of representation to which the film-maker might aspire, but it is also a mise en abyme of representation, with its final signified content always beyond reach. I would like to argue that the end point of the possession semiosis is the subjectivity of the Other, which thus resists cinematic representation along with its ideology of visibility.[22]

As such, Shaw's trance-like narration is a simulation of Reyes's interiority, which "remains outside the limits of visual knowledge." While Shaw's video recording of Reyes naturally constitutes an attempt at visual representation, the aural content of *Nailed* nonetheless underscores the impossibility of representing the faith healer's experience on the screen. I would even argue that the aural reenactment represents the videomaker's acknowledgment of the complicity and representational problematics that necessarily attend any representation of the Other.[23]

Indeed, this sense of complicity extends to the viewer of *Nailed*. Both the content and the form of *Nailed* configure the viewer's position as a kind of vacillating tension between witness and spectator. Here, it is important to distinguish between witness and spectator, the latter of which implies greater distance from the ethnographic subject and is more closely associated with the colonizing gaze. Russell distinguishes between the two terms in her analysis of the filming of possession rituals, which, like the crucifixion, are "community events intended to be witnessed, but they are not addressed to a spectator." Reyes's crucifixion clearly takes place within a communal, public space, filled by an organized chaos that renders long, stable camera shots impossible and that requires Shaw to change positions and angles hurriedly and frequently. Thus, the "automatic or fixed point of view" associated with the spectator becomes technically impossible for Shaw (Russell 235). On the other hand, Shaw's camera equipment and autoethnographic sensibility necessarily prevent her and the viewer of *Nailed* from becoming witnesses.[24]

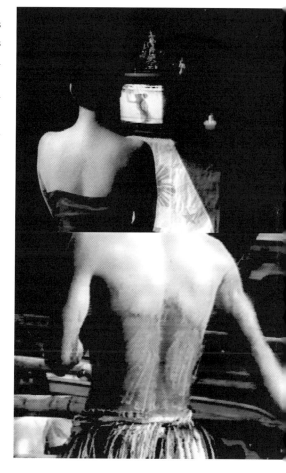

But, confronted with the visual confusion of *Nailed*, what retains the viewer's attention? If *Nailed* is a "hard story to hear," it is often very hard to watch but there is something that makes us try to witness. As painful as it is to watch and hear the act of injury, there is something compelling about the representation of violence. According to *Nailed's* editing sequence, the pig's slaughter prepares us for the documentary's central event. In a sense, the pig's pasyon compels us to watch further in anticipation of Reyes's crucifixion. *Nailed* capitalizes on the viewer's anticipation of the public crucifixion as much as possible, a use of suspense that propels and motivates the entire documentary. Suspense motivates the viewer; it keeps the curious viewer waiting and watching. With a mixture of guilt and desire, Shaw narrates her own impatience to see Reyes:

Angel Velasco Shaw, Scenes from *Nailed*, "Redemption"

> I was in such a hurry to get to the stage, this half-built stagewhere Lucy was going to be crucified, because I wanted to see whether or not she was going to suffer. I felt horrible about that because I think the majority of the people who were there also came for the same reason, partially—I mean, I think they believed in her. They believed in this reenactment. They believed that she had a calling and that she was special and that somehow she was a messenger from God. And I wanted to see signs of that.

Like the viewer, Shaw knows that Lucy will be crucified. Since we know what will happen, the suspense comes from not knowing exactly how it will happen, i.e., whether Reyes will suffer. Shaw seeks visible evidence of Reyes's suffering: "And I wanted to see signs of *that*" (my emphasis). But the ambiguity of the pronoun "that" raises another possibility: "that" may also refer to the other people in the crowd. In other words, Shaw's attraction to the stage reveals a desire to see evidence of the crowd's faith in Reyes as much as a desire to see Reyes's pasyon. In this way, Shaw's editing and narrating styles produce intensely personalized effects that nevertheless engage with a community of witnesses and viewers.

Moreover, Shaw's use of suspense affords her the space in which to experiment with an antilinear and fragmentary style of editing and mixing, without ever losing the viewer. That is, the overriding narrative or telos of Reyes's crucifixion allows the production of something anti-narrative. *Nailed* both refuses and relies on the power of linear narrative. Shaw's fragmentary editing style can be viewed as a series of wounds to the traditional, linear narrative. At the same time, this fragmented documentary feels so seamless and smoothly knitted together. While the juxtaposition of myriad images is relentless, spanning election campaigns, fiestas, church services, rice farms, and urban nightlife, Shaw's fragmentary editing style never lapses into incoherence. It is as if the "wide open eye" and cutting style of Shaw's camerawork and editing are bound together by the visual promise of yet another open wound, that represented by Lucy Reyes. Though it certainly risks bombarding the viewer, the constant shuffling of disparate images is bound together by Shaw's first-person narration and by the promise of a woman's voluntary crucifixion.

Nailed is a melancholic production both in the sense that it represents Filipina/American subject-formation as melancholic and that it produces an aesthetics of melancholia. As an experimental videomaker, Shaw makes explicit the connections between vision and violence in her critique of the colonizing gaze. But her identification with Reyes ("I want to embrace the 'Lucy' in me") indicates that there is another, significant dimension to this representation of the relationship between vision and injury that cannot be reduced to an oppositional stance against the colonizing gaze. Rather, Shaw's identification with Reyes's wounds suggests that Filipino/American subjectivity is impelled by a desire for parts, shards, and fragments, a gendered process that diverges radically from the search for unity and wholeness that drives colonial castration.

MELANCHOLIC JOKES AND IMPERIAL FORGETTING

Ralph Peña's play *Flipzoids* stages the Filipino/American encounter with American imperial forgetting. In *Flipzoids*, a particular mixture of humor and invective bridges the gap between melancholic loss and recollection, a combination that recalls the melancholic laughter of Ocampo's *Heridas*. One of the potential sites for the transfer of unofficial history (that is, memories and stories) occurs through a series of hurtful jokes. A rhetorical kind of "open wound," the melancholic joke reveals much that is painful or taboo. Indeed, the joke can expose forbidden or painful ideas in a way that is officially sanctioned precisely because it is, after all, only a joke. "Joke only," retorts Aying, one of the three characters, whenever anyone takes her odd pranks too seriously.[25] At the beginning of *Flipzoids*, though, hardly anyone listens to her stories and jokes, let alone takes them seriously.

An elderly, recent immigrant to the United States, Aying is engulfed by memories of the Philippines. Lonely and trapped in southern California, she pines for her village home Pagudpud, and she laments the emotional gulf between her and her daughter Vangie. Appalled at her daughter's blind yearning to assimilate into white suburban America, Aying insists on remembering and recycling stories of Pagudpud to anyone who will listen. Aying explains, "I can see things, all blue. But

maybe I should be blind. Where I come from, stories grow from trees" (43). To Aying, these stories grant a special kind of "blue" vision that enables her to "see things" and to tell stories. To Vangie, though, Aying's storytelling represents an inability to leave both the past and the Philippines behind. Frustrated by her mother's depressing ways, Vangie exclaims, "Aying. You know why you're like that? Why you feel sad and alone? Dejected. Despondent, and ah oh so very very blue. You know why? Because you won't get out of your grave. You insist on spending your days with the dead" (7). The "blue" Aying is paralyzed by the past and by a mournful nostalgia. Of course, Vangie's rejection of her mother's stories guarantees their obsolescence. Because Vangie refuses to listen, Aying's legacy—the stories and recollections that make up unofficial history—lack an audience and, therefore, a legatee. Until she befriends the unlikely Redford, Aying's stories are meaningless.

If Aying's unacknowledged legacy consists of stories that circulate pointlessly, Vangie's lexicon is made up of endless lists of memorized words. Clad in the stark white uniform of a nurse, Vangie methodically expands her English vocabulary by listening to a taped recording of Webster's dictionary on her ever-present Walkman: "You see that? I am putting Webster to memory. So far, I know every word from A to G. That's something, right? Not every nurse can say that [pause] I can." She wanders on and off stage, occasionally pausing her Walkman to parrot aloud wondrous new words in *Sesame Street* fashion: "Exercise One Fifty-Five. The letter D. Dainty. Dandelion. Dandruff. Decapitate. [She takes out a clothes pin and clips it onto her nose] Today's road to the promised land is brought to you by the letter D" (3-4). Vangie's mechanical approach to language is meant to counter her mother's depressing, "blue" storytelling. But Vangie's pinched nose results in a different kind of "blue," one that does not allow her to breathe and makes her go "blue" in the face from cultural asphyxiation.

Vangie's alliterative list of "D" words begins absurdly and innocently enough ("Dainty. Dandelion. Dandruff..."). However, both "dandelion" and "dandruff" summon images of the head: the flower invokes images of heavy yet fragile bobbing heads while dandruff falls off scalps. Both words anticipate the final reference to beheading, "decapitate," the utterance of which makes Vangie briefly pause and frown before donning the clothespin and continuing her lesson. Though baffling to Vangie, the abruptly violent end to her "D" list is fitting. Vangie's aural lessons

Ching Valdez-Aran as Aying in *Flipzoids*

389

in the English language , the dominant language of the American empire, cut off her ability to breathe. The clothespin signifies the suffocating effects of assimilation that accompany the acquisition of English. Unlike Ocampo's decapitated figure and amputated "lengua," Vangie's head remains atop her shoulders but the Walkman encasing her head does her another kind of violence. It forms a trap or cage that threatens to suffocate her. So while in Ocampo, the colonized (male) subject reverts to decapitation as an expression of the loss of language, Vangie represents the inassimilable (female) subject's reversion to suffocation as an expression of the cost and impossibility of acquiring language.

While Aying maintains that America smells like "bad pork" (7), Vangie manages the foul smell of America by closing off her olfactory senses, listening to the recorded version of the dictionary, and (ideally) speaking perfect, unaccented American English. In a way, Vangie attempts to transform American stench into American speech. In doing so, she shuns her mother and refuses her position as legatee. Vangie inadvertently announces her orphan status while reciting a new "M' word from the dictionary: "M. Maverick. Noun. A motherless calf" (39). Instead of "mother," "M" stands for "maverick," a calf that has lost its mother. The cost of assimilation is clear: the acquisition of English demands the renunciation of the mother, who in this case represents Vangie's link to memory, heritage, and the Philippines.

In a particularly telling aside to the audience, Vangie says of Aying: "I know you probably think, listening to her stories, that where she comes from is a magical place, well it's not. She says to me all the time, 'Evangelina, do not forget.' (pause) That's exactly what I've done" (39). Of course, Vangie's not forgetting is also a form of forgetting. According to Vangie's interpretation of her mother's directive ("Evangeline, do not forget"), not forgetting the Philippines entails forgetting and erasing any evidence of the Philippines in her speech and behavior. In other words, if imperial forgetting enacts a kind of psychic violence, certain forms of remembering seem necessarily associated with this kind of forgetting. Weirdly enough, Vangie's relentless forgetting is a form of not forgetting. Were Vangie truly able to forget the poverty and despair of her life in the Philippines, she would not expend so much energy distancing herself from memories of the Philippines and grasping at the material and cultural progress that white suburbia represents to her. Vangie's paradoxical amnesia takes on even greater significance when one considers the persistent cloud of obscurity surrounding the American colonization of the Philippines in both the American national imaginary and historiography. Vangie's racialized amnesia reflects not just the inferior status of racialized subjects in the United States but also the colonial status of the Philippines. Vangie's amnesia is constitutive of her identity as an assimilated Filipino/ American. Moreverover, Vangie's personal amnesia ironically functions as a metaphor for America's national amnesia about its imperial history and legacy. For at the level of national consciousness, America's amnesia is constitutive of its self-image as a nation of freedom and democracy.

A response to the numbing effects of imperial forgetting, Peña's characters use metaphors of physical aggression and injury—especially spitting, wounding, and itching—to describe their predicaments and their interaction with others. In one example of the play's biting dialogue, Vangie's and Aying's ambivalent relationship comes to a crisis in a crucial scene at the mall. Their intergenerational conflict about the meaning of language and the value of memory becomes a source of public embarrassment for Vangie when, "halfway between Eddie Bauer and Baccarat," Aying decides to perform a spiritual cleansing ceremony that includes spitting water at all other shoppers within range (31). Noticing Aying dancing and singing next to a water fountain, Vangie first tries to block out her mother from the idyllic image she glances in the mall mirrors of herself, apparently blending into white suburban anonymity. She says, "I noticed but denied. Who is that? She doesn't belong in my mirror" (33). Then Aying spews a stream of water out onto the "very classy, very confident shoulder of Miss Gucci," and Vangie's world of mall mirrors is shattered. Vangie is humiliated by Aying in front of the very people she hopes to emulate. Mortified and enraged by her mother's behavior, Vangie interprets the spitting as an act of murderous aggression against her, and she describes Aying as a poisonous snake: "[M]y mother's saliva. Her venom. It was intended for me. She wanted to bite me.... It worked. I died" (34). Vangie's references to aggressive orality and her own social death underscore the cruelty and viciousness—intentional or not—of the verbal and generational sparring between mother and daughter.

Redford (Ken Leung) meets Aying in *Flipzoids*.

Vangie blames her mother for her social and linguistic death at the mall. Vangie's mastery of English vocabulary and American accent immediately disappears as she tries to stop Aying and to apologize to Miss Gucci. Vangie's cries of protest are reduced to monosyllables: "AY! AY! AYING! DO NOT NOT NOT DO THIS NOT NOT THIS NOT HERE NOT NOW NOT NOT NOT HER. AYING!" (34). Then, on her knees before Miss Gucci, Vangie suddenly switches to a halting, heavy Tagalog accent:

> *Ma'am... ma'am... I am sorry... ma'am. Miss Gucci. Naku... ma'am. I... please... ma'am... you forgive ha? Please... you are so pretty ma'am... so fortunate... and blessed... let me touch your being, may I? Me... Pangit ako. Pangit. I am ugly. Yes. Can I clean you ma'am? I am humble... humble... forgive... ma'am... forgive. We are worthless... You like, I will clean your house? Kasi... Kasi... Misis... Where I come from... Doon... There is so many flies... so many flies... Kaya...* (34)

In this horrifying speech, Vangie pleads for forgiveness by offering several means of compensation to the drenched Miss Gucci that draw on cultural, class, and racial stereotypes of Filipina/Americans. Vangie mobilizes "pangit" stereotypes of Filipino/American women—as "ugly," "worthless," culturally backward, domestic workers—in order to mollify Miss Gucci. Ironically, in doing so, Vangie further negates her chances of assimilation because her self-denigrating attempts at obsequiousness only mark her distance from the privileged world of white suburbia.

Aying interrupts Vangie's kneeling plea for forgiveness, saying that there is "nothing to forgive," and she invites her daughter to participate in the cleansing ceremony: "Help me remember, Evangelina. Come. We will remember together" (34). But Vangie refuses to assist her mother, and as mall security approaches the dancing Aying, she asks them to shoot Aying: "YOU. YOU. THAT ONE. Mamang Pulis, Mr. Officer. YOU WITH THE GUN. STOP HER. MAKE HER STOP. SHOOT HER AND MAKE HER STOP" (35). In this vengeful response to Aying's presumed aggression, Vangie expresses her desire for her mother's death. To the mall security, Vangie denies that she has anything to do with Aying and then deliberately places a shopping bag over her head, literally blocking the sight and sound of her own humiliation and also symbolizing a kind of decapitation. Aying complies with Vangie's wishes, excuses herself as a "crazy old woman only," and quietly exits with the security escort, but not before pausing to explain her behavior to the headless Vangie: "Young people like you, it is very easy for you to forget. But when you are like me already, more hard to remember" (35). But Vangie rejects Aying's overtures, which cannot make up for the way she died at the mall. She compares her humiliating exposure with the butchering of an animal: "I was stripped naked before Miss Gucci and Mrs. Lauren... split open like a slaughtered cow" (36).

Even the most intimate moments in *Flipzoids* turn into teasing, cutting jokes that feature an underlying aggression that targets both the teller of the joke and his/her listener. Aware of the looming crisis in their relationship, Aying and Vangie make an attempt at reconciliation and begin to confess the way in which they fail and love each other as mother and daughter. Aying beckons Vangie to approach her and tenderly caresses Vangie's face. Carefully draping Vangie's arms around her shoulders, Aying sings a nonsensical Filipino nursery tune as Vangie awkwardly embraces Aying, a tender tableau of mother-daughter affection. But Aying shatters the fragile moment with a morbid joke that transforms Vangie's embrace into matricidal suffocation. She moves Vangie's hands around her neck and says, "Here. Now you press hard. Squeeze it" (24). Vangie draws back, horrified, then runs away as Aying calls after her: "Evangelina. You come back... Joke only." Just as jokes often reveal taboo desires, Aying's unexpected prank horrifies Vangie because it exposes her desire for her mother's death. In a sense, Aying gives Vangie what she wants, the ultimate sacrifice of parent for child, but this sacrifice is not completely altruistic. Indeed, Aying's joke contains a degree of malice for Aying must know that the sudden revelation of Vangie's prohibited matricidal impulses will upset Vangie. Aying's jokes hit much too close to home, and they hurt those she loves.

Aying repeats this pattern of hurtful humor with her new friend Redford, a queer, dyed-blonde, angst-ridden loner with self-mutilating tendencies whom she meets while wandering along a beach. Estranged from both his parents and his Filipino heritage, Redford usually lurks in the public toilet on the beach, where he holds barricaded conversations with anonymous, unsuspecting strangers in the adjoining stall. When Aying and Redford first meet, Aying is appalled to discover that Redford is also Filipino: "You? So you are Pilipino also? (pause) What happened?" It is not his clothes and dyed hair alone that prompt this brief interrogation. When he assures her that he is indeed Filipino, Aying says, "You don't look Pilipino," then asks, "Your parents? They look like you?" Redford answers that they do, and she matter-of-factly rejoins, "Then they do not look Pilipino also." The questions are racially motivated. Redford's light-skinned Chinese mestizo features cast doubt on his Filipino authenticity. Yet Aying's funny, if contemptuous, comments on Redford's mixed racial heritage serve as a way for him to begin remembering his cultural heritage.[26]

As we later learn, Redford lacks a sense of home or identity or, more accurately, a sense of continuity with the country of his childhood. Prompted by Aying's recollections of her father's stories, Redford describes his father's rejection of the Philippines and the

Redford listens to Aying in *Flipzoids*.

past, an attitude of conscious forgetting that recalls Vangie's amnesia: "I never once heard him talk about the past. It was always about what he was going to be in the future.... And there was never any residue, you know... I mean... he never left a trail behind. My father just kept moving forward. Behind him, there was nothing. He is what he is now, and nothing of him is what he was" (26). Rather than leaving no "trail behind," though, the father's deliberate forgetting inadvertently produces Redford's identity crisis. Redford's predicament is a residual, potentially dangerous product of his father's obsession with the future and utter rejection of the past.

Redford lacks the very memories and stories of the Philippines of which Aying has too many. He says to Aying: "Sometimes I'd be standing on a street corner, or be reading a book, or taking a shower, and my skin would begin to itch. Like I'm going to explode. And you know what keeps repeating in my head? Over and over. 'I want to go home.' I want to go home. Over and over. I want to go home" (26). Redford's nostalgia is quite literal. He is sick for home, a psychosomatic illness whose symptoms affect both body and mind. All too bluntly, Aying answers him, "This is your home" (26). As Redford learns from Aying, home is related to memory, an interior mapping of geography (see fig. 8). The Philippines, it seems, is in the heart. Redford's self-mutilating impulses recede as Aying's storytelling enables him to reconstruct memories of a lost childhood and a lost heritage. By the end of the play, Redford hesitantly begins to recall his own memories of his childhood in the Philippines, triggered by Aying's insistence on the past. He hesitantly recalls, "The only thing I remember... from the other side... maybe I was six... maybe seven... the only thing that survives... is a fuzzy picture... a small blue window over a bed. Maybe... over my bed. Lying down, I recall catching a slice of the sky outside and the rusted roof with its peeling blue paint" (47). Here, the color "blue" signifies neither the suffocating consequences of Vangie's assimilationist desires nor the despairing loneliness of Aying's nostalgia. It signifies the beginnings of a kind of visual memory ("fuzzy picture") that enables Redford to reconstruct that which was lost: a childhood, a heritage, and a nation.

In turn, Redford fulfills Aying's need for a listening audience, someone who will give meaning to her stories. Redford is somewhat uncomfortable in this role of surrogate 'son....I can't....I don't know how to process these parables... your allegories... whatever... into anything that will make a difference. They're wasted on me" (40). But Aying insists that Redford listen to her stories: "I will die soon. You listen to my stories. They will live with you" (27). With a combination of mirth, cruelty, and love, Aying passes on a legacy of stories in yet another series of jokes, and this time it works. Aghast at the fact that Redford cannot utter a word of his parents' language, she mischievously miseducates him when she teaches him his first words of Tagalog, ostensibly "I love you." First she again makes sure that he doesn't know any Tagalog. Deliberately mistranslating, Aying makes him practice over and over again, then loudly declaim the phrase, "Pangit ako!" ("I am ugly!"). The duped Redford finally gets to declare love by declaring himself ugly. And he's "pangit" in at least three ways. His mestizo features make him not-Filipino and, therefore, ugly. He obviously does not and cannot fit the image of his Hollywood namesake Robert Redford. Thirdly, he is "pangit" by virtue of his homosexuality. Redford's "pangit" status—of racial mixture, sexual marginalization, and cultural assimilation—gets declared only through the use of comic invective and self-denigration.

By mistranslating the phrase "Pangit ako!" to Redford, Aying rescripts Vangie's humiliating "Pangit ako" speech before Miss Gucci. With Redford, Aying transforms Vangie's self-denigrating phrase into an expression of love that nonetheless retains its self-injurious elements, and so the melancholic's self-abasement does not disappear completely. After Redford tells her "Pangit ako," she gently touches his face and replies, "Me also" (42). The "me also" response enables her expression of love for another, since Aying knows that Redford understands it as such. At the same time, in a typically twisted melancholic fashion, Aying declares that she too is ugly or "pangit." Furthermore, Aying's reciprocation of Redford's love occurs in the form of a joke that only the audience "gets," thereby demonstrating the melancholic's dependence on the presence of a third party. Both she and Redford become objects or victims of the joke. Redford has no idea that he is saying "I'm ugly," and so becomes the target of the audience's laughter. Too, though, Aying turns the joke on herself, acknowledging some of the blame for hurting others like Vangie and thereby expressing her love for her daughter. Here and throughout *Flipzoids*, the articulation of love involves hurting or defacing oneself and others. And yet there is a significant transformation, wherein the self-abasement is no longer entirely self-involved; instead, it can be directed outward toward others.

In the play's final scene, Redford drops to his knees, arms out wide, Christ-like, with the spotlight on him. Looking up at the sky, he shouts out, "Pangit ako!" A farewell to the now deceased Aying, Redford's final declaration of love for her propels him out of his melancholic com/plaining and desperate self-absorption. But this unconscious self-denigration has a certain significant effect on the audience as well. He unconsciously mocks himself and we in the audience laugh at him and his unknowing self-mockery. But in sympathizing or identifying with him, we end up laughing at ourselves in a way. So the melancholic triangulation of ego, object, and audience is still intact, but with a crucial difference: the individual's pain can now be taken up by the group. The pain of bodily self-mockery ("Pangit ako!") gets translated or changed into another kind of pain, something that enables one to feel and to bear the pain of colonial loss. *Flipzoids* insists on a delicate dependence on the audience and, in a larger sense, on community. This intimate interrelation between individual and communal loss saves the melancholic from self-destruction and from desperate self-involvement. Perhaps Aying and Redford point the way out of, or through, colonial melancholia. A way to name and remember the lost object, even though the object is loss itself.

COMMUNAL MELANCHOLIA AND EVERYDAY LAUGHTER

Clustering radically differing texts, a video, play, and paintings, this interdisciplinary study deliberately overreaches itself so as to underscore the wider, cross-media significance of a particular pattern of injury. In identifying an aesthetics of colonial melancholia in Filipino/American art, I of course do not claim that this is representative of all Filipino/American art. Indeed, at first glance, the three artists' works are almost incomparably different. Yet I juxtapose their work in this cross-media study because these texts share a distinct pattern of mutilation and injury that I call colonial melancholia. Colonial melancholia is a significant phenomenon in these texts, in Filipino/American art, and arguably in the lives of Filipino/Americans. These artists point toward constructive ways to represent and to theorize both the continuities and rifts amongst Filipino/Americans. These texts proffer definitions of community that, rather than based on affinity and the often homogenizing pressures of coalitionist alliances, are predicated on performative acts of injury. For both in these texts and in the everyday joking and banter that define Filipino/American communities, moments of healing, mourning, and resistance emerge during the performance of pain. This phenomenon suggests that Filipino/American art is embedded in a culture of presence, a "passional culture" that insists on the body as a vehicle for artistic, political, and religious expression. This cultural argument may sound reductive or dangerously essentialist to some, but the fairly stable status of Filipino/American history, art, and cultural production as absence (or, at best, as an irksome anomaly) in the United States speaks to the need for critical approaches that understand this insistence on the body as part of a combative engagement with imperial forgetting. Filipino/American art and cultural production reappropriate both the violence of Spanish and American colonization and the violence of American amnesia. In short, the process of Filipino/American decolonization is far from over. That the body is persistently represented as fragmented and mutilated attests to the vestiges of colonial trauma—colonial melancholia.

NOTES:

I am grateful to Catherine Ramirez, Karen Su, Vivian Chin, Emily Lee, Hiram Pérez, Yukari Yanagino, and my editors for commenting on earlier versions of this essay. I thank Manuel Ocampo, Ralph Peña, and Angel Shaw for indulging me in my critical attempts and for allowing me to reproduce images of their lyrical, always inspiring, work. I also thank the organizers of the 1999 "Vestiges of War" conference at New York University; and David Eng for the opportunity to participate in an illuminating panel on race and melancholia with Jani Scandura, Julie Barmazel, and Marlene Goldman at the Chicago 1999 Modern Language Association meeting. My deepest gratitude to Angel Shaw for her critical, artistic, and pedagogical vision.

1. I use the term "Filipino/American" to indicate both the presence of Filipinos in the United States and the imperial presence of the United States in the Philippines. This term encompasses minority racial status, colonial status, and the postcolonial legacy of invisibility produced by the amnesia that distinguishes U.S. history in relation to empire. Conceiving of the term Filipino/American solely as a designation of racial minority status risks repeating the erasure of a history of colonization, a massive omission that too typically characterizes many historical treatments of U.S. imperialism at the turn of the century. I would even argue that the terms "Filipino-American" and "Filipino American" are misleading and tautological, for being "Filipino" in some sense also means being "American," or, to be more precise, a racialized subject of a U.S. colony. (The asymmetry of the rhetorical relationship between "Filipino" and "American" becomes clear when one realizes that the inverse is ludicrous: being "American" emphatically does not always also mean being "Filipino.") While this claim has its limitations, I think it is important because it reveals the misleading effects of characterizing the relationship between the United States' rhetoric of democratic citizenship and the reality of its colonized subjects, as one of antithesis rather than of interdependence. More anecdotally, I regularly am confronted by various forms of the inevitable interrogation "Where are you from?" While much Asian Americanist deconstruction of this accusatory question rightly focuses on racial formation and on the perpetually alien status of Asians in America, it does not benefit fully from Filipino/American critical perspectives that might emphasize a legacy of colonization. That is to say, the response "I am an American" can be perceived as a declaration of citizenship that may or may not involve an embracing of assimilationist values. But what if the respondent is thinking, "I am an American (subject)," a subordinate subject not a citizen of the American empire?

2. *Flipzoids* (handbill), by Ralph Peña, dir. Loy Arcenas, May-Yi Theatre Ensemble, perf. Ching Valdes Aran, Mia Katigbak, and Ken Leung, Theatre for the New City, October 1997.

3. For a range of theoretical, anecdotal, and historical discussions of imperial forgetting, see Oscar Campomanes's "The New Empire's Forgetful and Forgotten Citizens: Unrepresentability and Unassimilability in Filipino-American Postcolonialities," *Critical Mass* 2.2 (1995); Ambeth R. Ocampo's "Bones of Contention: Relics, Memory, and Andres Bonifacio," *Amerasia Journal* 24.3 (1998): 45–74; Mia Blumentritt's "Bontoc Eulogy, History, and the Craft of Memory: An Extended Conversation with Marlon E. Fuentes," ibid.: 75–90; and Kimberly Ann Alidio's "'When I Get Home, I Want to Forget': Memory and Amnesia in the Occupied Philippines, 1901-1904" in *Social Text* 59, 17.2 (1999): 105-122.

4. Sigmund Freud, "Mourning and Melancholia," (1917). *General Psychological Theory: Theories on Paranoia, Masochism, Repression, Melancholia, the Unconscious, the Libido, and Other Aspects of the Human Psyche* (New York: Collier Books: Macmillan Publishing Company, 1963). All subsequent references to "Mourning and Melancholia" will use page numbers from this edition. Recently, critics like Anne Cheng, Judith Butler, Douglas Crimp, Jeff Nunokawa, and José Muñoz have used mourning and melancholia as a way to theorize subjectivity, especially in relation to sexual, racial, and gendered subordination. Other critics like Vicente Rafael, Anahid Kassabian, and David Kazanjian have used mourning and melancholia as a useful metaphor for national, transnational, and diasporic imaginings. What has been underexplored,

however, is the role of the body in melancholia. Naturally, critics typically have invoked the model of hysteria—especially with Freud's 1905 analysis of Dora—in order to theorize the repression of language and the reversion to the body as a means of voicing intensely repressed desire. The difference between hysteria and melancholia is subtle but significant. Whereas hysterical symptoms indicate the workings of repression, melancholia is about foreclosure. In other words, if hysteria is about the silencing of non-normative subjects, melancholia is about the utter loss of language. Thus, in melancholia the body not so much speaks as falls apart. Part of this distinction between hysteria and melancholia may depend upon the kind of power relation that exists between the subject and his or her society (or, as Kaja Silverman puts it, the "dominant fiction"). For example, the hysterical Dora is treated as a perverted subject (a lesbian), a retarded subject (a child), and an imperfect subject (a woman, hence, a man without a penis). Dora's inclusion within the dominant fiction depends upon her ability to follow the script of heterosexual femininity. Logically, then, her marginalization (she's hysterical, bisexual, etc.) indicates her refusal to follow the script. If we cast her cough as a symbol of this refusal to be a good girl, Dora's hysteria becomes social protest.

In colonial melancholia, the stakes and consequences change. According to Freud, his hysterical patients—white lesbians, gay white men, and straight white women—have either strayed from or refused their proper, normative roles within a civilized society. In contrast, the racially marked, colonized subject completely exceeds the bounds of humanity. Inhuman and bestial, Freud's "primitive" is frozen in time. Culturally deprived and depraved, the "primitive" is considered almost incapable of language. From the colonizer's perspective, the colonized subject can never have lost language since s/he is inherently incapable of language. If any communication occurs, it is only through the sheer physicality and painful presence of the dismembered, colonized body. Indeed, from the perspective of the colonized, the pain is often so overwhelming that the best one can muster is an incoherent scream. (Here, I borrow from Elaine Scarry's work on torture and the inexpressibility of pain; see Scarry's *The Body in Pain: The Unmaking and Making of the World* (New York: Oxford University Press, 1985).

5. One need not necessarily turn to psychoanalysis to understand the intrinsic connection between mental and physical wounds. In everyday usage, the term "trauma" denotes both emotional and bodily damage as *E.R.* and a host of other U.S. television hospital dramas demonstrate weekly. The etymology of "trauma" is informative: originally a Greek noun, trauma means "wound." Trauma also is linked to the Greek verbs *titroskein* and *tetrainein*, respectively "to wound" and "to pierce." So why psychoanalysis? I consider both the Filipino/American texts and the Freudian text as wonderfully unstable and richly layered. In juxtaposing them, however, I regard the Filipino/American texts as politically inspiring whereas Freud's writings are clearly authoritarian texts. To me, the use of Freud's writings (and Western psychoanalysis in general) forces an engagement with compulsory heterosexuality, whiteness, and imperial forgetting that reveals both their workings and their failures. Nothing works harder to reinforce and to undercut its own remarkably persistent grand claims than does Freudian psychoanalysis. Freud's canon is filled with hundreds of contradictions and awkward hiccoughs that interrupt the smooth delivery of a singular, authoritative voice and that threaten any sustained rationale for what Kaja Silverman has called the "dominant fiction." Though the term is risky, I attempt to cast Freudian texts as "fictive" because they seem to operate in the same ways that most compelling narratives and art do. They attempt to tell us, both prescriptively and descriptively, who we are.

6. Reynaldo Ileto, *Pasyon and Revolution: Popular Movements in the Philippines, 1840–1910* (Quezon City: Ateneo de Manila University Press, 1979).

7. This statement is monumentally reductive, but my intention here is to characterize the radical denigration of Philippine vernacular languages as an experience of violence and loss that is constitutive

of postcolonial subjectivity. As Vicente Rafael has argued in *Contracting Colonialism: Translation and Christian Conversion in Tagalog Society under Early Spanish Rule* (Durham, N.C.: Duke University Press, 1993), however, the heterogeneity of Philippine vernacular languages made it impossible for the Spanish to adopt and to codify a single language in its colonizing and Christianizing mission. Too, the geographical diversity of the archipelago and the relatively small Spanish population prevented the marginalization of Philippine languages. Rather, competence in Spanish (and later, with the advent of U.S. colonization, English) marked the formation of language-based class hierarchies, which continue to stratify metropolitan and rural life in the Philippines.

8. I must emphasize that I am not arguing that Ocampo's painting repeats the violence of colonization. Rather, the painting is a reenactment of colonial violence that contains powerful anti-colonial sentiment.

9. Judith Butler. *The Psychic Life of Power: Theories in Subjection* (Stanford, Ca: Stanford University Press, 1997) 162.

10. I adopt the term "disenfranchised grief" from a collection of essays titled *Disenfranchised Grief: Recognizing Hidden Sorrow*, edited by gerontologist Kenneth J. Doka. Doka focuses on radically unacknowledged kinds of bereavement and grievers, people who "experienc[e] a sense of loss but d[o] not have a socially recognized right, role, or capacity to grieve" (3). Doka's interest in both the "inter-social" and the "intrapsychic" aspects of disenfranchised grief is illuminating: "Disenfranchisement can occur when a society inhibits grief by establishing 'grieving norms' that deny such emotions to persons deemed to have insignificant losses, insignificant relationships, or an insignificant capacity to grieve. But... there is an intrapsychic dimension as well. The bereaved may experience a deep sense of shame about the relationship or they may experience emotions, perhaps reflecting societal norms, that inhibit the grieving process" (xv). Like traditional psychoanalysis, in grieving there are certain "norms" that determine not merely the line between normal and pathological but between normal and "insignificant." This social insignificance easily translates into a perceived innate inferiority or "incapacity," further pathologizing and harming sexual and racial minority communities precisely during crisis periods that require tremendous support and resources. While the authors in this collection primarily focus on the individual, the family, or other small social units, I argue that colonial melancholia is a communal, political form of disenfranchised grief.

11. For example, Apolinario de la Cruz founded the Cofradía de San Jose in 1832, a small religious organization in Tayabas, a Tagalog province in the Philippines that developed into a revolutionary, peasant-based movement against the Spanish. Ileto calls de la Cruz a "Tagalog Christ," who embodied the contradictory features of humility and authority associated with Jesus Christ and who both drew upon and diverged from Christian teachings in ways that the Spanish interpreted as politically threatening. By 1841, the Spanish had killed and imprisoned hundreds of Cofradía followers. According to Ileto, following a mock trial, de la Cruz was executed, "his body cut up into pieces, his head put in a cage and displayed atop a pole stuck along the roadside" (*Pasyon and Revolution*, 62).

12. Referring to the concept of *damay*—translated as participation, involvement, or empathy—Ileto argues that the significance of de la Cruz's and his followers' deaths lies in their acceptance of death and suffering: "Death at the hands of the 'establishment' was, after all, an event familiar to them through the story of Christ; it would have been one more act of damay for them to die for their cause. Apolinario taught the cofrades to accept suffering, even death, for the sake of their union. Perhaps he was right; perhaps those hundreds of deaths contributed to the survival of an ideal.... But even more than the memory of a specific man and a specific movement, it was the vitality of the pasyon tradition that made it possible for ordinary folk to recognize the appearance of other Christ-like figures, each

bringing the same message of hope that Apolinario brought. In this way did he live on in those that came after him" (62-63).

13. See Timothy Mitchell's *Passional Culture: Emotion, Religion, and Society in Southern Spain* (Philadelphia, Pa.: University of Pennsylvania Press, 1990) for a study of penitentiary rites, pain, and emotion in the southern Spanish context. See Peter Fraser's *Images of the Passion: The Sacramental Mode in Film* (Westport, Conn.: Praeger, 1998) for an eclectic series of analyses of major and minor films that evince what Fraser calls the "sacramental" or "incarnational" mode.

14. Mieke Bal, *Double Exposures: The Subject of Cultural Analysis* (New York and London: Routledge, 1996), 300.

15. However, there are two "whole" figures in *Heridas*: the floating, framed Madonna and child. The Madonna looks down at her child in a classic portrait of feminine nurturing. But her gaze could also extend farther, focusing attention downward to the wrapped, severed head carefully placed upright on the ground. I thank Benigno Trigo for insightfully noting that this thematic of maternal nurturing appears in most of the images I have selected for this essay, and that the image of Madonna and child seems to function as a counterpart or counterpoint to the fragmented, violent images of the pasyon.

16. Instead, the representation of the colony as female seems to stand in for the actual representation of female colonial subjects. In her essay "The Pasyon Pilapil: An-'other' Reading, *Women Reading Feminist Perspectives on Philippine Literary Texts*, Thelma B. Kintanar, ed. (Quezon City: University of the Philippines Press, 1992), 71-89, Priscelina Patajo Legasto emphasizes gender in her analysis of the *Pasyon Pilapil*, the traditional religious text that Reynaldo Ileto examines in greater length and detail in *Pasyon and Revolution*. Though the connections are rather briefly suggested, Legasto implies that the two "archetypal and contradictory" roles of Eve as the source of innate evil and corruption and of the Virgin Mary as the representative of goodness and purity are significant in the colonial context since the Pasyon was widely disseminated during Spanish rule and, hence, an important tool of Spanish colonization in the realm of signifying practices (85). Legasto then extends this analysis to the way in which imperialists and nationalists rely on very different but equally passive representation of the Philippines as female. Legasto writes, "The Philippine colony was imaged as woman prostituted by imperialists but held sacred by nationalists. In both valuations, however, the country, like woman, was represented as passive, immobile territory contested over by males" (87).

17. My attempt at narrating these visual signs is clearly influenced by Mieke Bal's interweaving of visual and narratological studies in her book *Double Exposures: The Subject of Cultural Analysis* (New York and London: Routledge, 1996). See, for example, Bal's analysis of vision and focalization in chapter eight "His Master's Eye," 255-288.

18. I began noticing the visual "logic" of blood after reading Mieke Bal's analysis of Michelangelo da Caravaggio's painting *Judith Beheading Holofernes*; see chapter nine "Head Hunting," *Double Exposures*, especially 292-293.

19. It is no accident, I think, that the "angels" of the dream coincide with the videomaker's first name "Angel."

20. The OED defines nostalgia as a "form of melancholia caused by prolonged absence from one's home or country." It is derived from the Greek words for "return home" and "pain." Literally a form of homesickness, nostalgia commonly denotes a wistful longing, a backward glance across time. In Shaw's case, this glance travels across space toward something that figures as home, or a lost home. But Shaw does not travel back in time, a crucial difference between her project and those of anthropologists and ethnographers who freeze the object of study in space (as exotic Other) and time (as primitive and backward). Shaw is sick for home, but the sickness is also about longing for a home that is not there. Again, in melancholic terms, the post/colonial subject mourns not the loss of an object that she once

"had" but the loss of a stolen object that she never had and that she has no right to have. The postcolonial, nostalgic glance at "home" is perhaps about reappropriation, about mapping memories on a landscape that has been stolen.

21. Mary Louise Pratt uses the term "autoethnography" in her influential *Imperial Eyes: Travel Writing and Transculturation* (London: Routledge, 1992) as does Françoise Linonnet in *Autobiographical Voices: Race, Gender, and Self-Portraiture* (Ithaca, N.Y.: Cornell University Press, 1989). More recent examinations of autoethnography can be found in the work of Catherine Russell; see chapter 10 "Autoethnography: Journeys of the Self" in her book *Experimental Ethnography: The Work of Film in the Age of Video* (Durham, N.C.: Duke University Press, 1999); and in the work of José Muñoz; see chapter three "The Autoethnographic Performance: Reading Richard Fung's Queer Hybridity" in his book *Disidentifications: Queers of Color and the Performance of Politics* (Minneapolis: University of Minnesota Press, 1999).

22. Russell, *Experimental Ethnography*, 194.

23. Here I respectfully disagree with Rolando B. Tolentino's reading of *Nailed* in his survey of the different "waves" of Asian-American and Filipino/American media production; see Tolentino's "Identity and Difference: 'Filipino/a American' Media Arts," *Amerasia Journal* 23.2 (1997): 137-161.

24. Russell, *Experimental Ethnography*, 194.

25. Ralph Peña's play *Flipzoids* is published in the anthology *Tokens? The NYC Asian-American Experience on Stage*, ed. Alvin Eng (New York: Asian-American Writers Workshop, 2000; distributed by Temple University Press). However, the published version was not available while I was writing this essay. Quotations from *Flipzoids* are based on Peña's copy of the play and are cited in the text.

26. Here I am indebted to Hiram Pérez for many conversations on memory, humor, and miscegenation. See Pérez's *On the Tip of Our Tongue: Topographies of Race and Forgetting in the Americas* (Ph.D. dissertation-in-progress, Columbia University).

Umbilical Cord

ANGEL VELASCO SHAW

VIDEO MAKER'S NOTE:

In 1998 I was an artist-in-residence at the University of the Philippines Film Center, sponsored by the Asian Cultural Council Residency Program in Asia. I conducted a six-month advanced-video workshop titled "Creating Presence for One Hundred Years of Absence: Filipino Women in History." The goal of the workshop was to highlight the roles of women during the Philippine revolution against Spain, the Philippine-American War, and its aftermath. Filipino women have played critical roles during the national struggle, and their contributions have largely been undocumented.

Inspired by the workshop participants and their projects, I set out to find women in Philippine history—searching for them in Philippine history books, in contemporary metropolitan everyday life—at the same time questioning my relationship to this history, these women, and the 1998 events I was witnessing (the commemoration of the centennial of the Philippine's liberation from Spain, presidential elections, the twelfth anniversary of the EDSA People Power revolution, economic depression, and El Niño). A central theme in the piece became an exploration of heroes and heroines, who they were, and how they were represented. We went out into the markets and malls of Metro Manila and conducted on-the-spot interviews with a diverse range of people, asking them who their heroes were, what a hero meant to them, what the centennial celebration meant to them, and how people saw the role of women today. I asked the workshop participants the same questions. The montage sequences consisted of these interviews, images from daily Manila life, archival photographs from the Philippine revolution against Spain, the Philippine-American War, historical monuments around Metro Manila, and personal family photographs.

I faced many challenges throughout the making of *Umbilical Cord*—how to connect individual history to collective history, negotiating language, my placement as a Filipino and displacement as an American, nationalist attitudes, and a plethora of intellectual and emotional questions I felt I needed to address as a Filipino/American woman. Because I speak very little Pilipino, most of the interviews were conducted in the native language by the workshoppers. Oftentimes, I would suggest follow-up questions that

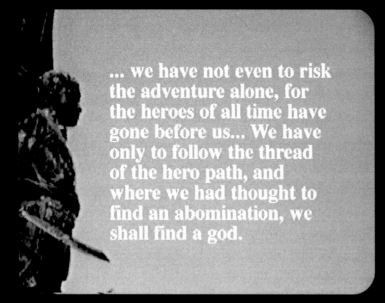

... we have not even to risk the adventure alone, for the heroes of all time have gone before us... We have only to follow the thread of the hero path, and where we had thought to find an abomination, we shall find a god.

were translated back to the interviewee, simultaneously revealing my identity as an American-born Filipino. This, of course, prompted surprise and, in many cases, further interaction. Translating the documentary into written form posed another challenge: other layers of meaning unfold that differ from the viewing experience that can be pondered upon at the reader's own pace, whereas in the video documentary many of the image and sound montages are fleeting and cumulative in meaning.

OPENING IMAGE: Camera pans down Monumento statue: side view of revolutionary leader Andres Bonifacio's profile to gun, and sword, end after a beat at the *Katipunan* flags/city traffic.	FADE UP MUSIC — *Pinikpikan Song* Superimpose Joseph Campbell quote *... And where we had thought to be alone, we will be with all the world.*
Series of Manila cityscapes dissolving into each other:	AUDIO 1 SYNC: Sound of train
- LRT train (Manila's light rail transit system) door closing. Train leaves the station.	AUDIO 2 — ANGEL'S VOICE-OVER Crawling through Manila traffic day after day,
- Heavy traffic in both directions on EDSA, the national highway.	
- Tracking shot of election posters (slow-motion)	all I can see as I pass miles of election posters,
- Medium Close-Up (MCU): the Philippine flag, camera pulls out to reveal the centennial site at the former Clark Air Base.	centennial flags,
- EDSA highway construction shot from inside a taxicab (rosary beads dangling from the rear view mirror).	construction,
- Long Shot (LS): handpainted movie bill boards.	billboards, and people is an umbilical cord...
- Children hanging out on the Pasig River	

bank against a graffitied wall.
- Photograph of my mother in her early twenties superimposed over the LRT train tracks.
- Hand-painted photograph of my grand-mother superimposed over the LRT train tracks.
- Hand-painted photograph of my great-grandmother superimposed over the LRT train tracks.
- Slow-motion of LRT train tracks, relief sculpture map of the Philippine Islands in Rizal Park.
- A baby picture of me holding on to a railing in Brooklyn superimposed over the LRT train tracks.
- My mother and I wearing matching sweaters superimposed over the LRT train tracks.

FADE TO BLACK
FADE UP A SERIES OF QUICK CUTS:
- A variety of candid photographs and studio portraits of my grandmother at ages ranging from her early teens to her eighties wearing different kinds of *saya*, native dresses.
- Two different photographs of my grand-mother and me in the Philippines.
- Photograph of my family with my grand-mother in the Botanical Gardens in the Bronx in 1969.

My mother's umbilical cord connects
to...
her mother's umbilical cord,

and her mother's umbilical cord—

on and on stretching across the water, across regional and national boundaries,

finally connecting to me,

and my unborn daughters.

AUDIO 1: ANGEL'S VOICE OVER:
The image in my mind is of my grandmother, but I cannot imagine her youthfulness.

I recall the last time I saw her. It was in December 1981, she was ninety years old. I was eighteen.
I'd met her only three times before,

DISSOLVE
- Photograph of my grandmother posing with my cousins and family in our house in the Bronx.

CAMERA PANS around a black and white portrait of my grandmother's ninety-year-old face close-up of face, forehead with a big mole in the center, of her eyes.
- MCU: photograph of her arthritic hands. Camera continues to pan her face: lips, eyes, forehead.

CAMERA PULLS OUT MCU: center of her face.
- Full portrait out-of-focus dissolves into portrait in focus.

FADE TO BLACK

Manila street: black and white image of Angel shooting street children playing basketball, with Ana doing sound.

FADE TO BLACK

QUICK CUTS: archival photographs of José Rizal's execution, and the statue of Rizal being built in Rizal Park.

CUT BACK TO: young boy bouncing a basketball, freeze-frame: statue of José Rizal in Rizal Park
- statue of Andres Bonifacio in front of the Manila post office.
QUICK CUTS OF ARCHIVAL PHOTO-GRAPHS (1896-1899) to the beat of the music: A *garrote* (Spanish torture device); portrait of a group of Spanish soldiers; camera pans a firing line of American soldiers positioned on the ground.
- Camera pans Gen. Gregorio del Pilar on a horse with Filipino troops during the revolution against Spain.
- Cartoon of Uncle Sam holding an African baby crying with a tag attached to its body "Philippines with compliments of Dewey."

and yet she was a goddess to me. A woman who possessed incredible powers. The many lines on her face,

the strength in her hands,

and the authority in her voice were affirmations of wisdom, her insatiable appetite for life. I could see the life breathing in her pores beginning to tire.

AUDIO 1 — THEME MUSIC STARTS — piano mixed with skipping record, and drums

AUDIO 2: ANGEL'S VOICE-OVER: To create presence, one must go back into darkness...

Ana: *Sino para sa iyo ang bayani?*
Subtitle: Who is your hero?
Street Kid: José Rizal
Street Kid: at Andres Bonifacio

into intervals of pain...

and joy...

denial...

American soldiers in the market with Pilipino children kneeling at their feet (c.1899)

- King Juan Carlos and Queen Sophia of Spain during their 1998 visit to Manila.
- Japanese occupation: the lowering of the American flag (1942).

UP Film Center: CAMERA PANS lecture room
— Professor Lumbera is talking to the "Creating Presence" workshop participants.

DISSOLVE INTO

QUICK CUTS: seven archival photographs of 19th-century Filipino women.

BREAK IN SEQUENCE

Slow-motion tracking: indoor market stalls and people in Nepa-Q Mart, Cubao.
— Angel shooting with her (back to camera) walking toward a large Philippine flag suspended from the rafters.

QUICK DISSOLVE of photographs and video

discovery...

and reconciliation.

FLASH UP CAPTION: *Spanish royals here for Centennial rites.*

Creating presence for 100 years of absence of Filipino women's history, what was I thinking?

MUSIC STOPS

AUDIO 1: ANGEL'S VOICE-OVER

AUDIO 2: THEME MUSIC

footage (to simulate blowing effect): statue of "Madre Filipinas" in Rizal Park; my mother in the 1950s in the Philippines; portrait of my grandparents in the 1920s; three archival photographs of *ilustrado* women; female vendor pushing a *halo-halo* cart down EDSA; giant statue of the Virgin Mary (shot through vines); Senator Enrile holding up a statue of the Virgin Mary during the twelfth anniversary of "EDSA revolution;" WWII photograph of the Manila post office riddled with bullets, WWII photograph of an American soldier carrying a wounded Pinay in wartorn Manila (nuns in the background); my parents on their honeymoon holding up a "Do Not Disturb" sign; MCU of Tandang Sora's (Melchora Aquino) statue/face; my two grandmothers in the 1950s, scene from Gerry de Leon's film *Sisa* screaming (slow motion), *Abanse Pinay* women demonstration line; photograph of American soldiers posing with three young Pinays (1899), portrait of martyred Martial Law youth activist, archival photograph of Secretary of Interior Dean Worcester posing with a naked Negrito woman, archival photograph of Pinays posing with long cigars; "EDSA Revolution" sculpture—MS of woman with outstretched arms/broken shackles;

PAN DOWN: a portrait of my mother's family taken in her late teens; pan across my mother's family portrait taken in the early 1950s.

Robinson's Mall: Ana and Olivier trying to interview a passerby, "Creating Presence" workshoppers shooting a scene of their documentary.

Camera zooms into a portion of the Monumento sculpture: a statue of a man blindfolded and tied

Blowing on the extinguishing embers, until they reignite all that we experience, day to day...

Blowing on the extinguishing embers until Filipino women's faces and their stories reappear in our imaginations...

FADE UP DOCUMENTARY TITLE:
UMBILICAL CORD
MUSIC STOPS

We ask—what is history?

How does it live?

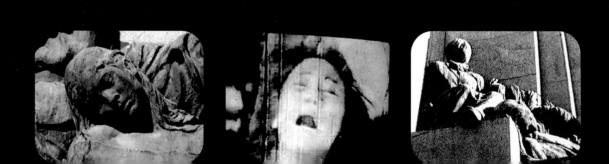

(garrote torture).
Monumento grounds: Centennial guards crossing in front of the monument (a tribute to the *Katipunan* and the 1896 Revolution).

Day-to-day on whatever level until it breathes.

QUICK CUTS: Archival photograph of a line of dead Filipino revolutionaries; University of the Philippines-Diliman statue of Andres Bonifacio; CU of the pyramid and eye on the dollar bill, Apolinario Mabini and Bonifacio on a ten-peso bill, President Quirino on a hundred-peso bill, President Quezon on a twenty-peso bill

Who are our heroes?

QUICK CUTS: MCU statue of Gabriela Silang (who led a revolt in a mid-18th century uprising in Ilocos Sur); a Filipino centennial Barbie wearing a Philippine flag dress, American Barbie dressed in pink; hand painted movie billboard of megastar Rosanna Roces looking like an Amazon queen with a spear.

Our heroines?

QUICK CUTS: *Philippine Daily Inquirer* headline announcing former action star Joseph Estrada as president of the Philippines; CU of General MacArthur statue in Quiapo.

Are they larger than life?

QUICK CUTS: Sheila, a workshopper in her mid-thirties playing with her two sons; photograph of Emman (workshopper) with his father; Angel posing with her baby sister; Angel and her two brothers playing with a Batman doll.

Are they our mothers, fathers, sisters, brothers,

Camera pans Quiapo market outside the church: female herb vendors stopping at a woman vendor talking on her cell phone.

neighbors? You and I?

CUT TO WHITE

Ana: *Ano po ba sa inyo ang isang bayani?*
Subtitle: What does a hero mean to you?
Porkman: *Ang isang bayani para sa 'kin ay isang makatao, makadiyos at mapagmahal sa kapwa.*
Subtitle: In my opinion, a hero is one who is compassionate, God-fearing, and loving toward all of humanity.

Nepa-Q Mart (indoors): a thirtyish heavyset man is slicing pork in a line of meat stalls dimly lit by hanging light bulbs. The man sharpens his knife while looking into the camera, camera zooms into pork ribs.

UP Film Center: MCU of Dang, a workshopper in her early twenties

Tandang Sora (Melchora Aquino) Memorial Tomb: Extreme Close-Up (ECU) relief sculpture of a dead soldier, pan up to a battle scene during the Revolution: medium shot of an elderly woman sweeping the streets in the commercial area of Cubao.

CUT BACK TO: Dang

Nepa-Q Mart (indoors): MS of a female vendor in her thirties. She goes about her business while talking to us.

- The woman hands change back to an unseen customer. Smiles.

CUT TO WHITE

FADE UP: MCU of a rice vendor in his twenties sitting in front of piles of different grades of rice for sale. (smiling as he talks).

AUDIO 1- SYNC: My hero ... (sighs) God...
Dang's Voice-Over: I don't want my hero to be doing big things...

but I just want my hero to be really who he or she is, like himself or herself...

SYNC: and say, this is what I am, and this is what I'm going to show the world.

Vendor: *Para sa 'kin, bayani ang tatay ko.*
Subtitle: For me, my father is my hero.
Ana: *Bakit po? Ano para sa inyo ang bayani?*
Subtitle: Why? What does a hero mean to you?

Vendor: *Kasi wala siyang bisyo. Wala siyang lahat. Nuong maliliit kami hindi kami nagkaroon ng problema. Hindi umi-inom ang tatay ko, walang babae. Ang alam namin hanggang paglaki namin, wala. Kaya alam namin ang lahat, kaya bayani ang tatay ko para sa amin.*
Subtitle: Because he has no vices and didn't cause us any trouble when we were young. We know he doesn't drink and is not a womanizer even until we were all grown up. That's why to us our father is a hero.

Riceman: *Kumander ko.*
Subtitle: My wife.

Ana: *Bakit? Hindi okay lang?*
Subtitle: Why?
Riceman: *Bayani dahil siya ang tagalaba, tagaluto, lahat. Siya'ng bayani ko, kumander ko.*
Subtitle: Because my wife does the laundry, cooks for us, does everything. She's my hero, my commander.

SYNC: To me, a hero is somebody who makes a

UP Film Center: MS of Nancy, a workshopper in her mid-thirties. The film "A Streetcar Named Desire" is playing on the TV in the background. CUT TO: A series of black & white portraits of the political Left. Text about each person is super-imposed onto each photograph.

- *Maria Lorena Barros. Poet and activist. "Makibaka" and "New People's Army." Ambushed and killed by the military in 1976 at age 28.*

(black frame like a slide projector flash)
- *Lean Alejandro. Student, leader, activist, "Bayan." Shot at close range in 1987 at age 27.*

(black frame flash)
- *Edgar Jopson. Student leader and political leader. "National Democratic Front." Killed in military raid in 1982 at the age of 34.*

(black frame flash)
- *Emmanuel Lacaba. Poet, teacher, activist. "NPA," "NDF" Killed in a military raid in 1976 at age 27.*

(black frame flash)
- *Abraham Sarmiento, Jr. Editor of student newspaper. Univ. of the Philippines. Imprisoned under harsh conditions later died of a heart attack in 1977 at age 27.*

CUT TO BLACK

BREAK IN SEQUENCE
Nicholas-Red Home: Sheila, a workshopper in her early thirties, is typing at the computer. The words she is reciting appear on the screen dissolve into a superimposition of the computer screen over Sheila waiting at a gate for her sons to get out of school.

QUICK CUTS: archival portrait of Tandang Sora, wall of election posters—"Vote Women Power," women in Quiapo Market playing cards, talking, and giving a pedicure.
- MS bronze statue of Tandang Sora ("mother of the 1896 Revolution")
- TV channel surfing: TV snow, scenes with

difference...

Nancy's Voice-Over: and somebody who, after having gone through a dark moment in his life comes back...

with something to give.

AUDIO 2: (MUSIC FADES UP) SOUND COLLAGE OF INDIGENOUS INSTRUMENTS AND ELECTRIC GUITAR (LIKE A MACHINE GUN)

MUSIC ENDS

AUDIO 1: FADE UP Pinikpikan song

AUDIO 2: Sheila's Voice-Over: Who is my *ate*, my heroine?
Who is she that can inspire me to be an equal?

Sheila's Voice-Over: So I will vote for her and gossip about her.

Is she a stone statue?

Is she too dead, or sensationalized and alive?

Valuable?

women on different channels.

- Josefa Escoda on the one thousand-
  peso bill.
- Hand-painted presidential election
  poster for Miriam Defensor Santiago.
- Monumento (sculptural tribute to the 1896
  Revolution against Spain): a statue of young girl.
- An old woman praying on her knees inside
  Quiapo Church.
- A *babaylan*/priestess performing a ritual on
  EDSA Day.
- Photographs of Cory Aquino (early 1980s)
  and Imelda Marcos (c. 1970s) giving public
  speeches.
- A female peanut vendor in Quiapo
  Market; Sheila interacting with her
  two sons; a torn poster of Pamela
  Anderson Lee with a gun.

QUICK CUTS: CU of a hand-painted movie
billboard depicting a young couple about to kiss;
1950s movie stills of revolutionary dramas;
archival portrait of Spanish soldiers, American
soldiers burying dead Filipinos (1899); WWII
movie poster—"Sunset Over Corregidor," WWII
photographs of bombed-out Manila, bones
scattered amongst soldiers' helmets.

- camera pans in slow motion to a man sitting
  on the Pasig River bank up to a squatter's
  home with a woman looking out.

BREAK IN SEQUENCE

Outside UP Film Center: Coreen, a workshopper
in her early twenties is sitting on a ledge while
talking into the camera.

TV channel surfing: Cartoons, Val Kilmer,
Mexican soap opera star; scene from Gerry de
Leon's *Sisa*—guardia civil's wife whipping *Sisa*
(insert); woman crawling on her knees in
Quiapo Church, dragging a bird cage (insert);
TV commercials, cartoons, the pope; Filipino
movie stills behind a bar grid.

Political?

Persecuted?

Religious?

Charismatic?

A *bida* or *contrabida?*
Subtitle: A protagonist or
antagonist?

Is she applicable to my reality?

Maria Lorena Barros
poet and activist
Makibaka and New Peoples Army

Emmanuel Lacaba
poet, teacher, activist
NPA, NDF

Before history gave us a common enemy, all
my *manangs* (sisters) fought against the
Spaniards, Americans, Japanese, or military
who held their men captive.

Now, poverty and ignorance are their invisible
enemy.

MUSIC ENDS

SYNC: Hero is someone you
try to follow...

Coreen's Voice-Over: you try to emulate at sig-
uro yong reason kaya ako walang (maybe the reason why I don't have a) hero is because, I don't
know what to do. Like me—I don't know what to
do. So sino pwede maging (who can be my)
hero, no one. MTV—walang...

SYNC: I'm still doing the search for the particular
person...

CUT BACK TO: Coreen

MTV: slick Mountain Dew commercial; Coreen greeting her grandmother during her group's project shoot, making a gesture of respect.

CUT BACK TO: Coreen gesturing with her eyebrows to emphasize her point.

QUICK CUTS OF PHOTOGRAPHS EDITED TO THE BEAT OF THE MUSIC: My brothers and five-year-old me posing with Mickey Mouse at Disneyland; my mother as a teenager with her mother; my mother and me in my twenties, my grandmother and me at 18, portrait of my grandmother at 90.
-   A girl peddling a pedicab passed the camera in the provinces.
-   Camera pans postcard paintings of revolutionary heroes and Philippine presidents.

QUICK CUTS: political cartoon of José Rizal with "Madre Filipinas," photograph of early 1900s Manila street scene (American flag prominent

in frame), *Manila Chronicle* headline "War Ends in Europe," WWII photograph of American flag being lowered.
-   Early 1900s photograph of the Pasig River dissolves into video footage of the polluted river today, sky scrapers in the back ground, dissolves into photograph of my grand mother, mother, and aunt (1969).
-   A series of photographs of my mother: in her early twenties in Manila, in a neighborhood in Pasay (early 1950s), with my father and colleagues in New York in 1957, sitting on a bench during her doctor's residency.
-   Jeepney traffic in Manila.

QUICK FADE TO BLACK

Camera pans slowly around a statue of heroine

Voice-over: *ng susundan* as I am myself still trying to figure out...

SYNC: what to do with my life.

AUDIO 1: THEME MUSIC

AUDIO 2: ANGEL'S VOICE-OVER
I was her grandchild from America, her youngest daughter's oldest female child. The day before I was to return to the States, I knelt at her feet.

She told me stories about the Philippines of her childhood. Every word carefully translated to me. The places and the events...

even the terrain that she spoke about are different.

Her Philippines that my mother left in 1957 for America is not the same place as now.

Gabriela Silang on a horse with her sword drawn, refocusing on the corporate skyscrapers behind the statue. Superimposed photographs are fading in and out of the buildings: portraits of my grandmother, ranging from a young single woman in her eighties, my grandmother with her grandchildren, portrait of my grandparents in their early twenties—camera pans back to the statue of Gabriela.

I want to be able to see these stories. See these landscapes. Experience them through her descriptions. Live with her through the telling of memories.

QUICK CUTS of family photographs: my grandparents in their forties, my great grand-mother at the turn of the century, three of my aunts as children in the early 1930s; reverse pan of "title" photograph—family portrait in the early 1950s.

My mother and my aunts remember what my grandmother can no longer relay to me. Some-times they cannot speak.

FADE TO WHITE

Nepa-Q Mart (Indoors): on-the-spot interview with a well-dressed woman in her fifties, marketing. (stalls and vendors in the background)

Ana: *Mayroon po ba kayong babaeng bayani?*
Subtitle: Do you have any female heroes?
Woman: *Babae? Wala, wala akong alam.*
Subtitle: Female? No, I don't know any.

BREAK IN SEQUENCE

Nepa-Q Market (indoors): on-the-spot inter-view with a middle-aged female vendor selling meat. A big animal tongue is hanging prominently in the foreground.

Woman: *Si Rizal, isang bayani*
Subtitle: He is a hero.

Nepa-Q Market (indoors): camera stops on a woman talking to a fish vendor (off camera). She is conscious of the camera in her face.

Woman: *Bayani? Hah?* (chuckles)
Subtitle: Hero? Who?
Woman: Rizal (chuckles)

Robinson's Mall: on-the-spot-interview with an elderly woman. She looks around nervously, thinking about how to respond to the question. She seems surprised by her own inability to think of more heroes.
-   EDSA (national highway): camera zooms into a wall of election posters to a hand written poster: "Vote... José Rizal for Senator."

Elderly Woman: Rizal... Aguinaldo... Ano pa?
Subtitle: Who else?

QUICK CUTS of images from the Revolution and Philippine-American War. CUT TO the beat of the music: portrait of Rizal, his execution;

SILENCE

AUDIO 1: THEME MUSIC
AUDIO 2: ANGEL'S VOICE-OVER:
My grandmother was five when the national hero, José Rizal, was executed by the Spaniards

Spanish soldiers, people standing beside Rizal's grave; firing line of American soldiers, Filipino soldiers with rifles, another picture of an American firing line, American officers wearing neat uniforms, Filipino officers wearing worn-out clothes, American soldiers resting.

Thomas Edison's reenactment film footage of a Philippine-American War battle scene: American soldiers advance into the center of the frame waving a big American flag.

CAPTION FADES UP: "The islands were not people. They were a geographical expression."

QUICK CUTS of images of the Philippine-American War: American soldiers digging a grave for a mutilated Filipino body, American soldiers posing in front of a nipa hut; pan photograph of smiling American soldiers sitting on a large tree trunk holding skulls and bones; a dead Filipino in a grave; political cartoon of an American soldier advancing toward a frightened Filipino with a bayonet sticking through a proclamation notice; political cartoon of the Statue of Liberty walking through water beside a boat with "U.S.A. Thomas" on the side;
- Portrait of Colonel Funston (the man who captured General Aguinaldo). The word "PREACH" is superimposed in faded red; portrait of Aguinaldo in uniform; political cartoon of Uncle Sam marching with a caricature of an African-looking Filipino— "July 4th" and "Spirit of 1776" are written on the cartoon.
- Camera pans to a photograph of a trenchful of dead Filipinos, a dead Filipino, American soldiers standing with a row of dead Filipinos.
- The word "PACIFY" is superimposed over a

in 1896. She was eight when the Philippine-American War broke out. A war written in indelible ink.

Not in American history books, only as paragraphs here and there in Philippine history books...

yet there are images of American soldiers standing on mounds of skulls and bones piled up in mass graves...

evidence of betrayal...

250,000 Filipinos dead... the official count.

Women raped.

photograph of women vendors. The word "COLONIZE" is superimposed over photograph of American soldiers with three young Pinays.

- Political cartoon of Uncle Sam playing with an African child (labeled "Philippines") and another child (labeled "Cuba").
- The word "PREACH" is superimposed over camera pan of a photograph of American soldiers with children kneeling at their feet.
- The word "PACIFY" is superimposed over a portrait of General Merritt, "COLONIZE" over Admiral Dewey, "PREACH" over President McKinley, "PACIFY" over General Bell.
- Camera pans over a group portrait of Aguinaldo and other revolutionary leaders in exile in Hong Kong (1897) as if searching for my great-grandfather. Camera stops on him (highlighted with a circle).
- Photograph of my grandparents, my grandfather's mother, and his sister (1950s).
- The word "COLONIZE" is superimposed over Admiral Dewey posing on his battleship in Manila Bay; illustration of a Spanish battleship, photograph of a sunken Spanish battleship in the Manila Bay with posing American soldiers; portrait of Filipino revolutionaries.
- American flag prominently hanging from a store front in Manila, Malolos Republic—rows of Philippine flags in the inaugural hall.
- Dead Filipinos, political cartoon of Uncle Sam trying to spoonfeed an African-looking infant.
- The word "WILD" superimposed over half-naked Negritos posing with top hats on; "TAMED" superimposed over Filipino boys; "CIVILIZED" superimposed over

Children casualties of American…

expansionism.

Sold for twenty million dollars.

Lolo Celestino was exiled to Hong Kong with Aguinaldo.

Exile is in the blood.

A mock battle, 1898.

Two flags are hoisted—American and Filipino.

Kindness turns to deceit.

(re) Christianizing the savages.

schoolchildren dressed in white; political cartoon of Uncle Sam holding an African/Filipino baby; split screen images of an indigenous Filipino boy "WILD" superimposed; and "TAMED" superimposed over a boy wearing Western clothes.

- Camera pans down a photograph of Secretary of Interior Dean Worcester posing with a bare-breasted Negrito woman; lounging American colonials; "CIVILIZED" superimposed over a provincial Filipino family in a horse-drawn cart; women washing in the Pasig River.
- A page from *The Spanish Official History of the Philippine Islands*; magazine cover illustration: "Game of the Philippines: Faces, Facts, and Figures. Know Our Empire" (Filipino revolutionary); a portrait of a provincial family posing in front of a vendor stall; Manila dock filled with goods; dead bodies in a trench; portrait of Aguinaldo with revolutionaries in exile; Macario Sakay with other freedom fighters; American officers with their wives eating.

FADE TO WHITE

BREAK IN SEQUENCE

EXCERPT FROM CENTRAL STATION
Apartment Interior: Bujo, a workshopper in her early twenties, is standing in front of a painting of three women.
- LS of a spectacular display of fireworks over Manila Bay for June 12th Centennial celebration; procession float with ethnic dancers passing through the frame; centennial site replica of Barasoain Church, same church on the back of a ten-peso bill.

CUT BACK TO Bujo

Quiapo Market: On-the-spot interview with a young man selling centennial flags.

My grandmother never told me these stories.

MUSIC ENDS

SYNC: Ah... the Centennial... um, okay...

Bujo's voice-over: It's a good thing that we're celebrating it. One hundred years of freedom, as they call it. But...I just feel sad that...

SYNC: people are not really that aware of what we are celebrating. It's like, do they know about the responsibility that comes with freedom?

Ana: *Bakit kayo nagtitinda ng mga* flag?
Subtitle: Why are you selling flags?
Flag Man 1: *Wala, pinaghahandaan lang natin ang araw ng kalayaan kasi matagal bago dumating ang 100 years.*

BREAK IN SEQUENCE

UP Film Center: interview with Nancy. Marlon Brando, in a scene from *A Streetcar Named Desire* is holding his head in despair in the background.
- MS of "Global City Site" billboard of the centennial site. Camera slowly pulls out to reveal a large construction area Superimposed text fades up:"Centennial Site: 3.1 billion pesos spent."

BREAK IN SEQUENCE

Robinson's Mall: on-the-spot interview with a well-dressed young male teenager with braces. He answers the question through a smile while his girlfriend, shyly leaning on him, giggles.

FREEZE-FRAME DISSOLVE

EDSA Day: an elderly man wearing a black beret is sitting against a wall of election posters animatedly talking to an unseen crowd, looking directly into the camera.

QUICK CUTS: pen-and-ink drawings
- Spanish galleon, conquistador Miguel Lopez de Legazpi, Spanish priests and soldiers meeting early Filipinos.

- drawing of a Filipino hanging from a noose with a crowd of people around, photograph of a large crucifix.

CUT BACK TO animated man, visibly excited and angry.

Monumento: Camera pans reproductions of the flags during the Revolution, hand-painted

Pagkatapos nito, year 2000 na naman bago dumating uli ito. Kaya nagtitinda kami nito. Hindi naman pinagbabawal.
Subtitle: We're preparing for independence day. It takes some time for another hundred years to come. After this, it'll be in the year 2000 before this happens again.

SYNC: Well, I think there are better ways of spending government monies because...

Nancy's Voice-Over: I think nationalism is not something you can work up by means of a media blitz or a presentation, or theme park. And as somebody said, it's not something you can really teach.

SYNC: Centennial? Well, I guess we're going to be free again, then something like that.

SYNC: *Kaya kayo, hindi niyo alam ang history.*
Subtitle: You don't know your history!

Beret Man's Voice-Over: *Sino'ng nagpapatay kay Rizal? Katoliko!*
Subtitle: Who killed Rizal? The Catholics!
Sino'ng nagpapatay kay Kristo? Romano! Julius Ceasar!
Subtitle: Who crucified Christ? The Romans!

SYNC: My golly! *Alam ko ang* (I know my) history. I was only a fifth grader. I never reached secondary school.

Man's Voice-Over: When I used to study, I look around. I open my eyes clear.

movie billboards in the background.

CUT BACK TO elderly man with beret.

UP Film Center: Dang is wearing a black costume veil over her face during the interview.

SYNC: I open my mind wide and that's it!
SYNC: I believe that we are because of our history and if you know your history really more or—and understand it really better than what is written or what you have studied, you understand more of your-self. And you become what you want.

BREAK IN SEQUENCE

CUT TO WHITE

AUDIO 1: THEME MUSIC

FADE UP IMAGE: passing LRT train, tracking view of passing landscape—relief map of the Philippines; dissolve into tracking wall of election posters blurring; dissolve into passenger tricycle moving away from camera—focus on a hanging banner "I Shall Go;" dissolve into tracking squatters lining the Pasig River banks; dissolve into a jeepney and van passing each other on a provincial road.

AUDIO 2: ANGEL'S VOICE-OVER
I depart and return again and again to the place of my soul, pulling on the invisible umbilical cord back to thousands of islands, until they become visible, until they become familiar...

QUICK CUTS (repetition of images seen throughout the piece): family photographs over the years; production of the workshop projects; various historical monuments; archival photo-graphs of the revolution, Philippine-American War; election posters; centennial images; people interviewed to slow-motion of a woman mouthing "Peace Be With You".

until my personal and collective history lives wherever I go.

UP Film Center: Bujo is sitting at an editing table.

- Nancy and Amy; Bujo and her workshop group researching in the library, meeting with their groups.

SYNC: The role of woman today is to be able to connect with her long lost self.
Bujo's Voice-Over: It's like we have been given this power before to assert ourselves and...

CUT BACK TO Bujo

SYNC: through all the colonizers that we have...

- Bujo shooting an interview for her group's documentary; camera pans to Sheila listening to the interview.

Bujo's voice-over: we have forgotten the strength and the importance and the voice.

BREAK IN SEQUENCE

Abanse Pinay demonstration (inside Philippine General Hospital): interview with Caridad, 83-year-old activist looking straight into the camera.

Portraits of Filipino women in history. An image of each woman is followed by text about their lives, laid out like a poem:

Teodora Alonzo y De Quintos

Mother of eleven, most prominent of whom is José Rizal. Graduated from the Colegio de Santa Rosa. Co-managed sugar, rice, and flour mills, a homemade hand press, dye factory, and drug-store. Exiled to Hong Kong with three of her daughters. Joined José Rizal during his exile in Dapitan. Died at the age of 84.

Josephine Bracken

Of Irish and Chinese ancestry. Common-law wife of José Rizal, suspected of being a Spanish spy. Lived in exile with Rizal in Dapitan. Crossed enemy lines in Cavite. After Rizal's execution, converted the Tejeros Estate into a field hospital. Took care of the sick and wounded revolutionaries. Married a Filipino, Vicente Abad. Died in Hong Kong at the age of 26.

Melchora Aquino (Tandang Sora)

Mother of the Revolution. Widowed, supported six children from her rice and sugar cane fields. Known as a medicine woman. Inspired and supported Katipuneros. Cared for the wounded. Arrested at the age of 84 for suspected sedition and rebellion. Exiled for seven years in Guam. Died at the age of 107.

Gregoria de Jesus

Looked after family's farm. Became a Katipunera the same day she married revolutionary leader Andres Bonifacio. Vice president of the women's chapter of the Katipunan. Risked her life concealing documents, ammunition, and the Katipunan seal. Fought in battles after Bonifacio's execution. Married Julio Nakpil in 1898. They had eight children. Died at the age of 68.

AUDIO 1: THEME MUSIC FADES UP

AUDIO 2: SYNC: And we have to honor these women before us because what we are today, we owe it to them, the unsung heroes.

Caridad's Voice-Over: There are many heroes, whom we do not know, because they just remain in the background, but they are the more heroic women that we do not know. That is why you are asking why no woman is in history…

You don't know history.

except those who fought behind the lines not only to give our country liberty but liberty and freedom to the people itself…

What is freedom to a country if the citizen is enslaved? And half of humanity, which is women are enslaved?

AUDIO 1: THEME MUSIC CONTINUES

AUDIO 2: ANGEL'S VOICE-OVER:

Breathe into the coals, until we spark the fires which are eternal… In a very humble way, we participate in this ritual which we strive to pass on to others as others have passed on to us.

Salome Siaopoco

Of Filipino Chinese descent. Collected funds for the Revolution. Fought in battles alongside husband General Llanera in Nueva Ecija. Endured the cruelty of the Spanish guardia civil. Was imprisoned many times—twice when she was pregnant, which prevented her from being executed. Had twenty-four children, but only five survived. Built the first moviehouse in Cabiao. Died at the age of 62.

Trinidad Tecson y Perez

Mother of the Philippine Red Cross in Bulacan. A member of the women's Masonic lodge, "Logia de Adopcion." Joined the Katipunan at the age of forty-seven. Dressed as a man with a wide-brimmed hat. Fought in twelve battles against Spain. When not in battle, nursed the soldiers in Biak-na-Bato. Seized arms and ammunition from a courthouse in Caloocan. Served as commissary of war of the short-lived Republic in Malolos, Bulacan. Died at the age of eighty.

Teresa Magbanua

Studied to become a teacher. Received a postgraduate teaching degree from the University of Sto. Tomas. Returned to the island of Iloilo in the Visayas. Managed a farm alongside husband, wealthy landowner Alejandro Balderos. A fine horse-woman and excellent sharpshooter. The only woman to lead combat troops in the Visayas. Fought valiantly in several battles against the Americans. Died in Zamboanga at the age of eighty-four.

Geronima Olaes Tolentino

My great-grandmother, born 1847. Traveled from town to town selling goods in the province of Nueva Ecija. She had twelve children. Only two reached adulthood. Widowed, she moved to Pasay City with her two children and opened a small vendor's stall. Died at the age of ninety-four.

Trinidad Tolentino San Agustin

My grandmother, born 1892. Went to school up

There are so many more stories to tell —the souls of our ancestors' voices are calling to us to continue...

to speak the struggle...

the rage...

the ecstasy...

the silence...

to third grade. Ran a small restaurant in Manila. Married Dionisio Alvarado San Agustin. Had nine children, seven survived. During World War II, she dug ditches with her bare hands to hide her children and grandchildren. All seven children graduated with professional degrees, for which she was named mother of the year by the University of the Philippines. Died at the age of ninety-two.

Mutya San Agustin Velasco Shaw
My mother, born 1934. Went to the U.S. in 1957 to study medicine. Returned to the Philippines, opened a clinic for the poor in Pasay City with her husband, Virgilio Velasco. Returned to the U.S., had three children, was widowed at the age of thirty-one. Remarried, had another child. Professor at Albert Einstein College of Medicine. Director of Primary Care, Montefiore Medical Center. Founder of the Philippine Ambulatory Pediatrics Association in the Philippines.

the complexity of being a woman.

Dedication: *For my mother: Mutya San Agustin Velasco Shaw; for my grandmother: Trinidad Tolentino San Agustin; for my great-grandmother: Geronima Olaes Tolentino.*

MUSIC ENDS

AUDIO 1: PINIKPIKAN SONG

CREDITS ROLL

Christina Quisumbing Ramilo

Tomboy Gang
1996
photos and tabloid cover
laminated on wood,
approx. 91.44 x 121.92 cm

422

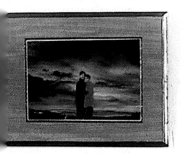

Maidens in the Philippines
1998
photos laminated on wood, coat rack
straw hats, Pinoy *komiks*
approx. 76.2 x 182.88 cm

Left: Details

Export Quality
1996
encaustic on canvas
121.92 x 182.88 cm

Mariano Del Rosario

Colonizado
1998
mixed media on canvas
223.52 x 182.88 cm

Right:
Help Me!
1998
mixed media on linen

Bottom:
Abaca
1990
mixed media on linen

ab•a•ca \ˌa-bə-'kä, 'a-bə-ˌ\
n [Sp abacá, fr. Tag abaká]
(ca. 1818) 1: a strong fiber
obtained from the leafstalk
of a banana (*Musa textilis*)
native to the Philippines —
called also *Manila hemp* 2: the
plant that yields abaca
used in packaging and weaving.
other products include: (ca.
1665) cat-o'-nine-tails; (ca.
1623) whip, rod or scourge for
flagellation.

Big Bee
1998
mixed media on linen
106.68 x 106.68 cm

(Untitled B) From *Made In USA* series
1990
mixed media on linen
106.68 x 106.68 cm

Third Station
1994
oil on canvas
116.84 x 193.04 cm

Top:
Manananggal: No Es Una Virgen 1
1998
oil on canvas
195 x 130 cm
Courtesy Galeria Soledad Lorenzo, Madrid

Top right:
Manananggal: No Es Una Virgen II
1998
oil on canvas
195 x 130 cm
Collection of Malou Babilonia
Courtesy Galeria Soledad Lorenzo, Madrid

top far right:
Creme de la Creme
1995
oil on canvas
182.88 x 152.4 cm
Collection of Gilles Fuchs, Paris
Courtesy Galerie Nathalie Obadia, Paris

bottom right:
Immigrant's Daughter
1997
oil and acrylic on linen
124 x 181.5 cm
Collection of Alfonso Pons, Miami
Courtesy Galeria OMR, Mexico City

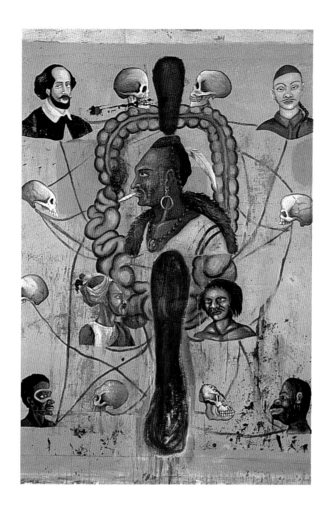

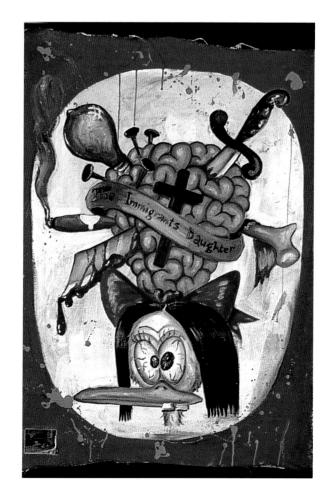

431

Santo Niño de las Narizas
1998
oil on canvas
156 x 122 cm
Private collection, Madrid
Courtesy Galeria Soledad Lorenzo, Madrid

Roberto Villanueva

Bulol
**performance and installation from "Pinoy Tok,"
a collaboration with Jessica Hagedorn at Exit
Art Gallery, NYC 1991**

Archetypes: Cordillera Labyrinth
Details of installation

Photographs by Angel Velasco Shaw

435

Archetypes: Cordillera Labyrinth
Detail of installation

Photograph by Angel Velasco Shaw

Japan Foundation

Archetypes: Cordillera Labyrinth
installation. Cultural Center of
the Philippines, 1989

Afterword: The Secret Archives

JOHN KUO WEI TCHEN

There is no document of civilization which is not at the same time a document of barbarism.
And just as such a document is not free of barbarism, barbarism taints also the manner in
which it was transmitted from one owner to another.

— Walter Benjamin[1]

This book embodies the obstinate act of recovery. It is a visceral, necessary, and ultimately futuristic challenge to systemic exclusions—to the abjection from the imperial dreamland. As is true with all histories, the past is reclaimed from this particular present. What is this particular moment? One pervaded by ignorance? Amnesia? Apathy? Repression?

Most Americans (of the United States) will look at the book's title and ask "What war?" and say they always thought Filipinos were somehow Spanish. Just as most people in the United States don't know much history, it is also true that most people in the Philippines and in the Filipino diaspora don't know much history. Yet we all know something about the past. We are supposed to memorialize the former. It's external. It's grand. It's important. It is the "business" of the historical profession. We live unsettled with the latter.[2] The U.S. war in the Philippines survives in an odd story *abuela* tries not to tell when the young ones are around, or discovering a photograph of any great-grand-uncle, virtually forgotten and killed "during the war," or in a threadbare piece of fabric worn in the escape and now kept in mothballs.

We (of whatever nation) have blind spots bound by regimes of power which limit gaining privy to other points of view and knowledge systems. In the U.S.-centric "world of tomorrow" we (of the Anglo-American "free market" world) tend to experience the omnipresent, all-consuming now. The past is gone. "Why dwell on it?" many say. And in this process life flattens. The spirits of people past living in our daily memories fade to the background, especially against the dazzling white noise of multimedia distractions.[3] This is part of the price paid for buying the Western modernist faith in progress and excess; at no extra charge comes the myopic historical narratives formulated by academics, by the media, by the victors.

The United States, the oldest surviving postcolonial nation, "won" this first "Vietnam-style" guerrilla war and subsequently repressed its ugly memory as invader from national consciousness. Any nagging doubts that a progressive civilization had become barbaric surely had to be banished from the psyche. This volume makes abundantly clear that the historical experiences of Filipino men and women in the Philippines, in the diaspora, and in the U.S. imperial dreamland have been discounted, if not ignored. After all, we are the "good guys," aren't we!?! The rhetoric of free trade and democracy masks and justifies being the world's moralizers and policemen. U.S. national interests displace the history of U.S. invasion and neocolonialism. The Pacific became an "American lake." Tourism in the Pacific and Asia has become the smiley face legacy.[4] Who counts as "we" and who doesn't? Naively, and ahistorically, most true believer Americans imagine we all are included, even though we know this has not been true. "We, the people" has been an ambivalent, contested, and multilayered identifier. Who counts as "white" at any given historical moment, for example Irish, Italians, and Jews, has been one indicator. Immigration exclusion/inclusion laws are another.[5]

This book boldly challenges this amnesiac confusion. It demands that readers imagine, feel, and understand why we don't know a critical part of U.S. history and Filipino history. This volume also does more. It challenges readers to go beyond a disinterested spectatorship ("This was not my people's, nor my family's war") to gain a deeper critical understanding of how colonial and imperial wars in the Pacific and in Asia have affected all of us. Can people once made aware of historical injustice cross the nationalistic miasma of narrow identity interests and find empathy, if not solidarity? Can Filipinos, for example, identify with Hawaiians, and with Puerto Ricans? Or can Euro-American academics find solidarity with their students of Asian and Latino/a heritage?

Strange, wonderful things can happen in the alchemy of the American dream. In the imperial shadows, fragments of the past survive. Hope survives in the scattered and buried, repressed and displaced. Each shard, if illuminated by the light of critical remembering, can disrupt the oblivious calm of the ever now. Paradoxically, the return of the repressed often reappears in the diasporic journey to the imperial heartland. U.S. foreign policy often drives refugee and immigration policies. The wealthy and those who sided with the United States are given special preferences— from compradores of the treaty port China to *ilustrado* elites of the Philippines to Hmong montagnards aiding the Central Intelligence Agency (CIA) to the high-tech professionals hired by U.S. multinationals.

But history and experience are complicated and paradoxical. In response to various European and Japanese colonialisms and imperial assaults (such as the U.S. involvement in the British Opium Wars against China or Coca-Cola's colonization of global markets and displacement of local drinks or the conspiracy of silence about Japanese military "comfort" women[6]), Asian nationalist identities arose to unify local/regional identities. Indeed, a central feature of the diasporic Asian-U.S., Third World-First World experience has precisely been the hopeful migrant seeking freedom and justice in the United States encountering racism and marginalization. Disillusioned, some return to their place of departure to join in a nationalist movement. Diasporic postwar experiences constitute special angles of vision, complex and irregular, into globalization processes. Vantages are often clearer from the margins. Each such person necessarily has to negotiate norms across two or more cultures, each culture marked by combinations of gendered, classed, sexualized, racialized, ethnicized, and other social positionings. Individual faith, desires, and actions become tested and retested. Questions of "Where is home?" and multiple citizenships and how historical experiences impact on choices we make today are all especially acute.

What is our present vantage onto this past? Can new understandings, new knowledges emerge? It is not simply Filipino/a, Filipino/a-American, nor American. Multiply this necessary dialogue many times. For each group from Asia and the diaspora, wars and colonialism mark points of devastation, departure, pilgrimage, aftershock, and research. The moment of arrival cannot be divorced from the trauma of departure. Psychic scar tissue, omnipresent yet invisible to the untrained eye, remains with the individual, the family, the generation, and the children. The surviving children living in postwar United States feel the aftershock of their parents' and ancestors' cross-cultural, postwar trauma. We/they bear silent witness, yet few hear explicit stories which would make these war experiences real, contextual, and meaningful. What we/they read in U.S. textbooks often aggravates the unreality. We/they can't gain a set of reflections which help to build our/their own sense of selves.7

The process of claiming the legacy of such wars is necessarily a painstaking, laborious, and costly constitutional act. This is the special role of students, poets, artists, writers, scholars, and those who are self-driven to puzzle the past (often unrecognized except in their own hearts). We improvise with whatever is around. The fragments are a good place to begin. If we can, we gather the time and funds to make a pilgrimage to the imperial archives and begin the re-searching process. The poet's inspired capture of a lost moment necessarily leads to the concerted acts of many devoted to a radical and healing historical re-narrativization.

Herein, then, lie the true archives — secreted from the victory of the omnipresent. Once fragmented, they are reassembled. They document the diverse lived fragments of the war and the postwar. Their existence is constituted by activist meaning-making and constitutive of more activist meaning-making. In this sense, archives-building embodies a people's reflexive self-creation.

In the hierarchies of what is studied and what is not (in U.S. history, American studies, East Asian studies, and even in the emergent field of Asian-American studies), the Philippines has been given scant attention. Why has this been true? It is not an imperial, warrior nation like Japan. It is not China or India, the centuries' sought-after trophy of European and U.S. wet dreams. As an archipelago of diversity and intermingled peoples, it is not perceived of as "pure" and it is not perceived of as descendants of a distinctive civilization. To study such histories is to study wealth and power, hence those nations which rival that of the United States and Europe. Unless, of course, one wants to look at "corruption" and "folly," then the Philippines is brought into the discourse. In this way, Filipino politics has been racialized and therefore trivialized, in a manner similar to Latin American and African governments.

We must shed such colonial conceits which structure our systemic misunderstandings. To study the history of the Philippines is to study the manifold ways in which four hundred years of European globalization and over a thousand years of intra-Asian globalization inform our cross-cultural decolonizing work now. It is precisely because of the multilayered, confounded, and ambivalent position of Filipino men and women in relation to the United States, Spanish colonialism, China, Japan, Asia, and Europe that makes this a central and generative area of study. The activist process of combing the various imperial, colonial, and trade archives is fundamental and critical to the decolonization of a people and the colonizers.

And yet we know this work is not enough. The various globalizations of the past need to be understood in relation to each other. Here in the U.S. imperial imaginary, various repressed archives can be assembled and claimed. Indeed, the migrant's sense of a nationalist (e.g., Korean or Indo-Caribbean) and local (e.g., Acehnese or Hmong or of Georgetown) self becomes further complicated by access to parallel and interlinked experiences of others with U.S. wars and "manifest destiny." In these struggles, new and unexpected communities of shared interests emerge. Double and triple critiques emerge — where neither the U.S. dreamland, nor the homeland of origin, nor the cosmopolitanism of international elite cultures can be complacently romanticized. This is the strength of the *Vestiges of War* vision. It is the call for a generosity of understanding and solidarity — a call for freeing ourselves from the conventional and limiting ways we've come to define ourselves — a call for critically engaging with peoples' living histories.

All the fractured contradictions of imperial modernity are contained in this book. And so are many possible decolonizing solutions. If only we can communicate, debate, and problem-solve together across so many divides.... The true "secret"? I believe it is the process of opening spaces for the voicing of the kinds of secreted experiences expressed in this book. I hope it sparks and sustains dialogues.

A few final words. This book-making process has been a labor of love and commitment. Such a visionary study has been a vision shared by many yet the initiative of one. Angel Velasco Shaw, artist, videomaker, teacher, and now editor, has been the driving force for the proposal that became the conference that became this book. I thank her first and foremost. Luis H. Francia must also be recognized. As coeditor and co-organizer, he has brought in his considerable expertise and wisdom to enrich the *Vestiges* project.

I also want to thank Thuy Linh Nguyen Tu, Aimy Ko, Liz Moon, and Nicol U for prompting me, unbeknownst to them, to think through the legacy of war on diasporic Asian families.

NOTES:

1. Walter Benjamin, "Theses on the Philosophy of History," *Illuminations: Essays and Reflections*, Hannah Arendt, ed. (New York: Schocken, 1969), 256.

2. Roy Rosenzweig and David Thelen, *The Presence of the Past: Popular Uses of History in American Life* (New York: Columbia University Books, 1998), 2-5; John Kuo Wei Tchen, "Back to Basics: Who Is Researching and Interpreting for Whom?," special issue, "The Practice of American History," *Journal of American History*, vol. 81, no. 3, December 1994, 1004-1011; John Kuo Wei Tchen, "Towards a Dialogic Museum," in *Museums and Communities,* Ivan Karp and Steven Lavine, eds. (Washington, D.C.: Smithsonian Institution Press, 1990), 285-326.

3. David Arkush and Leo O. Lee, *Land Without Ghosts: Chinese Impressions of America from the Mid-Nineteenth Century to the Present* (Berkeley: University of California Press, 1989).

4. Daisann McLane, "Sweet Déjà Vu in the Philippines," *Frugal Traveler* column, *New York Times,* January 23, 2000, 6, 20.

5. On European American "others" becoming "white," see: Karen Brodkin, *How Jews Became White Folks and What That Says About Race in America* (New Brunswick: Rutgers University Press, 1998); Matthew Frye Jacobson, *Whiteness of a Different Color: European Immigrants and the Alchemy of Race* (Cambridge: Harvard University Press, 1998); George Lipsitz, *The Possessive Investment of Whiteness: How White People Profit From Identity Politics* (Philadelphia, Pa.: Temple University Press, 1998); and John Kuo Wei Tchen, *New York Before Chinatown: Orientalism and the Shaping of American Culture, 1776-1882* (Baltimore: Johns Hopkins University Press, 1999). On the socio-legal history of "we, the people" and otherness, see: Benjamin B. Ringer, *"We the People" and Others: Duality and America's Treatment of Its Racial Minorities* (New York: Tavistock Publications, 1983).

6. Dai Sil Kim-Gibson, *Silence Broken: Korean Comfort Women,* video-documentary and book (1999).

7. Margo Machida, "Out of Asia," *Asia/America: Identities in Contemporary Art* (New York: The New Press, 1994), 69-109; Cathy Caruth, *Trauma, Narrative and History* (Baltimore: Johns Hopkins University Press, 1996).

ACKNOWLEDGMENTS

Vestiges of War: The Philippine-American War and the Aftermath of an Imperial Dream, 1899-1999 could not have happened without the support and collaborative efforts of a great many people. Our deepest gratitude goes to all of the contributors, and especially to John Kuo Wei Tchen, director of the Asian/Pacific/ American (A/P/A) Studies Program & Institute at New York University who never lost sight of the book's importance and without whom the Vestiges project would likely still be a dream. Karina Bolasco, editor in chief of Anvil Publishing, was a true believer from the start, generous in immeasurable ways, indispensable as well as indefatigable in overseeing the Manila phase of the book development. And Eric Zinner, Senior Editor at New York University Press, provided the final push for publication.

Since October 1997, the A/P/A staff—Christine Balance, Sheelagh Cabalda, Julian Esguerra, Pradnya Haldipur, Anne Lau, Elisa Paik, Masaki Yamagata—took on the daunting task of serving as the command center for the book and the events preceding it. Former Associate Director Risa Morimoto and former Events Coordinator Anthony Escobar exhibited a dedication to the project that went above and beyond their official duties.

For his yeoman's work in designing and laying out such a demanding book, John Woo—together with the invaluable assistance of Yun Zhou Wu, and A/P/A's Chris Nojima—deserves our measureless thanks. Shepherding the book through its various stages were project editor Ruth Roa of Balanghai Books; design consultant RayVi Sunico of Cacho Hermanos; copy editor Lorna Kalaw Tirol; and editorial assistants Jo Pantorillo of Anvil Publishing, Cecilia Feilla and Emily Park, of NYU Press. We thank as well Mercy Servida of the Lopez Museum Library for her generous assistance in photo research; Eric Gamalinda, Bonnie Poon, and Alma Villacorta for lightening our production workload; and Harold Schimdt and Gordon Kato, for helping us understand the complexities of publishing.

The *Vestiges* project spanning over nearly four years in various forms of production could not have come to fruition without the financial generosity of the following: former Program Officer Toby Volkman (Education, Media, Arts and Culture), and Janice Petrovich, Director, Education, Knowledge, & Religion at The Ford Foundation; Director Raymond Paredes, Deputy Director Lynn Szwaja, Associate Directors Joan Shigekawa, and Tomas Ybarra-Frausto of Creativity and Culture at The Rockefeller Foundation; the National Commission for Culture and the Arts of the Philippines; The International Visitors' Program, New York University; and NYU's Senior Vice President and Deputy Chancellor, the late Debra James of whom we have special memories; Loida Nicolas-Lewis; and Paul Poon.

We thank you all!

Angel Velasco Shaw's acknowledgments:
A project of this magnitude could not have been spiritually possible without the encouragement, love, and advice from very dear friends and colleagues.

I would like to extend a heartfelt thanks to the following people—the San Agustin, Shaw, and Velasco families; Sally Berger, Catherine Boyer, Carlos Celdran, Doreen Fernandez, Pat Hoffie, Marissa Ileto, Reynaldo Ileto, Suzanne Llamado, Margo Machida, Dr. Bernadette Madrid, Ami Miciano, Pascale Montedart, Mika Oshima, Paul Pfeiffer, Elizabeth Poulos, Sarita Echavez See, Karen Su, Lars Tragardh, and Maria Christina Villaseñor. An extra special one goes to friend and mentor, Jessica Hagedorn, for listening to years of *Vestiges, Vestiges, Vestiges.* There are those people who have inspired and influenced my pursuit to understand how history lives in the present on familial and collective levels. For this I must thank my brother Noel, my aunt, Mabini S.A. Gonzales and Antonio Perez who showed me actual vestiges. I would also like to acknowledge the late historian, Renato Constantino for his belief that Filipino Americans would someday contribute something valuable to the Philippines. The intense interaction with NYU students of my "Asian Americans and War" class (fall 1999) helped me to further understand the links between the major wars in Asia involving the United States. Without the generous support of Ralph Samuelson and the Asian Cultural Council, I would never have had the opportunity to further develop this project while in an artist residency in the Philippines. Jim Zwick's Web site (www.boondocksnet.com), dedicated to Philippine-U.S. relations, was a wonderful resource for me when I first became serious about researching the Spanish and Philippine-American Wars. Oscar Campomanes provided his expertise in Philippine/Philippine American Studies while putting together the Vestiges events of 1999. I am grateful to Anne-Marie Tupuola and Lok Siu for their valuable critical feedback on my introduction. *Maraming, maraming salamat* to my technical angels—Chris Bayani, Kidlat de Guia, R.J. Fernandez, Mark Gary, and Iday Marpa; to Ann Wizer and David Greene for offering me a sanctuary when I needed one most; and finally, to my Manila guardian angels—Neal and Susan Oshima, Nancy and Raul Rodrigo, and Ruth Roa for their unconditional friendship.

For my mother — Mutya San Agustin Velasco Shaw who taught me how to stand my ground even when it was shaking.

Luis H. Francia's acknowledgments:
I would like to thank my wife Midori Yamamura for her love, generous encouragement, patience, and support. Working on this book I kept thinking of three persons who irrevocably altered my views on the tangled web of relations between the Philippines and the United States: Daniel Boone Schirmer, who has always been a shining example of the passionate advocate for truth-telling, social change, and equality; Roque Ferriols, S.J., philosophy professor who opened my eyes to orthodoxy's pitfalls; and the late gifted poet and friend Emmanuel Lacaba, who willingly laid down his life for a vision of a truly democratic Filipino nation. And to all the many who have shown me, in astonishingly varied ways, that to question official definitions of history and to rethink one's views of the current milieu are necessary steps towards liberation and self-fulfillment, a heartfelt bow.

PERMISSION FOR REPRINTS

"An American Colonial State: Authority and Structure in Southern Mindanao," by Patricio Abinales, from P. Abinales's *Images of State Power: Essays on Philippine Politics from the Margins* (Quezon City: University of the Philippines Press, 1998), reprinted by permission of the author and the University of the Philippines Press.

"The Miseducation of the Filipino" by Renato Constantino, reprinted by permission of the author.

"Walls," by Luis H. Francia, from *Flippin': Filipinos on America* (New York: The Asian American Writers Workshop, 1996), reprinted by permission of the author.

"The Hills Are Still There" (originally titled "Epilogue") by Resil Mojares, reprinted from *The War Against the Americans: Resistance and Collaboration in Cebu: 1899-1906* (Quezon City: Ateneo de Manila University Press, 1999), by permission of the Ateneo de Manila University Press.

Poems by Alfrredo Navarro Salanga, reprinted from *Turtle Voices in Uncertain Weather* (Manila: The Cultural Center of the Philippines, 1989), by permission of Alice Salanga.

"U.S. Racism and Intervention in the Third World, Past and Present" by Daniel Boone Schirmer, reprinted from *The FFP Bulletin* 1994, by permission of the author, and here revised by the author.

PHOTOGRAPHY CREDITS

SECTION 1: THE OBJECT OF COLONIAL DESIRE

p.1
"Mount Albay"
Photo credit: Walter B. Townsend
Source: *Our Islands and Their People as Seen with Camera and Pencil*, ed. William S. Bryan. N. D. Thompson Publishing Co., 1899.

"The Future Civil Authorities in the Philippines"
Photo credit: J. D. Givens
Source: *Scenes in the Philippines* by J. D. Givens, 1898. The Lopez Memorial Museum Collection.

p.4
Harper's History of the War in the Philippines, edited by Marrion Wilcox. New York: Harper and Brothers, 1900.
Source: The Lopez Memorial Museum Collection.

p.59
The Baldwin Primer, by May Kirk, New York: American Book Company, c. 1900.

p. 87: "American soldiers posing in front of their encampment"
Photo by Walter B. Townsend
From *Our Islands and Their People as Seen with Camera and Pencil*, edited and arranged by William S. Bryan, N. D. Thompson Publishing Co. 1899.

p. 184
EDSA Event, Bencab. 1986, etching, 32 x 25 cm

p. 185
Marlboro Country, Bencab. 1975, etching/aquatint, 30 x 25 cm

p. 194
Conquest & Resistance, Bencab. 1999, acrylic-collage on canvas, 152.5 x 101.5 cm

444

p. 205

"View showing the new Jones Bridge and at right center the approach and one pier of the old Bridge of Spain. The Escolta District, 3.2.16 10 a.m."The Lopez Memorial Museum Collection.

"View from aeroplane looking northwest and showing the Army and Navy Club and Elks Club in foreground, the piers, Manila Hotel and Port Area district in background. New Luneta and Burnham green just in back of clubs." The Lopez Memorial Museum Collection.

"Holiday Time in The Philippines," F. Luis Mora (Illustrator) *Harper's Weekly*, Vol. XLIV, No. 2246,p. 15. 6 January 1990. Harper and Brothers, 1900. The Lopez Memorial Museum Collection.

p. 268

"Pagmulat/Awakening" © Genara Banzon from *Biyahe: Origin & Directions*, *KKK: Katarungan, Kalayaan, Kapayapaan* —Genara Bazon, KKK/Vestiges of War, 1999. "Amen! -Kulam" — Genara Bazon, Amen! Vestiges of War, 1999.

p.268

KKK.(Katarungan, Kalayaan, Kapayapaan)
Justice, Freedom, Peace
etched photo of installation detail of "Pag mumuni-muni: Katawan ng Kasaysayan":
L.: 1'.2 x W: 9": 1997-98.

p. 269

Pagmulat/Awakening
Paper work/collage, pastel painting, drawing & xerography: L: 3' x W: 2'4" (in site-specific mixed media installation): 1999.

p. 270

Amen! -Kulam
etched photo of installation "Likha" paper collage on wood: L: 2'3" x W: 1'6": 1997-98.

p. 275

"Delano, Ca. 1995"

"Watsonville, Ca.1995"
photo credits: Angel Velasco Shaw

pp. 319, 320, 321, 323, 325
Courtesy of the Diaz family
Reproduced by William Hernandez

p. 348
America is in the Heart, by Bencab. 1987, oil on canvas, 121 x 104 cm

p. 354
Pinoy Worker Abroad, by Bencab. 1975, etching, 30 x 25 cm

p. 359
San Juan Bridge, 2000.
Photo credit: Antonio Perez

Angel Velasco Shaw

pp. 402, 403, 405, 413, 420
Family photographs courtesy of Mabini S.A. Gonzales

p. 403
Images of Rizal portrait
p. 405
Uncle Sam with baby illustration
p. 412
Aerial shot of Manila bombed
p. 415
Row of dead Filipinos
Courtesy of The Lopez Memorial Museum Collection

p. 406
Still film frame from *Sisa,* directed by Gerardo de Leon, 1951.

p. 410
The portraits of Maria Lorena Barros and Emmanual Lacaba—Courtesy of Anvil Publishing,
Inc. from *Six Young Filipino Martyrs.* Edited by Asuncion David Maramba, 1997.

p.411
Movie poster — "Sunset Over Corregidor" from *The Golden Years: Memorable Tagalog Movie Ads
(1946-1956)* from the Collection of Danny Dolor. eds. Ronald K. Constantino and Ricardo
Lo. Danny Dolor Publications, 1994.

p.414
Images of women in a market, American soldiers with children, American soldier with
female prisoners, resting American soldiers, from *Our Island, and Their People as Seen with Camera
and Pencil,* edited and arranged by William S. Bryan. N.D. Thompson Publishing Co, 1899.
Photo credit: Walter B Townsend.

ABOUT THE CONTRIBUTORS

PATRICIO N. ABINALES is associate professor at the Center for Southeast Asian Studies, Kyoto University. He is author of *Images of State Power: Essays on Philippine Politics from the Margins* (University of the Philippines Press, 1998), and editor of *The Revolution Falters: The Left in Philippine Politics after 1986* (Cornell Southeast Asia Program, 1996). His book *Making Mindanao: Cotabato and Davao in the Formation of the Philippine State, 1900-1972* will be published by Ateneo de Manila University Press.

ERLYN RUTH ALCANTARA is publisher, publication consultant, and curator of The Sanctuary Gallery at Maryknoll in Baguio City. She has curated two photo exhibitions on Baguio and published the second edition of *CITY OF PINES: The Origins of Baguio as a Colonial Hill Station and Regional Capital* by Robert R. Reed, the first volume in *The Baguio Reader*. Among her recent publications are *Of Igorots and Independence* by William Henry Scott, *Cordillera Images* (volumes I & II), photographs by Tommy Hafalla, and *Prints: 1974-1986* by Ben Cabrera.

GENARA BANZON is an installation and mixed-media artist from Los Baños, Philippines; she now lives and works in Cambridge, Massachusetts. She received her Bachelor of Fine Arts from the University of the Philippines and her Masters of Fine Arts from Massachusetts College of Art in Boston. She has taught widely, conducted and assisted in field research amongst various ethnic groups in the Philippines; exhibited in museums and has given lectures in the Philippines, Japan, Australia, Canada, and the United States.

Philippine artist SANTIAGO BOSE is known for his paintings, installations, and performances both in Asia and North America He has had one-man exhibitions in New York City, Canada, Hong Kong, Singapore, and Indonesia. Bose has represented his country in major international exhibitions such as the 1996 Asia/Pacific Triennial. He is one of the founders of the Baguio Arts Guild, which promotes educational and cultural opportunities for young Filipino artists, and holds international arts festivals in Baguio City.

Born in the Philippines in 1942, BEN CABRERA (or **Bencab**, as he is better known) started his artistic career shortly after studying Fine Arts at the University of the Philippines. A painter and printmaker, he has exhibited widely in the Philippines and abroad. In a career spanning over three decades, he has received several major awards, including the 1992 Gawad CCP para sa Sining (Cultural Center of the Philippines Award for the Arts) and the 1997 ASEAN Achievement Award for Visual Arts. He lives and works in Baguio City.

OSCAR V. CAMPOMANES is a founding member of the Institute of Filipino Studies in Oakland, California, and associate professor of Literature at De La Salle University (Manila). He has held teaching appointments at Brown University, Yale University, Williams College, the University of California—Berkeley and San Diego, Ateneo de Manila University, and New York University. His essay in this volume is part of an envisioned longer study of the American soldier as imperial icon and agent in the U.S. neocolonization of the Philippines. His work on U.S. imperialism and Filipino-American cultural historiography has appeared in academic journals and critical anthologies in the United States.

RENATO CONSTANTINO (1919–1999) was a nationalist historian whose books *The Miseducation of the Filipino* (1968), *The Making of a Filipino* (1968), *Dissent and Counter-Consciousness* (1974), *Identity and Consciousness* (1974), and *The Philippines: A Past Revisited* (1975), and monographs, *Veneration without Understanding* and *Roots of Subservience* (both 1969) shaped the thinking of generations of activists, radically changing their way of looking at the events of Philippine history. He was thrice given a Nationalism Award, each by the University of the Philippines, the Civil Liberties Union of the Philippines, and the Quezon City local government.

MARIANO DEL ROSARIO holds an MFA in painting from the Maryland Institute College of Art and a BFA in painting from the University of the Philippines. He is a visiting artist at Moore College of Art and Design in Philadelphia and an art instructor at The Arts Students League of New York. He was recently awarded a Pollock-Krasner Foundation grant for the year 2000. Past grants and awards include: BCAT/Rotunda Gallery Residency Program, Brooklyn, New York; Asian Cultural Council fellowship, New York; Glassell School of Art, Houston Museum of Fine Arts; and Thirteen Artists Award, Cultural Center of the Philippines.

ANTIPAS P. DELOTAVO was born in Iloilo City in 1954. He started exhibiting his works with a group of socially conscious artists during the Marcos era. He has had eight one-man shows and several group exhibitions in the Philippines and abroad.

NICK DEOCAMPO is a prizewinning filmmaker, author, film curator, and director of the Mowelfund Film Institute. A graduate of New York University, his films have won international film awards, among them: *Oliver* (Grand Prize, Belgium), *The Sex Warriors and the Samurai* (Special Mention, Best Documentary, Tokyo) and *Private Wars* (Audience Prize, Yamagata). He has been scholar-in-residence at NYU Asian/Pacific/American Studies Program, artist-in-residence at the Walker Arts Center, and a Japan Foundation Fellow. An author of two books on cinema, he is currently finishing a book about the history of 100 years of Philippine cinema.

VICENTE DIAZ is Filipino/Pohnpeian (Federated States of Micronesia) who was born and raised on Guam. He recently joined the faculty in the Asia Pacific American Studies Program for American Culture as an assistant professor, at the University of Michigan, after spending ten years of teaching Pacific History and Micronesian Studies at the University of Guam.

BRENDA FAJARDO is both artist and teacher. She is the current head of the Philippine National Commission on Culture and the Arts' Committee on Visual Arts and the curator of the Vargas Museum at the University of the Philippines–Diliman, where she is also a Professor of Art Studies. Her works are at the Queensland Art Gallery, Brisbane, Museum of Contemporary Art in Tokyo, Fukuoka Art Museum in Japan, Singapore Art Museum, the National Museum in the Philippines, and the Metropolitan Museum of Manila.

DOREEN G. FERNANDEZ, professor at the Ateneo de Manila University and chair of the Department of Communications, teaches literature, composition, creative writing, and journalism. She writes on cultural, literary, theater and culinary history for scholarly and popular publications. On food and food history she writes in *The Philippine Daily Inquirer* and in *Food Magazine*; on books, a column in *The Philippine Journal of Education*. Among her books are: *The Iloilo Zarzuela, 1903-1930; Tikim: Essays on Philippine Food and Culture; Palabas: Essays on Philippine Theater*

History; Fruits of the Philippines; and in coauthorship with E. N. Alegre, *Writers and Their Milieu* (I and II); *Sarap: Essays on Philippine Food;* and *Kinilaw: A Philippine Cuisine of Freshness.*

LUIS H. FRANCIA, a Palanca Memorial Award for Poetry winner, has had two books of poetry published, *Her Beauty Likes Me Well* (1979, with David Friedman) and *The Arctic Archipelago and Other Poems* (1992). A collection of his essays, *Memories of Overdevelopment: Reviews and Essays of Two Decades,* came out in 1998. He has edited two anthologies of Philippine literature: *Brown River, White Ocean: An Anthology of Twentieth-Century Philippine Literature in English* (1993), and, with Eric Gamalinda, *Flippin': Filipinos on America* (1997). His latest work is the semiautobiographical cum travel reflections, *Eye of the Fish: A Personal Archipelago* (2001). He writes for *The Village Voice,* and Manila's *Sunday Inquirer Magazine,* and has taught literature at Sarah Lawrence College.

ERIC GAMALINDA recently published a collection of poems, *Zero Gravity* (Alice James Books, 1999). His novel, *My Sad Republic,* received the Philippine Centennial Prize in 1998. He teaches at New York University.

EMILIO GANOT grew up in Davao, Philippines and now lives in Salzburg, where he teaches photography. Keenly interested in the Filipino diaspora, he has had exhibitions in Austria, Italy, Germany, New York City, and Arizona, and has been a recipient of fellowships from the Austrian government.

GUILLERMO GOMEZ-PEÑA is a multimedia artist, cultural critic, and author. His performances have been presented at the Franklin Furnace and at Exit Art, New York; MOCA, Los Angeles, and the Walker Arts Center, Minneapolis; and at venues in Australia, Barcelona, London, and the former Soviet Union. He has received numerous awards including the Prix de la Parole and a MacArthur Foundation Fellowship. Gomez-Peña is the author of *Warrior for Gringostroika* (Grey Wolf Press, 1993), *New World Border* (City Lights Books, 1996), and *Temple of Confessions* (coauthored with Roberto Sifuentes; Powerhouse Books, 1997). He was born in Mexico City and came to the United States in 1978.

Poet, multimedia theater artist, novelist, and screenwriter, **JESSICA HAGEDORN** moved to the United States from the Philippines in her teens. Her novels include *Dogeaters,* nominated for a National Book Award, and *The Gangster of Love,* nominated for the Irish Times International Fiction Prize. She is also the author of *Danger and Beauty* and editor of *Charlie Chan Is Dead: An Anthology of Contemporary Asian American Fiction.* Hagedorn collaborated with photojournalist Marissa Roth on *Burning Heart: A Portrait of the Philippines* (1999) and is working with Angel Velasco Shaw on a documentary entitled *Excuse Me... Are You a Pilipino?* Multimedia theater pieces include the play version of *Dogeaters,* adapted by Hagedorn in 1998 for La Jolla Playhouse and subsequently staged at New York's Public Theater during the 2000-2001 season.

REYNALDO C. ILETO is a professor at the Australian National University, and the author of the award-winning book *Pasyon and Revolution: Popular Movements in the Philippines, 1840-1910* (winner of the 1989 Harry Benda Prize of the Asian Studies Association); *Filipinos and Their Revolution: Event, Discourse, and Historiography* (Ateneo de Manila University Press, 1998); and *Knowing America's Colony: A Hundred Years from the Philippine War* (Philippine Studies Occasional Papers Series No. 13, Center For Philippine Studies School of Hawaiian, Asian and Pacific Studies, University of Hawaii at Manoa, 1999). He has also written various seminal essays on subaltern historiography and Philippine cultural history/vernacular cultures. He is currently at work on American colonial representations of the Philippines. Professor Ileto was a scholar in residence at the Asian/Pacific/ American Studies Program at NYU in February 1999.

BIENVENIDO LUMBERA is professor of Filipino and Philippine/Comparative Literature at the University of the Philippines–Diliman. He is the author of among other works *Tagalog Poetry, 1576-1898*, a study of Tagalog lyric and folk poetry that is credited with initiating the vernacular turn in Philippine literary studies of the last thirty years, and *Philippine Literature: A History and Anthology*. He has written highly regarded essays on the literature of the Philippine revolution and anti-colonialism, and Filipino theater, popular culture, and cinema.

YONG SOON MIN is an artist whose works in a diverse range of media have been exhibited internationally. She is Associate Professor and Chair of the Studio Art department at the University of California–Irvine. Among her numerous grants is a National Endowment of the Arts' Artists Grant in New Genres (1989-90). She is a founding member of the Board of Directors of the Asian American Arts Alliance, Godzilla, and Seoro: Korean Artists Collective, and a national board member of the Women's Caucus for Art. She currently serves on the Board of Directors of the Korean American Museum and the College Art Association and was a commissioned curator for the Fourth Gwangju Biennale (2001) in Korea.

RESIL B. MOJARES has written numerous books and essays on diverse topics in Philippine culture and history. He holds a Ph.D. in Literature from the University of the Philippines; served as visiting professor at the University of Hawaii and University of Wisconsin–Madison; and is based at the University of San Carlos (Cebu City) where he teaches, served as founding director of the Cebuano Studies Center, and now acts as head of the university's publications program. His books include *Origins and Rise of the Filipino Novel* (1983), *House of Memory* (1997), and *The War Against The Americans* (1999).

NGUYEN QUI DUC was awarded the Overseas Press Club's Citation of Excellence for his reports about veterans and life in postwar Vietnam for National Public Radio in 1989. He is the author of *Where the Ashes Are: The Odyssey of a Vietnamese Family* (Addison-Wesley, 1994), and coeditor of *Vietnam: A Traveler's Literary Companion* (Whereabouts Press, 1995), and *Once Upon A Dream: The Vietnamese American Experience* (Andrews and McMeel, 1995). He translated the novella *Behind the Red Mist* by Hanoi novelist Ho Anh Thai (Curbstone Press, 1997). He hosts *Pacific Time*, a weekly public-radio show on San Francisco's KQED.

Painter **MANUEL OCAMPO** has shown at internationally recognized exhibitions such as *Documenta* in Kassel, Germany, the Saatchi Collection in London, and "Helter Skelter: LA in the 90s" at the Museum of Contemporary Art, Los Angeles. Ocampo was a fellow at the American Academy in Rome in 1995 and lived in Europe until 1999. He is represented by several galleries including Jack Shainman Gallery (New York), Galeria OMR (Mexico City), Galerie Nathalie Obadia (Paris), Soledad Lorenzo (Madrid), and Galerie Philomene Magers (Munich).

RENE G. ONTAL is a writer and community organizer based in New York City. Originally from the Philippine province of Negros Occidental, he began research on the David Fagen story in

1993. He has lectured on the Fagen saga at colleges and universities as well as venues for alternative education and politics. His articles on the subject have been published in African-American newspapers such as *The City Sun*, Filipino-American publications such as *Filipinas Magazine*, and in major Philippine daily newspapers. Ontal was a contributing writer to the American Friends Service Committee book, *Resistance in Paradise: Rethinking 100 Years of U.S. Involvement in the Caribbean and the Pacific*. He has written a feature-length screenplay based on the David Fagen story.

PAUL PFEIFFER is a New York-based visual artist. Recent exhibitions include, in New York City, "The Whitney Biennial 2000" at The Whitney Museum of American Art, "Greater New York," at the Institute for Contemporary Art, P.S. 1 Museum, "A Place Called Lovely" at Greene Naftali Gallery, and the solo show "The Pure Products Go Crazy" at The Project; in Chicago, "Out of Place" at the Museum of Contemporary Art; and in San Francisco, "At Home and Abroad" at the Asian Art Museum. He teaches at Parsons School of Design in Manhattan and was the first winner of the Baucksbaum Award given by the Whitney Museum in 2000.

VICENTE L. RAFAEL teaches at the University of California–San Diego. He is the author of *Contracting Colonialism: Translation and Christian Conversion in Tagalog Society Under Early Spanish Rule* (Durham, N.C.: Duke University Press, 1993), and *White Love and Other Events in Filipino History* (Durham, N.C.: Duke University Press, 2000). He has also edited *Discrepant Histories: Translocal Essays in Filipino Cultures* (Pasig City, Philippines: Anvil Publishing Inc., 1995) and *Figures of Criminality in Indonesia, the Philippines, and Colonial Vietnam* (Ithaca: Cornell Southeast Asian Studies Publications, 1999).

CHRISTINA QUISUMBING RAMILO is a Philippine-born visual artist based in New York City since 1985. She received her BFA in Editorial Design and Illustration from the University of the Philippines and her MA in Studio Art and Art Education from New York University. Her work has been exhibited in New York, Venice, Toronto, and Manila. Christina is codirector of a video documentary entitled *Sisterhood*, which explores the realities of Filipina lesbian lives in the Philippines and in North America.

ALWIN REAMILLO was born in Manila in 1964. He is currently based in Perth, Western Australia. "Humayo Kayo at Magparami" ("Go Forth and Multiply") was a recent site-specific installation at the Fremantle Cold Storage Building in May 1999, Feast of the Pentecost. He frequently works with Juliet Lea in a collaborative partnership called Reamillo & Juliet.

ALFRREDO NAVARRO SALANGA (1948-1988) was a political activist and detainee during the martial law regime of Ferdinand and Imelda Marcos. As a writer he wore different hats: journalist, poet, essayist, fictionist, and editor. Given the TOYM (Ten Outstanding Young Men) award in 1985, Salanga also garnered several Palanca Memorial awards in poetry, including first prize in 1980. Among his poetic works are *Poems 1969-1979*, *Portraits*, and *Turtle Voices in Uncertain Weather*. He wrote the novella *The Birthing of Hannibal Valdez*, and coedited *Versus: Philippine Protest Poetry 1983-1986*.

WIGAN SALAZAR grew up in the Philippines and Germany. He holds a master's degree in African/Asian History from the School of Oriental and African Studies (University of London), and a Ph.D. in History from the same university. His dissertation examined

German economic involvement in the Philippines from 1871 to 1918, and he has published work on German-Philippine economic relations and German trading houses in the Philippines. His current research projects include an exploration of the Philippine tobacco industry after the abolition of the tobacco monopoly in 1882 and a study of German pharmacies in colonial Philippines.

SARITA ECHAVEZ SEE, former Mellon postdoctoral fellow in Asian-American literature and culture at Williams College, is now an assistant professor in the English Department and Program in American Culture at the University of Michigan, Ann Arbor. She received her doctoral degree from Columbia University's Department of English and Comparative Literature. She is working on the manuscript form of her dissertation "'Our New Possessions': Race, Empire, and Postcoloniality in American Literature and Culture."

ANGEL VELASCO SHAW is film/video maker, educator, and a cultural activist. She has been developing a body of work around issues of identity politics, postcolonialism, and transnationalism from a Filipino American's perspective, working in the Asian and Filipino/ American communities in the United States, as well as the Philippines. Videos include *Umbilical Cord*, *Asian Boys*, *Nailed*, and *Balikbayan* ("Return to Home"). She has taught at The New School, Hunter College, Columbia University, and the Pratt Institute, and has been teaching media/cultural studies and community studies courses at NYU in the Asian/Pacific/American Studies Program since 1995.

A Harvard graduate, his MA and Ph.D. degrees from Boston University, **DANIEL BOONE SCHIRMER** taught U.S. history with a focus on the Philippines at Goddard College. He is the author of *Republic of Empire* (1972) and coeditor, along with Stephen R. Shalom, of *The Philippines Reader* (1987). In his adolescence, the Great Depression influenced him to work for the Communist Party of New England. He later dropped out but retained his socialist convictions. Convinced during the Marcos dictatorship of the need to oppose U.S. imperialism in the present as well as the past, he became a leading figure in Friends of the Filipino People, his life enriched by the Philippine movement for democracy and national independence.

MARK TWAIN (Samuel Langhorne Clemens, 1835-1910) was a novelist, satirist, journalist, and social observer, whose *The Adventures of Huckleberry Finn* (1884) is a beloved classic of American literature. He became the most compelling figure in the Anti-Imperialist League and wrote scathingly against American expansionism abroad and its war on the Philippines. His antiwar writings, excised from earlier posthumous collections of his works, were later reclaimed in the 1960s by activists against the American war on the Vietnamese.

JOHN KUO WEI TCHEN is a historian and cultural activist. His most recent book is *New York Before Chinatown: Orientalism and the Shaping of American Culture, 1776-1882*. He is an associate professor of the Gallatin School and the History Department at New York University. He is director of Asian/Pacific/American Studies Program at NYU and cofounder of the Museum of Chinese in the Americas.

DIONISIO VELASCO (a.k.a **Noel Shaw**) is an American-born Filipino writer and filmmaker who lives and works in New York City. He has written and directed short narrative and documentary films which have screened in festivals in the United States, Europe, and Asia. His research on the *"manong experience"*—the lives and struggles of Filipino migrant farm-workers—has taken him westward to Seattle, the San Francisco Bay area and California's Central Valley, and as far east as Pangasinan province in the Philippines.

A Cultural Center of the Philippines' annual 13 Artists awardee and winner of the Niigata Museum sculptural competition, Niigata, Japan, **ROBERTO VILLANUEVA** (1947-1994) was a Fine Arts graduate of the University of Santo Tomas. He participated in over 70 exhibitions in the Philippines and abroad. He was a founding member and vice president of the Baguio Arts Guild.

JIM ZWICK is the author of *Militarism and Repression in the Philippines* (1982), and editor of *Mark Twain's Weapons of Satire: Anti-Imperialist Writings on the Philippine-American War* (1992). A member of Friends of the Filipino People since the mid-1970s, he was editor of its *FFP Bulletin* from 1989 to 1994. Since 1995 he has highlighted the history of U.S. imperialism by placing hundreds of primary texts and graphics and historical analyses on the World Wide Web in the award-winning *Anti-Imperialism in the United States, 1898-1935* and sites at BoondocksNet.com. In 1997 he also created the Mark Twain site at About.com which hosts the Web's largest collection of Twain's writings about imperialism.

INDEX

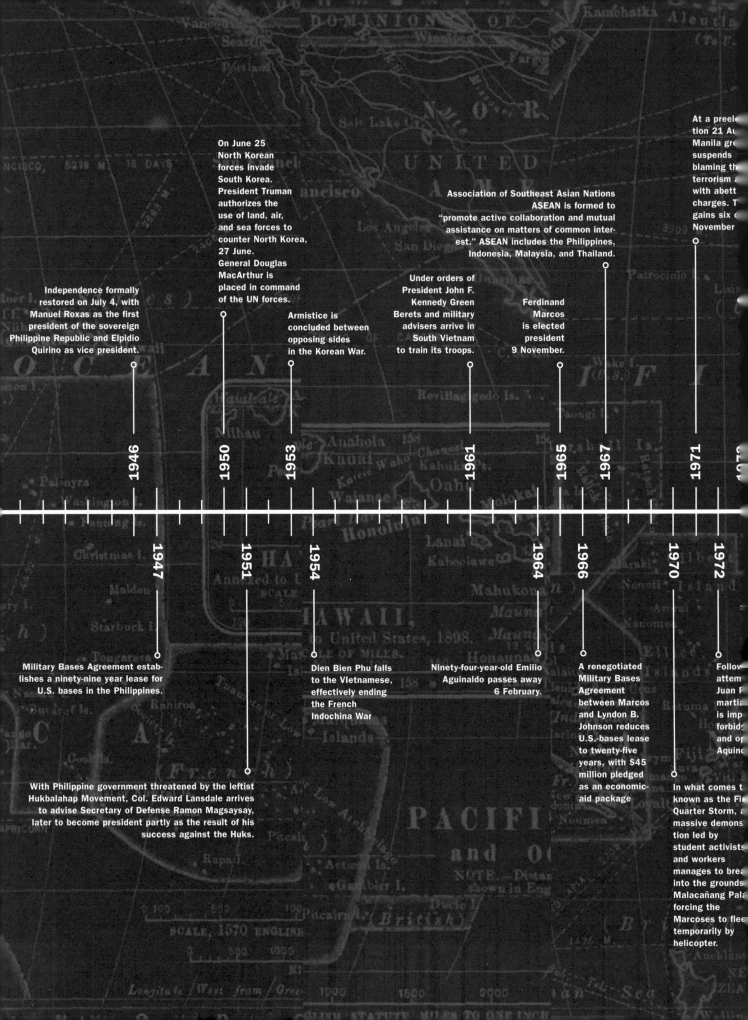

Independence formally restored on July 4, with Manuel Roxas as the first president of the sovereign Philippine Republic and Elpidio Quirino as vice president.

On June 25 North Korean forces invade South Korea. President Truman authorizes the use of land, air, and sea forces to counter North Korea, 27 June. General Douglas MacArthur is placed in command of the UN forces.

Armistice is concluded between opposing sides in the Korean War.

Association of Southeast Asian Nations ASEAN is formed to "promote active collaboration and mutual assistance on matters of common interest." ASEAN includes the Philippines, Indonesia, Malaysia, and Thailand.

Under orders of President John F. Kennedy Green Berets and military advisers arrive in South Vietnam to train its troops.

Ferdinand Marcos is elected president 9 November.

At a preelection 21 Au Manila gr suspends blaming th terrorism a with abett charges. T gains six c November

1946 **1950** **1953** **1961** **1965** **1967** **1971**

1947 **1951** **1954** **1964** **1966** **1970** **1972**

Military Bases Agreement establishes a ninety-nine year lease for U.S. bases in the Philippines.

With Philippine government threatened by the leftist Hukbalahap Movement, Col. Edward Lansdale arrives to advise Secretary of Defense Ramon Magsaysay, later to become president partly as the result of his success against the Huks.

Dien Bien Phu falls to the Vietnamese, effectively ending the French Indochina War

Ninety-four-year-old Emilio Aguinaldo passes away 6 February.

A renegotiated Military Bases Agreement between Marcos and Lyndon B. Johnson reduces U.S.-bases lease to twenty-five years, with $45 million pledged as an economic-aid package

Follow attem Juan F martia is imp forbid and op Aquino

In what comes t known as the Fi Quarter Storm, a massive demons tion led by student activists and workers manages to brea into the grounds Malacañang Pala forcing the Marcoses to flee temporarily by helicopter.

by the opposi-
iranda in
Marcos
as corpus,
or planned
iigno Aquino
o denies the
beral Party
seats in violent

ion, providing the
irect powers,
35 one.

On 30 April Saigon is cap-
by the North Vietnamese
s and the Vietcong, signalling
nd of the Vietnam War.

On 21 August
Aquino returns
to Manila but
is shot to death
at the Manila
International
Airport by alleged
assassin who is
immediately
killed by govern-
ment soldiers.
The Marcos
government
appoints a five-
judge panel to
investigate, while
denying official
involvement.

A 23 January *New York Times* article undermines Marcos's claim of anti-
Japanese guerrilla leadership and heroism during World War II. Elections on
7 February see thirty victims of violence. The People Power or EDSA
Uprising breaks out the weekend of 23 February with millions of citizens
turning out on metropolitan Manila's streets to support dissident military
factions and demonstrate their desire to see Marcos leave.

On 26 February he and his family flee for Hawaii. Mrs. Aquino takes over
the reins of government. The process of drafting a new constitution begins.

In Honolulu, Ferdinand Marcos dies in September. On 1
December the most serious of several coup attempts
against Pres. Aquino takes place. It fizzles out as U.S.
jets signal the U.S. government's intent to protect her.

General Fidel Ramos, Mrs. Aquino's Secretary
of Defense and former head of the Philippine
Constabulary under Marcos, succeeds her as
president. Former movie star and small-town
mayor, and ex-senator Joseph "Erap" Estrada
is his vice president.

Joseph "Erap" Estrada succeeds
Ramos as president.

Faced with overwhelming
evidence of corruption, protests
by crowds that recall People
Power, and the military's withdrawal of support, Estrada steps
down as president. Vice
President Gloria Macapagal
Arroyo takes over the presidency
of the country and orders the
arrest of Estrada.

On 11 September the World
Trade Towers are demolished in
a terrorist attack. In October
the U.S. declares war on
Afghanistan.

1983 **1986** **1989** **1992** **1998** **2001**

1980 **1985** **1987** **1991** **1999 - 2000** **2002**

assination
se Minister
arcos declares
mber. Curfew
monstrations
shut down,
rs, including

Benigno Aquino is
allowed by
Marcos to fly to
Texas on 8 May,
for heart surgery.
On November 4
Ronald Reagan
is elected
president.

3 November
Marcos
announces the
holding of "snap
elections."
Corazon Aquino,
Benigno's widow,
decides to run
against Marcos,
with Salvador
Laurel as her
vice president.

Voters approve a
new constitution,
which provides
for a single
six-year
presidential
term and gives
Congress a role
in determining
the fate of U.S.
bases.

The Philippine Senate votes not
to renew the U.S. bases treaty.
Mt. Pinatubo, a volcano near
Clark Air Field Base, erupts,
shutting down the base.

Visiting Forces Agreement is
forged between the Philippine
government and the United
States, allowing U.S. warships to use Philippine ports
and for joint sea, air, and land
military exercises between
the two countries.

U.S. troops arrive in the
Philippines to fight alongside
Filipino soldiers against the
Abu Sayyaf.